Lecture Notes in Computer Science 4039

Commenced Publication in 1973
Founding and Former Series Editors:
Gerhard Goos, Juris Hartmanis, and Jan van Leeuwen

Maurizio Morisio (Ed.)

Reuse of Off-the-Shelf Components

9th International Conference on Software Reuse,
ICSR 2006
Turin, Italy, June 12-15, 2006
Proceedings

 Springer

Volume Editor

Maurizio Morisio
Politecnico di Torino, Dip. Automatica e Informatica
Corso Duca degli Abruzzi 24, 10129 Torino, Italy
E-mail: maurizio.morisio@polito.it

Library of Congress Control Number: 2006926266

CR Subject Classification (1998): D.2, K.6, D.1, J.1

LNCS Sublibrary: SL 2 – Programming and Software Engineering

ISSN   0302-9743
ISBN-10   3-540-34606-6 Springer Berlin Heidelberg New York
ISBN-13   978-3-540-34606-7 Springer Berlin Heidelberg New York

Springer is a part of Springer Science+Business Media

springer.com

© Springer-Verlag Berlin Heidelberg 2006
Printed in Germany

Typesetting: Camera-ready by author, data conversion by Scientific Publishing Services, Chennai, India
Printed on acid-free paper   SPIN: 11763864   06/3142   5 4 3 2 1 0

Preface

Software reuse as an umbrella concept has been around for several decades. Over time, new techniques and approaches have been proposed to implement the concept, from libraries of reusable assets to product lines, to generative methods.

These latter techniques are mostly used in intra-organizational reuse, and require considerable formal knowledge over the evolution of technology and required functionality in a domain over several years.

On the other end of the spectrum, extra-organizational reuse is based on reuse of off-the-shelf (OTS) software (both open and closed source, acquired for free or for a fee). Here, a limited investment and immediate availability of the assets have widely spread the approach. On the other hand, the reusing organization has no control on the evolution of the functionality and assumptions of the asset. Even when the assets are open source, they are seldom modified.

The theme for this ninth meeting is the reuse of off-the-shelf (OTS) components and related problems:

* Documentation of OTS components
* Processes to identify and select OTS components
* Integration and evolution problems
* Reliability and security of OTS components and legal issues
* Interaction with the developer community or with the vendor

The proceedings you are holding cover these issues as well as development and use of product lines, variability modeling, aspect-based development, composition of components and services.

June 2006   Maurizio Morisio

Organization

Organizing Committee
General: Giancarlo Succi, Free University Bolzano/Bozen
Program: Maurizio Morisio, Politecnico di Torino

Workshops
Peter Knauber, Mannheim University of Applied Sciences, Germany

Tutorials
Birgit Geppert, Avaya Labs, USA

Steering Committee
Ted Biggerstaff, SoftwareGenerators.com
John Favaro, Consulenza Informatica
Bill Frakes, Virginia Tech
Ernesto Guerrieri, GTECH Corporation

Program Committee
Sidney Bailin, Knowledge Evolution
Len Bass, SEI
Ted Biggerstaff, SoftwareGenerators.com
Cornelia Boldyreff, University of Lincoln
Jan Bosch, Nokia
Christian Bunse, Fraunhofer IESE
Gerardo Canfora, Universita' del Sannio
Andrea Capiluppi, University of Lincoln
Paul Clements, SEI
Shalom Cohen, SEI
Reidar Conradi, NTNU Trondheim
Krzysztof Czarnecki, University of Waterloo
Ernesto Damiani, Università di Milano
Hakan Erdogmus, NRC Canada
Michel Ezran, Renault
Paolo Falcarin, Politecnico di Torino
John Favaro, Consulenza Informatica
Bill Frakes, Virginia Tech
Cristina Gacek, University of Newcastle upon Tyne
Birgit Geppert, Avaya
Hassan Gomaa, George Mason University
Ernesto Guerrieri, GTECH Corporation
Stan Jarzabek, National University of Singapore
Merijn de Jonge, Philips
Kyo Kang, Postech
Peter Knauber, Mannheim University of Applied Sciences

Charles Krueger, BigLever Inc.
Patricia Lago, Vrije Universiteit Amsterdam
Filippo Lanubile, Universita' di Bari
Juan Llorens, Universidad Carlos III Madrid
Mike Mannion, Glasgow Caledonian University
Michele Marchesi, University of Cagliari
Ali Mili, New Jersey Institute of Technology
Roland Mittermeir, University of Klagenfurt
Juergen Muench, Fraunhofer IESE
Markku Oivo, University of Oulu
Rob van Ommering, Philips
Witold Pedrycz, University of Alberta
Jeff Poulin, LockheedMartin
Wolfgang Pree, University of Salzburg
Rubin Prieto-Diaz, James Madison University
Stephen Rank, Lincoln University
Frank Roessler, Avaya
William Scherlis, Carnegie Mellon
Klaus Schmid, University of Hildesheim
Alberto Sillitti, Free University of Bolzano/Bozen
Ioannis Stamelos, Aristotle University of Thessaloniki
Marco Torchiano, Politecnico di Torino
Colin Tully, Middlesex University
Claudia Werner, University of Rio de Janeiro
Claes Wohlin, Blekinge Institute of Technology

Sponsors

Compagnia di San Paolo
Fondazione CRT
ICTeam
ISASE
Politecnico di Torino

Table of Contents

Reengineering Maintanance

Programming Languages and Retrieval

Aspect-Oriented Software Development

Approaches and Models

Components

Short Papers

Tutorials

A Goal-Oriented Strategy for Supporting Commercial Off-the-Shelf Components Selection

Claudia Ayala and Xavier Franch

Technical University of Catalunya
UPC-Campus Nord (Omega), 08034 Barcelona, Spain
{cayala, franch}@lsi.upc.edu

Abstract. The use of Commercial Off-The-Shelf (COTS) components is becoming a strategic need because they offer the possibility to build systems at reduced costs and within shorter development time. Having efficient and reliable COTS components selection methods is a key issue not only for exploiting the potential benefits of this technology, but also for facing the problems and risks involved. Searching COTS components requires to overcome several obstacles: the growing size and evolvability of the COTS marketplace, the dependencies from the components to be selected with others, and the type of descriptions currently available for those components. In this paper, we present a goal-oriented strategy for an effective localization, analysis and structuring of COTS components information. Our proposal is the GOThIC method, which provides methodological support to the construction of taxonomies. We present the seven activities that conform this method, which are illustrated with the case of real-time synchronous communication tools.

1 Introduction

Nowadays, the construction of systems based on pre-packaged solutions, usually known as Off-The-Shelf (OTS) components, is becoming an economic and strategic need in a wide variety of different application areas. The potential benefits of OTS technologies are mainly the reduced cost and shorter development time, while maintaining the quality [1]. Nevertheless, many challenges, ranging from technical to legal must be faced for adapting the traditional software engineering activities with the aim of exploiting these benefits.

One of the most critical activities in OTS-based systems development is the selection of the components that must be integrated therein. Selection is basically composed of two main activities, namely search of candidates and their evaluation with respect to system requirements.

However, most of the different existing methods for COTS selection -as those surveyed in [2] and [3]- (e.g. CAP, CARE, CEP, CRE, OTSO, PECA, PORE, QESTA, Scarlet, STACE, and Storyboard) focus on evaluation instead of search. This lack of specific proposals is a serious drawback that impacts in selection reliability: no matter how good is the evaluation process, selection may be wrong if the candidates chosen to be evaluated are not the right ones.

M. Morisio (Ed.): ICSR 2006, LNCS 4039, pp. 1 – 15, 2006.
© Springer-Verlag Berlin Heidelberg 2006

Searching candidate OTS components is not an easy task, especially in the case of Commercial-Off-The-Shelf (COTS) components, i.e. components that are acquired for a fee. On the one hand, COTS components are a class of reusable components, and it is well-known that one of the essential problems in reusing software components is locating and retrieving them from a large collection [4]. On the other hand, COTS search must cope with some challenging characteristics:

1. *Growing size of the COTS marketplace*: New and improved products and technologies are continuously offered. Thus, existing market segments offer more and more products, and new market segments are continuously emerging. Mobile technologies are a good example of both situations.
2. *Rapid changes in the COTS marketplace*: New versions of existing products are released every few months. Moreover, market segments frontiers move slightly over the years, making products to offer services that initially were seen as belonging to different segments. For instance, current mail server systems usually provide instant messaging facilities, even video-conferencing services.
3. *Dependencies among COTS components*: COTS components are not designed to work isolated, but in collaboration with others. Therefore many dependencies among them exist, either for enabling, enhancing or complementing their functionality [5]. For instance, document management systems need document imaging tools for scanning and storing paper documents.
4. *Type of descriptions available for COTS components*: COTS components suppliers do not provide the kind of structured information that would allow performing automated or at least assisted search. Moreover, it is not realistic to think that the situation will change in the future. This is especially true for coarse-grained COTS components such as ERP, CRM or CMS systems. The situation is aggravated by the fact that supplier information of course tends to highlight strengths and hide weaknesses of the licensed components.

Consequently, when carrying out a particular searching process, some practical questions may arise: Which are the market segments of interest for this particular context? Which are the relationships among the identified market segments and which are their implied needs? How can structured and trustable information be obtained for the COTS components available in the marketplace?

In this paper, we claim that an effective COTS search strategy shall rely on a thorough description of the COTS marketplace whose nature adapts to the above mentioned characteristics (diversity, size, evolvability, interoperability, lack of structure and subjectivity) and therefore provides real answers to the questions above. Therefore, we present a method called GOThIC (Goal-Oriented Taxonomy and reuse Infrastructure Construction) aimed at building a reuse infrastructure that may be used in COTS search processes by arranging marketplace segments as a taxonomy. The nodes of this taxonomy are characterized by means of goals and their relationships declared as dependencies. The method includes a domain analysis phase which faces the problem of unstructured and not validated information coming from lots of information sources. The rest of the paper is organized as follows. In section 2 we present our research method and previous work. Related work is presented in section 3. The core of the proposal, the GOThIC method, is presented from sections 4 to 11, illustrated with a case study on the category of real-time synchronous communication tools. Finally, in section 12 we give the conclusions and some future work.

2   Research Method and Previous Work

Our proposal relies on several industrial experiences which have been undertaken under action-research premises [6], as well as literature survey and grounded theory [7]. Furthermore, we have formulated in early work some preliminary proposals. This section provides details about both points.

The first industrial experience taken was in the context of an academic record management information system development which was planned to include some strategic business functionalities. We undertook a thorough analysis of the domain and experimented the problems mentioned in the introduction. As a result, we presented a first paper [8] proposing the use of taxonomies to structure the COTS business application marketplace. After this, we had other collaborations in the field of requirements management tools, telephony systems and others. We complemented these real cases with some academic ones. As a result, given that there is some evidence that goals are quite stable with respect to changes [9] and goal refinement provides a natural mechanism for structuring and exploring many alternatives [10], we incorporated the notion of goal to formalize the meaning of the nodes in the taxonomy making it domain-independent. Subsequently, we presented a goal-oriented method called GBTCM (*Goal-Based Taxonomy Construction Method*) which added the process dimension to our previous work [11]. It was inspired on GBRAM (Goal-Based Requirements Analysis Method) [10], a widespread method in the requirements engineering discipline. Although GBTCM was an improvement of our previous work, we have recently encountered some method design flaws, some due to the use of GBRAM in a different context, others due to our method as such. The flaws are:

- GBRAM is a requirements acquisition method; therefore the sources of information are mainly human beings, which is not the case in the COTS context.
- Furthermore, GBRAM lacks of proper mechanisms to deal with the huge amount of unstructured information of the COTS marketplace.
- GBTCM does not give the required importance to the analysis of the domain, which is more difficult than in a non-COTS context because expertise is needed not only on the domain itself but also on how this domain is represented in the marketplace.
- GBRAM is a one-shot method, with no orientation to knowledge reuse.
- GBTCM focuses on the market segments but did not consider the COTS components themselves.
- GBTCM definition was not oriented to having tool-support.
  The GOThIC method presented in this paper, aims at overcoming these flaws.

3   Related Work

Due to the highly applicable nature of the subject of our research, we find related work not only concerning scientific proposals but also in the way that the COTS marketplace is really organized nowadays. Profit and non-profit organizations define categories of services, products, and knowledge, usually structured in a hierarchical form. This type of organizations can be classified as follows:

- IT consultant companies such as Gartner [12] or Forrester [13] use these categories to structure their reports and services on IT technology.
- Commercial web-based companies such as ComponentSource [14] and Genium [15] group the products commercially available for facilitating the web browsing.
- Professional societies such as INCOSE [16] use hierarchies to organize systems engineering knowledge (often not related specifically to COTS issues).
- Portals with different registration procedures offer white reports, user's opinions [17], [18] or technical products from research projects [19].

In the academic world, organizations, teams and individuals have presented their own proposals that range from specific of one domain [20] to a wide range [4] [21] or even a field [22], being the extreme case proposals such as SWEBOK that acts as a body of knowledge of a particular discipline [23]. Nevertheless, it is well-know that the effort devoted to these activities is more valuable if the attributes can be reused; in this sense a wide range of works about COTS characterization exists [24-27] (see [28] for a recent survey).

However, such proposals do not provide proper mechanisms for facing the characteristics of the COTS marketplace mentioned in the introduction. Furthermore, sometimes, the meaning of a particular domain is not clear without further examining the items, especially if the domain is absolutely unknown to the user. Consequently the understanding, use, evolution, extension, and customization of the categorization proposal may be difficult. We have experienced in details these drawbacks in the case of Gartner and INCOSE, whose classifications were used as starting points in [8] and [11], respectively.

To sum up, we consider that there is a gap between the mentioned proposals and their applicability in the COTS search context that is considered an important open issue [29].

4   An Overview of the GOThIC Method

The GOThIC method has been structured into seven activities:

1. Exploration of information sources.
2. COTS marketplace domain analysis.
3. Identification, refinement, and statement of goals.
4. Establishment of dependencies.
5. Goal taxonomy structuring.
6. Taxonomy validation.
7. Knowledge base management.

Although presented as sequential for clarity, these activities may in fact be intertwined and iterated as required to obtain the target infrastructure incrementally. Furthermore, the GOThIC method does not depend on the extent and characteristics of the taxonomy built (e.g., a small part of the COTS marketplace such as photo processing software, or a huge portion like business applications).

The ultimate goal of the method is to populate a knowledge base with data according to the UML [30] conceptual model sketched in Fig. 1.

At the heart of this model lies the taxonomy composed of two types of nodes, market segments and categories, which are characterized by their goals. Market segments are the leaves of the taxonomy, whilst categories serve to group related market segments and/or subcategories (e.g., the category of communication infrastructure systems or financial packages).

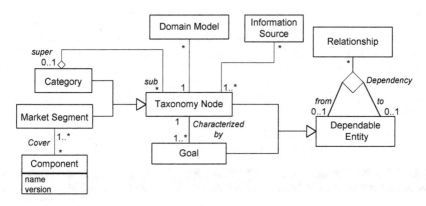

Fig. 1. Conceptual model for goal-oriented COTS taxonomies: overview

From a semantic point of view, market segments stand for the basic types of COTS components available in the marketplace (e.g., the domain of anti-virus tools or spreadsheet applications), i.e. atomic entities covering a significant group of functionality such as their decomposition would yield to too fine-grained domains. As a consequence, COTS components are associated with market segments and not with categories (although an indirect relationship exists, because market segments belong to categories). Components may cover more than one market segment. For simplification purposes, we are not distinguishing at the moment versions of components; two different versions are treated as two different products.

Dependencies among nodes provide a comprehensive view of the marketplace. In the case of dependencies among market segments, they stand for interoperability needs (e.g. mail server systems depend on anti-virus tools to support integrity). Concerning categories, more abstract relationships are modeled. In addition to taxonomy nodes, dependencies may involve goals, when the relationship can be established more accurately. The *Dependable Entity* superclass allows modeling this situation comfortably. Note that dependencies are represented by a ternary association, because they involve two elements (depender and dependee) and the relationship itself.

Finally, nodes have auxiliary artifacts bound, which are built during the domain analysis activity. Their construction is a result of the analysis of some information sources which are gathered, analyzed, and prioritized according to several characteristics.

In following sections, we provide details of the GOThIC method activities. To illustrate our approach, we use the Real-Time Synchronous Communication (RTSC) category. It means the various tools and technologies used to enable communication and collaboration among people in a "same time-different place" mode.

5   Exploration of Information Sources

This activity must be able to locate as much relevant information as possible, dealing with the diversity of its type, supporting media, cost, etc. We distinguish three related subactivities:

- *Gathering of sources.* Identification of the potential information sources for the domain of interest using information acquisition techniques (e.g., literature review, web screening, etc.). We have identified the following types of sources: existing hierarchies, taxonomies and ontologies; related standards; vendors information; independent reports (scientific, divulgation and technical); oral information; test of tools and systems; real experiences on the field; others.

Table 1. Information sources for the RTCS case

Information Source		Information Type	Language	Examples	Utility
Existing Taxonomies and Ontologies		Classifications; Categories; Glossaries	Natural Language (NL); Tree-like diagrams	Gartner, IDC, eCOTS, ComponentSource	They help not only for understanding domains and refining goals, but also for getting insights for organising goals.
Related Standards		Descriptions; Glossaries	NL	IETF-SIP ITU H.323 ISO 9126-1	They are considered the most confident of the sources, so the high-level goals are based on them.
Vendors Information		Brochures; Evaluation forms; Benchmarks	NL; Values for attributes	Microsoft	They are helpful to know functionalities, trends and interactions among components
Independent Reports	Scientific	Academic Events, Jounals Textbooks	Precise and rigorous descriptions	NL; Models; Formulas; Schemas	ICCBSS, ICSE, TSE	
	Divulgation	Magazines, Forums and Websites	Descriptions and tips for the general public	NL; Schemas; Tables	PCWorld, IEEE Software, COCOTS website,	
	Technical	White Papers, Surveys and Comparatives	Papers, Comparative tables	NL, Tables; Figures	Gartner, INCOSE, eCOTS	The information enclosed in this kind of sources, generally helps to understand domains and refining goals into sub goals.
Oral Information	Interviews		Knowledge; Tips; Practical Info.	NL	ICCBSS panels, SEI courses, Business luncheons	
	Talks, seminars and courses					
Test of Tools and Systems		Test results; User's manuals	Visual data; NL	ICQ, MSN Messenger, CommuniGate	
Real Experiences on the field		Knowledge; Technical reports	Knowledge; NL	Past projects made	
Others		Any	Any		

- *Analysis of sources.* Some techniques are applied to determine the relevant criteria to be used to rank the identified sources: reliability of the information; availability of the source; acquisition cost; timeliness; scope covered; and time needed to process the enclosed information. These criteria move along three dimensions: information source type, organization or people that created the information, and particular item of information.

- *Prioritisation of sources.* The analysed sources are ranked according to several characteristics of the taxonomy construction project, mainly: expected frequency of taxonomy use in future selection processes; resources allocated to the project, especially deadline, money and person/months; current and future knowledge of the domain and technical skills of the conformed team; expected criticality of the domain (and therefore required accuracy and completeness of the solution).

At the end of this phase we have a knowledge acquisition program which will allow extracting knowledge from the domain by reconciling the characteristics of the available sources with those of the taxonomy construction process. Table 1 is an excerpt of the information sources considered for the RTSC case and shows details of their utility and the kind of information therein. Fig. 2 shows an excerpt of some mechanisms and artifacts we used for analyzing sources.

	Name	Type	Author	Cost	...
1	Session Initiation Protocol	Standard	Engineering Task Force	Free	
2	H.323	Standard	International Telecommunication Union	±80€	
3	IMTC	Independent Report	International Teleconferencing Consortium	Free	
4	RTC-Gartner	Hierarchy	Gartner	Free	
:					

Example of Questionnaire

Determining Author reliability

Is it a reputable author or organization?
☐ Excellent ☐ Good
☐ Satisfactory ☐ Weak
Did you see this source listed in other sources?
☐ Yes   ☐ No
...

Fig. 2. Examples of the artifacts used for the information sources analysis

6 Domain Analysis

Domain analysis has been identified as a major factor in the success of software reusability [31]. Its goal is to identify the basic elements of the domain, organize an understanding of relationships among these elements, and represent this understanding in a useful way. Domain analysis is especially crucial in our approach because of two main reasons:

- One of the most endangering points in the COTS framework is the widespread information and lack of standard terminology, the same concepts are named different by different vendors or even worse, the same name may denote different concepts in different COTS components. Thus, using domain analysis principles we avoid syntactic and semantic discrepancies common in the COTS marketplace.
- The core elements of a domain and the relationships among them usually remain more stable, while the technologies and implementation environments are in continuous evolution.

Several proposals of domain analysis available in the literature may differ in the type of artefacts proposed to record the knowledge. In this work, we propose the following four artefacts:

- *Use Case Specification.* A UML use case diagram [30], arranged in packages if necessary, to provide an overall view of the services that the COTS components in the market segment or category offer. Individual specifications of use cases are recommended to be very abridged, for different reasons (evolvability of marketplace, avoid committing to behaviour of particular COTS components, etc.).
- *Class Diagram.* To keep track of the fundamental concepts in the domain, their attributes, associations and taxonomic relationships. Also in UML [30].
- *Quality Model.* A hierarchical representation of the quality factors applicable to the domain, such as those referring to efficiency and integrity, together with their metrics. For standardization issues, we propose the use of the ISO/IEC 9126 quality standard [32].
- *Glossary of terms.* It includes at least the names of elements in the class diagram and the quality model. The glossary must not include overloaded terms, although many definitions may exist for a single term (which should be semantically equivalent). We propose to use the Language Extended Lexicon (LEL) [33] for capturing the meaning and fundamental relationships of the particular symbols (words or phrases) of the domain.

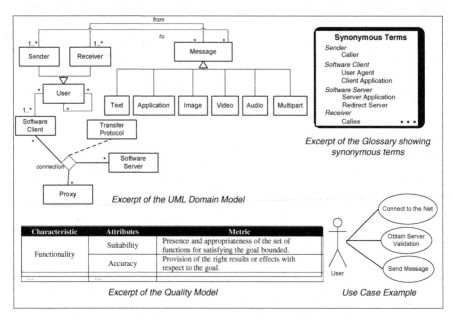

Fig. 3. Excerpt of models built for the RTCS case

It is important to remark that the models present some relationships when considering the nodes in the taxonomy. Contradictions when composing or joining models may arise and of course they should be detected and reconciled. In Fig. 3 we show excerpts of the four types of artifacts for the RTSC case.

7   Identification, Refinement and Statement of Goals

A goal is an objective that should be achieved and may be formulated at different levels of abstraction [9]. The activities performed in this stage are iterative and have the next objectives:

- *Identification* aims at extracting goals from available sources applying different goal-acquisition techniques [34] as scenarios and Inquiry Cycle (IC) approach [35].
- *Refinement* entails the goal refinement considering obstacles, scenarios to uncover hidden goals and mechanisms to discover synonymous or duplicated goals. Table 2 is an example of the use of scenarios for obtaining goals in the RTSC case.
- *Statement* consists on expressing the goals in a systematic way. We use a pre/post style for specifying these goals, i.e. stating which conditions are met when others hold, as showed in Table 3.

Table 2. A scenario excerpt of the RTSC case study

Action Initiator	Goal	Consumed Resources	Produced Resources	Action Addressed
Human User (Sender)	Message Sent	Message	Message, Receiver address	Requesting to Software Client
Software Client	Sent Request to the Server	Message, Receiver address	Sender address	Requesting to Software Server
Software Server	Messages Routed	Message, Sender and Receiver address	Routed Receiver address	Sending to Software Client (Receiver)
Software Client	Message Delivered	Message, Sender address	Message	Deliver to a Human User (Receiver)
Human User (Receiver)	Message Received	Message, Sender address	Message	Answering

Table 3. An example of goal statement

Goal:	Multiuser Textual Communication Established
Type	Achievement
Description	Provide RTSC in a Text Multi-user Environment
Agent	Software Client
Stakeholder(s)	Software Client, Software Server, Sender, Receiver
Precondition(s)	1) Users Communicated in Real Time; 2)Session Established; 3) Number of users >=2
Postcondition(s)	Multiuser Textual Communication Established
Subgoal(s)	1) Software Client Provided; 2) Software Server Provided

8   Establishment of Dependencies

We have identified that a COTS component may need another for:

- Enabling its functionality. For instance, in order to follow document life-cycles, document management tools need workflow technology to define them.
- Complementing its functionality with an additional feature, not originally intended to be part of its suitability. For instance, a web page edition tool can complement a web browser to facilitate the edition and modification of web pages.
- Enhancing its quality attributes. For instance, resource utilization can be improved significantly using compression tools.

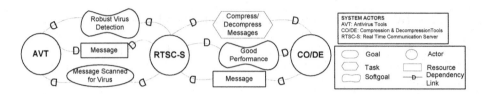

Fig. 4. *i** SD model representing some high level dependencies identified in the RTSC case

Fig. 4 shows some dependencies for the RTSC case. Relationships are gradually identified analyzing the goal information obtained in previous activities. These relationships are declared as dependencies using goal-oriented models, specifically *i** models [36]. Using this notation as proposed in [5], we represent market segments and categories as *i** actors, and establish dependencies that may be of four different types: goal dependencies, when an actor depend on another to attain a goal; task dependencies, when an actor requires another to perform an activity in a given way; resource dependencies, when an actor depends on another for the availability of some data; and soft goal dependency, when an actor depends on another to achieve a certain level of quality of service.

9   Goal Taxonomy Structuring

Taxonomic classification in the form of decision tree is the intellectual tool that helps us to organize goals in order to establish a structure and the locate/retrieve mechanisms. Our taxonomies are goal-driven, which means we provide semantics to the nodes expressing goals, giving a rationale for the decisions taken. The organization of goals comes from the analysis of pre and post-conditions stated for each goal. Goals are operationalized in terms of variables which, in the case of categories, represent classifiers (e.g., number of users of the system, data processing profile, ...). These classifiers may take values (e.g., for data processing profile, values are Acquisition, Storage, Preparation, Analysis), and for each possible value, a subcategory or market segment applies. Thus, *Goals* are defined over a set $X = \{x_k\}_n$ of independent variables that characterize the taxonomy. *Goal satisfaction* is defined by means of assignment to the variables, therefore for each assignment $ass = (x_1 \leftarrow v_1, ..., x_n \leftarrow v_n)$, the expression $sat_{ass}(G)$ yields true if the goal G evaluates to true for this assignment, otherwise false. Table 4 shows an excerpt of the departing goal hierarchy for the RTSC case as well as its variables assignment, considering that all the assignments are inherited downwards the hierarchy.

Table 4. Excerpt of the departing goal-oriented taxonomy for RTSC case

Goal /SubGoal	Variable	Satisfaction Values
Users Communicated in Real Time	TypeOfConnection	TypeOfConnection←RealTime
Intra-organizational Communication Established	Infrastructure	Infrastructure ←Intranet
Global Communication Established	Infrastructure	Infrastructure←Internet/WAN
...		

10 Taxonomy Validation

In order to be useful for driving COTS search processes, we require three conditions to the taxonomy: to be consistent, to be complete and to be not ambiguous. Also, we aim at leveraging its nodes to get similar levels of abstraction in the nodes of the same level. We have defined the process of taxonomy validation as the repeated application of some stated transformation rules (defined in terms of the goals pre and post-conditions) over the nodes to manipulate the hierarchy until reaching a stop condition. These transformations rules shall satisfy a precondition to be applied until completeness and correctness conditions with respect to the involved goals is assured, in such a way that a goal-oriented taxonomy is said to be correct and complete if it satisfies these invariant conditions. Specifically, this process has 4 steps each of them is aimed to ensure each condition:

- *Step 1* ensures the hierarchy of nodes is well-formed, which means that satisfaction of the goal of a node implies satisfaction of its parent goal.
- *Step 2* that the variable assignation provides a unique way for classifying COTS components, which means that there is no variable assignment which makes two siblings satisfy their goals simultaneously.
- *Step3* that any COTS related with the domain can always be classified using the taxonomy, i.e. that the taxonomy covers all the possible assignment of variables.
- *Step 4* was added for applying transformation rules in order to tailor the taxonomy to the particular (and subjective) taste of the designer with respect to the level of detail and organizational concerns.

This process and applicable transformation rules are detailed in [37]. Through this process we manipulated the nodes in a formal way to obtain the resulting taxonomy. For instance, in Table 4 we can see that the goal *Users Communicated in Real Time* was implying as subgoals 2 ways in which we can establish a communication; however in the resulting taxonomy showed in Table 5, 3 nodes are stated because the goal *Global Communication Established* was mixing 2 different concepts and func-tionalities that seems to be fashionable requirements demanded in the marketplace:

Table 5. Partial view of the RTSC Taxonomy

Categories				Market Segments
Level 1	Level 2	Level 3	Level 4	
a. Intranet Communication	d. Multi-user Communication	...	...	Multi-User Shared Applications
		j. Chat	o. Chat Client	Multi-user We-Based Chat Client Applications
				Multi-user No Web-Based Chat Client Applications
			p. Chat Server	Multi-user Chat Server Applications
		k. Video&Audio		Multi-user Video Applications
				Multi-user Audio Applications
	e. One-to-One Communication	...	...	One-to-One Shared Applications
		i. Chat	s. Chat Client	One-to-One We-Based Chat Client Applications
				One-to-One No Web-Based Chat Client Applications
			t. Chat Server	One-to-One Chat Server Applications
		m.Video&Audio		One-to-One Video Applications
				One-to-One Audio Applications
b. Internet Communication	f. Multi-user	...	...	...
	g. One-to-One	...	...	...
c. WAN Communication	h. Multi-user	...	...	...
	i. One-to-One	...	...	...

Internet Communication Established and *WAN Communication Established*; thus we applied a rule for showing explicitly this value preserving correctness and completeness properties. As a result of the process we have a high quality taxonomy in which the rationale for the classification is very clear and correctness and completeness are ensured by construction.

11   Knowledge Base Management

Many studies refer it is necessary to build a body of knowledge towards a knowledge-based framework for COTS components identification [29],[1]. The GOThIC method provides an efficient mechanism to maintain a repository of the obtained knowledge due to the UML class diagram that defines the form that this repository exhibits (see [38] for details). This knowledge base is the infrastructure support not only for an easy evolution and maintaining of taxonomies, but also for their suitability to specific organizational concerns.

12   Conclusions

In this paper we have presented the GOThIC method for facing COTS components search that is based on the notion of goal for building abstract, well-founded and stable taxonomies, which may evolve as the marketplace does. GOThIC is defined in a rigorous way, with a conceptual model that introduces all the concepts needed; and has been presented as a way to overcome the characteristics of the COTS marketplace mentioned in section 1:

- *Growing size of the COTS marketplace.* Proliferation of information is taken into account by prioritizing information sources in the bases of given criteria (time, money, reliability, ...). Appearance of a new market segment is easier to handle than in other approaches, since it requires to locate its place in the taxonomy using the defined classifiers, and once there even some useful artifacts are inherited (e.g., quality models and glossaries).
- *Rapid changes in the COTS marketplace.* We use a goal-oriented approach, in the belief that goals are stable concepts [9]. Also, the fact that taxonomy nodes do not stand for types of COTS components available but for related groups of functionalities, makes the taxonomy more robust with respect to the segment barriers movement effect mentioned in the introduction.
- *Dependencies among COTS components.* We represent explicitly these dependencies with a model built with *i**, a widespread and accepted notation in other disciplines (e.g., requirements engineering, agent-oriented development).
- *Type of descriptions available for COTS components.* We have identified two activities for collecting information sources and carrying out domain analysis to cope with the diversity, lack of structure and lack of reliability of information about COTS components. Also, our resulting taxonomy provides an external view that is: well-founded (with a clear rationale of the proposed structure), validated (sound, complete, pair-wise disjoint and balanced) and ready to browse (using the defined classifiers).

It is worth to think about applicability of the method. Basically, GOThIC requires the following characteristics to be applicable:

- The taxonomy addresses a category of market segments that is of general interest. This means that a great deal of organizations need to select COTS components from these segments. Some examples are: communication infrastructure (including the RTSC case used in this paper), ERP systems, security-related systems, etc. In these contexts, the number of selection processes that take place will be high and then reusability of the models likely to occur.
- The addressed market segments offer COTS components of coarse-grained granularity. This makes domain understanding more difficult, time-consuming and cumbersome and therefore domain analysis and taxonomy construction are helpful. Market segments such as CRM and ECM systems are typical examples, whilst time or currency converters are not. In these cases, having knowledge available and classifiers to know when a market segment is of interest is a great help. This last point is especially appealing in those selection contexts in which the organization that is interested in the selection does not have clear requirements about the kind of system needed.
- The COTS components search activity is monitored by an organization that accumulates experience from past selection processes. This organization will find valuable to have means to transfer knowledge from one experience to another and to assist their clients in the maintenance of their COTS-based software systems.

As a result, diverse actors may benefit from our approach:

- IT consultant companies offering assessment for business automation may structure their services better.
- Commercial web-based companies or portals may structure their offering in well-founded categories with a clear rationale behind.
- Medium and large-size companies with their own IT department may be more confident on their own selection processes.
- Software engineers which usually carry out COTS components selection may structure better their knowledge and may aim at a better return of investment.

At the time being, we have experimented our GOThIC method in the following fields: Real-Time Synchronous Communication Systems, Message-based Communication Systems, some sub-categories of Enterprise Applications (with emphasis with those related to Content Management) and Requirements Engineering Tools. The results are promising from the academic point of view, but we have not had the chance yet to make a proper validation involving an industrial partner, by means of some action-research collaboration as we have done in the past. Industrial validation is our main aim for future work. We also are going to tackle immediately development of tool support starting from the UML conceptual model detailed in [38].

References

1. Li, J., Conradi, R., et al. "Validation of New Thesis on Off-The-Shelf Component-Based Development" Proceedings 11th IEEE International Software Metrics Symposium, 2005.
2. Ruhe, G. "Intelligent Support for Selection of COTS Products" Proceedings Web Databases and Web Services 2002. LNCS 2593, pp. 34-45, 2003.

3. Morisio, M., et al. "COTS-based software development: Processes and open issues" Journal of Systems and Software 61(3):(2002)
4. Prieto-Díaz, R; Freeman, P. "Classifying Software for Reusability" IEEE Software. January 1987.
5. Franch, X., Maiden, N. "Modelling Component Dependencies to Inform their Selection" Proceedings 2nd International Conference on COTS-Based Software Systems (ICCBSS 2003).
6. Baskerville R., Wood-Harper A.T. "Diversity in Information Systems Action Research Methods" European Journal on Information Systems. Vol. 7 No.2, June 1998.
7. Martin, P., Turner, B. "Grounded Theory and Organizational Research" Journal of Applied Behavioral Science.1986; 22: 141-157.8.
8. Carvallo, J.P., Franch, X., et al. "Characterization of a Taxonomy for Business Applications and the Relationships among Them" Proceedings 3rd International Conference on COTS-Based Software Systems (ICCBSS 2004), LNCS 2959, 2004.
9. van Lamsweerde, A. "Goal-Oriented Requirements Engineering: A Guided Tour" Proceedings 5th IEEE International Symposium on Requirements Engineering. 2001.
10. Antón, A. I.. "Goal Identification and Refinement in the Specification of Software-Based Information Systems". Ph.D. thesis, Georgia Institute of Technology, June 1997.
11. Ayala, C.P., Botella, P., Franch, X., "On Goal-Oriented COTS Taxonomies Construction" Proceedings 4th International Conference on COTS-Based Software Systems (ICCBSS 2005), LNCS 3412, 2005. Bilbao, Spain.
12. Gartner Inc. www.gartner.com.
13. Forrester Research Inc. www.forrester.com
14. ComponentSource componentsource.com
15. Genium Software Development http://www.genium.dk/index. xml
16. INCOSE www.incose.org.
17. IT products guide. http://productguide.itmanagersjournal.com
18. eCOTS www.ecots.org
19. CBSE www.cbsenet.org/pls/CBSEnet/ecolnet.home
20. Arranga, E. "Cobol Tools: Overview and Taxonomy" IEEE Software, 17(2): 59-61, 2000.
21. Llorens, J; Astudillo, H. "Automatic Generation of Hierarchical Taxonomies from Free Text Using Linguistic Algorithms" Advances in OO Inf. Systems. LNCS 2426/2002. pp. 74-83.
22. Glass, R.L; Vessey, I. "Contemporary Application-Domain Taxonomies" IEEE Software July 1995.
23. SWEBOK www.swebok.org.
24. Ochs, M.A., Pfahl, D., et al. "A Method for Efficient Measurement-based COTS Assessment and Selection-Method Description and Evaluation Results" Proceedings IEEE 7th International Software Metrics Symposium, 2001.
25. Carney D., Long F. "What Do You Mean by COTS? Finally a Useful Answer" IEEE Software, 17 (2), March/April 2000
26. Bianchi, A; Caivano, D; et al. "COTS Products Characterization: Proposal and Empirical Assessment". ESERNET 2001-2003. LNCS 2765, 2003.
27. Erofeev, S; DiGiacomo, P. "Usage of Dynamic Decision Models as an Agile Approach to COTS Taxonomies Construction" International Conference on COTS-Based Software Systems (ICCBSS 2006). IEEE 2006.
28. Cechich, A., Réquilé-Romanczuk, A., et al. "Trends on COTS Component Identification and Retrieval" International Conference on COTS-Based Software Systems (ICCBSS 2006).

29. Réquilé-Romanczuk, et al. "Towards a Knowledge-Based Framework for COTS Component Identification" ICSE-MPEC 2005, USA. ACM 2005.
30. UML Specifications http://www.uml.org/
31. Prieto-Díaz, R., Arango, G. "Domain Analysis and Software Systems Modelling" IEEE Computer Society Press, 1991. p. 300.
32. ISO/IEC International Standard 9126-1 "Software Engineering-Product Quality-Part 1: Quality Model" 2001.
33. Leite, J.C.S.P. "Application Languages: A Product of Requirements Analysis" Informatics Department PUC-/RJ (1989).
34. Regev, G. "Where do Goals Come from: the Underlying Principles of Goal-Oriented Requirements Engineering" 13th IEEE Requirements Engineering Conference (RE 2005).
35. Potts, C., Takanashi, K., Antón, A. "Inquiry-Based Requirements Analysis" IEEE Software, 11 (2), March 1994.
36. Yu, E. "Modelling Strategic Relationships for Process Reengineering" PhD Thesis, University of Toronto, 1995.
37. Ayala, C., Franch, X. "Transforming Software Package Classification Hierarchies into Goal-Based Taxonomies" Proceedings 16th International Conference on Database and Expert System Applications (DEXA 2005). LNCS 3588. Copenhagen, Denmark. August 2005.
38. Ayala, C., Franch, X. "A process for Building Goal-Oriented COTS Taxonomies" LSI-Department. Technical University of Catalunya. 2006. Report Number: LSI-06-7-R.

A State-of-the-Practice Survey of Off-the-Shelf Component-Based Development Processes

Jingyue Li[1], Marco Torchiano[2], Reidar Conradi[1], Odd Petter N. Slyngstad[1], and Christian Bunse[3]

[1] Department of Computer and Information Science,
Norwegian University of Science and Technology (NTNU),
NO-7491 Trondheim, Norway
{jingyue, conradi, oslyngst}@idi.ntnu.no
[2] Dip. Automatica e Informatica, Politecnico di Torino
Corso Duca degli Abruzzi, 24, I-10129 Torino, Italy
marco.torchiano@polito.it
[3] Fraunhofer IESE, Fraunhoferplatz 1,
D-67663 Kaiserslautern, Germany
Christian.Bunse@iese.fraunhofer.de

Abstract. To gain competitive advantages software organizations are forced to develop systems quickly and cost-efficiently. Reusing components from third-party providers is one key technology to reach these goals. These components, also known as OTS (Off-the-Shelf) components, come in two different types: COTS (Commercial-Off-The-Shelf) and OSS (Open–Source-Software) components. However, the reuse of pre-fabricated components bears one major question: How to adapt development processes/methods with refer to system development using OTS components. To examine the state-of-the-practice in OTS component-based development a survey on 133 software projects in Norway, Italy and Germany was performed. The results show that OTS-based development processes are typically variations of well-known process models, such as the waterfall- or prototyping model, mixed with OTS-specific activities. One reason might be that often the process is selected before the use of OTS components is considered. Furthermore, the survey shows that the selection of OTS components is based on two processes: "Familiarity-based" and "Internet search-based". Moreover, it appears that the lifecycle phase to select OTS components is significantly correlated with a project members' previous familiarity with possible OTS candidates. Within this paper, we characterize the state-of-the-practice concerning OTS processes, using seven scenarios, and discuss how to decide or modify such processes and how to select OTS components.

1 Introduction

Software development with OTS components is becoming increasingly popular in research and industrial communities. The use of OTS components introduces new requirements, which again require revised development processes. Although researchers and practitioners have been dealing with such processes quite a time, most studies are based on military or aerospace projects [10], [15], or other large projects. To

M. Morisio (Ed.): ICSR 2006, LNCS 4039, pp. 16–28, 2006.
© Springer-Verlag Berlin Heidelberg 2006

propose and design cost-effective OTS-based development processes, it is necessary to investigate how such projects are performed in different domains and project contexts.

Within a first, exploratory study, we investigated the commonalities and differences between development processes in 16 COTS-based software projects in Norway [6]. The study summarized several variations in COTS-based development processes and concluded that the customization of such development processes crucially depends on the project context, such as familiarity with possible COTS components and flexibility of requirements. Due to the small sample size it is necessary to verify these conclusions with a larger and more representative sample.

The study presented in this paper investigated several conclusions about variations in development processes, based on the exploratory study. The results show that the actual OTS component-based development processes are typically variations of well-known process models. In addition, two OTS component selection processes, such as familiarity-based and Internet search-based, are widely used in practice. By summarizing the state-of-the-practice of OTS component-based development processes using seven scenarios, we give systematic proposals on how to adopt the OTS-based development and OTS selection processes based on the project context.

The remainder of the paper is structured as follows: Section 2 presents previous studies and their research questions. Section 3 presents selected samples and Section 4 presents the empirical results. Discussions on customizing OTS-based development processes are given in Section 5 and Section 6 separately. Possible threats to validity are discussed in Section 7. Conclusion and future research are in Section 8.

2   Related Work and Research Questions

There is a consensus that the use of COTS components implies changes in the software process [2]. Some studies focused on the whole software development lifecycle [1], [3], [10]. Others investigated the specific phase, especially in COTS component selection and evaluation [5], [8], [9], [11], [12], [13], [14].

2.1   Process of the Whole Software Development Lifecycle

Boehm et al. [3] regard both the waterfall model and evolutionary development as unsuitable for COTS-based development. In the waterfall model, requirements are identified at an earlier stage and COTS components chosen at a later stage. This increases the likelihood of COTS components not offering the required features. Evolutionary development assumes that additional features can be added if required. However, COTS components cannot be upgraded by one particular development team. The frequent lack of code availability hinders developers to adapt them to their needs. Therefore, Boehm et al. proposed that development models, which explicitly take risk into account, are more suitable for COTS-based development than the traditional waterfall or evolutionary approaches.

The National Aeronautic and Space Administration (NASA) has been developing systems using COTS components for many years (see [10] for the summary of experience made). Various processes, used across 15 projects, were examined and used as a basis for a common COTS-based development process.

The Software Engineering Institute developed the Evolutionary Process for Integrating COTS-based Systems (EPIC) [1]. EPIC integrates COTS component related roles and activities into a RUP process. The iterative and evolutionary nature inherent in EPIC allows developers to adjust the architecture and system design, as more knowledge is gained about the operations of the COTS components.

Our investigation on COTS-based development process in Norwegian IT companies, however, revealed that the main COTS-based development process is to customize the traditional development process to account for use of COTS components [6]. In addition, in all our investigated projects, the project members decided the main process before they started to think about using COTS components. To verify our findings, we needed more representative samples. Therefore, our first three research questions RQ1 to RQ3 are designed to examine the state-of-the-practice of the actual development process in OTS-based projects.

- **RQ1:** What were the actual development processes in OTS-based projects?
- **RQ2:** Was the actual development process decided before the make vs. acquire decision or after the make vs. acquire decision.
- **RQ3:** Who decided the actual development process?

2.2 COTS Component Selection and Evaluation Process

Based on case studies, researchers have proposed several COTS component selection processes and methods. Some of the direct assessment processes, such as OTSO [5], CAP [13], and CISD [8], assume that the requirements are fixed and select the COTS components by comparing how well the COTS component candidates satisfy the requirements. A formal decision-making process is usually used to select the "best" COTS component [12]. The formal decision-making process usually includes three basic elements: selecting evaluation criteria (factors), collecting and assigning values to these criteria, and applying formal decision-making algorithms such as MAUT [9], MCDA [11], and AHP [14]. However, both the study of Torchiano and Morisio [16] and our exploratory study [6] showed that these formal selection methods were seldom used. In fact, our exploratory study discovered two other popularly used selection processes. One is *familiarity-based selection process* and the other is *Internet search with trial-based selection process*. In addition, our exploratory study concluded that there are common new activities and that the possible variations are when and how to perform them, especially when and how to select COTS components. Therefore, research questions RQ4 to RQ6 are designed to investigate how OTS components were selected.

- **RQ4:** What was the actual selection process used?
- **RQ5:** When was the OTS component selected?
- **RQ6:** What was the relationship between the selection phase and the project context, such as the familiarities with the OTS component candidate and the importance of the OTS component candidate?

3   Questionnaire Design and Sample Selection

The general questionnaire design, sample definition and selection, and data collection procedures are reported in [4], [7]. This study extended the exploratory study in two dimensions. First, it included OSS components because they represent an alternative to COTS components. Second, this study included much larger samples from three countries - Norway, Italy, and Germany. In addition, the sample was selected randomly instead of by convenience as in the exploratory study.

We have gathered results from 133 projects (47 from Norway, 48 from Germany, and 38 from Italy) from 127 companies. In general, we selected one project from each company. However, we selected more than one projects in three Norwegian IT companies because those companies have many OTS-based projects and would like to share more experience to this study. In the selected 133 projects, 83 used only COTS components, 44 used only OSS components, and six used both COTS and OSS components. Profiles of collected companies and projects are reported in [7].

4 Empirical Results

4.1 RQ1: What Were the OTS Component-Based Development Processes?

The first research question **RQ1** is to investigate the actual development processes used in an OTS-based project. In the questionnaire, we asked the respondents to describe their development process in detail, whereby the answers were then summarized by different categories. The results are summarized in Figure 1 and show that the waterfall, incremental, XP [18], German V-model [19], and prototyping model are those mainly used in practice. Between these, the 'incremental with prototyping' model and XP was the most popular. The German V-model was also used widely in Germany as the OTS-based development process.

4.2 RQ2: When Was the Process Decision Made?

The second research question **RQ2** is to examine whether the actual development process was changed, considering the use of OTS-components. In the questionnaire, we asked the respondents to select whether the actual development process was decided before or after the make vs. acquire decision or after that. The results show that

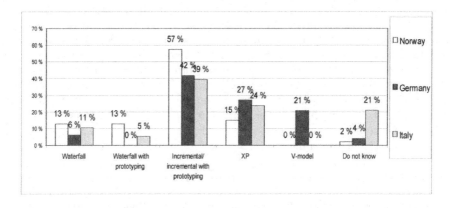

Fig. 1. The actual development process in the OTS-based project

most (75%) projects decided their main development processes *before* they started to think about using OTS-components.

4.3 RQ3: Who Was Responsible for the Process Selection?

The third research question **RQ3** is to identify the decision maker concerning the actual development process. Within the questionnaire, we listed five options, such as company/department rules, project manager, software architect, software developer, and customer. The respondents were asked to select *one or more* from the options. The answers reveal that in 29% of all projects the development process is predefined by global company or department rules. In addition, concerning 14% of the remaining projects the decision was at least affected by company/department rules. This trend is especially obvious in Germany as the company rules dominated the development processes in 65% of our studied projects.

4.4 RQ4: What Was the OTS Component Selection Processes?

The research question **RQ4** is aimed at summarizing the OTS selection and evaluation processes used in practice. Due to the length limitation of the questionnaire, we could not ask the respondents to fill in the details of every OTS component in their projects. Instead, they were asked to select one of the most important OTS components and fill in the details for this component, named **Comp.1**. Information provided for Comp. 1 was then used to investigate RQ5 and RQ6. To answer RQ4, we listed six possible activities as named a) to f) in the questionnaire:

    a. Searched Internet for possible OTS component candidates.
    b. Got recommendation of possible OTS component candidates from the customer.
    c. Got recommendation of possible candidates from a local colleague/OTS-expert.
    d. Used a formal decision-making method to compare possible OTS component candidates, e.g., with weighted evaluation criteria.
    e. Limited possible candidates into 1-3 components, by reading literature/documentation.
    f. Did "hands-on" try-out of 1-3 components, e.g., on a downloaded demo version.

The respondents were asked to fill in "yes", "no", or "do not know" for these options. The results are summarized in Figure 2 and show that activities *a, c, e*, and *f* were those mainly used. Thus, the familiarity-based selection process (activity c) and the Internet search, trial-based selection process (activity a, e and f) from the exploratory study are proved to be more popular than a formal processes (activity d) in general. However, the further analysis with *Chi-square* shows that there are significant differences of the activities *b* and *c* between countries. In Norway and Italy, very few projects used the activity *b*. However, activity *b* was popularly used in Germany. In addition, almost all German projects performed activity *c*, while it was used only in half projects in Norway and Italy.

4.5 RQ5: When Were OTS Components Selected?

From the exploratory study, we concluded that OTS components are selected in different development phases. Thus, research question **RQ5** was postulated to investigate the selection phase of OTS component. The respondents were asked to select one of five phases, ranging from pre-study to coding, as selection time. Figure 3 shows that OTS components were selected in the early stages, such as pre-study, requirement, and overall design, in most projects, especially in Germany.

4.6   RQ6: What Was the Influence of the Project Context?

RQ6 aims at investigating the correlation between the project context and the OTS component selection process. We investigated two project context variables. The first is the project members' familiarity with the Comp.1, measured by a five point Likert scale (i.e. very little, little, some, much, very much). The answers were coded into 1 to 5 (1 means very little and 5 means very much). The second variable is the importance of Comp.1 in the system, measured by the contribution (in %) of 'Comp.1' to the overall system functionality.

First, we investigated the correlation between the two context variables and the phase in which Comp.1 was selected. The selecting phases are treated as an ordinal variable and coded into the values 1 to 5 (1 means the pre-study phase and 5 means the coding phase). The importance of Comp.1 was also treated as an ordinal variable, although it is measured on a continuous scale. We then used the *Spearman correlation* test in SPSS 14.0 to investigate the correlation. The results are shown in Table 1 and reveal that the selection phase of Comp.1 was weakly (with correlation coefficient value -.356) correlated with the project members' familiarity with it. It means that the project members preferred to decide the familiar OTS components in the early stage of the project. However, there is no significant connection between the importance of an OTS component and the phase it was selected.

Second, we investigated the relationship between the two context variables with the selection and evaluation activities performed. Since possible answers on the selection and evaluation activity variable are "yes", "no", or "do not know", we treated the projects with "yes" and "no" answers as two independent samples and then compared the mean differences of the two context variables. For the project

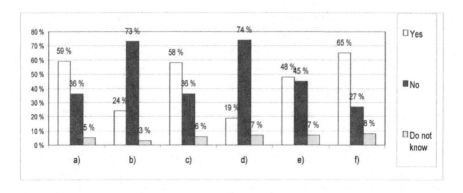

Fig. 2. What selection and evaluation actions were performed?

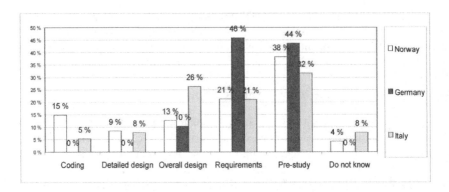

Fig. 3. When was the OTS component selected?

Table 1. The correlation between the selection phase and the context variables

Context variables	What phase was Comp.1 selected	
	Spearman correlation	
Project members' experience with the Comp.1	Correlation Coefficient	-.356
	Sig (2-tailed)	.000*
The importance of the Comp.1	Correlation Coefficient	-.132
	Sig (2-tailed)	.150
* P < .05		

Table 2. The relationship between selection activities and familiarity with the OTS component

Selection activities	Familiarity with Comp.1		
	Mann-Whitney	Z	Asymp. Sig (2-tailed)
a)	1263.000	-2.407	.016*
b)	1072.500	-1.622	.105
c)	1626.500	-1.043	.297
d)	964.000	-.533	.594
e)	1724.500	-.870	.385
f)	1481.500	-.913	.361
(Selection activities a) to f) are explained in Section 4.4)			
* P < .05			

members' familiarity variable, we used the *Mann-Whitney* test in SPSS 14.0 to compare their rank differences. Results, presented in Table 2, show that project members will search the internet for a possible candidate, if there is no proper or familiar candidate at hand.

For the importance of the Comp.1 variable, we used the independent *T-test* in SPSS 14.0 to compare mean differences, whereby the results are shown in Table 3. The overall result is that there is no significant relationship between the selection and evaluation activities performed with the importance of the OTS component.

Table 3. The relationship between the selection activities with the importance the OTS component

Selection activities	Importance of the Comp.1	
	t-test (equal variance not assumed)	Sig (2-tailed)
a)	.379	.706
b)	-.971	.337
c)	.804	.424
d)	-.436	.666
e)	1.543	.126
f)	1.096	.278
(Selection activities a) to f) are explained in Section 4.4) * P < .05		

5   How to Customize the OTS-Based Development Process

Concerning the conclusions drawn in another study [3], we agree that using OTS components in system development is bearing potential danger, especially when using unfamiliar OTS components. Although the risk driven processes proposed in [3] may give benefits, results of **RQ1** show, however, that most projects integrate OTS components successfully with traditional processes, such as waterfall, incremental with prototyping, XP, or V-model. Results of **RQ2** show that most actual development processes were decided before the decision of using OTS components was made. In addition, results of **RQ3** show that company rules pre-defined the main development processes in many OTS-based projects. According to the results of RQ1 to RQ3, we summarize the state-of-the-practice of OTS-based development processes into seven different scenarios. The classification of the scenarios is based on the phase of the make vs. acquire decision and the developers' familiarity with the OTS candidates.

5.1   Scenarios of Planned OTS-Based Software Development

In these scenarios (see Figure 4), project members prefer to evaluate the possibility of using OTS components right from the start. Due to the time-to-market, cost, or capacity issues, project managers realize that it is difficult, impossible, or not cost-effective to make everything from scratch. In these scenarios, the first step is to do a make vs. acquire decision (see step A in Figure 4). In case project members decide not to use OTS components, the development process will be the same as the non-COTS based development. If project members decide to use OTS components, they then need to decide the main development process (see step B in Figure 4). To decide the main development process, main issues are the traditional risks in a project, such as the stability of the requirements. One of the other issues is their familiarity with possible OTS candidates. According to the project members' familiarity with the OTS candidates, we define three scenarios from scenario 1 to 3.

   - *Scenario 1 – planned OTS-based project with unfamiliar OTS candidates.* In this scenario, the project members prefer to use OTS component to provide certain functionalities of the system. However, they are not familiar with the OTS candidate at all. To decide the main development process, the OTS relevant risks, such as the quality of OTS components and the vendor's support, should be seriously considered. In addition, project members should pay attention to other risks, which are not relevant to an OTS component but the overall project (e.g., which process is more suitable for projects with unclear or unstable requirements? Waterfall or an incremental with prototyping' model?).

- *Scenario 2 – planned OTS-based project with some familiar OTS candidates:* In this scenario, the project members have a certain experience on some of the possible OTS candidates. However, there are still certain candidates that they have never used before. In order to decide the main development process, the issues are similar with those of the scenario 1.
- *Scenario 3 – planned OTS-based project with familiar OTS candidates:* In this scenario, the project members are familiar with all possible candidate components. When deciding the main development process the OTS relevant risks are not as critical as in scenario 1 or 2. Other non-OTS relevant factors, such as company rules or requirement flexibility may be used to decide the main development process. In this scenario, the main development process can be any, such as waterfall, incremental, or XP. It may not need to be changed because the project members are very familiar with the OTS component candidates.

In our investigated projects, only 25% can be classified into scenario 1 to 3, because they decided their main development processes *after* they decided to use OTS components. In these projects, 67% can be put into scenario 3, because they used familiar OTS components.

The COTS-based development model in [10] illustrates the differences between COTS-based development and traditional software development, such as new, reduced, or modified activities. The underlying assumption of this model is that the rate or degree of using OTS components is fixed in the very early phases of a project and that the main development process has to be modified accordingly. The model can therefore be used as a reference in scenarios 1 to 3.

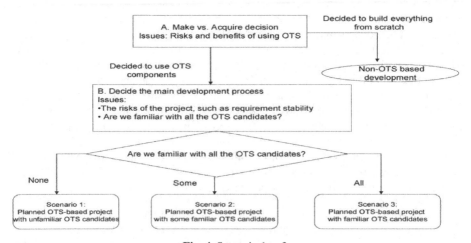

Fig. 4. Scenario 1 to 3

5.2 Scenarios of Unplanned OTS-Based Software Development

In these scenarios (see Figure 5), the decision of using OTS component was not planned or made in advance, i.e. there is no clear intention of using OTS components in the early phases of such a project. Project members decide on the main development process according to some non-OTS relevant factors, such as company rules and requirement stability. Due to the time-to-market pressure or internal capability, project members start to evaluate the possibility of using OTS components at certain stages of the project. At an industrial seminar [17], several industrial participants mentioned such conditions. According to the project members' familiarity with the OTS candidates, we classify three scenarios from scenario 4 to 6.

- *Scenario 4 – Unplanned OTS-based project with unfamiliar OTS candidates:* In this scenario, the project members decided to use OTS components in a late phase of the project, such as detailed design or coding. However, they do not have any previous experience with the possible OTS candidates. Therefore, the use of OTS components may bring several problems for the whole project. They need a second risk-evaluation to investigate whether the development process should be modified concerning the use of OTS components. For example, in projects with pure waterfall processes, the project members may need to add a short prototyping step to evaluate the OTS component and to negotiate the use of OTS component with their customer.

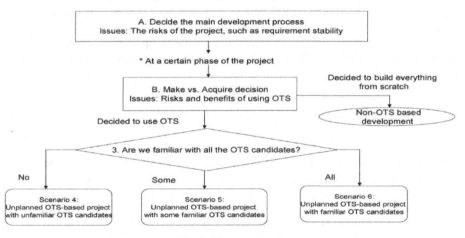

Fig. 5. Scenario 4 to 6

- *Scenario 5 – Unplanned OTS-based project with some familiar OTS candidates:* In this scenario, the project members decided to use OTS components in a late phase. However, they do not have previous experience with all OTS component candidates. In order to decide the main development process, the issues are similar with those of scenario 4.
- *Scenario 6 – Unplanned OTS-based project with familiar OTS candidates:* In this scenario, although the project members decided to use OTS components in a late development phase, they have enough experience on the OTS

component candidates or are able to hire a person with such experience. In case the project members have used the OTS component many times before, the OTS component can be regarded as comparable to in-house built components. Although the use of OTS component is a little risky due to the same reasons as described in scenarios 4 and 5, this scenario is less risky because of using familiar OTS components. It may not be necessary to do major changes to the current development process.

In our studied project, about 75% of them can be classified into scenario 4 to 6, because they decided their main development processes before they started to think about using OTS components. In these projects, 65% used familiar OTS components and therefore can be classified into scenario 6.

5.3 The Scenario of Semi-planned OTS-Based Software Development

This scenario is a mix of scenarios 1, 2, or 3 with scenarios 4, 5 or 6, whereby the use of OTS components is planned for some parts of the system. The main development process is decided according to the use of OTS components. However, in a late phase of the project, the project member may need to add some unplanned OTS component due to the same reasons as scenario 4, 5, or 6.

The EPIC approach [1], like the RUP, consists of four phases and each phase consists of one or more EPIC iterations. The information of four *spheres of influences*, such as stakeholders' needs, architecture design, risk, and marketplace, was gathered and evaluated in each iteration. The project management, customer requirements, and system architecture will be adjusted according to the trade-offs of the four *spheres of influences*. Since every iteration includes a complete sub-process to make the trade-off decision and select the OTS component, it is more flexible and suitable to be used as a reference in scenarios 4 to 7.

6 How to Select the OTS Components

The results of this study support our conclusion in the exploratory study [6], and shows that the familiarity-based and internet search-based processes are frequently used in practice. The results also confirm that OTS component selection can be performed in different development phases (requirements, design, or implementation), depending on the project context, especially on the familiarity with possible OTS components, and/or the flexibility of requirements [6]. In addition, results show project members aim at reusing familiar OTS components and selecting them in early phases. In our study, we measured the importance of an OTS component by their contribution on the functionality of the system. Although the results show no correlation between the OTS component's importances with the phase it was selected, we still suggest project members to select OTS in the earlier phases, especially if the OTS component has a tight coupling with other components.

In different scenarios shown in Section 5, different OTS component selection strategies and processes can be used. In scenarios 1, 2, 4, 5, and 7, some unfamiliar OTS component candidates are going to be used. The selection process for unfamiliar OTS components can either be an internet search with hand-on trial-based, or a formal selection process, such as processes shown in [5], [8], [9], [11], [13], [14]. In scenarios 3 and 6, all possible OTS component candidates have been used by the project members, the selection process could mainly be familiarity-based.

In scenarios 1 to 3, the use of OTS component is well-planned. In general, the OTS component will be selected in the early phase of the project in these scenarios. Selecting OTS component in the early phase can help to design the software architecture with consideration on constrains of the OTS components. Therefore, it is easier to avoid the mismatch between the OTS components and other components in the system.

In scenarios 4 to7, the OTS components are usually be evaluated at a phase which most of the other components are already integrated in the system. Since the goal is to integrate the OTS component into the current system and to check its integration thoroughly, integrate the demo version of the OTS component and do a hand-on trial is necessary. In case the OTS component was selected in the very late stage of the project, it is better to select a component that has a loose coupling with the other components. OTS components tightly coupled with existing components may impose a high number of changes onto the system.

7 Threats to Validity

To avoid possible threats to the construct validity of this study, we performed a pre-test to verify the questionnaire. In addition, we use a lot of effort to ensure the representative of the sample. Detailed discussion on other validities issue of this study are reported at [4], [7].

8 Conclusion and Future Work

This paper has presented a state-of-the-practice survey on the process issues in OTS-based development. We have studied 133 projects from Norway, Italy, and Germany. The main findings are:

1. The actual OTS-based development process was the traditional process with OTS-specific activities. The development process was dominated by the company/department rule instead of the decision of using OTS components.
2. The actual OTS component selection can be done in different phases. The main evaluation processes are familiarity-based or Internet search with hands-on-trial-based. The phase to select OTS component has relationship with the project members' familiarity.
3. The proposed software development process and OTS component selection process need further investigation to be suited to different project contexts.

The main limitation of this study is that it is a state-of-the-practice survey. We are going to perform more detailed case studies to get detailed information in projects with different contexts. The intention is to deepen our understanding the process improvement in OTS component-based development and to verify our proposals.

References

1. Albert, C. and Brownsword, L.: Evolutionary Process for Integrating COTS-Based System (EPIC): An Overview. Software Engineering Institute, Pittsburgh, (2002), http://www.sei.cmu.edu/publications/documents/02.reports/02tr009.html.
2. Brownsword, L., Oberndorf, T., and Sledge, C.: Developing New Processes for COTS-Based Systems. IEEE Software, July/August (2000), 17(4):48-55.
3. Boehm, B. W. and Abts, C.: COTS integration: Plug and Pray? IEEE Computer, Jan. (1999), 32(1):135-138.
4. Conradi, R., Li, J., Slyngstad, O. P. N., Bunse, C., Torchiano, M., and Morisio, M.: Reflections on Conducting an International CBSE Survey in ICT Industry. Proc. of the 4th Int. Symposium on Empirical Software Engineering, Noosa Heads, Australia, Nov. (2005) 207-216.
5. Kontio, J.: A Case Study in Applying a Systematic Method for COTS Selection. Proc. of the 18th Int. Conf. on Software Engineering, Berlin, Germany, March (1996) 201-209.
6. Li, J., Bjørnson, F. O., Conradi, R. and Kampenes, V. B.: An Empirical Study of Variations in COTS-based Software Development Processes in Norwegian IT Industry. Proc. of the 10th IEEE Int. Metrics Symposium (Metrics'04), Chicago, USA, Sept. (2004) 72-83.
7. Li, J., Conradi, R., Slyngstad, O. P. N., Bunse, C., Khan, U., Torchiano, M., and Morisio, M.: Validation of New Theses on Off-The-Shelf Component Based Development. Proc. of the 11th IEEE Int. Metrics Symposium (Metrics'05), Como, Italy, Sept. (2005) 26.
8. Tran, V., Liu, D. B., and Hummel, B.: Component Based Systems Development: Challenges and Lessons Learned. Proc. of the 8th IEEE Int. Workshop on Software Technology and Engineering Practice, London, UK, (1997) 452-462.
9. MacCrimmon, K. R.: An Overview of Multiple Objective Decision Making. Proc. of the Multiple Criteria Decision Making, University of South Carolina Press, (1973) 18-44.
10. Morisio, M., Seaman, C.B., Parra, A. T., Basili, V. R., Kraft, S. E., and Condon, S. E.: Investigating and Improving a COTS-Based Software Development Process. Proc. of the 22nd Int. Conf. on Software Engineering, Limerick, Ireland, June (2000) 31-40.
11. Morisio, M. and Tsoukias, A.: IusWare: a Methodology for the Evaluation and Selection of Software Products. IEE Proceedings-Software Engineering, June (1997), 144(3):162-174.
12. Ncube, C. and Dean, J. C.: The Limitation of Current Decision-Making Techniques in the Procurement of COTS Software Components. Proc. of the 1st Int. Conf. on COTS-Based Software Systems (ICCBSS'02), Orlando, FL, USA, Feb. (2002), LNCS Vol. 2255, Springer-Verlag Berlin Heidelberg New York 176-187.
13. Ochs, M., Pfahl, D., Diening, G. C., and Kolb, B. N.: A Method for Efficient Measurement-based COTS Assessment and Selection - Method Description and Evaluation Results. Proc. of the 7th IEEE Int. Software Metrics Symposium, London, England, Apr. (2001) 285-297.
14. Saaty, T. L.: How to Make a Decision: The Analytic Hierarchy Process (AHP). European Journal of Operational Research, (1990), 48(1): 9-26.
15. SEI COTS-Based Initiative Description. Software Engineering Institute, Pittsburgh, (2004), http://www.sei.cmu.edu/cbs/cbs_description.html
16. Torchiano, M. and Morisio, M.: Overlooked Facts on COTS-based Development. IEEE Software, March/April (2004), 21(2):88-93.
17. Li, J. Conradi, R. Slyngstad, O. P. N., Bunse, C., Khan, U., Torchiano, M., and Morisio, M.: Barriers to Disseminating Off-The-Shelf Based Development Theories to IT Industry. Proc. of the ICSE2005/MPEC workshop, St. Louis, Missouri, USA, May (2005), 1-4.
18. Kent, B.: Extreme Programming Explained: Embrace Change. (1999) Addison-Wesley.
19. German V-model: http://www.v-modell.iabg.de/#AU250

Automating Integration of Heterogeneous COTS Components

Wenpin Jiao and Hong Mei

Institute of Software, School of Electronics Engineering and Computer Science
Peking University, Beijing 100871, China
jwp@sei.pku.edu.cn, meih@pku.edu.cn

Abstract. Mismatches make COTS components difficult to be incorporated. In this paper, an approach is presented to eliminate mismatches among COTS components, which can truly consider COTS components as black boxes. In the approach, only the assembly description of components is required, based on which adaptors for resolving mismatches can be generated automatically. This paper also described an agent-based GUI implementation of the approach.

1 Introduction

Appropriate use of commercial-off-the-shelf products (i.e., COTS) is one of the remedies that might enable developers to acquire needed capabilities in a cost effective manner, and easy usage of COTS to interoperate properly within applications is crucial for component-based software systems.

Currently, many existing commercial component-oriented platforms address the interoperability of component-based software by using Interface Description Languages (IDL). However, in component composition using a specific configuration, mismatches may occur when the assumptions that a component makes about other components, or the rest of the system, do not match [16]. Even if the functionalities of components are matched and signature problems are overcome, the components are not assured of interoperating suitably.

First, at the component level, because of the ordering of exchanged messages and of blocking conditions [19], the mismatching interaction protocols may result in different behaviors of components. For instance, the order of messages exchanged and the sizes of data blocks transmitted between components may be different.

Second, at the architecture level, components at hand are usually supposed to support specified architectural styles and they may not interoperate properly in software systems with constraints of other architectural styles [8][15]. For example, components to be integrated based on method invocation may not be suitable to be directly integrated into software systems using the event-based architectural style.

Third, at the application domain level, COTS components are often involved in different naming spaces and the names for the same data entities may be discrepant.

Ideally, for integrating heterogeneous COTS components, approaches should at least satisfy the following requirements.

M. Morisio (Ed.): ICSR 2006, LNCS 4039, pp. 29–42, 2006.
© Springer-Verlag Berlin Heidelberg 2006

- Resolve naming and structuring discrepancies among interoperating components due to different ontologies of application domains;
- Enable components specific to different architectural styles to interact; and
- Incorporate components with mismatching interaction protocols.

In this paper, we adopt an agent-based approach to integrating heterogeneous COTS components. The main contributions of the paper are as follows.

We put forward an approach to incorporating COTS components with mismatches at different levels. Our approach neither limits the number of incorporating COTS components nor requires knowing any detailed information about what interaction protocols COTS components are supposed to support so that COTS components can truly be considered as black boxes in integrations.

Second, we describe an automated way to generate adaptors for resolving mismatches at interaction protocol level. By using the generated adaptors, data block mismatches and message-ordering mismatches can be eliminated automatically if components are incorporable.

Third, we present an agent-based implementation of the approach, in which agents can resolve the architectural style mismatches via transforming style specific interactions into uniform ACL (agent communication language) based communications and can automatically remove deadlocks potentially occurring in the interactions of COTS components even if components are not incorporable.

In the following context, Section 2 discusses the incorporability of COTS components and describes methods for eliminating mismatches involved in different levels. Section 3 and 4 describes the agent-based approach and its implementation, respectively. Section 5 discusses some related work and concludes our work.

2 Elimination of Mismatches

In our opinions, the premise that components can interact is that names can properly be mapped between input data and output data and interactions can be transformed from one architectural style specific to another style specific.

Definition 1. *Incorporability.* Components are *incorporable* if they satisfy the following conditions.

1. There is a name mapping, in which all input data entities (including their internal ingredient) imported by components are imaged (mapped) to output data entities exported by other components.
2. All style specific interactions can be transformed between different styles.
3. After names are properly translated and style specific interactions are well transformed, the components are *compatible* at the protocol level.

Nevertheless, it is very difficult to obtain the semantics of names and infer the mapping between names automatically even though there have been some ontology tools to specify names formally (e.g., [17]).

In addition, COTS components are usually only documented with the usage syntax of their interfaces when they are released, whereas architectural styles that COTS components are supposed to support are generally not specified explicitly.

Therefore, in this paper, we put forward the notation of *assembly* for specifying the interconnections of components, which describes the name mapping that components use to transmit data along interconnection links, the architectural styles that components support, and the intentions that components set up the interconnections.

By using the specifications of assemblies among components, we can implement an automated approach to resolving name conflicts and transforming mismatching architectural interactions.

2.1 Assembly Description of Components

In general, people know little about the interaction protocols of COTS components. To provide a generic solution for incorporating COTS components, we will not make additional assumptions about the information exposed by COTS components.

To describe the assembly of COTS components, we should first know what COTS components participate in the assembly. For example, an assembly involving a component playing the role of user and another component implementing the server can be described as follows.

```
<Assembly>
    <COTS name="User" />
    <COTS name="Server" />
</Assembly>
```

Then we need (and just need) know how COTS components are interconnected. In our opinions, connections among components are links for transporting data for different *purposes*, for instance, requesting services or calling methods. We assume that each connection is only used for unilateral data transportation. For each connection, there involve at least one source component and just one destination component and there is an *intention* (or purpose) of establishing the connection. In the establishment of a connection, the architectural style to which the source component is specific may be different from that of the destination component.

For example, the user sends a message containing *"username"*, *"email"* and *"password"* to authenticate itself to the server. Meanwhile, the server calls procedure *"authUsr(usr, pwd)"* to authenticate the legality of the user and returns *"yes"* for successful authentication or else the reason for failed authentication (fig. 1).

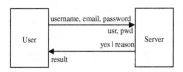

Fig. 1. Assembly of Components

In the assembly, there are two connections, one transports {*"username"*, *"email"*, *"password"*} for calling *"authUsr(usr, pwd)"* and the other returns the authentication result. In the figure, arrows represent data links through which upside data block is sent from the end to the head whilst the underside is being expected at the head. The connections between the two components can be described in the XML as follows.

```
<Assembly>
  <Connection>
    <connection-id> C_ID1 </connection-id>
      <source>
        <component-name> C1 </component-name>
        <data-block name = "D1",
            type = struct {username, email, password}/>
        <style> message-based </style>
      </source>
      <destination>
        <component-name> C2 </component-name>
        <data-block name = "usr", type = String />
        <data-block name = "pwd", type = String />
        <style> procedure-call </style>
      </destination>
      <intention>
        <signature-ref> authUsr(usr, pwd)
        </signature-ref>
      </intention>
      <data-item-mapping>
        <mapping  "C1.D1.username", "C2.usr" />
        <mapping  "C1.D1.password", "C2.pwd" />
      </data-item-mapping>
  </Connection>
  <!-- other connections -->
</Assembly>
```

Each connection has a unique identity. Within a connection, there is more than one *source* section. Each source section is related to a component and describes the data block(s) exported by the component. Differently, there is only one *destination* section that specifies the data block(s) imported to a destination component. In each source or destination section, the architectural style used to export or import the data block(s) is also required to be specified.

The *intention* section specifies what action the destination component will take after it receives the data exported by the source component(s). The intention can be specified via directly referencing a signature defined in the component's interface, for instance, "*authUsr(usr, pwd)*".

The *mapping* section specifies how exported data items will be used as imported data items. In principle, for all expected (*i.e.*, imported) data, there should exist the corresponding data exported from the sources (or else default values should be offered). Contrarily, for an exported data, it may not be expected by the destination so there may not exist a corresponding imported data.

2.2 Compatibility of Components

As mentioned above, two components are considered to be interoperable if they are compatible after naming discrepancies and architectural style mismatches have been resolved. Furthermore, we say components are *compatible* if the executions of all input actions occurring in the interactions are guaranteed, *i.e.*, components can obtain all of the required data (or arguments) before they provide services and can gain the results after they request services.

We can specify the interactions among components by using directed graphs, in which actions are nodes and arcs represent orders of actions. For any action, arcs fanning out from it will fan into other actions that should (or will) take place after it. According to the graph theory, we can prove that components are compatible if there is at least one action without fan-in arcs whenever actions happen in the interactions among the components.

In our definition, we do not restrict the incorporability to be related to only two components. In addition, we assume that components are distributed on different sites and there are no troubles with sharing resources. Therefore, the occurrences of deadlocks are merely due to interactions instead of resource contention.

Theorem 1. If components are incorporable, there must exist an additional component (*e.g.*, adaptor) that can incorporate the components together, *i.e.*, the adaptor can eliminate the data block mismatches and interaction protocol mismatches occurring in the interactions of the components.

We will not prove the theorem due to the space limitation. Anywhere, adaptors can automatically be generated for incorporating components.

Assume that naming conflicts and architectural style mismatches have been resolved by using the assembly specifications. Then the main tasks of the adaptor for incorporating two components include 1) resolving data block mismatches and 2) removing deadlocks occurring in the interactions.

To resolve the data block mismatches, we adopts a strategy by which the adaptor disassembles intercepted data blocks exported from source components into atomic data items (*i.e.*, the atomic ingredients of the data block) and re-assembles related atomic data items into expected data blocks imported by destination components.

To remove the deadlocks caused by synchronizations, we adopt a strategy using the message buffer that can be accessed randomly and concurrently.

Suppose the name mapping among components P_1, ..., P_n, is $\mathcal{M}$. Then, the adaptor can be divided into three parts.

1. *Disassembler.* Intercept data exported by components, disassemble it into atomic ingredients, and then rename them, for instance, d to $\mathcal{M}(d)$.
2. *Buffer.* Buffer the intercepted and disassembled data on one hand and then wait for the *Assembler* to take away the data.
3. *Assembler.* Transfer the buffered data to components that are importing data. To meet a component's expectation for data, the adaptor first obtains data ingredients from the buffer, then assembles them into the expected data block and at last transmits the block to the component.

The adaptor is actually defined as a composition of parallel finite automatons (FA). Corresponding to every export action occurring in the assembly, there is an FA generated, in which steps are states and actions are labels causing the interaction transiting from one step to another step.

For example, there are two components $P=\{-(a), +(b), -(c)\}$ and $Q=\{-(b), +(a, c)\}$, in which +/- represents data input/output (fig. 2a). Obviously, there is a data block mismatch and a deadlock between P and Q if the collaborative input/output actions should be synchronized. The adaptor will be generated for incorporating the two components as shown in fig. 2b.

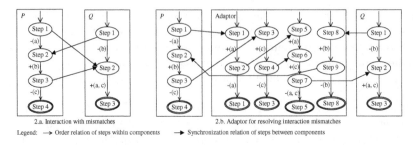

2.a. Interaction with mismatches   2.b. Adaptor for resolving interaction mismatches

Legend: ⟶ Order relation of steps within components   ⟶ Synchronization relation of steps between components

Fig. 2. Resolving Protocol Mismatches

According to the above description, for any export action occurring in the assembly, there must be a collaborative import action in the adaptor to accept the data coming from the source component and transmit the data into the buffer implemented in the adaptor. On the other hand, for any imported data block, if its ingredients have been buffered in the adaptor when the corresponding import action is going to fetch the data block, the import action will not be blocked. Therefore, if components involved in the assembly are incorporable they will be able to be incorporated properly via the adaptor.

As shown in the above example, because there is always at least one export action taking place during the interactions between P and Q, the deadlock is removable by using the adaptor (fig. 2b).

However, when components are not incorporable, deadlocks will be irremovable by just using the generated adaptors. For example, suppose $P=\{+(a), -(b)\}$ and $Q=\{+(b), -(a)\}$, there is a deadlock between P and Q and the adaptor cannot remove it because all finite automatons in the adaptor begin with import actions, too. To remedy this limitation, we will discuss how to implement agents to discover and remove deadlocks in the next section besides describing how to use agents to incorporate components.

3   Incorporation Using Agents

To resolve the mismatches between COTS components, we need adequate semantic information about components and their interactions so that we could transform style specific interactions (SSI) into homogeneous communications and could use name mappings for generating adaptors automatically. Therefore, we adopt an agent-based approach to implementing adaptors to incorporate COTS components.

In a distributed computing environment, it will be unacceptable to implement centralized adaptors to incorporate COTS components. A reasonable way is to resolve the mismatches locally and then interconnect COTS components together.

In our approach, the adaptor to incorporate components is partitioned into parts and each part is locally attached to a component and takes charge of the component's interactions. The responsibilities of the part at component P's side include:

1.   Disassemble data blocks coming from P and send them out.
2.   Buffer data received from other components.
3.   Assemble data ingredients into expected blocks and forward them to P.

The architecture by using agents to implement adaptors and incorporate distributed COTS components can be depicted as follows (fig. 3), in which agents are locally attached to the COTSs at the same sides.

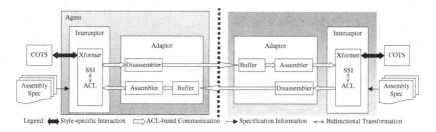

Legend: ◀▶ Style-specific Interaction   ⇨ACL-based Communication   ➔ Specification Information   ⟷ Bidirectional Transformation

Fig. 3. Architecture for Incorporation of COTS

The interceptors are responsible for 1) intercepting style specific interactions of components, transforming into ACL messages and forwarding to the adaptors, and inversely 2) receiving ACL messages from other agents, transforming into style specific interactions and interacting with the components. In addition, the interceptors are also in charge of 3) obtaining the specifications of the assembly, including the architectural styles and name mappings, and providing the agents for generating the adaptors automatically.

The adaptors take charges of taking actions specified in the finite automatons, which has been transformed into ACL-based communications.

As most agents do, our agents also use the FIPA ACL [14] as the agent communication language. In general, most of interactions among COTS components are to transport the values of variables. "*inform-ref*" and "*forward*" are two of the most frequently used performatives. "*inform-ref*" indicates a macro-action for the sender to inform the receiver the value that corresponds to a referential expression; whilst "*forward*" is used for the sender to ask the receiver to forward a message to another agent.

For example, an action involved in a connection is to send data block *d* from *P* to *Q*, then the ACL message corresponding to the action can be expressed as follows.

```
(inform-ref :sender P :receiver Q
      :content (Connection-Identity, d, value of d))
```

For convenience, we name the interceptor and the adaptor at *P*'s side as *interceptorP* and *adaptorP*, respectively.

For transforming architectural style-specific interactions and executing the adaptors, the agents will generate and trigger corresponding rules according to the specification of the assembly.

3.1 Transforming Style-Specific Interaction

To guarantee the transformation automated, we assume that any exported data is sent out for a unique intention. Thus, whenever an interceptor captures data out from a source component according to the architectural style supported by the source component, it can definitely make out where the data will be transmitted and what the component intents to do.

To transform bi-directionally between style-specific interactions and ACL based communications, interceptors use a group of rules.

When an interceptor locating at the source component side captures an exported data block from the component, it will trigger the following transformation rule.

```
Export action perceived → {
    1. Extract the data block transported by the export
       action;
    2. Retrieve the data block in the assembly specifi-
       cation and locate the connection in which the
       export action is involved;
    3. Compose an ACL message to forward the data block
       to the destination component via the adaptor.}
```

For example, suppose *interceptorP* perceives an export action of *P*, which is involved in connection *C* and is sending data *D* to *Q*. The corresponding ACL message is constructed as follows.

```
(Forward :sender interceptorP :to adaptorQ
    :receiver adaptorP :content <C, D, value of D>)
```

When an interceptor locating at the destination component side receives an ACL message from the adaptor, it will trigger the following transformation rule.

```
ACL message received → {
    1. Extract the data block and the connection iden-
       tity transmitted along with the ACL message;
    2. Obtain the intention of the connection via look-
       ing up the assembly specification;
    3. Take actions to realize the intention by using
       the received data according to the architectural
       style supported by the destination component.}
```

For example, suppose the intention is to call a procedure using the received data as arguments. Then the interceptor will make an invocation of the procedure.

3.2 Executing Adaptors

Since adaptors are composed of a group of parallel finite automatons, we implement adaptors using multiple threads, in which each FA is executed via a thread and controlled by a group of rules.

For an FA disassembling data, the corresponding thread uses the following rule.

```
ACL message from an interceptor received → {
    1. Extract the data block transported along with
       the message;
    2. Disassemble the data block into ingredients and
       rename them according to the name mapping speci-
       fied in the connection;
    3. Package every ingredient into an ACL messages
       and send it out sequentially.}
```

For example, when *adaptorP* receives the above message, it will first disassemble *D* and then transmit *D*'s ingredients to *adaptorQ* sequentially.

```
(Forward :sender adaptorP :to interceptorQ
    :receiver adaptorQ :content <C, M(D), value of D >)
```

For an FA assembling data, the corresponding thread uses the following rules.

```
D's ingredient is buffered in the adaptor's buffer → {
    1. Extract the ingredient from the ACL message.}
All of D's ingredients are obtained → {
    1. Assemble the ingredients;
    2. Generate an ACL message containing the data
       block and send it to the interceptor.}
```

For example, when *adaptorQ* receives a data block, it will generate the following message.

```
(Inform-ref :sender adaptorQ :receiver interceptorQ
    :content <C, D, value of D >)
```

For the FA buffering ingredients, the adaptor will also implement an independent thread to receive ACL messages and store them temporarily in a message buffer.

3.3 Removing Deadlocks

As we have mentioned that adaptors cannot remove all kinds of deadlocks. Therefore, we had to seek help from agents.

Since all FAs in adaptors begin with import actions, the interactions among components run into deadlocks must be because all actions currently occurring among components are import actions, too. Therefore, once agents find that they do not receive any messages for a while in the following situations, they can assert that there may be deadlocks occurring in the interactions.

1. An adaptor is blocked during accepting data ingredients in an FA assembling data block.
2. For some connection, the adaptors have not ever received any related data.

In both cases, the source components may be blocked so it cannot provide data for the destination component smoothly. In principle, a source component is blocked must be because it is also a destination component involved in another connection. Therefore, to break a deadlock (in fact, a waiting cycle), we need only let a component involved in the deadlock obtain what it is waiting for to force the component to get out from the waiting cycle. To achieve this, the agents will simulate source components to generate blank data blocks so that some destination component would not be stalled.

4 Implementation of the Agent-Based Approach

To make the description of the implementation more easily understandable, we first describe an application system as follows.

The system is designated to manage the dormitory information of students. When a new student is enrolled, the system should allot an accommodation to the newcomer, and while a student leaves, the system should de-allot the accommodation. In the system, there are two tables involved: one records the information about students and the other about the dormitories. These two tables are associated as follows (fig. 4).

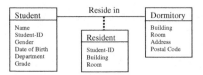

Fig. 4. Association between Students and Dormitories

There are four distributed COTS components available for constructing the system:

- A general-purpose table editor. The editor is an executable program that implements a GUI to edit relational data tables, including inserting new and deleting old records. The usage of the editor is specified as follows.

  ```
  EDITOR <table-name>
  ```

- A general-purpose table manipulator. It is implemented as a procedure and can be called to update relational data tables, including inserting new and deleting old records. The signature of the manipulator is specified as follows:

  ```
  void MANIPULATOR(String table_name, String re-
  cord_value, Integer operation);
  ```

  record_value contains the values of all fields of a record of the table, in which each field is a fixed length of string. *operation* indicates what manipulation the procedure will do, for example, *updating*, *inserting*, or *deleting* a record.

- A domain-specific procedure for allotting the dormitory to a newcome student according to the newcomer's *gender*, *department*, and *grade*. The dormitory information consists of the *building* and the *room* number.

  ```
  void ALLOTTER(String student_id, Integer gender,
  String department, Integer grade,String
  *building_no, String *room_no);
  ```

- A domain-specific console. The console browses information about students and their accommodations and calls *Editor* to edit students' information.

In the system, there are four interconnection links among these components:

1. *Console **calls** Editor* to enroll (or de-enroll) students.
2. When *Editor* inserts a record into *Student* table (a student is enrolled), *Allotter* will be **triggered** to allot an accommodation to the student.
3. After *Allotter* finishes the computation of allotting the accommodation, *Manipulator* will be **called** to insert a record into *Resident* table to store the accommodation information.
4. When *Editor* deletes a record (a student leaves), *Manipulator* will be **triggered** to remove the related accommodation from *Resident* table.

Among these connections, interaction 1 and 3 are *procedure-call based* while connection 2 and 4 are *event-based* and the architectural styles supported by the interactions are mismatched with the styles supposed by the COTS components.

For implementing the system via integrating COTS components, we developed a GUI (fig. 5) in the Java on the Borland JBuilder^{tm} platform to draw the assembly and generate the XML-based assembly specification. The GUI will also generate source codes for agent-based adaptors automatically. An adaptor is instantiated from an agent framework conformed to the FIPA specification [14], which integrates a rule engine for Java platform, Drools [9], using the Rete [13] algorithm to process rules.

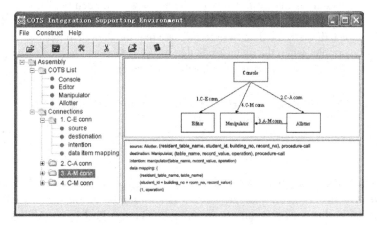

Fig. 5. GUI of the COTS Integration Environment

After the assembly is specified, the resource codes of agent-based adaptors can be generated automatically. For each connection, two agents are generated and reside separately beside the two connected components. For each agent, it will intercept interactions of its host component and resolve the mismatches of interactions.

For example, in the connection between *Allotter* and *Manipulator* (*i.e.*, the *A-M conn*), *Allotter* will call *Manipulator* after it finishes the computation of allotting the accommodation. Because *Allotter* will offer data items such as *table name*, *student id*, *building number* and *room number* separately, which are different from the parameters required by *Manipulator*, when it tries to call *Manipulator*, *Manipulator* syntactically cannot be called. By using the intentions and the data item mappings specified in the connection specification, the GUI can generate agents for eliminating mismatching interactions between *Allotter* and *Manipulator*. For example, the GUI will generate the code segments for the agent locating at the side of *Manipulator* as follows, in which each segment may correspond to a behavior rule of the agent.

1. Define a collection of Boolean variables corresponding to those expected data items. For example, if *Manipulator* is waiting for the table name, define *table_name_received* to record the state of the receival of the table name.

2. Initialize these Boolean variables. Initially, these variables are assigned with *false*. However, if an expected data item is provided with a default value in the name mapping section in the assembly specification, assign the corresponding Boolean variable with *true*.

```
table_name_received = false;
student_id_received = false;
building_no_received = false;
room_no_received = false;
operation_received = true;
```

3. Wait for data items from *Allotter*. The agent will frequently poll the buffer to find out whether an expected data item arrives. Once the agent receives a data item, it will mark the data item to indicate that the data item has been received. For example, when the agent finds that an ACL message in the buffer contains the *table name*, it will execute the following statements.

```
msg = getACLMessage();
if (msg.sender = "allotter") {
    item_name = msg.getDataItemName();
    if (item_name = "resident_table_name") {
        table_name_received=true;
        resident_table_name=msg.getDataItemValue();}}
```

4. Assemble data items into data blocks according to the name mapping if all data items received, and then call *Manipulator* based on the procedure-call style. In this code segment, *operation* is assigned with 1 by the GUI automatically though *Allotter* does not send any value of *operation* out.

```
if (table_name_received && student_id_received &&
    building_no_received && room_no_received &&
    operation_received) {
    table_name = resident_table_name;
    record_value = student_id+building_no+room_no;
    operation = 1;
    manipulator(table_name, record_value, opertion);}
```

After the agents are generated, they will behave as follows.

1. When *Console* tries to *call Editor* to enroll or de-enroll students, the agent residing beside *Editor* will capture the calling and fork a new process to *execute Editor*.

2. When *Editor* inserts a new student record into *Student* table, *Console* will dispatch an *event* out to notify that a new student is enrolled. When the agent along with *Allotter* captures the event, it will first *call Allotter* to allot an accommodation for the student and then *call Manipulator* to store the accommodation information into *Resident* table.

3. When *Editor* deletes a student record from *Student* table, *Console* will dispatch an *event* out to notify that a student leaves. And then, when the agent along with *Manipulator* captures the event, it will *call Manipulator* to remove the related accommodation information from *Resident* table.

5   Related Work and Conclusions

To eliminate mismatches among COTS components, people usually implement wrappers or adaptors while integrating them [12]. For instance, [4] and [10] explore means of implementing connectors to wrap and integrate components. [2] defines connectors as glue to connect components. [19] formally introduced the notion of adaptor as a software entity capable of letting two components with mismatching behaviors interoperate. In [5], a methodology is defined for the automatic development of adaptors. In [6], an adapter is presented to isolate, encapsulate, and manage a component's interactions outside the component.

Meanwhile, some formal approaches are presented for detecting interaction mismatches [7][15], and some techniques are proposed for dealing with architectural mismatches by means of analysis [8], removal [12] and tolerating [18]. In [3], an architectural approach is described for detection and recovery of incompatible interactions by synthesizing a suitable coordinator.

In addition, [11] presents an integration framework for adding notification and data synchronization facilities to COTS tools so that they can be integrated as active software components.

However, existing work is usually focused on behavior mismatches at the component level, whilst some coping with architectural level mismatches are mainly concerned with those special architectural constraints, called conceptual features [1]. Moreover, many approaches mainly discussed how two COTS components could be incorporated or one COTS component could be integrated into a system.

In this paper, we presented a very simple approach to incorporating COTS components with mismatches at different levels. To incorporate COTS components, we need only ask to provide the assembly description of COTS components, which specifies what interaction connections exist among components and why components build those connections. Based on the assembly specification, adaptors for resolving mismatches among components can be generated automatically.

Nevertheless, in our approach there are still limitations to be overcome in our future work.

First, we have assumed that every exported data was created for only one intention in an assembly.

Second, our approach will generate two agents for each connection. When the number of connections becomes larger, the scalability of the system may be affected because of a large number of agents generated. At the next stage, we will conduct more experiments to examine and improve the scalability of our approach.

Third, the transformations between style specific interactions and ACL messages are *ad hoc* implemented in agents. In the future, we will explore how to build the ontology of software architecture so that agents can make transformations automatically based on the understanding to the ontology.

Acknowledgements

This work is partially sponsored by the National Basic Research Program of China (973) (Grant No. 2002CB312003), the National Natural Science Foundation of China

(Grant No. 60233010, 60303004, and 90412011), and the National High-Tech Research and Development Program of China (863) (Grant No.2005AA112030).

References

1. Abd-Allah, A. Composing Heterogeneous Software Architectures, Doctoral Dissertation, Center for Software Engineering, University of Southern California (1996)
2. Allen, R., Douence, R., and Garlan, D. Specifying and Analyzing Dynamic Software Architectures. In Proceedings of 1998 Conference on Fundamental Approach to Software Engineering, LNCS 1382 (1998) 21-37
3. Autili, M., Inverardi, P., Tivoli, M. and Garlan, D. Synthesis of "correct" adaptors for protocol enhancement in component-based systems. Proceedings of SAVCBS'04 Workshop at ESEC/FSE (2004)
4. Balzer, R. and Goldman, N. Mediating Connectors. Proceedings of the 19th IEEE International Conference on Distributed Computing Systems (1999) 73-77
5. Bracciali, A., Brogi, A., and Canal, C. Systematic component adaptation. Electronic Notes in Theoretical Computer Science, 66(4) (2002)
6. Chiang, C.C. The use of adapters to support interoperability of components for reusability. Information and Software Technology, Vol.45, No.3 (2003) 149-156(8)
7. Compare, D., Inverardi, P., and Wolf, A. L. Uncovering architectural mismatch in component behavior. Science of Computer Programming, 33(2) (1999) 101–131
8. Davis, L., Gamble, R.F., Payton, J. The impact of component architectures on interoperability. Journal of Systems and Software 61(11) (2002) 31-45
9. Drools. http://drools.org/.
10. Ducasse, S. and Richner, T. Executable connectors: Towards reusable design elements. In ACM Foundations of Software Engineering, LNCS 1301. Springer (1997) 483–500
11. Egyed, A. and Balzer, R. Integrating COTS Software into Systems through Instrumentation and Reasoning. Automated Software Engineering, Vol.13, No.1 (2006) 41-64
12. Egyed, A., Medvidovic, N., and Gacek, C. Component-based perspective on software mismatch detection and resolution. IEE Proc.-Softw., 147(6) (2000) 225-236
13. Forgy, C.L. Rete: A Fast Algorithm for the Many Pattern/ Many Object Pattern Match Problem, Artificial Intelligence 19 (1982) 17-37
14. Foundation for Intelligent Physical Agents, http://www.fipa.org.
15. Gacek, C. Detecting Architectural Mismatches During Systems Composition---An Extension to the AAA Model. Technical Report USC/CSE-97-TR-502, Center for Software Engineering, University of Southern California (1997)
16. Garlan, D., Allen, R., and Ockerbloom, J. Architectural mismatch: Why reuse is so hard. IEEE Software, 12(6) (1995) 17–26
17. Gruber, T.R. A Translation Approach to Portable Ontologies, Knowledge Acquisition, vol. 5, no. 2 (1993) 199–220
18. de Lemos, R., Gacek, C. and Romanovsky, A. Tolerating Architectural Mismatches. In: de Lemos, R., Gacek, C. and Romanovsky, A. (eds.), Architecting Dependable Systems, LNCS 2677, Springer-Verlag, Berlin (2003) 175-194
19. Yellin, D. M. and Strom, R. E. Protocol specifications and components adaptors. ACM Trans. on Programming Languages and Systems, 19(2) (1997) 292–333

The Domain Analysis Concept Revisited: A Practical Approach

Eduardo Santana de Almeida[1], Jorge Cláudio Cordeiro Pires Mascena[1],
Ana Paula Carvalho Cavalcanti[1], Alexandre Alvaro[1], Vinicius Cardoso Garcia[1],
Silvio Romero de Lemos Meira[1], Daniel Lucrédio[2]

[1] Federal University of Pernambuco and C.E.S.A.R. – Recife Center for Advanced Studies
and Systems, Recife, Brazil
`{esa2, jccpm, apcc2, aa2, vcg, srlm}@cin.ufpe.br`
[2] Universidade de São Paulo
`lucredio@icmc.usp.br`

Abstract. Domain analysis has been identified as a key factor in the development of reusable software. However, for domain analysis to become a practical approach we need to understand the conceptual foundations of the process and to produce a unambiguous definition in the form of specific techniques. This paper presents a practical approach for domain analysis based on a well defined set of guidelines and metrics. A preliminary industrial case study was performed in order to identify the viability of the approach.

1 Introduction

Software reuse – the process of creating software systems from existing software rather than building software systems from scratch [1] – is a key factor for improving quality and productivity [2]. Through the years, several research works related to software reuse, including company reports [3, 4, 5, 6, 7], informal research [8] and empirical studies [9, 10, 11], have shown that domain analysis [12, 13] is a crucial factor for reusability.

The term domain analysis was first introduced by Neighbors [14] as "*the activity of identifying the objects and operations of a class of similar systems in a particular problem domain*." However, neither Neighbors' nor many other works [12, 13, 15] address the issue of "*how to perform*" domain analysis. These works focus on the outcome, not on the process. This issue can also be observed in the software reuse processes[1] [15], which present gaps in the domain analysis steps.

Thus, improvements related to domain analysis are necessary in the reuse processes, which conduct it in an ad-hoc manner and success stories are more exceptions than rules. The process of concept abstraction, from the identification of common features, is usually considered as an exclusive human activity and commonly associated with experience. However, little is known about the process involved in deriving and organizing such collections of abstract concepts. Gaining experience is a slow

---

[1] This work has analyzed eleven reuse processes involving domain engineering and software product lines. The processes correspond to the state-of-the-art in the area.

M. Morisio (Ed.): ICSR 2006, LNCS 4039, pp. 43–57, 2006.
© Springer-Verlag Berlin Heidelberg 2006

unstructured learning process. Similarly, domain analysis is a slow unstructured learning process that leads to the identification, abstraction, and encapsulation of objects in a particular domain [12].

Typically, knowledge of a domain evolves over time until enough experience has been accumulated and several systems have been implemented, so generic abstractions can be isolated and reused. In domain analysis, experience and knowledge are accumulated until it reaches a threshold. This threshold can be defined as the point when an abstraction can be organized and made available for reuse.

Thus, in order to truly exploit reusability in industrial environments, we need to develop systematic approaches for domain analysis. In this context, our goal with domain analysis, in concordance with Prieto-Diaz [12], (pg. 48) is: *"to find ways to extract, organize, represent, manipulate and understand reusable information, to formalize the domain analysis process, and to develop technologies and tools to support it."*

Our research is based on the following assumptions: **i.** problem domains exist; **ii.** problem domains evolve gradually; **iii.** there are companies that need to develop large numbers of similar systems within those domains; **iv.** there is expertise in building systems in those domains; and, finally, **v.** reusers follow systematic approaches to reuse. Our focus is on a practical approach that aims to: understand the conceptual foundations of the domain analysis process; produce a unambiguous definition in the form of specific techniques; and define a common notation for the process. Moreover, the approach should present a systematic set of principles, guidelines, metrics, roles, inputs and outputs.

2   A Practical Approach for Domain Analysis

2.1 Principles

The proposed approach is based on a set of Principles (P) in order to obtain a practical and effective way to perform domain analysis.

P_1. *Scoping:* project management activities for domain engineering and product lines are sometimes called product line scoping. The main goal of scoping methods and approaches is to identify the products that will belong to the product lines as well as to define their major features.

P_2. *Metrics:* metrics should be used whenever applicable, although not all the engineering activities can be carried out with metrics. So, if metrics are not applicable, the approach should provide guidelines rather than simply giving general principles.

P_3. *Flexibility:* features defined in the feature model can be used to parameterize domain architectures and components in the future. Thus, components can be developed almost free of design decisions by putting the features in the components as instantiation parameters.

P_4. *Commonality analysis:* the goal of commonality analysis is to identify which features (requirements) are common to all applications of the domain.

P_5. *Variability analysis:* the goal of variability analysis is to identify which features (requirements) differ among the applications, and to determine the differences precisely.

P6. Variability Modeling: this principle concerns with the modeling of variation points, variants, and their relationships.

P7. Traceability: traceability links, when well documented, can ensure the consistent definition of the commonality and the variability of the domain throughout all assets specified.

P8. Validation and documentation: one important consideration in any method or process is related to activities for validation and documentation of the developed assets, specially in the context of domains and product lines, where asset complexity and volume are enormous.

P9. Systematic sequence of steps: the last principle, but not less important, says that there must be a systematic sequence of steps, where the ordering of steps is logical and easy to apply in practice.

We are aware that this is not a definitive set. However, we believe that the identified principles constitute a solid basis for future work.

In this context, the main goal of domain analysis is to identify commonalities and variability of systems in a domain and represent them in an effective form. Our approach for Domain analysis consists of three steps, using SADT notation [16]: **Domain Planning, Domain Modeling** and **Domain Validation.** The next sections present each step in details.

2.2 Planning

The *first step* in the approach corresponds to a preparation phase. One of the goals in this step is to determine whether it makes good sense to invest in building a reuse infrastructure in a given domain.

Initially, the domain analyst – a person who conducts the domain analysis process – based on the chosen domain, performs the following activities:

- **Stakeholder analysis:** encompasses the identification of the stakeholders and their roles within the process. A stakeholder is someone who has a defined interest in the outcomes of the project;
- **Objectives definition:** corresponds to the definition of the stakeholder's desired objectives for the project;
- **Constraint definition:** comprehends the definition of the restrictions imposed by the organization and by market conditions, making clear what is beyond the process scope;
- **Market analysis** (*if applicable*)**:** this non-trivial activity – which can be performed or not, depending on costs, complexity and maturity of the organization in the domain – is the systematic research and analysis of the external factors that determine the success of the domain in the marketplace. It involves the gathering of business intelligence, competitive studies and assessments, market segmentation, customer plans, and the integration of this information into a cohesive business strategy and plan [17]; and
- **Data collection:** encompasses activities to elicit and examine existing knowledge about the potential domain in focus. It includes the analysis of all available documentation (project plans, user manuals, modeling, and data dictionary), existing applications and knowledge from domain experts.

It is important to highlight that these activities are not sequential and can be performed in parallel. After performing the above activities, the domain analyst starts to identify the features and to define the domain scope. These tasks are organized in four activities. The next sections present each activity in detail.

2.2.1 Map Application Candidates

This initial activity aims at identifying the characteristics that shall be supported by the future domain architecture. Thus, firstly, the domain analyst, based on system and stakeholder information, identifies the applications that might be supported by the domain sequentially.

Three types of applications can be distinguished: *existing applications* (i.e., applications that have been developed prior to the start of the domain analysis process), *future applications* (i.e., applications where the requirements are rather clear, but development has not yet started) and *potential applications* (i.e., applications for which no clear requirements exist yet, but are seen as relevant).

After understanding the relevant applications, the *list of features* is developed. The use of features is motivated by the fact that customers and engineers often speak of applications characteristics in terms of features that the application has and/or delivers [18]. This list provides a description of the different characteristics and identifies relations among them.

Identification of features involves abstracting domain knowledge obtained from the domain experts and other documents such as books, user manuals, design documents, and source programs [19]. However, the volume of documents and information to be analyzed tends to be too big in a domain. In this context, the guidelines (G) defined initially by Lee[2] et al. [19] (G_1 and G_3) can be very useful:

G_1. Analyze terminologies used in the domain to identify features. In some mature domains, experts usually use standardized terminology to communicate their ideas, needs, and problems. Thus, using standard terms for the feature identification can expedite communication between the domain analyst and information providers (domain experts and end-users).

Lee et al. categorizes the features in a feature identification framework. This framework organizes the features in four groups: *capability, domain technology, implementation technique, and operating environment.*

Capability features are characterized as distinct services, operations or non-functional aspects of applications in a domain. Services are end-user visible functionality of products offered to their users in order to satisfy their requirements. Operations are internal functions of applications that are needed to provide services. Non-functional features include end-user visible application characteristics that cannot be identified in terms of services or operations, such as presentation, capacity, quality attributes, etc.

Domain technology features are domain specific technologies that the domain analyst or architect uses to model specific problems or to implement service or operation features. These features are specific to a given domain and may not be useful in other domains.

---

[2] The guidelines originally defined by Lee et al. were proposed to software product lines. However, in our approach, we adapt it to work with the domain vision.

Implementation technique features are more generic than domain technology features and may be used in different domains. They contain key design and implementation decisions that may be used to implement other features. Some examples are: design patterns and architectural styles.

Operating environment features include domain contexts, such as computing environments and interfaces with different types of devices and external systems.

We believe that organizations starting to explore domain analysis in their projects, or in immature or unstable domains, should first concentrate just on capability features. Next, after achieving improvements in domain knowledge and analysis, the other kinds of features can also be used.

G_2. *Try to first find differences among existing applications in a domain and then, with this understanding, identify commonalities.* Applications in the same domain share a high level of commonality [20]. Hence, the commonality space would be larger to work with than the difference space, thus finding difference is much easier than finding commonalities. So, the strategy is, initially, to identify the existing applications (running systems), and then list different features that characterize each one. After this understanding, the identification of common features is more easily performed.

G_3. *Do not identify all implementation details that do not distinguish between applications in a domain.* A developer tends to enumerate all the implementation details and identify them as features, even though there are no variations among them. But it is important to note that a feature model is not a requirement model, which expresses the details of internal functions. For this reason, we recommend that this activity should be performed by a domain analyst, who will abstract implementation details.

At the end, the applications and features information are organized in the form of an *application map*. In this map, rows and columns are used to represent features and applications, respectively. Sometimes, it is common to divide a feature in a set of sub-features, when there is a relationship between them; for example, the feature *Search*, in a component repository domain, can be divided into five sub-features, such as: *active*, *passive*, based on *semantic*, *facets* and *keywords*. The same can happen for each sub-feature.

2.2.2 Develop Evaluation Functions

In this activity, based on the information that was previously produced, the domain analyst refines and operationalizes the business objectives that are relevant to the domain in the particular context.

This refinement is very important because initially (in the previous activity) the objectives are identified in a manner that is too generic for being directly used. Thus, our approach includes the concept of successively refining the business objectives towards more operational evaluation criteria, as also used in PuLSE methodology [21]. These criteria can be applied on a single application/feature combination. This refinement has the advantage that an explicit and traceable relation between the business objectives and the identified scope is established.

In this context, this activity starts when the domain analyst identifies the relevant stakeholders and elicits their objectives. Next, in order to make the goal more precise, a goal schema based on Goal Question Metric (GQM) [22] is used. The schema has the form of <purpose><Issue><Object><Context>, such as ***Minimize the effort*** *needed for **the development of new applications** from the viewpoint of **software engineers** in **the company**.*

After defining the goal, questions are used to elicit additional information about the objectives in order to capture them in a more effective way. Based on the objectives and questions, the domain analyst develops or reuses *evaluation functions*, which produces *benefit* and *characterization functions*. The *benefit functions* describe the benefit of introducing a certain feature into the reuse infrastructure relative to a certain business objective. The *characterization functions* are applied on single applications/features combinations and play a role that is analogous to metrics in the GQM approach. Table 1 presents a result of this activity (Develop evaluation functions) in the component repository domain.

Table 1. Develop evaluation functions

Objective	To attend most of the domain applications, maximizing the repository use and standardizing the characteristics that are available in the applications
Questions	1. How to define if the repository support or not an application? 2. How to evaluate the level of use from the repository by the applications? 3. How to determinate the deviation of a characteristic of an application in relation with the established pattern?

Characterization	• Is characteristic c necessary for the application a?
	  - $req(c,a)$ – 1:yes; 0:no
	• Similarity of the characteristic c_a with the standard characteristic c in the application a
	  - $sim(c,c_a,a)$ – 1:equal the standard; 0.5:next to the standard; 0:different of the standard

Benefit	• Proximity of the characteristic in the applications in relation with the standard
	  - $P(c,a) - \sum_{req(c,a)} x\ sim(c,c_a,a)$
	• Distance of the characteristic in the applications in relation with the standard
	  - $D(c) - \sum_{req(c,a)} x\ (1 - sim(c,c_a,a))$

2.2.3 Characterize Applications

In this activity, the characterization functions are applied on the *application map*. Usually this is done by stakeholders who provided the different objectives (e.g., the project leader for development can be useful to estimate effort, while a marketing expert can be useful to describe which features may be useful to gain market share), or other qualified person. It is, basically, a knowledge elicitation task centered on the characterization functions.

The difficulties that were found during knowledge elicitation for the characterization functions lead to modifications into the application map and the evaluations functions. Moreover, the scales used in the functions can also be changed. The information resulting from these iterations is entered into the application map and leads to the *documented application map*.

2.2.4 Benefit Analysis

The last activity of the domain planning is very important. At this point the information acquired is used to derive the *scope definition*. The first step is to identify the adequate values for the benefit functions. This is done by applying the definition functions on the values elicited for the characterization functions.

One important warning is related to difference scales. Some scales that are used for the characterization functions can be nominal or ordinal, thus, its definition should take this point in consideration, in order to allow arithmetic operations to be performed on these values.

After values are assigned to the benefit functions, it is possible to determine the scope that is aligned with the business objective. Some multi-objective decision techniques, described in literature, can be useful for this proposal [23]. In our approach, we use a weighting scheme to perform it.

Once candidate features are identified based on the described activities, these features should be organized into a domain model. The details of this step are described in the next section.

2.3 Domain Modeling

In the *Domain Planning* step, a domain was selected based on a strategic analysis of the stakeholders' interest on the process, which ensured a sufficient business case to develop a *domain model* for the selected domain. The purpose of the *Domain Modeling* step is to fill in the content within the domain itself. This means a shift of attention from scoping issues to structural issues and conceptual elements within the domain.

Thus, the resulting model should describe the commonality and variability within the domain. Rather than building a model for a single application in the domain, or even a generic model that may be applicable at a high level to a number of applications, the domain modeling task attempts to formalize the space of variations for individual applications in the domain.

In this approach, the domain model is represented through *feature models* [24]. The domain analyst groups the features that were identified in the previous step in a features model, a graphical AND/OR hierarchy of features, that captures logical structural relationships (e.g., composition and generalization) among features. Three types of relationships are represented in this diagram: "composed-of", "generalization/specialization", and "implemented by" [18]. Features may be "mandatory", "optional", "or features" or "alternative". *Composition rules* supplement the feature model with information showing mutual dependency and mutual exclusion relationships between variant features and variation point. It is used to verify the consistency and completeness of the selected features. In our approach, we consider three types of relationships (R):

R_1. *Variant Constraint Dependency*. A variant constraint dependency describes a relationship between two variants, which may be one of two types:

- *Variant requires variant.* The selection of a variant V_1 requires the selection of another variant V_2 independent on the variation points the variants are associated with.

- *Variant excludes variant.* The selection of a variant V_1 excludes the selection of the related variant V_2 independent on the variation points the variants are associated with.

R_2. *Variant to Variation Point Constraint Dependency.* The variant to variation point constraint dependency describes a relationship between a variant and a variation point, which may be of one of the two types:

- *Variant requires variation point.* The selection of a variant V_1 requires the consideration of a variant point VP_2.
- *Variant excludes variation point.* The selection of a variant V_1 excludes the consideration of a variation point VP_2.

R_3. *Variation Point Constraint Dependency.* A variation point constraint dependency describes a relationship between two variation points, which may be one of two types:

- *Variation point requires variation point.* A variation point requires the consideration of another variant point in order to be realized.
- *Variation point excludes variation point.* The consideration of a variation point excludes the consideration of another variation point.

Lee et al. [19] defines two useful guidelines that can be used to organize features:

G_4. *Do not organize features to represent functional dependencies, like a function call hierarchy, but organize features to capture and represent commonalities and differences.* Developers who are familiar with a structured development method often confuse a feature model with a functional call hierarchy. Thus they tend to identify all functions of applications as features and organize them similar to a functional call hierarchy. However, features should be organized so that commonalities and variabilities can be easily reorganized, rather than representing interactions among features, like a function call hierarchy.

G_5. *If many upper-level features are associated with a lower-level feature through the implemented-by relationship, reduce complexity of the feature model by associating the lower-level feature with the nearest common parent of its related upper-level features.* When upper-level features, in a feature model, are associated with several lower-level features through the implementation-by relationship, the implementation relationships between those features may be very complex. Since the primary concern of feature modeling is to represent commonality and variability in a domain rather than to model implementation relationships between features, complex relationships can be reduced by associating the lower-level feature with the nearest common parent of its related upper-level features. This guideline is useful in mature or stable domains where domain and technology features are identified. But in domains where only capability features are identified it is not applied.

Besides these guidelines, proposed by Lee et al., an important consideration (C) related to feature models must be considered:

C_1. *A feature model with AND-nodes at an upper level and OR-nodes at a lower level usually indicates a high level of reuse opportunity. On the other hand, alternatives (i.e., OR-nodes) at the upper level usually mean that applications in the domain do not share much commonality in terms of services and functions provided by them.* This indicates that the domain might not have much reuse opportunity at the application level, although there might still be opportunities for reuse at low level.

Additionally, *alternatives (OR-nodes) at a lower level indicate different ways of designing and implementing certain reusable information.*

Once feature models are organized in a coherent structure composed of features, common and variable points, relationships, and composition rules, the domain analyst performs the domain validation.

2.4 Domain Validation

Before the domain model is ready for being used, it is necessary to validate and document it; however, there are not many works in this direction. Addy [25] presents a framework that extends verification and validation from an individual application system to a product line of systems that are developed within an architecture-based software engineering environment. Nevertheless, Addy's work is very generic and does not discuss its task systematically, which makes difficult its practical usage.

Thus, in our approach, in order to achieve the domain validation, the domain analyst performs the following activities (*A*):

A₁. Document features. For this activity we use the template defined by Czarnecki and Eisenecker [26]. In this template each feature consists of:

- *Semantic description.* Each feature should have at least a short description describing its semantics;
- *Rationale.* A feature should have a note explaining why the feature is included in the model;
- *Stakeholders and client programs.* Each feature should be annotated with stakeholders (e.g., users, customers, developers, managers) who are interested in the feature and the client programs that need this feature;
- *Exemplar applications.* If possible, the documentation should describe features with known applications implementing them;
- *Constraints.* Constraints are hard dependencies between variable features. Two important kinds of constraints are *mutual-exclusion constraints* and *required constraints.*
- *Open/closed attribute.* Variation points should be marked as *open* if new direct variable subfeatures (or features) are expected. On the other hand, marking a variation point as *closed* indicates that no other direct variable subfeatures (or features) are expected; and
- *Priorities.* Priorities may be assigned to features in order to record their relevance to the process.

A₂. Check for synonyms. Once the semantic description has been defined, it is necessary to analyze each feature in order to find and eliminate *synonyms*, i.e., variant terms that appear to have the same domain-relevant meaning;

A₃. Check for homonyms. As a complementary activity to the search for synonyms, it is necessary to check each feature in order to find *homonyms*, i.e., the same literal term used with different meanings in different contexts;

A₄. Model Validation. After the features documentation, the check for synonyms and homonyms, the domain analyst performs the model validation. This activity corresponds to the matching of the requirements that were expressed by stakeholders and the domain model, in order to validate its completeness and accuracy; and

A5. *Document the domain.* The last activity of this step corresponds to the documentation of the domain. In this activity, we use the meta model defined in [27], which consists of the following information:

- *Domain description.* Defines the responsibilities of the domain;
- *Domain defining rules.* Includes decisions criteria about the inclusion and exclusion of domain membership and the logical relationships between these criteria;
- *Exemplar system selection.* Denotes a set of systems in the scope where the domain functionality occurs;
- *Documentation.* Describes a set of documents related to exemplar systems;
- *Domain Context (Relationship).* Describes the relation between the domain in focus and other domains;
- *Domain genealogy.* Encompasses information about the evolution and dependencies among systems within a domain; and
- *Feature.* Defines a set of features described in a domain.

3 Case Study

In order to validate our approach, we performed an industrial case study, which we analyzed from various view-points.

3.1 The Context

Our case study using the approach consisted of performing the domain analysis in the domain of repository systems. This project is part of the Reuse in Software Engineering (RiSE) project [28]. RiSE's goal is to develop a robust framework for software reuse, in conjunction with the industry, involving processes, methods, environment and tools. In the project, the role of the RiSE group[3] (researchers) is to investigate the state-of-the-art in the area and disseminates the reuse culture. On the other hand, the industry (and its project managers, architects, and system engineers), represented by Recife Center for Advanced Studies and Systems[4] (C.E.S.A.R.) is responsible for "making things happens" with planning, management, and necessary staff and resources. Recently, C.E.S.A.R. won, from Brazilian agencies, two important awards: best Innovation Institute and Research and Software System Company.

In the case study, we analyzed nine repository systems and component managers.

The subjects of this study were one senior system engineer and one senior software architect; however, the whole project (to develop our product line) includes: project manager (1), architect (1), team leader (1), analyst (2), system engineer (9), quality engineer (2), and configuration manager (1) and RiSE's staff.

---

[3] www.rise.com.br
[4] Currently, this company has more than 650 employees and is in preparation to obtain the CMMI level 3.

3.2 The Hypothesis

In this study, the following hypothesis was defined:

- **H$_1$: The proposed approach provides useful guidance to the domain analyst.**

3.3 Analysis of the Results

Analyzing the results of the approach applicability, we conclude that the approach offers considerable guidance through planning, modeling, and validation tasks. In the planning, the following benefits could be identified:

- *Guidelines.* The use of features in domain analysis is a key aspect. However, letting the process of feature identification and classification be performed in an ad-hoc way can compromise the domain reusability. In our approach, this problem is solved with the application of well-defined guidelines;
- *Documentation.* With the application map, the organization possesses a general picture of the domain, which comprehends its features and the set of applications (existing, future, and potential). This documentation can be useful for different stakeholders, such as the domain analyst and business and market staff;
- *Well-defined functions.* Using the GQM approach, the functions are defined according to the business objectives that were specified by stakeholders, which results in a more focused scope and in the development of a reuse infrastructure that conforms to organizational needs. Moreover, with the maturity of the organization using the approach, a base of functions can be developed and reused. On the other hand, the initial definition of the functions - a non-trivial task - demands a initial learning;
- *Scoping.* One of the problems with the domain analysis approaches and reuse processes [15] is the lack of support for the domain scoping activity. In our approach, we present a systematic way to achieve it, with inputs, outputs, guidelines and roles.

In the domain modeling task, the major benefit is the set of guidelines that can be applied on feature models. At the end, in the domain validation, the key aspect is the concern with feature and domain documentation.

Even with these benefits, the following drawbacks could be observed:

- *Domain selection.* In the approach, there is not an activity to determine if a domain is sufficiently mature to develop reusable assets. We assume that this characteristic can be initially defined by the organization. However, a better solution must be investigated;
- *Application existence.* In our approach, we assume that there are applications in the domain to perform the domain analysis process. However, in some situations the organization may not have applications of a specific domain. Thus, this issue must also be considered; and
- *Lack of tools.* In this case, we used a combination of tools such as style sheets, text editors, and tried others, such as modeling feature tools (FORM tool,

CaptainFeature[5] and XFeature[6]). However, these tools presented lack of support in some activities (scoping, documentation) and did not permit integration among them.

In this case study, about 70 features were identified in the repository systems domain, and the approach has proven to be useful and promissory.

4 Related Work

The domain analysis area is not new and some works in this area can be found. The work described in [29] is close to our Domain Scope activity; however, the most important difference from our approach is that Debaud et al.'s work is directed to software product lines. In a certain sense, the software reuse processes [15] served as an initial inspiration to the approach we present here, mainly, in its weak and strong points. However, others directions were also analyzed such as the works proposed by Frakes et al. [30], Bayer et al. [31], Kim et al. [32], Mei et al.[33] and Moon et al. [34].

Frakes et al. define a method and a CASE tool for helping in the achievement of systematic reuse through domain analysis. The aspect discussed in their work is the use of a prototype to automate the domain analysis process. The tool is used to extract knowledge from documents and source code and organize it to be reused. But, on the other hand, the method does not present improvements in the domain analysis area, since it does not discuss, for example, how to perform scope and validation domain, or modeling activities.

Bayer et al. present the Customizable Domain Analysis (CDA) method, which is a subset of the PuLSE methodology [21]. The CDA method was developed to be adapted to the project needs and provide guidance to be systematically applicable. It consists of three steps: *refine scope definition, elicit raw domain knowledge*, and *model domain knowledge*. The problem with this method is that its steps are very generic, lacking of details on how to perform it.

Kim et al. [32] propose a new direction in domain analysis with the use of goals, scenarios, and features. Their approach aims at offering a systematic and concrete method for identifying features and providing the rationale for the features and the commonality and variability analysis. The method is interesting in the domain modeling task. However, the task of scoping and domain validation is not considered. Moreover, the method does not systematically define inputs, outputs and roles, as in a more effective domain analysis process.

Mei et al. [33] define FODM, a feature-oriented domain modeling method, which explores FODA ideas. Moon et al. [34] propose a process of producing domain requirements where commonality and variability are explicitly considered. These approaches are very interesting, mainly the second one. However, our work is more complete due to the fact that we treat all the steps of domain analysis that are not considered in Mei and Moon's work. The first is mostly concerned with domain modeling, and the second does not treat planning and validation.

---

[5] http://sourceforge.net/projects/captainfeature/
[6] http://www.pnp-software.com/XFeature/

5 Concluding Remarks and Future Work

The domain analysis process is a key aspect for organizations to maximize the benefits of software reuse. However, the existing approaches present gaps and lack of support in some steps, difficulting their usage in an industrial environment.

In this paper, we present an approach for domain analysis to be performed in a practical way. The approach is based on a set of guidelines, metrics, roles, inputs and outputs. A preliminary case study was achieved and has shown the viability of using the approach.

As future work, we are developing a more robust case study in conjunction with the industry in order to refine the approach. Moreover, we are researching the domain architecture design area to define the mapping between domain analysis and domain design. Our goal is to define a domain architecture design process, which includes methods to identify, specify, design, document, and package components from a problem domain.

Acknowledgements. We would like to thank the members of Reuse in Software Engineering Group (RiSE) at C.E.S.A.R. for valuable suggestions for improving this paper. This research is sponsored by Brazilian Innovation Agency (FINEP (MCT/ FINEP/COMPGOV project).

References

[1] C.W. Krueger, Software Reuse, *ACM Computing Surveys*, Vol. 24, No. 02, June, 1992, pp. 131-183.

[2] V.R. Basili, L.C. Briand, W.L. Melo, How Reuse Influences Productivity in Object-Oriented Systems, *Communications of the ACM*, Vol. 39, No. 10, October, 1996, pp. 104-116.

[3] A. Endres, Lessons Learned in an Industrial Software Lab, *IEEE Software*, Vol. 10, No. 05, Sep., 1993, pp. 58-61.

[4] D. Bauer, A Reusable Parts Center, *IBM Systems Journal*, Vol. 32, No. 04, 1993, pp. 620-624.

[5] M.L. Griss, *Software Reuse Experience at Hewlett-Packard*, Proceedings of the 16th ICSE, , Italy, May, 1994, pp. 270.

[6] M.L. Griss, Making Software Reuse Work at Hewlett-Packard, *IEEE Software*, Vol. 12, No. 01, January, 1995, pp. 105-107.

[7] R. Joos, Software Reuse at Motorola, *IEEE Software*, Vol. 11, No. 05, September, 1994, pp. 42-47.

[8] W.B. Frakes, S. Isoda, Success Factors of Systematic Software Reuse, *IEEE Software*, Vol. 12, No. 01, January, 1995, pp. 14-19.

[9] D.C. Rine, *Success Factors for software reuse that are applicable across Domains and businesses*, ACM Symposium on Applied Computing, 1997, pp. 182-186.

[10] M. Morisio, M. Ezran, C. Tully, Success and Failure Factors in Software Reuse, *IEEE Transactions on Software Engineering*, Vol. 28, No. 04, April, 2002, pp. 340-357.

[11] M.A. Rothenberger, K.J. Dooley, U.R. Kulkarni, N. Nada, Strategies for Software Reuse: A Principal Component Analysis of Reuse Practices, *IEEE Transactions on Software Engineering*, Vol. 29, No. 09, Sep., 2003, pp. 825-837.

[12] R. Prieto-Diaz, Domain Analysis: An Introduction, *ACM SIGSOFT Software Engineering Notes,* Vol. 15, No. 02, April, 1990, pp. 47-54.

[13] G. Arango, *Domain Analysis – From Art Form to Engineering Discipline*, International Workshop on Software Specifications & Design, Pittsburgh, Pennsylvania, United States, May, 1999, pp. 152-159.

[14] J. Neighbors, *Software Construction Using Components*, Ph.D. Thesis, Department of Information and Computer Science, University of California, Irvine, 1981, pp. 75.

[15] E. S. Almeida, A. Alvaro, D. Lucrédio, V.C. Garcia, S.R.L. Meira, *A Survey on Software Reuse Processes,* IEEE International Conference on Information Reuse and Integration (IRI), USA, August, 2005.

[16] D. T. Ross, Structured Analysis (SA): A language for communicating Ideas, *IEEE Transaction on Software Engineering*, Vol. 03, No. 01, January, 1977, pp. 06-15.

[17] P.Clements, L. Northrop, *Software Product Lines*, Addison Wesley, USA, 2002, pp. 563.

[18] K. C. Kang, S. Kim, J. Lee, K. Kim, E. Shin, M. Huh, FORM: A Feature-Oriented Reuse Method with domain-specific reference architectures, *Annals of Software Engineering*, Vol. 05, January, 1998, pp. 143-168.

[19] K. Lee, K. C. Kang, J. Lee, *Concepts and Guidelines of Feature Modeling for Product Line Software Engineering*, Proceedings of the 7th International Conference on Software Reuse (ICSR): Methods, Techniques, and Tools, Austin, Texas, April, 2002, pp. 62-77.

[20] J. Coplin, D. Hoffman, D. Weiss, Commonality and Variability in Software Engineering, *IEEE Software*, Vol. 15, No. 06, November/December, 1998, pp. 37-45.

[21] J. Bayer, O. Flege, P. Knauber, R. Laqua, D. Muthig, K. Schmid, T. Widen, J. DeBaud, *PuLSE: A Methodology to Develop Software Product Lines*, Symposium on Software Reusability (SSR), 1999, pp. 122-131.

[22] V. R. Basili, G. Caldiera, H. D. Rombach, *The Goal Question Metric Approach*, Encyclopedia of Software Engineering, Volume II, September, 1994, pp 528-532.

[23] M. Mollaghasemi, J. Pet-Edwards, Making Multiple-Objective Decisions, *IEEE Computer Society,* 1997.

[24] K. C. Kang, S. C. Cohen, J. A. Hess, W. E. Novak, A. S. Peterson, *Feature-Oriented Domain Analysis (FODA) Feasibility Sudy*, Technical Report CMU/SEI-90-TR-21, Software Engineering Institute, Carnegie Mellon University, Pittsburgh, 1990.

[25] E. A. Addy, A framework for performing verification and validation in reuse-based software engineering, *Annals of Software Engineering*, Vol. 05, January, 1998, pp. 279-292.

[26] K. Czarnecki, U. W. Eisenecker, *Generative Programming: Methods, Tools, and Applications*, Addison-Wesley, 2000, p. 832.

[27] K. Schmid, S. Thiel, J. Bosch, S. Johnsson, M. Jaring, B. Thomé, Scoping, *Eureka 2023 Programme, ITEA project,* June, 2001, p. 67.

[28] E. S. Almeida, A. Alvaro, D. Lucrédio, V.C. Garcia, S.R.L. Meira, *RiSE Project: Towards a Robust Framework for Software Reuse,* IEEE International Conference on Information Reuse and Integration (IRI), USA, November, 2004, pp. 48-53.

[29] J. M. Debaud, K. Schmid, *A Systematic Approach to Derive the Scope of Software Product Lines*, USA, International Conference on Software Engineering (ICSE), May, 1999, pp. 34-43.

[30] W. B. Frakes, R. Prieto-Diaz, C. Fox, DARE: Domain Analysis and reuse environment, *Annals of Software Engineering,* Vol. 05, January, 1998, pp. 125-141.

[31] J. Bayer, D. Muthig, T. Widen, *Customizable Domain Analysis*, Proceedings of the First International Symposium on Generative and Component-Based Software Engineering (GPCE), Germany, September, 1999, pp. 178-194.

[32] M. Kim, H. Yang, S. Park, *A Domain Analysis Method for Software Product Lines Based on Scenarios, Goals and Features*, Tenth Asia-Pacific Software Engineering Conference (APSEC), Thailand, December, 2003, pp. 126-136.

[33] H. Mei, W. Zhang, F. Gu, *A Feature Oriented Approach to Modeling and Reusing Requirements of Software Product Lines*, 27th IEEE International Computer Software and Applications Conference (COMPSAC), USA, November, 2003, pp. 250-256.

[34] M. Moon, K. Yeom, *An Approach to Developing Domain Requirements as a Core Asset Based on Commonality and Variability Analysis in a Product Lines*, IEEE Transactions on Software Engineering, Vol. 31, No. 07, July, 2005, pp.551-569.

Feature Driven Dynamic Customization of Software Product Lines

Hassan Gomaa and Mazen Saleh

Department of Information and Software Engineering
George Mason University
Fairfax, Virginia 22030, USA
hgomaa@gmu.edu, mazensaleh@yahoo.com

Abstract. This paper describes a model driven development approach for software product lines based on Web services, in which feature selection drives the dynamic customization of the product line architecture and implementation to derive the application. During product line modeling, feature and their dependencies are described in a feature model. The product line architecture is based around a client/server pattern consisting of user interface objects interacting with Web services. During application engineering, features are selected by the application engineer and used to dynamically customize the product line architecture and implementation.

1 Introduction

The field of software reuse has evolved from reuse of individual components towards large-scale reuse with software product lines [Clements02, Weiss99]. A software product line (SPL) consists of a family of software systems that have some common functionality and some variable functionality. Parnas referred to a collection of systems that share common characteristics as a *family of systems* [Parnas79]. Applications are derived from the product line architecture and components by incorporating all the common features and some of the variable features.

Earlier papers and researches have described how this approach was carried out before [Gomaa96, Gomaa99] and after the introduction of the UML [Gomaa02, Gomaa04]. This paper describes how product line engineering can be carried out for product lines based on Web Services [Deitel03], which can be customized dynamically at run time. After the product line architecture has been modeled and implemented, dynamic customization can be carried out to derive the executable application. This process is driven by the feature model developed earlier. The customization uses white box reuse of the client user interface objects and black box reuse of Web services.

2 Evolutionary Software Product Line Engineering

The Evolutionary Software Product Line Engineering Process [Gomaa04] consists of two main processes, as shown in Fig. 1:

M. Morisio (Ed.): ICSR 2006, LNCS 4039, pp. 58–72, 2006.

a) Product line engineering. A product line multiple-view model, which addresses the multiple views of a software product line, is developed. The product line multiple-view model, product line architecture, and reusable components are developed and stored in the product line reuse library.

b) Application engineering. This process involves the configuration of target applications. A target application is a member of the software product line application. The multiple-view model for a target system is configured from the product line multiple-view model. The user selects the desired features for the product line member and the application is derived from the product line architecture and source code.

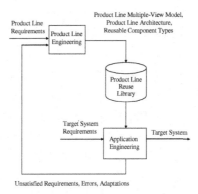

Fig. 1. Evolutionary Software Product Line Engineering Process

3 SPL Multiple View Modeling

During software product line engineering, a multiple-view model of the product line is developed. The multiple-view model defines the different characteristics of a software family [Parnas79], including the commonality and variability among the members of the family [Clements02, Weiss99]. A multiple-view model is represented using the UML notation [Rumbaugh04, Gomaa00] and considers the product line from different perspectives. Product line requirements modeling consists of use case modeling and feature modeling. Use cases and features complement each other. In particular, use cases can be mapped to features based on their reuse properties. Product line analysis modeling consists of static and dynamic modeling. Additional models that are particularly useful for modeling Web Services product lines are user interface navigation modeling, object interaction modeling, and activity modeling. Design modeling consists of developing the component-based software architecture [GomaaSaleh05]. This section describes the product line models that help particularly with modeling Web Services and customizing the product line models.

3.1 Feature Modeling

The feature model [Kang90, Cohen98, Griss98] is the main driver for the design of customizable software product lines. Software product line features are analyzed and categorized as kernel, optional, or alternative as given by the PLUS method [Gomaa04], and depicted as UML stereotypes:

- Kernel: Feature that exists in all members of the product line.
- Optional: Feature that may or may not exist in a given product line member.
- Alternative: One of a group of related alternative features is selected for a given SPL member.

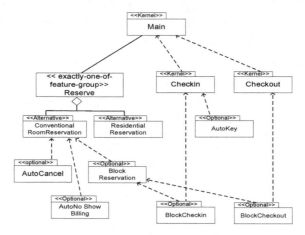

Fig. 2. Feature Dependency Model

Fig. 2 is a sample feature model for a hotel product line. It shows the kernel, optional, and alternative features in the product line. Feature groups can also be defined, which place constraints on feature selection, for example by not allowing two alternative features to co-exist in the same application. The emphasis in feature analysis is on the optional and alternative features, since they differentiate one member of the family from the others. Consider the two alternative features, Conventional Room Reservation and Residential Reservation; because they are in an exactly-one-of-feature-group, one of these features must be selected for any given application. Block Reservation is an optional feature, so it will be selected for some applications.

3.2   User Interface Modeling

Since this design method is based on a service-oriented architecture for the product line, it is important to show the navigation between user interface screens. Each user interface screen is supported by a user interface object, which is in turn associated with one or more Web services. After receiving inputs from the user, the user interface object interacts with the appropriate Web service.

Fig. 3 shows the system navigation from the user perspective. Each user interface screen is supported by a user interface class, which is categorized as kernel, optional, or alternative. Each class is depicted with two stereotypes, the role stereotype is <<user interface>> and the reuse stereotype, which is <<kernel>>, <<optional>>, or <<variant>>. The navigation model depicts the user interface classes that can be accessed from a given user interface class. Consider the realization of the features described in the previous section. From the Main Reservation kernel user interface class, either the Room Reservation variant class or Residential Reservation class can be reached, as well as the optional Block Reservation class. Based on the features desired for a given product line member, all kernel UI classes will be selected, some of the optional UI classes will be selected, and a choice is made among variant UI classes. Each user interface object interacts with relevant web services, which is shown in the dynamic model, as described in Section 3.3. The details of how a given user interface object can traverse to its neighbors is addressed by the activity modeling described in Section 3.4.

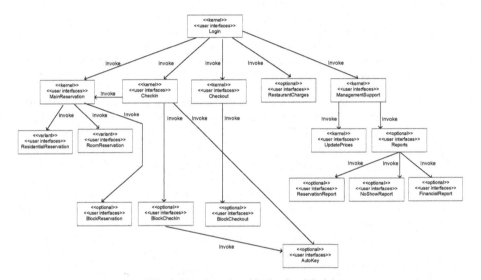

Fig. 3. User Interface Navigation Model

3.3 Dynamic Interaction Modeling

Each use case is supported by a user interface object, which is in turn communicates with one or more Web services. Fig. 4 is a communication diagram for the Room

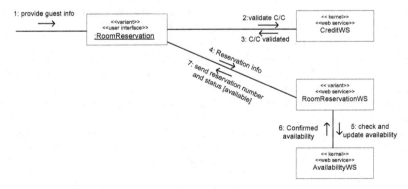

Fig. 4. Communication Diagram – Reserve single room

Reservation user interface object, which processes a reservation for a single room. This requires 3 web services: AvailabilityWS, CreditWS, and ReserveRoomWS. The user interface object accepts the user's information and directs the input to the appropriate web service as shown in Fig. 4.

3.4 Activity Modeling

The activity diagrams, in the SPL Service-Oriented approach, describe the workflow of interactions between the user interface objects and web services, based on events initiated by the user. Workflows have two major tasks:

- Invoke web services: Workflows show the sequence in which web services methods are called for processing a complete event.
- Invoke other user interfaces: Workflows show the navigation pattern in which other user interfaces are invoked.

The workflow for the SPL Service-Oriented architecture is customized during application engineering. Fig. 4 shows a customizable activity diagram for the Main Reservation kernel user interface object. As given by the feature model, Residential-Reservation UI and Room Reservation UI are mutually exclusive alternatives, where only one of them can be invoked by the user. During customization, a path will be selected for the application to identify which GUIs or web services will be invoked. Feature conditions are used for this purpose, where a feature condition is true if the feature is selected and false if not. For example, [feature = RoomReservation] and [feature = RoomReservation] are two feature conditions used in the activity diagram of Fig. 5 to show the mutually exclusive feature decisions in the workflow. Similarly the optional Block Reservation user interface is only provided if the Block Reservation feature condition is true. The customization of workflows is described later.

4 Dynamic Customization of Software Product Lines

After the product line architecture has been modeled and implemented, dynamic customization can be carried out to derive the executable application. This process is driven by the feature model developed earlier. The approach differs from other feature driven approaches [Gomaa96, Gomaa99, Griss98] in that the customization is done at run-time, However, the customization uses white box reuse of the client user interface objects and black box reuse of Web services.

The Dynamic Client Application Customization (DCAC) approach is based on the customization of client user interface objects at system run time based on the features selected for the application and values of parameterized variables. Fig. 6 shows a conceptual overview of the approach. It consists of the customizable SPL system architecture and the SPL environment.

The customizable SPL system architecture in Fig. 6 is based on the client/server architectural pattern, where the client application contain only user interface objects and a customizer object, and the server application contain all web services and database support.

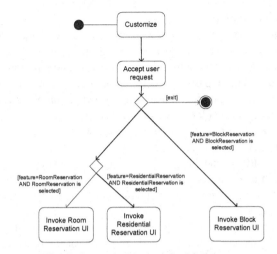

Fig. 5. Customizable Activity Model

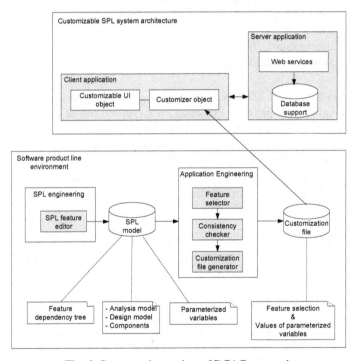

Fig. 6. Conceptual overview of DCAC approach

The software product line environment in Fig. 6, which is based on the PLUS method [Gomaa04], shows a conceptual overview of the approach from the SPL engineering phase to application engineering phase, as follows:

- SPL engineering phase:
  - SPL feature editor: Allows users to create a feature dependency model and define feature relations, create parameterized variables for each feature, and link each feature to related specifications, designs, test procedures, and in particular component implementations.
- Application engineering phase. The following components are based on concepts and tools developed earlier [Gomaa96, Gomaa99]:
  - Feature selector: Allows users to select desired features, and enters value of parameterized variables.
  - Consistency checker: This component is part of the feature selector. When a feature is selected, the consistency checker is invoked to verify selection by consulting the feature dependency model to ensure consistent feature selection.
  - Customization file generator: This component is responsible for generating a customization file that is required for the dynamic customization of client applications at system run time.
  - SPL model database: Contains feature model, feature relations, analysis model, design model, component implementations, and parameterized variables.
  - Customization file: Contains feature name, feature selection status (true/false) and values of parameterized variables.

The customizable SPL architecture uses the customization file produced in the application engineering phase to customize a target system at run time. The customizer object (Fig. 5) reads the customization file and stores all customization information in the customizer object's local storage (arrays, data table, etc.) to be used for customizing the client application user interfaces and their workflows. User interfaces are customized by enabling or disabling graphical user interface buttons, and by setting appropriate display variables. Workflows are customized by making decisions on which user interface to call or which web service to invoke.

The idea behind the DCAC approach is the development of dynamic client application that can be customized at system run time. The DCAC approach has two main processes, SPL Customization and Target application interaction.

4.1 SPL Customization

This step involves selecting desired optional and alternative features to be included in the target system. The feature selector component provides a capability to allow feature selection from a SPL model and run consistency checks to verify feature selections. Once features are selected, selection information will be stored in the customization file by the customization file generator. The dynamic client application is customized by reading the customization file at run time.

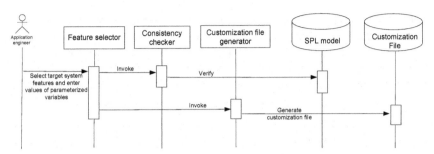

Fig. 7. SPL customization sequence diagram

The following scenario (Fig. 7) depicts the customization process of a target system:

- Application engineer selects desired features for an application using the feature selector.
- Consistency checker verifies feature selection, using the feature model in the SPL model.
- Generate a customization file to be used by the client application for dynamic customization.

4.2 Target Application Interaction

The Dynamic Client Application Customization approach divides the interactive application into three components, Customizer component, User interface component, and Web Service component.

Customizer component contains all customization information for a single target system. At run time, the customizer object reads the customization file and stores all customization information in the customizer object's local storage (arrays, data table, etc.) to be used for customizing the client application user interfaces and their workflows. Customization information consists of enabled or disabled features and parameterized variables.

User interface component is responsible for accepting input from users and allowing invocation of possible service requests. It involves the sequencing of web services invocation and handling of message communication based on the customizable workflow. It is also responsible for displaying results to users originating from the web service component.

Web Service component is a collection of functional methods that are packaged as a single unit and published in the Internet, Intranet, or Extranet in a private or public UDDI for use by other software programs, in this case the user interface component.

Once the target application features are selected in the SPL customization step, the application will be ready for execution. The application interaction process describes the two steps that occur at execution time: initialization of the customizer object and run time customization.

Step 1: Initialization of the customizer object at program startup (Fig. 8):
- Starts main client application program.

- Customizer object is invoked at main client application program startup.
- Customizer object reads customization information once from the customization file that is generated by the customization file generator.
- Customization information can be read by all user interface objects through the customizer object.

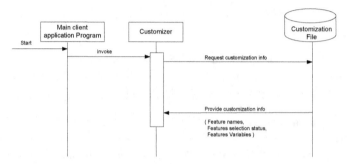

Fig. 8. Initialization of customizer object – sequence diagram

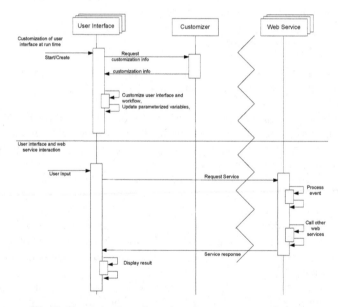

Fig. 9. Customization of user interface – sequence diagram

Step 2: Run time customization of user interface objects. It involves two phases: customization of user interface at run time and interaction of user interface objects with web services (Fig. 9).

Customization of user interface at run time
- User invokes a user interface.
- User interface requests customization information from customizer object.

- User interface reads the customization information to:
  - Customize user interface components
  - Define appropriate calls to web services based on selected features.
  - Define appropriate calls to other user interface objects.
  - Update parameterized variables.

  Customization is based on feature selection information stored in the customization file.

User interface and web service interaction

- User requests an activity by entering input data and clicking a button.
- User interface object passes the activity request and input data to a web service method(s).
- Web service processes the request and passes the results to the user interface object. A web service may also request services from other web services.
- User interface object displays results received from web service.

5   Development of the DCAC Approach

This section describes in more detail the dynamic customization of a product line with the DCAC approach, illustrated by two examples from the hotel software product line, the Main Reservation User Interface and the Reserve Room User Interface. The first example shows how alternatives and optional features are treated in the source code, while the second example shows how a service request is performed using web services. Both examples explain the transition from design into implementation.

The customizable activity diagram of Fig. 5, described in section 3.4, shows a customizable activity diagram for the MainReservation user interface. This diagram shows ResidentialReservation UI and RoomReservation UI as mutually exclusive alternatives where only one of them can be invoked by clicking the single reservation button of MainReservation user interface. (The Consistency Checker ensures that one and only one of these alternatives is chosen at feature selection). BlockReservation UI, on the other hand, belongs to an optional feature. It will be either enabled or disabled based on whether the BlockReservation feature is selected by the user.

The customizable SPL application uses the customization file generated in the application engineering phase to customize a target system, described in section 4.1. The customizer object reads the customization file once and stores all customization information in the customizer object's local storage (arrays, data table, etc.) to be used for customizing the client application user interfaces and their workflows. The Main-Reservation UI is customized by reading the feature selection and the value of parameterized variables from the customizer object to enable or disable GUI buttons and set appropriate display variables. Its workflow is customized by setting features to true or false and applying feature condition settings to user interface calls and web service invocations, as described in section 4.2.

Fig. 10 shows the actual implementation of the activity diagram depicted in Fig. 4. It shows how the MainReservation UI object can be customized at run time and how it interacts after the dynamic customization.

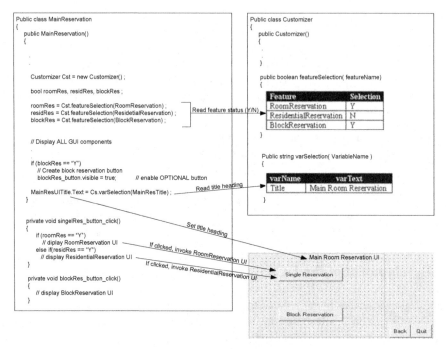

Fig. 10. Run time customization - Main Reservation UI

Customization of client application at run time:

- Object MainReservation is customized by reading the feature selections stored in the customizer object and storing them in local variables, where they will be used throughout by the MainReservation object. Each feature selection is are set to Y or N, depending on whether the feature is selected or not. Local feature variables roomRes, residRes, and blockRes store the RoomReservation, ResidentialReservation, and BlockReservation feature decisions respectively, which are set to Y, N, and Y in Fig. 10.

- During the customization process, optional GUI button Block Reservation is created if *blockRes* is equal to Y and ignored otherwise. In Fig. 10, because the Block Reservation feature is True, the GUI button is displayed, as given by:

  if (blockRes == "Y")
  // Create block reservation button
  blockRes_button.visible = true;

- During the customization process, the parameterized variable MainResTitle is read from the customizer object to set the appropriate header title of the MainReservation user interface.

  MainResUITitle.Text = Cst.varSelection(MainResTitle);

User interface object interaction:

After the dynamic customization process is complete, the MainReservation user interface is ready to accept user input.

- If Single Reservation button is invoked, either ResidentialReservation UI or RoomReservation UI will be called, depending on whether RoomReservation feature or ResidentialReservation feature is selected. Based on the feature selections in Fig.10, the former will be selected.

    if (roomRes == "Y")
        // display RoomReservation UI
    else if(residRes == "Y")
        // display ResidentialReservation UI

- If Block Reservation button is enabled and invoked, BlockReservation UI will be called.

    private void blockRes_button_click( )
    {
        // display BlockReservation UI
    }

- Since MainReservation UI has no service request to process, there will be no web services involved at this user interface.

The second example shows how a service request is processed in the RoomReservation UI. Once the RoomReservation UI is invoked, it initiates the dynamic customization process, described in the previous example. The user interface is now ready to accept user input and service requests. For the illustration, Make Single Reservation Service Request is explored.

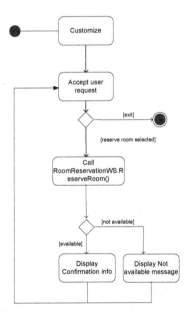

Fig. 11. Activity Diagram – RoomReservation UI

Fig. 11 is an activity diagram showing the workflow of processing a single reservation (Reserve button clicked).This interaction sequence follows that described in Section 3.3 and illustrated in Fig. 4:

- Customize RoomReservation UI object
- Accept user input that is required to make a single reservation, such as name, address, duration, and credit card, etc.
- Accept user request to process a single reservation.
- RoomReservationWS will be invoked (Fig. 4). Web service method ReserveRoom() will process the request.
- Web service method ReserveRoom() will invoke AvailabilityWS web service and call SetSingleAvailability() method. This method will attempt to update the room availability list in the database.
- Results will be returned to RoomReservation UI object.
- A confirmation message or a room unavailable message will be displayed to the user.

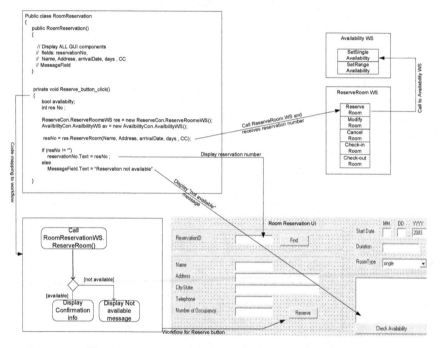

Fig. 12. Implementation of RoomReservation UI object

Fig. 12 is an implementation sample of the activity diagram for the RoomReservation UI object, depicted in Fig. 11:

- RoomReservation user interface object is responsible for all communication with RoomReservationWS methods. It passes input parameters entered by the user, through the graphical user interface, and calls ReserveRoomWS web service invoking ReserveRoom() method.
  ReserveCon.ReserveRoomWS res = new ReserveCon.ReserveRoomeWS();
  resNo = res.ReserveRoom(Name, Address, arrivalDate, days , CC);
- ReserveRoom() web service method of the ReserveRoomWS web service processes the entire service request. A web service may call one or more web

services methods. In this case, SetSingleAvailability() method is invoked from the AvailabilityWS web service.

- ReserveRoom() method returns a numeric reservation number, which is stored in the local variable *resNO* of the RoomReservation user interface and the database.
- RoomReservation user interface displays results received.
- Either reservation number or a room unavailable message is displayed to the user.

6   Discussion and Conclusions

The feature driven dynamic customization approach uses white box reuse of the client user interface objects and black box reuse of Web services. User interface objects have feature dependent code and feature based decisions, which dictate how the user interface code is tailored at runtime. Thus the graphical user interface and invocation of web services is dynamically modified corresponding to the features selected. Black box reuse of Web services is easier to manage; kernel web service components are always used, whereas optional and alternative web service components are invoked based on feature selection. White box reuse of client user interface objects is based on feature conditions and more easily managed since these objects are developed directly by the user organization.

Dynamic customization at run-time has several advantages over the more usual static customization for every member of the product line. First, there is only one code base, which incorporates all features, greatly simplifying the version control problem. Second, the code is only compiled once, instead of once for each application.

The disadvantages are greater code overhead, although for most product lines the cost of additional storage can be tolerated, and greater computation time to execute feature based decisions, which is also tolerable providing the applications are not time critical.

The feature driven customization approach was validated by developing two product lines, the hotel product line and a frequency management product lines. Both product lines were modeled using the PLUS method and implemented in C# in Microsoft Visual Studio .NET. For each product line, at least two applications were derived and tested using conventional approaches.

This paper has described an integrated model driven development and feature driven customization approach for software product lines, which has been used for product lines based on Web Services. The approach can be easily extended to other client/server applications. We are investigating how the concepts of separation of concerns and aspect-oriented development can be applied to product lines.

References

[Clements02]   P. Clements and L. Northrop, Software Product Lines: Practices and Patterns, Addison Wesley, 2002.

[Cohen98]   S. Cohen and L. Northrop, "Object-Oriented Technology and Domain Analysis", Proc. International Conference on Software Reuse, Victoria, June 1998.

[Deitel03]   Deitel, H. M., B. DuWaldt, et al. Web Services - A technical Introduction. Upper Saddle River, New Jersey, Pearson Education, Inc, 2003.

[Gomaa96]   H. Gomaa, L. Kerschberg, V. Sugumaran, C. Bosch, and I Tavakoli, "A Knowledge-Based Software Engineering Environment for Reusable Software Requirements and Architectures," *J. Automated Software Eng*, Vol. 3, Nos. 3/4, 1996.

[Gomaa99]   H. Gomaa and G.A. Farrukh, "Methods and Tools for the Automated Configuration of Distributed Applications from Reusable Software Architectures and Components", IEE Proceedings – Software, Vol. 146, No. 6, December 1999.

[Gomaa00]   H. Gomaa, "Designing Concurrent, Distributed, and Real-Time Applications with UML", Addison Wesley, Reading MA, 2000.

[Gomaa02]   H. Gomaa and M. Gianturco, "Domain Modeling for World Wide Web Based Software Product Lines with UML", Proc. IEEE International Conference on Software Reuse, Austin, Texas, April 2002

[Gomaa04]   H. Gomaa and M. E. Shin, "A Multiple-View Meta-Modeling Approach for Variability Management in Software Product Lines", Proc. International Conference on Software Reuse, Madrid, Spain, July 2004.

[Gomaa05]   Gomaa, H. Designing Software Product Lines with UML: From Use Cases to Pattern-based Software Architectures, Addison-Wesley, 2005.

[GomaaSaleh05] H. Gomaa and M.Saleh, "Software Product Line Engineering for Web Services and UML", Proc. 3rd ACS/IEEE International Conference on Computer Systems and Applications, Cairo, Egypt, January 2005.

[Griss98]   M. Griss, J. Favaro, M. D'Alessandro, "Integrating Feature Modeling with the RSEB", Proc. International Conference on Software Reuse, Victoria, June 1998.

[Kang 90]   Kang K. C. et. al., "Feature-Oriented Domain Analysis," Technical Report No. CMU/SEI-90-TR-21, Software Engineering Institute, November 1990.

[Parnas79]   Parnas D., "Designing Software for Ease of Extension and Contraction", IEEE Transactions on Software Engineering, March 1979.

[Rumbaugh05]   J. Rumbaugh, G. Booch, I. Jacobson, "The Unified Modeling Language Reference Manual," Addison Wesley, Second Edition, 2005.

[Weiss99]   D M Weiss and C T R Lai, "Software Product-Line Engineering: A Family-Based Software Development Process," Addison Wesley, 1999.

Inter-organisational Approach in Rapid Software Product Family Development — A Case Study

Varvana Myllärniemi, Mikko Raatikainen, and Tomi Männistö

Helsinki University of Technology
Software Business and Engineering Institute (SoberIT)
P.O. Box 9210, 02015 TKK, Finland
{varvana.myllarniemi, mikko.raatikainen, tomi.mannisto}@tkk.fi

Abstract. Software product families provide an efficient means of reuse between a set of related products. However, software product families are often solely associated with intra-organisational reuse. This paper presents a case study of Fathammer, a small company developing games for different mobile devices. Reuse at Fathammer takes place at multiple levels. The game framework and engine of Fathammer is reused by partner companies that in turn produce game assets to be reused by Fathammer while developing games for various devices. Very rapid development of games is a necessity for Fathammer, whereas maintainability of games is not important. The above characteristics in particular distinguish Fathammer from other case studies and practices usually presented in the product family literature. The results show the applicability and challenges of software product family practices in the context of multiple collaborating companies and a fast-changing domain.

1 Introduction

Software reuse is a means of enhancing the efficiency of software development. Several reuse techniques have emerged over the years, one of them being software product families. A *software product family* is a set of products that share a common, managed set of features [1], a common architecture and a set of reusable components [2].

Typically, the reuse that takes place in a software product family is intra-organisational. Recently, the possibility for more open family development has been identified. van der Linden *et al.* [3] note that some software product family organisations may cross company borders. Also the research challenges raised by the transition from closed system development towards open networks have been identified [4]. However, so far ideas rather than solid practices have been presented. Very few cases have been reported on software product family organisations that cross company borders.

This paper provides insight to a setting in which inter-organisational reuse takes place within a software product family. We present a case study Fathammer, a Finnish company that produces 3D games for various mobile devices. Fathammer develops X-Forge, a game framework and engine, on top of which

M. Morisio (Ed.): ICSR 2006, LNCS 4039, pp. 73–86, 2006.

game titles are built. Game title development is outsourced to partner development studios around the world. By reusing game titles, Fathammer derives several game instances each of which is targeted for a certain device and market. Thus the reuse takes place at multiple levels and across company borders.

In addition to the inter-organisational aspect, Fathammer displays a mix of characteristics that is not typically found in reported software product family case studies. The nature of the domain demands very short time-to-market and development cycles, and puts pressure towards cutting them down even more. However, tight schedules should not kill creativity. The case company is relatively small and *ad hoc* in its practices.

The above-mentioned characteristics are in contrast to the well-known case studies of successful product families in the domain of medical, automotive and telecommunication systems [5]. Further, software product family engineering originated from embedded systems development [3]. Therefore, a successful software product family often seems to be characterised by a stable domain, long-lived products, long development cycles and mature engineering practices inherited from embedded systems engineering.

Consequently, this case study indicates that software product family practices can be applied in the context of multiple collaborating companies and within a fast-changing domain. Hence this study refines the applicability of software product family practices. Further, the case study brings out challenges and issues that should be studied by the software product family research community.

The paper is organised as follows. Section 2 describes the research methods. Section 3 gives an introduction to the case company. Section 4 reports the results of the study. Section 5 compares the results to related research. Section 6 discusses the results and identifies lessons learned. Section 7 discusses the validity of results. Finally, Section 8 draws conclusions and suggests future work.

2   Research Method

The goal of the research is to study state of the practice of different kinds of software product families in the industry in order to sharpen the understanding of the feasibility of the different kind of software product family engineering. The study was carried out as a qualitative descriptive case study [6] at Fathammer. We applied the CASFIS framework [7], which is a framework designed for research on industrial software product families.

Fathammer was chosen to the study due to its unique mix of characteristics. We identified these characteristics when the R&D director and process manager of Fathammer gave us a brief overview of their current practices before the study. The overview also gave background information that enabled to tailor the CASFIS framework and focus the study.

The data collection was based on an interview, a validation session, documentation analysis, and a review. The primary data collection method was the interview of the process manager and derivation manager of Fathammer. The interview took about three hours. The interview questions of CASFIS [8] were

Fig. 1. A screenshot from one game title called *Stuntcar Extreme*. (Copyright Fathammer, reproduced with permission.).

slightly modified for the context of Fathammer. The interview was voice-recorded and transcribed, and notes were taken. A few months later, a validation session of roughly two hours was held, during which clarifying questions and uncertain issues were discussed. Documentation analysis covered Fathammer public and non-public documents that were identified to be relevant during the interview. Finally, the process manager reviewed this paper.

The analysis followed the principles of grounded theory approach using deductive coding of data [9]. The initial results were reported in the validation session. For the final analysis, data from the validation session was added. The data was analysed using ATLAS.ti [10], which is a software tool designed for qualitative data analysis.

3   Fathammer

This section presents an overall description of Fathammer, divided according to BAPO (Business, Artifact, Process, Organisation) [11] concerns.

3.1   Business

Fathammer (*www.fathammer.com*) is a Finnish company that produces 3D games for various mobile devices. The domain of mobile games requires very short time-to-market and development cycles. However, tight schedules should not outweigh creativity, since games must be addictive and fun to be successful.

Games are distributed either through device manufacturers, operators or game portals, which are called *sales channels* in this study. Fathammer has made a strategic decision to stay independent of sales channels. The approach has been multi-device from the start, which means that Fathammer provides support for all devices that are feasible technically and sales-wise.

The goal of Fathammer is to produce games on top of proprietary game technology. Towards this end, Fathammer has developed a technology platform called

X-Forge. X-Forge is licensed globally to third party development studios. Currently there are over 80 licensees of X-Forge around the world. Over 15 game titles that use X-Forge have been shipped.

3.2   Artifact

X-Forge is a C++ game development system and a multi-device game engine. Firstly, X-Forge provides functionality common to all games, such as graphics rendering, object world and physics. Secondly, X-Forge abstracts underlying hardware and operating system from games. Currently X-Forge comprises more than 150 KLOC (thousands of lines of code).

Game titles are built by reusing and extending the assets X-Forge provides. The game title architecture is largely determined by X-Forge. A large game title may include over 50 KLOC. Besides code, a game title includes graphics, sounds, and other auxiliary files.

The use of X-Forge alone cannot guarantee that the resulting game title is optimal for a certain mobile device. Further, some sales channels may require their own modifications, such as adding an operator logo to the game. Finally, many localisations and languages have to be supported.

Thus each game title is specialised into a number of game instances called SKUs (Stock Keeping Units). One SKU is targeted for certain device configuration and localisation settings, and is distributed through a certain sales channel. For each game title, approximately three to ten SKUs are produced—the exact number depends on market needs.

3.3   Process

The development process of Fathammer (Fig.2) is divided into X-Forge development and game development.

X-Forge is developed continuously. This includes extending the common functionality, providing support for new platforms, and correcting found bugs. Only rarely functionality implemented in a certain game title is merged into X-Forge.

The lower part of Fig.2 illustrates the development process for one game title and its SKUs. In the preproduction phase, the game concept and its feasibility are checked. In the production phase, the game title is developed iteratively. In the postproduction phase, SKUs are derived from the game title assets. In

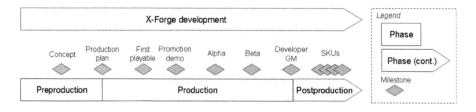

Fig. 2. A coarse-grained view of the development process at Fathammer. Preproduction and production combined take approximately 4 to 6 months.

some cases, the derivation consists of setting appropriate parameter values and configuration settings and re-compiling the code. Usually the derivation also requires a small amount of development or graphics design effort.

Fathammer does not maintain its game titles. Once a game title, i.e., its first SKU, is released, the game title is not developed anymore, other than to produce new SKUs when viable business opportunities emerge. New SKUs can be produced even years after the initial release.

In general, the evolution of X-Forge does not affect previous game releases. However, in a few exceptional cases, Fathammer has ported an old game title to a new version of X-Forge in order to produce an SKU to a new device.

3.4   Organisation

Currently the organisation of Fathammer comprises 36 employees. The organisation reflects the division of the development process. There are separate roles for those responsible of X-Forge development, preproduction, production and postproduction.

The development organisation crosses company borders. Development of one game title (production phase in Fig.2) is outsourced to a partner game development studio. These partner development studios are licensees of X-Forge, and they are located around the world.

4   Results

This section reports the results from the case study analysis and describes three interesting characteristics of Fathammer.

4.1   Inter-company Collaboration

Fathammer develops its software product family in a network of collaborative companies. Four types of co-operation relationships can be identified (Fig.3).

Firstly, Fathammer sells licenses to third party game development studios that wish to develop mobile games reusing X-Forge platform. However, due to Fathammer's recent decision to concentrate on game production, licenses are currently sold only to major publishers and game development studios used for outsourcing.

Secondly, Fathammer game title development is outsourced to partner game development studios, which are also licensees of X-Forge. Fathammer makes the final decisions concerning content of a game, budget and schedule of the development. A benefit of outsourced game development is that Fathammer can increase volume of its software product family without increasing its own size. Fathammer can concentrate on its core capabilities and yet produce a large game portfolio. Another benefit is that by outsourcing game development, Fathammer expands the network of licensed developers, and thus promotes the use of X-Forge as a game technology. However, Fathammer has met some major difficulties in

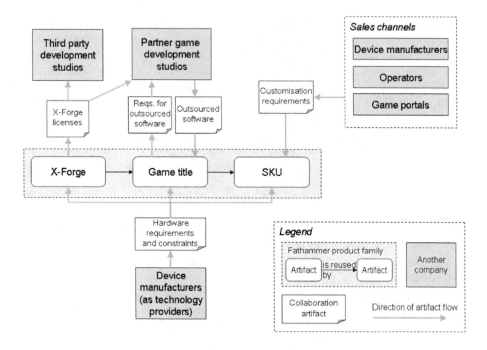

Fig. 3. Collaboration with Fathammer and other companies

outsourcing game title development. In particular, outsourcing development of software that supports variability has proved to be harder than expected.

Thirdly, device manufacturers form a major source of constraints and requirements, since the hardware and operating system underneath affects mobile games considerably. However, Fathammer cannot affect the properties of devices, but the software has to be adapted to device peculiarities. Sometimes the implementation of a device may contain a few surprises, causing difficulties in the game development.

Fourthly, the games are distributed through sales channels. These sales channels may require a customised version of the game, which essentially means producing a new SKU. As an example, an operator may want to distribute a game that portraits operator logos.

4.2   Hierarchical Software Product Family

Fathammer software product family artifacts have been organised hierarchically (Fig.4). There are two levels of reuse and three levels of artifacts in the hierarchy: game titles are built reusing X-Forge, while game titles provide means for rapid SKU production.

The software product family of Fathammer is hierarchical also from the organisational point of view. Further, this hierarchy crosses company borders. X-Forge is developed in-house. Then, X-Forge is reused by partner game development

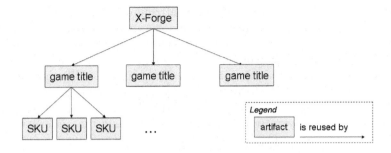

Fig. 4. Fathammer software product family is hierarchical in nature

studios during the game title development. Finally, Fathammer reuses the game title assets during SKU derivation.

The hierarchical model of software product family engineering has brought several benefits to Fathammer.

Firstly, the amount of variability Fathammer has to cope with is considerable. A hierarchical model eases the overall variability handling, provides a separation of concerns and eases derivation for each level.

Secondly, the hierarchical model is easily combined with the geographical distribution that stems from the outsourced game title development. This diminishes the inevitable overhead of distributed development.

Thirdly, a hierarchy eases managing entities with different life cycles. The long-lived and more stable part, X-Forge, is separated into its own layer of software product family, which can be maintained and developed more independently. Short-lived game titles and SKUs are developed separately.

However, a hierarchical approach brings also challenges. A hierarchy makes the organisation and development structure more complex, and weakens the link from the lower level to the upper level entities. However, since Fathammer is such a small organisation, these drawbacks do not have much overall impact.

4.3   Challenges of Rapid Variant Production

The main reason for Fathammer to reuse software is to enable rapid production of variants, since both game titles and SKUs must be produced in a short time frame. This can be achieved by efficient variability management and implementation.

The devices on which Fathammer builds its games vary drastically, ranging from cell phones and portable game consoles to PDAs and Pocket PCs. To cope with this variability, Fathammer has developed X-Forge as a multi-device platform that abstracts hardware away. However, X-Forge alone does not suffice, since some of the hardware-related variability must be taken care of during game title development and SKU derivation. As an example, game controls should be easy to use, regardless of the input controls of the device. Further, game graphics and menus have to adopt to varying display properties, such as resolution and orientation. The postponement of these issues slows SKU production down remarkably.

The varying hardware also causes quality attribute variability. The differences in the device computing resources might be enormous, and thus the software may need to vary its behaviour in order to provide the best perceived quality on all devices. In effect, this requires varying the performance level and memory consumption of software by tuning the game. Fathammer handles this variability in a straightforward manner: varying quality attributes are transformed into varying functionality. Since graphics form a major factor in the consumption of computing and memory resources, it is easy to tune the performance and memory consumption level by, e.g., changing the number of drawn polygons, the drawing algorithms, materials and applied textures.

To complicate the situation even further, game titles and SKUs are very short-lived; in fact they are not maintained at all after release. We call this kind of approach as a *disposable software product family*. A disposable software product family sets certain requirements for variability implementation and management. It is not feasible to build extensive variability mechanisms into game titles, since those mechanisms are used only for deriving a number of SKUs. The challenge is, how to implement variability mechanisms to game titles in a light-weight yet effective manner?

Further, building necessary variability mechanisms must be balanced with outsourcing. The initial approach was to outsource software without any variability. But when a game had not been designed to support variability, variability was really difficult to add afterwards. In other words, this approach accelerated the development of the first SKU, but delayed the development of further variants.

Therefore, Fathammer decided to explicitly specify some variability to outsourced development. However, it would have been infeasible to require implementation for all possible variability; this would have slowed down the game production too much. Therefore, *verification configurations model* was introduced. The game developers are given a number of separate device configurations that represent the range of existing mobile devices. These configurations specify the most critical aspects of the device, such as screen resolution and memory size. At the moment, the number of verification configurations used is three. A game is developed from the start to support these configurations. This enforces a game developer to identify variation points, i.e., the locations in the artifacts where the configurations differ from each other, and implement variation mechanisms for them.

To conclude, extending existing variation points with new variants is easier than creating new variation points from scratch.

5   Related Research

This section discusses related research, compares it with Fathammer practices, and identifies possible mismatch.

5.1   Intra-company and Inter-company Collaboration

Reported case studies of software product families tend to operate in closed, centralised structures of development [12]. Thus the notion of software product family development being comprised of networks of external interoperating component suppliers has not materialised as anticipated [12].

The concept of open networks is presented in product family evaluation framework [3]. BAPO-O, the organisation dimension of the framework, promotes level 4 as inter-company model, and level 5 as open business model. At level 4, software product family engineering takes place between several companies, while at level 5 the business is open for everyone who sees the advantage. However, to the best of our knowledge, there are no reported examples of level 5 approaches.

Even if the collaboration is intra-organisational, a software product family approach within a large company with separate divisions may raise conflicts that hinder the promotion of common interest [13].

Geographical distribution can bring its own challenges to software product family practices. Nokia has tried to answer this organisational challenge by organising its units to be aligned with product family development in order to minimise the overhead of distributed development [14].

Challenges of outsourcing and global software development [15] have been to some extent covered in software engineering research. However, outsourcing in the context of software product families has gained only little research. To the best of our knowledge, there is no research of outsourcing development of software that should support variability.

In comparison with related research, Fathammer software product family is relatively open. Four kinds of collaborations shape the software product family practices of Fathammer, and one of these collaborations involves global outsourcing.

5.2   Hierarchical Software Product Family

The hierarchical model of software product families is argued to be primarily suitable for large organisations with long-lived products [2, 16]. A considerable maturity with respect to development process and management is required [16]. According to Bosch [16], systems with relatively stable requirement sets and long lifetimes are substantially more suitable than products whose requirements change frequently and drastically, e.g., due to new technological possibilities.

Fathammer seems to be almost the exact opposite of the most optimal environment described in [16]. Despite this, Fathammer has succeeded in creating a hierarchical software product family model that suits its needs very well. However, there are a couple of success factors mentioned in [16] that apply to Fathammer case. Firstly, the geographical distribution that is due to outsourcing is easily combined with the hierarchical model of development. Secondly, the hierarchical model is especially suitable to situations where the amount of variability is large.

A drawback of the model is that agile reactions to changed requirements are difficult to make [16]. If an asset on the top level of hierarchy changes, the change must be propagated down all levels of hierarchy. However, this is not an issue for Fathammer, since game titles are not evolved after the release. Even if something changes at the upper level of hierarchy, i.e. in X-Forge, there is usually no need to accommodate existing game titles to these changes.

5.3   Challenges of Rapid Variant Production

For Fathammer, one of the biggest obstacles to rapid variant production is caused by varying hardware. *Hardware enforced variability* is software variability that depends on or is presupposed by the hardware configuration [17]. However, literature on variability most often refers to hardware neutral variability, assuming that variability originates purely from software [17].

Similar problems of hardware variability has been encountered at Nokia [14]. This is called *hardware challenge*, main sources of which consist of keys, display and scrolling, sound and backwards compatibility. Although in many respects Fathammer faces the same problems as Nokia, there are a few significant differences. Firstly, Nokia has control over the hardware and operating systems of the devices, whereas Fathammer does not. Secondly, Fathammer has to operate on many device manufacturers with many devices, which amplifies the differences between variants.

Hardware also creates a need for quality attribute variability at Fathammer. Although quality attributes have been studied quite extensively, surprisingly little research on quality attribute variability has been carried out. Only a few studies mention this phenomenon [18, 19]. However, it is possible that varying quality attributes are more difficult to handle than varying functionality. Unlike functionality, many qualities are architectural in nature [20]. Therefore, changing a quality attribute may require system-wide changes in the architecture.

Svahnberg *et al.* [21] point out that variability should not be introduced too early during the development, since the cost of managing and tracking variants throughout the variability implementation process may be too high. Since the short life span of Fathammer game titles require light-weight variability handling, the cost of early introduction would be even more severe. However, the difficulties with outsourced development indicate that variability shouldn't be introduced too late either.

5.4   Related Case Studies

One of the early pioneers of software product family development has been Nokia [14]. Many of the challenges faced by Nokia are similar to the ones faced by Fathammer. However, these companies are vastly different. Nokia is a huge organisation with very solid practices. Fathammer products are short-lived, and Fathammer has less control over their development. However, it is interesting to see that also Nokia regards openness to be vital for future success [4].

There are case studies of small to medium sized companies that have applied software product families successfully: MarketMaker [22] and Salion [23]. However, Fathammer operates in a domain that seems to require considerably more flexibility and shorter life cycles.

A recent study presented how Java mobile games could be re-engineered using aspect oriented techniques [24]. However, this study was not an industrial case study. It merely showed that it is technically feasible to construct a software product family from Java mobile games. In contrast, our case shows the feasibility, technically, organisationally and business-wise, of creating a software product family in such a domain.

6   Discussion and Lessons Learned

Based on the results of the case study (Section 4) and the comparison with related research (Section 5), we identify lessons that can be learned from Fathammer case.

Software product family engineering can be applied to small companies without matured engineering practices and to domains that are fast-changing and require short development cycles. Fathammer has successfully developed its products in a software product family. The benefits of this model of development have not been directly measured, but one indicator of the success is that Fathammer is currently building a similar game framework for Java mobile games. The drawback of this approach is that Fathammer games are not optimised for certain devices. However, Fathammer has made the strategic decision to serve many instead of focusing on a few devices only.

A software product family development can cross company borders. Game title development is outsourced to geographically distributed partners. Outsourcing is combined with selling licenses to X-Forge platform. To cope with the overhead involved in distributed development, Fathammer has organised its reuse hierarchy (see Fig.4) to match the outsourced development. The inter-organisational approach has been feasible even in a relatively small software product family. In fact, outsourcing is seen as a way of increasing volume without increasing company size.

Outsourcing development of software that is reusable and variable brings new challenges. The challenge lies in specifying the required variability for outsourced software. Extending existing variation points with new variants is easier than creating new variation points from scratch. It is not necessary to specify all possible variants, but it is essential to ensure that the outsourced software implements some mechanisms for all variation points. To address this issue, Fathammer is applying *verification configurations model* to its development.

Hierarchical software product families can be applied to small companies operating on fast-changing domains. Fathammer has regarded the hierarchical model to be very well suitable for organising its software product family engineering. The affecting factors were the need for distributed development, the large amount of variability, and the differences in the life spans of X-Forge platform, game titles and SKUs. The hierarchical model provides a separation of concerns that suits these needs well.

Hardware enforced variability can be a challenge to rapid variant production. Although X-Forge as a multi-device platform abstracts hardware away, there are inevitably some device-related issues that set challenges to rapid game title and SKU production. This is especially apparent when dealing with many device manufactures whose products differ from each other considerably. To conclude, a multi-device platform may not be enough to cover all hardware enforced variability.

Quality attribute variability can be resolved by transforming it to varying functionality. 3D games are very performance-intensive. When this kind of software has to be adapted to varying hardware, it is necessary to vary the performance level of software. Fathammer does this by transforming varying quality to varying functionality. However, there is one factor, namely graphics, which largely determines the quality. Without such a factor, it is possible that architectural means are needed. Further research on this topic is required.

Short life span of reusable assets requires light-weight variability mechanisms. A software product family with a very short life span requires light-weight yet effective ways of realising and implementing variability mechanisms. One Fathammer game title forms a *disposable software product family*. Therefore, effective variability implementation is far more important than effective variability management.

7   Validity and Reliability

We tried to ensure validity by using multiple sources of data i.e. the interviews, document analysis, and validation session; allowing an interviewee at Fathammer to review the report; and establishing a chain of evidence i.e. stored data and using as accurate data as possible, such as transcripts. The study contains also threats to validity: data collection took relatively short time although use of the methods was relatively efficient since the researchers were familiar with the research methods, had used the method in several studies before, and the method, in particular the interview questions, was tailored to Fathammer on a basis of initial understanding; only two persons were interviewed; no game developer partners were interviewed; and the study lacked longitudinal observations in which the Fathammer would have been observed over a period of time. Reliability was improved by following the publicly documented CASFIS framework [7].

We aimed to show that software product family practices can be applied in several different contexts. Consequently, research results on software product families may need refinement for applicability. While similar practices as at Fathammer could be applied with similar success, there are several context factors that should be taken into account. However, this requires further research.

8   Conclusions

We have presented a case study of Fathammer, a company developing a software product family of 3D mobile games. The domain requires flexibility, creativity and short time-to-market; yet it has been feasible to build a software product family on such a domain.

Fathammer case exemplifies the following. Firstly, software product family organisations can cross company borders. Secondly, software product family development can be outsourced, but this kind of outsourcing raises new challenges related to variability implementation. Thirdly, even small, immature companies requiring flexibility can develop a hierarchical software product family. Fourthly, a multi-device platform is not always enough *per se*, but hardware enforced variability needs to be taken care of during variant production, thus delaying the release. Finally, if the artifacts of the software product family are short-lived, light-weight variability management is required.

Although software product family development has helped Fathammer to produce games more efficiently, several challenges remain to be solved. Therefore, areas that need further research are identified.

Firstly, outsourcing combined to software product families requires further research. What are the situations in which outsourcing is applicable? How can one successfully outsource development of software that should support variability?

Secondly, hardware enforced variability has not gained much research attention. At Fathammer, varying hardware creates a need for quality attribute variability. If quality attribute variability cannot be easily transformed into functional variability, there is a need for other, possibly architectural means.

Acknowledgements

The authors acknowledge Ville Vatén and others at Fathammer who participated and aided our case study. The financial support of the 100-year Foundation of Technology Industries of Finland is acknowledged.

References

1. Clements, P., Northrop, L.: Software Product Lines—Practices and Patterns. Addison–Wesley (2001)
2. Bosch, J.: Design and Use of Software Architectures: Adapting and Evolving a Product-Line Approach. Addison–Wesley (2000)
3. van der Linden, F., Bosch, J., Kamsties, E., Känsälä, K., Obbink, H.: Software product family evaluation. In: Proc. of Software Product Line Conference. (2004)
4. Bosch, J.: Software product families in Nokia. In: Proc. of Software Product Line Conference. (2005)
5. Cohen, S.: Product line state of the practice report. Technical Report CMU/SEI-2002-TN-017, Software Engineering Institute (2002)
6. Yin, R.K.: Case Study Research. 2nd edn. Sage: Thousand Oaks (1994)
7. Raatikainen, M., Männistö, T., Soininen, T.: CASFIS–approach for studying software product families in industry. In: Proc. of the 2nd Groningen Workshop on Software Variability Management. (2004)
8. Raatikainen, M., Männistö, T., Soininen, T.: Case study questions for studying industrial software product families. Technical Report HUT-SoberIT-C10, Helsinki University of Technology (2004)
9. Strauss, A., Corbin, J.: Basics of Qualitative Research: Grounded Theory Procedures and Techniques. Newbury Park, CA: Sage Publications (1990)

10. ATLAS.ti: User's manual and reference, version 4.2. (2004)
11. van der Linden, F.: Software product families in Europe: The Esaps and Cafe projects. IEEE Software **19**(4) (2002) 41–49
12. Mannion, M.: Organizing for software product line engineering. In: Proc. of Workshop on Software Technology and Engineering Practice. (2002)
13. van Ommering, R., Bosch, J.: Widening the scope of software product lines—from variation to composition. In: Proc. of Software Product Line Conference. (2002)
14. Maccari, A., Heie, A.: Managing infinite variability in mobile terminal software. Software—Practice and Experience **35**(6) (2005) 513–537
15. Herbsleb, J., Moitra, D.: Global software development. IEEE Software **18**(2) (2001) 16–20
16. Bosch, J.: Software product lines: Organizational alternatives. In: Proc. of International Conference on Software Engineering. (2001)
17. Jaring, M., , Bosch, J.: A taxonomy and hierarchy of variability dependencies in software product family engineering. In: Proc. of Computer Software and Applications Conference. (2004)
18. Halmans, G., Pohl, K.: Communicating the variability of a software-product family to customers. Software and Systems Modeling **2**(1) (2003) 15–36
19. Hallsteinsen, S., Fægri, T.E., Syrstad, M.: Patterns in product family architecture design. In: Proc. of Workshop on Software Product-Family Engineering. (2003)
20. Bass, L., Clements, P., Kazman, R.: Software Architecture in Practice. Addison–Wesley (1998)
21. Svahnberg, M., van Gurp, J., Bosch, J.: A taxononomy of variability realization techniques. Software—Practice and Experience **35**(8) (2005) 705–754
22. Gacek, C., Knauber, P., Schmid, K., Clements, P.: Successful software product line development in a small organisation. Technical Report IESE-Report No. 013.01/E, Fraunhofer IESE (2001)
23. Clements, P., Northrop, L.: Salion, inc.: A software product line case study. Technical Report CMU/SEI-2002-TR-038, Software Engineering Institute (2002)
24. Alves, V., Matos, P.J., Cole, L., Borba, P., Ramalho, G.: Extracting and evolving mobile games product lines. In: Proc. of Software Product Line Conference. (2005)

Ontology-Based Feature Modeling
and Application-Oriented Tailoring

Xin Peng, Wenyun Zhao, Yunjiao Xue, and Yijian Wu

Computer Science and Engineering Department, Fudan University, Shanghai 200433, China
{pengxin, wyzhao, yjxue, wuyijian}@fudan.edu.cn

Abstract. Feature models have been widely adopted in domain requirements capturing and specifying. However, there are still difficulties remaining in domain model validating and application-oriented tailoring. These difficulties are partly due to the missing of a strictly defined feature meta-model, which makes it difficult to formally represent the feature models. Aiming at the problem, we propose an ontology-based feature modeling method supporting application-oriented tailoring. In this method features are classified into several categories and are all precisely defined in the OWL-based meta-model. Expression capacity of the feature model can be greatly improved due to the rich types of features. On the other hand the feature model can be easily converted into ontology model and be validated through ontology inference. Application-oriented tailoring can also gain support from the reasoning-based guidance. Finally, advantages of ontology-based feature modeling, especially for component and architecture design, are discussed with our conclusions.

1 Introduction

Domain analysis is an essential activity for successful reuse across applications in the same domain. Based on the domain model, domain assets, including DSSA (Domain-Specific Software Architecture) and domain components can be produced. When implementing a new system, products of domain analysis will be tailored to produce the specification and design of that system [1]. So, it is obvious that domain model is essential for domain and application-specific development.

To provide necessary supports for the domain and application development, the domain model should meet some requirements. First, it should provide sufficient business knowledge for the design of architecture and components. Second, it must offer the means to specify both features and their composition rules [2]. Then validation of the model can be performed on constraints. A domain model is valid if there is at least one set of single-system requirements that can be generated from it and satisfy the constraints [3]. An inconsistent domain model is meaningless for application development and will cause unnecessary investment waste in domain development. Third, it should present an applicable way for application engineers to configure the domain model according to product-specific requirements.

Nowadays, concept of feature model has been widely adopted in domain requirements capturing and specifying, since FODA [1] introduced it into domain engineering. However, a strictly defined feature meta-model is often missing, which makes

M. Morisio (Ed.): ICSR 2006, LNCS 4039, pp. 87 – 100, 2006.

feature models difficult to be formally represented. Thus, validation and application-oriented tailoring of domain models are also difficult due to the missing of a formal basis. Schlick [4] also indicated that a solid theoretical foundation is needed first.

Our research group is concerned with feature-driven domain and application development, including domain analysis, DSSA design, application-oriented tailoring and component-composition based application development. In these fields a strictly-defined modeling basis for features is essential, which should provide a mechanism to connect model elements in various development phases. Ontology related theory is a suitable way to achieve our goals. Ontology is a conceptualization of a domain or subject area typically captured in an abstract model of how people think about things in the domain [5]. Rubén [5] considers domain models as narrow or specialized ontology, and the main difference is that domain models define abstract concepts in an informal way and have no axioms. Because of the facilities for the generalization and specialization of concepts and the unambiguous terminology it provides [6], ontology has been widely used in domain knowledge representation and requirement modeling, reuse and consistency checking. For example, Sugumaran etc. [7] proposed a semantic-based approach to component retrieval, in which ontology and domain models are adopted for capturing application domain specific knowledge to express more pertinent queries for component retrieval. Girardi etc. [6] proposed GRAMO, an ontology-based technique for the specification of domain and user models in Multi-Agent Domain Engineering.

This paper proposes an ontology-based feature modeling method, in which features are divided into several categories (e.g. action, facet, and term) and defined as ontology concepts respectively. In this way, we can provide better support for domain modeling, and succeeding domain design and implementation. First, ontology-based feature model can be formally represented easily and validation of the model can be realized through ontology reasoning. Second, the ontology-based unambiguous terminology and faceted feature description provide precise and detailed semantic knowledge for the domain, so the feature model can also be adopted as the domain business model. The rich business information in it can be used as semantic infrastructure for component description and architecture design. Third, modularity can be supported by feature facets and dependency semantics. Finally, it provides a unified meta-model for both domain model and application model and a stepwise way for customization, which ease the application-oriented tailoring of feature models.

The remainder of this paper is organized as follows. Section 2 presents the ontology-based feature modeling architecture and the meta-model. Section 3 and section 4 discuss model validating and application-oriented tailoring respectively. Finally, we draw our conclusions with discussion of ontology-based feature modeling and future work in section 5.

2   Ontology-Based Feature Model

This section introduces the ontology-based feature modeling architecture and the feature meta-model first. Then some basic rules for feature modeling are introduced in 2.3, followed by an example of feature model in 2.4 for demonstration. Finally representation of complex constraints and the modularity mechanism are specially discussed in 2.5 and 2.6 respectively. Since OWL [8] is a W3C recommendation for ontology representation, we define the meta-model on OWL.

2.1 Ontology-Based Feature Model Architecture

Our ontology-based feature modeling architecture is presented in figure 1, which is based on a three-layer structure with an ontology level besides the traditional feature model level and meta-model level. The meta-model is strictly defined on OWL, so the feature model can be easily converted into OWL model. Constraints-related rules are also given in the meta-model level and then converted into ontology rules. By ontology reasoning we can perform both domain model validating and tailoring guidance, which are discussed in section 3 and 4 respectively.

The structure is similar to the XML-based three-layer structure in [2], while the main difference is that in our method domain model and application model share the same meta-model, only with different variability policy. Domain model contains domain-level variability, which will be specialized during application engineering to derive final products [4]. Even application model may still contain variability, which will be fixed at runtime by parameters or configuration files.

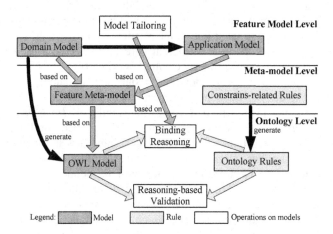

Fig. 1. Ontology-based feature modeling architecture

2.2 Feature Meta-model

Intuitively, a feature is a coherent and identifiable bundle of system functionality that helps characterize the system from the user perspective [9]. So operations with business semantics are basis of the feature model. In feature-oriented domain analysis, aggregation and generalization are applied to capture the commonalities among applications in the domain in terms of abstractions [1]. Differences between applications are captured in the refinements [1], mainly by decomposition and specialization.

In our method, features are divided into several categories. The basis is *Action*, which represents business operations. In order to provide more business details for actions, we introduce the concept of facet for actions, which can be construed as perspectives, viewpoints, or dimensions [5] and is a widely used classification scheme in library science. *Facet* is defined as dimension of precise description for *Action*. An action can have multiple facets and the facets can be inherited along with generalization relations between actions. Restricted value space for *Facet* is represented by *Term*. By *Facet* and *Term*, we can define a feature in more detail. This mechanism provides the "feature attributes" expressiveness, as proposed in [4].

In the ontology-based feature meta-model (depicted in figure 2) *Action* and *Term* are defined as OWL Class (*owl:Class*). *Facet* is defined as OWL property (*owl:Property*), domain (*rdfs:domain*) and range (*rdfs:range*) of which are *Action* and *Term* respectively. As OWL classes, *Action* and *Term* can form their own specialization tree by the relation *subClassOf*, which represents direct inheritance. All the *subClassOf* instances will be converted into *rdfs:subClassOf* in the OWL model, and the direct *subClassOf* relations will be reserved.

In figure 2, domain and range of OWL properties are represented by aggregation elements with solid and dashed lines respectively. *HasElement* is another important relation, which represents decomposition between certain action and its sub-actions.

Specialized and optional features are two basic mechanisms for variation [10]. In our method, the former is achieved by generalization between actions or terms, while the latter is denoted by the *IfOptional* property defined on *HasElement*. The range of *IfOptional* is the RDF data type *xsd:Boolean* and the value *True* means the sub-action is an optional element for its parent action. It should be noticed that the optional property is not defined on action itself but on the relation with its parent, so an action can have different optional property for different parents. In OWL, a property is also a class, so we can easily define a property on another property.

Three kinds of dependencies are identified in our method, namely *Use*, *Decide* and *ConfigDepend*. *Use* denotes the dependency on other features for its correct functioning or implementation [11], which is somewhat similar to *HasElement*. However, parent action in *HasElement* relationship can be seen as cooperation framework for its sub-actions, while a *Use* client often implements some actual function and assign certain part to the supplier. *Decide* indicates that execution result of an action can determine which variant of a variable action will be bound for its parent action (*HasElement*) or client (*Use*). So, the range of *Decide* includes *HasElement* and *Use*. *Use* and *Decide* embodies direct runtime functional dependencies, while *ConfigDepend* represents configuration constraints, which are static dependencies on binding-states of variable features [12]. Besides *Action*, the meta-model provides more precise expressiveness for elements of configuration dependencies by *FacetValue*. *FacetValue* itself is an OWL property from *Facet* to *Term* or *Boolean*, representing the facet value assumption of certain action.

The phase in the software life-cycle to decide whether a variation feature should be bound to or removed is called binding-time of features [13]. And the binding times will influence the design of system architectures [10]. So *HasBindTime* is defined on *HasElement* or *Use* relationships where the sub-action or use supplier action has variations (e.g. optional *HasElement* instance or abstract action with several variants). Typical binding times include reuse-time, compile-time, load-time, and run-time [1, 10]. However, only two binding times of *BuildTime* and *RunTime* are identified, since the main purpose of feature model is to support the tow development phases of domain engineering and application engineering. Intuitively, *BuildTime* binding variations should be implemented as abstract components, which are replaced by application components in product development, while *RunTime* binding variations should be implemented as domain components with variant-selecting proxy or interface parameters, which can determine the final semantics of the invoked service at runtime.

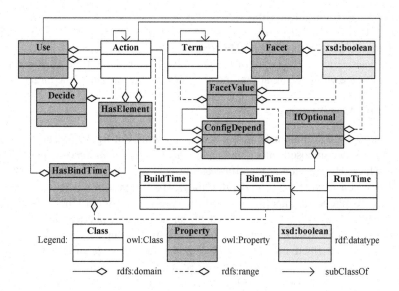

Fig. 2. Ontology-based feature meta-model

2.3 Basic Rules

There exist some basic rules for feature modeling. They act on the feature model directly and can be easily validated in modeling process. Because of the limited space, only three of them are listed here.

Definition 1. Facet set and facet value
$\forall action \in Action$, *FacetSet(action)* denotes all the effective facets for action. And for $\forall facet \in FacetSet(action)$, *action.facet* represents the value of *action* taken on *facet*. For example, there is *TextualDisplay.NeedProtocol=Telnet* in figure 3.

Property 1: Facet value restriction on sub-actions
$\forall a1,a2 \in Action, f \in FacetSet(a1)$, lets (*a2 subClassOf a1*), then $f \in FacetSet(a2)$ and (*a2.f subClassOf a1.f*).
    Note that in OWL a concept is a subclass of itself.

Property 2: Decomposition consistency
$\forall A1,A2 \in Action$, (*A2 subClassOf A1*), then for $\forall a1 \in Action$ and *A1-a1=(A1 HasElement a1)*:

If (*A1-a1 IfOptional False*), then $\exists a2 \in Action$, (*a2 subClassOf a1*), A2-a2=(A2 *HasElement a2*) and (*A2-a2 IfOptional False*).

This property states that all the mandatory elements of an action should be reserved in its variants. For the optional elements, the variants can have their own policies (removed, or reserved to be mandatory or optional).

Property 3: Decide binding time

$\forall a1, a2 \in Action$, a1-a2=(*a1 HasElement a2*) or a1-a2=(*a1 Use a2*), if $\exists a3 \in Action$ and (*a3 Decide a1-a2*), then (*a1-a2 HasBindTime Runtime*).

This property limited the target of *Decide* to have the binding time of *Runtime*: The source of Decide will execute at runtime to determine the variant of the target.

2.4 Feature Model Example

A segment of EBBS domain feature model is presented in figure 3. The top feature *BBSService* is decomposed into *UserLogin*, *MailService*, *BoadService*, and *MsgDisplay*, in which *MailService* is identified as optional element. Facet *HasFilePolicy* is defined between *BoardService* and *FilePolicy*, which represents whether file-upload is supported when posting and the allowed file types. According to the concept inheritance semantics in OWL, facets defined on an action are inherited by its variants. Furthermore, values of the facets are restricted by the super-action. For example, *NeedProtocol* is defined on *MsgDisplay*, so the facet values of *NeedProtocol* on *GraphicalDisplay* and *TextualDisplay* are restricted to be subclass of Protocol (*Http* and *Telnet* in figure 3). Besides abstract and optional actions (denoted by *subClassOf* and *IfOptional*), *Facet* also reserves variations for corresponding *Action* feature. For instance, *Facet HasStorageWay* defined on *FileTransfer* enables application engineers to make the decision of storing uploaded files in database or file system.

Fixing stages of all these variations are indicated by *BindTime*. For example, *BindTime* of the *HasElement* instance between *BBSService* and *MailService* is BuildTime, so the supported file policy of *BoardService* should be decided in application development and be fixed at runtime.

Two variants of *UserLogin* are identified in the model. *NormalLogin* means accepting and treating the request normally, while *RejectLogin* means rejecting the request. The binding time of them is *RumTime* and the binding is determined by *LoadEvaluate*. That means evaluating the system load and rejecting the login request when the load is heavy. *Decide* is similar to the *Modification* dependency in [11], which is interpreted as that the behavior of a feature can be modified by another feature. We consider *Decide* is clearer for dependency description in that the modifier is just a determining factor for variant-selecting of modifiee.

Both *BoardService* and *MailService* have *Use* dependencies on *FileTransfer*, and they are both optional. It can be seen from the *ConfigDepend* on *FileTransfer* that facet values of *BoardService* and *MailService* can determine the binding of *FileTransfer*. The *FacetValue* on *BoardService* can be interpreted as the situation of "*BoardService* having the value of *FileSupport* on the facet of *HasFilePolicy*". The appearance of that situation depends on the binding of *FileTransfer* and *GraphicalDisplay*.

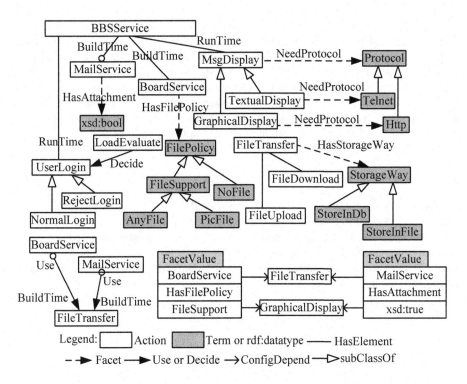

Fig. 3. Example of EBBS domain feature model

2.5 Complex Constraints

Constraints are a kind of static dependencies among binding-states of features [12], which provide a way to verify the results of requirements customization [13]. Three constraint categories, namely binary constraints, group constraints, and complex constraints, are identified in [12].

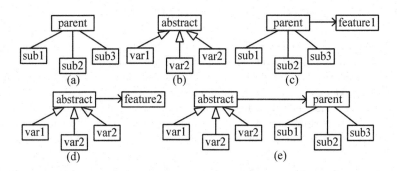

Fig. 4. Expression of complex constraints

In our method, constraints are represented by *ConfigDepend*, which is a kind of binary constraints defined between *Action* and *FacetValue*. By decomposition, specialization and binary constraints, we can also intuitively express most group constraints and complex constraints referred in [12]. Figure 4 shows the most usual cases. Figure 4a shows the common case of *all-bound* group constraints in that mandatory elements *sub1*, *sub2*... should be bound for *parent*. Figure 4b indicates that one and only one of the variants var1, var2... of *abstract* should be bound for it. Figure 4c-4e present common expressions of complex constraints. For example, 4e denotes that the binding of *abstract* (any of its variants) requires the binding of *parent* (all of its elements).

2.6 Modularity Mechanism

An applicable modularity mechanism is essential for feature modeling, especially when the model is large and complex. For example, the *feature macro* mechanism is proposed in [2] to split a large model into independent modules. A feature macro contains a feature node with all its sub-nodes, and can be extended in different instances by adding new features to its sub-tree. But this parameterized modularity mechanism has some shortages in flexibility and encapsulation.

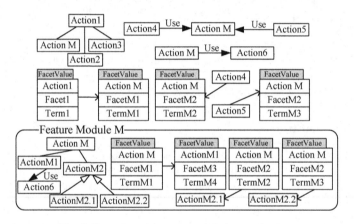

Fig. 5. Facet-based feature modularity mechanism

In our method, a module is a block box with a top feature and all its sub-features, which can be referred at different points of upper feature diagrams in different manners. The inner structure of the module is defined in its module feature diagram. Thus, a large feature model can be easily decomposed into modules at various layers. Figure 5 demonstrates the facet-based feature modularity mechanism, in which *Action M* is referred as whole by three actions and the inner structure of the module is defined in *Feature Module M*. Action1, Action4 and Action5 reuse *Action M* by the relationships of *HasElement* and *Use* with different parameters, which are expressed by those *ConfigDepend* instances on *Action M*. For example, *Action4* demands the facet *FacetM2* of *Action M* to be *TermM2*. Thus *Feature M* can be reused for different detailed demands as a black box, only its facets can be referred as "feature interface". Inner model of Feature M can be defined independently. In *Module M* (depicted in figure 5), *Action*

M is further described by its sub-features. Realization of various semantics of *Action M* depends on its sub-features. The dependencies are represented by the *ConfigDepend* instances between *Action M* and its sub-features. So we can see how various outer demands can be implemented by *module M* clearly. Besides, the sub-features can also employ those outer features provided by the top feature. For example, *Action M* has *Use* relationship with *Action6*, so *Action6* can be referred in *module M* by *ActionM1*. Thus, when developing the feature model of a module, one need only to consider how to meet various facet semantics of the top feature with outer resources provided by the top feature.

3   OWL-Based Formal Representation and Validation

Based on the meta-model over OWL we can transform a feature model into OWL model easily. Then reasoning-based validation can be performed on the ontology by inference engine. Jena [14] is a widely used Java framework for building semantic web applications, which provides a programmatic environment for RDF, RDFS and OWL, including a rule-based inference engine. In our implementation, it is adopted to generate the OWL file and reason on it.

3.1   OWL Representation of Feature Model

A segment of the OWL model for the EBBS domain feature model (depicted in figure 3) is presented in figure 6. *Action* features (e.g. *BBSService*, *MsgDisplay*) are defined as subclasses of *Action*. Facets (e.g. *NeedProtocol*) are defined as subproperties of *Facet* with various facets and terms. The decomposition relationship between *BBSService* and *MailService* is denoted by *BBSService-MailService*, which is a subproperty of *HasElement* with the *IfOptional* value "true". The OWL model can be generated by Jena API and be further processed with inference rules.

3.2   Constraints-Related Rules

This subsection introduces constraints-related rules for feature modeling. Constraints on variation features capture the binding relations with other features [10]. Validation of these rules is not as direct as the basic rules (see 3.1). So some methods are proposed to capture and validate on the constraints, such as propositional logic [10, 13], first-order logic [3] and XSL [2]. In our method, constraints are captured by inference rules and validated by ontology reasoning. So the constraints-related rules are described as Jena OWL rules here. A Jena rule has the format of:

[uncle: (?a fatheris ?b), (?b brotheris ?c) -> (?a uncleis ?c)].

This rule denotes a simple inference that a brother of one's father is his uncle.

For a variation feature, the binding-state can be *Bound*, *Removed* or *Undecided* [13]. Features with the state *Bound* or *Removed* are state-decided, while *Undecided* features remain to be variable. In our ontology-based feature model, the *Action* feature also has these three binding-states. However, there is still another binding type, i.e. specialization of *Facet* values. For example, the *Action FileTransfer* can be specialized to have the value *StoreInFile* in the application model. In order to describe the binding-state of Action features, we introduce a new ontology property *HasState* for *Action* with two possible value of *Bound*, *Removed* and *Conflict* (denotes the inconsistent state). And the existing property *Facet* can represent current state of *Facet* value binding. For example, in figure 3, when the *Facet HasFilePolicy* takes the value *FileSupport*, we will know *BoardService* is chosen to support file and *NoFile* has been negated. However, the binding of *AnyFile* or *PicFile* is still undecided.

For feature constraints, the basic relationships are *Require* and *Mutex*. They have the following semantics: (1) (*a Require b*) denotes that binding of feature *a* depends on the binding of feature *b*; (2) (*a Mutex b*) denotes feature *a* and *b* can not be bound at the same time. All constraints will be converted to these two basic relations and then be validated.

Property 4: Decomposition constraints
Description: Binding of an *Action* depends on the binding of its mandatory elements and *Use* suppliers.
Ontology Rule:
[(?a ?h ?b), (?h rdfs:subPropertyOf HasElement), (?h IfOptional false) -> (?a Require ?b)].
[(?a ?u ?b), (?u rdfs:subPropertyOf Use), (?u IfOptional false) -> (?a Require ?b)].

Property 5: Action specialization constraints
Description: If one and only one variant of an Action is bound, it is bound itself. Note that *subClassOf* denotes the direct inheritance defined in the meta-model (not the transitive *rdfs:subClassOf* in OWL).
Ontology Rule:
[(?a rdfs:subClassOf Action), (?a subClassOf ?b) -> (?a Require ?b)];
[(?c rdfs:subClassOf Action), (?a subClassOf ?c), (?b subClassOf ?c) -> (?a Mutex ?b)].

Property 6: Facet value constraints
Description: Binding of a *FacetValue* feature depends on the binding of the corresponding *Action* feature and those *FacetValue* features with more general value.
Ontology Rule:
[(?f rdfs:subPropertyOf Facet), (?a ?f ?t), (?t subClassOf ?m) -> (?a ?f ?m)];
[(?f rdfs:subPropertyOf Facet), (?a ?f ?t), (?v rdfs:subPropertyOf FacetValue), (?f ?v ?t) -> (?a Require v?)];
[(?v rdfs:subPropertyOf FacetValue), (?f ?v ?t), (?a ?f ?m) -> (?v Require ?a)].

Property 7: Configuration dependency constraints
Ontology Rule:
[(?b Decide ?a) -> (?a Require ?b)];
[(?a ConfigDepend ?b) -> (?a Require ?b)].

Property 8: Binding constraints
Ontology Rule:
[(?a Require ?b), (?a HasState Bound) -> (?b HasState Bound)];
[(?v rdfs:subPropertyOf FacetValue), (?f ?v ?t), (?a ?f ?m) -> (?a ?f ?t)].

Property 9: Removing constraints
Ontology Rule:
[(?a Require ?b), (?b HasState Removed) -> (?a HasState Removed)];
[(?a Mutex ?b), (?a HasState Bound) -> (?b HasState Removed)];
[(?a Require ?b), (?a Mutex ?b) -> (?a HasState Removed)].

```
......
<rdf:Property rdf:about="#HasElement">
    <rdfs:range rdf:resource="#Action"/>
    <rdfs:domain rdf:resource="#Action"/>
</rdf:Property>
<owl:DatatypeProperty rdf:ID="ifOptional">
    <rdfs:range rdf:resource="http://www.w3.org/2001/XMLSchema#boolean"/>
    <rdfs:domain rdf:resource="#Use"/>
    <rdfs:domain rdf:resource="#HasElement"/>
</owl:DatatypeProperty>
<owl:Class rdf:ID="BBSService">
    <EBBS:BBSService-MsgDisplay rdf:resource="#UserLogin"/>
    <EBBS:BBSService-MsgDisplay rdf:resource="#MsgDisplay"/>
    <EBBS:BBSService-BoardService rdf:resource="#BoardService"/>
    <EBBS:BBSService-MailService rdf:resource="#MailService"/>
    <rdfs:subClassOf rdf:resource="#Action"/>
</owl:Class>
<rdf:Property rdf:ID="BBSService-MailService">
    <rdfs:subPropertyOf rdf:resource="#HasElement"/>
    <EBBS:IfOptional>true</EBBS:IfOptional>
</rdf:Property>
<rdf:Property rdf:ID="Facet">
    <rdfs:range rdf:resource="#Term"/>
    <rdfs:domain rdf:resource="#Action"/>
</rdf:Property>
<rdf:Property rdf:ID="NeedProtocol">
    <rdfs:subPropertyOf rdf:resource="#Facet"/>
</rdf:Property>
<owl:Class rdf:about="#MsgDisplay">
    <EBBS:NeedProtocol rdf:resource="#Protocol"/>
    <rdfs:subClassOf rdf:resource="#Action"/>
</owl:Class>
......
```

Fig. 6. Segment of OWL representation for the EBBS domain model

3.4 Reasoning-Based Validation

Rules defined in 3.3 capture restrictions among features. In order to derive the validation conclusions from the model, we define the final rule for *conflict* as:

[(?a HasState Bound), (?a HasState Removed) -> (?a HasState Conflict)].

Besides the feature model, users should also specify the mandatory features in the model. These mandatory features (usually the top service features) will be represented by the relation of (*feature HasState Bound*). Then we can convert the OWL model into RDF statements and store them in a database (such as MySQL in our implementation) with Jena [14]. The conversion is executed along with the reasoning based on the inference rules, including basic rules (e.g. RDFS and OWL axioms) and user-defined rules.

After reasoning and RDF statements storage, we can get the validation result directly from the database by the RDF triples of (*a HasState Conflict*). If there is no such statement, then the model is valid. Otherwise, the model is inconsistent denoting an invalid original domain model or tailoring decisions. However, we can see in section 4 that the tailoring process can be guided by reasoning to avoid invalid decisions.

Besides *consistency*, *nonredundancy* and *necessity* are also identified as properties of well-formed domain feature models in [10]. These two properties can also be validated by reasoning: violation of *nonredundancy* means some variation features are set to be *Removed*, and violation of *necessity* means some variation features are set to be *Bound* (mandatory).

4 Application-Oriented Tailoring

The domain model needs to be customized in application engineering. In the instantiation process generic assets provided by the domain are configured to build a particular application [2]. After that, reuse decisions for domain assets and development of product-specific assets can be made. So application-oriented tailoring of the domain model is essential for successful product development. Two methods of requirement customization, free selection and discriminant-based selection, are identified in [15]. The former allows engineers to select requirements from the product line model freely, while the latter uses constraints and permits choices to be made only at discriminant points. In our opinion, free selection is likely to be used for immature domains, while discriminant-based selection looks fit for mature, steady and thoroughly-analyzed domains. Discriminant-based selection is chosen to be supported in our method, since it can ease the tailoring and strictly ensure the consistency between domain and application feature models.

Domain models in practice are often large and complex, so two mechanisms are provided to ease the tailoring. First, the model can be customized gradually with the hierarchical modules. When tailoring is executed in a hierarchy, only features or modules (see 2.5. Modularity Mechanism) in the same hierarchy are involved. After that, tailoring process is executed within each module involved in the upper hierarchy. It is obvious that well-designed hierarchy and modularity is essential for the effect of this principle. Second, the tailoring can be guided by identification of free variable for customization. A free variable means a variation feature on which no other variation feature depends for binding. Identification of active points is obvious: those variation features do not appear as the *object* of *Require* statements in the ontology. Also, in a well-designed model, free variables usually appear in upper hierarchies relative to passive variables.

5 Evaluation and Conclusion

A strictly-defined formal basis is essential for applicable feature modeling. In this paper, ontology is introduced as the definition foundation of the feature meta-model. Ontology has been widely adopted in domain knowledge modeling and has corresponding modeling language, such as OWL. So the feature model can be easily converted into formal ontology model. Furthermore, rule-based reasoning can be performed on the ontology model for model validating and tailoring guidance.

Establishing a mapping between domain model and the architecture is the objective of domain engineering [16]. However, there is a large gap between the problem space and the solution space. We can reduce the gap by establishing a smooth transition from elements in the domain model (i.e. features) to elements in the architecture model (i.e. components). In our research, domain ontology (i.e. the ontology-based feature model) is also representation basis for component semantics. We can first map the feature model to conceptual architecture, which defines business function assignments among components and semantic interactions between them. Then the conceptual architecture can be converted into the artifact architecture by combining technical factors (e.g. the component model and platform).

The ontology-based method has been implemented in OntoFeature (depicted in figure 7), an ontology-based feature modeling tool. It supports multi-view feature modeling and generation of the integrative feature diagram. Generation and validation of ontology model are also implemented by Jena APIs integrated in it. In the process of application-oriented tailoring, the tool provides a stepwise guidance through active-variations analysis.

Currently, our work is focusing on feature-driven DSSA design and architecture customization. Besides domain modeling and design, we are also interested in feature-oriented component composition, requirements trace and change management. Our final goal is to provide all-life-long support for feature-oriented domain and application development, including methods and corresponding tool set.

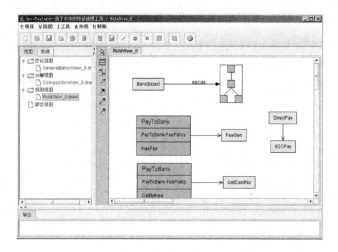

Fig. 7. Snapshot of OntoFeature tool

Acknowledgments. This work is supported by the National High Technology Development 863 Program of China under Grant No. 2004AA113030, 2005AA113120, the National Natural Science Foundation of China under Grant No. 60473061, the Science Technology Committee of Shanghai under Grant No. 04DZ15022. We would like to thank the members of the Feature Engineering group of our Software Engineering Lab, especially Jianhua Gu, Liwei Shen, Yiming Liu, etc.

References

1. Kang, Kyo C., Sholom G. Cohen, James A Hess, William E. Novak, and A. Spencer Peterson: Feature-Oriented Domain Analysis (FODA) Feasibility Study. Technical Report CMU/SEI-90-TR-21, Software Engineering Institute, Carnegie Mellon University, Pittsburgh, PA.

2. V. Cechticky, A. Pasetti, O. Rohlik, and W. Schaufelberger: XML-Based Feature Modelling. ICSR 2004, LNCS 3107, p.101–114, 2004. Springer-Verlag.
3. Mike Mannion: Using First-Order Logic for Product Line Model Validation. SPLC2 2002, LNCS 2379, p.176–187, 2002. Springer-Verlag.
4. Schlick, M., and Hein, A.: Knowledge Engineering in Software Product Lines. European Conference on Artificial Intelligence (ECAI 2000), Workshop on Knowledge-Based Systems for Model-Based Engineering, August 22, 2000, Berlin, Germany.
5. Rubén Prieto-Díaz. A faceted approach to building ontologies. Proceedings of IEEE International Conference on Information Reuse and Integration (IRI 2003). 2003: 458~465.
6. Rosario Girardi, Carla Gomes de Faria. An ontology-based technique for the specification of domain and user models in multi-agent domain. CLEI electronic journal, Vol.7(1), 2004.
7. Vijayan Sugumaran, Veda C. Storey. A semantic-based approach to component retrieval. ACM SIGMIS Database, Vol.34:pages 8-24, 2003.
8. Sean Bechhofer, et al. Owl Web Ontology Language Reference", http://www.w3.org/TR/owl-ref/, 2004-02-10.
9. Carlton Reid Turner, Alfonso Fuggetta, Luigi Lavazza, Alexander L. Wolf: A conceptual basis for feature engineering. Journal of Systems and Software 49(1): 3-15 (1999).
10. Hong Mei, Wei Zhang, Fang Gu: A Feature Oriented Approach to Modeling and Reusing Requirements of Software Product Lines. Proceedings of the 27th Annual International Computer Software and Applications Conference (COMPSAC'03).
11. Kwanwoo Lee and Kyo C. Kang: Feature Dependency Analysis for Product Line Component Design. ICSR 2004, LNCS 3107, p. 69–85, 2004. Springer-Verlag.
12. 12.Wei Zhang, Hong Mei, Haiyan Zhao: A Feature-Oriented Approach to Modeling Requirements Dependencies. Proceedings of the 2005 13th IEEE International Conference on Requirements Engineering (RE'05).
13. Wei Zhang, Haiyan Zhao, Hong Mei: A Propositional Logic-Based Method for Verification of Feature Models. ICFEM 2004, LNCS 3308, p. 115–130, 2004. Springer-Verlag Berlin Heidelberg 2004.
14. Jena home. http://jena.sourceforge.net.
15. M.Mannion, H. Kaindl, J. Wheadon: Reusing Single System Requirements from Application Family Requirements. Proceedings of the 1999 International Conference on Software Engineering, ICSE1999.
16. Kyo C Kang , Sajoong Kim , Jaejoon Lee , et al. FORM: A Feature-Oriented Reuse Method with Domain-Specific Reference Architectures. Annals of Software Engineering, 1998,5 :143~168.

The COVAMOF Derivation Process

Marco Sinnema, Sybren Deelstra, and Piter Hoekstra

University of Groningen, 9700 AV Groningen
{m.sinnema, s.k.deelstra}@rug.nl,
p.s.hoekstra@student.rug.nl

Abstract. The design, usage and maintenance of variability, i.e. variability management, is a very complex and time-consuming task in industrial product families. The COVAMOF Variability Modeling Framework is our approach to enable efficient variability management. As a practical realization of COVAMOF, swe developed the COVAMOF-VS tool suite, which provides several variability views on C#, C++, Java, and many other types of projects in Microsoft Visual Studio .NET. In this paper, we show how COVAMOF facilitates an engineer during product derivation, and what benefits are gained by it.

1 Introduction

A software product family is an approach to reuse that involves creating a collection of similar software systems from a reusable set of software artifacts [1][2][13]. As product families promise order of magnitude improvements in quality and productivity of software development, more and more organizations are adopting this approach [7].

The ability to derive distinct products from a product family is supported through variability, i.e. the ability of a software system or artifact to be extended, changed, customized or configured for use in a specific context. On the one hand, variability is enabled through variation points, i.e. the locations in the software that enable choice at different abstraction layers (features, architecture and implementation layer). Each variation point is associated with a number of options (represented by variants or values). On the other hand, the possible configurations that can be build with these variation points are restricted due to dependencies that exist between variants, and the restrictions that are imposed upon these dependencies.

Product derivation in software product families involves making a large number choices (up to ten thousands [4]) at variation points in the available artifacts (at feature [6], architecture, and implementation level). These large numbers make it hard to manage all variation points by humans. Even though it is absolutely necessary to handles these numbers effectively, however, there are even more complicated issues in managing variability.

In Sinnema et al. [11], for example, we discussed variability management issues that are the result of *complex dependencies*. Consider, for example, a design where the maximum processing time of data is constrained. The configuration of many variation points in the design influence this maximum processing time. The complex dependency (or value of the property) maximum processing time is the result of the combination of variants that is selected at each of these variation points. Determining

M. Morisio (Ed.): ICSR 2006, LNCS 4039, pp. 101–114, 2006.
© Springer-Verlag Berlin Heidelberg 2006

the value of this property is typically much more complicated than handling simple logical in- and exclusions.

The complications for complex dependencies are primarily caused by the fact that the knowledge that is available for these dependencies is often tacit (in minds of experts) [8], incomplete, and imprecise. In addition, complex dependencies suffer from dependency interaction, i.e. that due to the fact that several variation points are involved in multiple dependencies, trying to meet the constraints on a particular dependency value may influence other dependency values as well. For an extensive discussion on these issues, see Sinnema et al. [11].

Existing software variability modeling approaches and tools are inadequate to handle these variability management issues [10]. In response, we developed our own variability modeling framework COVAMOF [10]. This framework consists of modeling facilities that model the variation points and dependencies uniformly over different abstraction levels (e.g. features, architecture and implementation), and as first-class citizens. As part of our framework, we developed the COVAMOF-VS tool suite. The COVAMOF-VS tool suite is a set of Add-ins for Microsoft Visual Studio. NET [9]. It is designed for creating variability models of a product family, and using these models for configuration of individual products.

In earlier work [10], we focused on presenting the modeling concepts in COVAMOF. Before a modeling framework can be used to manage variability in a product family, however, it should be clear how the model needs to be created, maintained, and used. The purpose and contribution of this paper lies in showing how such a model is used during product derivation, and how COVAMOF facilitates a software engineer when he/she needs to derive a product from the product family.

In order to provide a concrete description of the COVAMOF Derivation Process, we discuss this process according to how the tool-suite is used, and provide initial results of the validation of COVAMOF. To present the derivation process in a concise manner, we first present a brief example that is used for illustrating our message. In section 3, we provide an introduction to COVAMOF and the COVAMOF-VS tool-suite. In section 4, we show the practical benefits of COVAMOF according to different steps in the derivation process. We revisit the core issues we mentioned above in section 5, and show how they are addressed by our approach. In section 6, we present a summary of empirical validation we gained by applying our approach at an industrial organization. We conclude this paper in section 7.

2   Example Case

To illustrate COVAMOF, we use an example in this paper (see also Fig. 1). This example originates from a product family that is built by the same organization from which we use empirical results to validate COVAMOF. The example involves a product family that is built on top of the product family we use in the validation. Most of the variability in this example has been abstracted away, or simply left out, so that the reader can easily grasp the example. The purpose of this small example is not to validate COVAMOF, but to explain some of the basic concepts.

The example involves a product family in the domain of license plate recognition on handhelds (PDAs, and smartphones). License plate recognition on handhelds involves automatically recognizing license plates on images captured through a camera.

These license plates are on- or offline checked against a white/blacklist using communication channels such as WAN, Bluetooth, GPRS, or cable. The products in this example are modules that a customer uses to rapidly build their own handheld recognition application. The modules for example offer a view-port for displaying camera images, an interface for a license plate recognition engine, as well as communication services.

Choice	Description	Examples of Variants
Hardware	Supported hardware with different CPU power, camera or amount of memory	HP iPaq 3715, Sony-Erisson P900, Symbol MC50
Viewport	Supporting view-ports (i.e. UI elements that display the camera stream) for different GUI libraries	MFC, UIQ, Nokia
Operating System	Supported operating systems	Windows CE, Windows Mobile, Symbian

Fig. 1. Example product family. This figure shows a picture of the HP iPaq 3715 running the application (left) and some examples of the variability (in terms of choices) provided by the product family (right).

3   COVAMOF

In order to support product family engineers, we developed the COVAMOF Variability Modeling Framework and the associated tool-suite for Microsoft Visual Studio .NET [9] (COVAMOF-VS). Although the focus of this paper is to explain how COVAMOF helps software developers to choose the right variants and settings that satisfy the constraints and functionality required for a new product, we first need to explain the basic concepts of COVAMOF. In the following sections, we discuss these concepts according to the two main views provided by the COVAMOF-VS tool-suite.

3.1 COVAMOF, Introduction

As we mentioned in section 1, COVAMOF is a framework for modeling variation points and dependencies uniformly over different abstraction levels (e.g. features, architecture and implementation), and as first-class citizens. This framework enables providing different views on the variability provided by product family artifacts. At this point, the tool-suite COVAMOF-VS provides two main graphical views, i.e. the variation point view, and the dependency view (see Fig. 2).

To provide these views, COVAMOF-VS maintains an integrated variability model. This model is constructed by reading variability information from the collection of files in the active Solution in Microsoft Visual Studio. The active Solution in MS Visual Studio contains the artifacts that constitute the software product family. The Solution can contain very different artifacts, e.g. XML-based feature models, start-up parameter specifications and C# source files.

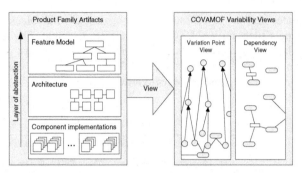

Fig. 2. COVAMOF Views. By treating dependencies and variation points as first-class citizens, COVAMOF enables providing a seperate dependency view on the variability provided by a product family.

The variability information in these artifacts is either directly interpreted from language constructs (such as #ifdef), or is based on special constructs from the COVAMOF variability language XVL. While we eventually strife for extending a programming language with these constructs, variability information in code files is currently inserted as comments. These constructs are inserted in the solution artifacts at the time they are under development, or afterwards using a variability modeling process as discussed in section 4.

The extraction of variability information is done by plug-in components that register themselves on one or more file types. These components convert the extracted variability to parts of the COVAMOF variability model. They are also responsible for feeding additions and changes in the views directly back into the files of the MS Visual Studio Solution.

Once the model is constructed, it can be viewed graphically in the variation point and dependency view. The variation point and dependency view each serve a specific purpose. In the following two sections, we discuss the entities in the COVAMOF model (see Fig. 3) according to these different views. In section 4, we discuss how these views are used during product derivation.

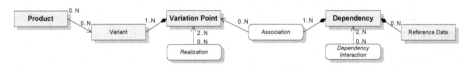

Fig. 3. The COVAMOF Meta-model

3.2   COVAMOF, the Variation Point View

The main purpose of the variation point view is to show to the engineer, which choices are available at different abstraction layers, how they realize each other across layers, and how choices depend upon each other. The variation point view contains the following entities: *Variation Point*, *Variant*, *Realization* and *Dependency* (see also Fig. 3). These entities are illustrated with a screenshot from the example case (see Fig. 4).

Variation Point: *Variation Points* in COVAMOF represent the location at which a choice is provided by the product family. A *Variation Point* entity has a number of properties, for example for storing the abstraction layer the choice is located in (abstraction layer), the moment in the lifecycle at which the choice is bound (binding time), and storing the reason why a choice is provided (rationale). The different options that are available for a choice are represented by a value, or by a set of variants that are associated to the *Variation Point*.

Variant: *Variant* entities represent the options that are available at a *Variation Point*. While values are used to represent parameters, *Variants* can represent anything from an object or class, to a file, or a code-block. The effectuation property of a *Variant* specifies the effectuation actions that should be executed in the product family artifacts when the variant is selected. Examples of such effectuation actions are the generation of a configuration file, the setting of compiler directives and the specification of libraries that have to be linked.

> **Example.** *The screenshot in Figure 4 shows a* Variation Point *'Supported OS', with* Variants, *'Symbian', 'Windows CE', and 'Windows Mobile 2003'. The* Variation Point *is situated in the feature layer. The information displayed here tells that a software engineer has the option to choose to derive a product that runs on one of these three operating systems.*

Realization: The *Variation Point* entities are hierarchically organized over abstraction levels. In this hierarchy, variation points in lower levels of abstraction realize the variability on a higher level abstraction. *Realization* relations specify *rules* that determine which variants or values at variation points at lower levels should be selected in order to realize the choice at variation points at higher levels.

The purpose of explicitly modeling these relations in the variability model is two-fold: first, as the realization relations capture the knowledge about *how* variation points realize other variation points, COVAMOF-VS can automatically infer choices on a higher level of abstraction to choices on a lower level of abstraction, reducing the human effort to configure products. Second, the hierarchical organization of variation points structures the variability in such a way that a software engineer does not have to consider all the variation points at once. Instead, he can just focus on one relevant subset of all the variation points. For example, he can just focus on the high level variation points that realize the overall product family variability, or just focus on the lower level variation points that together realize only one aspect of the product line variability. Therefore, it allows humans to manage the complexity caused by large numbers of variation points in industrial product families.

> **Example.** *In Figure 4, the* Realization *relation from 'CameraInterface Implementation' to 'Supported OS' specifies that different implementations for the Camera Interface realize the ability to choose between supported operating system. The rules at this Realization (not shown in Figure 4), specify which CameraInterface Implementation should be selected when a particular OS is chosen. An observing reader may note from other Realization relations that there is a strong coupling between Operating System, Device, and CameraInterface implementation.*

Dependency: The COVAMOF variability model captures both simple and complex dependencies (see also section 1). These dependencies are represented as *Dependency* entities in the variability model. They specify a mapping from the configuration of a set of *Variation Points* to a *value* in a specific 1-dimensional domain. In plain English, this means that if you select *Variants* or a value at *Variation Points* (called the configuration), the *Dependency* maps this selection to a *value* for a property (the target domain) such as maximum processing time or memory consumption. We refer to the set of *Variation Points* whose configuration influences the value as the *associated variation points*. The model combines two ways of capturing the knowledge about *how* the configuration of the associated variation points maps to a value in the target domain, i.e. by *Association* entities and *Reference Data* entities.

Association: The first way to capture this knowledge is by *Association* entities, which are part of a *Dependency*. These *Associations* refer to the *Variation Points* whose configuration affects the *value* of the *Dependency*. Each *Association* corresponds to the relation with one *Variation Point*. COVAMOF distinguishes between three types of *Associations*. In increasing order of completeness of the knowledge about the associations, these are Abstract, Directional, and Logical *Associations*. An Abstract *Association* means that experts only know that a relation between the *Variation Point* and *Dependency* exists, but have no way of predicting the effect of selecting a different *Variant* or value at the *Variation Point*. A Directional *Association* means that experts have an idea about the direction in which the value of a dependency will change when a different value or *Variant* is selected. In case of Logical *Associations* experts know

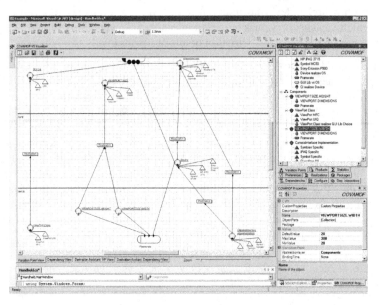

Fig. 4. A screenshot of the example case in COVAMOF-VS. This figure shows some of the variation points and dependencies that are involved to provide the variability of the example case we discussed in section 3.

exactly how the value of a dependency will change when a different _Variant_ or value is selected. Product family experts can enrich the _Associations_ with textual hints that explain how variation points can be reconfigured in order to obtain a certain _value_.

The type of associations of a _Dependency_ influences the type of the _Dependency_. In COVAMOF, we distinguish between Statically Analyzable and Dynamically Analyzable _Dependencies_. For Statically Analyzable _Dependencies_, the exact value can be calculated before running the system, which requires Logical _Associations_. The exact value of Dynamically Analyzable _Dependencies_ can only be determined by running and measuring the system, which is the case if the _Dependency_ contains Abstract and Directional _Associations_.

Reference Data: The second way of capturing the knowledge about how the configuration of the associated variation points maps onto the value of a dependency is modeling reference data. _Reference Data_ entities contain measurements of the _value_ of a _Dependency_ for specific configurations of the associated _Variation Points_. These measurements originate from tests of products that have been derived from the product family. These _Reference Data_ entities can in turn be analyzed to determine how single _Variation Points_ affect the _Dependency_. The results of this analysis are in turn stored in the _Associations_.

> **_Example._** _In Figure 4, the _Dependency_ 'Framerate' is associated to the three _Variation Points_ 'Device', 'VIEWPORTSIZE.HEIGHT', and 'VIEWPORTSIZE.WIDTH'. The first _Variation Point_ refers to the handheld device that can be chosen, while the latter two _Variation Points_ refer to configuration parameters that set a view-port size. The information displayed in Figure 4 therefore shows that the 'Framerate' of the application, i.e. the number of times/second an image is displayed, is dependent on the size of the view-port, and the selected handheld device. The Directional _Associations_ specify how the frame-rate depends on these _Variation Points_ (not shown in Fig. 4)._

3.3 COVAMOF, the Dependency View

The dependency view contains _Dependencies_ and _Dependency Interactions_ (see Fig. 3). The main purpose of this view is to show how dependencies interact with each other, and how an engineer can cope with these interactions.

Dependencies: _Dependencies_ in the dependency view are representations of the same dependencies that are represented in the variation point view. In the dependency view, however, they only show which dependencies exists, and do not show the relationships between variation points.

Dependency Interaction: In the introduction, we explained that dependency interaction occurs when variation points are part of multiple dependencies. Although the sets of dependencies that interact can be generated from the dependencies and their associations, COVAMOF also explicitly captures _Dependency Interaction_ entities in the variability model. These entities allow a software engineer to specify, for a set of dependencies, how to cope with the shared associated variation points during product derivation. This textual specification is documented by product family experts. It contains a strategy for developing a reasonable first guess during the initial phase, and a strategy to optimize the values in the iteration phase of product derivation.

4 COVAMOF Derivation Process

Product derivation is the construction of a software product that is built by selecting and configuring product family artifacts. With COVAMOF, products are derived by the COVAMOF Derivation Process. This process allows organizations to gain maximum benefit from COVAMOF and its associated tool support. This COVAMOF Derivation Process is divided into four steps, i.e. Product Definition, Product Configuration, Product Realization, and Product Testing. As visualized by Fig. 5, the last three steps can occur in one or more iterations. The following subsections describe these four steps respectively.

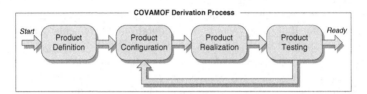

Fig. 5. The COVAMOF Derivation Process. This iterative process breaks down into four steps, i.e. Product Definition, Product Configuration, Product Realization and Product Testing.

4.1 Product Definition

The first step of the COVAMOF Derivation Process is called Product Definition. In this step, the engineer creates a new *Product* entity in the variability model. In response, COVAMOF-VS stores this product in the active Solution of Visual Studio. The properties of Product entities are the customer, a unique name for the product, and variation points that have been bound for the product. The latter are described by bindings of variation points, i.e. combinations of variation points together with their selected variants or parameter value. The engineer can directly fill in the customer and name property. For the bindings of the variation points, one or more iterations of the Product Configuration step are required.

4.2 Product Configuration

In order to start the Product Configuration step, the engineer selects the *Product* entity from the available products dropdown menu in the COVAMOF-VS toolbar. From that point, COVAMOF-VS is in configure mode and additional configuration information about the product at hand is shown in both variability views.

When the variation point view of COVAMOF-VS is in configure mode, the variation points that are bound for the product at hand are marked by a different color. During the Product Configuration step, the engineer binds one or more variation points to new values or variants based on the customer requirements. In order to bind these variation points, he marks the new variants or specifies the new values in the variation point view. The order in which variation points are bound is dynamically determined by the realization relations and dependencies in the variability model.

Meanwhile, the binding of a variation point is effectuated by creating or updating the relation between the *Product* entity and the *Variation Point* entity. Each variation point that is bound triggers the inference engine and the validation engine to work:

- **Inference Engine:** As described in section 3.2, the rules of *Realization Relations* define how variation points on a lower level of abstraction realize variation points on a higher level of abstraction (see also Fig. 4). These rules are used by the inference engine to automatically bind variation points on a lower level of abstraction. The binding of these variation points is based on the binding of the variation points on a higher level of abstraction. For each rule that the variation point is involved in, the consequences are recursively determined.
- **Validation Engine:** After a variation point is bound by the engineer and the inference engine has worked, the validation engine automatically checks whether no dependencies have been violated. The rule of each statically analyzable dependency is checked and for each dynamically analyzable dependency the reference data elements are checked. Based on the rules, the associations and the reference data, the dependencies in the variation point view are provided with the new estimated *value*. Any violations of these values with respect to the required values are immediately fed back to the engineer by marking the dependencies in the variation point view with the color red.

The customer requirements can be separated into functional requirements and non-functional requirements. Therefore, the engineer basically has two main concerns during product configuration. First, the right features and components should be selected so that the functional requirements are met. Second, the configuration is tuned and adapted to meet the non-functional requirements. The *Realization Relation* and *Dependency* entities in the variability model support the engineer in configuring a product that meets the functional as well as the non-functional requirements. *How* these two entities can be used is explained below. Note that in practice, the engineer has to take both into consideration at the same time.

- **Realization relations:** In order to select the right features and components, the engineer binds variation points in the feature layer. The variation points in the architecture layer can be bound using rules of the *Realization Relations* between the feature layer and the architecture layer. In case the inference engine was unable to automatically bind these variation points in lower layer of abstraction, the engineer has to bind them manually. Similarly, the variation points in the component layer can be bound by using the realization relations between the component layer and the architecture and feature layer.
- **Dependencies:** The dependency entities in the variability model support the engineer in binding variation points in such a way that the product is consistent and meets the non-functional requirements. When Product Configuration starts, the engineer specifies, for each of the dependencies the specific value or range that is required for the product at hand. The variation point view of COVAMOF-VS in configure mode shows the (estimated) value of each of the dependencies together with the required value or range. When the actual value is outside the required range, i.e. the *Dependency* is violated, the dependency in the variability view is colored red.

The goal of engineers is to (re)bind the variation points in such a way that none of the dependencies are violated. During iterations, the engineer therefore has to shift the *value* of each violated *Dependency* into the required range. The information in the *Associations* and the *Reference Data* of the *Dependency* entity are used to determine *how* the current *value* can be changed in order to meet the required range.

As Logical *Associations* specify exactly how the (re)binding of a variation point changes the *value*, this formalized knowledge can easily be used to change the value of the *Dependency*, and the effect is immediately visible in the variation point view. The documented knowledge in the Directional *Associations* can be used to increase or decrease the *value* in the right direction. However, a Product Test (section 4.4) is required to determine the new value of the *Dependency*. How Abstract *Associations* can be used can only be determined by any reference data available. Otherwise, the engineer has to use the tacit knowledge of an expert or even trial-and-error to change the *value* of the *Dependency*.

Note that the process of changing the *values* of *Dependencies* is a very complicated task. This is particularly due to the interaction between *Dependencies* like we described in the introduction. In such situations, the engineer uses the information of the corresponding *Dependency Interaction* entities in the dependency view (section 3.3). This information helps the engineer in making reasonable trade-offs between system properties and a strategy to accomplish the acceptable *values*, for example, which *Dependency* should be resolved first and which should be resolved later in the process.

Usually, the focus during the initial iteration of the COVAMOF Derivation Process is on satisfying the functional requirements, and, as the product functionality becomes more and more fixed, the focus gradually shifts to satisfying the non-functional requirements. This does not imply that functional requirements are more important. Functional properties are usually the easy aspect during product derivation, and generally have to be known in order to say something meaningful about the non-functional properties.

When the engineer is unable to bind additional variation points without testing the configuration at hand, the COVAMOF Derivation Process goes to the next step, Product Realization.

4.3 Product Realization

In order to get a complete software product, the *Product* has to be realized in the product family artifacts. In COVAMOF-VS, the product is realized by pressing the Realize button in the toolbar of COVAMOF-VS. As a result, COVAMOF-VS executes the effectuation actions for each of the variants that are selected for the Product entity (see also section 3.2).

Thereafter, Visual Studio builds the active Solution, resulting in the binaries that are used together with the configuration files to test the product in the next step.

> **Example.** The example in Figure 4 contains the <u>Variation Points</u> *'VIEWPORTSIZE.HEIGHT, and 'VIEWPORTSIZE.WIDTH'. When during the Product Configuration step these variation points both have been bound to 120, the following start-up parameters are specified in the configuration file* `mobileapp.ini`:
>
> ```
> [Viewport]
> Height=120
> Width=120
> ```

4.4 Product Testing

The goal of the testing phase is to determine whether the product meets both the functional and the non-functional requirements. When, during testing, the realized product appears to satisfy all requirements, the software product can be packed and shipped to the customer. Otherwise, one or more additional iterations of a Product Configuration and Product Realization steps are required.

In any case, the *values* of the dynamically analyzable *Dependencies* that have been determined during the test are fed back into the variability model as *Reference Data*. In this way, the COVAMOF variability model is gradually enriched and improved to provide better estimated *values* during Product Configuration steps in the future.

5 Benefits

COVAMOF and COVAMOF-VS were created to address the issues that are experienced by software engineers in many industrial families (see e.g. Deelstra et al. 2005 [4]). In section 3 and 4, we discussed the main entities in the COVAMOF meta-model (see also Fig. 3), and showed how they provide practicable benefits during product derivation. In this section, we summarize how the combination of COVAMOF and COVAMOF-VS addresses the variability management issues we discussed in the introduction.

1. Effectively handling complex dependencies. Instead of modeling dependencies between two variants, dependencies in COVAMOF group relations on the level of variation points. This allows specifying complex dependencies between multiple variants that would otherwise translate into a large amount of dependencies between variants. This grouping furthermore provides a more abstract view on relations between choices, thus reducing the overall complexity of the variability model. As the dependencies are first-class, COVAMOF is also able to provide a separate dependency view that shows the interaction between them.

2. Ability to use imprecise, tacit and documented knowledge. In addition to the formal specification of the variability model, COVAMOF explicitly deals with tacit, documented, and formalized knowledge through the different types of dependencies. Although tacit knowledge is not represented in a COVAMOF model (otherwise, it wouldn't be defined as tacit), COVAMOF deals with tacit knowledge by enabling references to the experts that possess this knowledge (e.g. through names, phone numbers, etc.). This may seem silly, but the importance should not be underestimated: it allows (less experienced) engineers to call-in the right assistance.

Documented and formalized knowledge are handled in several ways. The _Reference Data_ and _Associations_ at _Dependencies_ enable storing useful product derivation knowledge, e.g. in terms of links to documents, graphs, and formulas. The test results for a _Dependency_ in a particular configuration can be reused to know or estimate the value of a _Dependency_ in a new configuration. Multiple data points can be generalized to variants with specific properties, and the results can be stored into _Associations_. As we explained in section 4, these _Associations_ are used during the COVAMOF Derivation Process to estimate the impact of choices on dependencies.

All these facilities allow organizations to start with a minimal amount of formalization that can pay off immediately. This model can be gradually extended when organizational maturity grows and more precise knowledge becomes available, or when more benefits are perceived for the externalization.

3. Dependency interaction. To reduce the expert involvement and number of iterations, the problem of dependency interaction is addressed by explicitly capturing _Dependency Interaction_ entities. These entities specify a strategy that suggests to an engineer, which steps he/she should follow in trying to satisfy a particular set of interacting dependencies.

6 Validation

We are involved in a case study that introduces COVAMOF in an industrial setting. The subject of this case study is the Intrada product family of Dacolian B.V. Intrada is an industrial product family for complex intelligent traffic systems such as license plate reading, tolling, and parking applications [3]. At this point, the variability model has been integrated into the software product family. Dacolian B.V. is in the process of collecting data with respect to the use of COVAMOF, such as number of man-hours and iterations saved, as well as data on the experience of engineers with the tools. For each product derived, they keep track of which variation points are bound in the iterations of the COVAMOF Derivation Process, and how many hours are required to perform each step.

Although we cannot yet present the definitive quantitative results of this case study, Dacolian B.V. already provided interesting qualitative observations. First of all, Dacolian B.V. is convinced that COVAMOF saves an enormous amount of man-hours. Before the introduction of COVAMOF, the derivation of a typical product from the product family required about one day of work. Now, their engineers can derive the same product within a quarter of an hour. Below, we provide some detailed qualitative observation we received from Dacolian B.V.:

-   **Number of iterations reduced:** "The engineers are provided with much more useful information about the choices they have to make and dependencies they have to consider. As a result, the decision making of the engineers has improved and they are able to make better estimations for the variants and values that have to be selected. Therefore, the iterations required for a typical product derivation process has been reduced from 10-12 iterations to 0-2 iterations after the introduction of COVAMOF. This reduction of iteration, together with the automatic inference of bindings, resulted a dramatic reduction of required man-hours".

- **Finding Conflicts:** "Before we were able to implement the variability model of the product family, we had to externalize the variability information from the product family artifacts and the experts. During this externalization process, engineers and experts from our organization found many (previously unknown) conflicts in their own artifacts. This has, and will save us a lot of unforeseen problems".

- **Development and Evolution:** "A substantial part of the products of Dacolian B.V. are based on the automatic recognition of license plates. One key variation point for this family is the collection of countries of which license plates can be recognized. Before the introduction of COVAMOF only product line experts were able to extend the number of supported countries, i.e. implementing a new variant for this variation point. After COVAMOF has been implemented, with all major dependencies externalized, also engineers that are not involved in the product family are able to extend the number of supported countries. This reduced the workload of the product line experts".

7 Conclusion

Software variability management is an important factor in the success of a product family. It is also a complex task, where key issues such as handling complex dependencies, dealing with imprecise, tacit, and documented knowledge, and dependency interaction, are inadequately addressed by existing approaches [10].

In this paper, we discussed the COVAMOF Product Derivation Process. We described this process using the technical realization of COVAMOF in the form of the COVAMOF-VS tool-suite. We have shown how the different elements of COVAMOF address the key variability management issues during product derivation, and supported these claims with empirical results from an industrial application of COVAMOF.

References

1. Bosch, J.: Design and Use of Software Architectures: Adopting and Evolving a Product Line Approach, Pearson Education (Addison-Wesley & ACM Press), ISBN 0-201-67494-7, 2000
2. Clements, P., Northrop, L.: Software Product Lines: Practices and Patterns, SEI Series in Software Engineering, Addison-Wesley, ISBN: 0-201-70332-7, 2001
3. Dacolian B.V.: http://www.dacolian.nl
4. Deelstra, S., Sinnema, M., Bosch, J.: Product Derivation in Software Product Families; A Case Study, Journal of Systems and Software, Volume 74(2), pp. 173-194, January 2005
5. Deelstra, S., Sinnema, M., Nijhuis, J., Bosch, J.: COSVAM: A Technique for Assessing Software Variability in Software Product Families, Proceedings of the 20th IEEE International Conference on Software Maintenance (ICSM 2004), pp. 458-462, September 2004
6. Kang, K., Cohen, S., Hess, J., Novak, W., Peterson, S.: Feature Oriented Domain Analysis (FODA) Feasibility Study, Technical Report CMU/SEI-90-TR-021, 1990
7. v.d. Linden, F.: Software Product Families in Europe: The Esaps & Café Projects, IEEE Software, Vol. 19, No. 4, pp. 41-49, 2002

8. Nonaka, I., Takeuchi, H.: The Knowledge-Creating Company: How Japanese companies create the dynasties of innovation. Oxford University Press, New York, 1995
9. Microsoft Visual Studio .NET: http://msdn.microsoft.com/vstudio
10. Sinnema, M., Deelstra, S., Nijhuis, J., Bosch, J.: COVAMOF: A Framework for Modeling Variability in Software Product Families, Proceedings of the Third Software Product Line Conference (SPLC 2004), Springer Verlag Lecture Notes on Computer Science Vol. 3154 (LNCS 3154), pp. 197-213, August 2004
11. Sinnema, M., Deelstra, S., Nijhuis, J., Bosch, J.: Modeling Dependencies in Product Families with COVAMOF, Proceedings of the 13th Annual IEEE International Conference and Workshop on the Engineering of Computer Based Systems, March 2006
12. Spillman, W.J., Lang, E.: The Law of Diminishing Returns, 1924
13. Weiss, D. M., Lai, C.T.R.: Software Product-Line Engineering: A Family Based Software Development Process, Addison - Wesley, ISBN 0-201-694387, 1999

A Metamodel Approach to Architecture Variability in a Product Line*

Mikyeong Moon, Heung Seok Chae, and Keunhyuk Yeom

Department of Computer Engineering, Pusan National University
30 Changjeon Dong, Keumjeong Ku, Busan, 609-735, Korea
{mkmoon, hschae, yeom}@pusan.ac.kr

Abstract. Architecture describes the organizational structure of a system including components, interactions, and constraints. Reusable components, units of software systems, have been considered to support a considerable improvement in reducing development costs and time to market because their interfaces and functionality are explicitly defined. Instead of reusing an individual component, however, it is much more advantageous to reuse a whole design or architecture. A domain architecture, sharing a common software architecture across a product line, includes common components shared by all products and optional components exploited by a subset of the products. Variability, one of the key concepts in the development of domain architectures indicates the ability to derive various products from the product line. Clearly, we need to support variability during domain architecture development. In this paper, we suggest a metamodeling concept that enables a common under-standing of architecture variability. The domain architecture metamodel reflects the Object Management Group's (OMG^TM) Reusable Asset Specification (RAS) which addresses the engineering elements of reuse. We describe a domain architecture in which commonality and variability are explicitly considered.

1 Introduction

Product line engineering has been considered one of the promising approaches to successfully bringing products to the market [1]. Emphasizing an extensive reuse of softwares, software produce line engineering supports seamless reuse in the application development process. To enable reuse, explicit descriptions of variations among products of a product line should be specified. Thus, analyzing commonality and variability between products in a product line is one of the essential concerns that must be considered when building a product line. The variabilities that are identified at each phase of a product line development have different levels of abstraction. For instance, a variation at the architecture level would be more concretely refined than a variation at the requirements level. In the past, these variabilities have been handled in an implicit manner and without considering each core asset's characteristics.

---

* This research was supported by the MIC(Ministry of Information and Communication), Korea, under the ITRC(Information Technology Research Center) support program supervised by the IITA(Institute of Information Technology Assessment).

M. Morisio (Ed.): ICSR 2006, LNCS 4039, pp. 115–126, 2006.

This paper focuses on variability analysis of architectures in any software product lines development. The domain architecture captures the structuring rules of the domain, interaction between components, and the specification of the component. Each set of component variants and each optional component constitute a variability point at the architectural level of abstraction. We propose a metamodel that specifies a domain architecture where commonality and variability are explicitly considered. The proposed metamodel represents a comprehensive conceptual basis for variability of architectural models. The domain architecture supports the variation inherent in the product line by reflecting the Object Management Group's (OMG^TM) Reusable Asset Specification (RAS) [2]. RAS is a set of guidelines for the specification, development, and application of reusable software assets. We also describe the variability of the domain architecture by a case study with an e-Travel System domain.

The rest of this paper is organized as follows: Section 2 introduces our conceptual layered metamodel architecture. Section 3 describes a Reusable Asset Specification that is the basis for our domain architecture metamodel, which is presented in Section 4. In this section, the variabilities identified at the architecture level are categorized and explained. Based on the metamodel defined in Section 4, Section 5 describes a domain model for an e-Travel System domain. Related works, and conclusions and suggestions for future work are given in Sections 6 and 7, respectively.

2   Domain Assets Metamodeling Approach

The classical framework for metamodeling is based on a four-layered architecture [3]. The bottom level, M0, is the information layer, which is comprised of the actual data objects. The next level, M1, is said to hold a model of the M0 data. Level M2, which is referred to as a metamodel, holds a model of the information at M1. Finally, level M3 holds a model of the information at M2, and is called the meta-metamodel. As Fig. 1 shows, we adopt this basic metamodeling structure, where elements in a given conceptual layer describe elements in the next layer below.

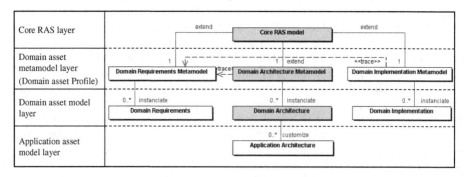

Fig. 1. Layered domain assets metamodeling

The domain assets metamodeling architecture comprises the following four layers:

1. ***Core RAS layer:*** The infrastructure for a metamodeling architecture. Defines the constructs for specifying our domain architecture metamodel. This describes a general representation of assets.
2. ***Domain asset metamodel layer:*** Provides the modeling constructs of our domain asset metamodel such as domain requirements metamodel, domain architecture metamodel, and domain implementation metamodel. This describes extensions to the fundamental elements of Core RAS. Therefore, this means Domain Asset Profile.
3. ***Domain asset model layer:*** Uses our domain assets metamodel to build the assets in a domain. Domain assets can be domain requirements, domain architecture, domain implementation, and other elements through domain analysis, domain design, and domain implementation processes. The models in this layer are instances of a metamodel.
4. ***Application asset model layer:*** Customizes a domain asset model and defines a specific application in a domain.

3   Reusable Asset Specifications

A *Reusable Asset Specification* (RAS) was recently adopted by the Object Management Group (OMG) and is now an open standard that can be used to manage any set of development artifacts. The scope of this specification is a set of guidelines and recommendations about the structure, content, and descriptions of reusable software assets [2]. RAS is described in two major categories: Core RAS and Profiles. Core RAS represents the fundamental elements of asset specification. The Profiles describe extensions to those fundamental elements. RAS defines three profiles, Default Profile, Default Component Profile, and Default Web Service Profile. Additionally, we extend the RAS to consider each domain asset's characteristics and explicitly define its variability. These definitions are called the Domain Asset Profiles. A domain architecture metamodel, which is one of the Domain Asset Profiles, is explained in the next section.

Fig. 2 shows a Core RAS Model. As the figure below indicates, Core RAS defines four major sections to an asset including the Classification section, Solution section, Usage section, and Related Assets section.

The classification section lists a set of descriptors for classifying the asset. The solution section describes the artifacts of the asset. An artifact is a work product that can be created, stored and manipulated by asset producers, consumers and tools. An artifact may have a relationship with another artifact. An artifact may have a variability point that is expected to be altered by the asset consumer, and which describes where and what in the artifact can be modified. An artifact may be relevant to a particular artifact context such as a requirement, design, implementation, or test context. An artifact context helps explain the meaning of the elements in the artifact. The usage section describes the activities to be performed for applying or using the asset. Some activities are for the asset in general whereas other activities are for a specific artifact within the asset, and other activities may be relevant to a particular artifact context. For each variability point, there must be at least one activity that describes how to bind that variability point. The Related Assets section describes this asset's relationship to other assets.

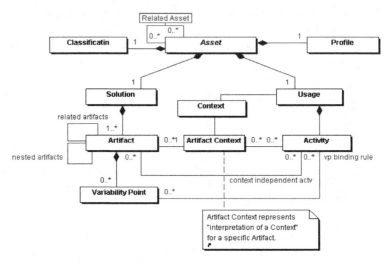

Fig. 2. The Core *Reusable Asset Specification (RAS)* Model

4   Metamodel of Domain Architecture

The notion of domain architecture is defined as "a reference model for a set of applications sharing similar functionality, behavior and structure" [4]. The domain architecture has two main roles: first, it must describe the commonalities and variabilities of the products contained in the software product line; and secondly, it must provide a common overall structure. In this paper, a metamodel of domain architecture is defined to establish an overall scheme for representing a domain architecture.

In this section, we present a domain architecture metamodel by extending the solution model of a Core *RAS* model in a domain design context. The primary responsibility of this layer is to define constructs for specifying domain architecture models in a specific domain. Fig. 3 shows an overview of our domain architecture metamodel. The Solution has one new element, domain architecture. Base constructs for representing domain architecture are domain component, domain component binding, interface, and operation:

- **Domain component:** a unit of computation or a data store with variation points that are built in or at least anticipated.
- **Domain component binding:** architectural building blocks used to model interactions between domain components.
- **Interface:** a set of defined operations that are accessible from outside the domain component and form the signature of the interface. The external behavior of a domain component is defined by its provided and required interfaces.
- **Operation:** an individual action that the component instance will perform.

Domain architecture has association with several classes including Model, Diagram, and Specification. Those may also be used to describe the domain architecture. A model may have multiple diagrams and specifications. There may be multiple models such as domain structure models, domain behavior models, and domain component specifications.

- **Domain structure model:** includes domain components and relationships between them (domain component bindings), and describes the static structure of the product line being modeled.
- **Domain behavior model:** describes how domain components interact with each other, or how interfaces will be used.
- **Domain component specifications:** include not only interface specifications that are specified by a set of operation specifications, but also constraints on the way the interfaces are to be implemented.

As Fig. 3 indicates, the context elements have variation as an attribute. The type of the variation is represented as a CV_property, which is defined as a property that can be common or optional. In a software product line, adding or changing requirements can cause a degeneration of the product line architecture. A CV_property is decided according to the existence of functionality, so it affects the existence of functionality in an application. Additionally, it affects the existence of the domain component, domain component binding, interface, and operations in the interface. The variation in the domain static and behavior models is influenced by the CV_property of the domain component, interface, or operation. The variation described in the domain component specification reflects the variations identified in internal domain components.

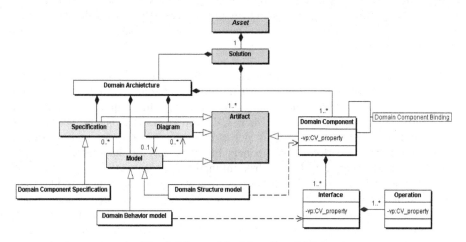

Fig. 3. Metamodel of domain architecture

4.1 Variability in Domain Architecture Constructs

The variations of domain architecture are classified as follows:

- *Domain Component CV_property* – A domain component implements functionality in a domain. Therefore, a domain component may or not appear in a domain architecture according to the domain functionality. This is defined as the property that the domain component can be common or optional.
- *Domain Component binding CV_property* – The variation of domain component binding occurs directly or indirectly. Direct variation occurs when domain relations between two domain components are added or deleted. Indirect variation occurs when domain components with the optional CV_property appear or not in the domain architecture. These domain component bindings depend on the CV_property of the domain components. If the relations between domain components are directly or indirectly varied, it conforms to the domain component binding CV_property at the architecture level. This variation type will be shown in the domain structure model.
- *Interface CV_property* – A domain component may have one or more interfaces that can be managed and evolved separately. The variation in an interface is defined as a property such that interfaces can be common or optional.
- *Operation CV_property* – Any function in a domain may be realized as an operation. Therefore, operations may appear or not in a domain component according to domain functionality. The variation of operations is defined as a property that operations can be common or optional.

4.2 Variability in Domain Architecture Model

Domain architecture models are composed of elements in the domain design context. Therefore, the variation of the domain architecture constructs in a domain causes domain architecture models to change. The variations of domain architecture model are classified as follows:

- *Domain Configuration Style* – The variations of domain configuration style can be identified in a domain structure model, a connected model of domain components and domain component bindings. These appear in a domain structure model according to their CV_properties. That is, the variation of domain configuration style is defined as an alteration in which domain components and domain component bindings may or may not appear in a domain structure model on the basis of their CV_properties.
- *Domain Component Interaction* – The variations of domain component interaction can be identified in a domain behavior model. Because the domain behavior model contains interaction models for each interface and operation, their CV_property cause interactions between domain components to alter. That is, the variation in domain component interactions is defined as an alteration in which an execution flow may or may not appear in a domain behavior model on the basis of the CV_property of the interface or operation.

- *Domain Component Specification* – A domain component specification describes an internal domain component. The information about domain types and domain object interactions that participate in realization of a domain component is given in detail. Therefore, a domain type and the operation of the domain type may have a variation point, and this is explicitly represented by stereotype <<v.p>>. These can be described using different detailed design representations like class diagrams and state charts. In this paper, we do not deal with variability of an internal domain component in detail.

5   Domain Architecture in the e-TS Domain

A domain architecture model is an instance of the domain architecture metamodel in a specific domain. In this section, we describe in detail the variations of domain architecture by illustrating a case study with e-Travel Systems (e-TS). An e-TS can be characterized as a family of B2C travel business applications that provide facilities such as e-travel catalogs, online reservations, secure e-payment systems, e-travel portal site services, and e-travel network/chain management on the Internet. e-TSs have commonality in many e-travel services such as accommodation, tour, car rental, travel activities, etc. Fig. 4 shows a partial Primitive Requirement (PR) [5] matrix of an e-TS domain, where the identified PRs are listed in the first column and the names of the e-TS systems are listed in the header row. The determination of whether a PR can be reused is based on its frequency of appearance in the PR matrix (i.e., the commonality ratio of the PR). The variation of domain architecture reflects properties such as commonality and variability that were identified from the requirements analysis step. Even though a single domain component may implement only one PR, mostly several related PRs are encapsulated as a domain component.

PR No	PR	RATIO(%)	eT Portal	Tourmall...	C-Com...	Joy View	Online-...	TourE...
PR1	Login	100	O	O	O	O	O	O
PR2	Logout	100	O	O	O	O	O	O
PR3	Register	100	O	O	O	O	O	O
PR4	Modify the member information	100	O	O	O	O	O	O
PR5	Withdraw	100	O	O	O	O	O	O
PR6	Search for vacation packages	100	O	O	O	O	O	O
PR7	Book vacation packages online	100	O	O	O	O	O	O
PR8	Confirm a trip reservation	100	O	O	O	O	O	O
PR9	Cancel a trip reservation	100	O	O	O	O	O	O
PR10	Review a trip reservation	100	O	O	O	O	O	O
PR11	Modify a trip reservation	100	O	O	O	O	O	O
PR12	Make a DIY travel planning	28	O	O	X	X	X	X
PR13	Customize trip plan	28	O	O	X	X	X	X
PR14	Add featured attraction and services	28	O	O	X	X	X	X
PR15	Search for flights	100	O	O	O	O	O	O
PR16	Make a flight reservation	100	O	O	O	O	O	O
PR17	Confirm a flight reservation	100	O	O	O	O	O	O
PR18	Cancel a flight reservation	100	O	O	O	O	O	O
PR19	Review a flight reservation	100	O	O	O	O	O	O
PR20	Modify a flight reservation	100	O	O	O	O	O	O
PR21	Search for Hotels	100	O	O	O	O	O	O

Fig. 4. A PR matrix

5.1   Variability in e-TS Domain Architecture Constructs

- **Domain Component CV_property** – Fig. 5 shows some of the domain components that are extracted in the e-TS domain. The *Customized Reservation Mgr* domain component that contains PR12, PR13, and PR14 has a variation point, explicitly represented by stereotype <<v.p>>, which indicates it may optionally appear in an application.

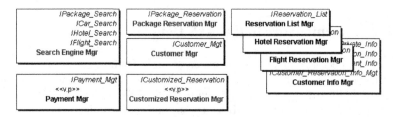

Fig. 5. Domain components in e-TS domain

- **Interface CV_property** – The *Customer Info Mgr* domain component provides functions for managing information about customers. Customer information about e-money, gift certificates, or coupons is necessary only when an application can support payment services such as payment by coupon or by e-money. Therefore, as Fig. 6 shows, an interface *ICustomer Supplement Info* in the *Customer Info Mgr* domain component has a variation point that indicates it may be optionally realized in an application component. The variation point is explicitly denoted by stereotype <<v.p>> on the interface name.

Fig. 6. Interfaces of *Customer Info Mgr* domain component

- **Operation CV_property** – The *Package Reservation Mgr* domain component provides functions for reservation, review, modification, and cancellation of vacation packages. As Fig. 7 indicates, the interface *IPackage Reservation* that the domain component provides has a variable operation *select_Package_option* for supporting a list of options for a vacation package. It is explicitly denoted by stereotype <<v.p>> because it can be optionally implemented in an application component.

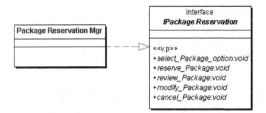

Fig. 7. Operations in *IPackage Reservation Interface*

5.2   Variability in e-TS Domain Architecture Model

- ***Domain Configuration Style*** – Fig. 8 and Fig. 9 show a partial domain structure model of the e-TS domain. When the domain structure model applies to an application system, it needs to be customized based on the variation points of the domain components and domain component bindings, so the configuration style will be changed. In Fig. 8, the *Car Reservation Mgr* domain component, the domain component binding connected with the *ICar Reservation* interface, and the *ICar Search* interface provided by the *Search Engine Mgr* domain component are explicitly denoted by stereotype <<v.p>> in the domain structure model. These are related to *Car Reservation* requirements. If an application system does not provide the functions of *Car Reservation*, these will be omitted from that model. This can be determined on the basis of a PR matrix, according to a property of the PR that can be common or optional.

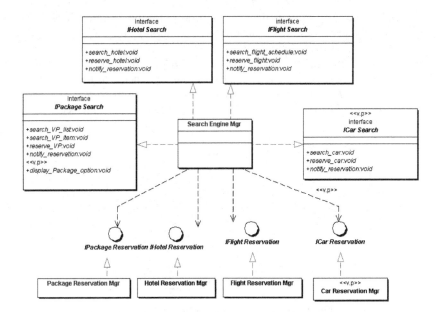

Fig. 8. Domain structure model related to *Search Engine Mgr*

- In Fig. 9, the *Payment Mgr* domain component and the domain component binding connected with the *IPayment Mgt* interface are explicitly denoted by stereotype <<v.p>> in a domain structure model. For example, a customer may pay a membership fee when he/she wishes to register to access some services. This function is one of several variations that the *Register* PR (PR3 in Fig. 4) includes. Thus, this can be determined on the basis of a PR specification, the detailed description for each PR.

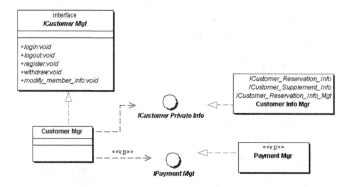

Fig. 9. Domain structure model related to *Customer Mgr*

- ***Domain Component Interaction*** – Fig. 10 shows the interactions between component instances for *Package Reservation*. As Fig. 7 indicates, an operation *select_Package_option* of the *IPackage Reservation* interface is variable one. Accordingly, the execution flows for the operation have variation points, which are explicitly denoted as condition [v.p]. Fig. 11 shows other interactions between component instances for *Package Reservation*. In Fig. 10, *IPackage Reservation* calls operations of *IReservation List* and *ICustomer Reservation Info* regardless of their message sequence. On the other hand, in Fig. 11, *IPackage Reservation* calls an operation of *IReservation List,* and then *IReservation List* calls an operation of *Reservation Info* in sequence.

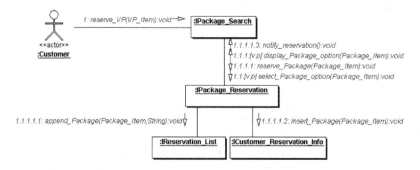

Fig. 10. Interactions 1 for *Package Reservation*

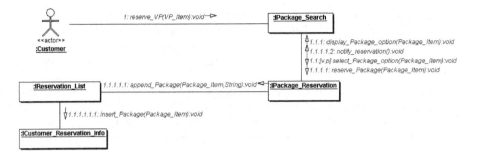

Fig. 11. Interactions 2 for *Package Reservation*

6 Related Works

Referring especially to domain architecture, an important task is to analyze the domain and to identify the commonalities and variabilities of components and operations of the domain. The FORM (Feature-Oriented Reuse Method) [6] was developed as an extension of the FODA (Feature-Oriented Domain Analysis) method [7]. The main characteristic of FORM is its four-layer decomposition, which describes different points of view on product development. However, this does not address explicitly the variations in the reference architecture, and entails complexity when many variants must be represented. In [8], variation is represented using patterns associated with discriminants. A discriminant has three types: single, multiple, and optional, and is closely related to the division of feature properties into mandatory, optional, and alternative. It does, however, not emphasize characteristics of variation at the design level. While requirements models are concerned with features and capabilities of the domain, design models focus on components, interfaces, and operations. Gomma explained the product line design phase in connection with features [9]. He strived to describe of design models with explicit variations in structural and dynamic views. However, all alternative variants appear in those models, so they are complex even in the simple case study. Because model elements that have common or optional properties may be modified when applied, variants should be managed separately at the detailed level. In our paper, the domain components, interfaces, and operations that have common or optional properties describe their variants in the domain component specification, i.e., at the detailed level.

7 Conclusions and Future Work

Domain architecture can play important role in managing the complexity of softwares and reducing cost of developing and maintaining them. However, well-designed domain architectures do often fail not because they are not effectively developed but because they are not properly described with regard to variability. To tackle the problems with variability of domain architecture, this paper has proposed a metamodeling approach to developing domain architectures in a product line. We adopt a layered metamodeling structure to establish an overall representation scheme of domain architecture. Based on the RAS model, the models of each layer are more specifically described in the below layer. We first classified the types of variation points that could be identified at the architecture level and then suggested a modeling approach to explicitly representing those variabilities in the domain architecture model.

Our future research activities include configuration management in a product line and development of a more concrete architecture for a specific domain. In the software product line context, adding or changing requirements can cause a degeneration of the domain architecture and components. In addition, because the impact of the changes in a product line can involve all the applications that are developed based on the product line, there should be more emphasis on configuration management than the conventional software. We also plan to build a more detailed metamodel of domain architecture for a specific domain, for example, automotive industry. This domain architecture for a specific domain can considerably contribute to developing and maintaining application by providing the more functionalities common to them and supporting their variabilities.

References

[1] D. Muthig and C. Atkinson, "Model-Driven Product Line Architecture," Proc. Second Software Product Line Conference, Aug. 2002.
[2] The Object Management Group (OMG), Reusable Asset Specification (RAS) Version2.2, http://www.omg.org/technology/documents/formal/ras.htm, Nov. 2005.
[3] The Object Management Group (OMG), Meta-Object Facility (MOF) Version 1.4, http://www.omg.org/docs/formal/02-04-03.pdf, 2003.
[4] D.J. Duffy, *Domain Architectures: Models and Architectures for UML Applications*, Wiley, 2004.
[5] M. Moon, K. Yeom, and H.S. Chae, "An Approach to Developing Domain Requirements as a Core Asset Based on Commonality and Variability in a Product Line," IEEE Transactions on Software Engineering, vol. 31, no. 7, pp.551-569, Jul. 2005.
[6] K.C. Kang, S. Kim, J. Lee, and K. Kim, "FORM: A Feature-Oriented Reuse Method with Domain Specific Reference Architectures," Annals of Software Engineering, vol. 5, pp.143-168, 1998.
[7] K. Kang, S. Cohen, J. Hess, W. Novak, and S. Peterson, "Feature-Oriented Domain Analysis (FODA) Feasibility Study," Technical Report CMU/SEI-90-TR-21, Software Engineering Institute, Carnegie Mellon University, Nov. 1990.
[8] B. Keepence and M. Mannion, "Using patterns to model variability in product families," IEEE Software, vol. 16, no. 4, pp.102-108, 1999.
[9] H. Gomma, *Designing Software Product Lines with UML, From Use Cases to Pattern-Based Software Architectures*, Addison-Wesley, 2004.

An Approach to Managing Feature Dependencies for Product Releasing in Software Product Lines*

Yuqin Lee, Chuanyao Yang, Chongxiang Zhu, and Wenyun Zhao

Computer Science and Technology Department, Fudan University,Shanghai 200433, China
li_yuqin@yahoo.com.cn, Yangcy9216@163.com,
{cxzhu, wyzhao}@fudan.edu.cn

Abstract. Product line software engineering is a systematic approach to realize large scale software reuse. Software product lines deal with reusable assets across a domain by exploring requirements commonality and variability. Requirements dependencies have very strong influence on all development phases of member products in a product line. There are many feature oriented approaches on requirement dependencies. However, most of them are limited to the problem domain. Among those few focusing on the solution domain, they are limited to modeling requirement dependencies. This paper presents a feature oriented approach to managing domain requirements dependencies. Not only is a requirement dependencies model presented, but a directed graph-based approach is also developed to analyze domain requirement dependencies for effective release of member products in a product line. This approach returns a simple directed graph, and uses an effective algorithm to get a set of requirements to be released in a member product. A case study for spot and futures transaction domain is described to illustrate the approach.

1 Introduction

One of the approaches to successfully realizing large scale software reuse is product line engineering. Its goal is to support the systematic development of a set of similar software systems by understanding and controlling their common and particular characteristics [1]. Analyzing requirements commonality and managing variability is an important activity for domain engineering (DE) and software product line engineering (SPLE). Managing requirements for a software product line(SPL) is a lot more complex and difficult than that for an individual application. Domain requirements commonality and variability are developed into reusable assets of a SPL. Obtaining a proper set of reusable requirements is the key to achieve successful DE activities, for these requirements are not only the inputs of subsequent steps in DE, but also help form requirement models for application engineering (AE) [2]. Many researchers

---

* Supported by the National Natural Science Foundation of China under Grant No. 60473061; the National High Technology Development 863 Program of China under Grant No.2005AA113120.

M. Morisio (Ed.): ICSR 2006, LNCS 4039, pp. 127–141, 2006.

have recognized that individual requirements are seldom independent of each other, and various kinds of dependencies exist among them [3, 4, 5, 6, 7, 8, 9].

Dependencies are essential elements among the requirements of a real software system, because of the cohesion of a system. The cohesion is a basic quality that is necessary for a system to be a system, and to achieve certain customer-desired goals [10]. A SPL deals with a set of member products, so dependencies exist among requirements of SPL. Otherwise the requirements would be unrelated and it would be unnecessary to use SPL to develop them. Dependencies among the requirements of a domain have not only positive but also negative effects. Positive dependencies are useful to achieve a requirements set for a member product from SPL, and guide the release planning for a software system. Negative dependencies will lead to requirement conflicts and inconsistencies. These conflicts and inconsistencies have to be managed during analysis phase and along with system evolution.

A feature is a set of tight-related requirements from the stakeholders' viewpoint. Features are not independent in a system. Feature dependencies reflect requirement dependencies. There are many feature oriented approaches on managing requirement dependencies. However, most of them are limited to the problem domain. Approaches focusing on the problem domain emphasize static relations among features. Dynamic relations and behavior characteristics of requirements are difficult to represent. Among those few focusing on the solution domain, they are limited to modeling requirement dependencies. Few of them deal with managing feature dependencies and getting requirement sets for a member product from a SPL.

Feature dependencies have to be represented in domain models. A feature dependencies model influences how effective to configure member products in a SPL. Tree structure can not represent feature dependencies, because not all feature relations are hierarchical. Representing the nonhierarchical dependencies relationships into a tree structure has left the current feature modeling methods with the possibility of either omitting dependencies or losing control over the feature model [11]. Feature dependencies relationships are a graph intuitively. The graph can be processed using a matrix or an adjoining table. It's the groundwork in achieving the concise graph representing feature dependencies.

The proposed method not only defines a classification of feature dependencies and presents a feature dependencies model, but also uses a directed graph to analyze domain requirement dependencies for effective release of member products in SPL. This approach returns a simple directed graph that includes only direct feature dependencies, and uses an effective algorithm to get the set of requirements which are to be released in a member product.

The paper is organized as follows: Section 2 discusses related work on feature dependencies. Section 3 defines a classification of feature dependencies in a SPL. Section 4 presents a feature dependencies model based on directed-graph, and provides an algorithm that generates the maximum connective dependencies graphs. It can be easily used to get the features set for a member product from a SPL, and detect conflicting dependencies. Section 5 illustrates and analyses our approach by an example of spot and futures transaction domain. Section 6 draws a conclusion and some suggestions for future work.

2 Related Work

Some different approaches exist on how to deal with feature dependencies. Most of them focus on feature dependencies modeling, and some of them deal with analysis or management of feature dependencies. The following are some approaches that deal with software release planning.

Claes Wohlin and Aybüke Aurum [20] presented an empirical study of the decision criteria when selecting a set of requirements to implement in a forthcoming project, and hence to postpone the implementation of other requirements to a later point in time.

Omolade Saliu and Guenther Ruhe [21] described ten key technical and non technical aspects impacting release planning, and evaluated seven existing release planning methods. They proposed a new release planning framework that considers the effect of existing system characteristics on release planning decisions.

Par Carlshamre and Bjorn Regnell [22] compared two independently developed industrial market-driven requirements engineering processes, which both apply continuous requirements management using state-oriented life cycle models in the fostering of requirements from invention to release.

Hassan Gomaa, Michael E. Shin [12] proposed a multiple-view meta-model for SPLs to describe how each view relates semantically to other views. The meta-model depicts life cycle phases, views within each phase, and meta-classes within each view. The relationship between the meta-classes in the different views was described. Consistency checking rules were defined based on the relationships among the meta-classes in the meta-model. The approach dealt with feature dependencies but did not go deep into it.

K. Lee and K. C. Kang [13] extended the feature modeling into analyzing feature dependencies that are useful in the design of reusable and adaptable product line components, and presented design guidelines based on the extended model. Although the structural relationships and configuration dependencies are essential inputs for product line asset development, they are not sufficient for development of reusable and adaptable product line assets. They gave out six types of feature dependencies which have significant influences on the design of product line assets. They emphasized on solutions to hide variable features from the client features which use them.

H. Ye and H. Liu [15] presented a matrix-based approach to model feature dependencies in a scalable way. Three hierarchical relationships and three non- hierarchical relationships were identified, but the dependencies in each class were not representative.

W. Zhang, H. Mei et al [10] identified static, dynamic feature dependencies. They also identified feature dependencies on the specification level. They emphasized feature dependencies modeling and interaction among different dependencies types. Dependencies on specification level are not sharing the same classification condition with the two other types of dependencies.

We define a classification of feature dependencies in a static and dynamic way, and propose a feature dependencies model. The directed graph is used to analyze domain requirements dependencies for effective configuration of member products in a product line. This approach returns a simpler directed graph, and uses an effective algorithm to generate the maximum of connective dependencies graphs. It can be used to get a set of requirements for a member product more easily. The characteristics make the approach more precise, easily understood and very effective for producing requirement set of a member product from a SPL.

3 Feature Dependencies

3.1 Feature Variability

Features in a SPL can be classified into two types: mandatory and variable features.

Mandatory features are those which must be present in all member products in a SPL.

Variable features are those that may not be present in all member products in a SPL.

3.2 Feature Dependencies

The dependencies among features can be classified into static and dynamic ones. Static feature dependencies show the intrinsic relations existing among features, such as whole-part relations and static constraints etc. Dynamic feature dependencies show the operational relations among features, such as sequential relation illustrates features that have to be active one after another. Each kind of dependencies will be discussed in detail. We use contiguous lines to represent static dependencies and broken lines for dynamic dependencies in the following figures.

3.2.1 Static Dependencies

The static dependencies reflect hierarchical feature relations and static constraints among features on the same level. They include decomposition, generalization, and static constraints. Static constraints include required and excluded. Decomposition and generalization reflects dependencies between parent and child features. Static constraints reflect dependencies between peer features, especially different variants in one variable point.

Decomposition: When a parent feature is decomposed into a number of children features, the relation between parent feature and child feature is called decomposition dependency. For instance, in spot and futures transaction product lines, a feature trade is decomposed into two features called order and match. The dependency between trade and order or match is decomposition. The figure 1 describes the decomposition dependency. We use rectangles to annotate feature, and diamonds to annotate decomposition dependency.

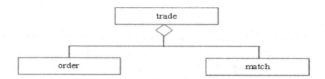

Fig. 1. Decomposition dependency example

Generalization: When a parent feature is generalized from a number of children features, the relation between parent feature and child feature is called generalization dependency. For instance, Match deal feature is generalized from forward, bidding, and auction etc.

We use triangles to annotate generalization dependency. The generalization dependency is illustrated in figure 2.

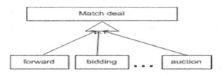

Fig. 2. Generalization dependency example

Static Constraints: If one feature is required or excluded by another feature to constitute a member product, the relation between the two features is called required or excluded. Required dependency is unidirectional. Excluded dependency is bidirectional. For instance, Cancel order feature requires Order feature, so Order feature is required by Cancel order feature. Local market feature can not coexist with Global market feature, so Local market feature is excluded by the Global market feature; meanwhile Global market is excluded by Local market. The static constraint dependencies are illustrated in figure 3.

Fig. 3. Static constraints dependency example

3.2.2 Dynamic Dependencies
In addition to static dependencies, there are several relations reflecting dynamic dependencies between features. Dynamic dependencies are described as following.

Serial: If two features should be active immediately one after another, the relation of the two features is called serial dependency. Serial dependency may represent precondition and post condition relations. The feature being active first is called precondition feature, the other is called post condition feature. For instance, Match deal and Create order form are serial features. Match deal should be active immediately after Create order form, so Create order form feature is the precondition of Match deal feature. Serial dependency can represent control flow and data flow operations. The serial dependency is illustrated in figure 4.

Fig. 4. Serial dependency example

`Collateral:` If two or more features should be active at the same time, the relation between these features is called collateral dependency. Collateral dependency is bidirectional. For instance, Order and Match should be active when the trading system is operating. Order feature will deal with order request related operations. Match feature will deal with matching order requests. The system is a real time transaction product, so the two features should be active at the same time during trading period. The collateral dependency is illustrated in figure 5.

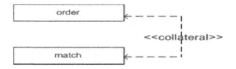

Fig. 5. Collateral dependency example

Synergetic: If two or more features should be synchronized sometime during their active period, the relation between them is called synergetic dependency. Synergetic dependency represents serial relation existing in concurrent operations. Synergetic dependency is bidirectional. For instance, in spot and futures transaction product line, feature Order and feature Match have to be active parallel, but Match has to wait to cooperate with Order by order queue. Synergetic dependency describes two or more features working concurrently to fulfill a task. The synergetic dependency is illustrated in figure 6.

Fig. 6. Synergetic dependency example

Change: If one feature can be changed by another feature, the relation between these two features is called change dependency. The feature changing other features is called changer, and the feature being changed by others is called changee.

Change dependency can be classified into the following kinds: state change, behavior change, data change, and code change.

State change dependency represents the relation that one feature can change another feature's state when they are active. For instance, a feature is changed from unbound to bound when it is needed by other features. In spot and futures transaction product line, Start match market feature will need Match trading feature to be bound to process the corresponding transactions, so Start match market feature has a state change dependency with Match trading feature. Likewise, close match market feature will change Match trading feature's state from bound to unbound, so Close match market feature has a state change dependency with Match trading feature. The state change dependencies are illustrated in figure 7-1.

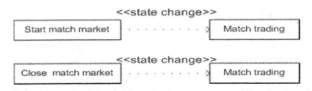

Fig. 7-1. State change dependency example

Behavior change dependency represents the relation that one feature may change another feature's behavior when they are active. For instance, when orders can't be matched, Match deal feature will be idle. When a client enters a new order, the new order will be added into the order queue, and Match deal feature will change from idle to run. So Create order form feature has a behavior change dependency with Match deal feature. The behavior change dependency is illustrated in figure 7-2.

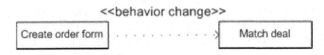

Fig. 7-2. Behavior change dependency example

Data change dependency represents the relation that one feature may change data when being used by another feature. For instance, one order may be matched partly when there is not enough suitable reversed order, e.g. partial match. So the matched and unmatched amount of the order is changed by Match deal. The matched and unmatched amount is not zero but less than the order amount. The Match deal feature has a data change dependency with order feature. The data change dependency is illustrated in figure 7-3.

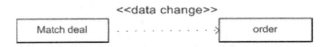

Fig. 7-3. Data change dependency example

Code change dependency represents a relation where one feature may change another feature's code. For instance, in the security model, Anti-trace feature will change Security protect feature's code. The code change dependency is illustrated in figure 7-4.

Fig. 7-4. Code change dependency example

4 Managing Feature Dependencies

Feature dependencies will influence how to get features set of a member product in a SPL, and how to release products in an incremental way. So how to represent feature dependencies in an understandable way is a challenge. We use directed graphs to represent feature dependencies, and assign an eigenvalue to each type of dependencies. In directed graph, eigenvalue of every directed path represents combined dependencies from one feature to the other.

4.1 Feature Dependencies Model

Among features in a SPL, usually majority dependencies exist among minority features. In order to decrease workload of feature dependencies analysis, we first set apart those features which have no dependencies with other features. These features are called isolated features. Then we analyze dependencies pair by pair.

Every type of dependency is assigned an eigenvalue. We use a byte to denote dependencies. Each bit of the byte represents a type of dependency. This method is used to represent combined dependencies easily and directly. If two features have more than one dependency, the eigenvalue of all dependencies between them is assigned a combined value with a corresponding bit representing a dependency. The eigenvalues of all dependencies are assigned in table 1.

Table 1. Eigenvalue of dependencies

Type of dependency	Assigned eigenvalue(binary)
decomposition	01000000 (0x 40)
generalization	00100000 (0x 20)
required	00010000 (0x 10)
excluded	10000000 (0x 80)
serial	00001000 (0x 08)
collateral	00000100 (0x 04)
synergetic	00000010 (0x 02)
change	00000001 (0x 01)

Table 2. Feature dependencies table

Feature(source)	Dependency	Feature(destination)
Feature1	decomposition (0x40)	Feature7
Feature2	Synergetic(0x02)	Feature1
Feature1	Synergetic(0x02)	Feature2
Feature3	required (0x10)	Feature4
Feature3	serial (0x08)	Feature4
Feature3	change (0x01)	Feature5
Feature5	Collateral(0x04)	Feature2
Feature2	Collateral(0x04)	Feature5
Feature6	excluded (0x80)	Feature1
Feature1	excluded (0x80)	Feature6

DependencyForestGenerator(T: in dependency table, F: out dependency forest)
F.TreeNo=0;
FeatureSet ; //feature set consists of all features;
While T not tableEnd
{
ReadOneRowFromTable(T, R);//T is the dependency table, R is the gotten row;
If R.sourceFeature exists in the dependency forest, and is the root of tree K
　Then If R.sourceFeature has a path to R.destinationFeature
　　　　　　Then eigenvalue of the path = + R.dependency
Else create a directed path from R.sourceFeature to R.destinationFeature with ei-
genvalue R.dependency in tree K;
　　　Else {
Create tree F.TreeNo++;
F.TreeNo.root= R.sourceFeature;
FeatureSet=FeatureSet – F.TreeNo.root;
}
}
While FeatureSet not empty //generate trees with only roots to represent isolated
features
{
　　　F.TreeNo ++;
　　　F.TreeNo.root= get a feature from FeatureSet;
FeatureSet=FeatureSet - F.TreeNo.root;
}
//end of algorithm DependencyForestGenerator.

Fig. 8. Algorithm for generating feature dependency forest

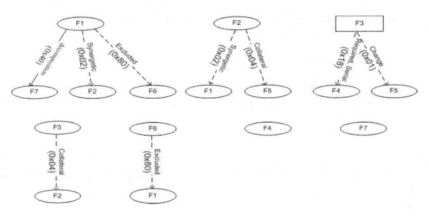

Fig. 9. Example of feature dependency forest generated

Rectangles are used to represent mandatory features, and ellipses are used to represent variable features. Directed path represents direct dependency from one feature to
another feature. Eigenvalue of each path represents combined dependencies eigenvalues from one feature to another feature.

MaximalConnectiveDependencyGraphGenerator(F: in dependency forest, G: out graph)
//generate maximum connective feature dependency graphs;
initial G is null;
initial F[i]=0, i=0..n, n is the number of features.
//F[i]=0 representing tree i has not be processed, the value will be 1 after processed;

Repeat
{
If a mandatory feature which is the root of one feature tree in the forest F exists, and F[i]=0
Then G.node =i ; //i is the mandatory feature number in feature set.
Else If a variable feature j which is the root of one feature tree in the forest F exists, and F[j]=0

   Then G.node =j ; //j is the variable feature number in feature set.
Else G.node = null;

While G.node not null and F[G.node]=0
{
Take feature tree G.node;
If G.node tree has a child Then NextNode = G.node.child;
      While NextNode not null
      {
            If NextNode is in G
Then
      Add NextNode to G;
Add a path from G.node to NextNode;
eigenvalue of the path= eigenvalue from G.node to NextNode in tree G.node;

If F[NextNode]=0 then insert NextNode to queue WaitingProcessedTrees;
If tree G.node has another child unprocessed
Then
NextNode = next child of tree G.node
Else   NextNode = null;
      } // tree G.node has been processed;
      F[G.node]=1; //tree G.node has been processed;
      If queue WaitingProcessedTrees is not empty Then G.node = the first node pop out of the queue;
      Else G.node = null;
}
// get one maximum connective dependency graph; the graph is directed, and two features may have
// bidirectional paths.

} until G.node is null;
// end of repeat; all maximum connective graphs returned.
// end of algorithm MaximalConnectiveDependencyGraphGenerator.

Fig. 10. Algorithm for generating maximum connective directed graphs

After analyzing dependencies between features in DE, we get a feature dependencies table. Each row in the dependency table represents a direct dependency between two features. The represented dependency is has a direction. Bidirectional dependency is represented by two rows; each feature of the dependency is the source feature in one row. In our classification, collateral, synergetic and excluded dependencies are bidirectional. A simple example is described in the following table 2. The example has seven features. Feature 3 is mandatory, and the other features are variable.

Based on feature dependency table, we design an algorithm DependencyForestGenerator to generate feature dependency forest. The feature dependency forest consists of n trees, where n is the number of features. Every feature is the root of one tree. The trees are called feature dependency trees. Only direct dependencies are presented in feature dependency trees, no implicit dependencies are presented in feature dependency trees. If there is more than one dependency between two features, all the dependencies are presented in one path by combined eigenvalue.

The algorithm DependencyForestGenerator is described in figure 8.

Using algorithm DependencyForestGenerator, the feature dependency forest in figure 9 below is generated.

The feature dependency forest describes feature dependencies clearly. Each feature dependency tree represent dependencies related with one feature. This approach is simpler and more straightforward than matrix-based and table-based methods. Only direct dependencies are represented on trees. Implied dependencies can be gained by transitional relations reasoning.

4.2 Managing Feature Dependencies

The feature dependency forest discussed above is a representation of direct dependencies. The forest only describes direct dependencies, but implied dependencies are not represented. When we want to get a feature set for releasing a member product, implied dependencies have to be used. Based on feature dependency forest, an algorithm generating maximal connective graphs is developed in the following figure 10. Implied dependencies can easily be gained from connective graphs.

Using algorithm MaximalConnectiveDependencyGraphGenerator, maximum connective feature dependency graphs of forest in figure 9 are generated in figure 11.

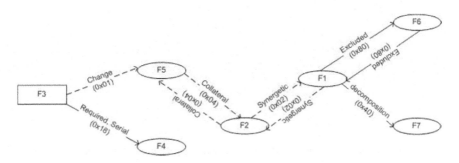

Fig. 11. Maximum connective dependency graphs generated from example above

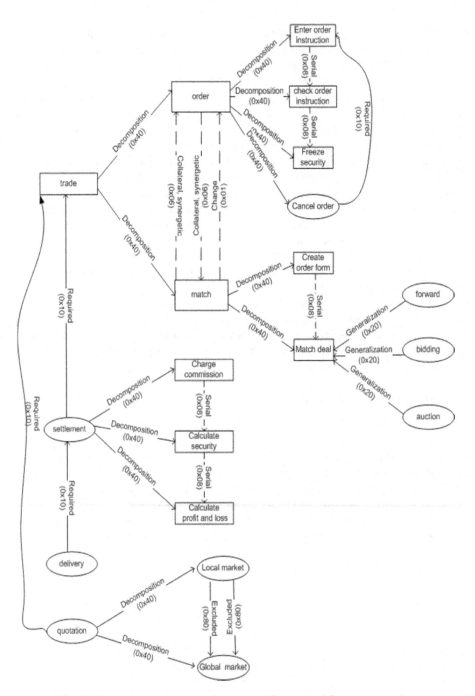

Fig. 12. Feature dependency graph generated for spot and futures transaction

The maximum connective dependency graphs are very effective for generating a features set for product release in SPL. Starting from a feature included in a product release, the features achieved by spreading maximum connective dependency graphs will constitute the member product. Only the graph consisting of the start feature need to spread, other maximal connective graphs can't be used. Until all required features are included in a set, generating process ends. From a few mandatory features, we can easily produce a features set of the product.

5 Case Study

We take the spot and futures transaction product line as an example. After analysis of domain requirements, we get a feature model and feature dependency model. The feature dependency model is the one we're concerned with here. In large SPL, there are a plenty hood of features, so the dependency forest will consist of many trees. A feature model can be included in a feature dependency model. We only describe the feature dependency graph generated in the following figure 12.

In figure 12, rectangles are used to represent mandatory features, and ellipses are used to represent variable features. Static dependencies are annotated by real lines, and dynamic dependencies are annotated by dashed lines. Every path is described by a dependency name and eigenvalue. From the dependencies graph, the relations of features are very concise and clear. For example, trade feature is mandatory in the product line, but settlement, delivery, and quotation are variable. If settlement is needed in a product release, its children features are needed. If settlement is included in a product release, trade feature is included implicitly. Similarly, delivery or quotation feature included in a product release implies that trade feature is included too. All kinds of feature dependencies are included in the figure, so children features of delivery feature are hidden to simplify the graph.

6 Conclusion and Future Work

Product line software engineering is a systematic approach to realize large scale software reuse. SPLs deal with reusable assets across a domain by exploring domain requirements commonality and variability. Domain requirements dependencies have very strong influence on all development phases of member products in a product line. Feature dependencies reflect domain requirement dependencies. How to manage feature dependencies will influence how to release products effectively.

A new feature oriented approach has been developed to model feature dependencies. Feature dependencies are classified as static and dynamic dependencies. Static dependencies reflect hierarchical feature relations and static constraints among features in the same level. They include decomposition, generalization, and static constraints. Dynamic feature dependency shows the operational relations among features. They include serial, collateral, synergetic, and change dependencies. Each kind of dependency is given a notation.

Each type of dependency is assigned an eigenvalue. The feature dependencies are analyzed in a dependency table, representing direct dependencies among features. The dependency table is transferred to a feature dependency forest. The forest is concise and easily understood. Each feature has a dependency tree whose root is the feature.

Based on feature dependency forest, maximal connective feature dependency graphs are achieved by an effective algorithm. The graphs may include more than one graph when the features have non connected parts. The graphs are useful for releasing products incrementally.

This approach is more effective than other approaches and provides a reasonable dependency classifying method. A feature dependency forest is used to annotate whole domain feature dependencies. Each feature has a tree to represent dependencies related within it. Based on the forest, maximum connective graphs are generated to represent united dependencies in the SPL. It is used to decide which features need to be included in a release.

Based on the feature dependencies model, we will research how different feature dependencies influence architecture design in a SPL, and how to detect and handle conflicts within dependencies.

References

1. Mikyeong Moon, Keunhyuk Yeom, "An Approach to Developing Domain Requirements as a Core Asset Based on Commonality and Variability Analysis in a Product Line", IEEE transactions on software engineering, vol. 31, no. 7, July 2005, pp551-569.
2. Hong Mei, Wei Zhang, Fang Gu, "A feature oriented approach to modeling and reusing requirements of SPLs", Proceedings of the 27th Annual International Computer Software and Applications Conference (COMPSAC'03),2003.
3. P. Carlshamre, K. Sandahl, M. Lindvall, B. Regnell, and J. Natt och Dag, "An Industrial Survey of Requirements Interdependencies in Software Product Release Planning", In Proceedings of Fifth IEEE International Symposium on Requirements Engineering, IEEE Computer Society, 2001, pp. 84-91.
4. A.G. Dahlstedt, A. Persson, "Requirements Interdependencies–Moulding the State of Research into a Research Agenda", In Proceedings of Ninth International Workshop on Requirements Engineering: Foundation for Software Quality, Klagenfurt/Velden, Austria, June 2003, pp. 55-64.
5. S. Ferber, J. Haag, J. Savolainen, "Feature Interaction and Dependencies: Modeling Features for Reengineering a Legacy Product Line", The Second Software Product Line Conference 2002, LNCS 2379, August 2002, pp. 235–256.
6. J. Giesen, A. Volker, "Requirements Interdependencies and Stakeholders Preferences", In Proceedings of IEEE Joint International Conference on Requirements Engineering, Sep 2002, pp. 206-209.
7. J. Karlsson, S. Olsson, and K. Ryan, "Improved Practical Support for Large-scale Requirements Prioritizing", Requirements Engineering Journal, Vol. 2, No. 1, 1997, pp. 51-60.
8. K. Lee, K.C. Kang, "Feature Dependency Analysis for Product Line Component Design", The Third Software Product Line Conference 2004, LNCS 3107, Aug 2004, pp. 69–256.
9. B. Ramesh, M. Jarke, "Toward Reference Models for Requirements Traceability", IEEE Transactions on Software Engineering, Vol. 27, No. 1, January 2001, pp. 58-93.
10. Wei Zhang, Hong Mei, Haiyan Zhao, "A Feature-Oriented Approach to Modeling Requirements Dependencies", Proceedings of the 2005 13th IEEE International Conference on Requirements Engineering (RE'05),2005.

11. Hein, A., Schlick, M., and Vinga-Martins, R.: 'Applying feature model in industry setting' 'SPLs – experience and research directions' (Kluwer Academic Publishers, Boston, 2000), pp. 47–70
12. Hassan Gomaa, Michael E. Shin, "A multiple-View Meta-modeling Approach for Variability Management in SPLs", ICSR 2004, LNCS 3107, pp274-185, 2004
13. Kwanwoo Lee, Kyo C. Kang, "Feature Dependency Analysis for Product Line Component Design", ICSR 2004, LNCS 3107, pp69-85, 2004
14. M. Sinnema, S. Deelstra, J. Nijhuis, J. Bosch, "Managing Variability in Software Product Families"
15. H. Ye and H. Liu, "Approach to modeling feature variability and dependencies in SPLs", IEE Proc.-Softw., Vol. 152, No. 3, June 2005, pp101-109.
16. P. Carlshamre, K. Sandahl, M. Lindvall, B. Regnell, and J. Natt och Dag, "An Industrial Survey of Requirements Interdependencies in Software Product Release Planning", In Proceedings of Fifth IEEE International Symposium on Requirements Engineering, IEEE Computer Society, 2001, pp. 84-91.
17. J. Giesen, A. Volker, "Requirements Interdependencies and Stakeholders Preferences", In Proceedings of IEEE Joint International Conference on Requirements Engineering, Sep 2002, pp. 206-209.
18. von Knethen, B. Paech, F. Kiedaisch, and F. Houdek, "Systematic Requirements Recycling through Abstraction and Traceability", In Proceedings of IEEE Joint International Conference on Requirements Engineering, Sep 2002, pp. 273-281.
19. Martin S. Feather, Steven L. Cornford, Mark Gibbel, "Scalable mechanisms for requirements interaction management", 2000, IEEE.
20. Claes Wohlin, Aybüke Aurum," What is important when deciding to include a software requirement in a project or release", 2005 IEEE,p246-255
21. Omolade Saliu, Guenther Ruhe, "Supporting Software Release Planning Decisions for Evolving Systems", Proceedings of the 2005 29th Annual IEEE/NASA Software Engineering Workshop (SEW'05)
22. Par Carlshamre, Bjorn Regnell, "Requirements lifecycle management and release planning in market-driven requirements engineering processes", 2000 IEEE, p961-965

Adaptation and Composition Within Component Architecture Specification

Luciana Spagnoli[1], Isabella Almeida[2], Karin Becker[1], Ana Paula Blois[1,2], and Cláudia Werner[2]

[1] Catholic University of Rio Grande do Sul
Av. Ipiranga, 6681 – Prédio 30 – Bloco 4 – ZIP 90619-900 - Porto Alegre – RS- Brazil
[2] Federal University of Rio de Janeiro
COPPE/UFRJ – System Engineering and Computer Science Program
P.O. Box 68511 – ZIP 21945-970 – Rio de Janeiro – RJ – Brazil
{lspagnoli, anapaula, kbecker}@inf.pucrs.br,
{isabella, anablois, werner}@cos.ufrj.br

Abstract. Component-Based Development (CBD) and Domain Engineering (DE) are important approaches for software reuse. In a DE process, components are specified in a high abstraction level, within a component architecture specification. When components are reused during an Application Engineering (AE), they are composed with each other and third-party components. However, conflicts usually occur and they must be considered as early as possible, otherwise they may jeopardize the defined architecture. This work proposes a set of functionalities for development with components, with focus on the support for the adaptation and composition functionalities. These were included in *Odyssey*, an environment that supports DE and AE processes. A preliminary study on the use of these functionalities is also reported.

1 Introduction

Component-Based Development (CBD) has become a major approach for reuse in software development. It focuses on the construction of new applications by the integration of components. It is expected that CBD results in better software quality and faster development, thus leading to a shorter time-to-market.

In a Domain Engineering (DE) process, components are specified in a high abstraction level, within a component architecture specification. Application Engineering (AE) deals with the reuse and integration of components to build a new application. Despite the potential benefits of component reuse, in practice component implementation technologies have received far more attention than component reuse itself. While there is a major concern with the development *of* components, support is still lacking for the development *with* components.

Developing with components involves the activities of component *selection*, *adaptation*, *composition* and *update* [1]. Component adaptation and composition are core activities in CBD. Adaptation involves structural and/or behavioral component modifications; composition means integrating components via some form of common infrastructure. These two activities are closely related since many adaptations are necessary to solve problems that appear within the composition activity.

M. Morisio (Ed.): ICSR 2006, LNCS 4039, pp. 142–155, 2006.

Frequently, component architecture modeling activity assumes the existence of third-party components, legacy systems and packages that will be used for provisioning the components specifications [2]. Adaptation and composition are core activities in component architecture specification for which support is required. Existing support is restricted to the provisioning phase (i.e. implementation), and it is often dependent on the implementation technology [3][4][5]. A critical issue is to match the services specified by the component architecture and the existing functionality while provisioning the solution. If component reuse aims at decreasing development efforts, it is required that CBD focus shifts from implementation to design, particularly architectural design. Hence, detecting and handling existing conflicts within the component architecture definition decreases the workload to adapt and compose components during the provisioning phase. If these issues are deferred to the implementation phase, their resolution may require extra work to adapt and compose components, possibly jeopardizing the defined architecture and requiring the selection of other components.

This work addresses the specification of component architecture by reusing available components, providing support to adaptation and composition activities. By considering these activities at architectural level, the focus is set on the definition of a conceptual solution for the system, to be detailed and implemented at the provisioning phase. The paper describes a set of functionalities for supporting adaptation and composition activities, and describes how these functionalities were implemented in *Odyssey-Adapt*, a plug-in of *Odyssey Environment* [6]. The paper also reports a preliminary study on the use of the proposed functionalities.

The remainder of this paper is structured as follows. Section 2 summarizes the key aspects of composition and adaptation activities within architecture specification. Section 3 details the proposed functionalities for supporting CBD, focusing in adaptation and composition at architectural level, and Section 4 describes how they were made available in *Odyssey-Adapt*. Section 5 describes a preliminary evaluation of *Odyssey-Adapt*. Finally, Section 6 presents some conclusions and future work.

2   Related Work

Adaptation refers to activities resulting in component modification to solve structural and/or behavioral problems (i.e., incompatibilities), so that it meets the requirements of a particular software application. Structural incompatibility includes all syntactic issues between the provided interface of a component and the required interface of another one: a) interfaces with different names; b) interfaces with different number of methods; c) interfaces with methods that differ in their signatures, and any combination of these [7][8]. Behavioral incompatibility refers to a semantic mismatch between the service provided by a component and the one required by another one. A hybrid incompatibility merges both structural and behavioral ones.

There exists a number of techniques proposed for adapting components [3][4]. Most frequently designers do not have access to component internals when reusing third-party components, legacy systems or packages. Wrapper and Proxy are common black-box adaptation techniques. Wrapper defines a container component that encapsulates the original one and forwards the requests to it. Proxy defines a component that mediates the communication between two components. It is possible to identify the correspondence between these techniques and known design patterns such as Adapter, Proxy, and Facade [9].

UML-based CASE tools have been suggested as CBD design environments, and this tendency may increase with the UML 2.0 features for component modeling [11]. Academic tools can be found in [12][13], which in addition explore design patterns to develop new components. All these design environments lack functionalities to support the modeling of applications *with* components in general, and therefore, do not fully address the requirements involving the search, adaptation and composition of available components. Wren [10] is an example of CBD prototype environment that supports components modeling, using an extended UML notation which is similar to UML 2.0. Wren focuses on component composition, by supporting the connection of provided and required interfaces, independent of any specific technology. However, the adaptation activity is not addressed at all. Other CBD tools addressing architectural level also do not have functionalities to support adaptation activities [5]. Hence, it is necessary to further detail the type of support required for the adaptation activity, and to develop environments that provide such support.

3   Functionalities for Component Architecture Specification

In this section we present a set of functionalities targeted at supporting adaptation and composition activities within component architecture specification. By specifying the problems to be addressed during these activities, it is possible to develop more comprehensive CBD support environments. Our approach focuses on handling conflicts during component architecture specification, with the goal to decrease the workload to adapt and compose components at the provisioning phase, as well as the need for architecture revision. These functionalities were proposed according to the following assumptions: a) adaptation and composition are entwined activities, since many behavioral or structural mismatches are identified when components are to be integrated through their required/provided interfaces; b) at architectural level, adaptation and composition activities define the structure of a solution, which is to be detailed and implemented during the provisioning phase; c) adaptation is the frequent and repetitive activity of applying standard solutions to recurrent problems, which are captured by widely known design patterns (e.g. Proxy, Adapter, Facade); d) it should be possible to identify and mark all behavioral and/or structural adaptations that are required, and to deal with them in the due time ; e) it should be possible to identify in the architecture which units were introduced to solve adaptation and integration problems. The proposed functionalities are:

-   **Component Architecture Modeling:** the component architecture modeling activity should be supported, according to some specific notation (e.g. UML 2.0). It should allow the creation of interfaces, components (with provided and required interfaces), as well as the connection of components through their interfaces. Components should be considered at any granularity level, ranging from (sub)systems to functions. In the following, we refer to the product of such an activity as the *Component architecture diagram* [2].

- **Component Search and Specification Inspection:** in a reuse perspective, it should be possible to search for potentially interesting existing components. The search for components is a complex task, particularly considering third-party components, and thus involves dealing with search engines and repositories that may be even out of the scope of the CBD environment. Search issues are addressed in [14][15], and are out of the scope of this paper. Once interesting components are identified, we assume their specifications are available in some repository for inspection, to which the CBD environment has access. At architectural level, the focus is on interface descriptions, disregarding whether a detailed design or implementation exists or is available. Component specification must include interface/methods/parameters names, parameters type, component and operation semantics (e.g. contracts, textual description), as well as any other type of additional documentation.

- **Component Composition:** this functionality aims to support designers in establishing dependencies between required and provided interfaces of components to compose the application architecture.

- **Mismatch Identification:** this functionality involves a fine-grained evaluation of incompatibilities among selected components. We distinguish between the identification of the incompatibility, and its resolution, which are two tasks that can be developed at distinct moments of the AE process. In addition, we assume that adaptation and composition are entwined activities. Hence, incompatibilities are most probably identified when trying to compose components. Thus, the designer should be able to mark both an interface and a dependency between interfaces as incompatible. The latter is referred to as incompatibility dependency, which marks and documents a mismatch between a required and a provided interface. As mentioned in Section 2, three types of incompatibilities should be considered: structural, behavioral and hybrid.

  Structural incompatibilities should be automatically discovered by a detection function that compares the specification of these interfaces. A structural incompatibility detection algorithm is trivial, and compares interfaces name, type (i.e. provided, required), number of methods in the interfaces, and methods signatures (method name, and number and type arguments). If at least one incompatibility is found, the interfaces should be considered structurally incompatible. This function should also document all structural incompatibilities found.

  On the other hand, the automatic identification of behavioral incompatibilities is much harder. Formal specification of component interfaces, including the semantics of operations, would allow some automatic detection of this type of incompatibility, but this is still an open research area [16]. A behavioral incompatibility refers to a specific provided interface and should be documented as well.

  To sum up, this functionality will only allow components composition if no incompatibilities are detected. Its aim is at supporting the marking/detection of behavioral incompatibilities, automatic detection of structural incompatibilities, and establishment of the appropriate dependency according to the type of incompatibility at hand.

- **Adaptation:** incompatibility dependencies merely highlight which connections between components require adaptation. This functionality should support the adaptation and actual composition of adapted components at architectural level, preferably by the automatic application of standard adaptation techniques. Adaptation at this level focuses on the structure of an architectural solution for the detection of incompatibilities, and the input of documentation that provide guidance for the later realization of this solution. The goal is to reduce as early as possible the critical mismatches between expected services and available assets, which puts at risk the defined architecture. The actual adaptation is to be carried out at the provisioning phase, when component implementation and infrastructure details (i.e. component framework) are considered.

– **Architecture/Component Alternative Views:** it should allow different views of components and component architecture, as well as the visual distinction between original and adapted components. Certain adaptation techniques (e.g. wrapper) result in complex components (grouping components), whose internal architectures include the original ones. This functionality should allow the designer to inspect the internal details of complex components. In this way, he could choose to view or hide component internal details, at any moment. Incompatibilities should be highlighted using different colors and icons, and all documentation should be available for inspection at any time.

4 Odyssey-Adapt

Odyssey is a reuse environment based on domain models that supports CBD in both DE and AE processes. The environment provides a kernel that contains basic tools to create and instantiate domain models. Other tools are available through plug-ins. *Odyssey-Adapt* was developed as a plug-in that supports the adaptation and composition functionalities discussed in Section 3. This section discusses how *Odyssey-Adapt* addresses these functionalities, illustrating their use in a hypothetical scenario of an online store application.

4.1 Component Architecture Modeling

Odyssey supports component diagrams according to UML 2.0. Fig. 1 illustrates *Odyssey* modeling environment interface, which is divided into two main windows. The leftmost window contains the Semantic Tree, where all the available artifacts are listed, including components and interfaces. The Modeling Area (right window) allows the creation of a logical component diagram. New interfaces and components can be created and edited using, respectively, the interface specification tab and the component specification tab (not visible in Fig. 1). The Modeling Area of Fig. 1 stresses the important constructs of UML 2.0 for the component architecture modeling: components, required and provided interfaces, and interface connectors. The latter can be either represented by assembly connectors (ball and socket direct connection) or by dependencies (dashed arrow) between required and provided interfaces. Fig. 1 illustrates a scenario in which the user has selected five components to constitute the component architecture: *ShoppingCart, Order, Customer, Account* and *Product*. All selected components were inserted in the Modeling Area, through drag and drop actions. It should be noticed that *Odyssey-Adapt* works uniformly at any level of component architecture specification. For instance, *ShoppingCart* component itself could be defined in terms of lower-grain components (*DollarExchange, EuroExchange, PaymentAuthorization, CartContentManager*, etc), as depicted in Fig. 2.

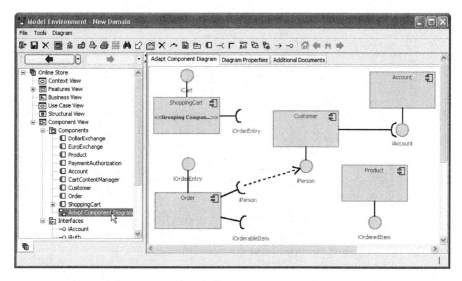

Fig. 1. *Odyssey* Environment with *Odyssey-Adapt* plug-in

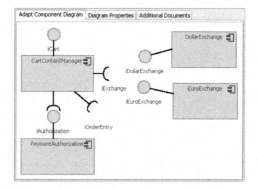

Fig. 2. *ShoppingCart* internal component architecture

4.2   Component Search and Specification Inspection

Odyssey-Search is a multi-agent system for component search and retrieval [17], which is not discussed here due to space limitations. When the user selects a component, either within the Semantic Tree or in the Modeling Area, he can inspect its details through the component specification.

The specification (Fig. 3a) indicates the provided and required interfaces of the component. Details about the interfaces methods (including names, return types and attributes) are available in the interface specification (Fig. 3b). Any additional documentation available on components or interfaces is also available (e.g. documents, contracts, etc).

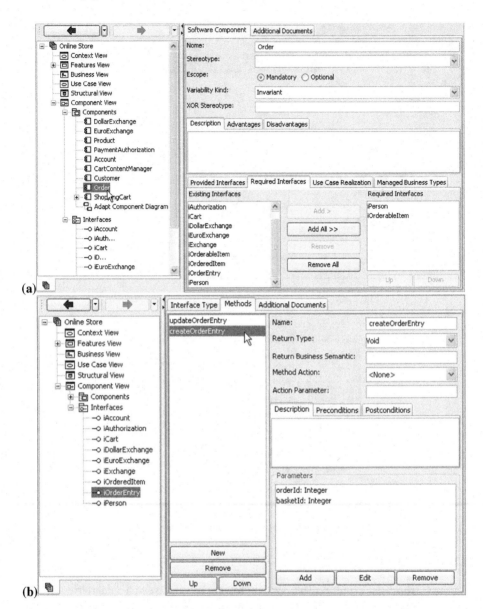

Fig. 3. (a) Component Specification and (b) Interface Specification

4.3 Component Composition

This functionality supports designers on the establishment of an assembly connector or a dependency between a pair of provided and required interfaces. Whenever a provided and a required interface are related, *Odyssey-Adapt* triggers the income-patibility detection function. If no incompatibilities are identified, the assembly connector/dependency is established. Otherwise, an incompatibility dependency is established between these interfaces, highlighting that these components require some kind of adaptation before their interfaces can be actually integrated. In the scenario of Fig. 1, the designer related *Order.iPerson* and *Customer.iPerson* using the dependency connector, and *Customer.iAccount* and *Account.iAccount* using the assembly connector. These connectors were created since no incompatibilities were detected.

4.4 Mismatch Identification

As mentioned, structural incompatibilities are automatically discovered by a detection function that compares the specification of the two interfaces to be connected. This function compares interfaces name, type (i.e. provided, required), number of methods in the interfaces, methods signatures (method name and arguments number and types). If at least one incompatibility is found, the interfaces are considered structurally incompatible. On the other hand, the identification of behavioral incompatibilities is in charge of the designer, due to the complexity of automatic detection. Hybrid incompatibilities are also automatically detected, provided that the behavioral incompatibility has been previously marked.

Currently, the designer marks a particular interface as behaviorally incompatible by selecting a provided interface and by using the respective popup menu. The incompatible interfaces are drawn using a darker color (Fig. 4), allowing the designer to immediately identify the ones that do not provide the expected services. The designer may document the behavioral problems using an Incompatibility Note as free format text. In our scenario, the designer realizes that although *Order* and *Account* are useful, they do not provide exactly the required services. Thus, he marks interfaces *Order.iOrderEntry* and *Account.iAccount* as behaviorally incompatible, and document the problems.

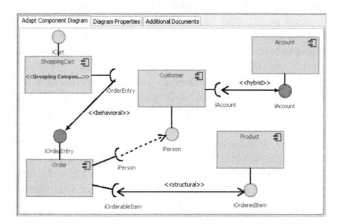

Fig. 4. Incompatibility dependencies

Incompatibility dependencies highlight connections between components that require adaptation. Three new stereotypes were created for dependency relationships that represent incompatibility dependencies (Fig. 4). Whenever the designer tries to relate interfaces using the assembly connector/dependency, *Odyssey-Adapt* searches for incompatibilities. If there no structural incompatibilities are found and the provided interface is not marked as behaviorally incompatible, the interfaces are related. Otherwise, it connects the interfaces using the appropriate incompatibility dependency (i.e. structural, behavioral or hybrid).

An incompatibility report is created whenever a structural/hybrid incompatibility is detected by *Odyssey-Adapt*. In case the incompatibility is hybrid, it merges the structural problems detected with the Incompatibility Note provided by the designer. The incompatibility report window (Fig. 5) presents the type of incompatibility, the name of connected interfaces, and details about all incompatibility problems.

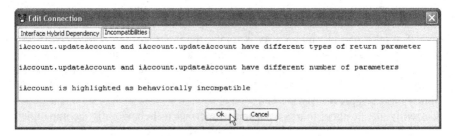

Fig. 5. Incompatibility report

4.5 Adaptation

This functionality supports the adaptation of components at architectural level by the automatic application of design patterns representing common adaptation techniques. Currently *Odyssey-Adapt* implements the patterns Adapter (Wrapper), Proxy, and two variations of Facade. Recall that adaptation at this level focuses on the structure of an architectural solution to detected incompatibilities, and the input of documentation that supplies detailed directions, guiding the effective realization of this solution. The actual adaptation is to be carried out in the solution provisioning phase, when component implementation and infrastructure details are considered.

Components, interfaces and dependencies with incompatibilities present in their popup menu an adaptation function. This function displays the *Components Adaptation Wizard*, in which the designer is presented with all candidate interfaces for adaptation, i.e. the ones related through an incompatibility dependency. By selecting a candidate interface, the window displays the interface(s) to which it is related and the applicable patterns. By evaluating all different choices on where to apply the adaptation, and through which technique, the designer is supported to make better decisions.

The user is also supported on the adaptation itself, since it concerns the straightforward application of a known technique. The user can solve one or more incompatibilities at a time. To do that, he iteratively selects an interface and a pattern among the applicable ones, and adds this selection to the adaptation tasks list. By the end of the interaction, the work list is applied, resulting in the creation of one or more components. Considering

Fig. 4, suppose that the designer decided to solve the behavioral incompatibility *Order.iOrderEntry* using a wrapper (adapter patter), and the structural incompatibility

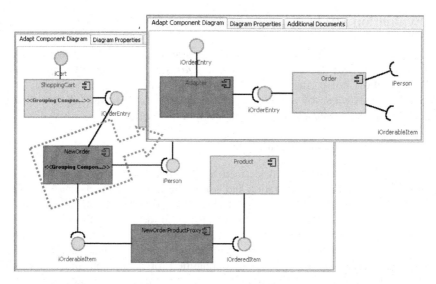

Fig. 6. Resulting component architecture and internal adapter architecture

involving *iOrderableItem* using a proxy. These two adaptations are added to the tasks list, and the result of their application is depicted in Fig. 6.

After adaptation takes place, the assembly connector replaces all handled incompatibility dependencies in the architecture. Adapter and FacadeAdapter patterns result in a complex component, which substitutes the original one. The internal architecture of this new component is modeled in a new, separate diagram. The Proxy and FacadeProxy patterns lead to the creation of a new component in the modeling window, which is related to the original ones. In Fig. 6., *NewOrder* is the result of applying the Adapter pattern to solve the behavioral incompatibility of *Order*, thus substituting this component in the architecture diagram. The details of *Order* can be inspected in a separate diagram on demand. *NewOrderProductProxy* is the component that solves the structural mismatch between *Order* and *Product*, according to the proxy pattern. The designer uses this functionality as many times as necessary: it provides a preliminary solution that needs to be refined and implemented. Designers should document all refinements that must take place during detailed component design and implementation.

4.6 Architecture/Component Alternative Views

All new components resulting from adaptation are displayed in the architecture diagram using a darker color, to allow the immediate realization of components inserted by adaptation activities. Their internal details can be visualized in a separate diagram (Fig. 6.). Incompatibilities are highlighted using different colors and stereotypes, and incompatibility documentation is available at any time for inspection.

5 Evaluation Study

The importance of empirical studies has been stressed in Software Engineering. A preliminary study was performed to evaluate *Odyssey-Adapt* support for adaptation and composition, comparing it with the modeling support available in *Odyssey*. To prepare the study plan, a five step process, as defined in [18], was followed: definition, planning, operation, analysis and presentation/packaging.

5.1 Study Definition and Planning

The objective of the study was defined as: "**analyze** *Odyssey-Adapt* and *ad-hoc* approaches for component adaptation and composition, **for the purpose of** characterization, **with respect to** viability and productivity, **from the point of view of** the researcher, **in the context of** graduate students in an academic environment". Two student groups would use *Odyssey* to adapt and compose components. The first group would use *Odyssey* basic component architecture modeling functionalities, and the second one would use the specific functionalities for adaptation and composition available through *Odyssey-Adapt* plug-in. Then, the study plan was detailed with the definition of the experiments questions, hypothesis, metrics and design. Three main questions with the related hypotheses were formulated:

Q1) Does the *Odyssey-Adapt* group detect more incompatibilities than the *Odyssey* group?
Q2) Does the *Odyssey-Adapt* group perform more adaptations over the detected incompatibilities than the *Odyssey* group?
Q3) Does the *Odyssey-Adapt* group adapt components faster than *Odyssey* group?

For all three questions, the hypotheses were defined in terms of the better performance of *Odyssey-Adapt* group, and the null hypotheses were the opposite. A toy problem in the mobile phone domain was defined for this experiment, as well as a set of metrics to answer these questions with regard to the toy problem, namely: number of correct incompatibilities identified number of correct component adaptations, the number of incompatibilities correctly solved and total time needed to detect and solve all incompatibilities. Subjects were randomly divided into the two groups, and metrics collected per subject.

5.2 Study Operation

Six graduate students from the Software Engineering Lab at Federal University of Rio de Janeiro were selected to participate in the study, which was in charge of the second author of this paper. All subjects received a quick training on adaptation and composition in *Odyssey*, but only the second group was trained to use the *Odyssey-Adapt* functionalities. After that, they had to compose eleven available components through eighteen interfaces to build a mobile phone application component architecture. These components presented structural incompatibilities that had to be detected and solved by adaptation. The subjects also filled in questionnaires to facilitate the analysis of quantitative results and enable qualitative evaluation.

5.3 Result Analysis, Presentation and Packaging

Descriptive analysis and Mann-Whitney hypothesis test [19] were used in the quantitative analysis of the results. The qualitative information was also analyzed. The most
interesting results are discussed in the remaining of this section.

From the total of 61 incompatibilities, *Odyssey* group subjects detected an average
of 40.7 incompatibilities, with a standard deviation of 6.5. *Odyssey-Adapt* group performed better, detecting an average of 46 incompatibilities, with a standard deviation
of 4. The number of correct component adaptations was very similar in both groups.
In the *Odyssey* group, only one subject incorrectly performed two adaptations, out of
the eight adaptations required. The adaptation errors made by the subjects are being
used to improve the *Odyssey-Adapt Components Adaptation Wizard*. The average
time to complete the task was also measured per subject, extracting the time spent
with the questionnaires. The *Odyssey-Adapt* group performed better, with an average
time of 49 minutes compared to the average 58 minutes from *Odyssey* group. The
standard deviations were 27 and 12, respectively.

Even with better results observed the *Odyssey-Adapt* group, the null hypothesis
(i.e. similar or inferior performance) could not be rejected, due to the low number of
subjects and the statistical test low power. Hence, despite the encouraging results,
more subjects are needed in order to statistically confirm the hypothesis of usefulness
and efficiency provided by *Odyssey-Adapt* functionality.

By examining the qualitative information provided by subjects in the questionnaires, it was possible to collect some interesting qualitative data. The three subjects
from *Odyssey-Adapt* group answered that they did not have difficulties to detect incompatibilities, whereas the ones from the *Odyssey* group stated the opposite. The
subjects that used *Odyssey-Adapt* also stated that they did not have difficulties for
using the tool (one of them claimed minor difficulties). All subjects were also asked
to make suggestions to improve the tool used in the experiment. The *Odyssey* subjects
suggested most of the features that are already available in *Odyssey-Adapt*. The suggestions from the *Odyssey-Adapt* group are under consideration and may be included
in the future, such as the possibility of manually mapping equivalent methods from
components interfaces.

This study was only a first step towards the evaluation of *Odyssey-Adapt*. Further
studies comparing it to different CASE or CBD tools, with greater number and more
experienced subjects, in real scenarios, are required to obtain conclusive results.

6 Conclusions

To effectively promote reuse, CBD must support selection, adaptation and composition of components as early as possible in the application development life-cycle. In
this paper, we presented a set of functionalities targeted at supporting adaptation and
composition activities during AE. Due to the focus on component architecture definition, these activities aim at defining the structure of an architectural solution. In later
phases, this solution must be refined and provisioned with detailed component design
and/or implementation. Our approach minimizes the risks of the late consideration of
mismatches between the services, as defined by the architecture, and the available

assets, which may require modifications of the architecture. It also reflects the practice of designing the architecture with the existing reusable assets in mind.

Current CBD environments do not provide explicit support to adaptation activity, which involves at least identifying mismatches and applying standard adaptation techniques. It is also useful to recognize in the component architecture which parts correspond to adaptations, as well as to be able to trace reused components into adapted components, and vice-versa. These issues are addressed by the proposed set of functionalities. *Odyssey-Adapt* is a plug-in of the *Odyssey* Environment that implements the proposed functionalities. *Odyssey-Adapt* can be improved in many ways, particularly in the (semi)automatic detection of behavioral incompatibilities, traceability and recommendation of adaptation techniques. Future work includes enhancements of the tool features, further evaluation studies for more conclusive results and coupling of the tool with a repository infrastructure.

References

1. Brown, A.; Short, K.: On Components and Objects: The Foundation of Component-Based Development. In: 5th International Symposium on Assessment of Software Tools and Technologies (1997) 112-121
2. Brown, A.: Large-scale component-based development. Prentice Hall (2000)
3. Bosch, J.: Superimposition: A Component Adaptation Technique. Information and Software Technology, 41(5), March (1999) 257-273
4. Heineman, G., Ohlenbusch, H.: An Evaluation of Component Adaptation Techniques. Technical Report WPI-CS-TR-98-20. Available in http://www.cs.wpi.edu/~heineman/classes/cs562/pdf/HO99.pdf
5. Cechich, A., Prieto, M.: Comparing Visual Component Composition Environment. In: 22nd International Conference of the Chilean Computer Society (2002) 217-225
6. The Odyssey Project Homepage, 2006. http://reuse.cos.ufrj.br/odyssey/index_en.html, accessed in 01/2006
7. Rine, D., Nada, N., Jaber, K.: Using Adapters to Reduce Interaction Complexity in Reusable Component-Based Software Development. In: Symposium on Software Reusability (1999) 37-43
8. Küçük, B., Alpdemir, M. N., Zobel, R. N.: Customizable Adapters For Blackbox Components. In: Nierstrasz, O. (Editor). International Workshop on Component-Oriented Programming (1998) Available in http://citeseer.nj.nec.com/article /kucuk98customizable.html
9. Gamma, E., Helm, R., Johnson, R., Vlissides, J.: Design Patterns: Elements of Reusable Object-Oriented Software. Addison-Wesley (1995)
10. Lüer, C., Rosenblum, D.: Wren - An Environment for Component-Based Development. In: 8th European Software Engineering Conference (2001) 207-217
11. UML 2.0 Superstructure Final Adopted Specification. Available in http://www.omg.org/cgi-bin/apps/doc?ptc/03-08-02.pdf
12. Keller, R., Schauer, R.: Design Components: Towards Software Composition at Design Level. In: 20th International Conference on Software Engineering (1998) 302-317
13. Yacoub, S., Xue, H., Ammar, H.: POD: A Composition Environment for Pattern-Oriented Design. In: 34th Technology of Object-Oriented Languages and Systems (2000) 263-272
14. Seacord, R., Hissam, S., Wallnau, K.: Agora: a search engine for software component. IEEE Internet computing 2-6, Nov/Dec (1998) 62-70
15. Meling, R., Montgomery, J., Ponnusamy, P., Wong, E., Mehandjiska, D.: Storing and retrieving software components: a component description manager. 12th Australian Software Engineering Conference (2000) 107-117

16. Zaremski, A., Wing, J.: Specification Matching of Software Components. ACM Transactions on Software Engineering and Methodology, 6(4), October (1997) 333-369
17. Braga, R. M. M., Werner, C. M. L., Mattoso, M. L. Q.: Odyssey-Search: A Multi-Agent System for Component Information Search and Retrieval. Journal of Systems and Software, Elsevier, 79(2), (2006) 204-215.
18. Wohlin, C., Runeson, P., Höst, M., Ohlsson, M., Regnell, B., and Wesslén, A.: Experimentation in Software Engineering: an introduction. Kluwer Academic Publishers, USA (2000)
19. Siegel S., Castellan N.J.: Non-parametric Statistics for the Behavioral Sciences, McGraw-Hill, 2 ed., New York (1988)

Re-engineering a Credit Card Authorization System for Maintainability and Reusability of Components – *A Case Study*

Kyo Chul Kang[1], Jae Joon Lee[1,*], Byungkil Kim[1], Moonzoo Kim[1],
Chang-woo Seo[2], and Seung-lyeol Yu[2]

[1] Software Engineering Lab. Computer Science and Engineering Dept.
Pohang University of Science and Technology, Pohang, South Korea
{kck,gibman, dayfly, moonzoo}@postech.ac.kr
[2] System Development Team and Quality Management Team, LG-Card Co.
118, Namdaemun 2 ga, Jung-gu, Seoul, South Korea
{cwseo, toto}@card.lg.co.kr

Abstract. A credit card authorization system (CAS) is a large information system performing diverse activities such as purchase authentication, balance transfer, cash advances, etc. One characteristic of CAS is its frequent update to satisfy the needs of customers and newly enforced governmental laws. Thus, CAS should be designed to minimize the effects of updates, for which high reusability of the CAS components is desired. In this paper, we present our experience of re-engineering CAS based on a feature model for improved reusability of components, which alleviates the difficulty of system maintenance. The result of this project has been successfully transferred to the company.

1 Introduction

A credit card authorization system (CAS) is one of the largest information systems used worldwide. CAS handles various types of transactions in large volume, such as purchase authentication, balance transfer, affiliated discount services, etc. One characteristic of CAS is its frequent update, and the maintainability of CAS is a crucial issue for credit card companies. Government frequently creates and enforces laws targeting the business of card companies. In addition, due to heavy competition in the credit card market, card companies are pressed to offer new services or change existing services frequently. For example, the discount rate on gas purchase for freight vehicles changes many times a year due to gas price changes and discount rate changes of other card companies. These situations cause constant revisions of CAS, which increases the complexity of system maintenance. Thus, in order to manage frequent revisions, CAS should be designed to accommodate changing requirements easily and isolate effects of updates as much as possible.

---

* Jae Joon Lee is currently at Fraunhofer Institute for Experimental Software Engineering, Fraunhofer-Platz 1, D-67663 Kaiserslautern, Germany (jaejoon.lee@iese.fraunhofer.de).

M. Morisio (Ed.): ICSR 2006, LNCS 4039, pp. 156–169, 2006.
© Springer-Verlag Berlin Heidelberg 2006

From the review of the CAS of LG Card Co. Ltd, we found several opportunities to enhance reusability of the CAS components. One manifest problem was that new services have been added to CAS by simply adding new components specially developed for those services without consideration of common/reusable characteristics of the services. This was caused by the lack of *proactive design* that anticipates updates of services based on market evolution. This ad-hoc way of evolution resulted in redundant code and difficulty of understanding program behavior. As a result, newly added services or updates of services easily affected unnecessarily large segments of CAS and caused high maintenance costs.

In this paper, we present our experience of improving reusability of the CAS components through *proactive re-engineering* based on a feature model. First, we reviewed the existing CAS code and the revision history with help of domain experts and extracted the legacy design. Then, we constructed a feature model of the CAS domain that captures variabilities of CAS from the revision history and a market analysis [1][2][3]. Based on the recovered legacy design and the feature model, we could re-design components of CAS to preplan adoption of future evolution, which enhanced system maintainability. This re-engineering task was conducted based on three re-engineering principles: encapsulation of variabilities, generalization of common processes, and separation of data-streams.

Section 2 describes related works briefly. Section 3 gives an overview of CAS and its corresponding feature model. Section 4 explains the three design principles we applied to the re-engineering task. In section 5, we explain details of the re-engineering task. Lessons learned from this re-engineering project are summarized in section 6. Finally, we conclude this paper with future works in section 7.

2   Related Work

There have been active researches for improving maintainability and reusability of software systems. One of difficult problems in software maintenance is that there exists duplicated code among multiple components that enlarges change efforts and, thus, increases the difficulty of maintaining systems. In order to alleviate this problem, in addition to applying fundamental software engineering principles such as decreasing component coupling and increasing functional cohesion [4], software metric [5], software visualization [6], and concept analysis [7] have been used.

There are several important classes of researches focused on reusability in the information systems domain. For information systems, process workflows should be designed with consideration of reusability of the components that handle business processes. The workflow management coalition [8] defines a standard architecture and component interfaces to design workflows conveniently. [9] studies reuse of existing workflows based on the characteristics of data dependency among processes. [10] proposes guidelines for architecture design and development processes for reusable business components, and [11] describes refactoring techniques focusing on improved system maintainability.

Although these works contribute to enhancing reusability and maintainability of business components and workflows, domain analysis to encapsulate variabilities and reuse commonalities must precede these activities in order to enhance the benefits further. We use a feature model for domain analysis, and apply the analysis results and re-engineering principles to make a proactive design for improved reusability and maintainability.

3   Overview of Card Authorization System

This section describes the background of the CAS domain. We explain the background of this project in section 3.1 followed by an overview of CAS in section 3.2. The feature model of CAS is given in section 3.3.

3.1 Background of the Re-engineering Project

In the year 2004, LG-Card Co. Ltd [12] adopted a component based development (CBD) method [13][14] and started to re-develop CAS by converting hard-coded business rules into a database and standardizing component interfaces. Moreover, to enhance the reusability of components, they continuously applied several component based management (CBM) programs [15][16] such as reuse rate measurement, component library construction, and component re-engineering. Nevertheless, they had difficulties in maintaining CAS. The developers added/updated components in an ad-hoc way at each update request, which brought about duplicated code and complex component interactions. As a result, this reactive maintenance caused high maintenance costs even with simple changes.

To solve these problems, LG-Card requested POSTECH in the year 2005 to evaluate and improve the *credit card* and *check card systems* that are the core of the entire CAS.   With the request, the POSTECH team studied the CAS domain and re-engineered CAS for six months to enhance maintainability by improving the reusability of CAS components.

3.2 Overview of CAS

Fig.1 shows an overview of CAS. The left part of Fig.1 shows CAS and its environment. CAS interacts with NET24, a middleware working as an interface between CAS and banks, point of sales (POS), and customer services. In addition, CAS communicates with a database system to retrieve and update transaction information. The Net24Main component of CAS directly interacts with NET24 and distributes transaction requests from outside to the credit card system or to the check card system accordingly. Each card system consists of four component layers: transaction classifier (TC), transaction flow manager (TFM), business process component (BPC), and interface component (IC).

The main task of TC is to classify transaction types and to call appropriate TFM components. The TFM components manage transaction flows by controlling business processes implemented in the BPC components. The IC components work mostly as data holders communicating with the database system. The component manager handles orderly creation of these components preventing redundant instantiation. Components of a higher layer control the components of a lower layer via call/return methods; a TC component calls appropriate TFM components, then a TFM component calls BPC components, etc.

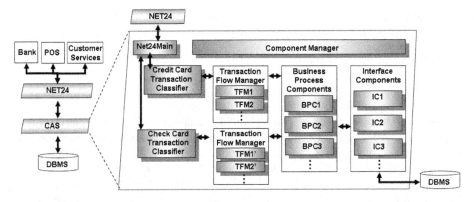

Fig. 1. Overview of CAS

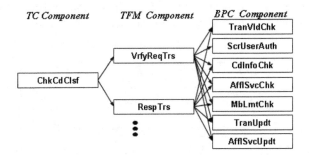

Fig. 2. Execution flow of the check card transactions

Fig.2 illustrates how these layers work in the check card system.[1] When a user purchases a product using his/her check card, a purchase authorization request is sent from the store to CAS. Then, ChkCdClsf, a TC component for classifying check card transactions, recognizes the type of the transaction and calls VrfyReqTrs, a TFM component, to check if the requested transaction is valid or not. VrfyReqTrs calls TransVldChk, ScrUserAuth, CdInfoChk, and others in sequence. TransVldChk identifies the place where the transaction occurs. If the transaction occurs at an online store, ScrUserAuth is called to check the user's identification and password. Otherwise, ScrUserAuth is not invoked. Then, CdInfoChk is called to verify whether the given card information, such as the expiration date and the name of cardholder, matches with the information in the CAS database. Similarly, other BPC components are also called according to the transaction flow encoded in VrfyReqTrs. Once VrfyReqTrs has finished authorization of the transaction, VrfyReqTrs sends a request to the bank that issued the check card to check if the bank account has enough balance for the purchase. After receiving that request, the bank sends to CAS a new

---

[1] The credit card system has 4 TFM components and the check card system has 5 TFM components. There exist 39 BPC components and 71 IC components shared by both systems.

transaction request that contains required information. Then, the request is passed to RespTrs, and RespTrs calls TransVldChk.[2]

3.3   A Feature Model of CAS

In order to improve the maintainability of CAS, we need to re-design CAS with consideration of potential service changes based on the revision history and market projections.   A feature model is a suitable tool to capture variability of services and make a proactive design for evolving services based on relationships among features. We analyzed commonalities and variabilities of the CAS domain first and developed a feature model shown in Fig. 3.[3]   CAS (the root node of Fig.3) consists of "Check Card Authentication" and "Credit Card Authentication" each of which corresponds to authentication features for check card and credit card respectively.   In addition, CAS has "*Affiliated Service*" feature that represents various affiliated services such as purchase discount, free service, etc.

Features that change frequently are named in italic font in Fig. 3.   For example, features related to "*Affiliated Service*" are indicated as frequently updated features.

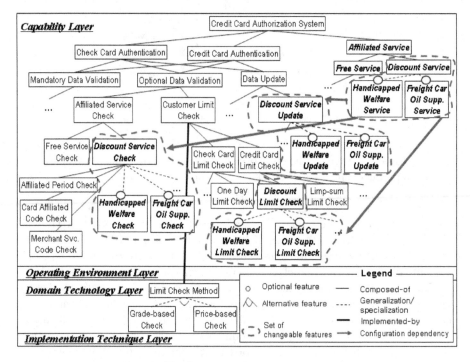

Fig. 3. A feature model of CAS

---

[2] Note that VrfyReqTrs and RespTrs share many BPC components because these two TFM components perform similar tasks. This redundancy problem comes from the legacy design of earlier CAS and has not been fixed yet due to risk of a large scale revision.

[3] Features corresponding to business processes are not shown in this paper.

Table 1 includes the revision history of CAS from July 2005 to August 2005. As can be seen in Table 1, there are frequent revisions due to newly added affiliated stores and changes of affiliated services. *"Discount Service"* (located at the top right corner of Fig.3) is an affiliated service for handling purchase discounts. This feature is specialized to *"Handicapped Welfare Service"* and *"Freight Car Oil Supp. Service"* features. *"Handicapped Welfare Service"* is a service that provides discount when a handicapped cardholder purchases daily necessities. *"Freight Car Oil Supp. Service"* provides discount to a freight vehicle driver for gas purchases. Changes of *"Discount Service"* affect *"Discount Service Update"*, *"Discount Service Check"*, and *"Discount Limit Check"* as indicated by the configuration dependency relationships.

As shown in Fig.3, changes in one feature (e.g., *"Discount Service"*) can affect several other features (e.g., *"Discount Service Update"* and *"Discount Service Check"*), which requires to modify related components altogether. This is a complex task without knowing explicit relationships between features. After we identified frequently changing features and related components, we could re-engineer these components to prepare adoption of future revisions by improving reusability of these components.

Table 1. CAS revisions between July 2005 and Aug 2005

Date	Revisions
Aug 16	Changed codes of refusing transactions for a family restaurant discount service. - If the service is not applicable to the card owner, return the refusal code 588. - If there was no transaction in the previous month, return the refusal code 593.
	Added an affiliated service code for the DW department store.
Aug 4	Added an affiliated service code for the KB department store.
	Added a business process to restrict a discount service for "LG BF" Card
July 13	If a welfare service for handicapped people is requested by a handicapped user using a family card, the transaction should be refused.
	Changed a business process for the oil discount service for freight vehicles - removed freight vehicle oil discount codes K002 and K003 - modified the codes between K011 and K020.
July 11	Added an affiliated discount service for DJ Zoo.
July 04	Added a business process for a discount service used by MIC

4 Re-engineering Principles

Based on the review of the design and the revision history of CAS, we propose three principles for making a *proactive system design* through re-engineering. These principles can serve as a primary design plan, which is indispensable in any engineering projects of sizable scale.

4.1 Principle 1: Encapsulation of Evolving Features

A complex system like CAS usually suffers from high degree of coupling among components. This problem often occurs when new components for the requested services are implemented by copying and modifying existing components without reorganizing/refactoring them. High coupling among components makes the behavior of the system difficult to understand and, thus, it is hard to revise and maintain the system, degrading evolvability.

To address this problem, we propose to encapsulate frequently changing features in a component. In other words, we group components for evolving features into a module that provides a common interface to the rest of the system. By this encapsulation, we can decrease the degree of component coupling and localize the effects of component update into a module. In addition, details of components can be abstracted away, which provides better system understandability.

4.2 Principle 2: Generalization of Common Processes

Information systems provide a large number of services some of which are similar with minor distinction. Thus, without careful anticipation of changes, multiple components with slightly different services easily prevail in the system. When a change is made to a common process, multiple components that implement the process should be modified altogether. In addition, it becomes hard to find which component is responsible for a specific behavior of the system, which degrades the maintainability of the system.

Therefore, it is highly desirable to make generalized components for common processes so that the degree of redundancy could be decreased. In addition, sequences of processing various transactions are valuable domain knowledge that should be reused to minimize the risk of creating wrong process sequences. Once common processes are identified, we can build generalized components for the common processes and then extend the components for specialized processes using inheritance and/or association mechanisms.

4.3 Principle 3: Separation of Upstream Data from Downstream Data

As typical of information processing systems, the main operations of CAS are to retrieve, process, and update data. Thus, clear and efficient handling of data is at the core of quirements. For this purpose, all data-streams among components must be clearly defined. In other words, the source and the destination of a data-flow must be identified clearly and patterns of data-flows must be visible. This clear identification of data-streams helps preventing unnecessary modification of multiple components that access a data-stream.

One way of achieving this goal is to classify data-flows explicitly based on its characteristic. CAS has a layered architecture consisting of TC, TFM, BPC, and IC components that process transactions in order. Thus, we could identify two separate data-streams as follows:

- TC→TFM→BPC→IC for managing transaction information (*downstream*)
- IC→BPC→TFM→TC for reporting result of transaction validation (*upstream*)

Based on this information, we could separate data-streams in two directions explicitly, which provided optimized data structures for each data-stream as well as localization of change effects when an update to data handling components happened.

5   Re-engineering CAS

In this section, we describe details of the re-engineering task. In section 5.1, we show how to encapsulate BPC components based on their characteristics.   Section 5.2 explains the design of generalized components. Finally, section 5.3 describes separation of an upstream data-flow from a downstream one.

5.1   Encapsulation of the BPC Components

In order to improve the reusability of CAS components, it is necessary to minimize the effects of updates as much as possible. The current layered architecture was designed to achieve this goal by embedding reusable business processes into the BPC components (i.e., components that embed business workflows are separated from the components of functional tasks) so that when a business process changes, its effects would be localized to the corresponding BPC component and the TFM components that control the BPC component directly. For example, in Fig. 2, suppose that AfflSvcUpdt BPC component is modified by changing a process of handling affiliated services. Then, all TFM components accessing AfflSvcUpdt, such as VrfyReqTrs and RespTrs, should be modified accordingly in the original design.

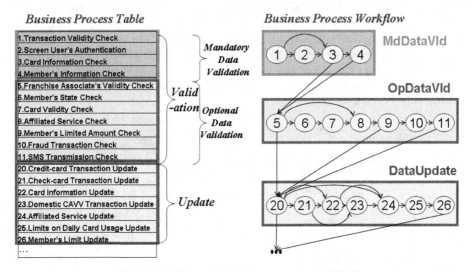

Fig. 4. Workflow of the business processes of CAS

Considering that most business processes of frequently changing services (e.g. affiliated services) are embedded in the BPC components, it is crucial to minimize update effects of the BPC components. We noted that effects of updating the BPC components could be reduced further by encapsulating BPC components. In other words, we grouped BPC components of similar characteristics into a module to minimize the change effects. For this goal, we studied the workflow of CAS carefully and grouped BPC components based on their data usage. Fig. 4 shows workflows of business processes of CAS. The table in the left part of Fig. 4 shows what these processes are and the flowgraph in the right part of Fig.4 shows how these processes are connected and executed in order.

First, we classified the business processes according to its type of data manipulation – validation (*read*) and update (*write*). Processes 1 through 11 are to validate transaction information and processes 20 through 26 are to update validation results into the CAS database. Second, we classified processes 1 through 11 further based on the type of data. Processes 1 to 4 validate mandatory transaction data that should be validated even for simple transactions such as purchase cancellation.[4] Processes 5 to 11 validate optional data such as data about affiliated services (process 8) and short message service (process 11). Based on this classification, we grouped processes 1 through 4 into the MdDataVld module, processes 5 through 11 into the OpDataVld module, and processes 20 through 26 into the DataUpdate module.

Fig. 5 shows the re-engineered component design. By encapsulating BPC components, we could localize the effect of updating a BPC component to only one module that incorporates the BPC component instead of multiple TFM components. In the original design, if AfflSvcUpdt BPC component is changed, all TFM components that directly access AfflSvcUpdt such as VrfyReqTrs and RespTrs need to be modified accordingly. In the new design, however, the effect of update is localized to the DataUpdate module only. In addition, this restructuring alleviated redundancy among the TFM components because common tasks among multiple TFM components to control BPC components were extracted into a new module. For example, task of controlling TransVldChk, ScrUserAuth, CdInfoChk is moved from TFM components, VrfyReqTrs and RespTrs, to the MdDataVid module. In the original architecture, when such a common task of TFM components is updated, we had to modify all related TFM components. In the new architecture, however, we need to modify only a corresponding module.

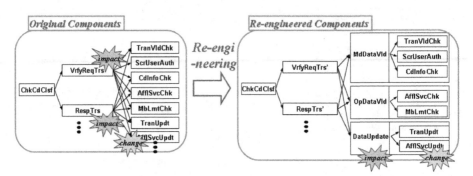

Fig. 5. Encapsulation of the CAS components

5.2 Generalization of the Common Business Processes

As can be seen in Fig. 2, the BPC components were designed to share common business processes for various transactions (even transactions of different systems – the

---

[4] In Fig.4, the workflow for purchase cancellation consists of processes 1-4, 5, and 20.

credit card system and the check card system). Existing BPC components were, how-ever, implemented without considering how the authorization processes could be changed. Accordingly, when new services were added, the CAS maintainer simply added new components for the services although these services could be provided with less effort by using a general component for the common processes of the ser-vices. This is a typical weakness of reactive maintenance without proactive design.

Let us look at an example. The feature model in Fig. 6 shows two sets of features for checking discount services, containing "Handicapped Welfare Check" (checking if welfare discount service is applicable) and "Freight Car Oil Supp. Check" (check-ing if a gas purchase discount for freight vehicles is available). These two sets of features were implemented in the HandiWelfareChk and FCarOilSuppChk BPC components respectively. These two BPC components share a same sequence of processes such as checking the affiliate service code first, then the period of affiliated service contract, then the merchant codes, etc.   This fact is reflected in the feature model in Fig.6 showing that these two features are specialized instances of the "Dis-count Service Check" feature that contains "Card Affiliated Code Check", "Affiliated Period Check", and "Merchant Svc. Code Check" features.

Considering the fact that services are added and changed frequently (see Table 1), ad-hoc addition of components for services (e.g. FCarOilSuppChk) should be avoided because it causes redundancy among components. Thus, we need to re-engineer components so that services of common characteristics should be pro-vided by generic components. Re-engineered components in Fig.6 show that

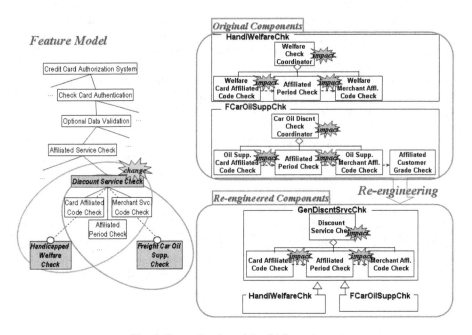

Fig. 6. Generalization of the CAS components

GenDiscntSrvcChk implements common processes of both HandiWelfareChk and FCarOilSuppChk (e.g. checking the affiliated card code, affiliated period, and affiliated merchant code) by generalizing these processes. Thus, HandiWelfareChk and FCarOilSuppChk are built as extensions of GenDiscntSrvcChk.

The re-engineered components have reusability benefits. Suppose that "Discount Service Check" feature is changed, e.g., the affiliated period should be checked first. With the original design, we need to update all BPC components that check discount services (e.g. HandiWelfareChk and FCarOilSuppChk). This is a burdensome job because there are many such services. In contrast, we only need to update GenDiscntSrvcChk in the new component design.

5.3   Classification of Data-Streams – Upstream vs. Downstream Data-Flows

In the original design, components communicate with each other using *valued objects* (VOs), which are global data objects containing the transaction information and the result of validation. A TC component writes down transaction information into VOs and passes reference pointers to the VOs to TFM components. The TFM components read the transaction information from the VOs. Similarly, a TFM component processes the transaction data (e.g. converting a card number into a format compatible with the database), writes the processed data (e.g. converted card number) into the VOs, and then passes the reference pointers to BPC components.

This way of communication is simple but problematic. First of all, as depicted in the left part of Fig.7, data-streams among components become obscure so that it is hard to visualize component interactions; it is not clear which components modify VOs and which components are affected by the modification because data-streams are implicitly constructed through VOs. In addition, cohesion of VO is low because VO serves multiple purposes of various components. Furthermore, once a component that accesses VO is modified, all components and VO should be modified accordingly because VO works as a medium for communications of different types without hiding information. Suppose that we modify a routine of updating VO in a BPC component. Then, VO as well as other TC, TFM, BPC, and IC components can be affected altogether.

We could solve these problems by separating data-streams into upstream data (containing result of transactions validation) and downstream data (containing transaction information) as depicted in the right part of Fig. 7. For downstream data, only TC and

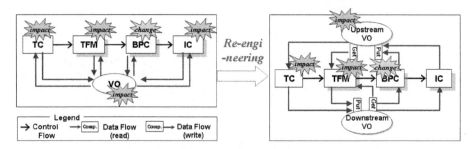

Fig. 7. Separated data-streams

TFM components write transaction data into the downstream VOs. BPC and IC components can read from the VOs, but do not write to the VOs. For the upstream data, IC and BPC components write the result of transaction validation and TFM and TC components read the result from the upstream VOs. Furthermore, we apply the facade pattern to both upstream and downstream VOs to hide internal modification of VOs.

As a result, each data-stream could have its own VO data structure optimized for its own purpose. Also, the data structure of the upstream VO is immune from changes of the downstream VO, and vice versa. Similarly, this separation localizes the effect of modifying a BPC component to the upstream VOs and TC/TFM components. Furthermore, component interactions became visible and the responsibilities of components became clear. Thus, we could anticipate easily which components should be modified at changes of services.

6 Lessons Learned

In this section, we share the lessons learned from this re-engineering project.

6.1 Necessity of Proactive Re-engineering

During the project, we are convinced that proactive re-engineering is essential, not optional in many ways. We found several poorly designed legacy CAS components that caused high maintenance costs. Due to lack of analysis on commonality and variability of services, developers tend to revise the system in an ad-hoc manner without considering how the system should be designed for better maintainability. This way of revision results in high degree of redundancy and component coupling, which degrades maintainability of the system severely as revisions are repeated. Therefore, proactive re-engineering should be enforced to preplan efficient adoption of future evolution of services by improving reusability of components. For this re-engineering activity, a feature model works as a very effective means for capturing variability of features and creating a proactive design.

6.2 Management of Commonality and Variability

We found that the company had difficulty in managing variabilities of services systematically. One of the goals in this project was to enhance adaptability of CAS to frequently changing services. Dependency relationships between features of the feature model helped us to recognize the effects of service changes/additions. In addition, generalization/specialization relationships helped us to encapsulate similar components into generalized ones and to adopt new services more conveniently (see section 5.2). Thus, the feature model expressed valuable information for identifying both variable services and the boundary of component reuse, which supported adoption of future service evolutions. Similarly, workflow analysis helped us to understand what processes should be mandatory or optional.

6.3 Broad Coverage of a Feature Model for System Analysis

In our experience, the feature model successfully provided guidelines for analyzing the target system in a broad way, from architectural issues to component refactoring.

This is because a feature model represents the domain of the target system *hierarchically*. In other words, features of higher level (near to the root of a feature tree) are related to system assets of a large scale such as an architecture or layers. In contrast, features at leaf nodes are mostly related to small objects of a system. Therefore, once a feature model is built carefully, the model can be used for analyzing a system in various levels of abstraction; the model can provide abstract views on the system domain as well as detailed views on relationships among concrete system entities.

7 Conclusion and Future Work

In this paper, we described our experience of re-engineering CAS for enhanced maintainability and reusability of components. Through the proactive re-engineering task based on the feature model, we could achieve this goal and the result was transferred to the company successfully. We believe that this case study can serve to promote the significance of proactive re-engineering based on a feature model, which can alleviate difficulties of system maintenance and reduce overall maintenance costs. As a future work, we will investigate systematic methods for validating re-engineering process, i.e., to show that re-engineered systems behave "equivalently" to the original systems.

References

1. J.Bergey, L.O'Brien, and D.Smith. Option Analysis for Re-engineering (OAR): A Method for Mining Legacy Assets (CMU/SEI-2001-TN-013). Pittsburgh, PA:Software Engineering Institute, Carnegie Mellon University (2001)
2. M.Kim, J.Lee, K.C.Kang, Y.Hong, and S.Bang. Re-engineering Software Architecture of Home Service Robots: A Case Study, International Conference on Software Engineering, Missouri, USA, pp.505-513 (2005)
3. K.C.Kang, M.Kim, J.Lee, and B.Kim. Feature-oriented Re-engineering of Legacy Systems into Product Line Assets, The 9th International Software Product Line Conference, Rennes, France, pp. 45 – 56 (2005)
4. C.Ghezzi, M.Jazayeri, D.Mandrioli. Fundamentals of Software Engineering 2nd ed., Prentice-Hall (2004)
5. B.Magdalena, M.Ettore, D.Michel, L.Bruno and K.Kostas. Measuring Clone Based Reengineering Opportunities, Sixth International Software Metrics Symposium (METRICS'99), p. 292 (1999)
6. D.E. Baburin et al. Visualization Facilities in Program Re-engineering, Programming and Computer Software Vol 27 No. 2, pp. 69-77 (2001)
7. G. Snelting and F. Tip. Re-engineering Class Hierarchies Using Concept Analysis, Proc. Foundations of Software Eng., pp. 99-110 (1998)
8. D. Holinsworth. The Workflow Reference Model, Workflow Management Coalition, TC00-1003, 1995
9. N.Russell, W.M.P. van der Aalst, A.H.M. ter Hofstede and D.Edmon. Workflow Resource Patterns: Identification, Representation and Tool Support, In the proceeding of the 17th Conference on Advanced Information System Engineering (CAiSE'05), Porto, Portugal, 2005
10. G. Baster, P. Konana, and J. E. Scott. Business Components: A Case Study of Bankers Trust Australia Limited, Communication of the ACM, Vol.44, No.5, 2001

11. C. J. Neill and B. Gill. Refactoring Reusable Business Components, IEEE Computer Society, 1520-9202/03, 2003
12. LG Card Co. Ltd homepage http://www.lgcard.com
13. D.D'sousz and A.Willi. Object, Components, and Frameworks with UML: The Catalysis Approach, Addison-Wesley (1998)
14. 14 K.C.Kang. Issues in Component-Based Software Engineering, Proceeding of the 21st International Conference Software Engineering (1999)
15. N.Boertien, M.Steen and H.Jonkers. Evaluation of Component-Based Development Methods, International Workshop on Evaluation of Modeling Methods in Systems Analysis and Design (2001)
16. S.A.Bohner. Extending Software Change Effect Analysis into COTS Components, Proceedings of the 27th Annual NASA Goddard/IEEE Software Engineering Workshop (2003)

Odyssey-CCS: A Change Control System Tailored to Software Reuse

Luiz Gustavo Lopes, Leonardo Murta, and Cláudia Werner

COPPE/UFRJ – Systems Engineering and Computer Science Program
Federal University of Rio de Janeiro – P.O. Box 68511
21945-970 Rio de Janeiro, Brazil
{luizgus, murta, werner}@cos.ufrj.br

Abstract. Software is constantly changing and these changes may occur at anytime in the software lifecycle. In order to avoid rework and information loss, among other problems, these changes must be controlled in a proper way. When changes affect reused components, possibly composed by other components, it is important to know who is responsible for implementing them. Some consequences of this problem, named Reuse Chain of Responsibility, is the misconception on rights and duties of teams that produce and reuse components. Aiming to solve this problem, we introduce Odyssey-CCS, a flexible change control system that allows the customization of a change control process to the specific needs of software reuse. Moreover, it keeps a reuse map that holds information about contracts between components producers and reusers. The reuse map is integrated to an existing component library and is queried by Odyssey-CCS within the impact analysis activity.

1 Introduction

Software is constantly changing, and these changes may occur at anytime in the software lifecycle. In order to avoid rework and information loss, among other problems, changes must be controlled in a proper way. Software Configuration Management (SCM), which is a discipline for controlling evolution of large and complex systems [11], is a critical element in the software maintenance process [13] and can be used to attenuate this problem. SCM is composed by a variety of systems. One of these systems, the Change Control System (CCS), supports the lifecycle of change requests, collecting, storing, and propagating related information.

Many successful software reuse projects apply some kind of SCM system [20]. However, the current CCSs are not properly designed to deal with specific idiosyncrasies of reuse-driven paradigms, such as Component-based Software Engineering (CBSE), which construct systems by reusing existing components [5]. The main drawbacks are related to the lack of information necessary for software maintenance, such as producers and consumers of a given component, together with the contracts established between them. Moreover, the current change control processes (CCPs) are not flexible enough to support scenarios where the change responsibility may be propagated to other development teams.

M. Morisio (Ed.): ICSR 2006, LNCS 4039, pp. 170–183, 2006.

It is difficult to know who is responsible for maintaining a given component in scenarios where components are composed by other components and developed by different teams. This problem can be attenuated if producers and consumers are identified, together with the contract that determines their rights and duties, and a change process tailored to CBSE is controlled in a proper way. This paper introduces an approach, named Odyssey-CCS, which allows CCP and template modeling for the specific needs of CBSE. These processes are bound together with templates and enacted by Odyssey-CCS via Web. Moreover, Odyssey-CCS keeps a reuse map that can be queried by specific activities of the CCP to detect the person/team who is responsible for maintaining each component.

It is important to notice that the focus of our paper is on the maintenance of components that are already stored in an existing controlled library. The search and retrieval of components available on the web [4], and discussions about existing library solutions [19] are out of the scope of this paper.

This paper is organized in six sections, including this introduction. Section 2 presents some background concepts of SCM and CBSE, together with the main challenges of applying CCS in the context of CBSE. Section 3 introduces the proposed approach to attenuate the discussed problems. Section 4 details a prototype constructed to automate the proposed approach. Section 5 describes the related work. Finally, some contributions and future work are presented in Section 6.

2 Background and Existing Challenges

SCM can be organized under two main perspectives depending on the role in the software development process. From the managers' perspective, SCM is composed by four main functions [14, 15]: configuration identification, configuration control, status accounting, and configuration audits and reviews. However, from the developers' perspective, SCM is composed by three main systems: CCS, version control system, and build and release control system.

This work is contextualized in the configuration control and status accounting functions when analyzed from the managers' perspective, and in CCS when analyzed from the developers' perspective. In the following, we present the main features of CCSs, the CBSE paradigm, and the existing challenges of using these systems to control the evolution of software developed according to the CBSE paradigm.

2.1 Change Control System

In the beginning, CCSs were mainly focused on corrective changes [25]. However, nowadays they are applied to any kind of change, including the ones regarding prevention, adaptation, and enhancement. In some cases, when the software development process emphasizes early releases, a CCS is used from the beginning of the project, acting as a process machine and being named request control system. Due to the success of process-based CCS, SCM has been recognized as one of the fields of software engineering in which process support has proven to be most successful [8].

One of the most known open-source CCS is Bugzilla [3]. It provides support for CCP execution, detailed queries over reported changes, establishment of links among changes, change state control, traceability among logical changes and affected artifacts, event notification, and textual and graphical reports regarding the status of the changes. Moreover, to achieve high performance they make use of a relational database and HTML interfaces. There are many other systems similar to Bugzilla [7]. We can cite Mantis [18], which allows information request configuration, and ClearQuest [30], a commercial system from IBM Rational which is one of the most flexible CCSs in terms of CCP and template customization. However, all these systems are focused on controlling changes over conventional systems. They are not prepared to deal with specific idiosyncrasies of the CBSE paradigm.

2.2 Component-Based Software Engineering

CBSE is a discipline of software development and maintenance that focus on reusing well defined components, produced via an independent process [5]. CBSE uses components, interfaces and connectors as first-class entities to structure software systems. Components, which are reusable software parts [9], make use of interfaces, described in a contractual manner, to interact with the remaining software elements [28]. Connectors are responsible for performing the binding among components.

When CBSE is in place, the software development teams can be classified by their roles in the process. Some teams are in charge of developing components. These teams, named producers, produce reusable components that serve to others. Other teams, named consumers, are in charge of developing systems by reusing existing components. Finally, there are some hybrid teams, which act as both producers and consumers. They reuse existing components to produce more other components.

The CBSE process is currently supported by a variety of methods. The most well known and adopted are Catalysis [9], UML Components [6], and KobrA [1]. However, besides the existence of these methods, the need for stable processes, standards, and supporting tools is still evident. For instance, when components are reused, they may evolve in parallel to their original version. SCM systems are responsible for keeping the traceability among original and reused versions of components, notifying producers and consumers when necessary [1].

Both SCM and CBSE aim to increase productivity and software quality, and to decrease the overall software cost [16]. However, they must be adopted in a consistent and integrated way to reach these goals.

2.3 Existing Challenges

The consumer team may detect that some reused component, made by other teams, needs maintenance when a client requests a change that affects this component. At this moment, the consumer team is supposed to choose the appropriate action: (1) ask the producer team to maintain the component, (2) maintain the component them-selves, or (3) acquire a new component from another producer team to replace the existing one. Some information, such as the producer team profile and reuse contract are vital to support this decision. A correct and well supported decision at this point can avoid judicial trials in the future.

In cases where the reuse contract guarantees that the producer team is responsible for the component maintenance, the consumer team requests a change to the producer team, asking for the component maintenance. The original change request will only be resumed after the producer team releases a new component version.

In some cases, the component under maintenance is also composed by other components, made by other producer teams, and the required maintenance may affect one of these components. In this case, the producer team acts as a consumer team, and the previous situation is repeated, recursively. This delegation scenario is repeated until the change request reaches the real responsible for the maintenance. When it occurs, the change request must be ranked in terms of how important it is to the other component consumers. For instance, almost all consumers can benefit from a bug fix. However, some enhancements may be important to just a few consumers.

After implementing and releasing a new component version, all consumers of that component should be notified, according to the status accounting function [14, 15]. This new component version may be provided free of charge or not, depending on the existing reuse contract clauses. If the released component version is part of other components, these components should also be released and their consumers notified. All in all, components may be composed by other components, recursively. For this reason, the list of consumers of a specific component may become complex, demanding support to responsibility detection and information propagation.

Another important aspect is related to legal issues regarding component maintenance. The producer should be aware of the details of the contracts established with each consumer. This knowledge is important to decide under which conditions the component is to be maintained. On the other hand, the consumer should also know all contracts established when the components were reused, to claim their rights.

Therefore, it is important to keep traceability links among components and their respective producers and consumers. For instance, it is important to know the producer's and the consumers' profiles, together with contractual information, for each component release available for reuse. The current CCSs do not take into account this problem, named in this paper as the *reuse chain of responsibility*.

Another challenge is regarding CCPs. Currently, there are some international standards [14, 15] that define CCPs for conventional software development. However, they do not deal with the CBSE issues discussed in this section. In conventional software development scenarios, these international standards are used as guidance. The CCP itself is adapted to the specific needs of the organization [29]. In the case of CBSE, the customization of the CCP is even more important due to the immaturity of the existing processes and the focus of existing standards on conventional CCP.

Moreover, CBSE scenarios demand for the gathering of some information that is neglected in conventional development. This information, related to component producers and consumers, contracts, and dependencies among components, is not a consensus in the CBSE community. Due to that, CCSs that support CBSE must allow the customization of templates for change request, impact analysis, evaluation, etc.

Some conventional CCSs allow the customization of CCPs and information gathering templates, such as IBM Rational ClearQuest [30] and JIRA [2]. However, they are usually focused on state machines, not allowing the modeling of products produced by SCM activities and multilevel sub-activities. These features are important even for conventional software development, and become essential when the CCP gets more complex, as in CBSE scenarios.

3 Odyssey-CCS

Considering the existing challenges to control changes over software developed using CBSE techniques, as discussed in Section 2.3, we introduce a change control approach tailored to this paradigm. Our approach, named Odyssey-CCS, is able to keep information regarding component reuse and make it available to producer and consumer teams when necessary. Moreover, our approach is flexible, allowing CCP and information template customization to the specific needs of different projects.

Fig. 1 presents an overview of our approach, depicting its main activities and components that support the activities (under the respective activity). In the following, we detail each of these activities.

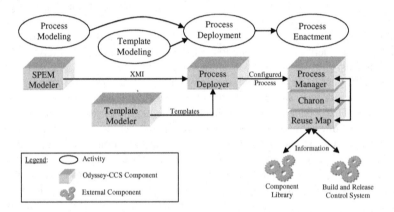

Fig. 1. Overview of Odyssey-CCS approach

3.1 Process Modeling

One of the challenges presented in Section 2.3 regards customization of CCPs to CBSE. As mentioned before, some commercial CCSs provide such support, but just a few provide graphical resources to support it. For this reason, the proposed approach provides a specific activity for CCP modeling.

The main goal of this activity is to model CCP using a standardized notation for software process modeling, which can be understood by many people and tools. Moreover, it is important to have some graphical support during process modeling to facilitate comprehension and the modeling itself. This graphical support avoids the necessity of source-code changes or complex XML files, found in other CCS approaches. It is also important to export the modeled process in a standard format.

This activity is supported by a process modeling component named *SPEM Modeler*. This component allows graphical process modeling according to the SPEM (Software Process Engineering Metamodel) notation [23], defined by OMG.

SPEM is a notation specifically designed for software process modeling and based on a standard meta-model, called MOF (Meta-Object Facility) [22]. The SPEM notation inherits some diagrams from the UML notation. For instance, the process workflow is modeled using an activity diagram and the relationship among process roles and process activities is modeled using a use case diagram. Since UML is a well known modeling language in the software engineering domain, it is expected that software engineers will comprehend the SPEM notation without difficulty.

The *SPEM Modeler* allows modeled processes to be exported according to the XMI (XML Metadata Interchange) specification [24]. This specification defines how MOF-based meta-models should be exported in XML format. Thus, other SPEM compliant systems are able to open the exported file.

3.2 Template Modeling

According to Section 2.3, in the same way, it is not possible to use a unique process for change control in the CBSE context, and it is not possible to gather a unique set of information independently of the process. For this reason, our approach proposes a specific activity for information template modeling. This activity allows the definition of which information should be collected in each CCP activity. This template modeling activity is supposed to be simple and graphical, avoiding the necessity of changes on the CCS source-code, as required by some existing systems.

A template is composed by a list of fields. Each field belongs to a specific field type, such as label, text-field, text-area, combo-box, check-box, file upload, link, etc. Moreover, each template may be bound to products produced by the CCP activities. When an activity is finished during process enactment, the templates associated to its produced products are presented to be filled in. The documents produced by the templates are attached to the change in progress and can be queried at anytime.

This template modeling activity is supported by the *Template Modeler* component. This component is a template composer infrastructure that allows graphical definition and on-the-fly visualization of the templates being created. In other words, this component supports the creation of user interfaces that are able to gather different types of information, according to the needs of the CCP for CBSE.

3.3 Process Deployment

Once the process is modeled, it should be deployed to be enacted. The process deployment activity is composed by the following four sub-activities, supported by the *Process Deployer* component: process importation, assignment of users to roles, assignment of templates to products, and notification configuration.

The process being imported should follow the SPEM notation and can be modeled by the *Process Modeler* component or any other tool compliant to the SPEM specification. An XMI file containing the process definition should be imported for each CBSE project controlled by Odyssey-CCS. This flexibility allows the assignment of different processes to distinct projects.

The imported processes are verified prior to enactment. This verification simulates the process enactment, searching for modeling mistakes that makes it impossible to start the real enactment. The next sub-activities are only available to the processes that succeed in this verification.

The assignment of users to roles consists in defining the users who are responsible for performing the existing roles. Each process activity has a set of associated roles.

Transitively, the assignment of users to roles indirectly defines which user is authorized to perform each process activity. This information is vital during process enactment, to identify authorized users to perform a given activity and users that should be notified after the execution of a given activity.

The assignment of templates to products consists in defining which templates will be presented to the user after the execution of a given activity. When an activity finishes, the products produced by this activity should be materialized by filling in the associated templates. For example, the impact analysis activity produces a product named impact report. This product is generated by an impact report template previously modeled as described in Section 3.2.

The last configuration regards notification sending. Some process activities demand notifying users after their execution. This feature is provided by a built-in template that can be associated to any product. This special template needs some information, such as the target e-mail addresses, the subject, and the message itself. For example, an e-mail product, associated to this built-in template, can be produced by the change request evaluation activity to notify the results to the user.

3.4 Process Enactment

The process enactment activity requires a workflow engine to control the process execution. This activity is supported by the *Process Manager*, *Charon*, and *Reuse Map* components. The *Process Manager* component is responsible for selecting the appropriate templates of each finished process activity, presenting the respective forms to be filled in by the users, and storing the documents produced by the forms.

The *Process Manager* component interacts with the *Charon* component, which is responsible for the enactment itself. The *Charon* component is a Prolog-based workflow engine compliant with the SPEM specification. It automatically loads the XMI file into a knowledge base, transforming SPEM elements into Prolog facts. Moreover, it makes use of intelligent agents to access the knowledge base and enact the process. The *Charon* component is able to detect pending activities and infer the next activities when an activity is finished.

As discussed in section 2.3, some process activities, such as impact analysis, need special support when CBSE is in place. In this scenario, it is important to provide information about producers and consumers of components, and the contract that define the rights and duties of both parts to detect the one responsible for maintenance. This information is stored by a *Reuse Map* component.

The *Reuse Map* component holds the profile of each team associated to the versions of components they produce or use. It is integrated to a component library. Aiming to facilitate the contract establishment among producers and consumers, a set of reuse licenses is made available to producers. These licenses, which describe in details reuse terms, are assigned by the producers to new components when they are added to the component library. At this moment, the producers define under which conditions the new components can be reused. These licenses are presented to consumers during component reuse and they can choose one of them to establish the reuse contract. The conceptual model of the *Reuse Map* component is shown in Fig. 2.

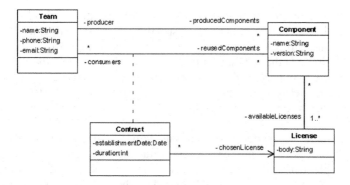

Fig. 2. Conceptual model of the reuse map

The information stored by the *Reuse Map* component allows producers and consumers to detect the real responsible for implementing a given change over a specific component. Moreover, it helps identifying other consumers that also reuse the component and are eligible for receiving a new version.

4 Prototype

Based on the approach described in Section 3, a prototype was implemented. This prototype is composed by a process modeling tool, available as a plug-in of the Odyssey environment[1], a template modeling tool, and a flexible CCS.

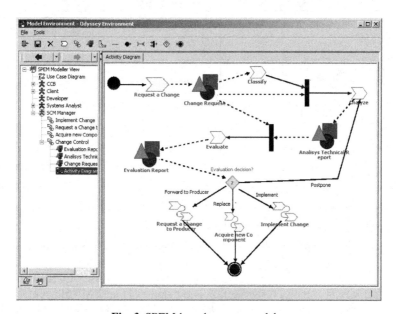

Fig. 3. SPEM-based process modeler

---

[1] URL: http://reuse.cos.ufrj.br/odyssey

The process modeler tool is based on the SPEM notation and allows graphical process modeling according to the SPEM specification suggested icons. It reuses the diagramming infrastructure of the Odyssey environment. Fig. 3 presents the SPEM Modeler in action. On the left hand side, there is a tree containing the SPEM process elements. On the right hand side, a CCP workflow is being modeled. For instance, the process being modeled is an adaptation of an existing CCP [14, 15] to the CBSE needs. Any process in the left hand side of Fig. 3 can be exported according to the XMI standard.

The CCP may be modeled considering activities performed in the software development process. For instance, after evaluating a change request, it may be decided to implement a software modification, or to replace the affected component, among other decisions, which are activities described in the development process. However, depending on the modeled CCP after the execution of these activities some information may be requested. For instance, the developer may be prompted to inform the time spent to perform the modification, the difficulties and problems found, the adopted solution, or any other information considered important for change control.

Both the template modeling tool and the CCS are Web-based applications. Fig. 4.a presents a change request template being modeled. This tool allows the inclusion of new fields and a fast preview of the whole template. Fig. 4.b shows a text area field that gathers change description information being configured.

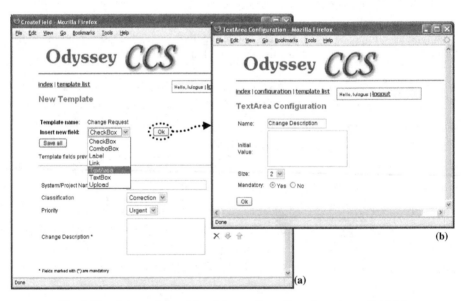

Fig. 4. Template modeling (a) and the configuration of a text area field (b)

At this moment, a new project can be created in Odyssey-CCS. The project creation activity is composed by the following steps: (1) an XMI file containing the modeled process is imported into Odyssey-CCS; (2) Odyssey-CCS users are associated to process roles, defined in the XMI file; (3) the modeled templates are associated to the products produced by process activities, defined in the XMI file. For instance, the change request template, shown in Fig. 4.a can be associated to the change request product, modeled in the process shown in Fig. 3; and (4) the notifications are configured to be automatically sent during the process enactment.

The process is ready to be enacted after this configuration phase. This task is performed by the *Charon* tool, which was originally designed to enact UML-based activity diagrams, and was evolved to be compliant to the SPEM specification. When a user logs in the Odyssey-CCS system, he is informed about his pending activities and decisions, as shown in Fig. 5.a.

When an activity is finished, the Process Manager presents the forms associated to its products to the user. For instance, Fig. 5.b shows a change request form being filled in during process enactment. The change request form is generated by Odyssey-CCS according to the change request template modeled in Fig. 4.a.

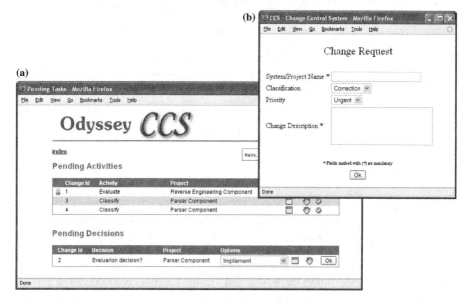

Fig. 5. Pending activities and decisions for a specific user (a) and template being filled in during process enactment (b)

The producer and consumer teams can access the reuse map during process enactment. Some common queries are "Who is the producer of component C?", "What are the components that compose component C?", "Which consumer teams reuse component C?", and "What are the contract conditions when component C is reused by team T?". These queries, when combined together and used in a recursive way, can support detecting the real responsible for a specific change. Fig. 6 shows, at the left hand side, the Analysis Technical Report form, which has a link to the Reuse Map. In the Reuse Map, the user can list the registered components and visualize their consumers. At the right hand side of the figure, the consumers of the Parser component are shown.

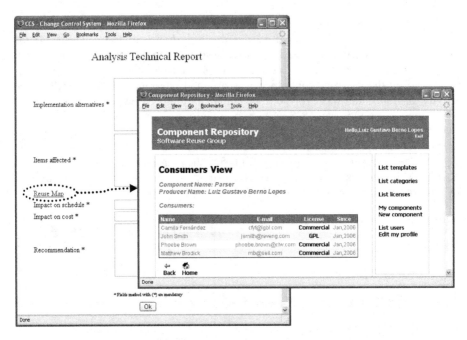

Fig. 6. Consumers View of the Reuse Map

5 Related Work

Currently, there is a lack of research on CCS applied to the CBSE paradigm. However, there are some few works on the boundary of this topic. Kwon *et al.* [16] defined the MwR (Maintenance with Reuse) process model. This process model uses software reuse to support software maintenance. It is implemented by a tool named TERRA, which provides the following activities: component recording and searching, change request recording, reuse report recording, and change approval recording. The process that guides the execution of these activities is hard-coded, and the tool has some pre-defined forms, also hard-coded, to collect and store information during the execution.

Moreover, MwR does not allow the identification of component versions and consumer teams during component recording. This information is necessary to define how the inner architecture of a given component (dependencies to other components) evolved overtime and which consumer reuses a specific component version. As discussed before, it is not possible to detect the real responsible for a change without such information. These problems were solved by our approach via a flexible mechanism for process and template definition, together with the reuse map.

Another important work involving maintenance of component-based systems is KobrA [1]. KobrA is an approach for product line that defines procedures for product line evolution and product generation from a product line. These procedures make use of change sets [27] to propagate changes among components. KobrA approach also keeps a cause relationship among changes. This cause relationship can be used to understand the effects of a given change.

Besides the effective support for component composition and change dependencies, KobrA approach does not support the responsibility detection dimension of the change control. It does not use producers and consumers information, together with the component composition information, to propagate a change request to other teams. Such feature can be found in our approach. Moreover, we could not find any computational tool that supports the KobrA approach.

Flashline Registry [12], Logidex [17] and Select Component Manager [26] are commercial component managers that maintain the reusable components information of an organization. This includes component consumption information and component interdependencies, assisting the resolution of the Reuse Chain of Responsibility problem, but with some limitations. They seem to consider that each component is reused under the same license type by all consumers. Nevertheless, some components may be available under more than one license type, which requires an association between a consumer and its selected license. In addition, they apparently do not list the components consumers to their producers, which is a valuable information when analyzing and evaluating change requests.

6   Conclusion

We presented in this paper an approach for change control tailored for CBSE. The main contributions of our work are:

- The identification of the main challenges on change control when the CBSE paradigm is being used;
- The identification of the current CCSs drawbacks regarding the identified challenges;
- The definition of an approach for change control focused on the specific problems of software reuse; and
- An implemented prototype deployed at http://reuse.cos.ufrj.br/Odyssey-CCS, integrated to an existing component library available at http://reuse.cos.ufrj.br/ brecho.

Our approach can be extended in the future to provide new functionalities, such as advanced queries summarizing the information gathered during process enactment. For instance, these queries could return high-level management charts showing how the gathered information evolved overtime, the average execution time of a given process activity, the average number of finished changes in a period of time, etc.

Our approach has also been useful for other projects. It has been integrated to a version control system (VCS) for UML models [21], which accesses some information from Odyssey-CCS, such as which process instances are in execution. This information is presented to the VCS users, who select the CCP instance in which they are working on. Thereafter, when they perform check in operations, the changed artifacts are associated to the selected process instance, composing change packages. Therefore, it is possible to know which artifacts were changed in each process instance context.

The Odyssey-CCS has also been used by the Odyssey-WI approach [10] to help contextualize traceability links among UML model elements with information gathered through CCP enactment. Odyssey-WI aims to answer the question: "When a given element is modified, which other elements are also usually modified?". Besides pointing the modified elements, Odyssey-WI presents who, when, where, what, why and how the modifications were done. Most of this information is found in Odyssey-CCS repository and can be accessed through an API, which is used by Odyssey-WI.

Although the technical indication that our approach can aid on controlling changes in the context of CBSE, we still need to perform some evaluation to quantify how useful is our approach in the software reuse scenario. Currently, we are designing this evaluation to be performed at the Brazilian Central Bank.

Acknowledgment

The authors would like to thank CAPES, CNPq, and the Brazilian Central Bank for the financial support.

References

1. Atkinson, C., Bayer, J., Bunse, C., Kamsties, E., Laitenberger, O., Laqua, R., Muthig, D., Peach, B., Wust, J., and Zettel, J.: Component-Based Product Line Engineering with UML. Addison-Wesley (2001)
2. Atlassian: JIRA - Bug tracking, issue tracking and project management software. In: http://www.atlassian.com/software/jira/docs/latest/, accessed in: 01/Feb/2006
3. Barnson, M.P, and Steenhagen, J.: The Bugzilla Guide - 2.17.5 Development Release. The Bugzilla Team (2003)
4. Braga, R. M. M., Werner, C. M. L., and Mattoso, M.: Odyssey-Search: A multi-agent system for component information search and retrieval. Journal of Systems and Software, Vol. 79, no. 2 (2006) 204-215
5. Brown, A. W.: Large Scale Component Based Development. Prentice Hall PTR (2000)
6. Cheesman, J. and Daniels, J.: UML Components: A Simple Process for Specifying Component-Based Software. Addison-Wesley (2000)
7. CMCrossroads: Defect Tracking Software. In: http://resources.cmcrossroads.com/cmcrossroads/search/browse/1715/1715.jsp, accessed in: 01/Feb/2006
8. Conradi, R., Fuggetta, A., and Jaccheri, M. L.: Six Theses on Software Process Research. European Workshop on Software Process Technology (EWSPT), Weybridge, UK, (1998) 100-104
9. D'Souza, D. and Wills, A.: Objects, components, and frameworks with UML: The catalysis approach. Addison Wesley (1998)
10. Dantas, C. R., Murta, L. G. P., and Werner, C. M. L.: Consistent Evolution of UML Models by Automatic Detection of Change Traces. International Workshop on Principles of Software Evolution (IWPSE), Lisbon, Portugal, September (2005) 144-147
11. Estublier, J., Leblang, D., Clemm, G., Conradi, R., Tichy, W., van der Hoek, A., and Wiborg-Weber, D.: Impact of the research community on the field of software configuration management: summary of an impact project report. ACM SIGSOFT Software Engineering Notes, Vol. 27, no. 5, September (2002) 31-39
12. Flashline: Flashline Registry. In: http://www.flashline.com, accessed in: 28/Mar/2006
13. IEEE: Std 1219 - IEEE Standard for Software Maintenance. Institute of Electrical and Electronics Engineers (1998)

14. IEEE: Std 828 - IEEE Standard for Software Configuration Management Plans. Institute of Electrical and Electronics Engineers (2005)
15. ISO: ISO 10007, Quality Management - Guidelines for Configuration Management. International Organization for Standardization (1995)
16. Kwon, O., Shin, G., Boldyreff, C., and Munro, M.: Maintenance with Reuse: An Integrated Approach Based on Software Configuration Management. Asia Pacific Software Engineering Conference, Takamatsu, Japan, December (1999) 507-515
17. LogicLibrary: Logidex. In: http://www.logiclibrary.com, accessed in: 28/Mar/2006
18. Mantis: Mantis Bug Tracker. In: http://www.mantisbt.org, accessed in: 28/Mar/2005
19. Mili, A., Mili, R., and Mittermeir, R. T.: A survey of software reuse libraries. Annals of Software Engineering, Vol. 5, no. 0 (1998) 349 - 414
20. Morisio, M., Ezran, M., and Tully, C.: Success and Failure Factors in Software Reuse. IEEE Transactions of Software Engineering, Vol. 28, no. 4 (2002) 340-357
21. Oliveira, H. L. R., Murta, L. G. P., and Werner, C. M. L.: Odyssey-VCS: a Flexible Version Control System for UML Model Elements. International Workshop on Software Configuration Management, Lisbon, Portugal, September (2005) 1-16
22. OMG: Meta Object Facility (MOF) Specification, version 1.4. Object Management Group. In: http://www.omg.org/technology/documents/formal/mof.htm, accessed in: 01/Feb/2006
23. OMG: Software Process Engineering Metamodel (SPEM), Version 1.1. Object Management Group. In: http://www.omg.org/technology/documents/formal/spem.htm, accessed in: 01/Feb/2006
24. OMG: XML Metadata Interchange (XMI) Specification, Version 2.1. Object Management Group. In: http://www.omg.org/technology/documents/formal/xmi.htm, accessed in: 01/Feb/2006
25. Pressman, R. S.: Software Engineering: A Practitioner's Approach. 6th. edn. McGraw-Hill (2005)
26. Select Business Solutions: Select Component Manager. In: http://www.selectbs.com, accessed in: 28/03/2006
27. Smds: Aide de Camp Product Overview. Software Maintenance & Development Systems (1994)
28. Szyperski, C.: Component Software: Beyond object-oriented programming. Addison-Wesley (2002)
29. Weber, D. W.: Requirements for an SCM Architecture to Enable Component-Based Development. Proceedings of Tenth International Workshop on Software Configuration Management (SCM 10), Toronto, Canada, May (2001)
30. White, B. A.: Software Configuration Management Strategies and Rational ClearCase: A Practical Introduction. Addison-Wesley (2000)

Case Study of a Method for Reengineering Procedural Systems into OO Systems

William B. Frakes, Gregory Kulczycki, and Charu Saxena

Computer Science Department, Virginia Tech, Falls Church, VA USA
frakes@cs.vt.edu, gregorywk@vt.edu

Abstract. This study evaluates a method for reengineering a procedural system to an object-oriented system. Relationships between functions in the procedural system were identified using various coupling metrics. While the coupling metrics used for analysis were helpful in identifying candidate objects, domain expert analysis of the candidate objects was required. The time taken at each step in the process was captured to help determine the effectiveness of the method. Overall the process was found to be effective for identifying objects.

1 Introduction

Many companies have large inventories of legacy code written in procedural languages. When these companies migrate to new object-oriented architectures, they do not want to start from scratch if it can be avoided. Therefore, a need exists for a methodology that can analyze existing procedural code and identify related functions and data that can be encapsulated into reusable objects in the application domain.

This case study extends the Pole method described in [1] with new metrics and uses it to identify potential reusable objects in the *ccount* metrics tool [3], which is written in C.

The steps in the method are described briefly along with the required metrics. The process and time taken for each step was captured and reported, and the data collected was used to determine the overall effectiveness of the method. The goal of this process is to identify reusable objects in the application domain. Once the code has been reengineered using these objects, traditional refactoring methods can be applied to further refine these objects and strengthen the design of the object-oriented code.

2 Reengineering Methodology

The method evaluated in this study proposes steps to be taken in reengineering a procedural system to an object-oriented system. The method delivers reusable objects from existing legacy code. It is based on the premise that program elements that exhibit certain kinds of coupling can be grouped together to form objects. The steps to be taken in the reengineering process are as follows:

1. **The domain expert creates a function stop list.** A stop list contains functions identified by the domain expert as utility functions that do not perform tasks specific to the domain.

M. Morisio (Ed.): ICSR 2006, LNCS 4039, pp. 184–202, 2006.

2. **A call graph is generated.** A tool or manual scanning of the code base is used to generate a call graph that shows the flow of control in the legacy code.

3. **Dependency and context lists are created.** A dependency list identifies all the functions invoked from a given function. A context list does the reverse—it identifies the functions that invoke or use a given function.

4. **Objects are identified.** In this step the metrics are calculated and the potential objects are identified. This step turned out to be the most involved step in the process. For clarity, we break its description into three sub-steps.

   (a) **Summary data is collected.** The summary data contains information for each function that is not in the stop list, such as the types and names of parameters, variables, and functions used in the given function.

   (b) **Metrics are calculated.** Different coupling metrics describe different relationships between functions, such as how many times one function invokes another or how many parameters are shared by the functions. In this study we used eight different coupling metrics and evaluated each one individually for its effectiveness in identifying objects.

   (c) **Candidate objects are identified.** The software engineer determines a threshold for each metric. If the metric for two functions is above the threshold, those functions are candidates to appear as methods in the same class.

5. **Domain expert chooses objects.** The domain expert examines candidate objects and determines whether they are reasonable. Variables common to two or more functions are examined for their appropriateness as object attributes. Leftover functions including the functions in the stop list can be converted into individual objects or packaged as utility objects.

Throughout the process of evaluating the proposed method, the following metrics were captured:

- The time taken at each step of the process.
- The number of domain specific objects and utility objects created.
- The number of functions and lines of codes in the legacy system.

3   Coupling Metrics

This section describes the metrics that we used in our methodology. Each metric describes a distinct relationship between any two functions in the legacy system. We call them *coupling* metrics because they are based on the various forms of module coupling, such as those given in [3], and because they indicate the dependency and the amount of communication that takes place between functions.

The metrics can be divided into three broad categories based on the kind of coupling that motivated them.

1. **Invocation metrics.** These metrics are based on routine call coupling as described in [6, p. 306]. They rank functions based on how often one function invokes another.
2. **Shared parameter metrics.** This category currently contains only one metric—the shared parameter metric. It is based on data element coupling as described in [3], which exists when data is passed from one function to another through a disciplined interface such as a parameter list.
3. **Shared variable metrics.** These metrics are based on data definition coupling as defined in [3]. Data definition coupling occurs when functions manipulate data of the same type.

Our goal is to use these metrics to determine if any two functions in the legacy system belong together in the same class when we move to an object-oriented system. We looked at many metrics because we did not know which ones would be the most effective in identifying objects. We discuss the effectiveness of the metrics we used and the prospect of finding additional metrics in Section 6 of this paper.

Table 1. Functions used in the definitions of the eight coupling metrics

Function	Definition
$\text{invocs}(f_1, f_2)$	Number of times that function f_2 is invoked in the body of f_1
$\text{params}(f_0)$	$\{\ v_{t,n}\ |\ v_{t,n}$ is a variable of type t with name n that appears in the parameter list of $f_0\ \}$
$\text{vars}(f_0)$	$\{\ v_{t,n}\ |$ variable $v_{t,n}$ of type t with name n appears in the body of $f_0\ \}$
$\text{source}(v, f_0)$	$\{\ v_{dec}\ |$ variable v appears in f_0 and v_{dec} is a declaration of variable v, or v is a formal parameter in f_0, and $v_{dec} \in \text{source}(v_1, f_1)$ where f_1 invokes f_0, and v_{dec} is the actual parameter in that invocation that corresponds to v $\}$
$\text{count}(v, f_0)$	Number of times that variable v appears in the body of f_0

The following subsections present eight different metrics—three invocation metrics, one shared parameter metric, and four shared variable metrics. Table 1 gives the definitions of several functions that are used in the definitions of these metrics. With the exception of the source function, these helper functions are self-explanatory. The source function gives the set of variable declarations associated with a particular variable, tracing back through calls if the variable is a formal parameter. We discuss the source function in further detail when we look at the shared variable metric.

3.1 Invocation Metrics

When a function f_1 calls another function f_2, it indicates that they perform related tasks and suggests that those functions should be considered for inclusion in the same object. When a method from one class invokes a method from another class, those classes are related by routine call coupling [6]. As the name implies, this form of coupling is routine in object-oriented programs. Nevertheless, when a function f_1 calls another function f_2 in a procedural program, it may indicate that f_2 can translate to a private method in same class that contains f_1. Therefore, these metrics may be considered helpful in identifying objects.

Direct invocation metric. This metric identifies the number of times that a function f_1 calls another function f_2. The metric is defined simply as

$$N(f_1, f_2) = \text{invocs}(f_1, f_2).$$

Indirect invocation metric. This metric identifies the number of times that a function f_1 indirectly calls a function f_2 by way of a third function f_{mid}. It is simply the sum of the direct invocation metrics for f_1 and f_{mid}, and f_{mid} and f_2. However, if either of the direct invocation metrics is zero, then no indirect invocation takes place, so the value of the indirect invocation metric is zero. The metric is defined in terms of the direct invocation metric as

$$N_{ind}(f_1, f_2) = N(f_1, f_{mid}) + N(f_{mid}, f_2) \text{ where } N(f_1, f_{mid}) > 0 \text{ and } N(f_2, f_{mid}) > 0$$

Recursive invocation metric. This metric identifies the number of times a function f_1 calls function f_2 and f_2 calls back to f_1. The value of the metric is the sum of the direct invocations from f_1 to f_2 and f_2 to f_1. Like the indirect invocation metric, the value of this metric is zero if no recursion exists. The metric is defined as

$$N_{rec}(f_1, f_2) = N(f_1, f_2) + N(f_2, f_1) \text{ where } N(f_1, f_2) > 0 \text{ and } N(f_2, f_1) > 0$$

3.2 Shared Parameter Metrics

Data element coupling occurs when modules access shared data that is passed in through a parameter list. If a client passes the same stack to functions in modules M_1 and M_2, then those modules exhibit data element coupling.

Shared parameter metric. This metric identifies the formal parameters that are common between two functions. It does this by counting the number of formal parameters that have the same type and same name. The metric is defined as

$$P(f_1, f_2) = |\, \text{params}(f_1) \cap \text{params}(f_2)\,|$$

3.3 Shared Variable Metrics

Shared variable metrics look at all variables—including parameters, global variables, and local variables—that are shared by functions. These metrics are based on data definition coupling [3]. Data definition coupling occurs when modules manipulate data of the same type. For example, if two modules modify a data structure of type stack, they exhibit data definition coupling.

There are two different kinds of shared variable metrics. The first, more sophisticated, metric considers variables to be shared only if they can be traced to a common declaration. For example, suppose variable x is declared in function f_0, which passes it to f_1 and f_2. Furthermore, suppose f_2 obtains x through a formal parameter y, which it then passes to f_3. Then functions f_0, f_1, f_2, and f_3 are all related, because they all use or manipulate a value that originated with a variable declared in f_0 (see Figure 1).

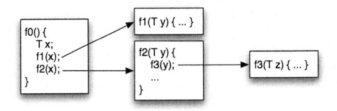

Fig. 1. The functions all use a variable that can be traced to the same source

Shared variable metric. This metric identifies variables in two functions that share a common source. The metric is defined as

$$V(f_1, f_2) = | \{ v \mid source(v, f_1) \cap source(v, f_2) | \neq \varnothing \} |$$

The function $source(v, f_1)$ gives the set of sources (variable declarations) for variable v in f_1. If v is not a formal parameter in f_1, then v will have a unique source. However, if v is a formal parameter, then v's source set includes the elements in the source sets of all corresponding actual parameters. Therefore, the size of v's source set may be greater than one.

The simpler version of the shared variable metric considers functions to be related if they share variables with the same type and the same name.

Shared type-name variable metric. This metric identifies all variables in two functions that have a common type and name. The metric is defined as

$$V'(f_1, f_2) = | vars(f_1) \cap vars(f_2) |$$

We also include a variation for each of these metrics in our analysis. The metrics above count declarations of variables rather than uses. For example, if the only variable shared by two functions was the global stack s, the shared variable metric for those functions would be one. Even if s appears three times in the body of the first function and four times in the body of the second function, the value of the metric is still one. The metrics below count the static occurrences (the *tokens* rather than *types*) of common variables.

Shared variable tokens metric. This metric counts the static occurrences of all variables in two functions that share a common source. The metric is defined in terms of the shared variable metric as

$$V_{tokens}(f_1, f_2) = \Sigma \; count(v, f_1) + count(v, f_2) \; where \; v \in V(f_1, f_2)$$

Shared type-name variable tokens metric. This metric counts the static occurrences of all formal parameters, global variables, and local variables that are common between two functions. The metric is defined as

$$V'_{tokens}(f_1, f_2) = \sum count(v, f_1) + count(v, f_2) \text{ where } v \in V'(f_1, f_2)$$

Table 2 summarizes the metrics and their definitions.

Table 2. Notations and definitions for the eight coupling metrics used in the study

Name	Notation	Definition
Direct Invocation Metric	$N(f_1, f_2)$	$invocs(f_1, f_2)$
Recursive Invocation Metric	$N_{rec}(f_1, f_2)$	$N(f_1, f_2) + N(f_2, f_1)$ where $\mid N(f_1, f_{mid}) \mid > 0$ and $\mid N(f_2, f_{mid}) \mid > 0$
Indirect Invocation Metric	$N_{ind}(f_1, f_2)$	$N(f_1, f_{mid}) + N(f_{mid}, f_2)$ where $\mid N(f_1, f_{mid}) \mid > 0$ and $\mid N(f_2, f_{mid}) \mid > 0$
Shared Parameter Metric	$P(f_1, f_2)$	$\mid params(f_1) \cap params(f_2) \mid$
Shared Variable Metric	$V(f_1, f_2)$	$\mid \{ v \mid history(v, f_1) \cap history(v, f_2) \mid \neq \varnothing \} \mid$
Shared Variable Tokens Metric	$V_{tokens}(f_1, f_2)$	$\sum_{v \in V(f_1, f_2)} count(v, f_1) + count(v, f_2)$
Shared Type-Name Variable Metric	$V'(f_1, f_2)$	$\mid vars(f_1) \cap vars(f_2) \mid$
Shared Type-Name Variable Tokens Metric	$V'_{tokens}(f_1, f_2)$	$\sum_{v \in V'(f_1, f_2)} count(v, f_1) + count(v, f_2)$

4   Example: Reengineering *ccount*

The procedural system analyzed in the study was *ccount*, a metrics tools implemented in C that reports counts of commentary and non-commentary source lines and comment-to-code ratios [3]. The ccount tool was initially written in K & R C and later converted to ANSI C. For the purpose of this study the ANSI C version was used.

The statistics collected for the ccount tool including the main function are:

- Number of non-commentary lines of code: 749
- Number of files: 7
- Number of functions: 17

The ccount metric tool was used because it is tractable for a small case study, but non-trivial, so that the case study is still relevant.

This section shows how the method was applied to ccount. We captured the process and time taken at each step. The authors acted as the domain experts.

4.1 Domain Expert Creates Function Stop List

For ccount the functions identified to be in the stop list were string manipulation and file manipulation functions that are provided by the standard C libraries. Since the system was relatively small, rather than providing the list as a starting point, we analyzed the output from the next step to help us come up with the functions to be placed in the stop list. The time taken for this step was 1 hour.

4.2 A Call Graph Is Generated

The cflow tool was used to identify the flow of control (call structure) of ccount. The output from cflow is in a text format, which we then converted to the graphical representation given in Figure 2. The cflow tool provides options to generate output in both a top-down and bottom-up manner. The graphical representation of the bottom-up output would simply be the call graph in Figure 2 with the arrows reversed. The time taken for this step was 2 hours.

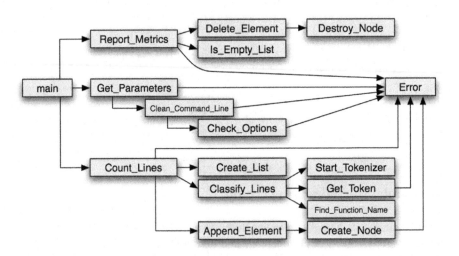

Fig. 2. Call graph for ccount tool.

4.3 Dependency and Context Lists Are Created

Using the call graph created in the previous step, the dependency list and the context list were created. The dependency list indicates the function that are invoked by a given function. For example, the function Classify_Lines uses functions Start_Tokenizer, Get_Token, and Find_Function_Name. The context list indicates the functions that invoke a given function. For example, Create_Node is used by Append_Element. In this example, the only function invoked by multiple functions is Error, which is used by seven other functions. The time taken for this step was 2 hours.

4.4 Objects Are Identified

This step was by far the most involved and the most time-consuming. Therefore, to make the presentation clearer we have divided it into three sub-steps: collection of summary data, calculation of metrics, and identification of candidate objects. The time taken for this step was 48 hours.

4.4.1 Summary Data Is Collected
To determine the various metrics, we first identified the variables and functions accessed by each individual function. The collection of the required data for each function was done manually. Lack of a tool for collecting the data made the process time consuming.

For each function the following data was collected.

- The parameters passed to it
- The local variables defined and accessed
- The global variables accessed
- The functions invoked along with the parameters passed to those functions
- The data type returned by the function

For each variable (parameters, local variables, and global variables) the following was captured.

- Its name
- Its data type
- Its scope
- The number of static accesses made to it

Shared variables were identified by looking at each file to determine global variables or local variables manipulated by a function. Ccount did not have any global variables, but it did have variables with file scope that were manipulated by functions in that file.

An example of the information collected in this step is given in Table 3. The function *Check_Options* has two parameters, *options* and *optionargs*. The parameter *options* is accessed twice in the body of the function, and *optionargs* is accessed once. The function also accesses the locally defined variable *ch_ptr* eight times, and it invokes the function *Error* twice.

Table 3. Summary data for functions Check_Options and Clean_Command_line

Summary Data Collection Table		
Check_Options (params.c)		
Parameters	char *options	2
	char *optionargs	1
Global variables		0
Local variables	char *ch_ptr	8
Functions invoked	Error	2
Clean_Command_Line (params.c)		
Parameters	char *options	2
	char *optionargs	2
	char **argv[]	9
	int *argc	6
Global variables		0
Local variables	char **new_argv	24
	char **files	9
	char *ch_ptr	11
	int new_argc	18
	int num_files	6
	int arg_index	16
	int file_index	4
Functions invoked	Check_Options(options, optionargs)	1
	Error(…)	8

4.4.2 Metrics Are Calculated

Once the summary data for each function was collected, the coupling metrics were calculated for each pair of functions, provided that neither function is in the stop list. For example, Table 4 gives the data invocation metric calculated for the ccount functions. Function pairs that had a metric value of zero were not included in the table.

Table 4. Non-zero direct invocation metrics for ccount

First function (f1)	Second function (f2)	N(f1, f2)
Main	Get_Parameters	1
Main	Count_Lines	1
Main	Report_Metrics	1
Get_Parameters	Clean_Command_Line	1
Get_Parameters	Error	1
Count_Lines	Create_List	1
Count_Lines	Error	1
Count_Lines	Classify_Line	1
Count_Lines	Append_Element	3
Report_Metrics	Error	2
Report_Metrics	Is_Empty_List	1
Report_Metrics	Delete_Element	1
Clean_Command_Line	Check_Options	1
Clean_Command_Line	Error	8
Classify_Line	Start_Tokenizer	1
Classify_Line	Get_Token	1
Classify_Line	Find_Function_Name	1
Append_Element	Create_Node	2
Delete_Element	Destroy_Node	1
Check_Options	Error	2
Get_Token	Error	1
Create_Node	Error	2

Most of the metrics can be calculated simply by inspecting the summary data for the two functions involved in the metric. The exceptions are the indirect invocation metric, the shared variables metric, and the shared variable tokens metric. Table 5 shows each of the eight metrics in which the first function (f1) is *Clean_Command_Line* and the second function (f2) is *Check_Options*. The following paragraphs indicate how to calculate each of these metrics.

Table 5. Metrics for f1 = Clean_Command_Line and f2 = Check_Options

$N(f_1, f_2)$	1
$N_{rec}(f_1, f_2)$	0
$N_{ind}(f_1, f_2)$	0
$P(f_1, f_2)$	2
$V(f_1, f_2)$	2
$V_{tokens}(f_1, f_2)$	7
$V'(f_1, f_2)$	3
$V'_{tokens}(f_1, f_2)$	26

Invocation metrics. From Table 3 we see that Clean_Command_Line calls Check_Options once, yielding a direct invocation metric of one. Since Check_Options never calls Clean_Command_Line back, the recursive invocation metric is zero. In fact, in this particular study all of the recursive invocation metrics turned out to be zero. The *indirect* invocation metric requires slightly more work. Looking at Table 3, we see that the only other function besides Check_Options that is called by Clean_Command_Line is the Error function, which is called eight times. If the Error function (whose record is not shown in Table 3) had called Check_Options n times, then the indirect invocation metric would have been $8 + n$. Since the Error function never actually invokes Check_Options, the indirect invocation metric is zero. Note that the direct and indirect invocation metrics are not necessarily symmetric. For example, we do not—in general—have $N_{ind}(f_1, f_2) = N_{ind}(f_2, f_1)$. However, the recursive invocation metric is symmetric.

Shared parameter metrics. We can also tell directly from Table 3 that functions Check_Options and Clean_Command_Line both have a parameter named *options* of type *char* and a parameter named *optionargs* of type *char*. For this reason, the value of the shared parameter metric is two. Note that, in this study, we ignored pointers when determining types—so variables declared with *char*, *char***, and *char[]* were all considered to have the same type.

Shared variable metrics. To calculate the shared variables metric we must determine which variables in Clean_Command_Line and Check_Options can potentially originate from the same source. From Table 3 we see that there are only three variables in Check_Options, so there are three candidates. The variable *ch_ptr* is declared in the body of Check_Options, so the only way that Clean_Command_Line can share this variable is if it is passed to Clean_Command_Line through some sequence of function calls. However, a quick look at the flow graph (Figure 2) tells us that although

Clean_Command_Line calls Check_Options, there is no call path from Check_Options to Clean_Command_Line. Therefore, even though Clean_Command_Line also has a variable named *ch_ptr* of type *char*, they are not considered shared for the purposes of this metric. On the other hand, both *options* and *optionargs* are formal parameters in Check_Options, and since Clean_Command_Line calls Check_Options, we know that Check_Options must share its formal parameters with the actual parameters passed to it by Clean_Command_Line. The fact that the actual parameters passed by Clean_Command_Line also happen to be named options and optionargs is unrelated to the calculation of this metric; the relevant fact is that the variables come from the same source. Thus, the value for the shared variable metric is two, and the value for the shared variable tokens metric is the sum of static occurrences for these variables in each function: 3 in Check_Options + 4 in Clean_Command_Line = 7.

The shared type-name variables metric is significantly easier to calculate. Both functions have variables with type-name combinations *char*/*options*, *char*/*optionargs*, and *char*/*ch_ptr*. Therefore the value of this metric is three, and the value of the shared type-name variable tokens metric is: 11 occurrences of these variables in Check_Options + 15 occurrences in Clean_Command_Line = 26.

4.4.3 Candidate Objects Are Identified

Once the individual metrics have been are calculated, a threshold is determined for each metric, and each metric is individually evaluated to come up with candidate objects. In this study, the following guidelines were taken into consideration.

- In C++ the function main is not part of any object, therefore the coupling metrics in relation to that function were not used.

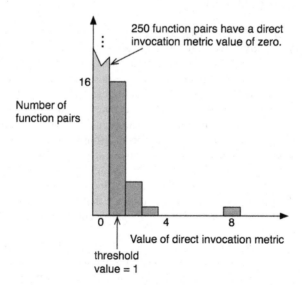

Fig. 3. Distribution of values for the direct invocation metric

- If the coupling metric for two functions was above or equal to the threshold value, both were placed in the same object.
- If a function f_1 has the same coupling metric with multiple functions in different objects, then this is used as an indication that f_1 should be placed in a separate object as it might be a utility function.

The decision of which threshold to use was empirical to ensure that functions don't cluster in one object. In the case of the direct invocation metric, the vast majority of function pairs had a metric value of zero, several functions had a value of one, and a few functions had a value greater than one (see Figure 3). A threshold value of one was chosen—a value of anything greater than one would have meant that too many functions would be in classes by themselves.

Using the guidelines outlined above, the main function was placed in a class by itself, and the Error function was identified as a utility function, so it was also placed in a separate class. This led to the following partitioning of the functions into objects.

Object 1	*Get_Parameters, Clean_Command_Line, Check_Options*
Object 2	*Count_Lines, Classify_Line, Start_Tokenizer, Get_Token,*
	Find_Function_Name, Create_List, Append_Element, Create_Node
Object 3	*Report_Metrics, Is_Empty_List, Delete_Element, Delete_Node*
Object 4	*Error*
Object 5	*Main*

The process of determining a threshold and finding candidate objects was repeated for all of the metrics, yielding the partitioning of functions in Table 7. The recursive invocation metric is not included because recursive calls did not occur in the application.

4.5 Domain Expert Chooses Objects

In this step the domain expert analyzed the objects for reasonableness. Each metric was analyzed individually, and the results of this analysis are given below. One of the criteria used in the analysis was whether the partitions corresponded to the modules in the C program, which exhibited good modular design in the first place. In particular, we were always interested to see if the candidate objects for a given coupling metric successfully identified the list data type. The time taken for this step was 16 hours.

The direct invocation metric provides a good breakup of the objects, but was unable to satisfactorily identify the list data type. It groups the functions that relate to extracting parameters since those functions invoke each other. However, the list functions do not necessarily invoke each other. The indirect invocation metric provides a breakup of objects very similar to the direct invocation metric. And similarly, it is not able to identify the list data type. This may indicate that these metrics will give similar results in general. If so, then the direct invocation metric should be used since it is easier to calculate.

The shared parameters metric is able to identify the list data type as it clusters all but one function in the same object. It places the functions Error and Report_Metrics in the same object as functions which classify lines. Since this metric only considers the parameter list of functions it does not always separate functions that have separate responsibilities.

Table 6. Candidate objects for each of the coupling metrics

Metric	Candidate Objects
Direct invocation	*Get_Parameters, Clean_Command_Line, Check_Options*
	Count_Lines, Classify_Line, Start_Tokenizer, Get_Token,
	Find_Function_Name, Create_List, Append_Element, Create_Node
	Report_Metrics, Is_Empty_List, Delete_Element, Delete_Node Error
Indirect invocation	*Get_Parameters, Clean_Command_Line, Check_Options*
	Count_Lines, Classify_Line, Start_Tokenizer, Get_Token,
	Find_Function_Name, Append_Element, Create_Node
	Report_Metrics, Delete_Element, Delete_Node
	Error, Create_List, Is_Empty_List
Shared parameters	*Get_Parameters, Clean_Command_Line, Check_Options*
	Count_Lines, Classify_Line, Start_Tokenizer, Report_Metrics, Error
	Delete_Element, Append_Element, Create_Node, Is_Empty_List,
	Create_List
	Destroy_Node, Find_Function_Name, Get_Token
Shared variables	*Get_Parameters, Clean_Command_Line, Check_Options*
	Count_Lines, Classify_Line, Start_Tokenizer, Get_Token,
	Find_Function_Name, Append_Element, Create_Node
	Report_Metrics, Delete_Element
	Error, Create_List, Is_Empty_List, Destroy_Node
Shared variable tokens	*Get_Parameters, Clean_Command_Line, Check_Options*
	Count_Lines, Classify_Line, Start_Tokenizer, Get_Token,
	Find_Function_Name, Append_Element, Create_Node
	Report_Metrics, Delete_Element, Destroy_Node
	Error, Create_List, Is_Empty_List
Shared type-name variables	*Get_Parameters, Clean_Command_Line, Check_Options*
	Count_Lines, Classify_Line, Start_Tokenizer, Get_Token,
	Find_Function_Name
	Report_Metrics, Create_Node, Append_Element, Delete_Element
	Error, Create_List, Is_Empty_List, Destroy_Node
Shared type-name variable tokens	*Get_Parameters, Clean_Command_Line, Check_Options*
	Count_Lines, Classify_Line, Start_Tokenizer, Get_Token,
	Find_Function_Name
	Report_Metrics, Create_Node, Append_Element, Delete_Element
	Error, Create_List, Is_Empty_List, Destroy_Node

The calculation of the shared variable metrics in general took up a substantial amount of time, but their results were not very different to the direct invocation metric. None of the shared variable metrics were able to identify the list data type; they all tended to have the functions related to the abstract data type either in the utility object or grouped with the Report_Metrics function.

Most coupling metrics placed the function Report_Metrics in a separate object. The task of reporting metrics (in ccount) follows that of counting and classifying lines, and hence it is best to use different classes for these to separate responsibilities.

If the list data type were already identified, the direct invocation metric would be the fastest and easiest to use to help determine objects. The shared parameters metric provides the best breakup of the objects; it comes closer than any other metric in identifying the list data type.

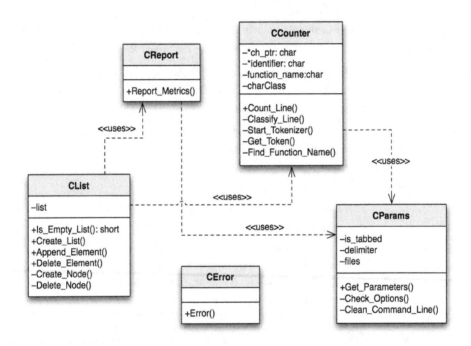

Fig. 4. Class diagram for object-oriented ccount application

Based on the above observations and using the candidate objects as references, we chose the following classes for coding the object oriented version of ccount. The list data type is identified and encapsulated in its own class. The functions main, Error, and Report_Metrics were each placed in their own class. Figure 4 gives a class diagram of the application.

Class::CError
Error()
Class::CCount
main()
Class::CReport
Report_Metric()
Class::CCounter
Count_Lines()
private:
   char *ch_ptr
   char identifier[MAX_IDENT+1]
   char function_name[MAX_IDENT+1]
   char_class charClass[128]
   Classify_Line()
   Start_Tokenizer()
   Get_Token()
   Find_Function_Name()
Class::CParams
Get_Parameters()
private:
   short is_tabbed
   char *delimiter
   char **files
   Check_Options()
   Clean_Command_Line()
Class::CList
Is_Empty_List()
Create_List()
Append_Element()
Delete_Element()
private:
   CElement *list
   Create_Node()
   Destroy_Node()

4.6 Coding

For coding in C++ the following guidelines were followed.

- Rather than using malloc and realloc functions to allocate memory, new was used.
- Rather than using #define, const was used.
- Some variables had to be renamed to adhere to C++ naming convention.

Otherwise, an effort was made to keep the function names the same and the algorithms the same. Due to the similar structure and syntax of the C and C++ languages, it was possible at times use the C functions with few changes.

The parameters extracted from the command line were placed as private variables in the class CParams and were accessed using public access get methods. The list was made a private variable in the CList class; only the methods in the CList class modified the list.

The global (file scope) variables accessed by the functions Get_Token, Start_Tokenizer, and Find_Function_Name were made private variables of the class CCounter.

To ensure that the code developed in C++ gave the same result as the C version, the 19 regression tests developed for C code in [3] were utilized. Abnormal inputs were provided to check if the code is able to handle them. And the output generated for the statistics of a valid C file was verified to ensure that it was accurate. The C++ version was found to perform satisfactorily and it passed all the test cases.

Time taken for the coding of ccount in C++ was 24 hours.

5 Process Variables Captured

The times taken for each step are shown in Table 7. The total time taken for the process was 93 hours. Though we did not record the times it took to calculate each metric in identify objects step, we estimate that we did not spend more than six hours calculating the direct invocation metric and the shared parameter metric—the two metrics that seemed to give the best results.

Table 7. Process Variables

Step	Time taken
Create stop list	1 hour
Create flow graph	1 hour
Dependency list	2 hours
Identify objects	48 hours
Domain expert analysis	16 hours
Coding	23 hours
Total	93 hours

The following data was captured for the ANSI C version and C++ version of ccount.

Statistics for the C version:

- Number of non-commentary lines of code : 749
- Number of files : 7
- Numbers of Functions : 17

Statistics for the C++ version:

- Number of objects : 6
- Number of real objects : 4

- Number of utility objects : 2
- Real objects with one function : 1
- Number of non-commentary lines of code : 679

6 Conclusion and Future Work

Coupling metrics provide a good starting point for identifying objects, but the metrics we used in this study had limitations. For example, they were not able to completely identify the list data type in ccount. Hence domain expert analysis is an important step in the process—it is necessary for finalizing the optimal objects from the candidate objects identified from the coupling metrics.

The largest amount of time spent in the process was in determining the coupling metrics. The direct invocation metric and shared parameters metric were found to provide reasonable objects very close to the objects finalized by the domain expert. The time taken to determine these two metrics was considerably less than the time it took to determine the shared variable metrics, since they do not require the collection of the detailed summary data shown in Table 3. Therefore, the process could be accelerated if only the direct invocation and shared parameter metrics were taken into consideration. Using a tool like the CIA (C Information Abstraction System) [4] would also help in speeding up the process.

Some things to consider for future case studies would be using the direct invocation and shared parameter metrics in conjunction to arrive at candidate objects. When more than one metric is used, one could either sum the metrics or assign a weight to each metric, indicating that one form of coupling is considered more relevant [5]. For example, we might calculate the combined direct invocation and shared parameters metric as 2 * direct invocation metric + 3 * shared parameters metric. In this case the higher weight attached to the shared parameters metric indicates a data definition coupling is more relevant than routine call coupling.

This case study presents a good first step in determining how to reengineer a legacy procedural system into an object-oriented system. The methodology we examined was found to be helpful in identifying objects. It can also serve as a framework that is usable with coupling metrics other than those presented here.

References

[1] Thomas P. Pole, *Pole Method for C to C++ Reengineering*. Personal Communication.
[2] William B. Frakes and Thomas P. Pole, "An Empirical Study of Representation Methods for Reusable Software Components," *IEEE Transactions on Software Engineering*. Vol. 20, No. 8, August 1990, pages 617–630.
[3] William B. Frakes, Christopher J. Fox, and Brian A. Nejmeh, *Software Engineering in the UNIX/C Environment*. Prentice Hall, Englewood Cliffs, 1991.
[4] Yin-Farn Chen, Michael Y. Nishimoto, and C. V. Ramamoorthy, "The C Information Abstraction System," *IEEE Transactions on Software Engineering*. Vol. 16, No. 3, March 1990, pages 325–334.

[5] Michael Whitney, Kostos Kontogiannis, J. Howard Johnson, Morris Bernstein, Brian Corrie, Ettore Merlo, James McDaniel, Renato De Mori, Hausi Muller, John Mylopoulos, Martin Stanley, Scott Tilley, and Kenny Wong, "Using Integrated Toolset for Program Understanding," in *Proceedings of the CAS Conference (CASCON 95)*. pages 262–274.

[6] Roger S. Pressman, *Software Engineering: A Practitioner's Approach*. Boston: McGraw-Hill, 2005.

Reconciling Subtyping and Code Reuse in Object-Oriented Languages: Using *inherit* and *insert* in SmartEiffel, the GNU Eiffel Compiler

Dominique Colnet[1], Guillem Marpons[2], and Frederic Merizen[1]

[1] LORIA (UMR 7503 CNRS-INPL-INRIA-Nancy2-UHP) - France
`colnet@loria.fr, merizen@loria.fr`
[2] Universitat Politècnica de Catalunya (UPC) - Spain
`gmarpons@lsi.upc.edu`

Abstract. SmartEiffel has been enjoying two different mechanisms to express subtyping and implementation inheritance for one year. After large scale practical tests and thanks to user feedback, this paper finalises the new typing policy of SmartEiffel, which combines two forms of multiple inheritance with genericity in one statically-checked, object-oriented language.

Having two forms of inheritance allows the designer to capture more design decisions in the source code. It is now straightforward to share reusable code between otherwise unrelated types. The new mechanism allows to reuse code from an existing class without polluting the reuser's interface. It also enables an elegant implementation of some design patterns.

Furthermore, this mechanism helps compilers to statically remove more dynamic dispatch code. It can also be used to add a no-penalty and no-risk multiple-inheritance-like construct to a single-inheritance language such as Java.

1 Introduction

The Eiffel language is intended to favour good software engineering practises. Its concern about building reusable software artifacts [10] should be stressed as the most salient trend of its design. The inheritance mechanism, in particular, was conceived as a powerful reuse mechanism with a panoply of adaptation facilities for inherited methods and attributes, and the possibility of multiple inheritance.

Still, subclassing and subtyping are strongly coupled in traditional Eiffel. Reusing code through inheritance is desirable for the great flexibility it provides and because of performance considerations. In spite of this, enforcing a subtyping relation when inheriting has a number of drawbacks. The problem is obviously not specific to the Eiffel world [3] and this coupling sometimes produces flawed designs (examples in section 4). The designers always have to balance these disadvantages with the hindrance of reusing code through other means than inheritance, or even not reusing code at all—the worst being copy-pasting. In fact, the designers of Eiffel have recognised this conflict, slightly relaxing the

M. Morisio (Ed.): ICSR 2006, LNCS 4039, pp. 203–216, 2006.

subclassing/subtyping relation. This has been done by allowing argument types to be covariantly redefined and method visibility to be restricted in subclasses, leading to the well-known type-safety problems of the language [11].

The SmartEiffel team [1] has been working on Eiffel tools, compilers and libraries for more than ten years [1, 2, 12, 16, 17]. In the remainder of this paper, we will use the unqualified term *"Eiffel"* as a shorthand for *"the Eiffel dialect of the SmartEiffel team"* [2]. This paper discusses an implementation-only inheritance language construct that we introduced in February 2005 (release 2.1 of the SmartEiffel compiler). This mechanism is conceived as a complement to the traditional Eiffel inheritance and gives the designer full control about which subtyping relations are actually established. To avoid confusion we use the terms *inheritance* or *inheritance mechanism* for the traditional Eiffel inheritance, and *insertion* or *insertion mechanism* for the recently devised language construct [3].

Since we first introduced the insertion mechanism, we have had the opportunity to extensively put it to use, on large scale programs and libraries, and with the feed-back of many SmartEiffel users. Thus, this paper is not only an *academic research work* but also a practical report. Practising the mechanism has helped us to clarify ideas about what kind of type-system we need to best fit the new mechanism into the language. SmartEiffel currently implements the type-checking rules presented here, with one restriction regarding expanded classes that will be lifted in the next release (SmartEiffel 2.3). We refactored SmartEiffel's 450 standard library classes to exercise the insertion mechanism, and the classes now make use of 350 inherit links and 300 insert links. Our work on the library clearly indicates that the new language construct favours the reconciliation between subtyping, static checking and reusability.

The paper is organised as follows. Section 2 introduces the insertion mechanism and some necessary background about Eiffel. The new typing policy is presented in section 3. Examples of how the insertion and inheritance mechanisms can be used together to remove certain specific design flaws and improve reuse opportunities are presented in section 4. Section 5 compares our work with papers or existing languages with similar aims. Section 6 concludes.

2   Adding the Insertion Mechanism to Eiffel

Eiffel is an object-oriented language that features multiple inheritance, static typing, (constrained) genericity and design by contract. As in Smalltalk [6] even basic entities such as small integers are true objects of some existing class. Uniformity in the type system helps to keep the language simple and to make all those facilities as broadly appliccable as possible. The language is well-suited for large software projects and teams.

---

[1] All authors of this paper are members of the current SmartEiffel team. This paper can be considered as the work of the whole SmartEiffel team.

[2] The reader might be aware that there are several dialects of the Eiffel language. The SmartEiffel dialect shares a common root with the ECMA standardisation attempt [4] but diverged from it in May 2005. Since then, SmartEiffel has made its own way.

[3] This mechanism has been known to Eiffel users as *non-conforming inheritance.*

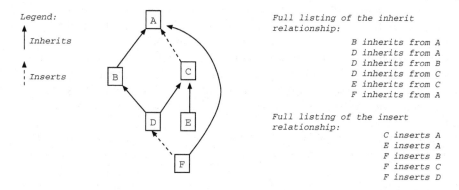

Legend:

Inherits

Inserts

Full listing of the inherit
relationship:

                    B inherits from A
                    D inherits from A
                    D inherits from B
                    D inherits from C
                    E inherits from C
                    F inherits from A

Full listing of the insert
relationship:
                    C inserts A
                    E inserts A
                    F inserts B
                    F inserts C
                    F inserts D

Fig. 1. The inherit and the insert relationships on a non-trivial example

2.1 Keeping inherit and Adding insert

The traditional inheritance mechanism introduced from the very beginning of
Eiffel is still present and unchanged. The inheritance relationship both induces
a subtyping relationship and introduces code reuse. The classes that a class
inherits from constitute a list of zero, one or more elements called the *inherit list*
of that class. Syntactically, the inherit list is introduced by the inherit keyword
if non-empty. In the remainder of this paper, "A inherits from B" means that
a path using only inherit links exists from A to B. Saying "A inherits directly
from B" means that B is syntactically a member of the inherit list of A.

In the new Eiffel syntax, a class can also have a second parent list introduced
by the new insert keyword. This is the relationship to be used when code has to
be inserted just for implementation purpose. The insert list can syntactically
have zero, one or more parents. In the remainder of this paper, "A inserts B"
means that a path using insert or inherit links exists from A to B, but A does not
inherit from B (i.e. at least one insertion link exists from A to B in every path).
The sum of the inheritance graph and the insertion graph must be an acyclic
directed graph. Saying "A inserts directly B" means that B is syntactically
a member of the insert list of A. Figure 1 summarises the inheritance and
insertion relationships on a non-trivial example.

The idea behind the insertion mechanism is simple: to complement the traditional inheritance mechanism with a new one that keeps the code reuse aspects
but discards the subtyping relationship. As we will see in section 3, the fact
that A inserts B does not allow us to assign an expression of type A into some
variable of type B. For such a polymorphic assignment to be legal, A must be a
subtype of B which can also be expressed as "A inherits from B".

2.2 The Special Status of the ANY Class

There is a special class in Eiffel, named ANY, somehow comparable with Java's
Object class, that has been traditionally seen as the universal ancestor of the
inheritance graph. A special rule still exists for class ANY, but now that we have

added the new insert relationship, the status of ANY is slightly different. Class ANY is the only class that has no direct ancestor at all: both its inherit list and its insert list are empty. All other classes must have at least one direct ancestor either through the **inherit** list or through the **insert** list. Class ANY is now the final ancestor of the inheritance / insertion graph. As a consequence, if a class X is not the ANY class itself, then X either inherits from or inserts ANY.

Actually, the ANY class contains important methods that all classes must have at runtime, including code necessary for object comparison, cloning and introspection support. Thanks to the rules we have just presented, we are sure that this code is part of all Eiffel classes.

2.3   Runtime Requirements

We do not only want a language dedicated to software engineering and specification, we also want Eiffel to keep the potential efficiency one can expect from a low-level language such as the C language[4]. A simple integer addition must be as efficient in Eiffel as in C. In Eiffel's runtime model, this goal is achieved by having two kinds of classes: normal classes and *expanded classes*. *Expanded objects* are the instances of expanded classes.

Most classes are normal (non-expanded). Normal objects are handled through a reference. When passed as an argument, a pointer to the object is copied onto the stack. Dynamic dispatch is enabled for such objects.

The machine's basic entities such as integers, floating-point numbers and booleans are defined by expanded classes. Users can create their own expanded classes using the **expanded** keyword. Expanded objects are directly represented as values and cannot be shared. Argument-passing is performed by copying the object's value onto the machine stack. There is no dynamic dispatch for expanded objects.

We require expanded classes to have an empty inherit list and never appear in another class's inherit list. In that way, rule 1 (section 3) is enough to express within the type system the fact that there is no polymorphism involving expanded objects.

2.4   Genericity

Eiffel has got generic classes from the very beginning. One of our design goals was to get the most constructive interaction possible between reuse through genericity and reuse through insertion.

A typical example of genericity at work is the class ARRAY[E_] where E_ is called the formal generic argument. The generic argument E_ may carry a constraint (see next paragraph), but it is not the case here so E_ can be replaced with any type (called an actual generic argument), including expanded types:

---

[4] The runtime efficiency of numerous languages is compared at the "Computer Language Shootout Benchmarks" (http://shootout.alioth.debian.org). Although we don't completely agree with the measuring scale, we want our Eiffel language to be able to sustain a good rank in this comparison.

ARRAY[STRING], ARRAY[INTEGER_8], ARRAY[ARRAY[INTEGER_16]] etc. are all valid types. Being able to directly use integers of the underlying machine as the element type of a generic class is an important benefit of having a very uniform typing policy.

Constrained genericity is the possibility to require a generic parameter to implement some existing class, generally an abstract class with just a few abstract methods. For example, the elements of a hash-based implementation of a set must implement the methods of class HASHABLE. This is denoted by giving the hashed set a constrained generic parameter: HASHED_SET[E_->HASHABLE]. In section 3 (rule 5), we claim that it is sufficient for the actual generic parameter to insert the constraint. An unconstrained generic parameter can be treated as a syntactic shortcut for a parameter constrained by the class ANY. For instance, the array class can be considered as defined as ARRAY[E_->ANY]. An important consequence is that expanded classes can be used as generic parameters although they cannot inherit from any class (including ANY).

3   Typing and Checking Policy

Because of space concerns, it is not possible to give the whole set of rules we apply to check Eiffel programs in this paper. We will focus on the main questions about our typing and checking policy in order to be able to answer the following crucial questions: What can be assigned into what? What type can be used when some method or attribute is overridden? What type can be used in case of a generic derivation? What about constrained genericity?

Rule 1 (Assignment). An expression of type A can be assigned into a variable of type B if and only if A and B are the same type or A inherits from B.

This first rule prevents an expression of one type from being assigned to a variable of another type if no subtyping relation exists between them. It directly follows that if A inserts B, the assignment is statically rejected and polymorphism is not possible. Since expanded classes cannot be at either end of an inheritance relationship (section 2.3), rule 1 is enough to forbid assignments from an expanded type to any other type.

Rule 2 (Argument Passing). An expression of type A can be passed as an argument of formal type B if and only if A and B are the same type or A inherits from B.

This second rule simply states that the same policy is used both for assignments (rule 1) and for argument passing (rule 2).

Rule 3 (Redefinition Under Inheritance). When overriding an inherited method or attribute, the types of any argument and/or of its result can be replaced covariantly with a type that inherits from the replaced type (i.e. a subtype).

Actually, for inheritance, the legacy covariant principle of Eiffel is kept unchanged: all types are treated the same way (both result type and argument types), the number of arguments cannot change; if the overridden signature has a result type, the new one must also have a result type. Thus, all legacy code can be reused as is.

Rule 4 (Redefinition Under Insertion). When overriding an inserted method or attribute, the type of any argument and/or of its result can be replaced covariantly with a type that inherits from *or inserts* the replaced type.

As in the case of rule 3, we assume that the overridden signature keeps the same number of arguments and that a result type cannot be discarded or added. Rule 4 is more permissive than rule 3 about the new type one can use because the overridden feature comes through a direct member of its `insert` list. Polymorphism between this inserted ancestor and the current type is not possible and it is thus safe to do so. This increased freedom is in fact beneficial and gives us more flexibility to adapt inserted code.

In a similar way, the exportation status of the inserted methods and/or attributes (i.e. from which other classes they are visible or can be called) can be freely changed. For example, we can insert a public attribute and convert it to a private one, or any other of the fine-grained intermediate possibilities that Eiffel offers. In traditional Eiffel this was also allowed under inheritance, but it creates type safety holes in the same manner as covariant argument changing [11]. Under insertion, the mechanism is safe and in fact plays an important methodological role as shown in section 4.2.

Rule 5 (Generic Derivation). When deriving an actual type from a generic class, we can instantiate each parameter using any class that ïnserts or inherits from the type that constrains the corresponding placeholder. The resulting fully instantiated type is only valid if statically proved correct (recursively) with respect to rules 1-5.

This rule allows to instantiate a generic class using a parameter that is not a subtype of the constraining type. Both inheritance and insertion are permitted here. This can be surprising at the beginning, but is type safe, because the replacement of the formal parameter by the actual one is done at compile time and the generic derivation obtained is statically checked. In fact, polymorphism is often not needed between the generic type constraint and the type that replaces it in a generic derivation. If the actual parameter is a subtype of the constraining type, the derivation will be statically valid. On the contrary, if the actual parameter only inserts the constraining type, the validity of the derivation must be checked by the compiler.

Rule 5 is meant to accept expanded types as any other parameter in classes such as ARRAY[E_->ANY]. In this way the insertion mechanism helps us to fit non-polymorphic and efficient basic types (i.e expanded types) in a very uniform type system that maximises type combining opportunities.

The insertion mechanism defined by those rules provides useful program design options, but it can also improve runtime and compile-time performance. Since insertion does not entail a subtyping relationship as inheritance does, there are less edges in the subtyping graph when insertion is used. Compilers that do type prediction [16] can predict smaller sets of possible dynamic subtypes for a given static type. This increased knowledge of static types can result in smaller dynamic dispatch functions or smaller virtual function tables. It would also be possible to extend single-inheritance based languages like Java with this mechanism, without changing the dynamic dispatch mechanism.

4   Examples of Code Reuse

The next examples are intended to show how the new insertion mechanism can help to reconcile reuse and other software engineering principles. We start with code sharing (section 4.1) because it is the most simple use of the insertion mechanism, although it is not the most illustrative of the benefits of insertion when—as in Eiffel—multiple inheritance is available. Many of the examples come from the SmartEiffel libraries and tools [1].

4.1   Sharing Methods and Attributes with Insert

Two or more classes will sometimes have a lot of commonalities in their *implementation*, while playing quite different *roles* in the design. The insertion mechanism allows those classes to share code without adding any spurious subtyping relations. For instance, in the SmartEiffel compiler the class CREATE_EXPRESSION is a specialisation of the abstract class EXPRESSION (a CREATE_EXPRESSION *is an* EXPRESSION), as shown in figure 2. Similarly, the class CREATE_INSTRUCTION is a specialisation of the abstract class INSTRUCTION. Because the implementation of the class CREATE_EXPRESSION is similar to the implementation of the class CREATE_INSTRUCTION, many common instance variables and methods are defined in CREATE_SUPPORT. The use of insertion (figure 2) emphasises the fact that CREATE_SUPPORT is just a useful place to share common code which is necessary to implement both CREATE_EXPRESSION and CREATE_INSTRUCTION and that there is no possible substitution of CREATE_EXPRESSION with CREATE_INSTRUCTION (or conversely). If inheritance was used (this would probably be the solution adopted with traditional Eiffel) this design decision would not appear in the code, making the role of each class more obscure.

Interestingly, the methods defined in CREATE_SUPPORT can be triggered due to dynamic dispatch although they are inserted (not inherited). For example, a shared method of CREATE_SUPPORT can be the implementation of an abstract method of the class CREATE_EXPRESSION. The class EXPRESSION has a lot of heirs and dynamic dispatch does work as expected. The fact that a method is inserted does not preclude using dynamic dispatch on that method.

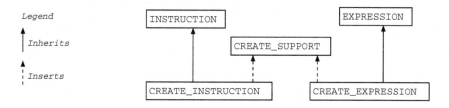

Fig. 2. Sharing code between unrelated classes. A routine storage example.

While this use of insertion appears all across our tools and libraries, and has contributed, in our opinion, to clarify the design, having this possibility would be even more beneficial to languages such as Java that do not have multiple class inheritance. Note that all three of CODE_SUPPORT, EXPRESSION and INSTRUCTION contain code, and reducing any of them to mere interfaces would result in significant code duplication. Furthermore, all three of them also have state (instance variables). It would not be reasonable, for instance, to move CODE_SUPPORT up in the hierarchy and turn it into a common ancestor EXPRESSION and INSTRUCTION, as this would clutter numerous non-creation-related instructions and expressions with useless attributes. Adding the insert mechanism to the Java language would solve this problem with little or no changes required to the runtime system. Particularly, since insertion does not create dynamic dispatch possibilities, the single-inheritance dispatch mechanism of the JVM could be kept intact.

As a special case of code sharing, the insertion mechanism can be used to share a set of related constant definitions. This effectively emulates the primary use of Java's "static import" mechanism.

4.2 Hiding Excess Methods

When inheritance is the only code reuse mechanism available, the benefits of reusing code will sometimes be mitigated by the fact that the interface of the child gets polluted by some public methods from the parent. Using the insertion mechanism, the programmer can effectively make those superfluous methods private, eliminating their impact on the child's interface.

For instance, in Java the class java.util.Stack extends java.util.Vector, where the class Vector is a resizable ordered collection of elements. This technique makes Stack very easy to implement and avoids duplicating Vector's code. Unfortunately, the spurious subtyping relationship between a Java Stack and a Vector makes it possible to use all methods of the class Vector on Stack objects as well. The class obtained is not a pure stack because one can directly peek or put elements at any position in the Stack.

In traditional Eiffel, the class STACK can hide methods and attributes inherited from the class VECTOR, but this protection is quite weak. If STACK inherited from VECTOR then a STACK object could be polymorphically assigned to a VECTOR variable and any method of VECTOR we wanted applied to the STACK object could be called (even with the assumption that some methods like put had been removed from its public interface). The following code is accepted by the compiler if STACK inherits from VECTOR:

```
local
  s: STACK
  v: VECTOR
  ...
do
  create s.make
```

```
...
v := s
v.put(an_element, a_position)
...
```

It is dangerous for an external client of an object to call methods that have been eliminated from its public interface because they can violate the invariant of the class and the object would have an unpredictable behaviour as from that point. In fact, code like that must be considered incorrect, even if current Eiffel compilers are not capable of discovering this situation in the general case. SmartEiffel avoids this problem by forbidding narrowing the exportation status of an inherited method or attribute.

On the contrary, the protection is effective if the class STACK reuses code from the class VECTOR by inserting it. With insertion it is no longer possible to assign an expression of type STACK into a VECTOR variable, so the previous code is rejected. It is always safe to narrow the exportation status of inserted methods and attributes because they can not be secretly called via a parent interface. This way we can easily implement a pure and safe stack.

Changing covariantly the type of an argument to an inserted method is also safe. If the class VECTOR had a binary method merge(other: VECTOR): VECTOR for getting a new vector containing the elements of two vectors merged in a particular order, it would be possible to redefine the method in class STACK so as to cope with stacks only. The STACK's version of the method would have signature merge(other: STACK): STACK, and as it could never be called through the VECTOR's interface, the compiler could guarantee that only stack objects were passed to the method. Covariant change of argument types is still useful also when inheriting, so the traditional rule, even if unsafe, has been kept.

As inheriting from ANY is no longer mandatory (see section 2.2), even its methods can be reliably hidden if the designer wants to. For instance, one may decide not to export the possibly slow equals comparison method. This is a way to promote the usage of the basic fast comparison operator (the built-in == in Java), and to favour the use of as much aliasing as possible [17].

Similarly, the universal clone inserted method can be hidden in some classes in order to make duplicating instances of that class a restricted operation. This is useful when implementing the Singleton and Flyweight design patterns [5]. The intent of the Singleton design pattern is to ensure that a class has only one instance, and to provide a global access point to it. The intent of the Flyweight design pattern is to use sharing to support large numbers of fine-grained objects efficiently. A maximal aliasing of flyweight objects is required and the developer does not want duplication methods to be called (except, maybe, for the Flyweight factory itself). Thanks to the insertion mechanism, the accidental duplicating of a Singleton or Flyweight object can be avoided safely.

4.3   Other Design Pattern Examples

Finally, we show how some common design patterns can be better implemented with insertion. The Class Adapter design pattern [5] (not to be confused with

Fig. 3. Using insertion for the Adapter design pattern

the *Object* Adapter) converts the interface of a class into another interface the clients expect.

Adapters let classes with otherwise incompatible interfaces work together. As shown on figure 3, an ADAPTER has multiple parents: typically, the class to be adapted, the ADAPTEE, and the interface we want to implement, the TARGET. Still, we *don't* want the adapter to be a subtype of the adaptee—that's why we are using the Adapter pattern in the first place. It is natural for the adapter to insert the adaptee.

As a side note, the UML diagram of the Class Adapter design pattern in [8] is annotated with an *implementation* tag for the inheritance link between the class ADAPTER and the class ADAPTEE, precisely the link for which we are using insertion.

The Template Method pattern [5] defines the skeleton of an algorithm in an operation, deferring some steps to subclasses. Template Method lets subclasses redefine some steps of an algorithm without changing the algorithm structure.

When all concrete classes that need to define the Template Method are subtypes of a common ancestor type, it is straightforward that the Template Method has to be stored in this common ancestor and that the insertion mechanism is not useful. However, in a situation similar to the one of figure 2, that is to say when the Template Method must be shared by classes that are by no other means related, insertion does help. Thus, the class CREATE_SUPPORT can contain Template Methods to be shared by CREATE_EXPRESSION and CREATE_INSTRUCTION. Again, the use of insertion emphasises the fact that the purpose of CREATE_SUPPORT is to share code.

5   Related Work

There have been many attempts to provide separate mechanisms for code reuse and subtyping. Most of those solutions also separate the unit of code reuse (modules, implementations, traits etc.) from the unit of subtyping (interfaces), while C++ and our solution rely on a single unit, the class.

5.1   ECMA Eiffel

Our proposal is rooted in the discussions for providing an insertion-like mechanism for Eiffel during the standarization efforts of the last years, discussions in which the SmartEiffel team has been involved. The ECMA final document [4] includes such a mechanism—with a different syntax—that at the time this is being written has not been implemented by any compiler. As, among other differences, the runtime model supported by ECMA Eiffel differs from the one of SmartEiffel (for example, expanded objects have a completely different meaning), the typing policy and the integration of the insertion mechanism with other features of the language have been specifically developed for SmartEiffel.

5.2 SCG Traits

Schärli *et al.* of the Software Composition Group present a mechanism called traits and discuss its implementation in Smalltalk [13]. Unlike classes, traits cannot have attributes and they cannot be part of an inheritance relationship, neither as parents nor as children. However, traits and classes can be *composed* of one or more sub-traits. Like insertion, the trait composition mechanism allows to reuse code without implying a subtyping relationship.

The trait composition mechanism avoids the most difficult issues of diamond inheritance, so the authors claim, thanks to traits not having attributes. In Eiffel, it is possible to insert a class even if it has attributes without suffering adverse effects. In the case of diamond inheritance, Eiffel's standard feature renaming mechanism allows the program to choose for each attribute if it is to be shared or replicated.

Because they do not take part in inheritance relations, traits enjoy the *flattening property*, which means that trait composition can be interpreted as simple textual substitution (with a few simple restrictions to take naming conflicts into account). Most importantly, if a class obtains a method that contains the **super** keyword through trait composition, that keyword's meaning does not depend on the trait where the keyword is written, but only on the class that contains the method through composition. The flattening property makes it possible to write traits that work as generic extensions. For instance, the authors show how to write a trait that can be used to make a synchronising stream from any input stream. We cannot hope to duplicate this result in a language with multiple inheritance such as Eiffel because, in the case of an inheritance diamond, the **Precursor** keyword must be complemented with the name of a parent class to avoid ambiguity. Of course, it is not possible to write the name of the parent class in a trait, since this name is only known in the classes that use this trait.

5.3 Mixins

In the mixin inclusion mechanism as illustrated by Ruby's [15] implementation, the unit of code reuse, called a *module*, can hold methods and define state variables. Mixin inclusion is similar to class insertion in the sense that a class or a module can include one or more modules to reuse their implementation without entering a subtyping relationship. Mixins differ from classes in the sense that classes cannot inherit from modules, and modules cannot inherit from anything. Moreover, modules cannot have direct instances. Technically, mixin inclusion is handled by language processors through anonymous classes and an underlying single inheritance mechanism, which requires the module inclusion graph to be linearised.

5.4   Sather's Class Inclusion

Sather has a mechanism for code reuse that is very similar to insertion [7]. Unlike Eiffel, Sather has a class/interface dichotomy just like Java. As their names suggest, classes can hold code while interfaces cannot. In Sather, interfaces can inherit from interfaces, and classes can implement interfaces. However, there is no such thing as inheritance between classes in Sather. Instead, a class can `include` another class. Sather's inclusion mechanism resembles Eiffel's insertion mechanism in that it handles multiple inclusion seamlessly, and allows the developer to restrict the availability of included methods or attributes, just like the technique discussed in section 4.2.

The main difference between our mechanism and Sather's is the fact that inheritance and insertion are handled uniformly by our mechanism, while Sather relies on a class/interface dichotomy. On another point, the designers of Sather did not reap the byproduct of safe covariant redefinitions through insertion. In Sather, only contravariant redefinitions of argument types are allowed.

5.5   Timor's Reuse Variables

The Timor language [9] separates interfaces from implementations in a way reminiscent of Sather.

Interfaces define types by listing the names and signatures of their methods, and they can take part in subtyping relationships by *extending* other interfaces. Interfaces can also *include* other interfaces, which allows them to inherit from interfaces without entering a subtyping relationship—a process that can be simulated in Eiffel by abstract classes inserting other abstract classes.

Implementations of a given interface supply actual code and attributes to support that interface's semantics. Implementations cannot play the role of a parent or a child in an inheritance relation. Instead, to achieve code reuse, implementations can have *reuse variables*, which behave like normal sub-objects with one exception. If an implementation lacks a method that is part of its interface, then that method is statically looked up in its reuse variables.

One interesting consequence of this model that completely decouples code reuse from inheritance is that the reused code does not pollute the reusing implementation. Its state variables are kept logically separate, and methods that are not needed to implement the reuser's interface are not included into it.

5.6   C++ Private/Protected Inheritance

The C++ mechanisms known as `private` and `protected` inheritance [14] bear a superficial resemblance with our insertion mechanism. However, they differ in one substantial way: the C++ mechanisms do not really prevent polymorphism. When a class B privately inherits from a class A, class B *is allowed* to perform polymorphic assignments of B objects to A variables. While other classes are not allowed to perform such polymorphic *assignments*, there is no mechanism to prevent B from letting pointers escape, so polymorphic *calls* can still happen even outside of B. As a corollary, when it comes to hiding inherited methods

C++ private or protected inheritance has the same problem as Eiffel inheritance. If B lets a pointer to itself of type A escape, that pointer can be used to access even `private`ly inherited methods.

6 Conclusion

During our work on the Eiffel language, we have exercised the insertion mechanism on a large scale project (the whole SmartEiffel compiler and tools as well as its large and numerous libraries [1]). This simple mechanism turns out to be valuable to capture more design information in the source code of applications. Code and design reuse opportunities then arise that were previously in contradiction with other design goals as type-safety, information-hiding, performance, or small memory footprint. Some design patterns can be implemented in a cleaner way with insertion. When inserting, covariant redefinition of arguments is no longer dangerous and does not incur type soundness problems. Exportation can also be tightened in subclasses without any problems.

The slight increase in complexity that this new mechanism entails is more than offset by the better match of efficient non-polymorphic types (expanded types) with the insertion mechanism. The uniformity of the type-system has been kept.

Acknowledgements

The research of G. Marpons is funded by the Ministerio de Educación y Ciencia and by FEDER under Grant TIC2004-06320-C03-01.

We want to acknowledge the work of Cyril Adrian and Philippe Ribet, the main architects of the compiler's new core. Many thanks to Marko Van Dooren for his feedback during the preparation of this paper. We are also grateful to all SmartEiffel users for their feedback and all their helpful comments during the practice of the insertion mechanism.

References

1. D. Colnet, P. Ribet, C. Adrian, V. Croizier, and F. Merizen. Web site of SmartEiffel, the GNU Eiffel compiler, tools and libraries. http://SmartEiffel.loria.fr.
2. D. Colnet, P. Coucaud and O. Zendra. "Compiler Support to Customize the Mark and Sweep Algorithm." 1st ACM SIGPLAN International Symposium on Memory Management (ISMM'98), pages 154-165, 1998, Vancouver, BC, Canada.
3. W. Cook, W. Hill, and P. Canning. "Inheritance is Not Subtyping." 17th ACM Symposium on Principles of Programming Languages, pages 125–135, 1990.
4. ECMA Normalisation group for the Eiffel language definition TC39-TG4, http://www.ecma-international.org/memento/TC39-TG4.html.
5. E. Gamma, R. Helm, R. Johnson, and J. Vlissides. "Design Patterns: Elements of Reusable Object-Oriented Software." Addisson-Wesley, Reading, Massachusetts, 1995. ISBN 0201633612.

6. A. Goldberg and D. Robson. "Smalltalk-80, the Language and its Implementation." Addison-Wesley, Reading, Massachusetts, 1983.
7. B. Gomes, D. Stoutamire, B. Vaysman, and H. Klawitter. "Sather 1.1: A language manual." http://www.icsi.berkeley.edu/~sather.
8. J. M. Jézéquel, M. Train, and C. Mingins. "Design Patterns and Contracts." Addisson-Wesley, 1999. ISBN 0201309599.
9. J. L. Keedy, C. Heinlein and G. Menger. "Reuse Variables: Reusing Code and State in Timor." International Conference on Software Reuse 2004, Vol. 3107 of LNCS, Springer Verlag, pages 205–214, 2004.
10. B. Meyer. "Reusable Software." Prentice Hall, 1994. ISBN 0132454998.
11. B. Meyer. "Beware of polymorphic catcalls." http://archive.eiffel.com.
12. P. Ribet, C. Adrian, O. Zendra and D. Colnet. "Conformance of agents in the Eiffel language." Journal of Object Technology (JOT), 2004, Volume 3. No 4., pages 125-143.
13. N. Schärli, S. Ducasse, O. Nierstrasz, A. Black. "Traits: Composable Units of Behavior." ECOOP 2003, European Conference on Object-Oriented Programming, vol. 2743 of LNCS, Springer Verlag, pages 248–274, July, 2003.
14. B. Stroustrup. "The C++ Programming Language." Addisson-Wesley, 2000. ISBN 0201889544.
15. D. Thomas and A. Hunt. "Programming Ruby: The Pragmatic Programmer's Guide." Addison-Wesley, Reading, Massachusetts, 2001. ISBN 0201710897.
16. O. Zendra, D. Colnet and S. Collin. "Efficient Dynamic Dispatch without Virtual Function Tables. The SmallEiffel Compiler." OOPSLA'97, 12th ACM Conference on Object-Oriented Programming Systems, Languages and Applications, pages 125–141, 1997.
17. O. Zendra and D. Colnet. "Coping with aliasing in the GNU Eiffel Compiler implementation." Software Practice and Experience (SP&E), Vol. 31 No 6, pages 601–613, 2001. J. Wiley & Sons.

Recommending Library Methods: An Evaluation of the Vector Space Model (VSM) and Latent Semantic Indexing (LSI)*

Frank McCarey, Mel Ó Cinnéide, and Nicholas Kushmerick

School of Computer Science and Informatics, University College Dublin,
Belfield, Dublin 4, Ireland
{frank.mccarey, mel.ocinneide, nick}@ucd.ie

Abstract. The development and maintenance of a reuse repository requires significant investment, planning and managerial support. To minimise risk and ensure a healthy return on investment, reusable components should be accessible, reliable and of a high quality. In this paper we concentrate on accessability; we describe a technique which enables a developer to effectively and conveniently make use of large scale libraries. Unlike most previous solutions to component retrieval, our tool, RASCAL, is a proactive component recommender.

RASCAL recommends a set of task-relevant reusable components to a developer. Recommendations are produced using Collaborative Filtering (CF). We compare and contrast CF effectiveness when using two information retrieval techniques, namely Vector Space Model (VSM) and Latent Semantic Indexing (LSI). We validate our technique on real world examples and find overall results are encouraging; notably, RASCAL can produce reasonably good recommendations when they are most valuable i.e., at an early stage in code development.

1 Introduction

Successful software reuse has been to shown to improve software quality and developer productivity whilst reducing defect density [1] and time-to-market [2]. Despite this, reuse has not been adopted widely. Ye et al. [3] identifies the significant cost and commitments required from an organisation to institute a reuse program. To maximise reuse, minimise risk and ensure a healthy return on investment, reusable components should be accessible, reliable and of a high quality. In this paper we concentrate on effective tool support to increase the accessibility and use of reusable libraries.

Poulin [4] suggests that the best libraries contain around 30, but in rare cases up to 250, components. In reality however, it is possible that a library could contain many thousand components; for example the Java 1.4 API library has 2,723 classes. To avail of all the reusable components in such a large library,

---

* Funding provided by the IRCSET under grant RS/2003/127.

M. Morisio (Ed.): ICSR 2006, LNCS 4039, pp. 217–230, 2006.

it is essential that adequate tool support be provided. Indeed it has been the inadequacy of conventional tools that has long hampered reuse. Frequently, the time taken to locate a component in a particular repository and the subsequent integration of that component with existing code will be perceived as too costly and outweighing any potential reuse benefits.

The importance of reuse support tools is reflected in the shift from initial software reuse research which focused on techniques to develop reusable components and component libraries to a focus on supporting reuse through intelligent storage and retrieval strategies, for example [5]. Each solution attempts to assist developers in discovering or locating components in which they are interested. These approaches share a common shortcoming though; the developer must initiate the retrieval process. Pragmatic issues such as time constraints, limited conversancy with the library and lack of developer motivation will determine the likelihood of a developer searching a library. In reality, if a developer believes a reusable component for a particular task does not exist or they do not anticipate the need to reuse such a component, then they are less likely to query the component repository; no retrieval schemes address this important issue.

In our work, we focus on complementing component retrieval with component recommendation. We describe a technique that can produce recommendations and we develop a reuse tool, named RASCAL, to investigate our approach. We believe recommendations will assist and encourage developers in making full use of large component libraries in an efficient manner and in turn will help to promote software reuse. RASCAL is a proactive tool; no additional requirements are placed on a developer and it is applicable to any existing code libraries.

Similar to many commercial recommenders, we produce a set of personalised recommendations for an individual. However, unlike other domains where perhaps a set of books or movies may be presented to a customer, RASCAL recommends a set of task relevant methods to a particular developer. Like most recommendation tasks, RASCAL recommends software components that the developer is interested in. Recommendation in our tool is complicated though because we wish to recommend components which we believe the developer may be unfamiliar with or unaware of. Another interesting distinction between our recommender system and most mainstream recommenders is that we are trying to predict, in order, the next likely items a developer will employ. Many typical recommender systems only predict a vote for items which the user has not yet tried. Our aim is to predict the next library method a developer should invoke; it is quite likely that the developer will have invoked this method previously.

We compare two information retrieval approaches commonly used in text retrieval and explain how these techniques can be adapted to our domain in order to produce recommendations. Firstly, we employ a Collaborative Filtering (CF) [6] algorithm using the popular Vector Space Model(VSM) [7]. We then compare this approach with recommendations produced using CF and the more advanced retrieval technique Latent Semantic Indexing (LSI) [7, 8, 9]. To validate our work we produce over 32,000 recommendations for almost 1500 open-source Java classes.

The remainder of this paper is organised as follows. In the next section we review related works. An overview of RASCAL's implementation is presented in section 3. In section 4 we detail our recommendation techniques followed by a comparative analysis of the experimental results in section 5. Finally we discuss how RASCAL can be extended and draw general conclusions in section 6.

2   Related Work

We discuss related research in software reuse tool support and recommender systems using information retrieval (IR), and we describe how IR techniques can be adapted to support software reuse.

2.1   Reuse Tool Support

The development of reusable components and component libraries has been an active research area for some time but this alone will not encourage reuse. "A classified collection is not useful if it does not provide a search-and-retrieval mechanism to use it" [10]. Mili et al. [11] classify traditional search and retrieval methodologies into four categories, namely *Keyword Search*, *Faceted Classification*, *Signature Matching* and *Behavioral Matching*. Each of these retrieval schemes has a number of limitations that result in less than adequate retrievals.

More recently, several *Semantic-Based* retrieval tools have been proposed; typically while querying the repository the developer specifies component requirements using natural languages which are interpreted using a language ontology as a knowledge base. Components in the repository will also have a natural language description. Both the developer query and component descriptions are formalised and closeness is computed. A set of candidate components can be ranked based on their closeness value. Unlike the approaches mentioned above, domain information, developer context and component relationships are all considered. Empirical results indicate that such schemes are superior to traditional approaches [12, 13].

Drummond et al. [14] present the use of a *learning* software agent to support the browsing of software libraries. The active agent attempts to learn the component the developer is looking for by monitoring the developers' normal browsing actions. Based on experimental results, 40% of the time the agent identified the developers' search goal before the developer reached the goal. By providing non intrusive advice that accelerates the search, this work is intended to complement rather than replace browsing.

A major disadvantage with all of the retrieval techniques above is that the developer must initiate the search process. However, in reality developers are not aware of all available components. If they believe a reusable component for a particular task does not exist then they are less likely to search the component repository; none of the above schemes attempt to address this important issue. Thus to effectively and realistically support component reuse it is tremendously important that component retrieval be complemented with component delivery/recommendation.

Ye and Fischer [3] identify the cognitive and social challenges faced by software developers who reuse and also present a tool named *CodeBroker* which address many of these challenges. *CodeBroker* infers the need for components and pro-actively recommends components, with examples, that match the inferred needs. The need for a component is inferred by monitoring developer activities, in particular developer comments and method signature. This solution greatly improves on previous approaches, however the technique is not ideal. Reusable components in the repository must be sufficiently commented to allow matching and developers must also actively and correctly comment their code which currently they may not do. Active commenting is an additional strain placed on developers which is likely to make the use of *CodeBroker* less appealing. Notably, Ye and Fischer remark that browsing and searching are passive mechanisms because they become only useful when a developer decides to make a reuse attempt by knowing or anticipating the existence of certain components.

2.2   IR and Recommenders System

Sarwar et al. [15] describe a collaborative filtering recommender system with Latent Semantic Indexing (LSI). Collaborative filtering works by matching customer preferences to other customers in making recommendations. LSI is a technique commonly used to infer meaning or concepts in texts. Recommendations are produced for two datasets: a movie dataset and a e-commerce dataset. Several limitations of CF algorithms are identified such as sparsity, scalability and synonymy. In an attempt to address these issues, LSI is applied; recommendations using this technique can be performed much faster than pure CF. Recommendations using the LSI approach performed less well than pure CF for the e-commerce dataset but in some cases performed better than CF on the Movie dataset.

LSI is commonly used in natural language domains though some of the properties of source code, such as comments and identifiers, make it suitable for LSI also. Marcus et al. [16] apply LSI to recover documentation-to-source-code links. LSI is used to extract meanings from documentation and source code, this information is then used to identify traceability links based on similarity measures. The results of this approach are promising; the LSI technique has performed at least as well as the traditional Vector Space Model (VSM) however much less preprocessing of the source and documentation is required. This work follows on from a LSI source code clone detection tool [17].

Our work is similar to a number of the techniques mentioned above. Like *CodeBroker* [3], our goal is to recommend a set of candidate software components to a developer; however our recommendations are not based on the developers' comments/method signature. In contrast we produce recommendations using collaborative filtering and LSI, akin to the work of Sarwar et al. [15] and Marcus et al. [16], however in a different context. Like Drummond et al. [14] we use an active agent to monitor the current developer though we are concerned with pro-actively recommending suitable reusable components as opposed to assisting the search process.

3   RASCAL Overview

RASCAL is currently implemented as a plugin for the Eclipse IDE, as illustrated in figure 1. As a developer is writing code, RASCAL monitors the methods currently invoked and uses this information to recommend a candidate set of methods to this developer. Recommendations are then presented to the developer in the recommendations view at the bottom right hand corner of the IDE window. At present, RASCAL recommends methods from the Swing and AWT libraries. An important consideration when implementing RASCAL is that recommendations must be produced in a real time environment; we discuss the implications of this in section 5. Below we describe the main components of RASCAL, as shown in figure 2.

We produce personalised recommendations for each individual **Developer**. When producing a recommendation, we only consider the content of the current

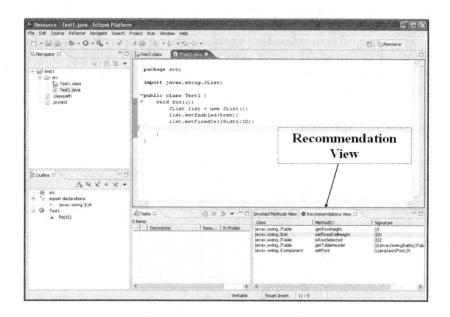

Fig. 1. Prototype implementation of RASCAL

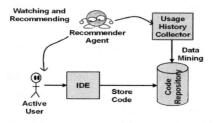

Fig. 2. RASCAL Overview

active method which this developer is coding. Recommendations are produced for and based on the current active method. For clarity in future sections, we introduce two terms:

User. The current active method which a developer is implementing.

Item. A reusable library method, ignoring signature, which is utilised by a user.

The **Code Repository** contains code from previous projects, external libraries, open-source projects etc; in our work we used the Sourceforge [18] repository. This repository will be continually updated as new classes/systems are developed. From such a repository, we can extract information about what reusable items exist and also knowledge about how these are used. The **Usage History Collector** automatically mines the code repository to extract item usage histories for all users. This will need to be done once initially for each user and subsequently when a new user is added to the repository. We extract this information using the *Bytecode Engineering Library* [19]. Item usage histories for all the users are then transformed into an item-user preference database, as detailed in section 4.1, which can be used to establish similarities between two users. Finally the **Recommender Agent** actively monitors the method that the developer is coding. The agent attempts to establish a set of neighbouring users who are similar to the active user; a set of ordered library methods is then recommended to the active user based on the neighbouring users.

4   Recommendations

In this section, we describe two information retrieval techniques; namely Vector Space Model and Latent Semantic Indexing. We explain how either of the retrieval techniques can be used by a Collaborative Filtering (CF) algorithm to produce recommendations. CF using the vector space model is commonly referred to as 'pure' CF; we will use this terminology in latter sections.

4.1   Information Retrieval

Vector Space Model. In text retrieval, the Vector Space Model (VSM) [7] is one of the most commonly used methods for representing a document as a vector of terms. A collection of documents is represented as a term-by-document matrix where the $[i, j]^{th}$ element indicates the association between the ith term and j^{th} document. This association reflects the ith term occurrence in document j. A term can represent different text units; most commonly a word. Each term can also be individually weighted allowing that term to become more or less important within a document or the entire document collection as a whole. We discuss weighting schemes below. The similarity between any two documents can be computed by determining the cosine of the angle formed by their vectors. This cosine will fall in the range [-1, 1]. A cosine of 1 indicates two documents are identical whereas -1 denotes no similarities.

In the context of our work, a document is representative of a user and a term represents an item. Table 1 displays an example item-user matrix derived using

Table 1. Non weighted Item-User matrix created using VSM

Item	User U1	User U2	User U3	User U4	User U5
JButton:getText	1	1	0	0	1
JButton:setText	2	1	0	0	0
JButton:setEnabled	1	0	1	0	1
JPanel:setLayout	0	0	3	4	0
JPanel:grabFocus	0	0	1	2	0

VSM. Given such a matrix, we can query this to find the set of users similar to user x. Firstly we need to create a query vector representative of user x. If a weighted scheme has been applied to the VSM matrix then each non-zero element in the query vector should be a weighted frequency. We can now calculate the similarity between user x and any other user by determining the cosine of the angle formed by their vectors.

Latent Semantic Indexing. Latent Semantic Indexing (LSI) is a vector space model approach to conceptual information retrieval. LSI is commonly used to overcome the synonymy and polysemy problem; it captures underlying latent semantic relationships between terms and documents. LSI achieves this by dimension reduction, selecting the most important dimensions from a term occurrence matrix, such as the matrix in table 1, using Singular Value Decomposition (SVD). In the natural language text domain, LSI has outperformed standard lexical retrieval techniques [20], classified texts [22] and been shown capable of extracting significant levels of meaning from words, sentences and documents [23].

SVD [7] is a powerful technique in matrix analysis. Once we have created a item-user m x n matrix A, as described earlier, a rank$-k$ approximation of that matrix ($k < min(m, n)$) to A, A_k is computed using SVD, as illustrated in figure 3. The SVD of the Matrix A is defined as the product of three matrices; $A = U\Sigma V^T$, where U represents the original row entries as vectors of derived orthogonal factor values, V represents the original column entities in the same

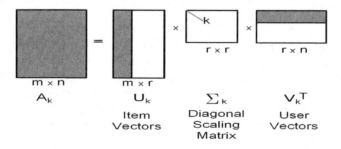

Fig. 3. Illustration of SVD. The shaded areas of U and V, as well as the diagonal line of Σ, represent A_k, the reduced dimension representation of the original item-user matrix.

way and Σ is a diagonal matrix containing scaling values such that when the three matrices are multiplied, the original matrix is reconstructed. As illustrated in figure 3, the first k columns of the U and V matrices and the first (largest) k singular values of Σ are used to construct a rank$-k$ approximation of A via $A_k = U_k \Sigma_k V_k^T$.

A_k is the $k-$dimensional approximation of the original item-user matrix. By reducing the dimensionality of this space, semantic relationships between users are revealed and much noise is thought to be eliminated. Thus care must be taken not to reconstruct A when choosing the dimensionality. The optimal dimension is an open question and is usually determined experimentally; in our domain we found 499 to be the most appropriate dimension. Like VSM, we can calculate the similarity between any two users by determining the cosine of the angle formed by their vectors.

Table 2. Original Item-User matrix with LSI SVD applied. The matrix has been reduced in dimensionality from 5 to dimension 2 ($A_2 = U_2 \Sigma_2 V_2^T$).

Item	User U1	User U2	User U3	User U4	User U5
JButton:getText	1.32	0.69	0.16	-0.11	0.53
JButton:setText	1.73	0.91	0.20	-0.16	0.69
JButton:setEnabled	1.04	0.54	0.48	0.40	0.42
JPanel:setLayout	0.01	-0.05	2.93	4.05	0.06
JPanel:grabFocus	-0.04	-0.04	1.29	1.79	0.01

In table 2 we briefly illustrate the power of the LSI SVD technique. We have constructed a 2-dimensional approximation of the original item-user matrix in table 1. Taking user $u4$ as an example, we see the original item values have changed. Items $setText$ and $getText$ have now both taken on negative values while $setEnabled$ now has a value of 0.40. This new value for $setEnabled$ can be viewed as an estimate of how many times it would be used by each of an infinite set of users who also use $setLayout$ and $grabFocus$. The negative values ensure user $u4$ will be less similar to users $u1$, $u2$ and $u5$ than may have previously been the case.

Queries are performed on the reduced dimension user vector, V_k; a smaller dimension can greatly increase query execution time. In the LSI model, queries are formed into *pseudo-documents* that specify the location of the query in the reduced document space [7]. Given a query vector q, identical to a VSM query vector, the pseudo-document, $\hat{q}$, can be represented by $\hat{q} = q^T U_k \Sigma_k^{-1}$.

Thus, the pseudo-document consists of the sum of the item vectors ($q^T U_k$) corresponding to the terms specified in the query scaled by the inverse of the singular values (Σ_k^{-1}).

Weighting. Term weighting is frequently applied in natural language processing; we investigate if such weighting is applicable to the source code domain. The most simple weighting scheme is a local weight. For non zero frequencies, this local weight is defined as tf_{ij} (frequency user i employs item j) dampened by the log function: local weight $= 1 + log(tf_{ij})$. In text documents, this reflects the fact that a term which appears in a document x times more than another term is not x times more important.

We extend this simple local weighting scheme to log-entropy weighting as recommended by [20]. Log entropy is local weighting times global weighting. Global weighting is defined as $1 - entropy$. The log-entropy item weight for item j by user i is:

$$log(1 + tf_{ij}) * \left[1 - \frac{\sum p \in I_j \left(\frac{tf_{pj}}{gf_j} * log\frac{tf_{pj}}{gf_j} \right)}{log(numUsers)} \right] \qquad (1)$$

where I_j is the set of all users who use item j, tf_{ij} is the frequency of use of item j by user i and global frequency gf_j is the total number of times item j is used in the complete user set.

4.2   Collaborative Filtering

The goal of a Collaborative Filtering (CF) algorithm is to suggest new items or predict the utility of a certain item for a particular user based on the user's previous preference and the opinions of other like-minded users [6]. CF systems are founded on the belief that users can be clustered. Users in a cluster share preferences and dislikes for particular items and are likely to agree on future items. Collaborative filtering algorithms are used in mainstream recommender systems such as *Amazon* [24]. In our work we use CF to recommend a candidate set of items to a user.

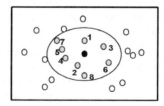

Fig. 4. Illustration of the k Nearest Neighbour formation. The similarity/distance between the target user query and all users in the item-user matrix is computed and k closest users are chosen as neighbours. $k = 8$ in this example.

Recommendation Algorithm. Recommendations are produced by examining the item-user matrix created using either VSM or LSI. Vote v_{ij} corresponds to the vote by user i for item j. The mean vote for user i is calculated as follows:

$$\overline{v}_i = \frac{1}{|I_i|} \sum_{j \in I_i} v_{i,j} \qquad (2)$$

where I_i is the set of items the user i has voted on. The predicted vote using CF for the active user a on item j, cf_{aj}, is a weighted sum of the votes of the other similar users:

$$cf_{aj} = \overline{v}_a + N \sum_{i \in kNN} sim\,(a,i)\,(v_{i,j} - \overline{v}_i) \tag{3}$$

where weight $sim(a,i)$ represents the correlation or similarity between the current user a and each user i. kNN is the set of k nearest neighbours to the current user, as illustrated in figure 4. A neighbour is a user who has a high similarity value $sim(a,i)$ with the current user. The set of neighbours is sorted in descending order of weight. For experiments we used a value of $k = 10$. N is the normalising factor such that the absolute values of the weights' sum to unity. From equation 3 we can now predict a users' vote for any item in the user-item preference database. Items are ranked based on their predicted vote and the top n items are recommended to the user. In our experiments, we use a value of $n = 7$.

We can calculate the similarity between the current user a and any user in the item-user matrix, $sim(a,i)$, by determining the cosine of the angle formed by their vectors, as detailed in [25]. If we are using LSI, we can efficiently perform vector similarity on the reduced user space, V_k.

5   Experiments

5.1   Dataset

We produced over 32,000 recommendations for 1410 Java classes taken from over 60 GUI applications mined from Sourceforge [18]. Recommendations were produced at the method level, and not the class level as in previous work [26]; in total there was 3038 methods (users) or approximately just over 2 methods per class. Further to this, each user had originally invoked on average 11 methods (items). The items which we recommended were Swing and AWT methods; in total there was 2407 items. Since we have the complete source code, we can automatically evaluate the recommendations.

For each user, several recommendations were made. For example, if a fully developed method had 10 Swing invocations, then we removed the 10th invocation from that user and a recommendation set was produced for the developer based on the preceding 9 invocations. Following this recommendation, the 9th invocation was removed from that user and a new recommendation set was formed based on the preceding 8 invocations. This process was continued until just 1 invocation remained. Each recommendation set contained a maximum of 7 items.

5.2   Evaluation

Precision and Recall are the most popular metrics for evaluating information retrieval systems. Precision is defined as the ratio of relevant recommended items to the total number of items recommended; $P = n_{rs}/n_s$, where n_{rs} is the number of relevant items selected and n_s is the number of items selected. This represents the probability that a selected item is relevant. An item is deemed relevant if it is used by the user for whom the recommendation is being sought. Recall is defined as the ratio of relevant items selected to the total number of relevant items; $R = n_{rs}/n_r$, where n_{rs} is the number of relevant items selected and n_r is the number of relevant items. This represents the probability that a relevant item will be selected. Several approaches have been taken to combine precision and recall into a single metric. The $F1$ measure, initially introduced by van Rijsbergen [27], combines both with an equal weight in the following form: $F_1 = 2PR/(P+R)$.

It is particulary important that RASCAL recommends items in a relevant order i.e. the invocation order. We will evaluate this using a simple binary Next Recommended (NR) metric; $NR = 1$ if we successfully predict or recommend the next method a developer will use, otherwise $NR = 0$.

5.3   Results

All results are displayed as a percentage value. A baseline result is included; these were produced by recommending the top 5 most commonly invoked items at each recommendation stage. We display the $F1$ metric combined with the NR metric for several different dimensions k in figure 5(a). This is the average $F1$ and NR result for various stages of recommendation, i.e. when $x\%$ of items are known. Without applying LSI SVD, the original dimension of the user-item matrix was 2407. We find that applying relatively low dimensions can produce

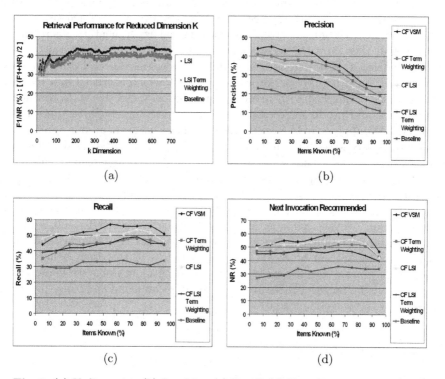

Fig. 5. (a) K dimension (b) Precision (c) Recall (d) Next Recommended (NR)

reasonable recommendations. The optimal value for k, based on our dataset, is 499; this is the value used in the below experiments. We notice from figure 5(a) that using term weighting has a negative effect on recommendations.

Figure 5(b) displays average Precision for four experiments; collaborative filtering with and without term weighting using either LSI or VSM. The pure VSM CF algorithm performs best, producing better results than the LSI model. Excluding, term weighting, the average CF VSM result is 36% compared with just 30% when using LSI. Precision, for all techniques, decreases as more items are known; we discuss this in the following section. Both LSI and VSM produce significantly better precision values than our baseline technique. We present Recall in figure 5(c). Like precision, the CF VSM produces the best retrieval, averaging at 52%. The result is followed closely by LSI where the average recall value is 50%. Term Weighting performs poorly. Figure 5(d) displays Next Recommended (NR). Again, the CF VSM produces the best retrieval, averaging at 55%. LSI performs well here with an average NR value of 52%.

5.4 Discussion

We make several interesting observations from these experiments. Firstly we note that applying the log-entropy term weighting scheme to the item-user matrix has a consistent negative effect on the recommendation results. This suggests that items which are used by many users are as important as items which are used by only a small number of users. To verify this, manual experimentation is required. We also find that pure CF recommendations consistently outperform CF LSI recommendations. However, it is important to recognise several other benefits of using LSI; most notably performance efficiency which is crucial in a realtime recommender. Using LSI with reduced dimension $k = 499$, RASCAL initialises twice as fast and produces recommendations approximately three times faster than the VSM approach. This will be important as we scale up our application.

Generally, we notice two different trends in precision and recall. Precision tends to decrease as we know more information about a user while recall tends to increase. This result perhaps requires clarification. Consider a user who uses in total 10 items. When we make a recommendation for that user when they have only used 1 item, there is a set of 9 possible items to recall. The chances of recalling all relevant items is quite low and hence the recall result is low in earlier recommendations. However, when this user has used 9 items and there is only 1 possible item to recall, then the chances of this item being in the recommendation set is quite high. In contrast, the more items we know about the current user, the fewer there are to correctly recommend and hence precision decreases in latter recommendations.

6   Conclusions

Just as people can be clustered in terms of their preferences for various items, Java methods may also be clustered based on the methods they invoke. To clusters methods, we investigated and compared two information retrieval techniques, namely the vector space model and latent semantic indexing and found the VSM most effective. Unlike many retrieval schemes, we found that preprocessing or weighting of items negatively impacted retrieval. We also noted some of the limitations with using VSM such as scalability and performance times, and we explained how LSI can overcome these challenges.

Further work is needed to enhance RASCAL. Using LSI, we will investigate significantly increasing the size of the library; we would expect this to improve precision and recall whilst having a small impact on performance times. We will also investigate the use of probability models to produce recommendations. RASCAL offers unsolicited advice and we must be sensitive to this in our delivery of recommendations. We will extend our Eclipse plugin, complementing and extending the existing context-sensitive list of methods recommended by the Eclipse IDE. Our overall goal is to develop a recommender that seamlessly integrates with the Eclipse IDE but more importantly allows reuse to become a natural and convenient part of a developers daily routine.

Recommender systems are a powerful technology that can cheaply extract knowledge for a software company from its code repositories and then exploit this knowledge in future developments. We have demonstrated that RASCAL offers real promise for allowing developers discover and easily access reusable library components. When little information is known about the user we can nevertheless make reasonably good recommendations and it is our belief that future work will strengthen both recommendation accuracy and performance.

References

1. Mohagheghi, P., et al.: An empirical study of software reuse vs. defect-density and stability. In: ICSE '04: Proceedings of the 26th International Conference on Software Engineering, Washington, DC, USA, (IEEE Computer Society) 282–292
2. Yongbeom, K., Stohr, E.: Software reuse: Survey and research directions. Management Information Systems 14(4) (1998) 113–147
3. Ye, Y., Fischer, G.: Reuse-conducive development environments. International Journal of Automated Software Engineering 12 (2005) 199–235
4. Poulin, J.: Reuse: Been there done that. Communications of the ACM 42(5) (1999)
5. Inoue, K., et al.: Component rank: relative significance rank for software component search. In: ICSE '03: Proceedings of the 25th International Conference on Software Engineering, Washington, DC, USA, IEEE Computer Society (2003) 14–24
6. Sarwar, B.M., Karypis, G., Konstan, J.A., Reidl, J.: Item-based collaborative filtering recommendation algorithms. In: World Wide Web. (2001) 285–295
7. Letsche, T.A., Berry, M.W.: Large-scale information retrieval with latent semantic indexing. Inf. Sci. 100(1-4) (1997) 105–137
8. Landauer, T., Foltz, P., Laham, D.: An introduction to latent semantic analysis. Discourse Processes 25 (1998) 259–284
9. Deerwester, S., et al.: Indexing by latent semantic analysis. Journal of the American Society for Information Science 41 (1990) 391–407
10. Prieto-Diaz, R., Freeman, P.: Classifying software for reuse. IEEE Software 4(1) (1987) 6–16

11. Mili, A., Mili, R., Mittermeir, R.T.: A survey of software reuse libraries. Annals of Software Engineering **5** (1998) 349–414
12. Sugumaran, V., Storey, V.C.: A semantic-based approach to component retrieval. SIGMIS Database **34**(3) (2003) 8–24
13. Girardi, M., Ibrahim, B.: Using english to retrieve software. Journals of Systems and Software **30**(3) (1995) 249–270
14. Drummond, C.G., Ionescu, D., Holte, R.C.: A learning agent that assists the browsing of software libraries. IEEE Trans. Softw. Eng. **26**(12) (2000) 1179–1196
15. Sarwar, B.M., et al.: Application of dimensionality reduction in recommender systems–a case study. In: Proceedings of ACM WebKDD Workshop. (2000)
16. Marcus, A., Maletic, J.I.: Recovering documentation-to-source-code traceability links using latent semantic indexing. In: ICSE '03: Proceedings of the 25th International Conference on Software Engineering, Washington, DC, USA, IEEE Computer Society (2003) 125–135
17. Marcus, A., Maletic, J.I.: Identification of high-level concept clones in source code. In: ASE '01: Proceedings of the 16th IEEE International Conference on Automated Software Engineering, Washington, DC, USA, IEEE Computer Society (2001) 107
18. Ebert, J.: Storm - a user story tool. http://xpstorm.sourceforge.net. (2002)
19. Apache: Apache software foundation - bytecode engineering library (2002-2003). http://jakarta.apache.org/bcel/index.html. (2003)
20. Dumais, S.: Improving the retrieval of information from external sources. Behavior Research Methods, Instruments and Computers **23**(2) (1991) 229–236
21. Dumais, S.: Latent semantic indexing (lsi) and trec-2. The Second Text REtrieval Conference (TREC2), National Institute of Standards and Technology Special Publication 500-215. (1994) 105-116
22. Zelikovitz, S., Hirsh, H.: Using lsi for text classification in the presence of background text. In: CIKM '01: Proceedings of the tenth international conference on Information and knowledge management, New York, ACM Press (2001) 113–118
23. Berry, M.: Large scale singular value computations. Int. Journal of Supercomputer Applications **6** (1992) 13–49
24. Bezos, J.: Amazon.com plc. seattle, wa 98108-1226, usa www.amazon.com. (2004)
25. Breese, J.S., Heckerman, D., Kadie, C.: Empirical analysis of predictive algorithms for collaborative filtering. In: Proceedings of the Fourteenth Annual Conference on Uncertainty in Artificial Intelligence. (1998) 43–52
26. McCarey, F., Cinnéide, M.O., Kushmerick, N.: Knowledge reuse for software reuse. In: Proceedings of the 17th International Conference on Software Engineering and Knowledge Engineering. (2005)
27. van Rijsbergen, C.: Information Retrieval. Butterworths, London (1979)

Improving Extensibility of Object-Oriented Frameworks with Aspect-Oriented Programming

Uirá Kulesza[1], Vander Alves[2], Alessandro Garcia[3], Carlos J.P. de Lucena[1], and Paulo Borba[2]

[1] PUC-Rio, Computer Science Department, Rio de Janeiro - Brazil
{uira, lucena}@inf.puc-rio.br
[2] Informatics Center, Federal University of Pernambuco, Recife - Brazil
{vra, phmb}@cin.ufpe.br
[3] Lancaster University, Computing Department, Lancaster - United Kingdom
garciaa@comp.lancs.ac.uk

Abstract. Object-oriented frameworks are nowadays a common and useful technology used in the implementation of software system families. Despite their benefits, over the last years many researchers have described the inadequacy of object-oriented mechanisms to address the modularization and composition of many framework features, thus reducing the extent to which a framework can be extended. The crosscutting nature of many framework features is identified as one of the main causes of these problems. In this paper, we analyze how aspect-oriented programming can help to improve the design, implementation, and extension of object-oriented frameworks. We propose the concept of Extension Join Points (EJPs) as a way of designing and documenting existing crosscutting extension points. EJPs improve framework extensibility, including superior composability of the framework core functionality with other modules or frameworks. Four case studies of frameworks from diverse domains are presented to illustrate our proposal. This paper also discusses lessons learned on the application of our approach to the development and extension of these frameworks.

1 Introduction

Framework technology plays nowadays a central role in the development of software product lines. Object-oriented (OO) frameworks enable systematic reuse-in-the-large by modularizing and composing one or more recurring features of a given domain, and by offering predictable extension options to the target applications. Framework extension is achieved in different ways, ranging from the selection of optional and alternative features to its integration with other complementary components and frameworks. However, some researchers [2, 18, 19] have recently described the inadequacy of OO mechanisms to address the modularization and composition of many framework crosscutting features, thus reducing the framework variability and integrability. This crosscutting phenomenon manifests itself in several manners: both in the core and variable parts of a framework, and also in the features being integrated as the system evolves.

M. Morisio (Ed.): ICSR 2006, LNCS 4039, pp. 231–245, 2006.

Hence all framework benefits are hindered if there is no systematic approach to support the encapsulation and extension of crosscutting framework features through their development and instantiation processes. With the emergence of aspect-oriented programming (AOP) [12], it is important to investigate the suitability of AOP mechanisms to promote enhanced variability and integrability of OO frameworks. AOP supports the encapsulation of crosscutting features into new modular units – the *aspects* – and their composition through the notion of *join points*. Recent work [1, 9, 14, 16] has started to explore the use of aspects to improve the isolation of crosscutting features encountered in the design of frameworks and product lines. Other authors have also examined the influence of AOP on different software integrability scenarios, such as COTS [17] and design patterns [3, 11]. However, there is no methodological foundation to support framework designers while using aspect-oriented mechanisms to improve the variability and integrability of their frameworks in the presence of crosscutting features.

This work briefly revisits well-known problems relative to OO framework modularity (Section 2). We then perform a systematic analysis of how AOP can help to address them, and enhance the framework implementation and extensibility. In particular, we present a systematic approach, based on the concept of Extension Join Points (EJPs), as a unified way of designing and documenting existing crosscutting extension points (Section 3). EJPs provide new means for extending framework core functionality, introducing optional and alternative crosscutting features, and integrating the framework elements with other components and frameworks. We further present a categorization of framework aspects that support the encapsulation of distinct types of crosscutting features. We describe four case studies of frameworks from different domains to illustrate the applicability of our proposal (Section 4). Lessons learned on the design and implementation of these frameworks are also discussed (Section 5).

2 Modularization Problems in OO Frameworks

We now briefly describe three major problems, previously discussed by other authors, showing how they negatively affect framework extensibility from different perspectives. We also illustrate representative symptoms of these problems in the design of the JUnit framework, which is a classical example in the framework literature.

Complexity of Object Collaboration. An OO framework defines a set of abstract and concrete reusable classes implementing a software family architecture. Complex collaborations between these classes must be implemented. These collaborations represent the common functionalities shared by several applications in the framework domain. Each framework class in general has to play different roles, which means that they need to collaborate with different classes in order to implement their different responsibilities [5, 22]. Therefore, understanding and maintaining the framework classes become a difficult task. Moreover, further introductions of framework variations and compositions with other software modules are hindered, as each class role cannot be treated as a separate framework feature as the framework evolves.

In the JUnit framework, for example, the primary purpose of the main classes is to execute a set of test suites and cases, and return a testing report. However, they have to play an additional role: a different feature related to the tracking of the execution of test cases and suites by those classes is superimposed in their code in order to notify GUI classes about the execution state (started, failed, ok, finished) of test cases.

Riehle et al [22] analyze the problems of complex object collaborations and their impact on framework design and integration. They show how the complexity of an OO framework increases when its internal classes play different roles. The authors, however, propose the use of role modelling [22], which only partially addresses the plastering of multiple roles into classes as it is focused on the design level.

Inability to Modularize Framework Optional Features. Batory et al [2] discuss the difficulties of the framework technique to modularize optional features. An optional feature is a framework functionality that is not used in every framework instance. They illustrate some alternatives developers typically adopt to deal with this problem, such as: (i) to implement the optional feature in the code of concrete classes during the framework instantiation process; and (ii) to create two different frameworks, one addressing the optional feature and the other one without it. Accordingly, many framework modules need to be replicated just for the sake of exposing optional features. To summarize, the authors argue that frameworks are usually "overfeatured" [5], which means that several non-general functionalities can inevitably be part of the framework.

An analysis of available frameworks (such as JUnit and JHotDraw) makes it evident that the most common practice adopted in the implementation of framework optional features is the use of inheritance mechanisms to define additional behavior in the framework classes. These classes represent an existing framework feature to be extended. In the JUnit framework, for example, inheritance relationships are used to define a specific kind of test case as well as additional extensions to test cases and suites.

Crosscutting Feature Compositions in Frameworks Integration. Mattsson et al [18, 19] have analyzed the problems and causes related to the integration of OO frameworks. For each problem presented, they have also proposed several OO solutions. A combination of two frameworks, as described by the authors, can also be seen as the composition of a new set of features (represented as a framework) in the structure of another framework. As an example, suppose we need to extend the JUnit framework to send specific failures that occur to software developers. A specific test failure report could be send by e-mail to different software developers, every time a specific and critical failure happens. Imagine we have available an e-mail framework to support our implementation. The problem here is how we could implement this functionality in the JUnit framework. It involves the integration of the JUnit and e-mail frameworks. This composition could be characterized as crosscutting since we are interested to send a failure report by e-mail during the execution of the tests.

We have analyzed [16] the framework integration solutions presented by Mattson et al [18, 19]. Many of their OO solutions are invasive and bring several difficulties to the implementation, understanding and maintenance of the framework composition code. Our analysis was based on a case study with feature compositions involving four OO frameworks of varying complexity and addressing concerns from distinct horizontal and vertical domains [6]. The analysis has showed that from the 9 solutions described by those authors, 6 solutions have poor modularity and a crosscutting nature, and require invasive internal changes in the frameworks code.

3 Improving Framework Extensibility with Aspects

This section presents our approach to design and implement OO frameworks with aspects. Our approach deals with the framework modularization problems presented previously (Section 2.1) by using AOP and the notion of extension join points (EJPs). EJPs also support the disciplined specification of additional opportunities for framework extensions. Sections 3.1 – 3.3 present the proposed approach by respectively describing the central concept of EJPs, describing different uses of aspects to improve framework extensibility, and presenting the achieved benefits. Section 3.4 presents an example of the approach applied to the JUnit framework.

3.1 Extension Join Points

The extension points or hot-spots of an OO framework are typically implemented as abstract classes or interfaces [7]. They allow extending the common collaboration behavior provided by the framework by providing specific implementations for their abstract methods. One of the difficult problems of framework development is that it requires dealing with many common and variable features pertaining to a domain. We can thus notice an increase on framework complexity and on many modularization and composition problems, such as those presented in Section 2.

In our approach, an OO framework specifies and implements not only its common and variable behavior using OO classes, but it also exposes a set of *extension join points* (EJPs) which can be used to also extend its functionality. The idea of EJPs is inspired by Sullivan et al's work [24, 10] on specification of crosscutting interfaces (XPIs). Similar to XPIs, EJPs establish a contract between the framework classes and a set of aspects extending the framework functionality. However, unlike XPIs, EJPs are adopted as a means to increase the framework variability and integrability. Thus, we propose to use the XPI concept in the context of framework development. EJPs can be used to three different purposes:

(i) to expose a set of framework events that can be used to notify or to facilitate a crosscutting integration with other software elements (such as, frameworks or components);
(ii) to offer predefined execution points spread and tangled in the framework into which the implementation of optional features can be included;
(iii) to expose a set of join points in the framework classes that can have different implementations of a crosscutting variable functionality.

In this context, EJPs document crosscutting extension points for software developers that are going to instantiate and evolve the framework. They can also be viewed as a set of constraints imposed on the whole space of available join points in the framework design, thereby promoting safe extension and reuse. A key characteristic of EJPs is that framework developers and users do not need to learn totally new abstractions to use them, as they can mostly be implemented using the mechanisms of AOP languages (Section 5.1).

3.2 Framework Core and Extension Aspects

Our approach promotes framework development as a composition of a core structure and a set of extensions. A framework extension can be: (i) the implementation of optional or alternative framework features; or (ii) the integration with an additional component or framework. The composition between the framework core and the framework extensions is realized by different types of aspects. Each aspect defines a crosscutting composition with the framework by means of its exposed EJPs. Next, we describe the main elements of our approach:

(i) *framework core* – implements the mandatory functionality of a software family. Similar to a traditional OO framework, this core structure contains the frozen-spots that represent the common features of the software family and hot-spot classes that represent non-crosscutting variabilities from the domain addressed;

(ii) *aspects in the core* – implement and modularize existing crosscutting concerns or roles in the framework core. They represent the traditional use of AOP to simplify the understanding and evolution of the framework core;

(iii) *variability aspects* – implement optional or alternative features existing in the framework core. These elements extend the framework EJPs with any additional crosscutting behavior;

(iv) *integration aspects* – define crosscutting compositions between the framework core and other existing extensions, such as an API or an OO framework. These elements also rely on the EJPs specification to define their implementation.

Figure 1 shows the design of an OO framework with aspects following our approach. As we can see, both variability and integration aspects can only act in the EJPs provided by the framework and they must respect all the constraints defined by them. This brings systematization to the framework extension and composition with other artifacts.

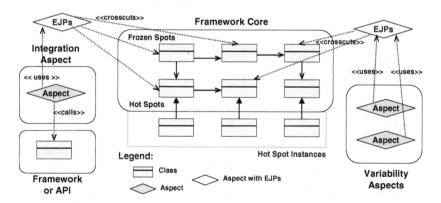

Fig. 1. Elements of our Framework Development Approach

3.3 Benefits

Table 1 describes the benefits brought by each type of aspect in our framework development approach. It also indicates how the core, variability, and integration aspects address each of the modularization problems in framework development and evolution discussed in Section 2. As pointed out in the table, the use of internal framework aspects also has a positive impact on the framework variability and integrability. They facilitate the specification of EJPs because core aspects promote modularization of the internal class roles. Therefore, they offer additional join points to be exploited in extension scenarios.

Table 1. Framework Development Approach Elements

Approach Element	Benefits	Modularization Problem Addressed
Aspects in the Core	- Simplify the understanding and evolution of the framework core • Modularize existing crosscutting concerns or roles in the framework core. - Facilitate the design of EJPs	Crosscutting Roles and Concerns
Extension Join Points	- Systematize the framework extension and composition by promoting safe framework reuse • Enable the composition between framework core and extensions. • Encapsulate the framework and exposes only proper join points.	Tight Coupling between Core and Extensions
Variability Aspects	- Facilitate the framework reuse and extension. • Modularize optional and alternative framework features. • Make it possible to plug and unplug optional or alternative features.	Optional or Alternative Features
Integration Aspects	- Facilitate the framework reuse and composition. • Modularize the framework composition with other extensions. • Make it possible to plug and unplug crosscutting framework composition.	Crosscutting Framework Compositions

3.4 JUnit Example

This section illustrates the use of the proposed approach in the context of the JUnit framework. Although JUnit presents a well-modularized architecture, we have found some modularization problems [15] hindering its future extension/evolution. In the context of other complex and large-scale frameworks, these problems can cause architecture erosion after a while. Due to space limitation, we have briefly mentioned JUnit problems in Section 2.

The main purpose of the JUnit framework is to allow the design, implementation and execution of a set of test suites and cases for any Java application. It is especially useful to implement unit tests, but it can also be used to implement integration tests between modules. The JUnit framework implementation is composed of the following components:

(i) **Tester**: defines the framework classes responsible for specifying the basic behavior to execute test cases and suites. The main hot-spot classes available in this component are `TestCase` and `TestSuite`. The framework users extend these classes in order to create specific test cases to their applications;

(ii) **Runner**: this component is responsible for offering an interface to start and track the execution of test cases and suites. JUnit provides three alternative implementations of test runners: a command-line based user interface (UI), an AWT based UI, and a Java Swing based UI;

(iii) **Extensions**: responsible for defining functionality extending the basic behavior of the JUnit framework. Examples of available extensions include: a test suite to execute tests in separate threads, a test decorator to run tests repeatedly, and a test setup class that allows specifying initial and final configuration of specific tests.

Following our approach, in the JUnit OO framework we can consider the classes of the Runner and Tester components as the *framework core* (Figure 2). They provide the main functionalities needed to execute the test cases and suites, as follows: (i) the definition of a test case or suite to be executed; (ii) the execution of a selected test case or suite; and (ii) the collection and visual presentation of the test results. The JUnit core offers three abstract classes (`TestCase`, `TestSuite` and `BaseTestRunner`) representing traditional extension points of the framework.

The JUnit framework core must expose its extension join points in order to allow the composition of crosscutting extensions into its basic functionality. Figure 2 presents the `TestExecutionEvents` aspect, which exposes a set of EJPs of the JUnit framework. It exposes the following join points: (i) test case execution; (ii) test suite execution; and (iii) initialization of test runners. We have chosen these join points because they represent relevant events in the test execution functionality of the JUnit core that can be of interest to framework extensions.

Different extensions can be implemented to add new functionality into the JUnit EJPs. We can assume that the tracking of the test case execution by the Runner component is not initially addressed by the framework core. It is necessary to codify an *aspect in the core* working as an observer. Since this is an aspect in the core, it can be codified to intercept directly framework classes (such as presented in Figure 2) or it could reuse the join points exposed by the `TestExecutionEvents` aspect mentioned above and notify the instance of the Runner executing about the current state of the test case (initiated, finalized, failed). Figure 2 shows three aspects (`Observer-TestExecution`, `AWTUIObserver`, `TextUIObserver`) addressing this functionality considering different Runner classes available.

The implementation of the functionality of the original JUnit Extension component can also benefit from its EJP. Different variability aspects, as presented in Figure 2, can be codified to add the testing extensions into the JUnit EJPs, such as: (i) to run test cases or test suites repeatedly (RepeatAllTest aspect); (ii) to execute them in separate threads (ActiveTestSuite aspect); and (iii) to introduce some additional behavior before or after the test case or suite (TestCaseDecorator and TestSuite-Decorator aspects). In this case, we could implement easily these aspects by reusing the join points exposed in the aspect TestExecutionEvents. It is also possible to codify aspects to affect just specific test cases or suites defined to test an application. Finally, the JUnit EJPs can also be used to compose it with other OO frameworks. Figure 2 shows, for example, the MailNotification integration aspect responsible for monitoring the test execution, building specific test reports and sending them by e-mail to specific developers. An e-mail framework could be composed with the JUnit framework to provide that functionality by means of an integration aspect.

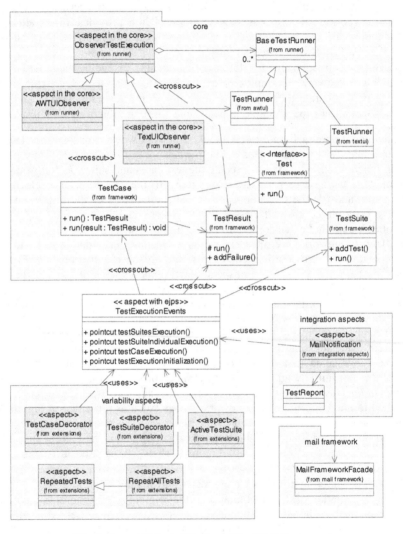

Fig. 2. Aspect-Oriented Design of the JUnit Framework

4   Case Studies

Our approach has emerged from our experience in different domains, through a process of continuous interaction and refinement between case studies and the approach itself. In this context, the approach was employed in the development of frameworks in the following domains: (i) J2ME games [1]; (ii) multi-agent systems (MASs) [9, 14]; and (iii) measurement support for product quality control [16]. Table 2

Table 2. Case Studies Overview

Domain	Framework Core	EJPs	Variability and Integration Aspects
J2ME Games	*Game engine*, a state machine defining the game core structure and workflow, including: (i) handling of user interaction and elapsed time: (ii) game actors state update; (iii) game actors rendering; (iv) game screen management.	- Image initialization and usage; - Drawing of specific images; - Game startup and changing screens.	Variability and Integration aspects were defined to implement: (i) *croma* optional feature; (ii) alternative drawing feature; (iii) optional image loading optimization feature.
MASs	Our AspectT agent framework implements the core internal structures and behaviors of autonomous software agents, including: (i) the knowledge elements – beliefs, actions, plans, goals; (ii) the management of goals and plan execution; (iii) the thread scheduling; (iv) adaptation of agent knowledge.	- Reception and sending of messages; - Reception of external stimulus; - Initialization of goals; - Exceptions in plan executions; - Initialization and finalization of plan/action executions.	Integration aspects were defined to integrate the framework core with: (i) 2 alternative inter-agent communication platforms; (ii) 2 alternative code mobility platforms; Variability aspects were included to enhance the agent behavior with: (i) optional learning capabilities; (ii) different roles and collaboration protocols.
Measurement for Quality Control	The Measurement Framework defines a process for quality control composed of the following steps: (i) product data collection phase; (ii) data analysis and product categorization phase; (iii) actuation phase – actions are performed over the products according to their categorization.	- Activation of triggers (event of product processing initialization); - Activation of sensors (event of product data collection); - Activation of actuators (event of product processing finalization).	Different integration aspects were defined to compose the measurement framework with other ones, as follows: (i) a GUI framework presenting visually information about the measurement process; (ii) a Statistical framework calculating statistical data about the measurement process; and (iii) a Persistence frame-work storing infor-mation about the items processed and the statis-tical data.

summarizes the framework core, EJPs, variability and integration aspects of the three case studies. Due to space limitation, in this section we describe our experience only in the domain of J2ME Games. For a complete description of the implementation of EJPs and framework extensions for these case studies, please refer to [15].

4.1 J2ME Games

J2ME games are mainstream mobile applications of considerable complexity [1]. Their overall structure and behavior are defined by a framework known in this domain as the *game engine*. Essentially, this is a state machine whose state change is driven by elapsed time and user input through the device keypad. State changes affect the state of various drawing objects (*game actors*) and how they interact. Then, these objects are drawn again after such state changes. Typical hot-spots of this framework include some abstract classes defining basic drawing capability for game actors.

The game engine must also expose its EJPs in order to allow the composition of crosscutting extensions in its basic functionality. Some interesting EJPs are the following: (i) how images are initialized and used; (ii) drawing of specific images; (iii) game startup and changing screens. We have chosen these EJPs because they represent relevant events that can be of interest when extending the game engine core workflow.

Based on these EJPs, we provide implementations for optional and alternative features. For example, EJP (i) can be composed with a *variability aspect* to implement the *croma* optional feature (decorative images of the game screen, for example clouds rolling in the background). This feature is optional in the product line comprising a number of devices, since some are resource-constrained and thus this feature should not be selected for such devices. Accordingly, in the game assets, such feature amounts to images files in the resource directory; in the code, they are declared, and loaded into fields, which are updated in their state, and then drawn, this comprising a number of different code blocks in different classes. Therefore, the implementation of this optional feature is crosscutting. By exposing this crosscutting nature within EJPs and implementing the feature within a variability aspect, we provide an appropriate way to document this crosscutting in design and to implement it modularly.

As another example, EJP (ii) can be composed with integration aspects to implement the alternative features for drawing some images. Specific images may be drawn at various locations and, under certain circumstances, may be transformed (rotated, flipped), which may be accomplished by using fresh new images or by transforming the original ones by calling device proprietary drawing API. By exposing these EJPs and composing them with integration aspects, we provide modular implementation for the interaction between the core game and the device-specific API.

Lastly, EJP (iii) can be composed with variability aspects to implement an optional optimization feature: images are loaded on demand when changing to the next screen. This is also a policy for resource-constrained devices; other devices just load all images at once during game startup. By exposing these EJPs, we can explicitly show where the optional optimization might be composed.

5   Discussion and Lessons Learned

This section provides some discussion and some lessons learned based on our experience on applying our proposed approach (Section 3) to several frameworks [1, 3, 9, 14, 15, 16], such as those ones described in Section 4.

5.1   EJPs Documentation

An important issue to consider when developing the framework EJPs is how to document them. The way they are documented can help developers to implement more easily their framework extensions. Different ways of documentations can be used which complement each other. We advocate the use of a combination of programming language, textual and visual documentation to make EJPs explicit.

The XPI proposed approach presents the documentation of exposed join points of an application using AspectJ [13] source code directly [10] or a textual representation of elements composing the XPI [24]. The documentation based on AspectJ source-code defines aspects declaring public pointcuts that expose the join points of an application. Many invariants that must be respected by the extensions can also be codified in AspectJ to guarantee their automatic verification [10]. This way of documentation for the EJPs is very useful because developers that are interested in extending the framework can directly reuse those public pointcuts. Besides, the syntactic specification of the invariants also helps to control inappropriate interactions between the framework and extensions in the EJPs. In the JUnit example in Section 3.4, the `TextExecutionEvents` aspect represents the syntactic specification of the framework EJPs specifying a set of public pointcuts related to the testing execution in the framework core. The documentation of EJPs based on source code can be complemented with textual based representation. Sullivan et al [24] present a XPI textual representation which can also be used to document our EJPs.

Although Sullivan et al [10, 24] XPI proposal can be useful to document the EJPs, new properties must also be considered in their documentation. A framework crosscutting extension can be codified to affect only join points of specific hot-spot instances. In the JUnit framework, for example, only specific test cases or test suites of a framework instance can be considered to be extended. In order to address these situations, we also need to document specific join points that will be completely available only after the framework instantiation. The pointcuts specifying these join points need be customized with the name of framework instance classes. Thus, it is necessary to distinguish between EJPs allowing changes to the framework internal classes and those ones allowing direct extensions of concrete implementations of hot-spots in a framework instance. The source code based documentation, for instance, can present examples of how the pointcuts that affect directly hot-spot classes can be adapted to affect only specific hot-spot instances.

Many OO framework documentation techniques (such as, cookbook approaches) emphasize the use of examples to show how to instantiate the framework extension points. In the case of EJPs, we believe it is also fundamental to present examples in how they can be used to compose any additional functionality in the framework. First, because AOP has not became a widely adopted technology yet. Second, because crosscutting composition is supposed to be more difficult to understand than composition based on inheritance. Section 5.2 explores the documentation of examples of framework crosscutting extensions using implementations based on traditional design patterns. Finally, the documentation of EJPs could also offer any visual representation to make them more explicit. Currently, we are analyzing if it is possible to use aSideML crosscutting interfaces [4] to offer a UML-based notation to represent the EJPs.

5.2 Implementation of Variability and Integration Aspects

In our approach, all framework crosscutting extensions are attached to the framework core using integration and variability aspects. Each aspect introduces a crosscutting behavior in a specific set of EJPs. The aspects play a specific role related to the way they extend the framework. They can, for example, play the role of observers of internal framework events to notify any external OO extension. They can mediate the communication between the framework classes and other OO extensions on particular EJPs. They can also decorate EJPs with new and optional implementation of features. Thus, many aspects can play the role of traditional design patterns [8] with the aim of extending the framework core.

Hanneman & Kiczales [11] have demonstrated how the implementation of many design patterns can be well modularized using aspects. The implementation of many integration and variability aspects can follow the Hanneman & Kiczales' guidelines based on the played role by the framework extension being composed. In the JUnit example showed in Figure 2, the variability aspects decorate the execution of test suites and test cases with new optional features, whereas the `MailNotification` integration aspect mediates the communication between the framework testing elements and a mail framework. Examples of aspect implementations based on design patterns can work as an effective documentation of the available ways to extend the EJPs.

Other issues relative to the implementation of variability and integration aspects deserve attention but are not explored in this paper due to space limitation, such as: (i) the composition of aspects on the same EJPs – since different aspects can add new functionality on the same EJPs, it is necessary to determine if there is any execution order of them or any conflict on their composition on the same points; and (ii) the modularization of the common and specific code of aspects [16] – also a clear separation between the extensions affecting directly the framework and those affecting only specific framework instances could be done.

5.3 Finding EJPs

One of the main difficulties in the development of OO frameworks is to find their flexible points or hot-spots. Domain analysis methods [6] and experience on the development of applications in the same domain are techniques used to find commonalities and variabilities of a framework. EJPs can also be considered framework hot-spots. They represent flexible points in the execution of specific framework scenarios that can have a crosscutting extension inserted. EJPs are modeled as events or transition states occurring during the execution of the framework functionalities. Thus, these events or transitions states are dependent on the domain and functionalities being addressed by the framework. Table 2 shows a set of EJP examples derived from our case studies in different domains.

While some heuristics to find EJPs such as the identification of relevant events and transition states in the framework functionalities can help, we believe that current domain analysis methods and techniques need to be extended to support the modeling of crosscutting relations between features in early development stages. This can anticipate the modeling of EJPs. An EJP could be modeled as the integration point of the crosscutting relationship between two features [15].

6 Related Work

Our concept of EJPs is inspired by Sullivan et al's work [24] on specification of crosscutting interfaces (XPIs). XPIs abstract crosscutting behavior, isolating aspect design from base code design and vice-versa. Continuing this work, Griswold et al show how to represent XPIs as syntactic constructs [10]. EJPs play a similar role to XPIs, but specifically in the context of framework development, by exposing a set of framework events for notification and crosscutting composition, and by offering predefined execution points for the implementation of optional and alternative features.

Feature oriented approaches (FOAs) have been proposed [23] to deal with the encapsulation of program features that can be used to extend the functionality of existing base program. Batory et al [2] argue the advantages that feature-oriented approaches have over OO frameworks to design and implement product-lines. Mezini and Ostermann [20] have identified that FOAs are only capable of modularizing hierarchical features, providing no support for the specification of crosscutting features. These researchers propose CaesarJ [21], an AO language that combines ideas from both AspectJ and FOAs, to provide a better support to manage variability in product-lines. The work of those authors has a direct relation to our work, since we believe that the design of product-line architectures may benefit from the composition and extension of different frameworks using integration and variability aspects.

In the middleware domain, Zhang and Jacobsen [25] propose the Horizontal Decomposition method (HD), a set of principles guiding the definition of functionally coherent core architecture and customizations of it. The core is customized with aspects implementing orthogonal functionality. Unlike our approach, which uses EJPs to achieve bi-directional decoupling of the core from its extensions in the framework context, HD has a principle explicitly embracing obliviousness, whereby the core should be completely unaware on the aspects.

7 Conclusions

In this paper we presented an approach for the design and implementation of traditional OO frameworks with aspects. Our approach addresses the modular implementation of framework optional features and enables framework crosscutting composition with other OO extensions. The exposition of only specific framework join points brings systematization to the process of extension and composition of the framework. We have presented some case studies that demonstrate the benefits brought by the approach. Furthermore, some initial guidelines to the use and adoption of the approach were discussed. As a future work, we plan to refactor other existing object-oriented frameworks to validate quantitatively the benefits of our approach.

Acknowledgements. We would like to thank the members of Software Productivity Group at Federal University of Pernambuco for valuable suggestions for improving this paper. This research was partially sponsored by FAPERJ (grant No. E-26/151.493/2005), CNPq (grants No. 552068/2002-0, 481575/2004-9 and 141247/2003-7), MCT/FINEP/CT-INFO (grant No. 01/2005 0105089400), and European Commission Grant IST-2-004349: European Network of Excellence on AOSD (AOSDEurope).

References

[1] V. Alves, P. Matos, L. Cole, P. Borba, G. Ramalho. "Extracting and Evolving Mobile Games Product Lines". Proceedings of SPLC'05, LNCS 3714, pp. 70-81, September 2005.

[2] D. Batory, Rich Cardone, and Y. Smaragdakis, Object-Oriented Frameworks and Product-Lines. 1st Software Product-Line Conference (SPLC), pp. 227-248, Denver, August 1999.

[3] N. Cacho, et al. Composing Design Patterns: A Scalability Study of Aspect-Oriented Programming. Proceedings of AOSD'06, Bonn, Germany, 2006.

[4] C. Chavez, A. Garcia, U. Kulesza, C. Sant'Anna, C. Lucena. Taming Heterogeneous Aspects with Crosscutting Interfaces. Journal of the Brazilian Computer Society, 2006 (to appear).

[5] W. Codenie, et al. "From Custom Applications to Domain-Specific Frameworks", Communications of the ACM, 40(10),October1997.

[6] K. Czarnecki, U. Eisenecker. Generative Programming: Methods, Tools, and Applications, Addison-Wesley,2000.

[7] M. Fayad, D. Schmidt, R. Johnson. Building Application Frameworks: Object-Oriented Foundations of Framework Design. John Wiley & Sons, September 1999.

[8] E. Gamma, et al. Design Patterns: Elements of Reusable Object-Oriented Software. Addison-Wesley, 1995.

[9] A. Garcia. From Objects to Agents: An Aspect-Oriented Approach. PhD Thesis, Computer Science Department, PUC-Rio, April 2004.

[10] W. Griswold, et al, "Modular Software Design with Crosscutting Interfaces", IEEE Software, Special Issue on Aspect-Oriented Programming, January 2006.

[11] J. Hannemann, G. Kiczales. Design Pattern Implementation in Java and AspectJ. Proceedings of OOPSLA'02, 2002, pp.161-173.

[12] G. Kiczales, et al. Aspect-Oriented Programming. Proc. of ECOOP'97, Finland, 1997.

[13] G. Kiczales, et al, "Getting Started with AspectJ," Comm. ACM, vol. 44, pp. 59-65, 2001.

[14] U. Kulesza, et al. "A Generative Approach for Multi-Agent System Development". In "Software Engineering for Multi-Agent Systems III". LNCS 3390, pp. 52-69, 2004.

[15] U. Kulesza, et al. "Implementing Framework Crosscutting Extensions with XPIs and AspectJ", Technical Report, PUC-Rio, Brazil, April 2006.

[16] U. Kulesza, A. Garcia, F. Bleasby, C. Lucena. "Instantiating and Customizing Product Line Architectures using Aspects and Crosscutting Feature Models". Proceedings of the Workshop on Early Aspects, OOPSLA'2005, San Diego,2005.

[17] U. Kulesza, A. Garcia, C. Lucena. "Composing Object-Oriented Frameworks with Aspect-Oriented Programming", Technical Report, PUC-Rio, Brazil, April 2006.

[18] A. Kvale, et al. A Case Study on Building COTS-Based System using Aspect-Oriented Programming. Proceedings of SAC'2005, pp. 1491-1498.

[19] M. Mattson, J. Bosch, M. Fayad. Framework Integration: Problems, Causes, Solutions. Communications of the ACM, 42(10):80–87, October 1999.

[20] M. Mattsson, J. Bosch. Framework Composition: Problems, Causes, and Solutions. In [7], 1999, pp. 467-487.

[21] M. Mezini, K. Ostermann: "Variability Management with Feature-Oriented Programming and Aspects". Proceedings of FSE'2004, pp.127-136, 2004.

[22] M. Mezini, K. Ostermann. "Conquering Aspects with Caesar". Proc. of AOSD'2003, pp. 90-99, March 17-21, 2003, Boston, Massachusetts, USA.

[23] D. Riehle, T. Gross. "Role Model Based Framework Design and Integration". Proceedings of OOPSLA'1998, pp. 117-133, Vancouver, BC, Canada, October 18-22, 1998.

[24] Y. Smaragdakis, D. Batory. Mixin Layers: An Object-Oriented Implementation Technique for Refinements and Collaboration-Based Designs, ACM TOSEM, 11(2): 215-255 (2002).

[25] K. Sullivan, et al. Information Hiding Interfaces for Aspect-Oriented Design, Proceedings of ESEC/FSE´2005, pp.166-175, Lisbon, Portugal, September 5-9, 2005.

[26] C. Zhang, H. Jacobsen. "Resolving Feature Convolution in Middleware Systems". Proceedings of OOPSLA'2004, pp.188-205, October 24-28, 2004, Vancouver, BC, Canada.

Comparing White-Box, Black-Box, and Glass-Box Composition of Aspect Mechanisms*

Sergei Kojarski and David H. Lorenz

University of Virginia, Charlottesville, VA 22904, USA
{kojarski, lorenz}@cs.virginia.edu

Abstract. The manifestation of miscellaneous aspect-oriented extensions raises the question of how these extensions can be used together to combine their aspectual capabilities or reuse aspect code across extensions. While white-box composition of aspect mechanisms can produce an optimal compound mechanism, as exemplified by the merger of ASPECTJ and ASPECTWERKZ into ASPECTJ 5, it comes with a high integration cost. Meanwhile, generic black-box composition can compose arbitrary aspect mechanisms, but may result in a compound mechanism that is suboptimal in comparison to white-box composition. For a particular family of aspect extensions, e.g., ASPECTJ-like mechanisms, glass-box composition offers the best of two worlds. Glass-box may rely on the internal structure of, e.g., a pointcut-and-advice mechanism, without requiring a change to the code of the individual mechanisms. In this paper we compare white-, black-, and glass-box composition of aspect mechanisms. We explain subtle composition issues using an example drawn from the domain of secure and dependable computing, deploying a fault-tolerance aspect written in ASPECTWERKZ together with an access-control aspect written in ASPECTJ. To compare the three composition methods, we integrate a TinyAJ extension with a TinyAW extension, and compare the results of running the aspects in a black-box framework and in a glass-box framework to the result of running these aspects in ASPECTJ 5.

1 Introduction

Various aspect extensions exist today and more are being developed [1, 2]. Many of those extensions follow the example set by ASPECTJ [3] in providing a join point model, pointcuts, and advice. These extensions belong primarily to a family of aspect mechanisms called pointcut-and-advice (PA) [4]. In this paper we focus on integrating PA mechanisms, ignoring for the sake of clarity any secondary (static) mechanisms, such as the Open Classes (OC) mechanism in ASPECTJ.

A current phenomenon in aspect-oriented software development (AOSD) is the integration of popular PA aspect extensions. ASPECTJ 5 [5] is an example of integrating ASPECTJ 1.2 [3] and ASPECTWERKZ [6]. Another planned integration is that of ASPECTJ 5 and Spring [7]. This begs the question: can the method of integration scale up and the cost of integration be reduced to also support on-demand integration of less popular or domain-specific PA mechanisms?

---

* This work is supported in part by NSF's Science of Design program under Grants Number CCF-0438971 and CCF-0609612.

The current major integration efforts are motivated by the need to combine forces of existing AOSD communities [8]. The desire to integrate aspect mechanisms is also motivated by the foreseen need to reuse aspect libraries across extensions [9]. But the potential benefit is much greater [10, 11, 12, 13, 14]. Reducing the integration cost and supporting on-demand integration of aspect mechanisms will allow developers to combine future and custom-made PA extensions at will.

1.1 Integration Approaches

In considering the integration of aspect mechanisms, there are three general composition approaches: white-box, black-box, (and a whole spectrum of gray shades in between), and glass-box (which is different than gray-box).

- In white-box composition [15] the internal code of the individual mechanisms is visible at an arbitrary level of detail and open for modifications. This lets the integration accommodate highly customized composition semantics. For example, ASPECTJ 5 can be characterized as white-box composition of traditional ASPECTJ and ASPECTWERKZ. However, white-box composition is not easily extensible. For example, it would be difficult to extend ASPECTJ 5 to accept aspects from extensions other than ASPECTJ and ASPECTWERKZ.
- In black-box composition [15] only the interface to the individual mechanisms is visible, without the code. This keeps the integration highly modular, letting arbitrary aspect mechanisms to be composed as long as they conform to the interface. For example, Pluggable AOP [9] is a method that can be characterized as black-box composition of dynamic aspect mechanisms. However, because black-box composition cannot rely on internal structure, it can only support a fixed composition semantics that might be too restrictive. For example, ASPECTJ 5 is not the result of black-box composition [9].
- In glass-box composition, internal knowledge of what the aspect mechanism is may guide the composition, but the integration remains modularized and non-invasive. White-box composition maximizes integration power in terms of workable semantics, by exposing everything and hiding nothing. Black-box composition also aims to maximize integration power, but in terms of modularity and reuse, by hiding almost everything (about the internal part of the aspect mechanism) and exposing almost nothing (except the observable ability to weave). Glass-box composition supports black-box extensibility while achieving customizable white-box composition semantics (Table 1). Hence, glass-box composition takes the best of the two worlds, trading some reuse (namely, limiting the applicability to only PA mechanisms) for improved composition semantics.

Table 1. Property-based comparison of composition approaches

Property	White-Box	Black-Box	Glass-Box
Target set of mechanisms	Selected	Heterogeneous	Homogeneous
Extensible	No	Yes	Yes for PA
Customizable	Yes	No	Yes for PA

1.2 Evaluation Method

In order to evaluate the three composition approaches, we apply them to ASPECTJ and ASPECTWERKZ. We built a black-box and a glass-box evaluation frameworks using:

- a simple object-oriented JAVA-like language named TinyJ,

and two PA mechanisms for TinyJ:

- an ASPECTJ-like aspect mechanism named TinyAJ; and
- an ASPECTWERKZ-like aspect mechanism named TinyAW.

The choice of focusing on the integration of ASPECTJ and ASPECTWERKZ as a case of study is driven by several considerations. First, composing PA mechanisms is the most practical specialization of the general composition problem.

Second, ASPECTJ 5 is the only case for which a white-box composition of two PA mechanisms is readily available. We can run ASPECTJ code in ASPECTJ and in TinyAJ. We can run ASPECTWERKZ code in ASPECTWERKZ and in TinyAW. We can run code written partly in ASPECTJ and partly in ASPECTWERKZ in ASPECTJ 5. This gives us a reference data point for what the preferred behavior should be. We can therefore evaluate different composition approaches by checking whether or not their behavior is consistent with ASPECTJ 5.

Third, ASPECTJ and ASPECTWERKZ are both general-purpose mechanisms. The functionality of a general-purpose mechanism normally ranges over many domain-specific mechanisms. For example, ASPECTJ may be used to express aspects written in the domain-specific language COOL [16]. We can therefore expect the methods for combining these general-purpose extensions to be applicable also for combining domain-specific PA mechanisms.

Finally, we note that ASPECTWERKZ and ASPECTJ are highly similar in syntax and semantics. While this similarity poses a concern in deriving from this example conclusions about any two PA mechanisms, it is mostly a limitation for generalizing a white-box composition method, less so for black-box and glass-box compositions. Specifically, in our evaluation we take care not to rely on these similarities beyond what can be expected in any PA mechanism.

2   White-Box Composition: A Benchmark Example

In this section, we defer to ASPECTJ 5 for the preferred semantics for integrating AS-PECTJ and ASPECTWERKZ. We study the ASPECTJ 5 composition behavior by example. The example is taken from the domain of secure and dependable computing and comprises code in JAVA, ASPECTJ, and ASPECTWERKZ.

2.1 Service in JAVA

The JAVA part consists of three classes: Client, DataSource, and Main. Client (List. 1.1) and DataSource (List. 1.2) are classes of objects located on a quote server.

A client is identified by name and can request a quote. The getQuote method redirects the request to the *main* database (using the DataSource class). The DataSource

Listing 1.1. code/example/base/Client.java

```
public class Client {
 private String name;
 public Client(String name) {this.name=name;}
 public String getName() {return name;}
 public String getQuote(String request) {
  System.out.println("Client.getQuote: client="+name+", req="+request);
  return new DataSource("main").getData(request);
 }
}
```

Listing 1.2. code/example/base/DataSource.java

```
public class DataSource {
  private String src;
  public DataSource(String src) {this.src = src;}
  public String getData(String request) {···}
  public static boolean isAvailable(String src) {···}
}
```

Listing 1.3. code/example/base/Main.java

```
public class Main {
  public static void main(String[] args) {
    Client client = new Client("regular");
    System.out.println("Requesting quote for regular client");
    System.out.println(client.getQuote("<quoteName>")+"\n");
    Client root = new Client("root");
    System.out.println("Requesting quote for root client");
    System.out.println(root.getQuote("<quoteName>"));
  }
}
```

class is an abstraction over databases. Each database is identified by a source string
(`DataSource.src`). The `getData` method provides a way of retrieving data from the
database.

The method `Main.main` (List. 1.3) simulates client-side activity. Specifically, it requests <quoteName> quotes on behalf of two clients, namely *client* and *root*.

2.2   Access Control and Billing in ASPECTJ

As the quote database grows in size, it may include sensitive data. The `AccessControl`
aspect (List. 1.4) protects the data against unauthorized access. The aspect imposes
advice around executions of `DataSource.getData` that are in the control flow of a
`Client.getQuote` execution. Depending on the client object and request string, the

Listing 1.4. code/example/aj/AccessControl.java

```
1 public aspect AccessControl {
2  pointcut request():
3   execution(String Client.getQuote(String));
4  pointcut access():
5   execution(String DataSource.getData(String));
6  String around(Client client, String request):
7   access() && cflow(request() && this(client)) && args(request){
8     System.out.println("AccessControl: jp="+thisJoinPoint);
9     if (isTrusted(client,request)) {
10      System.out.println("AccessControl: access granted");
11      return proceed(client,request);
12    }
13    else {
14      System.out.println("AccessControl: access denied");
15      return "ACCESS DENIED";
16    }
17  }
18  private boolean isTrusted(Client client, String request) {···}
19 }
```

Listing 1.5. code/example/aj/Billing.java

```
1 public aspect Billing {
2  pointcut request():
3   execution(String Client.getQuote(String));
4  before(Client client, String request):
5   request() && target(client) && args(request) {
6     System.out.println("Billing: jp="+thisJoinPoint);
7     ...
8  }
9 }
```

advice either grants or denies access to the database. In the former case, the advice proceeds to execute DataSource.getData. In the latter case, the advice returns an *ACCESS DENIED* string.

As the quote service gains popularity, the company that owns the quote server decides to bill clients for every request. This policy change is then implemented in an aspect-oriented manner, using a Billing aspect (List. 1.5). The Billing aspect executes advice before each execution of Client.getQuote. The advice charges a fee to the client's account.

2.3   QoS and Fault Tolerance in ASPECTWERKZ

Once clients start paying for requests, a quality of service (QoS) aspect becomes important. To ensure continuous service, the company decides to replicate the information on

Listing 1.6. code/example/aw/FaultTolerance.java

```
1  @Aspect
2  public class FaultTolerance {
3    @Around("execution(String Client.getQuote(String)) && args(request)")
4    public Object toleranceAdvice(ProceedingJoinPoint joinPoint,
         String request) {
5      System.out.println("FaultTolerance: jp="+joinPoint);
6      if (DataSource.isAvailable("main")) {
7        System.out.println("FaultTolerance: using main");
8        return joinPoint.proceed();
9      }
10     else {
11       System.out.println("FaultTolerance: using mirror");
12       return new DataSource("mirror").getData(request);
13     }
14   }
15 }
```

the *main* server with a second *mirror* server. Whenever the *main* server is overloaded or down, the *mirror* server takes over and serves clients' requests. The FaultTolerance aspect (List. 1.6), written in ASPECTWERKZ, implements the new QoS strategy. At each execution of Client.getQuote, the aspect checks if the *main* database is available. If so, the aspect proceeds to the original method execution. If not, the aspect redirects the request to the *mirror* database.

2.4   Testing

We test the collaborative behavior of these aspects by playing out four scenarios (Table 2). In the first two scenarios, the *main* database is available, and, in the last two, unavailable. In the first and third scenario, the AccessControl aspect denies access. In the second and fourth scenario, AccessControl grants the access. The outputs are shown in Listings 1.7, 1.8, 1.9, and 1.10.

2.5   Analysis

Running this example in ASPECTJ 5 exhibits two important behaviors that this white-box composition of ASPECTJ and ASPECTWERKZ preserves:

- All three aspects affect each of the four scenarios;
- Billing and FaultTolerance apply to the same join point, and Billing is always applied *first*.

The first observed behavior suggests that the ASPECTJ and ASPECTWERKZ aspects *observe* the program execution through a coherent join point view. Note that in the third and fourth scenario, the ASPECTWERKZ's FaultTolerance aspect does *not* proceed

Table 2. Four scenarios

Scenario	List. 1.7	List. 1.8	List. 1.9	List. 1.10
Database	Available	Available	Unavailable	Unavailable
Access	Denied	Granted	Denied	Granted

Listing 1.7. Main available; access denied

```
1  Requesting quote for regular client
2  Billing: jp=execution(String base.Client.getQuote(String))
3  FaultTolerance: jp=execution(String base.Client.getQuote(String))
4  FaultTolerance: using main
5  Client.getQuote: client=regular, req=<quoteName>
6  AccessControl: jp=execution(String base.DataSource.getData(String))
7  AccessControl: access denied
8  ACCESS DENIED
```

Listing 1.8. Main available; access granted

```
1  Requesting quote for root client
2  Billing: jp=execution(String base.Client.getQuote(String))
3  FaultTolerance: jp=execution(String base.Client.getQuote(String))
4  FaultTolerance: using main
5  Client.getQuote: client=root, req=<quoteName>
6  AccessControl: jp=execution(String base.DataSource.getData(String))
7  AccessControl: access granted
8  REQUESTED DATA
```

Listing 1.9. Main unavailable; access denied

```
1  Requesting quote for regular client
2  Billing: jp=execution(String base.Client.getQuote(String))
3  FaultTolerance: jp=execution(String base.Client.getQuote(String))
4  FaultTolerance: using mirror
5  AccessControl: jp=execution(String base.DataSource.getData(String))
6  AccessControl: access denied
7  ACCESS DENIED
```

Listing 1.10. Main unavailable; access granted

```
1  Requesting quote for root client
2  Billing: jp=execution(String base.Client.getQuote(String))
3  FaultTolerance: jp=execution(String base.Client.getQuote(String))
4  FaultTolerance: using mirror
5  AccessControl: jp=execution(String base.DataSource.getData(String))
6  AccessControl: access granted
7  REQUESTED DATA
```

to the `Client.getQuote` execution. Instead, the aspect invokes the `DataSource-.getData` method directly from the advice body. Nonetheless, the ASPECTJ's `Access-Control` advice identifies subsequent `DataSource.getData` executions to be *in the control-flow* of the `Client.getQuote` execution. That is, the `getQuote` method execution join point is observed by *both* ASPECTJ and ASPECTWERKZ aspects as soon as it "occurs," regardless of what advice is run. Thus, at any point in the program execution, ASPECTJ and ASPECTWERKZ aspects have the same join point view of the program execution.

The second observed behavior suggests an advice ordering rule that should be preserved across aspect extensions. In particular, **before** advice written in one extension apply (at the same join point) *before* any **around** advice that is written in another extension. Similarly, it can be demonstrated that **after** advice must always apply *after* any foreign **around** advice.

These behaviors allow us to evaluate a compound ASPECTJ/ASPECTWERKZ mechanism. In fact, this example is useful for evaluating the behavior of a composition of any two PA mechanisms. We use it to compare and contrast black-box and glass-box composition of `TinyAJ` (a simplified ASPECTJ) with `TinyAW` (a simplified ASPECTWERKZ).

3 Black-Box Composition

Black-box composition (Fig. 1) supports the integration of arbitrary third-party aspect mechanisms. Essentially, a third-party aspect mechanism is a transformer of a base language interpreter (base mechanism). The aspect mechanism *overrides* some of the base mechanism's operations, and *extends* the base mechanism with new operations [9].

More specifically, black-box composition integrates a base mechanism **B** with aspect mechanisms $\mathbf{M}_1, \ldots, \mathbf{M}_n$ into an AOP interpreter $\mathbf{A}_n$. **B** realizes the expression evaluation semantics for the base language, and each $\mathbf{M}_i$ realizes the semantics for a corresponding PA extension to that language. $\mathbf{M}_i$ is designed to realize *only* its respective aspectual functionality, while all base operations are delegated to **B**.

Multiple aspect mechanisms compose in a chain-of-responsibility [17], pipe-and-filter architecture [18]. In the composition, each aspect mechanism performs some part of the evaluation and forwards other parts of the evaluation to the next mechanism using delegation. If an expression is delegated by all mechanisms then it is eventually evaluated in **B**. The mechanisms *expose* selected advice by evaluating them in $\mathbf{A}_n$.

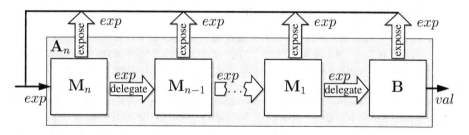

Fig. 1. Black-box Composition of PA mechanisms

Listing 1.11. Main available; access denied

```
1   Requesting quote for regular client
2   FaultTolerance: jp=execution(String base.Client.getQuote(String))
3   FaultTolerance: using main
4   Billing: jp=execution(String base.Client.getQuote(String))
5   Client.getQuote: client=regular, req=<quoteName>
6   AccessControl: jp=execution(String base.DataSource.getData(String))
7   AccessControl: access denied
8   ACCESS DENIED
```

Listing 1.12. Main available; access granted

```
1   Requesting quote for root client
2   FaultTolerance: jp=execution(String base.Client.getQuote(String))
3   FaultTolerance: using main
4   Billing: jp=execution(String base.Client.getQuote(String))
5   Client.getQuote: client=root, req=<quoteName>
6   AccessControl: jp=execution(String base.DataSource.getData(String))
7   AccessControl: access granted
8   REQUESTED DATA
```

Listing 1.13. Main unavailable; access denied

```
1   Requesting quote for regular client
2   FaultTolerance: jp=execution(String base.Client.getQuote(String))
3   FaultTolerance: using mirror
4   REQUESTED DATA
```

Listing 1.14. Main unavailable; access granted

```
1   Requesting quote for root client
2   FaultTolerance: jp=execution(String base.Client.getQuote(String))
3   FaultTolerance: using mirror
4   REQUESTED DATA
```

3.1   Semantics of Black-Box Composition

In this section we re-run the benchmark example in a black-box composition of TinyAJ and TinyAW. W.l.o.g., we assume that TinyAW takes precedence over TinyAJ, i.e., it dominates the composition. In other words, the TinyAW mechanism intercepts all invocations of the AOP interpreter $\mathbf{A}_n$, and delegates evaluation to the TinyAJ mechanism; the TinyAJ mechanism delegates the evaluation to the TinyJ evaluator function. Both mechanisms expose pieces of advice by evaluating them in the AOP interpreter $\mathbf{A}_n$.

Interestingly, the output is different from the output obtained with ASPECTJ 5. In Listings 1.11 and 1.12, all TinyAJ and TinyAW aspects get executed. However, the

TinyAJ Billing aspect is executed after the TinyAW FaultTolerance aspect. In Listings 1.13 and 1.14, only the FaultTolerance aspect runs, while all the TinyAJ aspects are disabled. In the last two scenarios, users are not billed. Moreover, in List. 1.13 an unauthorized user gains access to the protected data.

The benchmark example illustrates that the observed behavior in a black-box composition is different than ASPECTJ 5:

- There are scenarios that some of the aspects do *not* affect;
- The Billing advice is never applied first.

A more careful look at the black-box composition method reveals that:

- A black-box PA mechanism observes *only* the evaluation of expressions that are delegated to that mechanism;
- A mechanism *never* delegates the evaluation if it advises a join point with an around advice that does not proceed;
- If M_i delegates the evaluation to M_{i-1}, then all M_{i-1} pieces of advice are dynamically "nested" within (run in the control flow of) M_i's **around** advice.

The first two points explain why different black-box PA mechanisms may (and generally do) reflect in their join point stacks *different* views of the program execution. Consider the two scenarios shown in Listings 1.13 and 1.14. At the Client.getQuote method execution join point, the TinyAW mechanism reflects the join point in its join point stack, selects and runs the FaultTolerance aspect. Since the *main* database is unavailable, FaultTolerance does *not* proceed, and the Client.getQuote method body expression never reaches the TinyAJ mechanism. Consequently, TinyAJ:

- does *not* run the Billing **before** advice;
- does *not* reflect the Client.getQuote method execution join point in its join point stack;
- does *not* run the **around** advice of the AccessControl aspect.

The third point explains why **before** advice of the Billing aspect does not apply before the FaultTolerance **around** advice. Consider the two scenarios shown in Listings 1.11 and 1.12. At the Client.getQuote method execution join point, both Billing and FaultTolerance aspects take effect. However, the **before** advice of the Billing aspect runs only *after* the FaultTolerance.toleranceAdvice advice proceeds.

4 Glass-Box Composition of PA Mechanisms

The *Pluggable AOP* [9] is a framework implementing a semantical model [19] of an AOP language in which the PA extension semantics is defined separately from semantics of the base language. The model defines semantics of a PA extension as an AOP interpreter $\mathbf{A}$, which comprises a base mechanism $\mathbf{B}$ and an aspect mechanism $\mathbf{M}$. $\mathbf{B}$ realizes the expression evaluation semantics for the base language, and $\mathbf{M}$ realizes the semantics for a PA extension to that language.

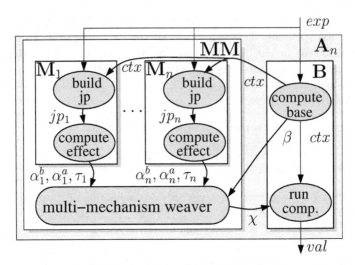

Fig. 2. Glass-box Composition of PA mechanisms

Elsewhere [19, 20] we introduced an extension of the PA mechanism model that supports a *parallel* glass-box composition of PA mechanisms (Fig. 2). The model defines the base mechanism $\mathbf{B}$ as a computation *constructor*, and the mechanism $\mathbf{M}$ as a computation *transformer*. $\mathbf{B}$ constructs a base computation β, and a computation's context ctx by interpreting an input expression exp. $\mathbf{M}$ selects pieces of advice by matching them against ctx, and *weaves* them by transforming β into an *advised computation* χ, which replaces β in the program execution.

The PA mechanisms $\mathbf{M}_1, \ldots, \mathbf{M}_n$ compose into a *multi-mechanism* $\mathbf{MM}$. For each base computation β, $\mathbf{MM}$ passes the currently evaluated expression exp and a computation context ctx to all the PA mechanisms $\mathbf{M}_1, \ldots, \mathbf{M}_n$. Each PA mechanism $\mathbf{M}_i$ then constructs a join point, computes an aspectual effect, and passes it to the multi-mechanism weaver. The weaver combines the aspectual effects of all the mechanisms, and wraps them around the base computation β.

While black-box composition does not impose any requirements on an aspect mechanism design, the glass-box composition requires the following design conventions to be met:

1. The PA mechanism $\mathbf{M}_i$ must provide its aspectual effect via three functions, namely a before computation α_i^b, an after computation α_i^a, and an around computation transformer τ_i. Intuitively, α_i^b, τ_i, and α_i^a provide meaning for **before**, **around**, and **after** pieces of advice that were selected by the mechanism, respectively.
2. A multi-mechanism is a computation transformer (but not an expression evaluator transformer);

The multi-mechanism weaver composes all constructed effects together into the result computation χ. χ is built by sequencing three multi-effect computations, namely a before computation α_χ^b, an around computation α_χ^{ar}, and an after computation α_χ^a:

$$\chi = \alpha_\chi^b \triangleright \alpha_\chi^{ar} \triangleright \alpha_\chi^a$$

where $\triangleright$ denotes a left-to-right execution order for the sequenced computations: χ first executes α_χ^b, then α_χ^{ar}, and finally α_χ^a. More specifically, let γ be a composite computation defined as:

$$\gamma = \gamma_1 \triangleright \ldots \triangleright \gamma_m$$

Then the execution of γ runs the subcomputations $\gamma_1, \ldots, \gamma_m$ one by one, starting from γ_1 through γ_m. All subcomputations are passed the same context as that passed to γ. The value computed by γ is the value returned from γ_m.

α_χ^b sequences the before computations that are produced by the aspect mechanisms in the index-ascending order:

$$\alpha_\chi^b = \alpha_1^b \triangleright \ldots \triangleright \alpha_n^b$$

α_χ^a sequences the after computations in the index-descending order:

$$\alpha^a = \alpha_n^a \triangleright \ldots \triangleright \alpha_1^a$$

The around transformers $\tau_1, \ldots, \tau_n$ are composed sequentially, in the following index-descending order. First, τ_n produces the around computation α_n^{ar} by transforming the base computation β. The τ_{n-1} then produces α_{n-1}^{ar} by transforming α_n^{ar}. The process repeats until τ_1 produces α_1^{ar} by transforming the output of τ_2:

$$\alpha_\chi^{ar} = \alpha_1^{ar} = \tau_1(\tau_2(\ldots(\tau_n(\beta))\ldots))$$

The composition of the around transformers allows aspects written in one extension to proceed to the aspects written in another extension. α_1^{ar} proceeds to α_2^{ar}, α_2^{ar} proceeds to α_3^{ar}, and so on. β is executed only if all the around computations proceed.

The glass-box approach enables PA mechanism compositions that exhibit the desired behavior. The parallel architecture allows the composed mechanisms to observe the same exact sequence of computation contexts and expressions. The multi-mechanism weaver is capable of ordering the advice appropriately.

As a proof of concept, we applied glass-box composition to integrate TinyAJ and TinyAW. When we run the benchmark example in the constructed glass-box composition, we get the same output as ASPECTJ 5.

5   Conclusion

White-box composition of aspect mechanisms involves the aspect mechanisms' code being opened, inspected, modified and merged. It hides nothing; exposes everything. This is a powerful composition technique for a one-time customized composition like the one applied to create ASPECTJ 5, but it does not scale up to integrating multiple mechanisms or to handling repeated integrations.

Black-box composition, in contrast, supports third-party composition of aspect mechanisms [9]. It hides the internal parts of the aspect mechanism; exposes only the ability to wrap. Conceptually, black-box composition is similar to mixin inheritance.

A glass-box composition method [20] for integrating PA mechanisms hides *how* the PA mechanisms work but exposes some information on *what* they do. It trades little extensibility for added composition power.

In this paper, we compare white-box, black-box, and glass-box composition of PA mechanisms using the integration of ASPECTJ and ASPECTWERKZ as a benchmark example. We present a set of aspects in ASPECTJ and ASPECTWERKZ, drawn from the domain of secure and dependable computing, that display different behavior depending on whether they are deployed in a compound mechanism integrated using black-box or white-box composition. We then present a glass-box framework for composing PA mechanisms. The glass-box framework supports a composition that exhibits the behavior observed in ASPECTJ 5.

Although the glass-box composition cannot be applied to integrate non-PA mechanisms, it can be combined together with other approaches. A general strategy to achieve composition of any domain specific extensions is to partition the space of extensions to classes of homogeneous extensions. The glass-box integration method can be applied to each homogeneous subset of mechanisms, and the classes can then be integrated once using a white-box or black-box composition.

References

1. Kersten, M.: AOP@Work: AOP tools comparison, part 1. developerWorks (2005)
   `http://www.ibm.com/developerworks/java/library/j-aopwork1/`.
2. Kersten, M.: AOP@Work: AOP tools comparison, part 2. developerWorks (2005)
   `http://www.ibm.com/developerworks/java/library/j-aopwork2/`.
3. Kiczales, G., Hilsdale, E., Hugunin, J., Kersten, M., Palm, J., Griswold, W.G.: An overview of AspectJ. In Knudsen, J.L., ed.: Proceedings of the 15th European Conference on Object-Oriented Programming. Number 2072 in Lecture Notes in Computer Science, Budapest, Hungary, ECOOP 2001, Springer Verlag (2001) 327–353
4. Masuhara, H., Kiczales, G.: Modeling crosscutting in aspect-oriented mechanisms. In Cardelli, L., ed.: Proceedings of the 17th European Conference on Object-Oriented Programming. Number 2743 in Lecture Notes in Computer Science, Darmstadt, Germany, ECOOP 2003, Springer Verlag (2003) 2–28
5. Colyer, A.: AOP@Work: Introducing AspectJ 5. developerWorks (2005)
   `http://www.ibm.com/developerworks/java/library/j-aopwork8/`.
6. Bonér, J.: What are the key issues for commercial AOP use: how does AspectWerkz address them? In Lieberherr, K., ed.: Proceedings of the 3rd International Conference on Aspect-Oriented Software Development, Mancaster, UK, AOSD 2004, ACM Press (2004) 5–6
7. Colyer, A.: Joining interface21. The Aspect Blog (2005)
   `http://www.aspectprogrammer.org/blogs/adrian/2005/09/joining_interfa.html`.
8. Colyer, A.: The new holy trinity. The Aspect Blog (2005)
   `http://www.aspectprogrammer.org/blogs/adrian/2005/03/the_new_holy_tr.html`.
9. Kojarski, S., Lorenz, D.H.: Pluggable AOP: Designing aspect mechanisms for third-party composition. In Johnson, R., Gabriel, R.P., eds.: Proceedings of the 20th Annual Conference on Object-Oriented Programming Systems, Languages, and Applications, San Diego, CA, USA, OOPSLA'05, ACM Press (2005) 247–263
10. Courbis, C., Finkelstein, A.: Towards aspect weaving applications. In: Proceedings of the 27th International Conference on Software Engineering, St. Louis, Missouri, USA, ICSE 2005, ACM Press (2005)

11. Czarnecki, K., Eisenecker, U.: Generative Programming: Methods, Tools, and Applications. 1st edn. Addison-Wesley (2000)

12. Hugunin, J.: The next steps for aspect-oriented programming languages (in Java). In: NSF Workshop on New Visions for Software Design & Productivity: Research & Applications, Vanderbilt University, Nashville, TN, National Coordination Office for Information Technology Research and Development (NCO/IT R&D) (2001) White Paper.

13. Lopes, C.V., Dourish, P., Lorenz, D.H., Lieberherr, K.: Beyond AOP: Toward Naturalistic Programming. ACM SIGPLAN Notices **38**(12) (2003) 34–43 OOPSLA'03 Special Track on Onward! Seeking New Paradigms & New Thinking.

14. Wand, M.: Understanding aspects (extended abstract). In: Proceedings of the 7th ACM SIGPLAN International Conference on Functional Programming, Uppsala, Sweden, ACM Press (2003) Invited talk.

15. Szyperski, C.: Component Software, Beyond Object-Oriented Programming. 2nd edn. Addison-Wesley (2002) With Dominik Gruntz and Stephan Murer.

16. Lopes, C.V.: D: A Language Framework for Distributed Programming. PhD thesis, Northeastern University (1997)

17. Gamma, E., Helm, R., Johnson, R., Vlissides, J.: Design Patterns: Elements of Reusable Object-Oriented Software. Professional Computing. Addison-Wesley (1995)

18. Shaw, M., Garlan, D.: Software Architecture, Perspectives on an Emerging Discipline. Prentice-Hall (1996)

19. Kojarski, S., Lorenz, D.: Modeling aspect mechanisms: A top-down approach. In: Proceedings of the 28th International Conference on Software Engineering, Shanghai, China, ICSE'06 (2006)

20. Lorenz, D.H., Kojarski, S.: Parallel composition of aspect mechanisms: Design and evaluation. In Brichau, J., Chiba, S., Volder, K.D., Haupt, M., Hirschfeld, R., Lorenz, D.H., Masuhara, H., Tanter, E., eds.: AOSD 2006 Workshop on Open and Dynamic Aspect Languages (ODAL), Bonn, Germany (2006)

Achieving Smooth Component Integration with Generative Aspects and Component Adaptation

Yankui Feng, Xiaodong Liu, and Jon Kerridge

School of Computing, Napier University, Edinburgh, UK
{y.feng, x.liu, j.kerridge}@napier.ac.uk

Abstract. Due to the availability of components and the diversity of target applications, mismatches between pre-qualified existing components and the particular reuse context in applications are often inevitable and have been a major hurdle of component reusability and successful composition. Although component adaptation has acted as a key solution of eliminating these mismatches, existing practices are either only capable for adaptation at a rather simple level, or require too much intervention from software engineers. This paper presents a highly automatic approach to component adaptation at adequately deep level. The adaptability and automation is achieved in an aspect-oriented component reuse framework by generating and then applying the adaptation aspects under designed weaving process according to specific adaptation requirements. An expandable library of reusable adaptation aspects at multiple abstraction levels has been developed. A prototype tool is developed to scale up the approach.

1 Introduction

Component-Based Development (CBD) has been proved as an effective technology in supporting community-wide reuse of software assets [6][12][13]. Under the methodology of CBD, both Commercial-Off The Shelf (COTS) [6] components and in-house components can be integrated to build a range of target applications, including traditional systems and most modern applications such as web services in a service-oriented architecture.

However, in many cases mismatches between pre-qualified available components and the specific reuse context of particular applications are inevitable and have been a major hurdle of wider component reusability and smooth composition. Component adaptation has been researched over the years as a key solution to the above problem [3][8][9][17]. Due to the complex nature of the mismatch problem, available approaches are either only capable for adaptation at simple levels such as wrappers [3], or inefficient to use as a result of lack of automation in their adaptation process [8][17].

In this paper, a Generative Aspect-oriented component adaptatIoN (GAIN) approach is proposed to achieve adaptation at a deeper level, in terms of functionalities and non-functional features, rather than limited at component interface level like wrappers [3]. The approach is based on the successful points in a few technologies, i.e., Aspect Oriented Programming [10][16], Software Product Line [2][5] and

M. Morisio (Ed.): ICSR 2006, LNCS 4039, pp. 260–272, 2006.
© Springer-Verlag Berlin Heidelberg 2006

Generative Component Adaptation [1][4] the GAIN approach, component adaptation is carried out within an aspect-oriented component reuse framework by generating and then applying the adaptation aspects under designed weaving process according to specific adaptation requirements. The generation absorbs the variation concept of software product line and assures the perfect suitability of adaptation aspects for the specific adaptation requirements of aimed reuse context. Compared with traditional AOP, the weaving process of aspects in GAIN supports more complex control flow, i.e., not only sequence, but also switches, synchronization and multiple threads, to make the adaptation more accurate and efficient for components reused in more complicated environments such as concurrent dynamic applications. To facilitate the reusability of adaptation knowledge, an expandable library of reusable adaptation aspects at multiple abstraction levels has been developed. A prototype tool is developed to scale up the approach.

The reminder of the paper is organized as follows: Section 2 discusses related work with critical analysis. Section 3 describes the approach framework. Section 4 presents how to generate and apply reusable adaptation aspects under the designed weaving process. Section 5 introduces the prototype tool, and section 6 presents an example to demonstrate the approach. Finally, section 7 presents the conclusion.

2 Related Work

2.1 SAGA Project

Scenario-based dynamic component Adaptation and GenerAtion (SAGA) [8][17] at Napier University developed a deep level component adaptation approach with little code overhead through XML-based component specification, interrelated adaptation scenarios and corresponding component adaptation and generation.

SAGA project focused mainly on generative component adaptation at binary code level, i.e., the adapted part of the component will be generated as new blocks of binary code and these blocks will then be composed with other unchanged blocks of code to form a new adapted component.

SAGA project achieved deep adaptation with little code overhead in the adapted component; however, automation is a challenge in the SAGA approach because it is always complex to generate blocks of code according to scenarios and original component code. To reach high automation, a large set of adaptation rules and domain knowledge has to be developed to support the process, and probably the application domains have to be restricted as well.

2.2 Binary Component Adaptation

Binary Component Adaptation (BCA) [9] has been proposed by R. Keller and U. Hölzle to support component adaptation in binary form and on-the-fly (during program loading). BCA rewrites component binaries before (or while) they are loaded, requires no source code access and guarantees release-to-release compatibility. That is, an adaptation is guaranteed to be compatible with a new binary release of the component as long as the new release itself is compatible with clients compiled using the earlier release.

However, together with the binary code adaptation, especially with "online" (on-the-fly) adaptations, extra processing time is required. As a result, the load-time overhead is a major problem. Consequently, when more adaptation processes are required, the load-time will be the bottleneck of the system performance.

2.3 Superimposition

Superimposition [3] is a novel black-box adaptation technique, which is proposed by J. Bosch at University of Karlskrona/Ronneby. In Superimposition, software developers are able to impose a number of predefined, but configurable types of functionality on reusable components.

The notion of superimposition has been implemented in the Layered Object Model (LayOM), an extensible component object language model. The advantage of layers over traditional wrappers is that layers are transparent and provide reuse and customizability of adaptation behaviour.

Superimposition uses nested component adaptation types to compose multiple adaptation behaviours for a single component. However, due to lack of component information, modification is limited at simple level, such as conversion of parameters, and refinement of operations. Moreover, with more layers of code imposed on original code, the overhead of the adapted component increases heavily, which degrades system efficiency.

2.4 Customizable Components

Customizable Components [11], as part of the COMPOSE project, is an environment for building customizable software components, it is an approach to expressing customization properties of components. The declarations enable the developer to focus on what to customize in a component, as opposed to how to customize it. Customization transformations are automatically determined by compiling both the declarations and the component code; this process produces a customizable component. Such a component is then ready to be custom-fitted to any application.

In this work, the customized components generated for various usage contexts have exhibited performance comparable to, or better than manually customized code, however, component adaptation is limited to pre-defined optional customization, and deeper adaptation is not supported.

2.5 JAsCo

JAsCo [14][15] is an aspect based research project for component based development, in particular, the Java Beans component model. JAsCo combines the expressive power of AspectJ [10] with the aspect independency idea of Aspectual Component [7].

The JAsCo language introduces two concepts: aspect beans and connectors. An aspect bean is used to define aspects independently from a specific context, which interferes with the execution of a component by using a special kind of inner class, called a hook. Hooks are generic and reusable entities and can be considered as a combination of an abstract pointcut and advice [14][15]. Because aspect beans are described independently from a specific context, they can be reused and applied upon a variety of components. A connector allows specifying precedence and combination strategies between the aspects and components.

However, JAsCo is not suitable for specific modification requirements since it does not provide a mechanism for conducting users' requirements. In addition, the way to apply aspects on target components / systems is based on traditional AOP process, and therefore, may result in lower readability, maintainability and performance. Moreover, the current implementation of JAsCo has been bounded to Java, which means it can not be used in a heterogeneous system including different programming language implementations.

2.6 Summary

Due to the complex nature of the mismatch between reuse requirements and components, available component adaptation approaches are either only capable for adaptation at simple levels such as wrappers, or inefficient to use as a result of lack of automation in their adaptation process. Deep level component adaptation can be achieved through AOP.

Some AOP based frameworks have been developed to achieve reusable aspects. However, an AOP platform independent framework is still desired in a heterogeneous distributed environment to solve crosscutting problem since a common model for AOP is still missing. Furthermore, current AOP techniques only support weaving aspects sequentially. To cope with complex adaptation, it often requires weaving aspects in more sophisticated control flow, e.g. dynamically deciding whether to invoke a particular aspect, and synchronizing in multi-thread applications.

3   The Approach Framework

The general process of our approach is given in figure 1. We presume that a component has been found potential suitable to be used in a component-based application, however, the application developer indicated some mismatches of the component and wishes to have it adapted.

The mismatches will be eliminated by applying aspect-oriented adaptation to the original component. At start, the component is analyzed with the component analyzer, which analyzes the source or binary code of the component and extracts component specification information, e.g. class names and method signatures. The component specification will be used to guide component adaptation. If the component already has well defined specification, this step can be skipped.

Then based on the adaptation requirements, a Process-based Component Adaptation Specification (PCAS) will be composed by selecting aspects defined at the abstraction level of Abstract Aspect Frames (AAF). The selection of aspects is actually the process to determine functional variation of a specific adaptation. An AAF is considered as a template to coin out specific aspects. The composition of PCAS is supported by an interactive IDE called PCAS Editor, which supports both graphical and XML source view of the PCAS.

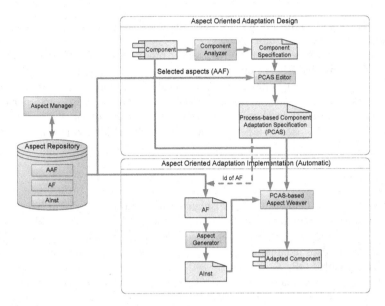

Fig. 1. The Generative Aspect-oriented component adaptatIoN (GAIN) framework

A PCAS is an XML formatted document, which includes the details of component adaptation, such as the target component, the weaving process, and the abstract aspects to be applied. In a PCAS, sequence and switch structure are supported to achieve flexible adaptation on components. In PCAS, the adaptation process is depicted with only the ID of the selected aspects. Full details of the aspects are still kept in Aspect Repository.

Based on PCAS and the lower level aspect definition, namely Aspect Frame (AF) in the aspect repository, executable aspects instances (AInsts) are generated by the aspect generator according to different AOP implementation specifications. As result, platform variation is achieved during aspect generation. The input for the aspect generator is AF and the output is AInsts.

Reusable aspects are defined at different abstraction levels and kept in the repository as AAF, AF, and AInst. The reusable assets in the repository include both primitive and composite aspect types, which comes from the adaptation process in PCAS. The saved aspects, particularly composite aspects are potentially reusable for component adaptations in other applications. While the framework is used, the repository will be populated with more and more aspects incrementally. Therefore, the aspect repository supports highly and incrementally reusable aspects.

The aspect manager is a tool to manage reusable aspects in the aspect repository, and to present graphical views of aspects at various abstraction levels.

The generated executable aspects are finally applied to the component by the aspect weaver. A new adapted version of the component is then created through the aspect weaving. Since current AOP platforms like AspectJ do not support complicated flow control such as switch in weaving process, post-processing is applied to enable process-based weaving in our framework. The basic idea of post-processing

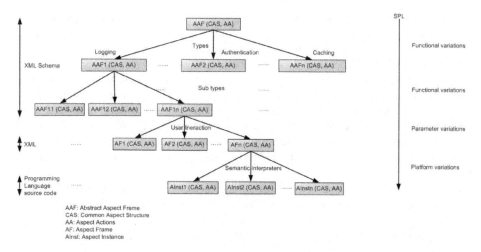

Fig. 2. Multiple abstraction levels of reusable aspects in Software Product Line view

based weaving is to revise the binary code of AInst generated by normal AOP compiler such as AspectJ compiler, and add more process control to it according to PCAS.

4 Aspect-Oriented Generative Adaptation

4.1 Capturing Adaptation Knowledge in Aspects

In our approach, the adaptation knowledge is captured in aspects and aims to be reusable in various adaptation situations. As shown in figure 2, to achieve automated and
precise adaptation, these aspects are defined at three abstraction levels, i.e., Abstract
Aspect Frames (AAF), Aspect Frames (AF), and Aspect Instances (AInsts).

The three abstraction levels of aspects facilitate the reusability of adaptation aspects as they realize different variations of these aspects, including functional variations, parameter variations and platform variations. At each level, a pair, namely
(CAS, AA) is used to describe Common Aspect Structure (CAS) and Aspect Actions
(AA). Common core assets are defined in Common Aspect Structures and variations
are defined in Aspect Actions.

CAS provides the basic information of an aspect, e.g. which component to be
adapted (target component), pointcut name, etc. All aspects have the same CAS at
AAF level no matter how different these aspects are in functionality and implementation platform.

On the other hand, Aspect Actions provide the information of the variations of different aspects of the same or different aspect types. For instance, for an aspect of
logging type, an output file name must be provided; similarly an authentication aspect
must be supplied with an authentication type.

Abstract Aspect Frames are the fundamental and the most abstract level of the Aspect Repository. As XML schema files, AAFs are used to define the structure of different aspects. According to the functionality, the AAFs form a hierarchical structure
that reflects functional variations of different adaptations. Adaptation aspects are

modelled into different types, for example, logging, caching, authentications, etc. Each aspect type is then refined into a group of sub-types. For example, aspects about authentication may consist of operating-system-based authentication and database-based authentication.

AAFs are a hierarchical aspect type system defined in XML schema format. This type hierarchy includes many levels of aspect types and sub-types, which capture various functionalities of the adaptation aspects. The Aspect Repository, assisted with the Aspect Manager, can adjust its aspect type structure to accommodate aspects with any functionality as long as they are defined in the required AAF formats.

Each AAF may have many Aspect Frames. AFs are the second abstraction layer in aspect definition. AFs are the instances of related AAFs. Compared with its AAF, an AF has the details of a concrete aspect populated into it by assigning a value to the parameters. User interaction is required in the tool to provide necessary information for creating an AF from an AAF. All information gathered from the tool will be described in (CAS, AA) pair. Defined in XML format, AFs are independent from concrete AOP platforms such as AspectJ.

An AF is not executable until it is mapped onto a concrete AOP platform. The result of this mapping is a family of Aspect Instances based on various AOP platforms. An Aspect Instance is executable and specific to a concrete AOP platform, and it reflects platform variations of an aspect on different AOP platforms. The agent to generate Aspect Instances from their AF is called Semantic Interpreter. The generation process is fully automatic.

4.2 Process Based Component Adaptation Specification (PCAS)

To satisfy the adaptation requirements for a particular reuse context, it often requires performing complex adaptations to multiple components with a set of generated aspects applied to these components under a specially designed process containing conditions, synchronization and other flow controls. Process-based Component Adaptation Specification is developed to describe the above complicated adaptation details.

The elements in a PCAS include target component(s) ("Host"), information of aspect(s) to be applied such as aspect id, type, and level ("Apply-aspect"), and process control information, such as flow controls ("Sequence", "Switch", "Case"), conditions, and synchronization support ("synchronized"). Flow control elements are used to provide advanced weaving process, and synchronization support enables multiple accesses to the same resource such as a file or a database from different aspects. A sample of PCAS is given in figure 5.

If a PCAS is found common and reusable in the future, its process control part can be regarded as a composite aspect type. Composite aspects are supported in AAF level to achieve advanced reuse in typical aspect using cases.

To implement PCAS in weaving process, a post-weaving technique is developed. The post-weaving tool gets class files for aspects generated by AOP platform such as AspectJ as input, and then modifies those class files to generate new class files that support complicated flow control and synchronization according to PCAS.

5   The Prototype Tool

A CASE tool has been developed to scale up the proposed approach. The tool provides a visual environment for component users to adapt components with the proposed approach.

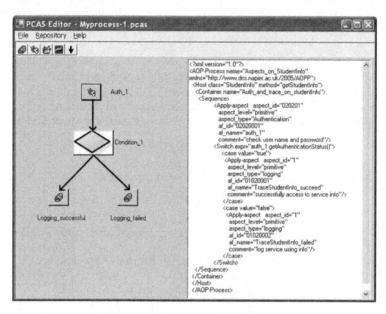

Fig. 3. A screen dump of PCAS Editor

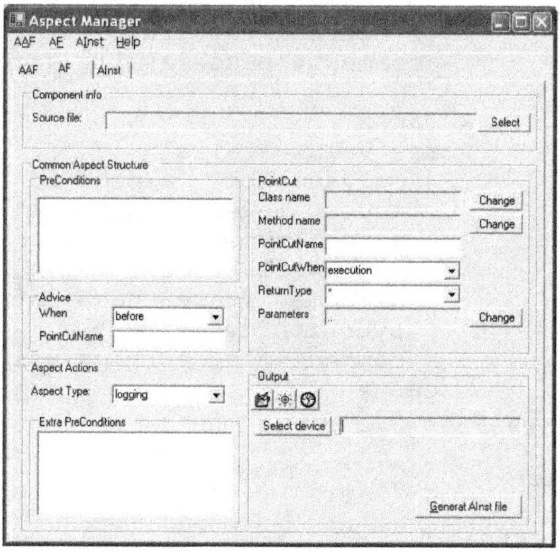

Fig. 4. A screen dump of Aspect Manager

The tool includes the following parts: 1) *Component Analyzer*, which analyzes component and gets necessary information such as the class names and method names, for component adaptation. 2) *PCAS Editor*, which provides an edit environment for PCAS both in graphical interface and at XML level. A screen dump is shown in figure 3. 3) *Aspect Manager*, which supports the management of reusable aspects in Aspect Repository and the graphical view of different levels of aspects. Aspects at different levels can be created, removed, and edited in Aspect Manager, either in the graphical user interface, or at XML level. A screen dump of Aspect

```xml
<?xml version="1.0"?>
<AOP-Process name="Aspects_on_StudentInfo"
xmlns="http://www.dcs.napier.ac.uk/2005/PCAS">
  <Host class="StudentInfo" method="getStudentInfo">
    <Container name="Auth_and_trace_on_studentInfo">
      <Sequence>
          <Apply-aspect   aspect_id="020201"
              aspect_level="primitive"
              aspect_type="Authentication"
              af_id="02020001"
              af_name="auth_1"
              synchronized="false"
              comment="check user name and password"/>
          <Switch
expr="auth_1.getAuthenticationStatus()">
                <case value="true">
                  <Apply-aspect   aspect_id="1"
                    aspect_level="primitive"
                    aspect_type="logging"
                    af_id="01020001"
                    af_name="TraceStudentInfo_succeed"
                    synchronized="true"
                    comment="successfully access to ser-
vice info"/>
                </case>
                <case value="false">
                  <Apply-aspect   aspect_id="1"
                    aspect_level="primitive"
                    aspect_type="logging"
                    af_id="01020002"
                    af_name="TraceStudentInfo_failed"
                    synchronized="true"
                    comment="log service using info"/>
                </case>
          </Switch>
      </Sequence>
    </Container>
  </Host>
</AOP-Process>
```

Fig. 5. The Process-based Component Adaptation Specification

Manager is shown in figure 4. 4) *Semantic Interpreters*, which translate AFs to AInsts based on selected specific AOP platform and aspects. If there are m different AOP platforms and n different aspects in the tool, there will be m×n different interpreters. 5) *Aspect Generator*: based on AFs and corresponding Semantic Interpreters, executable aspect instances will be generated by Aspect Generator. The result executable aspects will be saved into aspect repository as AInsts. 6) *Aspect Weaver*, which is used to generate new components by weaving generated AInsts into original components.

6 Example

The proposed approach has been applied to the construction of a student record system as a case study to test its correctness and capability. The following example is taken from the case study to demonstrate how the proposed approach works. In the case study, a component is found from a previous system providing access to student information. The component user has found the component is potentially suitable for the new application and wishes to integrate it into the new system. However, the

```
<?xml version="1.0" ?>
<Aspect name="TraceStudentInfo_succeed">
 <!-- Core asset -->
 <CommonCoreAsset>
  <PointCut>
    <Name>traceMethods</Name>
    <When>execution</When>
    <ReturnType>*</ReturnType>
    <ClassName>StudentInfo</ClassName>
    <MethodName>getStudentInfo</MethodName>
    <Parameters>..</Parameters>
  </PointCut>
  <Advice>
    <When>before</When>
    <PointCutName ref="traceMethods" />
  </Advice>
 </CommonCoreAsset>
```
→ CAS

```
 <!-- Variations -->
 <Variation type="logging">
  <ExtraPreConditions>
   <ExtraPrecondition/>
  </ExtraPreConditions>
  <Output>
   <Device>
    <File>D:\tmp\student_info_aop.log</File>
   </Device>
   <Messages>
    <Message>Access to StudentInfo.getStudentInfo
              successfully on </Message>
    <Date/>
    <Message>at </Message>
    <Time/>
   </Messages>
  </Output>
 </Variation>
</Aspect>
```
→ AA

Fig. 6. An Aspect Frame

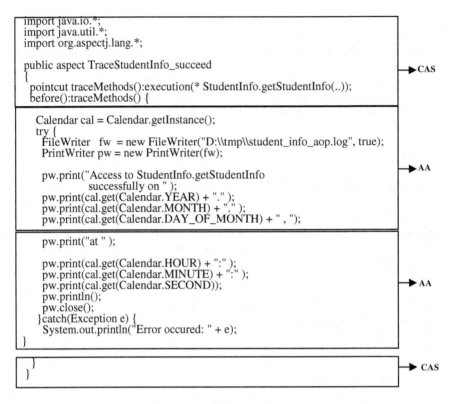

```
import java.io.*;
import java.util.*;
import org.aspectj.lang.*;

public aspect TraceStudentInfo_succeed                          ➤CAS
{
  pointcut traceMethods():execution(* StudentInfo.getStudentInfo(..));
  before():traceMethods() {

    Calendar cal = Calendar.getInstance();
    try {
      FileWriter  fw = new FileWriter("D:\\tmp\\student_info_aop.log", true);
      PrintWriter pw = new PrintWriter(fw);

      pw.print("Access to StudentInfo.getStudentInfo              ➤AA
              successfully on " );
      pw.print(cal.get(Calendar.YEAR) + "." );
      pw.print(cal.get(Calendar.MONTH) + "." );
      pw.print(cal.get(Calendar.DAY_OF_MONTH) + " , ");

      pw.print("at " );

      pw.print(cal.get(Calendar.HOUR) + ":" );
      pw.print(cal.get(Calendar.MINUTE) + ":" );
      pw.print(cal.get(Calendar.SECOND));                        ➤AA
      pw.println();
      pw.close();
    }catch(Exception e) {
      System.out.println("Error occured: " + e);
}

  }                                                               ➤CAS
}
```

Fig. 7. A simple Aspect Instance

component user wants to restrict the access to the student information only to the approved users, and wishes to monitor the access by logging the usage time.

To respond to the above need, the component user plans to add authentication to this component prior to using it. According to the result of authentication, the detail of access activity to the component will be recorded.

An authentication aspect is applied to this component first, followed by the application of corresponding logging aspects depending on the result of authentication aspect.

The adaptation actions are then described in a Process-based Component Adaptation Specification (PCAS) shown in figure 5. As shown in figure 4, the specification is created with the PCAS Editor by finding appropriate AAFs, i.e., either primitive types or composite types of aspects, and putting these AAFs into an adaptation process. Functional variation of adaptation is implemented through the composition of PCAS.

The specification in PCAS is at a rather overview level and does not contain the details of individual aspects. Developers need to provide parameter value for each aspect. Common AFs can be saved into Aspect Repository for further reuse. In this example, three AFs will be generated: AF for authentication, AF for logging if authenticated successfully, and AF for logging if authenticated unsuccessfully. Due to the structural similarity of AFs of different aspects, we only give the AF for logging if authenticated successfully in figure 6 as an example.

From AFs, Aspect Generator generates aspect instances (AInsts) that are specific to a selected AOP platform. The generated AInst of the AF in figure 6 is given in figure 7.

The Aspect Weaver weaves the generated aspect instances into the original component according to the PCAS. The final adapted component source code is invisible to the developer. By deploying the adapted component, the new application is built and released to the targeted user.

7 Conclusions

Despite the success of component-based reuse, the mismatches between available pre-qualified components and the specific reuse context in individual applications continue to be a major factor hindering component reusability and smooth composition. The work presented in this paper is based on the observation that existing reuse approaches and tools are weak in providing a mechanism to adapt components at adequately deep level and meanwhile with sufficient automation.

The proposed approach applies aspect-oriented generative adaptation to targeted components to correct the mismatch problem so that the components can be integrated into the target application smoothly. Automation and deep level adaptation are the benefits of the approach. This is achieved with the following key techniques in an aspect-oriented component reuse framework: 1) the generation of adaptation aspects based on specific adaptation requirements and selected abstract aspects as template; 2) the advanced aspect weaving process definition mechanism that supports switch and synchronization; 3) an expandable library of reusable adaptation aspects at multiple abstraction levels.

The GAIN technology enables application developers to adapt the pre-qualified components to eliminate mismatches to the integration requirement of specific applications. The benefits of the approach include deeper adaptability, higher automation and therefore smooth component composition and wider reusability. As consequence, the target component-based systems will have better quality. Our case studies, partly described in section 6, have shown that the approach and tool are promising in their ability and capability to solve the mismatch problem.

References

1. Batory, D., Chen, G., Robertson, E., & Wang, T.: Design Wizards and Visual Programming Environments for GenVoca Generators, IEEE Transactions on Software Engineering, May 2000, pp. 441-452.
2. Batory, D., Johnson, C., MacDonald, B., & Heeder, D. V.: Achieving Extensibility Through Product-Lines and Domain-Specific Languages: A Case Study, ACM Transactions on Software Engineering and Methodology (TOSEM), April 2002, Vol. 11(2), pp. 191-214.
3. Bosch, J.: Superimposition: a component adaptation technique, Information and Software Technology, 1999, 41, 5 pp. 257-273.
4. Cleaveland, J. C.: Building application generators, IEEE Software, July 1998, pp. 5(4): 25-33.

5. Diaz-Herrera, J.L., Knauber, P., & Succi, G.: Issues and Models in Software Product Lines, International Journal on Software Engineering and Knowledge Engineering, 2000, 10(4):527-539
6. http://www.sei.cmu.edu/cbs/
7. Lieberherr, K., Lorenz, D., & Mezini, M.: Programming with Aspectual Components, Technical Report NU-CCS-99-01, March, 1999.
8. Liu X., Wang B., & Kerridge J.: Achieving Seamless Component Composition Through Scenario-Based Deep Adaptation And Generation, Journal of Science of Computer Programming (Elsevier), Special Issue on New Software Composition Concepts, 2005, pp. 56, 2.
9. Keller, R., & Hölzle, U.: Binary Component Adaptation. Proceedings of the 12th European Conference on Object-Oriented Programming, July, 1998.
10. Kiczales, G., Hilsdale, E., Hugunin, J., Kersten, M., Palm, J., & Griswold, W.: Getting Started with AspectJ, Communications of the ACM, October 2001, pp. 59-65.
11. Kucuk, B., & Alpdemir, M.N.: Customizable adapters for blackbox components, Proceedings of the 3rd International Workshop on Component Oriented Programming, 1998, pp.53-59.
12. Samentinger, J.: Software Engineering with Reusable Components, Springer Verlag, 1997.
13. Sommerville, I.: (2004) Software Engineering (7th ed.). Addison-Wesley. ISBN: 0-321-21026-3
14. Suvee, D., Vanderperren, W., & Jonckers V.: JAsCo: an Aspect-Oriented approach tailored for component Based Software Development, Proceedings of the 2nd international conference on Aspect-oriented software development, Boston, USA, 2003, pp. 21-29.
15. Vanderperren, W., Suvée, D., Verheecke, B., Cibrán, M.A., & Jonckers, V.: Adaptive programming in JAsCo, Proceedings of the 4th international conference on Aspect-oriented software development, March, 2005.
16. Viega, J., Voas, J.: Quality time - Can aspect-oriented programming lead to more reliable software?, IEEE SOFTWARE, Nov-Dec, 2000, 17(6), pp. 19-21.
17. Wang, B., Liu, X., & Kerridge, J.: Scenario-based Generative Component Adaptation in .NET Framework, Proceedings of the IEEE International Conference on Information Reuse and Integration, Las Vegas, USA, November, 2004.

A Tactic-Driven Process for Developing Reusable Components*

George Kakarontzas and Ioannis Stamelos

Department of Informatics
Aristotle University of Thessaloniki
54124 Thessaloniki, Greece
gkakaron@teilar.gr, stamelos@csd.auth.gr

Abstract. True reusability of components assumes that they not only offer the functionality prescribed by their APIs, but also that they conform to a well-defined set of quality attributes so that we know if a component can be successfully reused in a new software product. One of the problems with quality attributes however is that it is hard to identify the characteristics of components that contribute to their emergence. End-user quality attributes are versatile and difficult to predict but their occurrence is not of an accidental nature. In this paper we propose a methodology for the exploration of candidate architectural tactics during component analysis and design for the achievement of desirable quality effects. Our approach is based on executable specifications of components that are augmented with the required tactic-related parameters to form a testbed for quality-driven experimentation. We believe that the proposed approach delivers both reusable components as well as reusable models.

1 Introduction

Succesful component reuse requires careful consideration in relation to the quality attributes that a component should satisfy and formal verification of these attributes for an actual component design. Quality or extra-functional properties are often viewed from different perspectives. For example the ISO/IEC 9126-1 standard for software product quality [1] suggests that there are internal quality requirements used to specify the quality of interim products used at the various stages of development of a software product and external quality requirements that specify the required product quality from an external view, including the required quality requirements of end users (quality in use). This standard classifies internal and external quality properties into six characteristics which are further subdivided into sub-characteristics. Another classification of quality properties is a realization-oriented classification [2] that relates component properties with

---

* This work has been partially funded by the project MISSION-SPM which is co-funded by the European Social Fund and Hellenic national resources (EPEAEK II/Archimedes II program).

M. Morisio (Ed.): ICSR 2006, LNCS 4039, pp. 273–286, 2006.
© Springer-Verlag Berlin Heidelberg 2006

system quality properties. This classification suggests that there are five different classes of quality properties according to their composition characteristics (directly composable properties, architecture related properties, derived properties, usage dependent properties, and system environment context properties). Classifications such as those mentioned above are useful and indicative of the need to move closer to the realization of the fundamental properties of software artifacts that contribute to the emergence of system level properties, as these properties are perceived from the final users of a system. To put it differently it is essential to realize what the driving forces of end system quality are. However this is a difficult issue. As mentioned in [1]: *"as the current state of the art does not provide the support necessary for the purposes of prediction, more technology should be developed to show the co-relation between internal quality, external quality and quality in use"*. A similar observation is made in [2] that mentions: *"(a problem) specific to component-based systems, is the difficulty of relating system properties to component properties"*.

An important problem is therefore the identification of the component properties that relate to specific system quality properties. What sort of features a component should posses in order to support higher system availability or better system performance so that we can safely assume that it is suitable for reuse in a given product?

Viewing the same issue from the opposite direction we are faced with the problem of the absence of the closed-world assumption [3]. The component developer is asked to produce components of high-quality to be reused in various systems. However the component developer cannot assume a closed world for his/her components. If the component is to be truly reusable in future systems requiring various quality properties and varying degrees of support for the same quality properties the obvious question is how it should be built to achieve that. The component developer cannot make the required assumptions and furthermore he/she cannot test the final product (the component) under specific system requirements, since the system is absent when the component is built.

A theory for the identification of component responsibilities relevant to a specific quality attribute is the theory of *architectural tactics*[9, 4, 6]. One possible way to address the closed-world assumption problem is the construction of a *model program*[5]. Model programs are system specifications written in a suitable (usually formal) specification language. The model program, among other things, can be used to simulate the conditions under which the component is to be used and its execution can offer substantial insight as to what architectural tactics should be applied to make the component more reusable in a number of possible contexts. In other words model program execution provides the oracle for the decision whether the model satisfies the requirements and whether the selected architectural tactics solve quality-related problems or not.

In the following Sect. 2 we provide a short introduction to architectural tactics and model programs and describe the steps of our process that uses these two theories and related tools. In Sect. 3 we provide a small illustrative example on the application of our process to a server component. Sect. 4 presents related work and compares our approach to other approaches. Finally in Sect. 5 we provide future research directions and conclude.

2   The Tactic-Driven Process

Before describing the tactic-driven process in detail we first provide a short introduction on the two theories that are the cornerstones of our approach: namely architectural tactics and model programs.

2.1   Architectural Tactics

A recent definition of architectural tactics from [6] is the following: "An architectural tactic is a means of satisfying a quality-attribute response measure by manipulating some aspect of a quality attribute model through architectural design decisions". Architectural tactics are based on quality attribute models that determine what is important in relation to the quality attribute under consideration. For example if we are interested in performance then relevant quality attribute models include scheduling theory and queuing theory. A quality attribute model has a number of independent parameters that determine the values of a number of dependent parameters. Choosing among the available quality attribute models depends on which are the dependent parameters of interest. For example if we are interested in worst-case latency then scheduling theory is more appropriate than queuing theory. The application of one or more architectural tactics can satisfy the required quality-attribute response.

2.2   Model Programs

A definition of a model program given in [5] is the following: "A model program P declares a finite set of action methods and a set of (state) variables. A model state is a mapping of state variables to concrete values.". Model programs are developed in a suitable formal language which is executable. In the case of the tool described in [5] model programs can be developed in the Abstract State Machine Language (AsmL), a formal language based on the theory of Abstract State Machines [7]. This is the language that we use for the illustration of our process in this paper.

2.3   A Description of the Tactic-Driven Process

The steps of our proposed process are those depicted in the activity diagram in Fig. 1. The steps are the following:

1. *Create a tentative formal model or modify an existing model by including the relevant independent and dependent parameters*: This is the first step of the tactic-driven process and in this step the designer creates a tentative model for the component under implementation using a suitable formal language. The model provides abstractions for the environment around the component

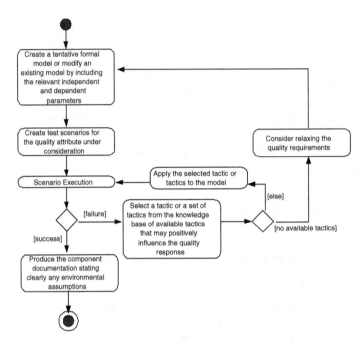

Fig. 1. The steps of the tactic-driven process

under implementation. It also includes the relevant parameters (independent and dependent) for the quality attribute of interest. It is assumed that in a pre-process step the designer determined what the suitable quality attribute model for the quality attribute under examination is. This might be achieved with a process similar to that described in [6].

2. *Create test scenarios for the quality attribute under consideration*: Here the designer applies expertise and judgment to instrument test scenarios that are relevant to the quality attribute under consideration. These scenarios should be conclusive in nature: they should act as oracles for the decision whether the quality attribute response is achieved or not.

3. *Scenario Execution*: After the construction of the scenarios the designer can execute them to decide whether the model satisfies the quality response desired or not. The output of this step will indicate if further manipulation of the model is necessary.

   (a) *[If the scenario execution was unsuccesful] Select a tactic or a set of tactics from the knowledge base of available tactics that may positively influence the quality response*: At this step the designer having failed to achieve the desired quality response selects a tactic from the available tactics that may have a positive impact on the desired quality response. It may be the case that the designer needs to select a set of tactics instead of just one, since some tactics require the application of others. For example fault recovery tactics (e.g. active or passive redundancy) require that some fault detection tactics are applied first (e.g. heartbeat).

Depending on whether or not there are more available tactics to consider this step may have two possible outcomes:

    i. *[If there are available tactics] Apply the selected tactic or tactics to the model*: At this step the designer applies the selected tactic or tactics to the model and repeats the "Scenario Execution" step.

    ii. *[If there are no available tactics] Consider relaxing the quality requirements*: If all the set of available tactics in relation to the quality response under investigation is exhausted and the designer still cannot achieve the desired quality response, he/she may consider relaxing the quality requirements and repeat the first step of the process by modifying the model.

(b) *[If the scenario execution was succesful] Produce the component documentation stating clearly any environmental assumptions*: The model itself is the most valuable deliverable that the process produces. It states clearly the conditions under which the component achieves the required quality response (the environmental assumptions). The model may be augmented with explanations on the rational of the decisions taken in the form of text, pictures etc. If the modeling language used supports literate programming (as AsmL does) then the explanations and the model can be part of the same executable document.

After the documentation step the process ends. The designer may repeat the whole process again considering this time other quality properties of interest.

3   Server Component Example

To illustrate our proposed process we will follow the steps of the process for a small model of a server component. The component serves a number of requests that arrive in the server's component queue. The component offers an interface with two methods: a `Compute` method and a `ComputeAndUpdateDB` method. The first method performs a computation that takes approximately 10 milliseconds to complete, whereas the second method performs the same computation but at the end also updates a database. The database step of the second method is an expensive operation compared to the computation step and requires approximately 100 milliseconds to complete. The arrival rates of the two methods follow the exponential distribution with an arrival mean of 100 ms for both methods. Internally the component uses a queue where requests are placed while the compute engine part of the component is busy. When the compute engine is idle it selects a request from the queue and services the request. Pictorially this is depicted in Fig. 2.

For this example we are interested for the performance of our component. Our main concern is latency: the time it takes for the service of a request including the waiting queue time and the service time. We require that the component performs the first method with a latency no more than 40 ms in average. On the other hand the method that performs the expensive database operation should also be close to the average service time of the operation. These are the quality requirements that our model should satisfy.

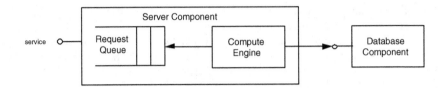

Fig. 2. The server component example

3.1   Create a Tentative Formal Model or Modify an Existing Model by Including the Relevant Independent and Dependent Parameters

In this step we construct a model program for the system under implementation. The model program is a simplification of the component for simulation, testing and exploration. We have used the Abstract State Machine Language (AsmL) [8] for this example. AsmL is a language based on the theory of Abstract State Machines [7]. It is an executable specification language and is fully interoperable with the other languages of the .NET platform. AsmL generates assemblies that can be executed from the command line or packaged as COM components and AsmL programs can also be explored with test exploration tools [10] such as the AsmL Test tool or Spec Explorer [5]. These tools can also generate tests that can be used for the conformance checking of an actual implementation of the model.

We have a number of agents executing in parallel in our model. A Distributed Abstract State Machine involves a number of agents executing in parallel. AsmL doesn't provide at the moment support for true concurrency, it is however possible to simulate it with interleaving as described in detail in [11]. To achieve this we introduce an abstract base class `Agent` with an abstract `Proceed()` method and several agents extend this class providing their own implementation of `Proceed()`. All these agents fire at each step of the execution of the machine and execute their respective `Proceed()` method.

```
abstract class Agent
   abstract Proceed()


class Clock extends Agent
class Arbitrator extends Agent
class Server extends Agent
class ComputeClient extends Agent
class DBClient extends Agent
```

The `Clock` agent simulates the clock of our model. The `Arbitrator` agent selects a request for service from the incoming queues and assigns it to a `Server` component for execution. The `Server` agent simulates the server component. The two client agents (`ComputeClient` and `DBClient`) simulate the clients of the component producing requests for the `Compute` and `ComputeAndUpdateDB` methods respectivelly.

A `Request` is a placeholder class for a request that clients make to the server component. Each request has a status recording the current state of the request and a type: it can either be a request for the `Compute` method or a request for the `ComputeAndUpdateDB` method. We declare enumerations for the state and the type of a request. We also embed in this class variables to record the execution times of each request for performance analysis.

```
enum Status
    Compute
    Blocked
    DBUpdate
    Finished
enum RType
    ComputeType
    DBType
class Request implements System.IComparable
    var whenArrived as Double
    var rtype as RType
    var whenStarted as Double = 0.0
    var whenFinished as Double = 0.0
    var whenToUnblock as Double = 0.0
    var status as Status = Compute
    Request(whenArrived' as Double, rtype' as RType)
        whenArrived = whenArrived'
        rtype = rtype'
    public CompareTo(obj as System.Object) as Integer
        match obj
            r as Request:
                return whenArrived.CompareTo(r.whenArrived)
```

A client generates requests according to an exponential distribution. In our example both types of requests arrive with a mean arrival rate of 100 ms. The client at each step generates a request and if the time has arrived for the generated request it places it in an incoming queue of requests (a `Set` of requests). Each client has its own queue. We show here the code for the `ComputeClient` agent. The code for the `DBClient` agent is similar. We also record the number of incoming requests.

```
var incomingCQ as Set of Request = {}
class ComputeClient extends Agent
    var exp as Exponential = new Exponential(100)
    var nextArrival as Request = null
    var inc as Integer = 0
    override Proceed()
        if nextArrival = null
            let when = clock.Now()+exp.NextValue()
            nextArrival := new Request(when, ComputeType)
```

```
    else
        if nextArrival.whenArrived <= clock.Now()
            add nextArrival to incomingCQ
            inc += 1
            nextArrival := null
```

The `Arbitrator` agent at each step chooses an idle server (one that currently processes no requests) and if there is a request in the union of the two sets containing the arrived requests, it selects the first request that arrived and assigns it to the idle server. The choice of the server, if we have more than one, is non-deterministic. The selection of the first arrival is done with the `min` selector of a set comprehension clause on all arrived requests. To use the `min` selector we had to make requests comparable in relation to their arrival time by implementing the `System.IComparable` interface of the .NET Framework SDK.

```
class Arbitrator extends Agent
    override Proceed()
        choose s in servers where s.currentRequest = null
        if s <> null
            let allRequests = {x | x in incomingCQ+incomingDBQ}
            if not allRequests.IsEmpty
                let r = (min x | x in allRequests)
                s.ProcessRequest(r)
                r.whenStarted := clock.Now()
                if r.rtype = ComputeType
                    remove r from incomingCQ
                else
                    remove r from incomingDBQ
```

Finally the `Server` agent has a `ProcessRequest` method that allows the arbitrator to assign requests to it. In its `Proceed` method it performs either a `ComputeNextStep` or a `ComputeAndUpdateDBNextStep` depending on the actual type of the current request. The two methods are similar, blocking the current request as required by the description of the durations for each step of the methods. When a request finishes the `Server` agent places the request in an outgoing set and assigns null to its current request so that it becomes selectable again by the `Arbitrator`.

```
class Server extends Agent
    var currentRequest as Request = null
    var exp10 as Exponential = new Exponential(10)
    var exp100 as Exponential = new Exponential(100)
    public ProcessRequest(request as Request)
        currentRequest := request
    override Proceed()
        if currentRequest <> null
            if currentRequest.rtype = Compute
```

```
                    ComputeNextStep()
            else
                ComputeAndUpdateDBNextStep()
    ComputeNextStep()
        match currentRequest.status
            Compute:
                currentRequest.whenToUnblock :=
                    clock.Now()+exp10.NextValue()
                currentRequest.status := Blocked
            Blocked:
                if currentRequest.whenToUnblock <= clock.Now()
                    currentRequest.status := Finished
                    currentRequest.whenFinished := clock.Now()
                    add currentRequest to outgoingComputeRequests
                    currentRequest := null
    ComputeAndUpdateDBNextStep()
        match currentRequest.status
            Compute:
                currentRequest.whenToUnblock :=
                    clock.Now()+exp10.NextValue()
                currentRequest.status := Blocked
            Blocked:
                if currentRequest.whenToUnblock <= clock.Now()
                    currentRequest.status := DBUpdate
                    currentRequest.whenToUnblock :=
                        clock.Now()+exp100.NextValue()
            DBUpdate:
                if currentRequest.whenToUnblock <= clock.Now()
                    currentRequest.status := Finished
                    currentRequest.whenFinished := clock.Now()
                    add currentRequest to outgoingDBRequests
                    currentRequest := null
```

3.2   Creation of Test Scenarios and Scenario Execution

Our test scenario requires that we run the program with the agents described
and measure the actual latency achieved by the component. We define variables
for each of these agents and the main execution step of the machine calls the
Proceed() method on all of them in parallel until the end of the simulationTime
constant.

```
var clock as Clock = new Clock()
var server as Server = new Server()
var servers as Set of Server = {server}
var arbitrator as Arbitrator = new Arbitrator()
var cclient as ComputeClient = new ComputeClient()
```

```
var dbclient as DBClient = new DBClient()
var agents as Set of Agent =
   {clock, server, arbitrator, cclient, dbclient}
Main()
   step while clock.Now() <= simulationTime
      forall a in agents
         a.Proceed()
```

After the simulation finishes we calculate the average latency for each type of request. Executing the simulation with these particular values for the independent parameters (event rate, service duration etc.) for 10000 ms gives an average latency of both types of requests in the area of 1000 ms. This shows that requests wait for a long time until they receive service. The scenario execution is therefore considered to be a failure and we proceed with the next step of selecting tactics that may positively influence the quality response.

Performance tactics from [4] and [9] include those depicted in Fig. 3.

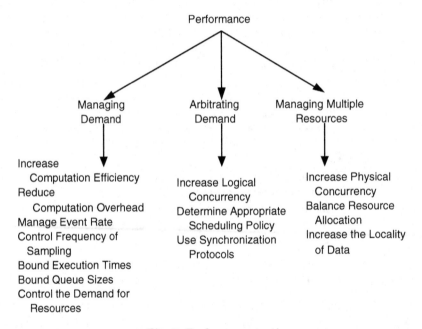

Fig. 3. Performance tactics

As we described in Sect. 2 this step of the process can be applied many times until we are satisfied with the system quality response or until we are convinced that the quality response cannot be met. For this example we carried out two such process steps.

The first step was to apply the *"Bound Queue Sizes"* tactic. We bounded the incoming queue sizes to four requests each and we measured the latency again and the number of rejected requests. This required modifications in the client agents who now placed requests in the incoming queue only if the queue sizes where less than four. The application of this tactic reduced the latency to one third of what we had before. It resulted however in rejections of incoming requests that were increasing as the simulation time increased. This showed that the system was becoming unstable as the time passed.

The second step was to apply the *"Bound Execution Times"* tactic. It is clear that the problem is the long database update request that causes other requests to queue for long periods or in the bounded queue size design leads to losses of large number of requests. To remedy this we applied a buffering scheme in which incoming requests that were updating the database were buffered. We used a buffer size of 5 requests. Now the method calls to the `ComputeAndUpdateDB` method update the buffer instead of the database. This is a much less expensive operation that requires 5 ms in average. Only every five requests the actual database update takes place and this requires again 100 ms in average. Notice that the introduction of this buffering scheme bounds the execution times of the expensive database update method and improves performance but the penalty is reduced reliability. If the server component crashes before the actual update takes place, the buffered updates will be lost. Assuming however that this is acceptable in this case the resulting latency converges for the first type of requests to 40 ms in average and for the second kind of requests to 50 ms. Also the number of the rejected requests are near zero for both types of request. The result was the same for increasing simulation times showing that the system is stable.

We could have applied other tactics to achieve the same or better results. For example an obvious candidate would be to increase the physical concurrency introducing multiple processors. Assuming however that this was not an option we turned our attention to other tactics. The important point here is that the tactics catalogue provides a knowledge base from which the designer can choose the appropriate solution that is acceptable. The designer can even produce multiple models satisfying different requirements and therefore provide different versions of the same component suitable for reuse in systems with different requirements.

3.3 Produce the Component Documentation Stating Clearly Any Environmental Assumptions

At this step the component developer documents the component design stating clearly any environmental assumptions. In the example given the environmental assumptions include the mean arrival rates of the requests as well as the fact that the reduced reliability should be acceptable. It also includes the performance guarantees given by the component designer for these assumptions. The model itself can serve as the formal definition of the component explaining in detail the actual implementation decisions adopted by the designers. With this information any future user of the component will be in a more informed position to decide whether or not he/she can use the component for an actual system, than merely knowing the interfaces of the component and the services that it offers.

4   Related Work

Quality has received considerable attention from the component community since it is the single most important issue for the successful reusability of components. Some recent relevant works to ours include the following.

In [12, 13] detailed queuing theory models are presented that can be used for the prediction of the performance of Java 2 Enterprise Edition (J2EE) applications. The models capture with details the important factors of delay in a J2EE container and can be used to guide the designer of J2EE applications. Detailed quality models such as these, can provide the basis for the development of accurate environment models that can be reused for the modeling of components for these environments with our proposed methodology.

In [14] a prediction-enabled component technology (PECT) is presented. A PECT comprises a construction framework and one or more reasoning frameworks used for the interpretation of PECT. The construction framework comprises an Abstract Component Technology (ACT) and tools (editors, constraint checkers, repositories etc). PECT is a very ambitious project that tries to address several long-lasting issues related to quality in component assemblies. One particular difficulty with PECT relates to the use of multiple reasoning frameworks. Issues such as the substitutability or the compatibility of reasoning frameworks are difficult to address. The interested reader can refer to section 6 of [14] for more details on this issue.

The Attribute-Driven Design method [15, 9] is a method for designing software architectures that also uses architectural tactics as a driver. Whereas ADD aims at the design of software architectures and is essentially a top-down approach, our method assumes an environment (e.g. component framework or product line architecture) and aims at designing a component so that it fits in this environment.

Architectural tactics are not specific to performance but cover instead a large and ever-growing body of quality characteristics including some of the less well understood. For example in [16] a list of tactics for usability is presented along with the usability benefits by the application of each tactic. Also in [9] tactics are given for controlling availability, modifiability, performance, security, testability and usability.

Abstract State Machines have been used extensively for the modeling of complex systems both software and hardware. The interested reader can refer to the Abstract State Machines website [17] for more information. In [18] AsmL is used for conformance checking of an actual component implementation against its specification. Conformance checking is an important next step to the process described here since it can prove or disprove the claim that a component actually conforms to a given model.

5   Conclusion and Future Research Directions

In this paper we have presented a tactic-based process for the development of reusable components that is based on quality requirements and experimentation using a model of the component and the environment in which it is to be placed. Although the small example presented is about performance, the process can be applied to other quality attributes as well, with the requirement that their quality properties can be calculated by algorithms.

The choice of Abstract State Machines for performance modeling is not the most obvious choice. Various others formal notations and their respective tools, such as the Performance Evaluation Process Algebra [19], are arguably more appropriate for modeling performance since they were made specifically for that. Our choice of ASM comes from the fact that our proposed process is not only concerned with performance. We want to be able to model a variety of arbitrary quality properties and validate the model response to them. Furthermore this validation must take place incrementally yet at the end simultaneously for all the required quality properties since very often the satisfaction of a quality response for one quality property renders the validation of another false (as the performance/reliability tradeof in our example). Also the ASM community has been very active in providing formal semantics for the UML metamodel and the various UML models (e.g. [20]). Mapping of UML constructs to ASM provides the opportunity to construct CASE tools that will hide the complexity of writing ASM (and in general formal) specifications from the average developer and software engineer. The developers will instead use (possibly a well-defined subset of) UML and the tool will provide the necessary mappings to ASM and the subsequent verification of the design. Finally, a specific to AsmL and .NET benefit is that AsmL is a first class citizen of the .NET language runtime. The interoperation of AsmL specifications and .NET components opens the possibility of mixed executable systems where some components are executable models and some are specifications. We can imagine very useful applications of this including the construction of reusable specifications of arbitrary environments where actual component implementations for them can be tested as well as the reverse where the environment exists and the component under implementation can be specified and tested prior to the implementation effort.

In the future we plan to move to two directions. The first is the use of our methodology for quality attributes less well understood than performance, such as modifiability and the application of our process to large projects. The second is the investigation of ways to make the process as automated as possible. One first step in this direction that we plan to investigate is the construction of a tool that will use a repository of architectural tactics and the model as input to guide the designer in the choise of the architectural tactics that might be useful in improving the quality response.

References

1. ISO/IEC 9126-1: "Software Engineering - Product Quality - Part 1: Quality Model". ISO/IEC Standard, ISO/IEC 9126-1:2001(E), 2001
2. Ivica Crnkovic et. al.: "Concerning Predicatbility in Dependable Component-Based Systems: Classification of Quality Attributes". in R.de Lemos et. al. (Eds.): Architecting Dependable Systems III, LNCS 3549, pp. 257-278, 2005.

3. Clemens Szyperski: "Component technology: What, Where, and How?". Invited talk in ICSE '03: Proceedings of the 25th International Conference on Software Engineering, IEEE Computer Society, pp. 684–693, 2003.
4. Felix Bachmann et. al.: "Illuminating the Fundamental Contributors to Software Architecture Quality". Technical Report, CMU/SEI-2002-TR-025, Software Engineering Institute, Carnegie Mellon University, 2002.
5. Margus Veanes et. al.: "Online testing with model programs", SIGSOFT Softw. Eng. Notes, vol. 30, no. 5, pp. 273–282, ACM Press, 2005
6. Felix Bachmann et. al.: "Deriving Architectural Tactics: A Step Toward Methodical Architectural Design", Technical Report, CMU/SEI-2003-TR-004, March 2003
7. Yuri Gurevich: "Evolving Algebras 1993: Lipari Guide", Specification and Validation Methods, ed. E. Borger, Oxford University Press, pp. 9–36, 1995
8. AsmL Website: http://research.microsoft.com/fse/asml, 2005
9. Len Bass, Paul Clements and Rick Kazman: "Software Architecture in Practice, 2nd ed.", Addison-Wesley, 2003
10. Mike Barnett et. al.: "Validating Use-Cases with the AsmL Test Tool", in proc. of the Third International Conference On Quality Software (QSIC03), p. 238, IEEE, 2003
11. Uwe Glässer, Yuri Gurevich and Margus Veanes: "Abstract Communication Model for Distributed Systems", IEEE Transactions on Software Engineering, vol. 30, no. 7, pp. 458-472, July, 2004
12. Yan Liu and Ian Gordon: "Performance Prediction of J2EE Applications Using Messaging Protocols", in proc. CBSE 2005, LNCS 3489, pp. 1-16, 2005
13. Yan Liu et. al.: "Predicting the Performance of Middleware-based Applications at the Design Level", in proc. of the 4th international workshop on Software and performance (WOSP'04), pp. 166–170, ACM Press, 2004
14. K. C. Wallnau, "Volume III: A Technology for Predictable Assembly from Certifiable Components", Carnegie Mellon University Software Engineering Institute, TECHNICAL REPORT CMU/SEI-2003-TR-009, Apr. 2003
15. Len Bass et. al.: "Quality Attribute Design Primitives and the Attribute Driven Design Method", in proc. of the 4th International Workshop on Software Product Family Engineering (PFE 2002), LNCS 2290, pp. 169–186, 2002.
16. Len Bass and Bonnie E. John: "Linking usability to software architecture patterns through general scenarios", Journal of Systems and Software, vol. 66, no. 3, pp. 187–197, 2003
17. ASM website: http://www.eecs.umich.edu/gasm/, 2005
18. Mike Barnett and Wolfram Schulte: "Spying on Components: A Runtime Verification Technique", OOPSLA 2001 Workshop on Specification and Verification of ComponentBased Systems, 2001
19. J. Hillston: "A Compositional Approach to Performance Modelling", Cambridge University Press, 1996
20. Alessandra Cavarra, Elvinia Riccobene and Patrizia Scandurra: "Integrating UML Static and Dynamic Views and Formalizing the Interaction Mechanism of UML State Machines", in proc. of the ASM 2003, LNCS, pp 229-243, 2003

Does Refactoring Improve Reusability?

Raimund Moser[1], Alberto Sillitti[1], Pekka Abrahamsson[2],
and Giancarlo Succi[1]

[1] Center for Applied Software Engineering, Free University of Bolzano-Bozen,
Piazza Domenicani 3, Italy
{rmoser, asillitti, gsucci}@unibz.it
[2] VTT Electronics, Oulu, Finland
pekka.abrahamsson@vtt.fi

Abstract. The improvement of the software development process through the development and utilization of high quality and reusable software components has been advocated for a long time. Agile Methods promote some interesting practices, in particular the practice of refactoring, which are supposed to improve understandability and maintainability of source code. In this research we analyze if refactoring promotes ad-hoc reuse of object-oriented classes by improving internal quality metrics. We conduct a case study in a close-to-industrial, agile environment in order to analyze the impact of refactoring on internal quality metrics of source code. Our findings sustain the hypothesis that refactoring enhances quality and reusability of – otherwise hard to reuse - classes in an agile development environment. Given such promising results, additional experimentation is required to validate and generalize the results of this work.

1 Introduction

In Extreme Programming (XP) much emphasis is given on an agile, iterative and customer oriented way of how to develop software. Among the top priorities of XP are (a) customer satisfaction through continuous delivery of valuable software and (b) embracing changing requirements (http://agilemanifesto.org). The practices of XP are tailored to achieve such goals: iterative and informal planning, simple design, continuous refactoring of the code, pair programming, test first and continuous integration – just to mention a few [3]. Most of these practices are intended to be used during development and maintenance and seem to keep at least in part their promises [21].

However, XP does not address explicitly the issue of software reuse as one of its practices. This may wonder since many believe that software reuse provides "the key to enormous savings and benefits in software development" [24], [13]. XP *per se* does not aim at developing software for possible future reuse in order to avoid overhead during development. Keep it simple and develop only what the customer really wants is one of the key principles of XP.

On the other hand we think that XP – compared to more traditional development methodologies - intrinsically guides software engineers to develop software, which is of high quality and therefore suited for ad-hoc reuse. In particular the practice of continuous refactoring may improve internal quality metrics and affect reusability of a software system in a positive way [7]. Reusability is a rather high-level quality metric

M. Morisio (Ed.): ICSR 2006, LNCS 4039, pp. 287–297, 2006.
© Springer-Verlag Berlin Heidelberg 2006

that consists of several internal and external properties of the software and of the development process [15]. Poulin [24] introduces a possible taxonomy of reusability metrics: He differentiates between empirical and qualitative methods and gives an overview of several models to assess reusability. Dandashi and Rine [11] decompose reusability into direct and indirect quality attributes, namely: adaptability, completeness, maintainability, and understandability. Refactoring seems to enhance particularly the last two quality attributes [5], [25]: In his book on refactoring [16] Fowler stresses over and over that one of the key points of refactoring is to make the code easier to understand and to read. We believe this should affect in a positive way also ad-hoc reuse of otherwise not reusable pieces of software.

A proven way to measure reusability is to analyze how often parts (classes, methods, etc.) of a software system are reused in a product. Such reusability frequency and amount of reuse metrics are proposed and used by several researchers [13], [10], [17]. In this research we do not follow this approach, as we do not have such data. Our idea is to analyze whether refactoring enhances reusability by analyzing its impact on some of the internal reusability metrics proposed and validated in the work of Dandashi et al. [11]. Thus, in order to assess reusability we employ only a restricted set of internal product attributes that are available and monitored during development. We do not take into account any external and high-level product or process metrics. In doing so we risk failing in characterizing properly software reusability. However, we think that our approach is in part justified by the findings of other researchers, in particular by [8], [2], and [11].

The paper is organized as follows: In Section 2 we present our research methodology and define the research question; in Section 3 the results of a case study are presented and discussed; in Section 4 we refer to some issues regarding the limitations of our approach and future plans. Finally, conclusions and implications of the investigation are drawn in Section 5.

2   A Methodology for Evaluating the Impact of Refactoring on Code Quality

In this section at first we describe the metrics we use for assessing code quality - with particular focus on reusability. Afterwards, we develop a model for evaluating how refactoring may affect internal quality metrics, which are used to assess reusability of the software system during development. Finally we state our research questions.

2.1   Internal Quality Metrics That Affect Reusability

Our research question is to assess whether refactoring facilitates the development of high-quality code and as a consequence ad-hoc reusability or not. To answer such question first we have to define carefully what we mean by high-quality and reusability and how we measure it. Code quality is a rather vague term for describing certain quality attributes of a software system and can be decomposed in different ways into lower-level metrics [15]. In this research we focus on internal properties of the software that are considered to be relevant for its reusability. In particular, we follow the approach proposed by Dandashi and Rine [11] and use two different sets of metrics:

- One for micro level measurements (measurements at a method level)
- And one for macro level measurements (measurements at a class level)

For the micro level measurements we employ McCabe's cyclomatic complexity of a method [23] and the number of Java statements per method. To arrive at a measure for the whole class, the highest measure is used as a representative measure of the corresponding class measure. For the macro level measurements we use the Chidamber and Kemerer (CK) set of object-oriented metrics [8].

The motivation for choosing this set of metrics is twofold: First, some of them such as the CK metrics are among the best-understood and validated metrics for object-oriented systems and therefore we can be more confident in their expressiveness [2]. Second, the tool we use for collecting these metrics is able to collect them in an automatic and non-invasive way - a fundamental requirement for data collection in an XP process [19].

Several empirical studies put the CK metrics into relationship with software quality, in particular with maintainability, reusability, and reliability. Li and Henry [22] for example show that the CK metrics are useful to predict maintainability. Basili *et al.* [2] investigate the relationship between the CK metrics and code quality: Their findings suggest that 5 of the 6 CK metrics are useful quality indicators. However, such studies are rare in XP-like environments and they do not analyze how the evolution of the CK metrics during development is affected by refactoring. Table 1 summarizes the metrics we use in this research as indicators for reusability.

Table 1. Selected internal product metrics as indicators for reusability

Metric name	Level	Definition
MAX_LOC	Class	Maximum number of Java statements of all methods in a class
MAX_MCC	Class	Highest McCabe's cyclomatic complexity of all methods in a class
CBO	Class	Coupling Between Object classes (CK)
LCOM	Class	Lack of Cohesion in Methods (CK)
WMC	Class	Weighted Methods per Class (CK)
RFC	Class	Response Of a Class (CK)
DIT	Class	Depth of Inheritance Tree
NOC	Class	Number Of Children

Dandashi and Rine [11] find in their research a correlation between the CK and complexity measures and external high-level quality attributes for reusability. In this work we rely on their findings, as we do not analyze directly the impact of refactoring on external reusability measures. However, we are well aware that we conduct a study in a very different environment; the fact that we consider only a restricted set of internal product metrics for assessing reusability limits to some extent the validity of our findings and has to be addressed in a future study.

2.2   An Approach to Assess the Impact of Refactoring on Internal Quality Metrics During Development

In section 2.1 we choose a set of metrics, which is known to be useful as internal measures for quality of a software system. However, we do not know a priori the range of values of these metrics that would indicate good or bad quality. Analyzing historical data or several similar projects can only – if at all – derive such thresholds [4]. We follow a different strategy, as we do not seek to associate absolute values of the metrics in Table 1 to different classes of quality, but rather analyze the changes of them during development.

Our approach is the following: First, we identify a set of candidate classes that are likely to be considered for reuse. Afterwards, we monitor the daily changes of our quality metrics for each class during development. Finally we compare the average of these daily changes with the change each class gains after it has been refactored. This allows us to quantify the impact of refactoring on internal quality metrics compared to their overall evolution during development.

A bit more formally we can define our method as follows.

Let $M_i \in M=\{MAX\_MCC, MAX\_LOC, CBO, RFC, WMC, DIT, NOC, LCOM\}$ be one of the quality metrics listed in Table 1. In a first step we average their daily changes for each candidate class over the whole development period not including days when the class has been refactored. We denote this average value for metric M_i by ΔM_i. N in equation (1) is the total number of development days; Δt is a time interval of 1 day and R is the set of all days during which developers have refactored a particular class.

$$\Delta M_i = \frac{\sum_{\substack{k=1 \\ k \notin R}}^{N} M_i(k \cdot \Delta t) - M_i((k-1) \cdot \Delta t)}{N - |R|} \tag{1}$$

By ΔR_i we denote the average of the daily changes of quality metric M_i only for the days ($k \in R$) in which a class has been refactored. To assess whether refactoring improves quality of a class we compute its ΔR_i and ΔM_i values and compare them with each other: If ΔR_i is negative and significantly lower than ΔM_i we may conclude that refactoring improves quality metric M_i compared to its standard evolution during development.

In order to apply our method to a real system we not only need to collect the daily evolution of source code metrics but also to identify a set of candidate classes and refactoring activities. Regarding the first issue we proceed as follows: We analyze the design document and use the description provided by developers and our own experience to find classes, which are either explicitly developed for reuse or at least are promising to be reused in the same or similar products. We exclude any classes that are highly dependent on the specific application such as classes dealing with the user interface, product specific data representation/processing or classes holding hard coded data (constants). The identification of candidate classes is a subjective process and therefore we may not identify all relevant classes. However, in an XP process development is not targeted specifically to reusability and in principle every class that is not tightened too much with a particular application feature could be reused in an ad-hoc manner.

The second issue we have to address is: How can we identify days in which a class has been refactored? Currently we are working on a method that extracts such information automatically from a CVS repository by using source code change metrics information (for the basic idea see [12]). This work is still in an early phase and cannot be used for this research. However, for the case study we present in section 3 developers have created user stories for refactoring activities and by analyzing them we know which classes have been refactored when.

To summarize our method for assessing the impact of refactoring on quality and reusability we stress again that it has to be taken with a grain of salt, as we do not include many important factors such as experience of developers, development tools, or the stability of the application domain. However, we think that by analyzing the change of important internal quality metrics induced by refactoring we can indicate whether refactoring - by delivering easy to reuse and maintain code - supports ad-hoc reuse or not.

2.3 Research Question

The goal of this research is to determine whether refactoring improves code quality and as a consequence supports ad-hoc reuse. Our objective is to present evidence that will allow us to reject the null hypothesis:

- H_0: The changes of quality metric M_i induced by refactoring (ΔR_i) are not different from the average changes during development (ΔM_i) for classes that are likely to be reused in an ad-hoc manner.

And to accept the alternative hypothesis:

- H_1: The changes of quality metrics M_i induced by refactoring (ΔR_i) are different (preferably lower) from the average changes during development (ΔM_i) for classes that are likely to be reused in an ad-hoc manner.

In section 3 we present a case study we run in order to reject or accept the null hypothesis stated above.

3 Case Study

In this section we present a case study we conducted in a close-to industrial environment in order to analyze quality enhancement and promotion of ad-hoc reuse by refactoring in a software project developed using an agile, XP-like methodology [1]. The objective of the case study is to answer our research question posed in section 2: First, we collected in a non-invasive way the metrics listed in Table 1; afterwards, we analyzed their time evolution and fed them into equation (1) in order to compute their values for ΔM_i. Then we selected candidate classes for reuse and collected their change metrics after they have been refactored (ΔR_i). Finally, we used a statistical test to determine whether or not it is possible to reject our null hypothesis.

3.1 Description of the Project and Data Collection Process

The object under study is a commercial software project developed at VTT in Oulu, Finland. The programming language in use was Java. The project was a full business success in the sense that it delivered on time and on budget the required product, a production monitoring application for mobile, Java enabled devices. The development process followed a tailored version of the Extreme Programming practices [1], which included all the practices of XP but the "System Metaphor" and the "On-site Customer"; there was instead a local, on-site manager that met daily with the group and had daily conversations with the off-site customer. Two pairs of programmers (four people) have worked for a total of eight weeks. The project was divided into five iterations, starting with a 1-week iteration, which was followed by three 2-week iterations, with the project concluding in a final 1-week iteration.

The developed software consists of 30 Java classes and a total of 1770 Java source code statements (denoted as LOC). Throughout the project mentoring was provided on XP and other programming issues according to the XP approach. Three of the four developers had an education equivalent to a BSc and limited industrial experience. The fourth developer was an experienced industrial software engineer. The team worked in a collocated environment. Since it was exposed for the first time to the XP process a brief training of the XP practices, in particular of the test-first method was provided prior to the beginning of the project.

To collect the metrics listed in Table 1 we used our in-house developed tool PROM [26]. PROM is able to extract from a CVS repository a variety of standard and user defined source code metrics including the CK metric suite. Not to disrupt developers we set up the tool in the following way: Every day at midnight automatically a check-out of the CVS repository was performed, the tool computed the values of the CK and complexity metrics and stored them in a relational database. In this way we obtained directly the daily evolution of the CK metrics, LOC and McCabe's cyclomatic complexity.

3.2 Results

We were able to collect the daily evolution of the metrics in Table 1 for the entire period of development, which was 8 weeks, apart from 3 days. In these days developers apparently did not check-in the source code and therefore we had to omit them from our analysis.

The design of the developed system is based on the MVC pattern [6], the Broker architectural pattern [6] and several standard design patterns described in [18]. We think that some basic classes of these patterns – their importance is also emphasized by the design document – are particularly interesting to be considered for reuse. Out of them we choose a subset of classes, which have been refactored during development. We can infer this information from two user stories that have been implemented specifically for refactoring tasks and comments added in the respective classes.

We select in total five candidate classes and compute in a first step the daily changes of the metrics for each of them omitting the days when they have been refactored. We denote the five classes by A, B, C, D, and E. After we compute the average of these changes for all days in which a class has been refactored (the considered classes have been refactored at most on two different days during development). Table 2 shows the results: For each metric and candidate class we indicate the average changes during development (without refactoring), ΔM_i, the average changes induced by refactoring, ΔR_i, and whether or not we can reject our null hypothesis, H_0. We accept or reject H_0 by applying a one-sample Wilcoxon rank sum test [20]: We test whether a sample of changes for metric M_i has a median ΔR_i or not. For the test we use a significance level of $\alpha=0.05$.

Table 2. Average daily changes of quality metrics in case of refactoring (ΔR) and development (ΔM). A **1** in the column with heading H means that we can reject the null hypothesis for the particular class and metric, 0 means that we cannot reject the null hypothesis. Values are rounded to their closest integer.

Class	CBO			RFC			WMC			LCOM		
	ΔM	ΔR	H	ΔM	ΔR	H	ΔM	ΔR	H	ΔM	ΔR	H
A	0	0	0	0	1	1	1	-1	1	0	-1	1
B	1	-4	1	1	-4	1	0	0	0	0	0	0
C	1	0	0	2	-5	1	4	0	0	1	0	0
D	1	-1	1	1.4	-2	1	2	0	0	1	0	0
E	1	-1	1	3.5	-2	1	2	3	1	0	0	0
	MAX_MCC			MAX_LOC			DIT			NOC		
A	0	-1	1	0	0	0	0	0	0	0	0	0
B	0	0	0	2	-2	1	0	0	0	0	0	0
C	3	0	0	6	-46	1	0	0	0	0	0	0
D	3	-2	1	0	0	0	0	0	0	0	0	0
E	1	0	0	10	-20	1	0	0	0	0	0	0

The interpretation of the numbers in Table 2 is straightforward: For every candidate class there are at least two quality metrics that improve significantly after it has been refactored (compared to the average evolution during development). In particular classes A and E show a notable enhancement: These two classes provide general interfaces to the user interface and database and it is likely that they will be reused in a similar application.

By investigating the different metrics we notice that not all of them are affected in the same way by refactoring: The metrics related to inheritance and cohesion for example are not at all or only in a negligible way changed by the refactorings applied in the project. This could be explained by the fact that the software under scrutiny is relatively small: It does not use deep inheritance hierarchies and only in a limited way inheritance as a mechanism for reuse. Therefore, it is quiet obvious that no refactoring dealing with inheritance has been applied (it was not necessary to restructure code due to complexity caused by inheritance). As for LCOM several researchers have questioned its meaning and the way it is defined by Chidamber and Kemerer [9]; the impact of LCOM on software reusability is little understood by today and therefore we do not analyze it further in this research.

The highest benefit of refactoring show the CBO and RFC metrics: They express the coupling between different classes and the complexity of a class in terms of method definitions and method invocations. We believe that these two metrics are strong indicators for how difficult it is to reuse a class: A high value of RFC makes it difficult to understand what the class is doing and a high value of CBO means that the class is dependent on many external classes and difficult to reuse in isolation. Both situations prevent it from being easily reused. For three out of the five candidate classes refactoring improves significantly both the RFC and CBO values and as such clearly makes them more suitable for ad-hoc reuse.

Refactoring seems also to lower method complexity: In all the classes either the method with the maximum lines of code or the one with the highest cyclomatic complexity have gained a notably improvement after refactoring. Again, classes with less complex methods are easier to reuse.

Summarizing our results we can reject hypothesis H_0 for several metrics M_i (in particular for the RFC and CBO metric) but not for all of them (like the inheritance related metrics) and not for all classes we selected. We can conclude that refactoring improves for every class we analyze at least two internal metrics that are important for reusability; moreover, for most of them it lowers significantly coupling and method invocation complexity – two "code smells" [14] that often prevent classes from being reused in an ad-hoc manner. Overall the results of this case study give strong evidence that refactoring supports ad-hoc reuse in an XP-like development environment.

4   Threats to Validity and Future Work

This research addresses the question whether refactoring supports ad-hoc reuse or not. We try to answer it by analyzing and comparing the evolution of quality metrics of a software system during "traditional" development and after phases of refactoring. Our approach considers only a set of internal product metrics that may be useful and important as reusability indicators. Of course, this is only half of the story and a complete model should also consider external product and process metrics that characterize reusability.

Regarding the internal validity of this research we have to address the following threats:

- The subjects of the case study are heterogeneous (three junior and one experienced developers) and use for the first time an XP-like methodology. This could affect seriously our findings, as for example junior developers may behave very different than experienced ones. Also the kind and application of refactorings depend highly on the experience of a developer and could lead to different results in other environments. Moreover, a learning effect could be visible and for example influence the evolution of reusability metrics during the project.

- We do not validate the approach we propose and use in this case study. I.e. we do not analyze if refactored classes that show an improvement of internal quality metrics are reused more often and more easily in the same or similar projects. Such validation has to be addressed in a future study.

- Finally, the choice of candidate classes, quality metrics and the time interval we use to compute their changes is subjective. Although we tried to motivate our choices we plan to consider variations in metrics and time interval in future experiments in order to confirm or reject the conclusions of this research.

Altogether, as with every case study the results we obtain are valid only in the specific context of the experiment. In this research we analyze a rather small software project in a highly volatile domain. A generalization to other application domains and XP projects is only possible by future replications of the experiment in such environments.

5 Conclusions

Although agile processes and practices are gaining more and more importance in the software industry much more work has to be done to convince managers to introduce new and innovative development concepts in their companies. This research focuses on whether refactoring, a key practice of XP, supports ad-hoc reuse or not. Software reuse is a key success factor for software development and should be supported as much as possible by the development process itself. We believe that refactoring supports and enhances ad-hoc reuse in a software project, which does not address reusability as one of its primary goals.

The contribution of this research is twofold: First, we propose a methodology for assessing if refactoring improves quality and therefore promotes ad-hoc reuse of object-oriented classes during development. Second, we conduct a case study in which we apply our methodology and which allows us to provide in a quantitative way and in a close-to industrial environment an answer to our research question.

The main conclusion of this research can be summarized as follows:
Refactoring seems to improve significantly important internal measures for reusability of object-oriented classes written in Java. Therefore, we can sustain our claim that refactoring has a positive effect on reusability and for sure promotes ad-hoc reuse in an XP-like development environment.

Of course refactoring as any other technique is something a developer has to learn and to train. First, managers have to be convinced that refactoring is very valuable for their business; this research should help them in doing so as it sustains that refactoring – if applied properly – intrinsically delivers code, which is easier to reuse than code which has not been refactored. Afterwards, they have to provide training and support to change their development process into a new one that includes continuous refactoring. Agile Methods already use refactoring as one of their key practices and could be a first choice for developing code in a way that supports - among other benefits such as good maintainability - also reusability.

References

1. Abrahamsson, P., Hanhineva, A., Hulkko, H., Ihme, T., Jäälinoja, J., Korkala, M., Koskela, J., Kyllönen, P., and Salo, O.: Mobile-D: An Agile Approach for Mobile Application Development. Proceedings of the 19th Annual ACM Conference on Object-Oriented Programming, Systems, Languages, and Applications, OOPSLA'04, Vancouver, British Columbia, Canada (2004)

2. Basili, V., Briand, L., and Melo, W.L.: A Validation of Object-Oriented Design Metrics as Quality Indicators. IEEE Transactions on Software Engineering, **22**(10): 267-271 (1996)
3. Beck, K.: Extreme Programming Explained: Embrace Change. Addison-Wesley (2000)
4. Benlarbi, S., El Emam, K., Goel, N., Rai, S.: Thresholds for Object-Oriented Measures. Proceedings of 11th International Symposium on Software Reliability Engineering (ISSRE'00), p. 24 (2000)
5. Bois, B. D., Demeyer, S., Verelst, J.: Refactoring – Improving Coupling and Cohesion of Existing Code. Belgian Symposium on Software Restructuring, Gent, Belgium (2005)
6. Buschmann, F., Meunier, R., Rohnert, H., Sommerlad, P., and Stal, M.: Pattern oriented software architecture. Volume 1: A System of Patterns. John Wiley & Sons (1996)
7. Caballero, R., and Demurjian, S.A.: Towards the Formalization of a Reusability Framework for Refactoring. Proceedings of the 7th International Conference Software Reuse: Methods, Techniques, and Tools, ICSR-7, Austin, TX, USA (2002)
8. Chidamber, S., Kemerer, C.F.: A metrics suite for object-oriented design. IEEE Transactions on Software Engineering, **20**(6): 476-493 (1994)
9. Counsell, S., Mendes, E., Swift, S.: Comprehension of object-oriented software cohesion: the empirical quagmire. Proceedings of the 10th International Workshop on in Program Comprehension, Paris, France (2002) 33 – 42
10. Curry, W.E., Succi, G., Smith, M.R., Liu, E., and Wong, R.W.: Empirical Analysis of the Correlation between Amount of Reuse Metrics in the C Programming Language. Proceedings of the 1999 Symposium on Software Reusability (SSR'99), Los Angeles, Ca, USA (1999)
11. Dandashi, F., and Rine, D.C.: A Method for Assessing the Reusability of Object-Oriented Code Using a Validated Set of Automated Measurements. Proceedings of 17th ACM Symposium on Applied Computing (SAC 2002), Madrid (2002)
12. Demeyer, S., Ducasse, S., Nierstrasz, O.: Finding Refactorings via Change Metrics. Proceedings of the 15th Annual ACM Conference on Object-Oriented Programming, Systems, Languages, and Applications, OOPSLA'00, Minneapolis, USA (2000)
13. Devanbu, P., Karstu, S., Melo, W., and Thomas, W.: Analytical and Empirical Evaluation of Software Reuse Metrics. Proceedings of the 18th International Conference on Software Engineering, Berlin, Germany (1996)
14. van Emden, E., and Moonen, L.: Java Quality Assurance by Detecting Code Smells. Proceedings of the 9th Working Conference on Reverse Engineering, IEEE Computer Society Press (2002)
15. Fenton, N., and Pfleeger, S.L.: Software Metrics A Rigorous & Practical Approach. PWS Publishing Company, Boston (1997) pp. 408
16. Fowler, M.: Refactoring Improving the Design of Existing Code. Addison-Wesley (2000)
17. Frakes, W., and Terry, C.: Reuse Level Metrics. Proceedings of the 3rd International Conference on Software Reuse, Rio de Janeiro, Brazil (1994)
18. Gamma, E., Helm, R., Johnson, R., and Vlissides, J.: Design patterns: Elements of Reusable Object-Oriented Software. New York, Addison-Wesley (1995)
19. Johnson, P.M., Disney, A.M.: Investigating Data Quality Problems in the PSP. Proceedings of the Sixth International Symposium on the Foundations of Software Engineering (SIGSOFT 98) (1998)
20. Hollander, M., Wolfe, D.A.: Nonparametric statistical inference. New York: John Wiley & Sons (1973) 27-33
21. Layman, L., Williams, L., Cunningham, L.: Exploring Extreme Programming in Context: An Industrial Case Study. Agile Development Conference (2004) 32-41

22. Li, W., Henry, S.: Maintenance Metrics for the Object Oriented Paradigm. Proceedings of the First International Software Metrics Symposium, Baltimore, MD (1993) 52-60
23. McCabe, T.: Complexity Measure. IEEE Transactions on Software Engineering, 2(4): 308-320 (1976)
24. Poulin, J.S.: Measuring Software Reusability. Proceedings of the Third Conference on Software Reuse, Rio de Janeiro, Brazil (1994)
25. Ratzinger, J., Fischer, M., Gall, H.: Improving Evolvability through Refactoring. Proceedings of the 2nd International Workshop on Mining Software Repositories (MSR'05), Saint Louis, Missouri, USA (2005)
26. Sillitti, A., Janes, A., Succi, G., Vernazza, T.: Collecting, Integrating and Analyzing Software Metrics and Personal Software Process Data. Proceedings of the EUROMICRO 2003 (2003)

Using the Web as a Reuse Repository

Oliver Hummel and Colin Atkinson

University of Mannheim, Chair of Software Technology
68159 Mannheim, Germany
{hummel, atkinson}@informatik.uni-mannheim.de
http://swt.informatik.uni-mannheim.de

Abstract. Software reuse is widely recognized as an effective way of increasing the quality of software systems whilst lowering the effort and time involved in their development. Although most of the basic techniques for software retrieval have been around for a while, third party reuse is still largely a "hit and miss" affair and the promise of large case component marketplaces has so far failed to materialize. One of the key obstacles to systematic reuse has traditionally been the set up and maintenance of up-to-date software repositories. However, the rise of the World Wide Web as a general information repository holds the potential to solve this problem and give rise to a truly ubiquitous library of (open source) software components. This paper surveys reuse repositories on the Web and estimates the amount of software currently available in them. We also briefly discuss how this software can be harvested by means of general purpose web search engines and demonstrate the effectiveness of our implementation of this approach by applying it to reuse examples presented in earlier literature.

1 Introduction

It has long been recognized that reuse is the key to making software development a fully fledged engineering discipline [19] in which quality systems are built at low cost in a dependable and predictable manner. In principle, almost all assets that are produced during a software development process such as domain knowledge, requirements, design and source code are potentially reusable. Traditionally, however, reuse initiatives have focused on the reuse of software in binary or source-code form [1]. Even reuse in this sense is an umbrella term for many different concepts that can range from ad-hoc copying of a few lines of code to the architecture-centric usage of large parts of a software product line [12]. In this paper our focus is on software components, but not in the sense of Szyperski [13] which emphasizes binary software units, rather as source code units that can be used independently. This can range, in the simplest case, from a class that contains a stateless method, to a variety of classes that depend on some shared libraries. Unfortunately, these more complex forms of components are difficult to retrieve since common programming language do not make their required interfaces explicit.

There has been an ongoing discussion in the literature (see e.g. [3], [6]) over whether a component repository is a necessary condition for a successful reuse program or not. Failure mode analyses have established that to be reused a component

M. Morisio (Ed.): ICSR 2006, LNCS 4039, pp. 298–311, 2006.
© Springer-Verlag Berlin Heidelberg 2006

must at the very minimum be available and findable, and component repositories are certainly one way of achieving this [24]. It has often been argued that typical reuse collections are small and hence do not need library support, however, intuition suggests that the bigger the component collection the higher the probability it contains a matching artifact [30]. Given this observation it makes sense to study the ability of repository organization and retrieval techniques to handle large component collections. To date Mili et. al.'s well known survey [17] gives the best overview of this topic. After their study Mili et. al, like Seacord [6], were rather pessimistic that there will be a solution to the so-called "repository problem" in the foreseeable future. They argue that currently "(...) *no solution offers the right combination of efficiency, accuracy, user-friendliness and generality to afford us a breakthrough in the practice of software reuse"*.

In addition to these academic studies of software reuse, there have been numerous attempts to establish commercial component "marketplaces" in recent years. However, these have also had limited success. Two of the most well known, ComponentSource.com and Flashline.com, have had to merge recently. Moreover, the Universal UDDI Business Registry (UBR), the high profile industry repository for web services, rarely contained useful material (as we will show later) and was finally shut down in January 2006[1]. Likewise, most other initiatives have had very limited impact. These stated approaches have essentially all been based on a standard "e-retail" model in which components are offered in an informal catalogue-like style as if they were mainstream consumer products. Trying to discover a component at ComponentSource is therefore still much like browsing for a book on Amazon. It is a very informal, unpredictable process with a highly uncertain outcome. Of course, searching tools are provided, but these are very simple, typically text-based technologies which essentially look for keywords in a component's documentation.

1.1 The Opportunity

Naturally the rise of the Internet as a public library for almost everything has raised the reuse community's interest in utilizing it for their purposes (see e.g. [17], [6] & [9]). In recent years there have been a growing number of research projects that have made initial steps towards this goal. The earliest known approach that utilized the Web together with a general purpose search engine was Agora [6]. Other researchers and commercial websites have crawled publicly available CVS repositories to build their own source code search engines (SPARS-J [25], Koders.com, Codase.com) or for other research purposes (for instance [15]). Others have recently experimented with the use of general search engines (such as Google and Yahoo) to search for components. However, [25] did this only in a rudimentary way by augmenting queries with the terms "java" and "source" while [29] questioned the feasibility of doing this. Despite this pessimism, we have succeeded in developing a reuse approach called Extreme Harvesting that we first introduced in [2] that can successfully retrieve components from the Web. The basic idea is to use the whole Web itself as the underlying repository, and to utilize standard search engines as the means of discovering appropriate software assets. Since the Web, by its very nature, is a very unstructured and

---

[1] The official rationale is that the UBR has been successful as a proof of concept, though.

unruly place that was not designed to store software source code this is not always easy. However, we have shown it is indeed possible to automatically harvest all kinds of valuable components by means of general search engines.

As the main purpose of this paper is to assess the size and quality of the Web as a software repository we give only a brief overview of our Extreme Harvesting approach in the next section. Section 3 surveys specialized service and software search engines on the web and evaluates their efficiency. In section 4 we compare these results with the outcome of our Extreme Harvesting experiments and give our assessment of the Web's potential to serve as a ubiquitous software repository. Finally, in section 5 we conclude and discuss potential future directions of the work.

2   Component Retrieval Basics

For the reader to understand why it makes sense to search the Web for usable software components despite the problems described in [29] and above we briefly introduce our Extreme Harvesting approach. Based on the lessons learned from Mili et al.'s survey [17] and our own experiments we created this new hybrid semantics-driven retrieval engine by integrating some of the techniques outlined there. As stated in the survey, a retrieval process typically has to cover two criteria because a candidate component can fulfill the matching condition of one specific retrieval technique but may not necessarily match a user's relevance criterion. Consider the above mentioned keyword-based search technique, for instance. Such a search engine might retrieve a number of components that contain the word Stack somewhere (maybe they use a Stack), but only very few of them implement the appropriate data structure. In other words, a single matching criterion is too weak to guarantee satisfactory precision.

Applying more than one matching criterion essentially represents a filtering process that iteratively shrinks the number of acceptable components in a repository search until only acceptable components are left. In our current tool we apply three filtering stages, namely linguistic, syntactic and semantic filtering. The linguistic filtering is basically a keyword search as described above. After that a signature matching step is applied [22]. Then, thirdly, we check the semantic compliance of components by sampling their behavior [7]. As we have focused our current research on Java we chose quasi standard JUnit [23] test cases to represent this information. Unfortunately, behavior sampling of this from is only a limited substitute for complete semantic checking, but it is the only practical way at present, because to find out whether a code unit complies to a given formal description is equivalent to solving the halting problem [28].

The cost of applying these filtering steps grows in the order they are introduced. For this reason the combination of the three steps is the only practical way to retrieve components with reasonable precision from very large repositories like the web. In other words, it would never be computationally possible to apply a semantic relevance check to millions of components. Figure 1 below provides a schematic summary of the main steps involved in the practical implementation of our approach as originally introduced in [2]:

a) define syntactic signature of desired component
b) define semantics of desired component in terms of test cases
c) search for candidate components using the APIs of standard web search engines with a search term derived from (a)
d) find source units which have the exact signature defined in (a) or try to create appropriate adapters
e) filter out components which are not valid (i.e. not compilable) source units, if necessary find any other units upon which the matching component relies for execution
f) establish which components are semantically acceptable (or closest to the requirements) by applying the tests defined in (b)

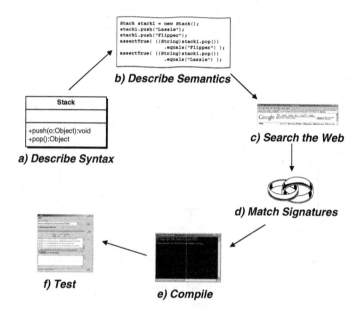

Fig. 1. Schematic process overview

We currently have a Java-based prototype which implements the above approach and is able to harvest Java components and web services from the web. Extending the tool to handle other programming languages is a straightforward matter. Since our three step filtering process has proven to be very effective in our experiments and our tool has the capability to adapt search results into the form required in (a) automatically, a developer can integrate any accepted search result right away in his/her development project.

3 Internet-Based Repositories

This section briefly reviews the component and service search engines available on the Internet or reported in the literature. Since one of the reasons for the recent excitement around web service technology is that its search technology UDDI [16] is supposed to bring together service providers and service requestors we start our overview with web services that are available for third-party (re-)use. UDDI is advertised as a flexible brokering technology that allows component developers to "publish" their software as services, and potential component users to find suitable services automatically through formalized syntactic descriptions of their requirements (in the form of WSDL documents). Even semantic composition capabilities for web services are becoming available (e.g. with the help of OWL [8]). Since so much industry investment has been pumped into the Universal UDDI Business Registry (UBR) one would expect a sizeable index of services to now be available. However, as table 1 demonstrates, the UBR (and other service repositories) failed to reach a critical mass of entries and a large proportion of the entries contained in the repository were out of date. Many entries did not even point to valid WSDL descriptions and of those that did, only a small proportion were actually working. The UBR's shutdown in early 2006 was a logical consequence.

Table 1. Number of WSDL files within reach at various websites (July 2005)

Search Method	API	Claimed number of links to WSDL files	No of actual links to valid WSDL files
UDDI Business Registry[2]	yes	770 (790 [11])	400 (430 [11])
BindingPoint.com	no	3900	1270 (validated)
Webservicelist.com	no	250	unknown
XMethods.com	yes	440	unknown
Salcentral.com[2, 3]	yes	~800	all (validated)

We can only speculate about the reasons for the disappointing performance of such repositories. However, the main problem with this concept in our opinion is not a technical one, it is the overhead involved in the manual creation and maintenance of the repository. The effort involved in entering a complete service profile into the UBR should not be underestimated. In addition, there is the effort of updating or removing the (possible many) entries when a server is moved or closed down. Interestingly, the UBR followed exactly the three-phase reuse progression (empty, filled with garbage or too general) that Poulin reported in [30] from his practical experience at IBM over ten years ago (although we would argue that the UBR actually never reached the third phase).

Since the Web in its current form is still relatively new there have been few attempts to date to utilize it as a source of components for mainstream software engineering. The most well known attempt is Agora search engine [6] mentioned above. Agora was developed at the Software Engineering Institute (SEI) as a special purpose search engine with its own index of Java applets and ActiveX components which has

---

[2] As of March 2006 this website is no longer available.
[3] Salcentral copied the entries of UDDI and XMethods, the values were estimated from active UDDI and XMethods entries.

been filled using a general purpose search engine. However, this project was discontinued probably due to the high effort involved in setting up the index. In addition to this approach, focused on black-box components, the recent advent of open source software has also made it possible to look – at least manually – for white-box components – that is, publicly available source code on the Web [26].

Another idea, utilized by a number of papers in the 2004 and 2005 ICSE workshops on mining software repositories, is to crawl the CVS servers of Sourceforge.net or similar sites (see e.g. [15]) and analyze the content in some way. However we are not aware of an approach that explicitly aims to reuse this material. As Sourceforge does not offer search capabilities for the code it stores, the approach of Koders.com, a fairly new commercial site, makes a lot of sense. They download and index source codes from publicly available CVS repositories and then support text based searches on these assets through a Google style search interface. Codase.com has built a similar index that offers limited support for syntactic searches constrained to method names or parameter types. Krugle.com is a similar site that is scheduled to come on line early in 2006. The following table provides an overview of the sites known to us at the time of writing. We did not consider software retailers like Component-Source.com or Jars.com in this overview as they typically offer very large packages or complete applications which are beyond the scope of our approach and do not offer access to source code.

Table 2. Overview of specialized source code search engines (January 2006)

URL	No. of Languages supported	API	Supported Search Methods	Indexed Lines of Code	No. of Java classes
Koders.com	30	RSS	Linguistic	225,816,744	330,000
demo.spars.info [25]	1	no	Linguistic & Syntactic	n.a.	180,000
Kickjava.com	1	no	Linguistic	20,041,731	105,000
Codase.com	3	no	Linguistic & Syntactic	250,000,000	95,000
Csourcesearch.net	2	no	Linguistic & Syntactic	283,119,081	n.a.
Sourcebank.com	8	no	Linguistic	n.a.	> 500
Planetsourcecode.com	11	no	Linguistic	11,276,847	230

In contrast to general web search engines the listed sites are specialized for source code searches. Hence, they all offer the opportunity to limit searches to a specific language, but only Koders.com fulfills another important requirement for being accessible with our tool, namely an API for programmatic access. Their API is based on Amazon's Opensearch format which in turn is based on RSS. As illustrated by the table above, none of the listed sites provides a form of semantic evaluation for the searches and only a few support the constraining of queries to given syntactic elements (such as method names or parameter types). The estimates we provide for the size of the repositories are the number of indexed lines of code (where this is specified on the site) and the number of Java classes available (by searching for the term "class" in Java files).

4 The Web as a Component Repository

In section 2 we described how a suitable combination of well known techniques and heuristics can effectively harvest components from the web when the desired kind of component is present. However, as with any component repository, it cannot deliver components if there are no suitable ones in the repository. As discussed in section 3, this has been highlighted by web services, the most recent attempt to make third party software components discoverable and accessible via the Internet. As shown in table 1 the Universal UDDI Business Repository has fallen far short of the original predications. Other specialized source code search engines are better, but still only deliver a small part of the Web's potential as we will demonstrate below.

The effectiveness of the retrieval mechanism is only one prerequisite for a practically useful reuse technology. The other is the availability of a repository with a rich and extensive collection of components which covers a large proportion of the kinds of components that users are likely to require [6]. In this section we discuss and evaluate the extent to which the web is able to fulfill this need. As briefly mentioned above, search engines are appropriate for integration in an automated approach like ours if two prerequisites are satisfied. First, a search engine must have an API that allows computational access to its index and second – and this is very important for general search engines as Google and Yahoo – there must be a way to (pre-) filter searches according to a given programming language. To date we have found these features in three engines, namely the two market leaders for general web searches Google and Yahoo where we are able to exploit an undocumented feature of their "filetype" filter, and the specialized engine from Koders.

4.1 Repository Volume

To illustrate the magnitude of the accessible code resources on the web the following table shows the numbers of Java files that could be retrieved using Google, Koders and Yahoo search engines during our experiments in 2004 and 2005. Two sets of values are shown for the Google entries – the first giving the number obtained using the regular human HTML interface and the second (bracketed) giving the number obtained using the Web-API for automated access. Unfortunately, the latter delivers only a fifth of the results available using the former.

The italicized value in the last row stems from the query *"filetype:java" class OR –class*. One should assume that a search with *"filetype:java" -class* only delivers Java interfaces and no classes but actually this is not the case. Manual inspections revealed a high percentage of class files. One explanation for this strange result may be that Google does not completely index some files. The numbers in the table represent the mean value of several samples per month whereas individual values can vary even

Table 3. Number of Java files indexed by search engines on the Web

Month	Google (Web API)	Koders	Yahoo
08/2004	300,000	-	-
01/2005	640,000	-	-
06/2005	950,000 (220,000)	310,000	280,000
08/2005	970,000 (220,000) *1,510,000 (367,000)*	330,000	2,200,000
11/2005	2,212,000 (190,000) *4,540,000 (410,000)*	330,000	2,200,000

from one request to the next within just a few minutes (for Google and Yahoo). However, the growth trend illustrated by the numbers is unmistakable. In August 2005 a similar request for various C-style languages (filetypes: c, cpp and cs) revealed a total of about 1.6 million source files in Google's index, 2.7 million from Yahoo and 500,000 from Koders.

The overlap between Google and Yahoo seems to be rather low - it is typically below 20% (5 out of 24) for our isLeapYear example (see table 6) and for the first 250 results of each engine for our Matrix example from table 7, 47 out of 500 overlap. This observation tallies with other reports for general HTML searches [14]. Unfortunately, it is not possible to estimate a URL-based overlap between Koders and Google/Yahoo because Koders stores the contents with proprietary URLs. With the numbers presented above, we estimate that our system currently has access to about 3 million Java files. This is – to our knowledge – the most comprehensive source-code collection reported in the literature so far. Inoue et. al. [25] has access to roughly 180,000 classes and Agora to around 10,000 (black-box) applets [6].

Similar to Agora, Yahoo allows a search to be limited to pages that contain Java applets (*feature:applet*), delivering the impressive number of 95,000,000 results, or to ActiveX components (*feature:activex*), resulting in an astonishing 750,000,000 pages. Although our tool focuses on white-box components at present, it should be possible to use mechanisms like Java's reflection capability to utilize this large number of black-box components as well. Initial experiments in this direction have already demonstrated promising results: we were able to populate a database with more than 4500 JAR files containing almost 500,000 classes.

Google and Yahoo could also be helpful for the web service community since they are also able to retrieve WSDL files. As the next table illustrates, they are actually better at discovering WSDL files than the web service repositories from table 1.

Table 4. Number of WSDL files delivered from search engines

Search Engine	API	Claimed no. of links to WSDL files	No. of actual links to valid WSDL files
Google	yes	9000 (1700)	794 out of first 1000
Yahoo	yes	13400 (1900)	425 out of first 1000

The values in brackets show the number of results returned through the APIs. This indicates that the search results could be better were not it for the artificial limitation imposed on automated queries. Both search engine APIs allow access to only the first 1000 results returned in response to a query. This is not usually a problem when searching for a specific functional component since the number of retrieved candidates rarely exceeds a few hundred. To conclude this subsection, we summarize the results of our investigations in the following table. This reinforces our belief that the Web has a high, but so far neglected potential as a software repository.

Table 5. Summary of investigated component types that are accessible via an API

Type	Estimated number	Applicable search engines
.java	3,000,000	Google, Yahoo, Koders
.c, .cpp, .cs	4,000,000	Google, Yahoo, Koders
.wsdl	10,000	Google, Yahoo, UDDI, BindingPoint, XMethods
.jar	600,000	Yahoo
Applets	95,000,000	Yahoo
ActiveX	750,000,000	Yahoo

4.2 Repository Scope

Beyond the shear number of components the functional scope of the components in a repository is another interesting characteristic which is a widely unexplored issue in the reuse literature. Most reuse approaches published to date provide some kind of estimate of their tool's power. Typically, however, the underlying repositories used in such evaluations only contained up to a few thousand classes with very limited scope. Furthermore, their comparability is very low since most evaluations were based on proprietary repositories supporting some special features tailored to the employed retrieval technique. Moreover, in order to get any results from these experiments researchers had to give tasks to their subjects that were indeed solvable with the repositories contents. As one possible solution for this issue we propose the definition of reference collections of the kind commonly used in information retrieval research to evaluate "standard" retrieval systems. However, due to the high complexity of, and large variations in, software solutions it is clear that this will not be easy.

Another issue arises with the assessment of uncontrolled repositories like the Web. It is very likely – as confirmed by our experiments – that large numbers of components with common functionality appear on the Web. This is of course ideal for reuse. However, it compounds the problems involved in comparing retrieval techniques and estimating the scope of a software repository. Our solution for this problem was to take examples from comparable reuse experiments to (a) get an impression of the quality of our combination of retrieval techniques and (b) to estimate the scope of the Web as a repository. Another insight into the demand for component searches was provided by the Koders' search statistics[4]. The table below gives an impression of the capability of our tool and shows that it compares favorably to other approaches. The table presents various stateless components that offer typically used algorithms. The first column presents the method names that we used for the search, the second column shows the signature that we entered into our system. Columns three, four and five show how many results passed the filtering process and the last column shows the source which provided the inspiration for the example. Due to space restrictions we cannot show the test cases for the semantic checking here. It should be enough to know that we used about three to five test cases per example as they are typically applied for unit testing in non-reuse processes.

Table 6. Query results from June and July 2005

Names	Signature	Koders	Yahoo	Google	Source
getRandomNumber	int x int: int	3	6	2	[5], [25]
sort	int[]: void	1	12	15	Koders
reverseArray	int[]: void	0	10	6	-
copyFile	String: void	2	1	0	Koders
isPrime	int: Boolean	1	8	14	[18]
sqrt	double: double	2	9	5	[7]
isLeapYear	int: Boolean	1	29	24	[5]
replace	String x String: String	14	10	22	Koders
gcd[5]	int x int: int	3	68	10	[10]
md5	String: String	3	1	0	Koders
lcs[6]	String x String: String	0	0	2	[10]
quicksort	String[]: void	4	3	2	[25]

Due to the heuristics implemented in our prototype, results with slightly different names were adapted to the original signature and also accepted, like `getRandomInt` instead of `getRandomNumber` and so on. Furthermore, the autoboxing capabilities of Java 1.5 came handy for the `BinaryTree` example from the table below which illustrates more complex and typically stateful components. Interestingly, we were not able to retrieve a single functioning web service for any of the examples from table 6 above, and we were only able to find the `CreditCardValidator` from table 7 with more complex classes below. We describe the interfaces of these examples in the form of UML class diagrams:

---

[4] http://koders.com/info.aspx?page=LanguageReport
[5] Greatest common divisor.
[6] Longest common substring.

Table 7. Exemplary stateful components

Component's UML diagram	Koders results	Yahoo results	Google results	Source
BinaryTree +BinaryTree(value:int, left:BinaryTree, right:BinaryTree) +height():int	0	4	7	[17]
Stack +push(o:Object):void +pop():Object	6	13	33	[25] & similar to [22]
Matrix +Matrix(rows:ints, cols:int) +set(row:int, col:int, val:double):void +get(row:int, col:int):double +add(m:Matrix):Matrix +sub(m:Matrix):Matrix +mul(m:Matrix):Matrix	1	1	3	[21]
CreditCardValidator +CreditCardValidator(type:int) +isValid(no:String):boolean	1	1	1	[20]
Deck +shuffle():void +deal():Card → Card +toString():String	-	20	17	[5]

4.3 Component Quality

The most pressing question still to be answered is of course the quality of components downloaded from the Web. So far we found that most components that passed our tests were of reasonable quality, and some minor problems (e.g. with the isLeapYear example or the size of harvested Stack classes) could have been avoided with better test cases. This directly leads to the realm of reliability measurement and the evaluation of components to certain levels of confidence. Even when a component passes all tests defined by a developer it is not certain that it will perform with 100% reliability since unit tests are incomplete in most practical situations. As this is also the case for non-reuse components, further acceptance tests would certainly follow in either case.

However, as harvesting typically delivers multiple results for a search request the idea of back-to-back testing [27] (i.e., comparing the results of functionally identical components for the same random input) is a good starting point to estimate the reliability of retrieved components. This naturally leads to another area of enhancement which relates to the issue of ranking components. At present the result of our selection process is a list of components which have passed all the filtering steps and thus qualify as "working" components. However, this set is not ordered in any way. The next logical extension of the approach is to present the components in a ranked list similar to that of Google and Spars-J [25]. There are many possible ways of doing this like depending on non-functional attributes of a component such as its estimated reliability or code metrics to mention just a few.

4.4 Extensibility

One way of estimating the size of the World Wide Web as a component repository is to inject known components into and determine how easily they can be detected. One way of doing this is to insert files into the CVS repository of a big open source site like Sourceforge since these are almost immediately made available on the Web. Another approach would be to simply store source files on a web server, link them via a HTML file and submit everything to the crawlers of one of the big search engines. We did exactly this in early 2006 with some Java projects. However, the results were not encouraging. Google had not indexed any of them in our eight week observation period and via Yahoo our index page was accessible for a few days but was then removed again. A possible explanation might be that the big search engines focus on human readable material and hence try to avoid including source code in their index. Koders also appears not to have updated its index for many months. These observations make it clear that contributing to the ubiquitous repository World Wide Web in a controlled fashion is not practical at present.

We have also investigated whether the common peer-to-peer (P2P) platform Gnutella is useful for component distribution, as P2P systems are typically a place where all kinds of files can be easily shared with almost no effort. However, the results are – at least currently – not encouraging. For instance, there are only about 2,500 Java source files available in the Gnutella network on average. And as P2P systems simply search in the name and not in the content of files they offer only the most simplistic search support and hence offer not much incentive for developers to use P2P systems for this purpose. These investigations show that there is plenty of room for a dedicated P2P or web search system that makes it easy contribute code, perhaps in the same way that CVS plug-ins for common CASE tools function.

5   Conclusion and Future Work

There have been many notable attempts during the history of computer science to make software reuse a more integral part of industrial software engineering, but to date they have all foundered on the problem of creating and maintaining a sufficiently rich and large repository of components. This includes the UDDI-based Universal Business Registry which despite the relative newness of the technology was full of unusable material before it has been closed down recently.

In contrast to this experience, the contribution of this paper is to show that (1) the Web has become sufficiently large and stable to serve as a self-maintaining component repository and (2) that it is possible to build an engine which can harvest components from this repository in an efficient and dependable way. Since we are still in a fundamental research stage there is a whole host of other issues to be addressed. The security problem associated with executing unknown software from the Web is one example, of course. Hence, we are working to extend the capabilities of our prototype tool in this and several other directions. Support for some kind of ontology or thesaurus technology is one important idea. Another is the inclusion of proactive recommendation technology in the spirit of CodeBroker [25]. Although our approach originated from agile development approaches we also aim to provide tight integration into modern component development methodologies like KobrA [12]. Closely related to this aspect is the problem that common programming languages do not make components they rely on explicit- that is, their required interface is typically hidden inside the source code. Although, we have made good progress in resolving the required interfaces of components (i.e. the imports of Java files) there is still a long way to go. Finally, there are lots of ethical and legal aspects related to the harvesting of software from the Web that could also influence the usability of a component. However, as with most other Internet technologies including search engines and peer-to-peer file sharing systems, the technology usually comes first and the legal issues are sorted out afterwards. Therefore, we hope the work described in this paper will provide a new impulse to software reuse and will help bring closer the day when automated access to a rich library of software components is the rule rather than the exception.

References

1. McIlroy, D.: Mass-Produced Software Components. Software Engineering: Report of a Conference sponsored by the NATO Science Committee, Garmisch (1969)
2. Hummel, O., Atkinson, C.: Extreme Harvesting: Test Driven Discovery and Reuse of Software Components, Proceedings of the International Conference on Information Reuse and Integration (IEEE-IRI), Las Vegas (2004)
3. Frakes, W. B., Fox, C.J.: Sixteen Questions about Software Reuse. Communications of the ACM, Vol 38 Issue 6 (1995)
4. Beck, K.: Extreme Programming Explained: Embrace Change. Addison-Wesley (1999)
5. Ye, Y., Fischer, G., Reuse-Conducive Environments. Journal of Automated Software Engineering, Vol. 12, Iss. 2, Kluwer (2005)
6. Seacord, R.: Software Engineering Component Repositories, Proceedings of the International Conference of Software Engineering, Los Angeles (1999)
7. Podgurski, A., Pierce, L.: Retrieving Reusable Software by Sampling Behavior. ACM Transactions on Software Engineering and Methodology, Vol. 2, Iss. 3 (1993)
8. Sirin, E., Hendler, J., Parsia, B.: Semi-automatic composition of web services using semantic descriptions. In Web Services: Modeling, Architecture and Infrastructure workshop in ICEIS 2003, Angers (2003)
9. Frakes, W.B., Kang, K.: Software Reuse Research: Status and Future. IEEE Transactions on Software Eng., Vol. 31, No. 7 (2005)
10. Cormen, T., Leiserson, C., Rivest, R., Stein, C.: Introduction to Algorithms, 2nd Edition. MIT Press (2001)
11. Dong, X., Halevy, A., Madhavan, J., Nemes, E., Zhang, J.: Similarity Search for Web Services. Proceedings of the 30th VLDB Conference, Toronto (2004)
12. Atkinson, C., Bayer, J., Bunse, C., Kamsties, E., Laitenberger, O., Laqua, R., Muthig, D., Paech, B., Wüst, J., Zettel, J.: Component-based Product Line Engineering with UML. Addison Wesley (2002)
13. Szyperski, C.: Component Software, Addison-Wesley, 2nd Edition, 2002
14. Dogpile.com: Different Engines, Different Results, Technical Report, (2005): http:// comparesearchengines. dogpile.com/ OverlapAnalysis.pdf (accessed 09/08/05).

15. Amin, R., Ó Cinnéide, M. and Veale, T.: LASER: A Lexical Approach to Analogy in Software Reuse, Proceedings of the International Workshop on Mining Software Repositories, Edinburgh (2004)
16. Belwood, T., Clément, L., Ehnebuske, D., Hately, A., Hondo, M., Husband, Y., Januszewski, K., Lee, S., McKee, B., Munter, J., von Riegen, C.: UDDI Version 3.0. Oasis Committee Specification (2002)
17. Mili, A., Mili, R., Mittermeir, R: A Survey of Software Reuse Libraries. Annals of Software Engineering 5 (1998)
18. Hall, R.J.: Generalized behavior-based retrieval. Proceedings of the International Conference on Software Engineering, Baltimore (1993)
19. Mili, A., Yacoub, S., Addy, E., Mili, H., Toward an engineering discipline of software reuse. IEEE Software, Vol. 16, No. 5 (1999)
20. Vitharana, P., Zahedi, F., Jain, F.: Knowledge-Based Repository Scheme for Storing and Retrieving Business Components. IEEE Transactions on Software Engineering, Vol. 29, No. 7 (2003)
21. Czarnecki, K., Eisenecker, U.W.: Generative Programming: Methods, Tools, and Applications. Addison Wesley (2000)
22. Zaremski, A.M. Wing, J.M.: Signature Matching: A Tool for Using Software Libraries. ACM Transact. on Software Engineering and Methodology, Vol. 4, No. 2 (1995)
23. Beck, K., Gamma, E., JUnit: A Cook's Tour. Java Report (August 1999)
24. Frakes, W.B., Fox, C.J.: Quality Improvement Using A Software Reuse Failure Modes Model. IEEE Transactions on Software Eng., Vol. 22, No. 4 (1996)
25. Inoue, K., Yokomori, R., Fujiwara, H., Yamamoto, T., Matsushita, M., Kusumoto, S.: Ranking Significance of Software Components Based on Use Relations. IEEE Transactions on Software Eng., Vol. 31, No. 3 (2005)
26. Brown, A.W., Booch, G.: Reusing Open-Source Software and Practices: The Impact of Open-Source Software on Commercial Vendors. In C. Gacek (Ed.): LNCS 2319, Springer (2002)
27. Vouk, M.A., Back-to-Back Testing. Information & Software Techn., Vol. 32, No. 1 (1990)
28. Edmonds, B., Bryson, J.: The Insufficiency of Formal Design Methods - the necessity of an experimental approach for the understanding and control of complex MAS, Proc. of the 3rd Intern. Joint Conf. on Autonomous Agents & Multi Agent Systems, New York (2004)
29. Yao, H., Etzkorn, L.: "Towards a Semantic-based Approach for Software Reusable Component Classification and Retrieval", Proceedings of the 42nd annual Southeast Regional Conference, Huntsville (2004)
30. Poulin, J.: "Populating Software Repositories: Incentives and Domain-Specific Software", Journal of Systems and Software, Vol. 30 (1995)

A UML2 Profile for Reusable and Verifiable Software Components for Real-Time Applications

V. Cechticky[1], M. Egli[1], A. Pasetti[1], O. Rohlik[1], and T. Vardanega[2]

[1] Institut für Automatik, ETH-Zentrum, Physikstr. 3,
CH-8092 Zürich, Switzerland
{eglimi, pasetti, rohlik}@control.ee.ethz.ch
[2] Dept. of Pure and Applied Mathematics, University of Padua
Via Belzoni 7, 35131 Padova, Italy
tullio.vardanega@math.unipd.it

Abstract. Software frameworks offer sets of reusable and adaptable components embedded within an architecture optimized for a given target domain. This paper introduces an approach to the design of software frameworks for real-time applications. Real-Time applications are characterized by functional and non-functional (e.g. timing) requirements. The proposed approach separates the treatment of these two aspects. For functional issues, it defines an extensible state machine concept to define components that encapsulate functional behaviour and offer adaptation mechanisms to extend this behaviour which warrant preservation of the functional properties that characterize the framework. For timing issues, it defines software structures that are provably endowed with specific timing properties and which encapsulate functional activity in a way that warrants their enforcement. A UML2 profile is defined that formally captures both aspects and allows the proposed strategy to be deployed at design level.

1 Introduction

A *software product family* is a set of applications that can be built from a pool of shared software assets. *Software frameworks* [1] offer a way to organize the shared assets behind a product family. They define an architecture optimized for applications in a certain domain and offer predefined components that support its instantiation. During the instantiation process the framework assets are tailored to suit the specific requirements of the target application. To this end, a software framework defines a number of *adaptation points* where application-specific behaviour can be inserted. Most contemporary software frameworks are *object-oriented* in the sense that their reusable assets consist of encapsulated software components and their adaptation mechanisms are based on class extension and interface implementation.

Although software frameworks have proven very successful at fostering a reuse-driven approach in business and desktop applications, they have so far failed to penetrate the realm of hard real-time (HRT) applications. HRT applications are characterized by non-functional (timing) requirements that impose severe constraints on the timing behaviour of the application and that often are mission-critical.

M. Morisio (Ed.): ICSR 2006, LNCS 4039, pp. 312–325, 2006.

Presently the prevalent paradigm in the real-time world is bases on *model driven architectures*. With this approach, the requirements of the target applications are expressed in a formalism that allows an implementation to be automatically generated from the specification.

Both the reuse-driven and model-driven approaches have strengths and weaknesses. The model-driven approach holds the promise of completely automating the software development process. Additionally, the formal definition of the requirements facilitates formal verification of correctness, for example using model-checking techniques [2]. On the downside, the model-driven approach is intrinsically limited by the expressive power of the modeling language of choice. Model-driven tools also are very costly to develop and their development is only justified for applications that have sizable markets. The reuse approach can be more flexible both because reusable building blocks can, in principle, be provided to cover as wide a range of functionalities as desired, and because it can be applied in an incremental way with repositories of reusable building blocks built up over time. The main drawback with this approach is that the adaptation process is difficult to formalize and developers of critical applications are reluctant to adopt components that they did not develop (the well-known "not-invented-here syndrome") and over whose characteristics they may have little visibility. Furthermore, adaptation techniques are in effect geared to functional requirements only and adaptation to real-time requirements remains poorly understood.

In this paper, we propose a design approach for HRT applications that combines reuse- and model-driven flavours. The proposed approach is reuse-driven in the sense that it sees an application as an instance of an object-oriented software framework. It is model-driven in the sense that a modeling language is defined to describe both the framework components (in terms of their interfaces as well as their behaviour) and their adaptation mechanism. The component implementation is automatically generated from their models. Our approach also allows for the definition of *formally verifiable properties* upon the framework. Since our focus is on real-time applications, we cover both functional and timing properties. Functional properties formalize logical relationships on the variables that define the state of an application. This logical relationship may also be sequential in that it may relate past and present values of the state variables. Timing properties define constraints on the arrival time of external events and on the completion times of application activities.

We regard an object-oriented software framework as a set of interacting components that can be adapted through class extension[1]. The components encap-sulate the commonalities of the applications within the framework domain. Their adaptation allows application-specific behaviour to be added to the default behaviour defined at framework level. Figure 1 shows our proposed development process for a framework. We break the process up in three main phases. The *domain analysis phase* defines the target domain of the framework and the functionalities it must provide [3]. This phase is not discussed further in this paper. In the *domain design phase*, the framework components are designed. The output of this phase is a model of the framework. Two

---

[1] The second adaptation mechanism of object-oriented frameworks – adaptation through interface implementation – is seen as a special case of the first as an interface can be represented by an "empty" class (a class with only abstract methods)

views of this model are constructed. The *functional view* defines the framework from a functional point of view. It consists of class diagrams that define the functional architecture of the framework (the component interfaces and their mutual relations) and state charts that define the internal *behaviour* of each component. The functional model also identifies the extension points of the components. The *timing view* defines the HRT characteristics of the framework by identifying and characterizing the threads and the synchronization points and data structures that may be used by applications instantiated from the framework. Finally, in the *domain implementation phase* the components are implemented. For the most part this latter stage is attained by automatic code generation from the component models.

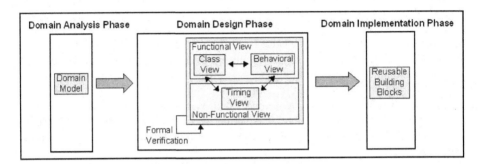

Fig. 1. Framework Development Process

In this paper we discuss the functional and timing views. Notably, these two views do *not* form two separate models. Rather, they provide two different representations of the *one and the same* underlying model. The value of our approach is that it allows these two views to be defined independently of each other, so that conceptually they can be treated in isolation. The concerns arising from each view are merged during the code generation process after verifying the feasibility of the timing view and the correctness of the functional view of the system. The framework model is then processed and the code for the framework components is automatically generated for both the functional and timing dimensions.

The association of verifiable properties to models is typical of model-driven architectures. In a framework context two levels of properties must be distinguished (cf. figure 2). Framework-level properties formalize the commonality of behaviour of applications within the framework domain. These properties must be satisfied by all applications instantiated from the framework. Additionally, each individual application may be endowed with application-specific properties. The adaptation process through which the framework components are tailored to the needs of a target application is constrained to guarantee that the application-level components still satisfy the framework-level properties. The framework instantiation process can thus result in new properties being added but will *never* result in the violation of the framework-level properties.

In keeping with the standard approach in the model-driven community, the framework modeling language is expressed as a UML2 profile that we name the *FW (framework) Profile*. The bonus of this choice is that UML2 environments are now

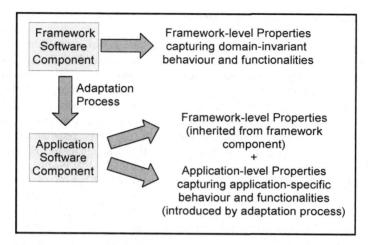

Fig. 2. Framework- and Application-Level Properties

available that can be customized to enforce a user-defined profile during the design process. Most application developers are familiar with UML-based design. The transition to our approach can therefore take place naturally and at minimal costs.

The remainder of this paper is organized as follows. Sections 2 and 3 describe the design approach for, respectively, the functional and timing aspects of a framework. Section 4 presents the code generation approach. Section 5 describes a case study, discusses related work, and concludes the paper.

The full definition of our framework profile and associated development process can be found in [4]. A plug-in for the Eclipse UML2 platform to enforce the profile during the design process is available from [5].

2 Functional Design

The functional design of the framework consists in the definition of its functional view. The functional view describes the framework architecture, the functional behaviour of the framework components, and the component adaptation mechanisms. The framework architecture is described in terms of the external interfaces of the framework components and their mutual interconnections. The framework architecture is represented through UML2 class diagrams. The adaptation mechanism is also defined on the class diagrams by identifying the class methods that are either abstract or virtual. The functional behaviour of the components is represented through UML2 state charts. Advanced support of state charts is the main reason of choice of UML2 over older versions of UML.

The FW Profile defines the rules that constrain the way UML2 class diagrams and state charts are built. The description of the FW Profile is best given in terms of three elements: (i) the restriction of the UML2 state machine model; (ii) the component extension mechanism; (iii) the action language to define the actions associated to the state machines.

2.1 UML2 State Machine Restrictions

The rationale for restricting the UML2 state machine model stems from our intent to use state machines solely to describe the functional part of the behaviour of a class. Behaviour that is time-related (e.g. waiting for an event) or that implies interaction across thread boundaries (e.g. engaging a synchronization with a thread of control in another class) is modelled in the timing view using other mechanisms discussed in section 3. Accordingly, the FW Profiles stipulates that state transitions can only be triggered by calls on the operations defined by the class associated to the state machine. Other types of transition mechanisms (through signals or time triggers) are forbidden. By the same token, no events are allowed by the FW Profile.

In practice, the state machines are only used to model behaviour *inside* threads. Removing the time dimension from the state machine models is important because it removes all the semantic ambiguities that plague the UML2 state machine model and that make other attempts to use state machines to model behaviour unwieldy [15, 16].

The second driver for the restrictions on the UML2 state machine model is simplicity and elimination of unnecessary features. This helps us streamline the model validation and the code generation processes. UML2 allows for three kinds of states: simple states, composite states, and submachine states. Only simple and composite states are allowed by the FW Profile. UML2 also defines several kinds of pseudo-states but the FW Profile only retains the initial pseudo-state and the choice pseudo-states. Finally, UML2 allows *entry*, *do* and *exit* actions to be associated to states. The *entry* and *exit* actions are retained but the *do* action is not necessary since the FW Profile state machines are purely reactive: they only do something when they are triggered by a call to a trigger operation defined on the class to which they are associated.

2.2 Component Extension Mechanism

At class level, component extension is modelled through class extension. The main constraint on the extension mechanism is that it must allow new properties to be defined on the extended component while preserving the properties defined on the base component (see figure 2).

Figure 3 illustrates the proposed mechanism. Class Base represents a component provided by the framework. Class Derived represents the adapted component constructed during the framework instantiation process. The framework-level properties capture aspects of the Base state machine topology and of its state transition logic. The FW Profile ensures that these properties are preserved by constraining the extension to define the internal behaviour of one or more of the states of the base state machine without altering its topology and transition logic. This is illustrated in the figure where the derived state machine differs from the base state machine only in including an embedded state machine that adds to the base states. The derived state machine defines the internal behaviour of a state that was initially defined as being a simple state.

The FW Profile adopts the extension process of figure 3 and forbids all other kinds of state machine extensions that are allowed by UML2 (redefinition of transition, definition of new transitions between existing states, definition of new states, etc).

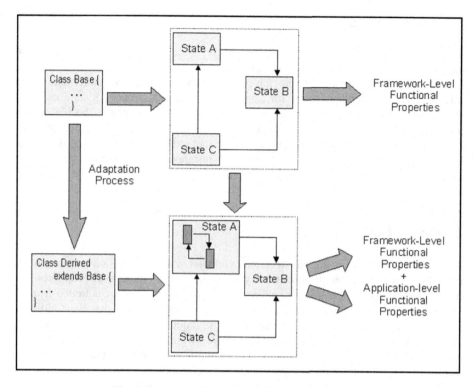

Fig. 3. Framework Component Extension Mechanism

In order to freeze the transition logic of a state machine, the FW Profile stipulates that the trigger operations that control the state transitions must be defined as final (i.e. they cannot be altered during the class extension process).

In order to ensure the preservation of properties defined on the base state machine, the two state machines – the base state machine and the state machine embedded in one of its states during the extension process – must be decoupled: trigger operations defined on the derived class must act on one and only one of the two state machines, and the embedded state machine must not be allowed to trigger transitions in the base state machine.

The extension mechanism enforced by the FW Profile, though very simple, corresponds to a realistic situation that often arises in framework design. This is the case described by the well-known template design pattern where a class defines some skeleton behaviour that offers hooks where application-specific behaviour can be added by providing implementation for abstract methods. The behaviour encapsulated in the skeleton, however, is intended to be invariant. In terms of the FW state machine model, the invariant skeleton behaviour is encapsulated by the base state machine whereas the variable hook behaviour is encapsulated by the nested state machines added by the derived class.

2.3 Action Language

The FW Profile stipulates that state machines are used to model the behaviour of a class. At its most basic level, the link between a class and its associated state machine is defined by the trigger operations (the class operations that trigger transitions in the state machine). In order to allow for a more complete link between a state machine and its associated class, the profile also defines an action language. The FW action language is introduced to define: transition guards, transition effects, and state entry and exit actions. It allows manipulation of class methods, class attributes of integer or boolean type, and references to associated class instances. It thus allows a guard to be expressed as a Boolean expression combining the above elements and transition effects.

3 Timing Design

A software framework is not an executable application and hence it cannot in general be subject to timing requirements. By arguing that a framework supports the instantiation of HRT applications, we maintain that applications instantiated from it are "aware" of the timing requirements imposed upon them and that their ultimate feasibility can be statically analyzed against those requirements. The latter property is of course crucial to the mission critical domain of our interest. Our goal is thus to offer a design approach that guarantees that all applications instantiated from a certain framework are statically analyzable for their timing properties.

The approach we take to this effect is centered on a reuse-geared adaptation of the HRT-UML design method [7,8,9]. A distinct prerogative of HRT-UML is that it adopts a concurrent computational model based on the Ravenscar Profile [10].

TheRavenscar Profile amounts to a set of restrictions placed on the concurrent behaviour of a system. Notably, such restrictions are genuinely orthogonal to the FW Profile presented in this paper since they do *not* concern the functionality that can be expressed by the sequential part of target programming languages, but only the concurrent behaviour of the application. All concurrent applications designed in compliance with the restrictions of the Ravenscar Profile are statically analyzable for their timing behaviour at run time by construction.If the Ada programming language [6] is used, Ravenscar compliance can be proven *a posteriori* on the source code submitted to the compiler. This assurance is an important asset for model-based code generators, since code accepted by a Ravenscar-aware compiler is guaranteed to behave at run time exactly as assumed by static analysis. Yet HRT-UML adds considerable value to this assurance by elevating the Ravenscar restrictions to the design level, so that the model space itself warrants structural compliance with them by construction, that is *a priori*.

HRT-UML does so by placing rigorous restrictions (which all emanate from the Ravenscar Profile) on the ontology and the taxonomy of the allowable elements of a model. Ontological restrictions specify the semantic nature of model elements (hence what they are for and how they can be used). Taxonomical restrictions define the allowable relations that can be placed among model elements (hence how they can interconnect to one another). It is out of the scope of this paper to provide an exhaustive presentation of HRT-UML. In the following we will simply illustrate the basic principles of HRT-UML design that are relevant for illustration of the FW Profile presented in this paper. For further details on HRT-UML the reader is referred to the relevant literature [7,8,9,10].

3.1 Brief Ontology of HRT-UML Model Elements

Each element of an HRT-UML model is a cohesive aggregate of:

- one **Provided Interface** (PI), which publishes: (i) the signature of the services (operations) that the element is capable of executing on request from the outside environment; (ii) the constraints placed on invocation of its operations (the *invocation protocol*); and (iii) the time bound (WCET) stipulated on the execution of the required operation
- one **Object Control Structure** (OBCS), which is the agent responsible for execution of the invocation protocol attached to the invocation of PI operations
- one **Thread** that associates an autonomous run-time behaviour to the element; such Thread is associated to a thread of control whose run-time behaviour amounts to a non-terminating iteration revolving around a *single* activation event arising from either a hardware interrupt (a clock or some other device with a stipulated behaviour) or software
- one **Operation Control Structure** (OPCS) per operation published in the PI, which provides the functional specification of the operation; as a direct consequence of the Ravenscar restrictions, such functional specifications must involve *no* internal concurrent action and *no* voluntary suspension
- one **Required Interface** (RI), which publishes to the outside environment: (i) the signature of the operations that the element needs to use for carrying out its own duties; (ii) the execution protocol that the element is willing to accept for their invocation; and (iii) the execution time bound (WCET) that warrant the preservation of the corresponding bounds on the PI.

Not all model elements need to possess all of the above internals. Specific ontological rules determine the internal composition of each model element and the nature of each internal constituent. Intrinsic to the hierarchical nature of HRT-UML design, the primary ontological distinction is to be made between non-terminal and terminal elements.

Non-terminal elements are "capsules" that hide their inner detail to the outside and only present PI and RI (both of which can be void). Terminal elements are fully resolved and allow/require no further decomposition. A non-terminal entity is created by either top-down decomposition of a parent element into a set of child elements or by bottom-up aggregation of independent sibling elements into a containing, hierarchically superior, element. Hierarchical decomposition requires that the PI of the parent element be *delegated* to matching PI of child elements. Hierarchical aggregation permits to *promote* selected items of the PI of the aggregated elements to the PI of the aggregating element and hide all others. Decomposition and aggregation must preserve respectively respect the ontology of model elements. In other words, specific semantic rules determine the legal decompositions and the allowable aggregations.

A further ontological rule on the composition of model entities stipulates that only "active" terminal elements include a Thread. In fact, terminal elements that include a Thread are denoted Cyclic or Sporadic. The former implies that the thread of control associated at run time to the Thread entity of the Cyclic element takes its activation event from a fixed-rate clock event. The desired rate can be changed at run time by the application logic (as it would occur during a "mode change" situation) as long as the PI of the corresponding Cyclic element publishes an operation to that effect. The latter implies that the source of the activation event be other than time, however requiring a guaranteed minimum separation between two subsequent arrivals of it. This property is assumed at model level and warranted by the model transformation rules that inform automated code generationA few words are in order on the ontology of the internal constituents of HRT-UML model elements. The PI of a terminal element is delegated to the PI of the element's OBCS, which may hold further operations to match any of those appearing in the RI of the element's Thread, if any. While having an empty PI, the Thread's RI includes the operations to fetch service requests from the OBCS as well as the invocation of those services in the PI of the corresponding OPCS. The element's OPCS, finally, has both PI and RI, the latter because the execution of a service charged to the element may need to use the services provided by other visible elements of the system. Figure 5 illustrates these notions by depicting the ontology of a Cyclic element.

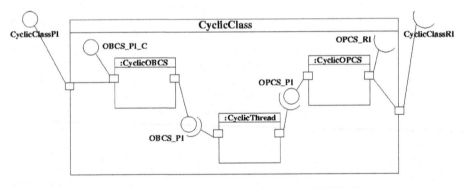

Fig. 4. The ontology of a Cyclic element in HRT-UML

3.2   Brief Taxonomy of HRT-UML Model Elements

The HRT-UML invocation protocols address two dimensions of critical relevance to concurrent computing: (i) the guarantee of mutual exclusion on access to element internals on execution of a given PI operation; and (ii) the suspension of the call until the element internal state permits to execute it. The former caters for controlled access to shared resources. The latter corresponds to placing a state-dependent conditions akin to Dijkstra guards on the servicing of PI operation [12] HRT-UML draws from the Ravenscar Profile the restrictions on the use of these invocation constraints.

Firstly, it assumes that the locking policy in force in the execution environment be based on Immediate Priority Ceiling Inheritance [11,12]. Secondly, it prescribes that no more than *one* state-dependent invocation constraint should ever appear in the PI of a terminal element so as to avoid the non-determinism that would incur from multiple guard conditions becoming open simultaneously on one and the same PI. Thirdly, it requires that no more than one call should ever queue at any one time awaiting access to a state-constrained operation. The intent of this very severe restriction is to *constructively* avoid the non-determinism that would arise from call queuing. HRT-UML takes a very straightforward approach to enforcing this particular restriction: it stipulates that state-constrained operations should only be invoked by the Thread of Sporadic elements. In essence, PI invocation protocol of a Sporadic element would specify how a given sequence of PI invocations would produce the activation event of the element's Thread.

3.3 Integration with the FW Profile

HRT-UML defines the concurrent architecture of the framework. That architecture may include components defined to the level of terminal elements, as either fully developed object instances or plain classes. Other components may be left to the stage of non-terminal elements, hence simply described by the corresponding PI and RI (either of which may be empty).

The FW Profile defines the functional components of the framework architecture. As discussed above, HRT-UML stipulates that such functional specifications pertain to the PI, along with the applicable invocation protocol, to the RI, and to the OPCS components of model elements.

In practice, the FW Profile imports the HRT-UML constraints on those ontological components and guarantees that they are respected throughout design and instantiation. On these conditions, verification on the model can safely be performed for the timing and the functional aspects in isolation, while code generation can also be undertaken separately for the structural (concurrent) and the functional part.

4 Code Generation

The core of the approach proposed in this paper is a UML2 profile that allows functional and timing behaviour of extensible components to be expressed in a manner that permits the inclusion of components in HRT applications. Automatic generation of the component code from its profile-compliant models is a natural extension to this objective.

We do not deem it appropriate to define a *single* code generator for our profile. Different domains have different coding rules and must interface to different middleware or operating systems. The code generator must therefore be framework-specific. The *code generating approach* can, however, be generic.

The approach we propose propagates the split between functional and non-functional issues down to code level. We have found it convenient to have two code generators (cf. Figure 5). The first one processes the timing view of the framework model and generates a set of *structural containers* that enforce the timing constraints.

In practice, these containers implement HRT-UML entities (sporadic, cyclical or protected elements) with no functional behaviour attached to them. The second code generator processes the functional view of the framework model and generates the classes that implement the state machine logic, which encapsulates the functional behaviour of the framework components. Each state in a state machine is mapped to an instance of a generic `State` class. There is an aggregation relationship between a class and the states of the associated state machine. Any state can embed further state machines and thus embedded states (cf. figure 6). Triggers are mapped to parameterless operations that operate on a state by calling operations `unmarkAsCurrent()` and `markAsCurrent()` on `State` objects. Guards, transition actions and state entry and exit actions are expressed in the model using the action language associated to the FW Profile. The action language syntax is simple and compatible with most mainstream object-oriented languages.

The two code generators are integrated in the sense that the functional code is designed to be embedded within the structural containers.

One can imagine that the non-functional code generator generates a set of non-functional containers, whereas the functional code generator fills the containers with the functional code.

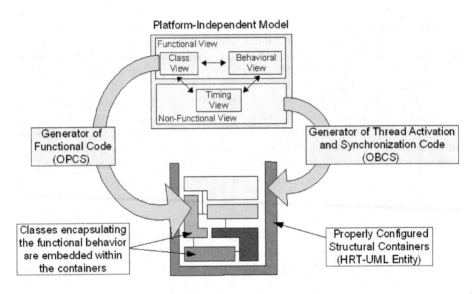

Fig. 5. Code Generation Approach

The Eclipse Java Emitter Templates (JET) is the basic technology for our code generator. JET is an open source tool for code generation. It is a generic template engine that permits to generate any type of source code. A model-to-code generator for Java has been implemented and the development of a generator for Ada 2005 [6] is now under way, which builds on the work described in [13,14]. Both generators are distributed as plug-ins for Eclipse and for IBM RSM [5].

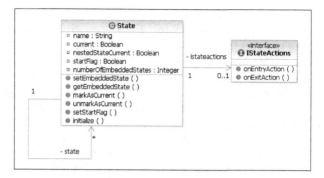

Fig. 6. Hierarchical State Machine Implementation

5   Case Study and Conclusions

We are using our approach to construct a software framework for satellite on-board applications. These applications form a good case study since they are subject to HRT constraints and are mission-critical. Our framework covers the handling of *tele-commands*, namely the commands that are sent to a satellite by the ground station.

Telecommands are characterized by timing requirements that define the minimum inter-arrival time of consecutive telecommands and the maximum execution time of each telecommand. At a functional level, telecommands are characterized by some requirements that apply to all satellite applications, and by others that are specific to each satellite application. Examples of the former are the requirements that telecommands must report the outcome of their execution to the ground station; that they must perform an acceptance check that may lead to their being rejected before their execution starts; or that their execution can be aborted by the ground station; etc.

In accordance with the process proposed in this paper, we designed the framework in two steps. In one step, we defined the timing view to implement the timing requirements. This was done by defining a set of HRT-UML sporadic structural containers to hold groups of telecommands with the same timing constraints. This architecture ensures that timing requirements are satisfied, independently of the functional content of the telecommands. In the other step, we defined the functional view of the framework by defining a set of reusable components. Their behaviour was described by state machines. The state machine logic ensures that the application-invariant functional requirements of the telecommands are satisfied. Since the design complies with the FW Profile, the application developer can extend these components to implement the application-specific behaviour in the knowledge that properties such as reporting of execution outcome, or implementation of an acceptance check will be preserved.

The case study demonstrated the four decisive advantages of our approach over rival approaches to framework-based software reuse. Firstly, the functional and non-functional aspects of the framework are defined separately from each other and are only merged when the models are translated into code. This simplifies the design process. In fact, functional and non-functional design can be entrusted to two different teams (as was in fact done in our case study). Unlike other authors who have attempted to use state charts to model both the functional and non-functional behaviour of real-time applications [15,16], we use two different modelling vehicles for functional and non-functional issues and thus avoid the semantic uncertainties and complexities of the UML2 state machine concept.

Secondly, the encapsulation of our approach in a UML2 profile means that compliance with the approach can be enforced at design time using standard software design tools. It also means that translation to code can be easily automated since there are standard ways of building code generators for UML2-based models.

Thirdly, compliance with our FW Profile ensures that functional and timing properties defined at framework level are preserved when the framework components are reused to instantiate a particular application. This is an essential pre-requisite for software reuse in mission-critical applications and we are not aware of other methodologies that provide the same guarantee.Finally, the formulation of functional properties on profile-compliant UML2 models opens the way to their formal verification at model level. This is an avenue that we are currently exploring in a follow-on project. The final objective is to arrive at a reuse methodology where reusable components are provably endowed with functional properties whose preservation be provably guaranteed throughout the adaptation process.

Acknowledgments

The definition of HRT-UML design method is the result of the collective effort of several people. The authors of this paper gratefully acknowledge the considerable contributions by Daniela Cancila and Enrico Mezzetti from the University of Padua (Italy), and Silvia Mazzini, Stefano Puri and Maria Rosa Barone from Intecs (Italy).

References

1. Pasetti, A.: Software Frameworks and Embedded Control Systems, LNCS Vol. 2231, Springer-Verlag, 2002
2. Wang F.: Formal verification of timed systems: A survey and perspective. Proceedings of the IEEE, 92(8), pages 1283-1305. August 2004.
3. Cechticky, V., Pasetti, A., Rohlik, O., Schaufelberger, W.: XML-Based Feature Modelling, in Bosch, J., Krueger, C. (eds), Software Reuse: Methods, Techniques, and Tools (ICSR), LNCS Vol. 3107, Springer-Verlag, 2004.
4. Cechticky, V., Pasetti, A., Rohlik, O., Vardanega, T: Automated proof-based System and Software Engineering for Real-Time Applications: Framework Design Report. Technical Report, 2005. Available at ASSERT project website: http://www.assert-online.org/
5. Cechticky, V., Pasetti, A., Rohlik, O.: The Model-to-Code Transformation Project website http://people.ee.ethz.ch/~ceg/assert/model2code/
6. ISO SC22/WG9: Ada Reference Manual. Language and Standard Libraries. Consolidated Standard ISO/IEC 8652:1995(E) with Technical Corrigendum 1 and Amendment 1 (Draft 16). (2006) Available at http://www.adaic.com/standards/rm-amend/html/RM-TTL.html.
7. Mazzini S., D'Alessandro M., Di Natale M., Lipari G., Vardanega T.: Issues in Mapping HRT-HOOD to UML. In: Proc. 15th Euromicro Conference on Real-Time Systems, IEEE, 221-228, July 2003 (ISBN: 0-7695-1936-9).

8. Mazzini S., D'Alessandro M., Di Natale M., Domenici A., Lipari G., Vardanega T.: HRT-UML: Taking HRT-HOOD onto UML, Reliable Software Technologies Ada Europe 2003, Springer Verlag. LNCS(2655): 405-416, June 2003 (ISBN: 3-540-40376-0).
9. Vardanega T., Di Natale M., Mazzini S., D'Alessandro M.: Component-Based Real-Time Design: Mapping HRT-HOOD to UML, IEEE CS Press, In: Proc. 30th Euromicro Conference, pp. 6-13, September 2004 (ISSN: 1089-6503).
10. Vardanega T., Zamorano J., de la Puente J.A.: On the Dynamic Semantics and the Timing Behaviour of Ravenscar Kernels, Real-Time Systems, 29(1):5989, 2005. Kluwer Academic Publishers (ISSN: 0922-6443).
11. Goodenough, J., and Sha, L. The priority ceiling protocol: a method for minimizing the blocking of high priority Ada Tasks. Technical Report SEI-SSR-4, Software Engineering Institute, Pittsburgh, Pennsylvania, 1988.
12. Dijkstra, E. 1975. Guarded commands, nondeterminacy and formal derivation of programs. CACM 18(8): 453– 457.
13. M. Bordin, T. Vardanega: Automated Model-based Generation of Ravenscar-compliant Source Code, In: Proc. 17th Euromicro Conference on Real-Time Systems, July 2005, IEEE, 69–77 (ISBN: 0-7695-2400-1, ISSN:1068-3070).
14. Bordin M., Vardanega T.: A New Strategy for the HRT-HOOD to Ada Mapping, Reliable Software Technologies – Ada-Europe 2005, Springer. LNCS(3555):51–66, June 2005 (ISBN: 3-540-26286-5).
15. Ober I., Graf S., Ober I.: Validating timed UML models by simulation and verification. In STTT, Int. Journal on Software Tools for Technology Transfer, Springer 2005.
16. Latella D., Majzik I., Massink M.. Automatic verification of a behavioral subset of UML statechart diagrams using the SPiN model-checker. Formal Aspects of Computing, (11), 1999.
17. Packet Utilization Standard, European Space Agency, ESA PSS-07-101, (ECSS version ECSS-E-70-41). Available from: http://www.ecss.nl/forums/ecss/_ templates/default.htm? target = http://www.ecss.nl/forums/ecss/dispatch.cgi/standards/showFolder/100004/def/ def/a492

Formalizing MDA Components

Liliana Favre and Liliana Martinez

Universidad Nacional del Centro de la Provincia de Buenos Aires
Comisión de Investigaciones Científicas de la Provincia de Buenos Aires (CIC)
Argentina
{lfavre, lmartine}@exa.unicen.edu.ar

Abstract. The Model Driven Architecture (MDA) promotes the use of models and model transformations for developing software systems. The idea behind MDA is to manage the evolution from Platform Independent Models to Platform Specific Models that can be used to generate executable components and applications. The concepts of metamodels and metamodel-based model transformations are critical in MDA. In this paper, we propose a metamodeling technique to reach a high level of reusability and adaptability of MDA components. In particular, we analyze how to define reusable components for the standard design patterns in a way that fits MDA very closely. To define families of reusable components we describe a "megamodel" that refers to metamodels and model transformations organized into an architectural framework. We propose a "megamodel" formalization that focuses on interoperability of formal languages in Model Driven Development (MDD).

1 Introduction

The Model Driven Architecture (MDA) is an initiative of the Object Management Group (OMG) that promotes the use of models and model transformations for developing software systems. MDA distinguishes at least three kinds of models: Platform Independent Model (PIM), Platform Specific Model (PSM) and Implementation Specific Model (ISM). A PIM is a model that contains no reference to the platforms that are used to realize it. A PSM describes a system in the terms of the final implementation platform e.g., .NET or J2EE. An ISM refers to components and applications using specific languages such as Java or Eiffel. The idea behind MDA is to manage the evolution from PIMs to PSMs that can be used to generate ISMs [14].

Metamodeling has become an essential technique to support model transformations. In MDA, metamodels are expressed using MOF (Meta Object Facility) that defines a common way for capturing all the diversity of modeling standards and interchange constructs [16].

The success of MDA depends on the definition of model transformations and component libraries which make a significant impact on tools that provide support for MDA. MDA is a young approach and several technical issues are not adequately addressed. For instance, existing MDA-based tools do not provide adequate support to deal with component-based reuse [5].

M. Morisio (Ed.): ICSR 2006, LNCS 4039, pp. 326–339, 2006.

In this light, we propose a metamodeling technique to reach a high level of reusability and adaptability of MDA components. In particular, we analyze how to define reusable components for the standard design patterns with the MDA approach.

[2] analyzes the popular Gamma et al´s design patterns [11] to identify which ones can become reusable components in an Eiffel library. Their work hypothesis is that "design patterns are good, but the components are better" because they are reusable in terms of code. Our work takes up these ideas and contributes a metamodeling technique to build reusable design pattern components in a MDA perspective.

We propose a "megamodel" to define families of design pattern components by means of PIM-, PSM- and ISM-metamodels and their interrelations. Instances of the "megamodel" are reusable components that describe specific design patterns at different levels of abstraction (PIMs, PSMs and ISMs). They can be viewed as "megacomponents" that allow defining in a concise way as many components as different pattern solutions can appear. We analyze metamodel transformations of both PIMs into PSMs, and PSMs into ISMs.

Developing reusable components requires a high focus on software quality. In this direction the traditional techniques for verification and validation are still essential to achieve software quality. In this paper, we describe foundations for constructing formalizations of design pattern component. We define a "megamodel" formalization, in particular, we show how to formalize MOF-metamodels and metamodel-based model transformations by using the metamodeling notation NEREUS that can be viewed as an intermediate notation open to many other formal languages [8], [9]. We illustrate our MDA-based approach by using the *Observer* design pattern.

This paper is organized as follows. Section 2 describes a "megamodel" to define MDA components and Section 3, how to specify design pattern components in a MDA perspective. Section 4 presents formalization for MOF-metamodels in terms of the NEREUS language. Section 5 describes how to build automatically a formalization of components (that are instances of the "megamodel"). Section 6 deals with related work. Finally, Section 7 considers conclusions and future work.

2   A "Megamodel" for Defining MDA Reusable Components

We propose a metamodeling technique to define MDA components. In the MDA, modeling languages and model transformations are defined in the same way through MOF-based metamodels. A metamodel is an explicit model of the constructs and rules needed to build specific models. MOF-based metamodels use an object modeling framework that is essentially a subset of the UML core [20]. The 4 main modeling concepts are "classes, which model MOF metaobjects; associations, which model binary relations between metaobjects; Data Types, which model other data and Packages, which modularize the models" [16, pp. 2-6]. OCL (Object Constraint Language) can be used to attach consistency rules to metamodel components [17]. The UML metamodel can be viewed as an instance the MOF. OMG is working on the definition of a QVT (Query, View, Transformations) metamodel for expressing transformations as an extension of MOF [18].

To define families of reusable components we describe a "megamodel" that refers to metamodels and model transformations organized into an architectural framework.

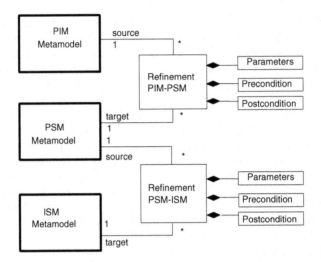

Fig. 1. A "megamodel" for MDA components

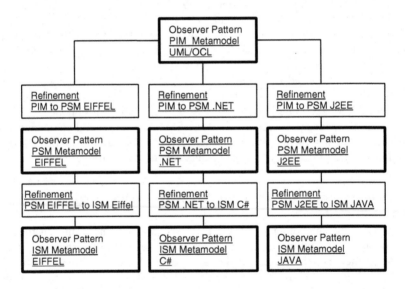

Fig. 2. An instance of the "megamodel"- The Observer Pattern Component

Fig.1 depicts a "megamodel" that associates a set of classes linked to metamodels and refinements. The class *PIM-Metamodel* describes a family of PIMs, and the class *Refinement PIM-PSM* a family of refinements among PIM- and PSM- metamodels. Vertical refinements refine a source model into a target model at a different abstraction level (PIM to PSM, PSM to ISM). In this context, a refinement is a more detailed specification that conforms to another which is more abstract. It is associated to a source metamodel and a target metamodel and is composed by parameters, local operations, preconditions and postconditions. The precondition states the conditions that must be hold whenever the transformation is applied. The postcondition states the properties that the transformation guarantees when it was applied. OCL contracts describe conditions that must be met for a refinement step to be consistent.

In Fig. 2 we show an instance of the "megamodel" that   refers concrete instances of an *Observer* pattern metamodel, refinements and, links between metamodels and refinements. It can be viewed as a "megacomponent" defining a family of reusable components that integrate instances of PIMs, PSMs and ISMs.

3   Specifying Design Pattern Components with MDA

In this section we analyze how to specify design patterns with MDA. We illustrate our MDA-based approach by using the *Observer* design pattern. It "defines a one-to-many dependency between objects so that when one object changes state, all its dependents are notified and updated automatically" [11, pp. 293]. We show how to build PIM-and PSM- metamodels and how to define refinements between them.

3.1   PIM-Metamodel of the *Observer* Pattern

The *Observer* pattern metamodel at PIM level specifies the structural and behavior views of this pattern in a platform independent pattern model. It specifies the classes that participate, its operations and attributes and the relation between classes. The specialized UML metamodel of the *Observer* pattern is partially shown in Fig. 3. The shaded metaclasses correspond to metaclasses of the UML metamodel, whereas the remaining corresponds to the specialization of the UML metamodel of the *Observer* pattern. Fig. 4 partially shows some well-formedness rules in OCL for the metamodel.

In Gamma et al´s design pattern there are four essential participants: *Subject*, *Observer*, *ConcreteSubject* and *ConcreteObserver* [11]. So, these four classes must be specified in the metamodel, as well as the relation between them and their interactions. The PIM metamodel involves the following participants linked to them:

AbstractObserver: This metaclass specifies the characteristics of class *Observer* inside the *Observer* pattern. It should have at least an operation with the characteristics of *Update*. Each instance of this metaclass can be an abstract class or an interface. If the instance is an abstract class, a concrete observer inherits its behavior, therefore there is an inheritance relation with the concrete observer. If the instance is an interface, there is a realization relation with the concrete observer.

ConcreteObserver: This metaclass specifies the characteristics of a concrete observer. It knows the subject (or the subjects), then it is associated to *ConcreteSubject* through a unidirectional association navigable away from that end.

AbstractSubject: Each instance of this metaclass can be an abstract class or an interface and it has at least three operations specified by *Attach*, *Detach* and *Notify*. If the instance of this metaclass is an abstract class, all concrete subjects inherit its behavior, therefore there is an inheritance relation with the concrete subject. If the instance is an interface, there is a realization relation with the concrete subject. If the instance of *AbstractSubject* is an abstract class, it is associated to an instance of *AbstractObserver* through a unidirectional association navigable away from that end.

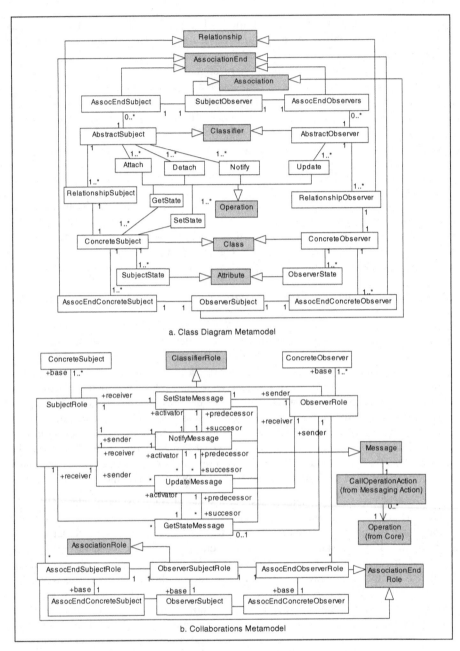

Fig. 3. A simplified PIM-Metamodel of the Observer Pattern

ConcreteSubject: This metaclass specifies the characteristics of a concrete subject. It has at least two operations specified by *GetState* and *SetState* and its internal state is specified by the *ObserverState* metaclass.

context *AbstractSubject* **inv:**
(self.oclIsTypeOf(Class) and self.isAbstract = #true) **or** self.oclIsTypeOf(Interface)
      and self.oclIsTypeOf(Interface) **implies** self.assocEndSub ->isEmpty( )

context *AssocEndConcreteSubject* **inv:**
self.isNavigable= #true and (multiplicity.range.lower >= 0)
and (self.multiplicity.range.upper > 0 **or** self.multiplicity.range.upper = #unlimited)

context *AssocEndSubject* **inv:**
self.isNavigable= #false **and** (multiplicity.range.lower >= 0)
and (self.multiplicity.range.upper > 0 **or** self.multiplicity.range.upper = #unlimited)

context *Attach* **inv:**
self.isQuery= #false **and** self.parameter->notEmpty() **and** self.parameter->
select(param |param.kind= #in **and** param.type= oclIsKindOf(AbstractObserver)) -> size( ) = 1

context *ConcreteObserver* **inv:**
 self.oclIsTypeOf(Class) **and** self.isAbstract = #false

context *ConcreteSubject* **inv:**
 self.oclIsTypeOf(Class) **and** self.isAbstract = #false

context *RelationshipObserver* **inv:**
self.oclIsTypeOf(Generalization) **or**
(self.oclIsTypeOf(Abstraction) **and** self.stereotype.name= 'realize')
and self.oclIsTypeOf(Generalization) **implies** (self.parent.oclIsKindOf(Class) **and**
  self.parent.oclIsTypeOf(AbstractObserver) **and** self.child.oclIsTypeOf(ConcreteObserver))
and self.oclIsTypeOf(Abstraction) **implies** (self.supplier.oclIsKindOf(Interface) **and**
  self.supplier.oclIsTypeOf(AbstractObserver) **and** self.client.oclIsTypeOf(ConcreteObserver))
...

Fig. 4. OCL rules- Class Diagram Metamodel

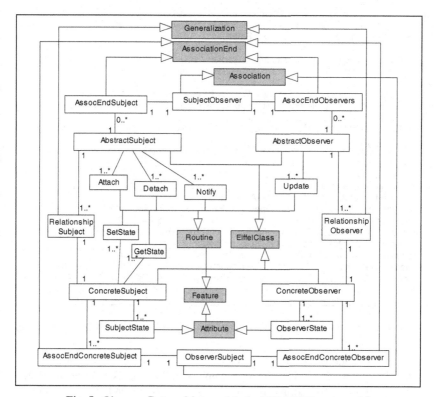

Fig. 5. Observer Pattern Metamodel: An Eiffel PSM-metamodel

3.2 PSM-Metamodel of the Observer Pattern

For each design pattern at the PIM level there are a number of metamodels corresponding to different platforms at the PSM level. The metamodel of the *Observer* pattern in an EIFFEL platform is described below. Fig. 5 partially shows an UML specialized metamodel of the *Observer* pattern in the Eiffel platform (structural view). The shaded metaclasses correspond to metaclasses of the Eiffel metamodel.

3.3 Specifying Metamodel-Based Model Transformations

A model transformation is a specification of a mechanism to convert the elements of a model, that are instances of a particular metamodel, into elements of another model which can be instances of the same or different metamodels. Metamodel transformations are a specific type of model transformations that impose relations between pairs of metamodels. They can be used in the specification stages of the MDA-based developments to check the validity of a transformation.

```
Transformation PIM-UML TO PSM-EIFFEL {
parameters
sourceModel: Design Pattern Metamodel :: Package
targetModel: Design Pattern Metamodel-EIFFEL :: Model
local operations
equivalentType (a_type: Design Pattern Metamodel::Classifier,
    another_type: Design Pattern Metamodel-EIFFEL::Classifier): Boolean...
pre: sourceModel.importedElement → isEmpty
post:
sourceModel.ownedElement → select(oclIsTypeOf(Class) or oclIsTypeOf(Interface) )→ size() =
    targetModel.ownedElement → select(oclIsTypeOf(EiffelClass))→ size()
post:
sourceModel.ownedElement → select(oclIsTypeOf(Class))→ forAll ( sourceClass /
targetModel.ownedElement->select.(oclIsTypeOf(EiffelClass))→ exists ( targetClass /
sourceClass.name = targetClass.name   and
sourceClass.generalization.parent = targetClass.generalization.parent  and
sourceClass.specialization.child = targetClass.specialization.child   and
sourceClass.templateParameter = targetClass.templateParameter   and
sourceClass.feature → select (oclIsTypeOf(Attribute)) → forAll ( sourceAtt /
    targetClass.feature → select (oclIsTypeOf(Attribute)) → exists ( targetAtt /
    sourceAtt.name = targetAtt.name  and  sourceAtt.visibility = targetAtt.visibility  and
    equivalentType(sourceAtt.type, targetAtt.type)  ))     and
sourceClass.feature → select (oclIsTypeOf(Operation)) → forAll (sourceOp /
    targetClass.feature → select (oclIsKindOf(Routine)) → exists (targetOp /
    targetOp.name = sourceOp.name and equivalentType (targetOp.type, sourceOp.type) and
    sourceOp.parameter → size() = targetOp.parameter → size()  and
    Sequence {1..( sourceOp.parameter→size())} → forAll ( index:Integer /
        targetOp.parameter→at(index).name = sourceOp.parameter→at(index).name and
        equivalentType(targetOp.parameter→at(index).type, sourceOp.parameter→at(index).type)) ))
)) ... }
```

Fig. 6. Specifying refinements in OCL: From PIMs to PSMs

We specify metamodel-based model transformations as OCL contracts that are described by means of a transformation name, parameters, preconditions, postconditions and additional operations. In Fig. 6, we partially exemplify a transformation *Observer* Pattern component from a PIM to an Eiffel-based PSM.

The definition of the transformation from PIM to PSM uses both the specialized UML metamodel of the *Observer* pattern and the UML metamodel of an Eiffel platform as source and target parameters respectively. The source metamodel describes a family of packages whose elements are only classes and associations. The postconditions establish correspondences among classes, their superclasses, parameters, operations, and associations. The transformation specification guarantees, for instance, that for a class *sourceClass* in the source model exists a class *targetClass* in the target model, both of them with the same name, the same parent classes, the same child classes and so on.

4 Formalization of MOF-Metamodels

Formalisms can be used to detect inconsistencies in MDDs whether in internal models or between a source model and a target model that has been obtained through model transformations. A formal specification clarifies the intended meaning of metamodels and metamodel-based model transformations helping to validate them and providing reference for implementation. In this direction, we propose the metamodeling notation NEREUS and, a system of transformation rules to transform MOF-based metamodels into NEREUS. Most of the MOF-based metamodel concepts can be mapped to NEREUS in a straightforward way. MOF is based on UML and OCL which are too imprecise and ambiguous when it comes to simulation, verification, validation and forecasting of system properties.

NEREUS consists of several constructs to express classes, associations and packages and a repertoire of mechanisms for structuring them. Fig. 7 shows the syntax of NEREUS specifications.

```
CLASS className [<parameterList>]          ASSOCIATION <relationName>
IMPORTS <importsList>                      IS <constructorTypeName>
INHERITS <inheritsList>                     [...: Class1;...: Class2; ...: Role1; ...:
IS-SUBTYPE-OF <subtypeList>                 Role2;...: mult1; ...: mult2; ...: visibility1;
GENERATED-BY <basicConstructors>           ...: visibility2]
ASSOCIATES<associatesList>                 CONSTRAINED-BY <constraintList>
DEFERRED                                   END
TYPES <typesList>
FUNCTIONS <functionList>                   PACKAGE packageName
EFFECTIVE                                  IMPORTS <importsList>
TYPES <typesList>                          INHERITS  <inheritsList>
FUNCTIONS <functionList>                   <elements>
AXIOMS <varList>                           END-PACKAGE
<axiomList>
END-CLASS
```

Fig. 7. The NEREUS syntax

NEREUS distinguishes inheritance from subtyping. Subtyping is like inheritance of behavior, while inheritance relies on the module viewpoint of classes. The DEFERRED and EFFECTIVE clauses declare new types or operations that are incompletely or completely defined.

Operations are declared in FUNCTIONS clauses. NEREUS supports higher-order operations. In the context of OCL *Collection* formalization, second-order operations are required. NEREUS provides a taxonomy of constructor types that classifies binary associations according to kind (aggregation, composition, association, association class, qualified association), degree (unary, binary), navigability (unidirectional, bidirectional), connectivity (one-to one, one-to-many, many-to-many). New associations can be defined by the ASSOCIATION construction. The PACKAGE construct groups classes and associations and controls its visibility (see Fig. 7).

We define semantics by giving a precise formal meaning to each of the constructs of the NEREUS language in terms of the CASL language [4]. A detailed description may be found at [8].

```
PACKAGE ObserverMetamodel
IMPORTS Core
CLASS AssocEndSubject
IS-SUBTYPE-OF AssociationEnd
ASSOCIATES
<< AssocEndSubject-SubjectObserver >>,
<< AssocEndSubject-AbstractSubject >> ...
END-CLASS

CLASS SubjectObserver ...END-CLASS

CLASS AssocEndObservers ...END-CLASS

CLASS AbstractSubject
IS-SUBTYPE-OF Classifier
ASSOCIATES
<<AssocEndSubject-AbstractSubject>>,
<< AbstractSubject-RelationshipSubject >>,
 <<AbstractSubject-Attach>>,
<<AbstractSubject-Detach>>,
<<AbstractSubject-Notify>> ...
AXIOMS s:AbstractSubject;..
(oclIsTypeOf(Class,s) and isAbstract (s)) or
oclIsTypeOf(Interface, s)
oclIsTypeOf (Interface,s) implies
isEmpty (assocEndSub (s))
END-CLASS

CLASS AbstractObserver
IS-SUBTYPE-OF Classifier
ASSOCIATES
<< AssocEndObservers-AbstractObserver>>,
<<AbstractObserver-Update>>,
<<AbstractObserver-RelationshipObserver>> ...
END-CLASS

CLASS Attach
IS-SUBTYPE-OF Operation
ASSOCIATES <<AbstractSubject-Attach>> ...
FUNCTIONS...
AXIOMS at:Attach
(isQuery (at ) = False) and
notEmpty (
get_formalParameter (Operation-Parameter, at)
and size (select_param (
get_formalParameter (Operation-Parameter, at),
[equal(kind (param),´in´) and
equal (type(param),
oclIsKindOf(AbstractObserver,at)]) = 1
END-CLASS
```

```
CLASS Detach... END-CLASS

CLASS Notify ... END-CLASS

CLASS Update... END-CLASS

CLASS RelationshipObserver
IS-SUBTYPE-OF Relationship
ASSOCIATES
<<AbstractObserver-RelationshipObserver>>,
<< RelationshipObserver-ConcreteObserver>>
...
AXIOMS r:RelationshipObserver;...
oclIsTypeOf(Generalization, r) or
(oclIsTypeOf(Abstraction, r) and
equal (get_name(stereotype( r ), ´realize´)
oclIsTypeOf(Generalization,r)implies
oclIsKindOf(Class, r)
END-CLASS

CLASS ConcretSubject ... END-CLASS

CLASS ConcreteObserver ... END-CLASS

CLASS AssocEndConcreteObserver ...
END-CLASS

ASSOCIATION
AssocEndSubject-SubjectObserver
IS Bidirectional-1 [AssocEndSubject: Class1;
SubjectObserver: Class2; assocEndSub:role1;
sub-obs:role2; 1:mult1; 1:mult2; +:visibility1;
+:visibility2]
END

ASSOCIATION
AssocEndSubject-AbstractSubject
...
ASSOCIATION
AbstractSubject-RelationshipSubject
...
ASSOCIATION
AbstractObserver-RelationshipObserver
IS Bidirectional-3[AbstractObserver:Class1;
RelationshipObserver:Class2; absObs:role1;
relObs:role2; 1:mult1;1..*:role2;+:visibility1;
 +:visibility2]
END

ASSOCIATION AbstractSubject-Attach ...
END-PACKAGE
```

Fig. 8. Specifying MOF-metamodels in NEREUS: The Observer Pattern Metamodel

Fig. 8 partially shows the NEREUS specification of the simplified UML meta-model shown in Fig 3-a. In this example, the association names refer to the names of the associated classes, for instance *AbstractObserver-RelationshipObserver* denotes an association between *AbstractObserver* and *RelationshipObserver*. The axioms of *Attach* and *RelationshipObserver* classes are linked to the OCL well-formedness rules of Fig. 4.

5 Formalization of Instances of the "Megamodel"

The formalization implies formalizing metamodels, refinements and links among them. We describe how to transform metamodels and metamodel-based refinements.

5.1 Constructing Metamodel Formalizations

MOF-metamodels and NEREUS have similar constructs and structuring mechanisms. Then, every package in a metamodel is translated into a package in NEREUS. Also,

RULE	OCL	NEREUS
1	v. operation (v') v->operation (v')	operation (v, v')
2	**context A** object.rolename	get_ rolename (a, object) *Let a:A*
3	OCLexp1 = OCLexp2	Translate NEREUS (OCLexp1) = Translate NEREUS (OCLexp2)
4	e.op	op (Translate NEREUS (e))
5	collection->op(v:Elem|bool-expr-with-v) op ::=select| forAll| reject| exists	**LET** **FUNCTIONS** f: Elem -> Boolean **AXIOMS v : Elem** f (v)=Translate NEREUS (bool-expr-with-v) **IN** op (collection, f) **END-LET** ---------------------------------- op$_v$ (collection, [Translate NEREUS (bool-expr-with-v)] *Equivalent concise notation*

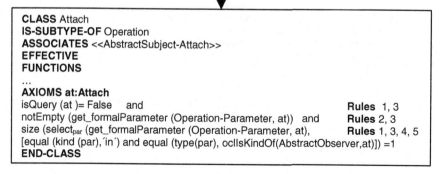

CLASS Attach
IS-SUBTYPE-OF Operation
ASSOCIATES <<AbstractSubject-Attach>>
EFFECTIVE
FUNCTIONS
...
AXIOMS at:Attach
isQuery (at)= False   and   **Rules** 1, 3
notEmpty (get_formalParameter (Operation-Parameter, at))   and   **Rules** 2, 3
size (select$_{par}$ (get_formalParameter (Operation-Parameter, at),   **Rules** 1, 3, 4, 5
[equal (kind (par), ´in´) and equal (type(par), oclIsKindOf(AbstractObserver,at)]) =1
END-CLASS

Fig. 9. Constructing the Class Attach in NEREUS

every class or association in a metamodel is translated into a class or an association in NEREUS. A detailed analysis may be found at [8].

The transformation process of OCL specifications to NEREUS is supported by a system of transformation rules. In metamodels, OCL specifications can appear as preconditions, postconditions or invariants of classes, attribute constraints, association constraints and transformation contrats. Analyzing OCL specifications we can derive axioms that will be included in the NEREUS specifications. Preconditions written in OCL are used to generate preconditions in NEREUS. Postconditions and invariants allow us to generate axioms in NEREUS. An operation can be specified in OCL by means of pre- and post-conditions. Fig. 9 shows how to transform the class *Observer*. Let Translate$_{NEREUS}$ be functions that translate logical expressions of OCL into first-order formulae in NEREUS.

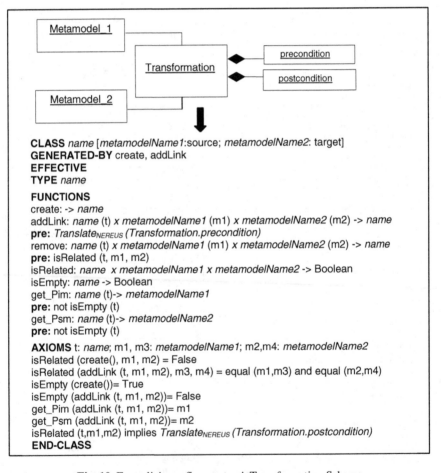

Fig. 10. Formalizing refinements- A Transformation Scheme

5.2 Formalizing Refinements

Instances of refinement classes are translated into NEREUS specifications by instantiating reusable schemes. Fig. 10 depicts the scheme for translating refinements into NEREUS. Following, we show an instantiation of the scheme for the transformation *PIM-UML TO PSM-EIFFEL* (Fig. 6):

> [name: PimToPsm; metamodelName1: PimMetamodel; metamodelName2:
> PsmMetamodel; precondition: OCLexp1; postcondition: OCLexp2]

where *OCLexp1* and *OCLexp2* are the OCL expressions following the "pre:" and "post" in Fig. 6 respectively.

$Translate_{NEREUS}(OCLexp1)$ and $Translate_{NEREUS}(OCLexp2)$ are the expressions in italic following the *"pre:"* and *"isRelated (t, m1,m2) implies "* in Fig. 10 respectively:

> $Translate_{NEREUS}(OCLexp1) =$
> isEmpty(get_importedElements(ElementImport-PackageableElement, m1))
>
> $Translate_{NEREUS}(OCLexp2) =$
> size(select $_s$(get_ownedElement(Element-Element, s),
>   [oclIsTypeOf(Class,m1) or oclIsTypeOf(Interface, m1)]) =
> size(select $_e$ (get_ownedElement(Element-Element,m2),
>   [oclIsTypeOf(EiffelClass,c)])   and
>   forAll $_{sourceClass}$(select $_{source}$ (get_ownedElement(Element-Element,source),
>   [exists $_{targetClass}$ (select $_{tc}$ (get_ownedElement(Element-Element), tc),
>   [oclIsTypeOf(EiffelClass, tc)]),
>   [name(sourceClass) = name(targetClass)] and...

6   Related Work and Discussion

[1] describes how a metamodel can be used to obtain a representation of design patterns and how this representation allows both automatic generation and detection of design patterns. The contribution of this proposal is the definition of design patterns as entities of modeling of first class. The main limitation of this approach concerns the integration of the generated code with the user code.

[12] describes an approach to rigorous modeling of pattern-based transformations that involves specializing the UML metamodel to characterize source and target models.

[10] presents a technique to specify pattern solutions expressed in the UML. The specifications created by this technique are metamodels that characterize UML design models of pattern solutions. The patterns specification consists of a Structural Pattern Specification that specifies the class diagram view of pattern solutions, and a set of Interaction Pattern Specification that specifies interactions in pattern solutions.

Component-based approaches have been proposed to reuse [3], [7], [15], [19]. [3] summarizes lessons from several projects related to component-based development and MDA and examines the pragmatic use of today's MDA tools.

Several specification of UML, metamodels and model transformations have been proposed. [13] compare and contrast two approaches to model transformations: one is graph transformation and the other is a relational approach. In [6] a taxonomy for the classification of several existing and proposed model-to-model transformations approaches is analyzed. The taxonomy is described with a feature model to compare them.

Currently, there are not many of CASE tools that provide some support for MDA. Some of them are OptimalJ, ArcStyler, AndroMDA, Ameos, Codagen among others [5]. Techniques that currently exist in UML CASE tools provide little support for analyzing consistency of model transformations.

In contrast to other work, our approach is the only one focusing on interoperability of formal languages in component-based model-driven development. We define NEREUS to take advantage of all the existing theoretical background on formal methods in different stages of MDD. NEREUS would eliminate the need to define formalizations and specific transformations for each different formal language. In a Model Driven Development (MDD) different tools could be used to validate/ verify models at different abstraction levels (PIMs, PSMs, or implementations).

Our motivation was to integrate design patterns components with MDA-based forward engineering processes [8]. The following advantages between our approach and some existing ones are worth mentioning. A design pattern metamodel allows detecting the presence of a pattern in a family of models. If there were no metamodels, a library of models specifying each one the ways in that the design pattern can appear should be necessary (this is expensive). Also, it should be necessary to compare the model that is analyzed with the models of the library to see if matching exists. On the other hand, the specification of the metamodels in the three levels allows us to refine pattern model step-by-step in a MDA perspective.

7 Conclusions and Future Work

In this paper we analyze a metamodeling technique to reach a high level of reusability and adaptability of MDA-based design pattern components. We propose a "megamodel" for defining families of reusable design pattern components. The idea is to describe them through PIM-, PSM- and ISM-metamodels and metamodel-based refinements. We use our approach to specify standard design patterns.

Rather than requiring developers to manipulate formal specifications, we want to provide rigorous foundations for MDDs in order to develop tools that, on one hand, take advantage of the power of formal languages and, on the other hand, allow developers to directly manipulate the MDA-based models that they have created. However, meta-designers need to understand metamodels and metamodel-based transformations. We foresee to integrate our results in the existing MDA CASE tools experimenting with different platforms [5].

References

1. Albin-Amiot H., Guéhéneuc Y.: Meta-modeling Design Patterns: application to pattern detection and code synthesis. In Tekinerdogan, B. (ed.). Proceeding of ECOOP Workshop on Automating Object-Oriented Software Development Methods (2001)
2. Arnout, K.: From Patterns to Components. Ph. D. Thesis, Swiss Institute of Technology (ETH Zurich) (2004)

3. Bettin, J.: Practicalities of Implementing Component-Based Development and Model-Driven Architecture. Proceedings of Workshop Process Engineering for Object-Oriented and Component-Based Development, OOSPLA 2003, USA (2003)
4. Bidoit, M., Mosses, P.: CASL User Manual- Introduction to Using the Common Algebraic Specification Language. Lecture Notes in Computer Science 2900. Springer-Verlag, Berlin Heidelberg New York (2004)
5. CASE TOOLS www.objectbydesign.com/tools (2005)
6. Czarnecki, K., Helsen, S.: Classification of Model Transformation Approaches. In: Bettin J. et al. (eds). Proceedings of OOSPLA'03 Workshop on Generative Techniques in the Context of Model-Driven Architecture. www.oopsla.acm.org/oopsla2003 (2003)
7. D´Souza, D., Cameron Wills, A.: On Components, and Framework with UML. Addison-Wesley (1999)
8. Favre, L.: Foundations for MDA-based Forward Engineering. Journal of Object Technology (JOT). Vol 4, N° 1, Jan/Feb (2005) 129-153
9. Favre, L.: A Rigorous Framework for Model Driven Development. In: T. Halpin, J. Krogstie and K. Siau (eds.). Proceedings of CAISE´05 Workshops. EMMSAD ´05 Tenth International Workshop on Exploring Modeling Method in System Analysis and Design Porto, Portugal: FEUP Editions (2005) 505-516
10. France, R., Kim, D., Ghosh, S., Song, E.: A UML-Based Pattern Specification Technique. IEEE Transactions on Software Engineering. Vol. 30, N° 3, March. IEEE Computer Society (2004) 193-206
11. Gamma, E., Helm, R., Johnson, R., Vlissides, J.: Design Patterns. Elements of Reusable Object-Oriented Software. Addison-Wesley (1995)
12. Judson, S., Carver D., France, R.: A metamodeling approach to model transformation. OOPSLA Companion 2003 (2003) 326-327
13. Kuster, J., Sendall S., Wahler M.: Comparing Two Model Transformation Approaches. In: Bezivin, J. et. al (eds.). Proceedings of OCL and Model Driven Engineering Workshop. Lisboa, Portugal. http://www.cs.kent.ac.uk/projects/ocl/oclmdewsuml04 (2004)
14. MDA: The Model Driven Architecture www.omg.org/mda (2005)
15. Meyer B.: The Grand Challenge of Trusted Components. Proceedings of the 25th International Conference on Software Engineering, Portland, Oregon (2003) 660-667
16. MOF: Meta Object facility (MOF ™) 1.4. formal/2002-04-03 www.omg-org/mof (2005)
17. OCL: OCL Specification. Version 2.0. Formal document: ptc/03-10-14 www.omg.org (2005)
18. QVT: Revised submission for MOF 2.0 Query/Views/Transformations RFP. Version 1.1. OMG Adopted Specification. ptc/05-11-01 www.omg.org (2003)
19. Szyperski, C., Gruntz, D., Murer, S.: Component Software. Beyond Object-Oriented Programming, Second Edition. Addison-Wesley and ACM Press (2002)
20. UML: UML 2.0 Superstructure Specification. OMG formal/05-07-04   www.omg.org (2005)

A Component-Oriented Substitution Model

Bart George, Régis Fleurquin, and Salah Sadou

VALORIA Lab., University of South Brittany, France
{Bart.George, Regis.Fleurquin, Salah.Sadou}@univ-ubs.fr

Abstract. One of Software Engineering's main goals is to build complex applications in a simple way. For that, software components must be described by its functional and non-functional properties. Then, the problem is to know which component satisfies a specific need in a specific composition context, during software conception or maintenance. We state that this is a substitution problem in any of the two cases. From this statement, we propose a need-aware substitution model that takes into account functional and non-functional properties.

1   Introduction

Component-oriented programming should allow us to build a software like a puzzle whose parts would be units "subjects to composition by a third party" [17]. Examples of such units are COTS (*Components-Off-The-Shelf*), which are commercial products from several constructors and origins. When one develops and maintains a component-based software, some problems occur, and we will notice two main ones: how to select, during conception of such a software, the most suitable component in order to satisfy an identified need ? And during a maintenance, if this need evolves, will the chosen component remain suitable, or shall we replace it ?

We think that these problems are related to a substitution problem. In fact, when one conceives or maintains an application, some needs appear. And to describe them, the designer or the maintainer can imagine *ideal components*. These are virtual components representing the best ones satisfying these specific needs. Then the problem is to find the concrete components which are the closest to the ideal ones. In other words, trying to compose or maintain components means trying to make concrete components substitute ideal ones.

However, composition doesn't concern only the functional aspect. Most components are "black boxes" which must describe not only functional, but also non-functional properties. As every software needs a certain quality, one can't think about composing components whose non-functional properties are unknown, and at the same time hope having its quality requirements satisfied anyway. This is why substitution must take functional and non-functional properties into account.

So, how to substitute ? Some may say we just have to use subtyping, as some object-oriented languages made it a general way of substitution. However, an ideal component describes more than general needs: it describes the application's

M. Morisio (Ed.): ICSR 2006, LNCS 4039, pp. 340–353, 2006.

context, a notion that is absent from objects. Let us explain what we mean by
"context". If we take a need, modeled by an ideal component, we will try to find a
concrete one to substitute it. Now, let us suppose that we already found a suitable
component. We may need to check if there isn't another one better than the first
one. However, trying to substitute the old candidate by a new one would be a
mistake, because the key notion isn't the candidate, but the need it is supposed
to satisfy. Plus, if this need changes, a former candidate may no longer remain
suitable. So substitution of an ideal component by a concrete one is performed
only into the context of the need modeled by the ideal component. This is why
a candidate component can replace another one without any subtyping relation
between them, as every candidate is compared only to the ideal component.

In this paper, we consider a generic component model and a quality model
(section 2), and into this framework we define a component-oriented substitution
model, including substitutability rules for every functional and non-functional
element of our model (section 3). In order to illustrate the possibilities of such
a model, we describe the different substitution cases during the life cycle using
a short application example (section 4). Then, before concluding, we describe
some related works (section 5).

2   Component and Quality Models

Definitions given in this paper are placed in the following framework: one component model, holding a type system such as Java for EJB, and one quality model
such as ISO 9126 standard [12]. In this framework, we suppose the existence of
metrics to measure non-functional properties (such as those defined in [19]), so
that our contribution will focus only on the substitution model definition.

2.1   The Generic Model

Our goal is not to give yet another definition of what a component is, or what
non-functional properties are. It is to define a component-oriented substitution
that we can apply on many existing component and quality models. That is
why we prefer to give generic models, on which we can apply our substitution
concepts.

The generic component model includes component **artifacts**, representing the
component's architectural elements, which are common to most existing component models, and which have non-functional properties. As shown in figure 1, we
chose to keep three kinds of component artifacts: components themselves, interfaces, and operations. A component contains provided and required interfaces,
and interfaces contain operations. In the remaining of the paper, we refer to **candidate component** and **substitutable component** when the first one tries to
substitute the second one. Their elements are called respectively **candidate elements** and **substitutable elements**. When we find the best candidate for the
substitution, we say the substitutable component or element can be **replaced**
by this candidate.

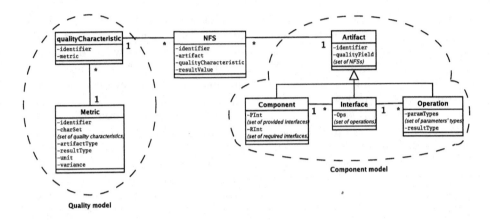

Fig. 1. Our generic model

Beside the component model, we define a generic quality model. Its elements are quality characteristics (such as those from ISO 9126 [12]), and metrics. We use existing metrics to evaluate and compare non-functional properties (see [9] for a survey). But why metrics ? In the literature, several methods for defining and evaluating non-functional properties already exist (see [1] for a survey). But such methods usually focus on one specific property, or family of properties, for example quality of service, which is only a part of the whole software quality. Metrics may be applied to many families of properties, and allow comparisons. This is why we think that in our case, metrics represent the best method for comparing different non-functional properties.

A component's quality properties are based on our generic quality model. We start by describing elements of this quality model in the next subsection, before introducing their link with the elements of the component model.

2.2 Elements of the Quality Model

This quality model is composed of two elements: quality characteristics which represent non-functional properties, and metrics, which measure these characteristics (see left part of Figure 1). For the remaining of this paper, we consider that a metric may measure several quality characteristics (as proposed in the IEEE standard 1061-1998 [11]), but each characteristic is measured by only one metric. Elements of the quality model are defined as follows:

Quality characteristics. A quality characteristic, or simply characteristic, represents a given quality property, preferably a fine-grained attribute (such as latency), because of our statement that only one metric can measure such a characteristic.

Metrics. A metric holds a set of quality characteristics it measures. It also holds a set of artifact types on which it can be calculated (for example: {component, interface}), the result's type, and its unit. The metric's variance explains the relation between the metric's result and the evaluated quality characteristic. For example, if a metric calculates an execution time, the variance stipulates that the lower the value is, the better it is.

Two metric values are *comparable* only if they are from the same metric. So having two "comparable metric values" M_1 and M_0 means that we have the same metric M, and we try to compare the value of M on the candidate artifact A_1 with the value of M on the substitutable artifact A_0. Having two comparable metric values M_1 and M_0, we can check if M_1 is *superior to M_0 according to the variance*. For example, if the metric type is an integer representing the execution time in milliseconds, then its variance is decreasing. In this case, if M_1 is greater than M_0 according to integer comparison, M_1 is in fact inferior to M_0 according to M's variance.

2.3   Non-functional Specifications

A component artifact is linked to a quality element using a **non-functional specification** (noted **NFS**). An artifact may be related to several quality elements, so several NFSs belong to only one artifact. An NFS describes the effect of a quality characteristic on the artifact it belongs to, and uses the metric applied on the latter. Several NFSs of a same component artifact may share the same metric, but not the same characteristic.

In Figure 1, the *resultValue* attribute of an NFS is given by the metric's measurement on the artifact. In the case of an ideal component, this attribute value is given by the application's designer.

Two NFSs are comparable if the artifacts they belong to are of the same kind and comparable (see next subsection for comparison definitions), and if they refer to the same characteristic. Two NFSs are equal if they are comparable and their *resultValue* attributes are equal.

2.4   Artifacts

The main element of our generic component model is the artifact. All artifacts, whatever their kind is, have a *quality field*, which is a set of NFSs. Two artifacts' quality fields are comparable if, for each NFS of one quality field, there is at least one comparable NFS in the other quality field. Two quality fields are equal if for at least one NFS of one quality field, there is an equal NFS in the other quality field, and *vice versa*.

Let us now describe the different kinds of artifacts:

Operations. An interface's operation is defined by its *signature*, also called a *type*. An operation's type is defined by the set of its parameters' types $(\alpha_1, \ldots , \alpha_n)$[1] and its result's type β. It is noted $(\alpha_1, \ldots , \alpha_n) \longrightarrow \beta$.

Two operations are comparable if their signatures are comparable. Two operation signatures T and U are comparable if they are equal modulo the renaming

---

[1] For reasons of simplicity, in the current version of our model we do not take into account parameters' order.

of the type names, or if there exists a type substitution relationship V so that $V.T$ equals to U, or T equals to $V\ U$, modulo the renaming of the type names.

For example, $\alpha \longrightarrow \alpha$ equals to $\beta \longrightarrow \beta$ if we rename α by β, but $\alpha \longrightarrow \alpha$ is not equal to $\beta \longrightarrow \gamma$.

And if we consider Java's *Object* type, signature *Object* $\longrightarrow$ *Object* may be replaced by *Integer* $\longrightarrow$ *Integer* if we let *Integer* substitute *Object*. It corresponds to Zaremski and Wing's exact and generalized signature matching for functions [20].

Two operations are equal if their signatures are equal modulo the renaming of the type names, and if their quality fields are equal.

Interfaces. A component's interface is defined by a set of operations.

A candidate provided interface PI_1 is comparable to a substitutable provided interface PI_0 if for each operation of PI_0 there exists a comparable operation in PI_1. A candidate required interface RI_1 is comparable to a substitutable required interface RI_0 if for each operation of RI_1, there exists a comparable operation in RI_0. Two interfaces (provided or required) are equal if their quality fields are equal and if, for each operation of one interface, there exists an equal operation in the other interface, and *vice versa*.

Components. A software component is defined by a set of provided interfaces and a set of required interfaces.

A candidate component C_1 is comparable to a substitutable component C_0 if for each provided interface of C_0 there exists a comparable provided interface of C_1, and for each required interface of C_1, there exists a comparable required interface of C_0. If C_1 is not comparable to C_0, it can not pretend to substitute C_0.

3   Our Substitution Model

For each NFS, we attach a **weight** (or comparison weight) noted $Comparison_S$, and a **penalty** noted $Penalty_S$ (S being the NFS). These two values define the NFS's importance for the artifact it belongs to. The higher these two values are, the more important this NFS is, in the whole substitutable component. If a substitutable artifact owns an NFS and a candidate artifact owns a comparable one with a superior value, the candidate's chances increase proportionally with the comparison weight. Else, the penalty will be used to sanction this lack. A candidate component may also bring his own new NFSs that the substitutable component doesn't have. These new elements will be evaluated by the ideal component designer.

The **substitution distance**, or distance, is defined using these weights, penalties, and NFS' *resultValues*. This distance will inform on the substitutability of an NFS or an artifact. The best candidate for substitution is the one with the lowest distance. If the distance is negative, the candidate element can be considered as "better" (in terms of quality) than the substitutable one, according to the current context. If the distance is positive, then the candidate is worse. If the distance equals to 0, then the two compared elements are "equivalent" each to the other, but it doesn't mean that they are equal.

For each component, there is a **maximal distance** for substitution, fixed by its designer. Let us consider a component C_1, a candidate for the substitution of another component C_0. If the substitution distance between C_1 and C_0 is bigger than the maximal distance associated to C_0, then C_1 will be rejected.

3.1   Substitution Distance Between Artifacts

Here, we will define a calculus that will give the distance separating a candidate component C_1 from a substitutable component C_0 in a given context. This context is defined by the weight and the penalty allocated to the NFSs of C_0's artifacts. So, before talking about distance between artifacts, let us present the distance between their quality fields.

We will suppose that there exists a relation $MIN_{x \in E} \; f(x)$, which selects an element x from the set E so that the function $f(x)$ has the lowest value.

Distance between artifacts' quality fields. Let us consider a substitutable artifact A_0, a comparable candidate one A_1, and their quality fields (denoted Q_{A_1} and Q_{A_0}). The substitution distance between these quality fields (denoted QD) is defined as follows:

$$QD(Q_{A_1}, Q_{A_0}) = \sum_{S_0 \in Q_{A_0}} QDSpec(Q_{A_1}, S_0) - \sum_{S_1 \in Q_{A_1}} QDBonus(S_1, Q_{A_0})$$

with:

$$QDSpec(Q_{A_1}, S_0) = Comparison_{S_0} * (resultValue_{S_0} -_{Variance} resultValue_{S_1})$$
  if $\exists \; S_1 \; in \; A_1$ that is comparable to S_0; else, $Penalty_{S_0}$.

and:

$$QFBonus(S_1, Q_{A_0}) = 0 \; if \; \exists \; S_0 \in Q_{A_0}$$ that is comparable to S_1; else, a value
  given by C_0's designer.

To measure the distance between the quality fields, we try to find for each S_0 a comparable NFS S_1 in A_1 (there can be only one, as NFSs of a same artifact cannot share the same characteristic). Substituable NFSs without any comparable S_1 are taken into account through their penalty value $Penalty_{S_0}$. Candidate NFSs without any comparable S_0 are taken into account through a value given by C_0's designer.

$resultValue_{S_0} -_{Variance} resultValue_{S_1}$ is a subtraction between $resultValue_{S_0}$ and $resultValue_{S_1}$ depending on their metric's variance. For example, if its type is integer or float and variance is increasing, the measurement will equal to: $resultValue_{S_0} - resultValue_{S_1}$. If variance is decreasing, it will equal to: $resultValue_{S_1} - resultValue_{S_0}$.

Distance between incomparable artifacts. If two artifacts are incomparable, there will not be any substitution distance measurement between them.

Distance between comparable operations. Let us consider a substitutable operation O_0 and a comparable candidate operation O_1. The substitution distance between them (denoted OpD) is defined as follows:

$$OpD(O_1, O_0) = QD(Q_{O_1}, Q_{O_0})$$

As long as O_1 and O_0 are comparable, the distance between them is in fact the distance between their quality fields.

Distance between comparable provided interfaces. Let us consider a substitutable provided interface I_0, a comparable candidate provided interface I_1, and their sets of operations Ops_{I_1} and Ops_{I_0}. The substitution distance between I_1 and I_0 (denoted PID) is defined as follows:

$$PID(I_1, I_0) = \sum_{O_0 \in Ops_{I_0}} MIN_{O_1 \in Ops_{I_1}} OpD(O_1, O_0) -$$
$$\sum_{O_1 \in Ops_{I_1}} POBonus(O_1, I_0) + QD(Q_{I_1}, Q_{I_0})$$

with:

$POBonus(O_1, I_0) = 0$ if $\exists\ O_0 \in Ops_{I_0}$ that is comparable to O_1; else, a value given by C_0's designer.

To measure the distance between the interfaces, we take into account only the lowest found distance for each O_0. Candidate operations without any comparable O_0 are taken into account through a value given by C_0's designer.

Distance between comparable required interfaces. Let us consider a substitutable required interface I_0, a comparable candidate required interface I_1, and their sets of operations Ops_{I_1} and Ops_{I_0}. The substitution distance between I_1 and I_0 (denoted RID) is defined as follows:

$$RID(I_1, I_0) = - \sum_{O_0 \in Ops_{I_0}} MIN_{O_1 \in Ops_{I_1}} OpD(O_1, O_0) -$$
$$\sum_{O_0 \in Ops_{I_0}} ROBonus(I_1, O_0) - QD(Q_{I_1}, Q_{I_0})$$

with:

$ROBonus(I_1, O_0) = 0$ if $\exists\ O_1 \in Ops_{I_1}$ that is comparable to O_0; else, a value given by C_0's designer.

The principle of distance between required interfaces is the same as for provided ones, except that it is symmetrical. For provided interfaces, it is better to have I_1 providing better quality than I_0, whereas for required interfaces, it is better to have I_1 requiring less quality than I_0.

Distance between comparable components. Let us consider a substitutable component C_0, a comparable candidate component C_1, their sets of provided interfaces $PInt_{C_1}$ and $PInt_{C_0}$, and their sets of required interfaces $RInt_{C_1}$ and $RInt_{C_0}$. The substitution distance between C_1 and C_0 (denoted CD) is defined as follows:

$$CD(C_1, C_0) = \sum_{PI_0 \in PInt_{C_0}} MIN_{PI_1 \in PInt_{C_1}} PID(PI_1, PI_0) + \sum_{RI_1 \in RInt_{C_1}}$$
$$MIN_{RI_0 \in RInt_{C_0}} RID(RI_1, RI_0) - \sum_{PI_1 \in PInt_{C_1}} PIBonus(PI_1, C_0) -$$
$$\sum_{RI_0 \in RInt_{C_0}} RIBonus(C_1, RI_0) + QD(Q_{C_1}, Q_{C_0})$$

with:

$PIBonus(PI_1, C_0) = 0$ if $\exists\ PI_0 \in PInt_{C_0}$ that is comparable to PI_1; else, a value given by C_0's designer.

and:

$RIBonus(C_1, RI_0) = 0$ if $\exists\ RI_1 \in RInt_{C_1}$ that is comparable to RI_0; else, a value given by C_0's designer.

To measure the distance between the components, we take into account only the lowest found distance for each PI_0 and for each RI_1. Candidate provided (resp. substitutable required) interfaces without any comparable PI_0 (resp. RI_1) are taken into account through a value given by C_0's designer.

4   Substitution in Practice

Now let us take the example of an application that requires a Digital Video ("DV") camera component, with an interface for video stream and another one for camera control. It must also conform to the DV standard. This video camera example is taken from [3].

4.1   Modeling an Ideal Component

The above requirements could be expressed by an ideal component called *videoCamera*. The latter contains a provided interface *videoStream* (with an operation *outputVideoFlow*), a provided interface *cameraControl* (with basic operations such as *on*, *record* and *eject*[2]), and a required interface *DVFormat* (with an operation *inputDVFlow* that asks for a DV tape).

The needs are not just about functional part, but also about non-functional properties and their respective importance. For example, we suppose that a high level of reliability for *record* and *eject* operations is required (so that the camera does not crash while recording, nor refuse to eject a video tape). We also assume that a high image quality, such as a 1 million pixels (1 MPixels) screen resolution, is required for *videoStream* interface. According to the quality model of Figure 2, we use the following characteristics: *reliability* and *imageQuality*. Their respective metrics are: *MeanTimeToFailure* (*MTTF*) and *screenResolution*. Then we attach to the ideal component several NFSs. To each operation of the *cameraControl* interface, we attach an NFS using *reliability* characteristic (*onReliability* for *on* operation, *recordReliability* for *record* operation, and

---

[2] For simplicity and brevity reasons, we limit this provided interface to only three operations.

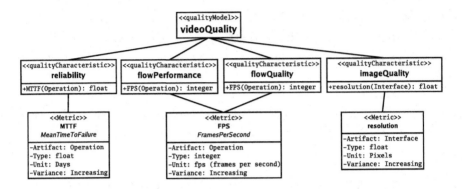

Fig. 2. Example of quality model

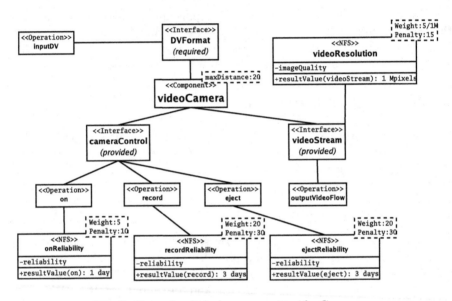

Fig. 3. Example of ideal component: *videoCamera*

ejectReliability for *eject* operation). To *videoStream* interface, we attach the NFS *cameraResolution*, using the characteristic *imageQuality*.

Finally, the designer fixes expected *resultValues*, weights and penalties for each NFS, and also fixes a maximal distance for the ideal component *video-Camera*. On Figure 3, we see that the expected value for *cameraResolution* is 1 million pixels, and the expected values for NFSs using *reliability* characteristic vary from operation to operation. The values required for *recordReliability* and *ejectReliability* are higher than those for *onReliability*. The penalties attached to *cameraResolution*, *recordReliability* and *ejectReliability* are very high in order to enforce candidate components to contain these NFSs. *cameraResolution* has a low comparison weight, which means that a big difference on the image quality is not very important. However, *recordReliability* and *ejectReliability* have higher weights, which means that a big difference on the reliability measurements of *record* and *eject* is very important. The maximal distance is fixed at a low level, so that the lack of one of these three NFSs in a candidate component will hardly be accepted.

4.2   Component Lifecycle and Substitution Cases

Now that our ideal component is modeled, we can look for the best concrete candidate one to substitute it. Here are the different substitution cases:

First composition. Trying to plug a component into an application (in order to satisfy a given need) means trying to make this concrete component substitute the ideal one (corresponding to this need). Let us take the video camera example. Now that we modeled an ideal camera component, we have to check which concrete camera is the best candidate to substitute it.

First, according to our substitution model, a candidate must meet all the functional requirements, i.e. it must have all the ideal component's provided services (interfaces and operations), and must not bring more required ones. Otherwise, it will be rejected even if it has a higher quality. For example, let us consider a *VHSCamera* component meeting all functional requirements, except one (it requires VHS tapes instead of DV ones). No matter its quality, we need a camera that requires only DV tapes, and this candidate adds a required interface, so it is rejected.

Then, a candidate, like the *fluidCamera* component on Figure 4, may add new NFSs unanticipated by the ideal component designer. For example video flow's number of frames per second. That corresponds to the metric *FPS*

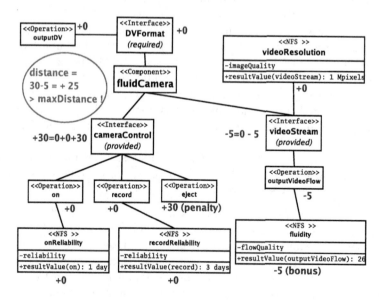

Fig. 4. Example of rejected candidate: *fluidCamera*

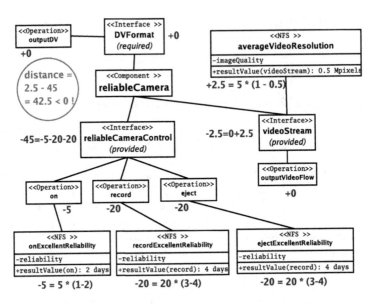

Fig. 5. Example of accepted: *reliableCamera*

(for Frames Per Second), which measures *flowPerformance* and *flowQuality* characteristics (all of them are shown in Figure 2). It may be interesting to have a new NFS using *flowQuality* characteristic on the *outputVideoFlow* operation, but the candidate (*fluidCamera*) lacks an important NFS. The penalty is so high that it is rejected.

We can also have candidates providing at the same time some lower qualities, and other higher ones, than ideal component. In this case, a candidate component would rather have good "scores" in the most important NFSs. For example, let us take a candidate *goodImageCamera* which has an excellent image quality (2 million pixels instead of 1 million) and an average reliability (2.5 days instead of 3 for operations *record* and *eject*), while candidate *reliableCamera* shown in Figure 5 has an average image quality and an excellent reliability. We are not directly comparing them to find which one is "better" than the other. We are comparing each one of them, separately, with the ideal component, in order to find if it is an acceptable candidate. If we consider this ideal component, and the distance obtained for each one of the candidates, we can say that both are acceptable (distance with candidate *goodImageCamera* would equal to +15), but the *reliableCamera* is the best one.

Maintenance. The application now has its camera component, but it could have a "better" one. If the needs are the same, the ideal component that models them is exactly the same, but we can have new candidates. So we have to compare each one of them to this ideal component, ignoring the previous candidate. If the needs change, this implies that the ideal component changes too. Thus, we must compare each candidate (including previous accepted one) with the new ideal component. In both cases, we are back to the first composition schema.

5   Related Work

We said in introduction that substitutability was a well-known problem in object-oriented languages which include typing [5] and subtyping [13]. It is also an industrial problem, as referred in [18], who asks how to make sure that changes on a component won't affect existing applications of a component, and try to answer by setting rules based on subtyping. It was tempting for us to base on subtyping too, in order to substitute components [16]. But we took critics of typing [15] and subtyping [17] into account. Especially the one which said that they were too rigid and too restrictive for componentware, and couldn't deal with context. This is why we preferred to try a more flexible approach.

Premysl Brada has explored the notions of deployment context and contextual substitutability [4]. A deployment context of a component is a sub-component that contains the used part of its services (provided and required services that are bound to other components). So Brada's contextual substitutability consists in comparing a candidate component with this sub-component, rather than the whole one. Although these notions seem close to ours, we work at a different level. Brada's approach consists in finding an "architecture-aware" form of substitutability, his context concerns a concrete component, and depends on its deployment in global architecture. Our approach is rather "need-aware", and our context considers an ideal component (modeling a need) and a concrete one which could substitute it.

As we said, our substitution model was inspired by Zaremski and Wing's specification and signature matching for library components [20, 21]. Their matching takes into account some substitution schemes that subtyping doesn't include. We were close to this approach, but we went further, by taking context and non-functional properties into account, and applying our substitution rules on generic component models. Beside Zaremski's and Wing's approach, there are other notable works in software reuse and component retrieval [14]. For example, our notion of weights can be compared to Scott Henninger's tools [10]. These tools parse a source code, extract "components" from several keywords, then put them into a library where a valued network between words and components is created. So, when we search a word or a component in this library, a weight is calculated for each component with the nodes' values, and the selected candidate is the one which has the biggest weight. Our approach is at a different level, because we search and select candidates, not from keywords, but from components' structure. It can be used in such retrieval mechanisms in order to refine component search, and create more trustable libraries.

For our quality generic model, we were inspired by quality standards like ISO-9126 [12] and metrics standards like IEEE-1061 [11]. Example of existing metrics that could be used with our model can be found in [9, 19]. But the quality part of our model can also be used with quality of service contracts languages (based on Antoine Beugnard's fourth level of component contracts [2]), such as the ones modeled in QML [7] and QoSCL [6]. In particular, our concern about substituting non-functional properties can be compared to Jan Aagedal's CQML language [1], that deals with the substitutability of QoS "profiles". However, contrary to

CQML, which, like most QoS languages, doesn't take functional aspects into account, our model combines functional and non-functional ones. And while Aagedal separates primitive component substitutability and composite component one, we deal with contextual substitutability of two components, no matter their internal structure.

6   Conclusion and Future Work

We proposed a substitution model including several elements: i) a generic quality model, able to use existing quality metrics and QoS languages. ii) a generic component model, able to use existing research and industrial approaches. iii) a substitution distance, able measure the substitutability of a candidate component. We also introduced the notion of ideal component, that models functional and non-functional conceptual needs and takes composition context into account.

In our current framework, we chose to consider one component model using existing quality characteristics and metrics from one quality model. There are two reasons for such a limitation : i) in the actual research and industrial schemes, composition concerns mainly components that come from a same component model; ii) the problem of comparing components from different models is orthogonal to the substitution problem. Both can be treated separately.

Right now, we have a tool [8] that allows us to check if a component can substitute another one according to our substitution distance measurement. This tool aims to help designers to find the best candidates for their needs.

References

1. J. Aagedal. *Quality of Service Support in Development of Distributed Systems.* PhD thesis, University of Oslo, 2001.
2. A. Beugnard, J.-M. Jézéquel, N. Plouzeau, and D. Watkins. Making components contract aware. *IEEE Computer*, 32 (7), 1999.
3. G. Blair and J.-B. Stefani. *Open Distributed Processing and Multimedia.* Addison-Wesley, 1997.
4. P. Brada. *Specification-Based Component Substituability and Revision Identification.* PhD thesis, Charles University in Pragues, 2003.
5. L. Cardelli. Type systems. In A. B. Tucker, editor, *The Computer Science and Engineering Handbook*, chapter 97. CRC Press, 2004.
6. O. Defour, J.-M. Jézéquel, and N. Plouzeau. Extra-functional contract support in components. In *Proceedings of 7th International Symposium on Component-Based Software Engineering (CBSE 7)*, May 2004.
7. S. Frolund and J. Koistinen. Qml : A language for quality of service specification. Technical report, Hewlett-Packard Laboratories, Palo Alto, California, USA, 1998.
8. B. George. Substitute tool. http://www-valoria.univ-ubs.fr/SE/Substitute/, 2006.
9. M. Goulao and F. B. e Abreu. Software components evaluation : an overview. In *CAPSI 2004*, November 2004.
10. S. Henninger. Constructing effective software reuse repositories. In *ACM TOSEM 1997*, 1997.

11. IEEE. *IEEE Std. 1061-1998 : IEEE Standard for a Software Quality Metrics Methodology*, ieee computer society press edition, 1998.
12. ISO Int. Standards Organisation, Geneva, Switzerland. *ISO/IEC 9126-1:2001 Software Engineering - Product Quality - Part I : Quality model*, 2001.
13. B. Liskov and J. Wing. A behavioral notion of subtyping. In *ACM Transactions on Programming Languages and Systems 1994*, 1994.
14. D. Lucrédio, A. Prado, and E. S. D. Almeida. A survey on software components search and retrieval. In *EUROMICRO*, 2004.
15. D. E. Perry and A. L. Wolf. Foundations for the study of software architecture. *ACM SIGSOFT Software Engineering Notes*, 17 (4):40–52, October 1992.
16. J. C. Seco and L. Caires. A basic model for typed components. In *ECOOP*, 2000.
17. C. Szyperski. *Component Software : Beyond Object-Oriented Programming*. Addison-Wesley / ACM Press, second edition, 2002.
18. R. Van Ommering. Software reuse in product populations. *IEEE Transactions on Software Engineering*, 31 (7):537–550, july 2005.
19. H. Washizaki, H. Yamamoto, and Y. Fukazawa. A metrics suite for measuring reusability of software components. In *Metrics 2003*, 2003.
20. A. Zaremski and J. Wing. Signature matching : a tool for using software libraries. In *ACM TOSEM 1995*, 1995.
21. A. M. Zaremski and J. Wing. Specification matching of software components. In *ACM TOSEM 1997*, 1997.

Building Reflective Mobile Middleware Framework on Top of the OSGi Platform

Gábor Paller

Nokia Research Center, Köztelek str. 6, Budapest 1092, Hungary
gabor.paller@nokia.com

Abstract. The literature on mobile middleware is extensive. Numerous aspects of the mobility's effect on middleware have been analysed and the amount of previous work allowed to identify the most important patterns. Although the notion of "most important middleware" depends on the application supported by the middleware, there are traits that can be discovered in most of the connected mobile applications. Based on the experience of several authors, these traits are context-awareness, reflectivity, support for off-line operation and asynchronous (message-based) communication.

This paper presents a mobile middleware system built to support these patterns and demonstrates, how the OSGi service platform can be used to realize these patterns. It will be demonstrated that although OSGi was built to support manageability requirements, the resulting platform is suitable for implementing the 4 major middleware patterns too. The paper presents the components of this context-aware, reflective middleware framework and evaluates its footprint.

1   Introduction

The literature about mobile middleware is extensive and goes back to about 10 years. Mobile middleware is normally categorized as nomadic and peer-to-peer, the first being server-based with temporarily disconnected clients, the second having no privileged node with constant, high-bandwidth availability at all. There were several attempts to survey the entire middleware space (e.g. [1],[2]) and there seems to be a growing consensus that there are 4 major patterns differentiating mobile middleware from the traditional middleware supporting connected workstations. These patterns are the following.

Context-awareness. Traditional middleware is strictly layered meaning that it shields the applications from events concerning the lower level of the stack. Context-awareness means that there is no such shielding and the application is aware of the environment situation. Context changes are inherently asynchronous and are often delivered in the form of events. It is important to note that only the application can decide what context events are important and how to handle them. For example when a business application notices that its cheap and fast proximity connection is no longer available, the application can revert to using slower and more expensive cellular connection.

M. Morisio (Ed.): ICSR 2006, LNCS 4039, pp. 354–367, 2006.

The same option may not be available for a game which is not allowed to use more costly bearer and in case of disconnection, an error should be sent to the end user or the application may switch to standalone mode.

Reflection. Reflection generally means that the program is able to make computations on its own structure during its execution (retrieve the current structure, evaluate the structure against environmental constraints then update the structure if necessary). Reflection is a crucial technique in mobile computing, especially, if the application is expected to be context-aware. Even moderate number of context states can yield large number of context state combinations. If the application and the middleware are built in monolithic fashion, the application and middleware code must be prepared for *all possible context state combinations* which quickly becomes intractable. Also, the memory footprint of the monolithic middleware increases with each context state combination handled. In order to keep the footprint minimal and the design of the system clear, the middleware needs to be decomposed into a collection of smaller components. The application chooses just the components it needs and composes the middleware that serves the application the best. In case of context changes, the application evaluates the context transition and possibly changes the instantiated components and/or their configuration.

Off-line access. Disconnection is an inherent property of mobile computing. The reason for disconnection can be physical (no coverage) or social (mobile access is too expensive or not acceptable in the given situation). In order to provide acceptable user experience, operation in disconnected mode must be available. The key technology to achieve disconnected operation is the relocation of relevant data and code to the mobile device. Data relocation can be achieved by pretty established data synchronization techniques.

Asynchronous communication. Networked computing is dominated by solutions following Remote Procedure Call (RPC) semantics. RPC mimics the procedure call on a single processor, the calling procedure is suspended for the duration of the call and execution continues in the called procedure. Therefore RPC is inherently *synchronous*. Mobile transport networks are characterized by long and variable delays and frequent transmission errors. In this environment communication must be asynchronous (event-based or message-based terms are also used for the same concept). This affects the communication semantics the middleware uses. Instead of procedure call semantics, communication-related events are delivered to the application.

It is important to note that middleware patterns are in no way restricted to the 4 patterns mentioned above. These 4 patterns, however, can be identified in almost all connected mobile applications.

In this paper, it is presented how a middleware framework built on these patterns can be implemented using the 4th release (R4) of the OSGi framework[1].

---

[1] http://www.osgi.org

2   Overview of OSGi R4

OSGi used to mean Open Service Gateway Interface but according to the current position of its host organization, OSGi Alliance, OSGi is just a 4-letter technical name. This is due to the fact that the original OSGi business model concentrating on household service gateways (e.g. pay-per-view TV set-top box) has been extended significantly over the existence of OSGi and now includes application platforms for vehicle systems and mobile devices.

OSGi is a Java-based interface specification between management-aware applications and the management platform itself. Key principle of OSGi is asynchronous ("hot") management which means that running applications must be prepared to react immediately to management interactions. For example one software component may be upgraded to a newer version and applications using the component must be able to gracefully migrate from the old component to the new one. This property makes OSGi a dynamic environment. Applications and the platform are involved in extensive event communication and well-behaving OSGi application uses these events to coordinate with the platform in case of asynchronous management actions.

As of Release 4 (R4), the OSGi software stack has the following layers.

Security layer. This layer specifies how to sign OSGi artifacts. This layer builds heavily on Java JAR signing and the bundle concept (see module layer).

Module layer. This layer is responsible for the management of the installable software modules called *bundles* in OSGi parlance. A bundle is a collection of resources (Java class files and/or static files) and metadata that are added or removed by one operation. Bundles can export and import Java packages creating a dependency web among bundles.

Lifecycle layer. Bundles can be started and stopped, clearly demarcating the operational and maintenance mode of the bundles. When a bundle is taken into use, it is often started. This shows that the bundle can start exposing its services (see service layer) or launch processing tasks associated with the bundle. Before management of the bundle begins, the bundle is stopped. At this point, the bundle should stop exposing its services and stop any processing associated with the bundle.

Service layer. Services are key abstractions in OSGi. An OSGi service is much reminescent to a component port: it is associated to a Java type (preferably interface type) and has meta information attached to it. Services are registrated in the *service registry* and the platform provides flexible ways to look up services based on type or meta-information. The standard OSGi service implementation is lightweight. Service providers instantiate an object implementing the service interface type and register this object in the service registry. This object can be looked up and its methods can be invoked directly over the service interface. In the simplest case there is no service invocation overhead. The specification, however, does not prevent the implementation of more complex service invocation schemes inter-process service or remote service invocation.

OSGi specifies a wealth of standard services on top of the core framework, most of them are optional.

3   Implementing Reflective Middleware with OSGi R4

Reflection is a vaguely defined term. One common definition of reflection is that reflection allows the program to access, reason about and alter its own interpretation [1]. In the problem domain of mobile middleware, reflection becomes important if the mobile system is exposed to diverse and highly variable environmental conditions - short-range wireless connections and location-dependency are two, often identified areas causing environmental variability. Reflective approach means that the mobile system reacts to environmental changes by adapting its own program structure.

This adaptation can happen in many forms (e.g. dynamic aspects [23]). Due to its predictability, the most commonly used approach is the *dynamic component system* where dynamic refers to the ability to create and destroy components and change the connections among them at run-time.

OSGi services have provided the kernel of dynamic components since the beginning of OSGi's existence. Services can be substituted for *component ports* because they are typed, can be introspected and meta-information can be associated to them. In addition, they are dynamic which allows for the creation of a component that changes its port structure.

Prior to R4, multi-port components were not made explicit in OSGi, the component semantics were hidden in bundle code. One significant addition in R4 is the *Service Component Runtime (SCR)*. SCR allows for describing components in declarative way. Bundles using SCR contain *component descriptors*. These descriptors specify the services the component provides and consumes and SCR connects the services automatically, based on the constraints in the descriptor files. The constraint language is quite expressive and can take into account the Java type associated to the port and the port meta-information. The component may have properties and services registered as component ports will have the same properties as the component does.

The consumed services can be dynamically bound. The component descriptor defines, which service can satisfy the service reference and SCR looks for the appropriate service if the previously bound service is unregistered. Components became first-class entities in OSGi and have life-cycle of their own that is tied to the life-cycle of the bundle containing the component. The component life-cycle is manipulated by the SCR. Components are activated and deactivated depending on their constraints.

Programmatic manipulation of the component network is also possible. It is possible to programmatically enable and disable components. Disabled components are ignored by SCR when it binds components therefore it is possible to reconfigure the component network by enabling/disabling components. Additionally, it is possible to define component factories which allow programmatic creation of components. Note that it is still the SCR that binds, activates and deactivates components created by the component factories. Analysis of how OSGi supports reflective requirements is provided below.

- **The mobile application and middleware is able to discover its internal composition and recompose itself [10],[1].** SCR dynamically recomposes components when the component relationships change. This can happen due to enabling/disabling components, dynamically changing meta-information of the services provided by the component or creating/disposing components by means of component factories. When the component network is recomposed by SCR, the component network may not be functional because all the necessary connections may not exist during the reconfiguration phase. This creates "blackout effect"; short period of time during which the application is not available.
- **It is possible to assign separate meta-spaces to applications [11].** Middleware and application components are created and wired in application-specific way. For example one application would like to communicate only over proximity connection (WLAN, Bluetooth, etc.) while the other application running on the same platform may use any bearer, including e.g. GPRS. One logically separate meta-space is populated with the components belonging to one particular application (including application and middleware components). OSGi's support for meta-spaces will be discussed below.
- **The integrity of the middleware and the applications using it is preserved in spite of the reflection mechanisms.** Recomposing the system when it potentially serves requests is a complicated task and can be solved only if the application logic supports the reflective system. SCR supports static and dynamic binding. In case of static binding, the component being reconfigured is deactivated and reactivated after the bindings are updated. This creates a "blackout" in the component's operation. In case of dynamic binding the component is not deactivated when it is rebound and it is the responsibility of the component logic to handle the problems that may arise from dynamic reconnection and partially reconnected component network.

Our framework extends the OSGi component model by only some usage conventions. These are the following.

- Every component is generated by their component factories. This guarantees that separate component instances are created for each application meta-space.
- Every component is tagged by mwfw.app.id whose value is a string unique for each application. Components with the same mwfw.app.id property belong to the same meta-space. The filter expression of every component in the application meta-space includes a match of the mwfw.app.id property. This guarantees that components can be connected only to other components in the same meta-space.

These conventions can function only in case of cooperating applications. Nothing prevents a malicious or faulty application to create a component with erroneous mwfw.app.id property disrupting the component network of another application.

Analysing the requirements convinced us that OSGi R4 is suitable as a platform to build reflective middleware with the following problematic areas identified.

- OSGi R4 component model is not hierarchical which may yield inacceptable reconnection times in case of large component networks [3]. For example if the component network supports hierarchical composition, entire parts of the component network can be moved as one unit.
- Application separation which is a general concern in case of OSGi. SCR adds to the problem because components generated dynamically by component factories do not belong to any application. Therefore the limited OSGi application separation mechanism offers no protection against erroneous applications that leak components and disrupt the component network of other applications.

In the following sections I will present how the context, synchronization and asynchronous communication subsystem can be built on top of the reflection layer provided by the SCR.

4   Context Subsystem

Context-awareness is generally defined as the ability of the application to adapt itself to changing environmental conditions. Context is defined formally in [5] as the following: "context is the set of environmental states and settings that either determines an application's behavior or in which an application event occurs and is interesting to the user". One particular aspect of the environment affecting the application is called *context element* and the set of all context elements is called *context*. Some context elements are for example: location, end user-related information (e.g. language), presence of available communication link (e.g. enterprise WLAN access), etc. Obtaining and processing context information comprises two steps.

- Obtaining environmental information from software or hardware sensors like network cards, file system monitors, etc. These context elements are commonly called *low-level context*.
- Calculating high-level context elements suitable for applications. For example the context element "device from the same group nearby" can be generated from "Bluetooth device in range" low-level context element if the Bluetooth device is recognized as a device belonging to some application-defined group.

Much more complex context systems have been described where devices publish their context interest using ontologies [7],[6].

The most common solution is to consume the context information in the form of events. Calculating high-level context requires querying context elements.

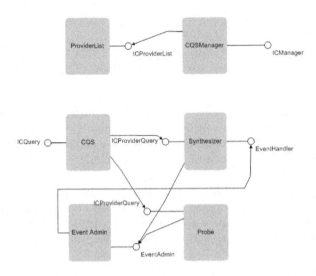

Fig. 1. Context framework

A high-level context element is often calculated from low-level ones. This requires that the state of the context elements can also be queried.

Considering the requirements above, the following context subsytem was designed (see figure 1). Context elements are arranged into a tree. Context information is made available to applications by two services: OSGi R4 Event Admin distributes context events and Context Query Service (implemented as part of our middleware framework) provides query access. Event Admin is a standard publish-subscribe service in OSGi R4. Event Admin provides publication and consumption of events in hierarchically named topics. Our framework adds only the convention to Event Admin that context events are published under topics whose root is mwfw/ (e.g. mwfw/network/status).

Context element sources can be *probes* (low-level context elements) and *synthesizers* (high-level context elements) [4]. In both cases, context element source publishes context events directly by Event Admin and registers context query interface with Context Query Service (CQS). CQS really acts only as a switchboard: when it receives a context query request, it finds the probe or synthesizer responsible for the context element subtree and forwards the request to the appropriate handler. OSGi favors the implementation of this structure with the so called whiteboard pattern [24]. Upon registration of a context subtree query interface, CQS is notified by the service registry which takes the newly registered subtree provider into use. The coding of this logic is greatly simplified by SCR where CQS can declare its interest in context subtree services and provide registration and unregistration callback methods.

One particular concern of context element providers is their potentially large number. Our middleware framework allows probes to be disabled after installation and enabling them only if applications require them. SCR has a feature of disabling and enabling context providers from applications. The Context

Provider Management component (CQSManager) enables/disables context providers based on their subtree. The implementation is more complex than one would think because OSGi R4 SCR does not have centralized component directory. Enabling/disabling components is possible only for other components in the same bundle. Therefore, each bundle containing context providers that can be enabled/disabled must expose a directory component that is enabled by default (ProviderList). This directory component has two functionalities: it provides a list of all the context provider components in the bundle and it enables/disables these context providers on behalf of the Context Provider Manager.

5   Synchronization Framework

Significant research happened in the area of file synchronization that can also be extended to synchronization of other structured data items, e.g. database tables [13],[14]. The literature analysis identified the following key requirements regarding data synchronization.

- Although time-stamp-based synchronization is the most common technique, the solution must be able to incorporate alternative sync engines. Particularly, full backup/restore (slow sync) and CPISync [9] were identified as interesting candidates for more special scenarios.
- The solution must be able to incorporate multiple sync protocols like SyncML DS [22], ActiveSync, etc. [8].
- It must be possible to use any network bearer for the synchronization. In addition, it must be possible to change the bearer during a synchronization session by first suspending the synchronization then resuming it on the new bearer.
- The storage abstraction must be flexible enough to incorporate databases, plain files and applications acting as data sources.
- Application must be able to provide their own conflict handling logic to resolve synchronization conflicts.
- The synchronization system may hide the sync logic behind an object-oriented front-end. This means that synchronizable data items are hidden behind access objects [12].

The following component set was designed (see figure 2).

- The transport layer is abstracted by the *protocol adapter* component. This is a simple component that is able to send packets to given URI (where URI can identify any transport, not just HTTP) and receive packets.
- Synchronization protocol adapter components abstract the synchronization protocol. Client version of this component is able to initiate synchronization sessions, server version is able to handle an incoming synchronization session.
- Synchronization engine component abstracts the synchronization method (e.g. bidirectional time stamp-based synchronization engine).
- Storage component abstracts the data storage to synchronize.

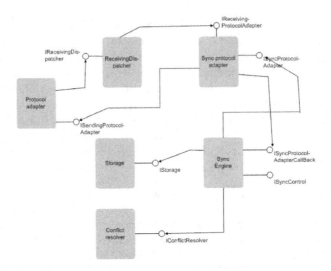

Fig. 2. Synchronization component network

6 Asynchronous Communication

RPC-based communication models don't work well in mobile network due to the high latency and unreliable nature of wireless bearers. Asynchronous communication is a term used for a solution where the application hands over a data packet to the middleware and continues executing. The application is notified by events about arrival of data packets the application registered to. Application programming in the asynchronous model is more complicated than in the synchronous RPC-model but the volatile wireless bearers most often don't allow the luxury of RPC. As the programming model delivers invocations as events, this model is also called message-based or event-based communication [18].

Asynchronous approaches can be divided into two categories: queues and tuple spaces. Queues may use explicit addressing (when the sender specifies the target along with the queue entry) or they may rely on the publish-subscribe pattern [19],[20],[21]. Tuple space is a distributed hash table [15],[16],[17]. The communication is achieved by placing key-value pairs in the hash table. Replication mechanisms ensure that local copies of the hash table get replicated to other nodes. Tuple spaces and queues are close to each other, a queue fuctionality can be implemented by using tuple spaces and vice versa. The first implementation of our framework provides queue-based communication with explicit addressing (figure 3 and 4).

- Protocol adapter is the same as in the synchronization solution. Typically the queue and the synchronization component network use a separate instance of protocol adapters but this depends on the protocol.
- Queue protocol adapter is the software component responsible for queue item coding to and decoding from the packets sent to and received from the protocol adapter.

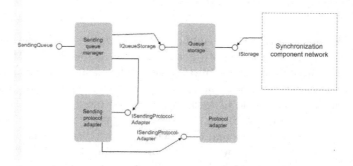

Fig. 3. Sender queue network

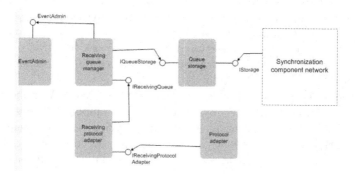

Fig. 4. Receiver queue network

– Queue storage component is an extension of the synchronization storage
  component. In addition to the interface required by the synchronization engines, the queue storage component implements one additional interface for
  queue management functions. These include placing an entry into the queue
  and consuming an entry from the queue. The fact that queue storage components are also synchronization storage components allows the queue to work
  in synchronization mode as well when the queue storage component is linked
  with a synchronization component network. This allows queues to work in
  batch mode when the queue entries are updated by the synchronization engine instead of the queue managers.
– There is a pair of queue managers, one for the sending queue and one for the
  receiving queue. The sending queue manager scans the sending queue and
  if there are queue entries, sends them over the queue protocol adapter to
  the peer. The receiving queue manager scans the queue storage and delivers
  queue entries as OSGi events by Event Admin.

Only explicitly addressed queues are supported by our framework. In order to
provide really comprehensive functionality, publish-subscribe mechanisms and
tuple space middleware should also be integrated into the framework.

7   Implementation and Results

Basic component set and a simple application was implemented. The component set contains HTTP- and Bluetooth-based protocol adapters, SyncML DS synchronization components, timestamp-based synchronization engine and queue components for both the sender and receiver side. The application is a simple contact manager that is able to work in networked mode as well. The contact application can be paired with the same contact application on another device. When the peer device is detected, the devices synchronize automatically. After synchronization contact changes are exchanged immediately, using the queue system as long as the devices have network connection to each other. The communication patterns of this simple application can be identified in many real world applications. Figure 5 presents the component set of the application.

The system is benchmarked in two setups, both using OSGi R4 reference implementation (available from osgi.org). In the first setup two instances of the same application are run on the same OSGi framework instance. The two instances are run independently (both use their own component set) and communicate over local HTTP connection.

The uncompressed class file sizes are the following. MWFW framework core + interface classes: 55231 bytes. SyncML DS sync component implementation: 86857 bytes. Contacts application, PC setup: 71748 bytes. Note that parts of the framework can be deployed separately and only the MWFW core bundle is required. This allows component sets to be deployed incrementally, according to application needs.

The first setup is executed on Linux 2.4.21 with standard JRE 1.4.2_08-b03. The dynamic memory (RAM) footprint of the application, the middleware framework and the OSGi framework is the following. Initiator after sync: 2567248

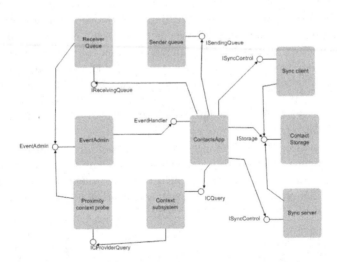

Fig. 5. Components in the sample application

bytes. Server after sync: 2691064 bytes. Initiator with disabled server components: 2551312 bytes. The footprints were measured in the final phase of a succesful synchronization session. The sync initiator and server instances were run in two JVMs and the footprint shown was obtained as the difference returned by java.lang.Runtime totalMemory() and freeMemory() methods. It can be clearly seen that even the OSGi Reference Implementation instantiates services lazily. The initiator would have been able to function as server as well but as this functionality was not used, the related service object were not instantiated. This function can yield even more significant footprint reduction in more advanced OSGi R4 implementations. Further footprint reductions can be achieved when the server components are not instantiated at all in the initiator, as shown in the table.

The second setup is executed on IBM's J9 virtual machine preinstalled on the Nokia 9500 Communicator. The purpose of this demo was to demonstrate the suitability of the dynamic component-based approach for short-range wireless bearers. Unfortunately, the Personal Profile implementation in the the 9500 does not support JSR-82 (Bluetooth API) therefore the Bluetooth support was implemented only as non-functional stubs. The footprint numbers presented here are only informative therefore. The total static footprint was 11708791 bytes (total size of files installed on the phone including OSGi framework elements, standard OSGi services, middleware framework and the demo application). The RAM footprint was measured with the Spy application available from forum.nokia.com. When the application's launch process finished and the application's opening screen appeared, the J9 process occupied 5898 kBytes in the phone's RAM memory. These numbers are realistic for a device having 64 MBytes total RAM and 80 MBytes total flash disk space but may be problematic to squeeze into a smaller device.

8   Conclusions

Reflective model is attractive in the mobile application space because of its low footprint and easy adaptability to changes in the environment. This paper aimed to demonstrate that the OSGi R4 component model can be efficiently used to implement reflective middleware. OSGi R4 provides a powerful component system which is made even more interesting by its dynamic component wiring capabilities. Dynamic wiring, if not used carefully, may cause "blackout" in the operation of the system. This blackout effect must be considered when designing the application.

OSGi R4 as it is provides weak application separation that depends on classloaders in many implementations. There are many ways to exploit this protection system and malicious applications are able to disrupt other applications. Our reflective middleware framework is built on component factories that complicate the separation problem further because components created by component factories do not belong to applications. Therefore even the weak OSGi application separation mechanism can be overridden. The framework presented here depends on cooperative applications. Further study is needed on application separation issues.

The value of the reflective approach was demonstrated by the footprint measurements. It is definitely harder to develop, debug and test in the dynamic component model supported by OSGi R4 than using the monolithic approach. OSGi R4-based applications have realistic footprint for PDA-class devices and smartphones.

References

1. C. MASCOLO, L. CAPRA, W. EMMERICH, Mobile Computing Middleware, *NET-WORKING 2002 Tutorials, pp. 20 - 58*
2. A. GADDAH AND T. KUNZ, A Survey of Middleware Paradigms for Mobile Computing, *Carleton University, Systems and Computer Engineering, Technical Report SCE-03-16, July 2003*
3. G. PALLER, Framework for Dynamic and Automatic Connectivity in Hierarchical Component Environments, *Fractal Workshop, Middleware2005 conference, Grenoble, France, 2005 Nov.*
4. G. CHEN AND D. KOTZ, Context Aggregation and Dissemination in Ubiquitous Computing Systems *Proceedings of the Fourth IEEE Workshop on Mobile Computing Systems and Applications, 2002*
5. G. CHEN AND D. KOTZ, A Survey of Context-Aware Mobile Computing Research, *Technical Report: TR2000-381, Dartmouth College, Hanover, NH, USA, 2000*
6. R. POWER, D. LEWIS, D. O'SULLIVAN, O. CONLAN AND V. WADE, A Context Information Service using Ontology-Based Queries, *First International Workshop on Advanced Context Modelling, Reasoning And Management, UbiComp 2004*
7. H. CHEN, T. FININ AND A. JOSHI, An Ontology for Context-Aware Pervasive Computing Environments *Special Issue on Ontologies for Distributed Systems, Knowledge Engineering Review, 2003.*
8. S. AGARWAL, D. STAROBINSKI AND A. TRACHTENBERG, On the Scalability of Data Synchronization Protocols for PDAs and Mobile Devices, *IEEE Network (Special Issue on Scalability in Communication Networks), Vol. 16, No.4, pp.2228, July/August 2002.*
9. A. TRACHTENBERG, D. STAROBINSKI AND S. AGARWAL, Fast PDA Synchronization Using Characteristic Polynomial Interpolation, *IEEE Infocom 2002*
10. R. HAYTON, A. HERBERT AND D. DONALDSON, Flexinet: a flexible, component oriented middleware system, *Proceedings of the 8th ACM SIGOPS European Workshop: Support for Composing Distributed Applications, Sintra, Portugal, 7-10 September 1998.*
11. G. S. BLAIR ET AL., Reflection, Self-Awareness and Self-Healing in OpenORB, *Proceedings of the first workshop on Self-healing systems, 2002*
12. N. H. COHEN, A Java Framework for Mobile Data Synchronization, *Cooperative Information Systems: 7th International Conference, September 2000*
13. M. SATYANARAYANAN, J. KISTLER, P. KUMAR, M. OKASAKI, E. SIEGEL AND D. STEERE Coda: A Highly Available File System for a Distributed Workstation Environment, *IEEE Transactions on Computers, 39(4), 447-459, 1990*
14. M. SATYANARAYANAN, Mobile Information Access, *IEEE Personal Communications, 3(1), 1996*

15. G. Picco, A. Murphy and G. Roman, LIME: Linda meets mobility, International Conference on Software Engineering archive, *Proceedings of the 21st international conference on Software engineering, 1999.*
16. JavaSpaces specification, *http://java.sun.com/products/jini/2.0/doc/specs/html/ js-spec.html*
17. T. Lehman, S. McLaughry and P. Wyckoff, T Spaces: the next wave, *IBM Systems Journal, 37 (3): 454– 474, 1998.*
18. Ren Meier, Communication Paradigms for Mobile Computing, ACM SIGMO-BILE Mobile Computing and Communications, Volume 6, Issue 4, 2002
19. M. Caporuscio, A. Carzaniga, A. Wolf, Design and Evaluation of a Support Service for Mobile, Wireless Publish/Subscribe Applications, *IEEE Transactions on Software Engineering, December 2003 (Vol. 29, No. 12)*
20. B. Segall and D. Arnold, Elvin has left the building: A publish/subscribe notification service with quenching, *Proceedings AUUG97, Brisbane, Australia, September 1997.*
21. Y. Chen, K. Schwan and D. Zhou, Opportunistic Channels: Mobility-aware Event Delivery, *Proceedings of the 4th ACM/IFIP/USENIX International Middleware Conference (Middleware2003), June 2003.*
22. SyncML Data Synchronization Specifications, Version 1.1, *http://www. openmobilealliance.org/tech/affiliates/syncml/syncmlindex.html*
23. M. Pinto, L. Fuentes, M. E. Fayad and J. M. Troya, Separation of coordination in a dynamic aspect oriented framework, *Proceedings of the 1st international conference on Aspect-oriented software development, Enschede, The Netherlands, April, 2002*
24. Listeners Considered Harmful: The "Whiteboard" Pattern, *Technical Whitepaper, OSGi Alliance, http:// www.osgi.org/ documents/ osgi_technology/ whiteboard.pdf*

Goal-Oriented Performance Analysis of Reusable Software Components

Ronny Kolb[1], Dharmalingam Ganesan[1], Dirk Muthig[1],
Masanori Kagino[2], and Hideharu Teranishi[2]

[1] Fraunhofer Institute for Experimental
Software Engineering (IESE)
Fraunhofer-Platz 1, 67663 Kaiserslautern, Germany
Tel .: +49 (0) 631 – 6800-2195
{kolb, ganesan, muthig}@iese.fraunhofer.de
[2] Ricoh Company, Ltd.
1-15-5 Minami-Aoyama, 107-8544 Minatoku, Tokyo, Japan
hideharu.teranishi@nts.ricoh.co.jp

Abstract. To establish software reuse successfully in the long run, it is crucial for providers of reusable components to continuously react on problems or future trends arising around their component. In practice, however, many providers of reusable components are not able to do so due to insufficient feedback and details from reusers. Additionally, they often have too little knowledge on system context and constraints that may lead to major deficits of the reusable component especially with respect to non-functional aspects. This paper presents an approach for systematically engineering performance of reusable components that has been validated in an industrial context.

1 Introduction

With software reuse, organizations aim at improving efficiency of the development process and quality of the developed products. Improving efficiency depends on smaller cost for reusing an existing artifact than creating one newly from scratch. The reuse process thereby encompasses the identification of reuse candidates, their evaluation and selection, as well as their tailoring and adaptation to the specific context and the final integration into the product developed [3].

Product line engineering is a strategic reuse approach aiming primarily at efficiency improvements [1, 4]. It firstly minimizes the effort for the first part of the reuse process by enabling a straight forward selection via a smart organization of the reuse repository, that is, the product line infrastructure is strictly aligned with results from scoping and domain analysis. Secondly, product line engineering optimally supports tailoring of product line assets within the defined scope boundaries and thus also minimizes the need for adaptations.

Some adaptations, however, are still necessary in many cases. Even if the adaptation effort is small, it is hard to determine its effects on product quality. In practice, quality assurance is thus typically performed by each project individually. Such an approach, however, negatively affects the efficiency of the overall organization. Hence

M. Morisio (Ed.): ICSR 2006, LNCS 4039, pp. 368–381, 2006.
© Springer-Verlag Berlin Heidelberg 2006

organizations try to engineer quality properties of artifacts in a reusable way as well so that artifacts are adaptable also with respect to quality requirements of the reusing context. In order to do so, however, it is necessary but rather difficult for teams that maintain and evolve reusable artifacts to get a sufficient understanding of (potentially future) reuse contexts and existing constraints.

On the one hand, it is difficult by nature because future scenarios cannot be envisioned fully and in all detail in advance, as well as because most quality requirements are system-wide requirements. System-wide requirements can only be achieved by collaborations of sets of components according to rules defined by the system architecture. Looking only at single components does typically not lead to optimal system qualities. For example, assembling components that have been made as fast as possible from local, system-independent viewpoints, does not necessarily result in systems with optimal performance.

On the other hand, detailed information on former reuse contexts and usage scenarios can be of great help to developers of reusable artifacts. In practice, however, there generally is a lack of communication between reusers and providers of reusable artifacts. Hence, providing technical mechanisms that automatically generate information on the exact scenarios reusing components in the context of real products may support goal-oriented improvements of reusable components also for future contexts. This paper will thus present such a mechanism that focuses on performance requirements which play a central role in determining the overall quality and usability of many systems. Especially in embedded systems, performance problems are observed after field release including system performance degradation or problems handling required real-time constraints. The practical application of the approach is illustrated using a case study in the context of an industrial system product line.

The remainder of this paper is structured as follows. Section 2 introduces the goal-oriented approach for measuring and analyzing the performance of reusable software components. In Section 3 then results and experiences of applying the approach to an industrial product line component are presented. Section 4 closes the paper by providing some final conclusions.

2   Approach

The analysis and measurement of performance in software systems in general has been addressed by some researchers (e.g., [6], [7], [8], and [10]) and there are numerous tools and methods available. Despite the importance and increasing interest in industry, however, there has been very little research published in the area of software performance measurement for reusable software components (e.g. in [5], [9], [11],). Most research in component-based software engineering and product lines has focused on the design and implementation of components and their functional aspects so far, with relatively little reported on performance issues. Also, the fundamental challenges for performance analysis in the context of embedded systems have not been addressed adequately so far. Therefore, an approach is proposed in the following to efficiently analyze the performance of reusable components in the context of embedded systems. First, the basic ideas of the approach are presented. Then, an overview of the underlying process is provided and the individual steps are discussed.

2.1 Basic Ideas

Major problems with current available methods and tools for measuring the performance of components or systems are the large amount of generated data and the overhead caused by unfocused and excessive instrumentation. Not only is it difficult and time-consuming to analyze the amounts of data, but also often infeasible to effectively analyze the data and to derive concrete suggestions for improvements. Furthermore, the unreasonable instrumentation causes memory overhead and often has a significant influence on the behavior that is generally not acceptable for embedded systems. Also, resulting executables may be unsuitable for a production environment due to the tremendous performance penalty incurred.

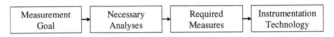

Fig. 1. Principle of the approach

The basic ideas of the approach are therefore to perform a selected instrumentation, to do performance measurement focused and on demand, and to base measurement and instrumentation on clearly defined goals. Because of the latter, the approach is called goal-oriented. As shown in Figure 1, the concrete measurement goal determines the necessary analyses which then determine the required measures. The required measures finally determine the applied instrumentation technology. In order to address specific characteristics of the component or system and to measure different metrics, different instrumentation technologies are used. To limit the amount of data generated, only a few key functions, classes, or parts are instrumented instead of the complete component or system. The instrumented functions or classes are identified based on the measurement goals. The rationale for this approach is that the identification of useful and relevant measures reduces effort for analysis and interpretation of collected data and hence a more reasonable usage of available resources. Further, it reduces the overhead associated with instrumentation and hence the influence on the behavior of the system.

2.2 Process

Figure 2 shows the process for measuring and analyzing the performance of a system in general and a reusable component in particular. As the figure shows, the process includes five steps. In general, the steps are executed in sequential order, starting with "Plan" and finishing with "Improve". It is, however, also possible to go from the step "Analyze" back to the steps "Plan" or "Instrument" to adapt the measurements according to the analysis results. In general, a performance measurement using the process is performed in an iterative manner. In the following, the individual steps are described in detail.

Plan. In this first step, the performance measurement and analysis of the component or system is planned. In particular, the concrete measurements and analyses that should be performed are defined, the instrumentation strategy is selected, and the

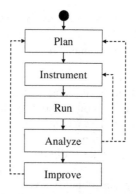

Fig. 2. Process for performance analysis

team and infrastructure for performing the measurement and analysis are set up. The step is typically performed by a project manager or developer responsible for performance measurement. It is started once performance problems have been encountered or information about performance issues requested. The step consists of the following activities: 1) Set Measurement Goals, 2) Plan Analyses, 3) Determine Measurements, 4) Define Instrumentation Strategy, and 5) Prepare Team and Infrastructure. As the approach is goal-oriented, the first activity is to define together with stakeholders the goals of the performance measurement. Examples of stakeholders are component users, customers, marketing, designers, and developers. The goals are preferably defined using the Goal-Question-Metric (GQM) approach[1] 1. At the beginning, high-level measurement goals are stated which are then transformed into formal GQM goals. If there is more than one goal, a limited number of goals which finally have to be achieved by the planned performance measurement are selected. According to the defined measurement goals, the analyses that should be performed on the data collected during execution of the component or system are defined. The analyses help to find the reason of problems and provide the input for improvement activities. Based on the measurement goals and the planned analyses, then measurements are defined. Measurements define the type of data that should be collected and how often the data is collected. Examples of measurements are response time for functions in milliseconds, number of function calls, latency, and throughput. According to the defined analyses and measurements, an instrumentation strategy is defined next. An instrumentation strategy specifies:

- which instrumentation technology will be used,
- how the instrumentation technology will be customized to the concrete context,
- which parts (e.g. subcomponents, collection of classes) of the investigated component or system should be instrumented,

---

[1] GQM is a method for performing goal-oriented software measurement and defining measurable goals. Abstract high level goals are refined into questions and these questions are further refined into metrics which help to answer the questions in a measurable way.

- what constructs should be instrumented (e.g., statements, functions, methods, classes, external components), and
- when the component will be instrumented (e.g., preprocessor, compile-time, link-time, run-time)

The selection of an instrumentation technology not only depends on the planned measurements and analyses, but also on constraints such as the availability of source code, personnel skills, and costs. The technology of choice can also depend on the hardware features and instrumentation tools available. For example, some methods require special hardware features like a digital output port, while other techniques require a specific software application or measurement instrumentation to be available. In some cases, the required hardware or tools can be quite expensive and the cost and lack of availability can prevent using a particular method. Once the instrumentation technology has been selected, the parts for instrumentation are determined. The decision of what should be instrumented can be supported by a static analysis of the source code or by expert feedback. Experts are particularly used to identify certain key locations inside the component or system for instrumentation. The last activity in the planning step is the preparation of the measurement infrastructure and the set up of a team performing the measurement and analysis. The team size depends on the complexity of the analyzed component or system, the instrumentation strategy, and the planned analyses.

Instrument. In this step, the investigated component or system is instrumented according to the previously defined instrumentation strategy. The step is typically performed by person(s) having detailed knowledge about the selected instrumentation technology. A developer of the component supports this step by providing detailed knowledge about the internal structure of the component as well as the domain. The instrumentation also includes checking the correctness of the measurement code and the correct behavior of the modified component. After the step, the component or system is ready to run and can be integrated and used.

A common way to measure performance is to automatically or manually insert measuring code into the source code of the investigated component or system. This provides the ability to capture the metrics of interest, and the analyst has the possibility of taking the measurements in the most appropriate places. A problem of manual instrumentation, however, is that for all but trivial systems, it is very labor-intensive and in consequence often time-consuming and costly. In the case of component-based systems, furthermore, the source code of a component might not always be available. Whether instrumentation is done manually or automatically, a sound understanding of the design and implementation of the system is required to ensure that all appropriate measurement sites are instrumented, and that no bugs are introduced. Besides code level, instrumentation can also be performed as part of compilation or directly on the executable either before or during execution. The problem, however, is that there are generally differences between development and production environment of embedded systems. Different compilers and tools as well as different hardware platforms make it difficult to analyze and compare measurement data and to draw conclusions.

Run. The instrumented component or system is executed in the same way as the original version. Depending on the planned analyses, the component is executed one or more times using clearly defined usage scenarios. Depending on the nature of the component or system, another component or a user interacts with the component or product according to defined scenarios. During each of the executions, the previously injected code collects measurement data that is either persistently stored directly or at the end of the run. The executions of the component or system lie mainly in the responsibility of the product developers, component users or customers. In case of problems with the instrumented code or the measurement data collection, they are assisted by the instrumentor.

Analyze. After the instrumented component or system has been executed and all the measurement data collected a post-mortem analysis with respect to the measurement goals and with the goal of giving detailed interpretations of the collected data is performed. The analysis is performed by one or more specialists in data analysis. As a first step, the collected data is assessed for reasonableness and correctness. If any problems regarding the validity of the data are found, the reason has to be determined. Depending on the identified reason, either the planning or the instrumentation has to be revisited and performed again resulting in new measurement data. Once the validity of the collected has been confirmed, the initially planned analyses are conducted. The results are interpreted to identify and understand problems in the investigated component or system. Based on the analysis results, preliminary conclusions and improvement suggestions are derived. If it is necessary, for example to gain confidence in the results or to draw sound conclusions, additional measurement and analyses passes are conducted. This might also include improving measurement definitions, data collection procedures, and analysis techniques as needed to ensure meaningful results that support measurement goals. To prevent misunderstandings of the analysis results and rework, initial and final results should be reviewed with all relevant stakeholders. Once the final analysis results are available, relevant stakeholders should be assisted in understanding and interpreting the results.

Improve. In this final step, the analysis results are used by the developers to perform improvements and to remove agreed upon defects and detected bottlenecks. After all the problems have been removed, typically the previous performance measurement is performed again to check whether all problems have been resolved. If this measurement shows no further problems, the process is finished. Otherwise, a new performance measurement with different goals and analyses is planned and conducted.

3 Case Study

This section illustrates the practical usage of the goal-oriented performance measurement process by means of a case study. After giving an overview of the context of the case study, the section provides some results of the component's performance measurement and summarizes experiences and lessons learned in applying the proposed approach.

3.1 Context

The case study presented in this paper is based on a reusable software component called User Interface Component (UIC) which is used in Ricoh's current products of office appliances. Ricoh is one of the world's leading developer and producer of digital office equipment, including copiers, printers, scanners, facsimiles, and multifunctional peripherals (MFPs). All these products are embedded systems with limited hardware resources and increasingly complex software as most innovative features are realized by software nowadays. Because of the very large number of similar products and the need to reduce development and maintenance costs, Ricoh is interested in applying Fraunhofer PuLSE™ (Product Line Software and System Engineering)[2] to systematically tackle variability and reusability issues. In this context, the issue of systematically measuring and improving performance of reusable software components was addressed.

As one of the most important parts in an office device is the user interface and already a reusable component with performance problems was available, the user interface component was selected for the case study. In the following, a brief overview of the component is provided.

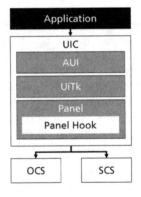

Fig. 3. Overview of the UIC

The user interface component is a reusable component that provides features for easily realizing the graphical user interfaces of Ricoh's products. It is used by the developers of concrete products to build the user interfaces that provide access to the various functions of the different products. The component abstracts from the underlying hardware and capabilities of the various input and output devices used in Ricoh's products. Currently, the component supports four-line LCD, VGA and WVGA output panels with function keys and touch screens as input devices. Potential variabilities had been analyzed and considered in design and implementation in advance. The component is realized as a C++ framework with hook methods for variabilities. In total, it consists of about 100,000 lines of code.

---

[2] PuLSE™ is a registered trademark of Fraunhofer Institute for Experimental Software Engineering (IESE), Kaiserslautern, Germany.

To realize the required functionality, the component uses other components, namely OCS and SCS, as shown in Figure 3. These components have been developed by different units so that their source code is not available. Internally, the user interface component is structured into three layers. The top-most layer, called AUI, is responsible for the connection between an application and its data to the component. The UiTk layer realizes the display and control of various widgets on a panel. The panel layer at the bottom is responsible for controlling the underlying hardware by using the device drivers controlled by OCS and SCS. The adaptation to the different input and output devices is realized in the so called panel hook. For every new device, a specific implementation of the panel hook has to be provided.

The user interface component is developed iteratively. To effectively test the different variants of the component, an emulation environment was created to perform automatic tests and simulation of various input and output devices. Component developers can thus create user interfaces and simulate the usage of their component by products. These activities focused on assuring correct functioning of the component. Non-functional aspects such as time behavior and resource consumption were not addressed. After successful testing, the component is released to development units reusing the component for building products.

Product development thereby includes activities assuring quality of the whole product, such as black-box testing that uncovered occasionally that some user interface requests, such as a transition from one screen to another, had an unusual long (e.g. several seconds) response time. Naturally, product teams conjectured that problems regarding the low performance might be caused by the user interface component. Since the problems did not show up in the emulation environment, however, the component development team refused to take responsibility for the low performance and conjectured that the problems might be caused by the external components used by UIC. To resolve this issue, performance properties of the reusable component must be analyzed in detail.

3.2 Activities

This section discusses some of the activities performed in the case study according to the individual steps of the goal-oriented performance measurement approach.

Define Instrumentation Strategy. According to the defined analyses and measurements and taking into account project constraints an instrumentation strategy was then defined. Because of the usage of C++ as programming language and the availability of source code of the user interface component it was decided to selected automatic source code instrumentation. As the source code of the external components was not available for any modifications, instrumentation was done at call sites in the UIC. Instrumentation was limited to calls to external functions provided by OCS and SCS in the panel hook of the component. Note that the panel hook is adapted to the different hardware devices supported by a product. Therefore, the panel hook of the emulation is slightly different than the product version. The external functions acquired by UIC and the call sites have been identified using static code analysis. In total, 16 functions provided by the components OCS and SCS have been identified to be used by the UIC.

Instrument. According to the defined instrumentation strategy the source code of the user interface component was automatically instrumented by the Fraunhofer IESE using custom tools. At all the sites in the code with calls to functions provided by the external components OCS and SCS, additional code to collect and store timing information was automatically inserted before and after a function call. For recording the start and end time of a function and also to relate the time to a particular function, an instrumentation library developed by Fraunhofer IESE has been used. The library provides a number of simple macros such as PERMEAS_FUNC_START and PERMEAS_FUNC_END for storing events, time stamp, and name of an entity in a very compact log file. To keep the overhead of the measurement code to a minimum, the library does not compute the duration of functions or methods nor increments a counter for the respective function. However, it enables to customize the data storage mechanisms to the particular context. In case of the emulation environment, the measurement data was written directly to a file on the hard disk whereas in case of the product environment a special hardware mechanism provided by Ricoh was used to efficiently store and transmit the data. The mechanism enables to store data without much overhead and even if there is no persistent memory in the product available.

In addition to the automatic instrumentation, some minor manual instrumentation of specific aspects was done by Fraunhofer IESE and Ricoh. For example, the code was adapted manually to collect start and ending time of test scenarios in the auto test environment. Also, the Ricoh developers did some instrumentation for certain component-internal methods they wanted to include the measurement.

Run. The instrumented component was integrated with other components and then executed in the emulation environment and in two concrete products. To have comparable measurement results, two specific usage scenarios have been defined and used for interaction with the user interfaces realized using the component. In case of the emulation environment, the automatic test capabilities have been used to easily and repeatable stimulate the component according to the test scenarios. In the product environment, the stimulation was done manually by pressing respective keys and buttons.

Analyze. Once the measurement data had been collected by running the component in the emulation environment and in a concrete product, a post-mortem analysis of the data was started. As a first step, the measurement data stored in the log files was preprocessed in order to have a better basis for the analyses. In particular, the duration of function calls was calculated from the start and ending time stored for each function in the log file using a small Java program. The preprocessing resulted in comma separated values (CSV) files containing the function name and the duration of the function in milliseconds. After preprocessing, the files have been imported to Excel for performing the pre-planned analyses. Examples of the performed analyses and their results are provided in Section 3.3.

Because of the analysis results which indicated that the performance problems are not caused by the external functions but internal methods of the user interface component, a further cycle plan, instrument, run, analyze was done after performing the originally planned analyses. In particular, the measurement goal was extended to finding internal methods of the user interface component that cause the identified performance problems.

3.3 Results

In this section, some results of the measurement of the user interface component in the emulation environment and two concrete products are summarized. Note that due to confidentiality reasons all the names of functions have been anonymized and there is also no information about the actual response time of functions.

As shown in Figure 4, the percentage of calls to external functions in the emulation and product environments are relatively similar. In particular, the results for the different products show only minor differences. The results also showed that some functions are never called or are only executed in one of the environments.

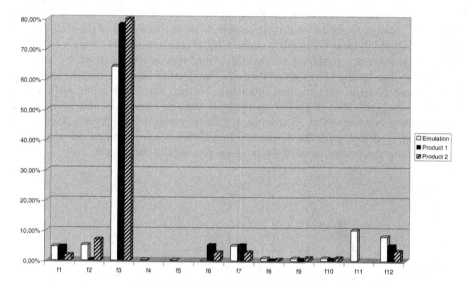

Fig. 4. Percentage of function calls

Even though the distribution of the function calls is comparable in the emulation and product environments, there are significant differences regarding the total time spent in the individual functions as shown in Figure 5. Whereas in the product most of the time is spent in function f3 for both usage scenarios, more than 90% of the total time is spent in function f7 in the emulation environment. As more detailed analyses have shown this is caused by large differences between the response times of the functions in the emulation and product environment. For function f7, for example, the average response time is 87% higher in the emulation environment than in the product even though the emulation is running on a much faster processor. As with knowledge about the different hardware platforms this result was very surprising, an effort investigating the cause was initiated. It eventually showed that in the emulation environment much overhead is caused by the way the emulations of the external components OCS and SCS are technically realized. A major influencing factor was the fact that both OCS and SCS are realized as dynamic link libraries which are dynamically loaded whenever a provided function is requested.

In the product environments and the emulation environment function £3 is called very often. However, in the emulation environment it has very short response time resulting in very small percentage of the total time. Conversely, in the product environment the percentage of time is proportional to the percentage of calls for this and many other functions.

Figure 6 shows the ratio of time spent in functions provided by OCS and SCS (i.e., External functions) in comparison to the percentage of time spent in the user interface component itself. As can be seen the component spends in the emulation environment, on average 54% of the total time in functions provided by OCS and SCS. This result lead to the preliminary conclusion that the performance problems with the user interface component are indeed caused by the external components. In the concrete products, however, only 2% and 11% of the time is spent in external functions. Analogous, in the product environment up to 98 percent of the total time of a usage scenario is spent exclusively inside UIC. Hence, the results strongly indicated that the performance problems of the UI component are not caused by external components but by the UI component itself. The detailed analysis showed that most of this time is spent in just three methods. Furthermore, only minor differences regarding the performance of the component variants reused in the investigated products have been observed. In order to significantly improve the performance of the component, therefore, only the three identified methods have to be modified without compromising the performance of the products reusing the component.

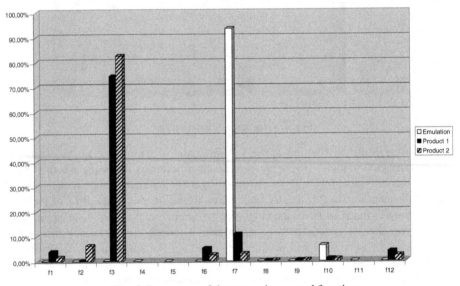

Fig. 5. Percentage of time spent in external functions

The major problem identified by the performance measurement is the significantly different behavior of the emulation environment in terms of performance. Especially the emulation of the external components OCS and SCS does not resemble the behavior of the original components. Therefore, the current emulation environment can be used for testing functional correctness of the user interface component, but not

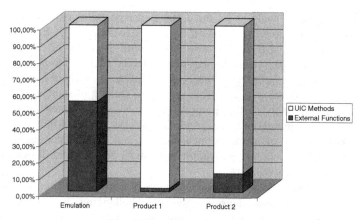

Fig. 6. Percentage of spent times

to realistically predict the performance in the product environments. By adapting the time behavior of the emulation components to that of the original components used in the products an early detection and resolution of performance problems in the UIC would be possible. Without waiting for feedback from the product teams, performance bottlenecks could be detected and the performance of the component in a particular product demonstrated to interested product teams. This also would result in a higher level of confidence in the quality of the component by product teams thus increasing the willingness to reuse the component.

3.4 Lessons Learned

This section summarizes some experiences and lessons learned in applying the performance measurement approach to a reusable software component. It also presents some limitations and discusses the main points that should be considered when planning and performing a performance measurement.

In general, the presented approach enabled to efficiently and effectively measure and analyze the performance of a reusable software component. Due to the goal-orientation and the selective instrumentation the amount of data that had to be analyzed was reduced significantly without reducing the quality of the analysis results. Furthermore, the influence of the measurement code on the behavior was kept to a minimum and there was no visible performance degradation observed. The key to success, however, was to identify the right (i.e., most promising) places in the component to add measurement code, to use the same – or at least very similar – usage scenarios for collecting measurement data. Also, the adaptation of the code collecting and storing the measurement data to the different environments was crucial. Furthermore, the iterative approach and the adaptation of measurement goals and planned analyses after having analyzed the collected measurement data enables to improve the quality of the analyses and to achieve the required goals in shorter time.

Despite its success, the case study showed that there are still possibilities for improvement. First of all, most of the analyses have been done manually, making them time-consuming, tedious, and cumbersome to do. At least for some default analyses, therefore, automation would be an important issue. Another problem is the selection of appropriate analyses for the defined measurement goal. In the case study, the selection was done intuitively based on prior experiences. To make the process more explicit and to also enable developers with little or no knowledge and experience in performance measurement to effectively analyze the performance of a component, however, a well-defined process and information about possible analyses is required. Ideally, developers are provided with a catalog of standard analyses that describes for each analysis the purpose, the context to which it applies, the prerequisites, the required measures, and the process of performing the analysis. Similarly, an overview of available measurement and instrumentation technologies together with prerequisites for application and known benefits and drawbacks would support inexperienced developers.

Another important issue that has to be addressed is ensuring the correctness of the collected measurement data. This is especially challenging in the case of multi-threaded systems and asynchronous function calls which are typical for embedded systems. For asynchronous functions the simple approach of measuring the time before and after a function call does not work as the function usually just sends a message to another thread and then immediately returns resulting in very short execution times. The actual execution time of the functions, however, is much longer and needs also measurement of the function responding to the message in another thread. As the user interface component and the used external components, however, are all single threaded and asynchronous functions are not used, the problem has not been addressed so far.

Finally, the selection of appropriate usage scenarios requires domain knowledge and determines the reliability of the measurement results for all instances of a reusable component. To make detailed recommendations for improvement domain knowledge and knowledge about the internal structure of the component is necessary. It is also important to analyze the impact of any change to the component on the different products.

4 Conclusions

This paper motivated that establishing successful reuse of components requires also their careful engineering of relevant quality properties in a reusable way. It in particular has addressed the problem of measuring and analyzing performance of reusable components by a goal-oriented measurement approach, whose practical applicability was validated in an industrial context.

In contrast to existing approaches, the presented technique focuses on well-scoped usage scenarios and qualities so that much less data must be collected and enables therefore a selective instrumentation that minimizes side effects of measurement code on the behavior of the system. Additionally, analyses must process less data. As shown in the case study, the approach uncovers problem areas and thus enables significant improvements without much overhead or large effort.

In the future, we want to apply the presented approach to other components, quality attributes, as well as environments.

Acknowledgements

This work could not have been carried out without the cooperation and assistance of the developers of both the Ricoh UIC team as well as the product team using the component who applied the approach and delivered the essential measurement results. In particular, we would like to thank Mr. Matsui and Mr. Hatakeyama for their support in integrating the instrumented component and collecting the measurement data. Finally, we would like to thank the management of Ricoh Ltd., Tokyo for their permission to publish the results.

References

1. Atkinson, C. et al. Component-based Product Line Engineering with UML. Addison-Wesley, 2001.
2. Basili, V. R., Caldera, G., and Rombach, H. D. Goal Question Metric Paradigm, In J. J. Marciniak (ed.) Encyclopedia of Software Engineering (vol. 1), John Wiley & Sons, 1994, 528–532.
3. Basili, V. R. and Rombach, D. Support for Comprehensive Reuse. IEEE Software Engineering Journal, Volume 6, Number 5, 1991.
4. Clements, P., and Northrop, L. M. Software Product Lines: Practices and Patterns. Addison-Wesley, 2001.
5. Ganesan, D., Maurer, U., Ochs, M., Snoek, B., Verlage, M. Towards Testing Response Time of Instances of a Web-based Product Line. In Proceedings of International Workshop on Software Product Line Testing (SPLiT 2005), Rennes, France, September 2005, 23–34.
6. Metz, E., Lencevicius, R. Efficient Instrumentation for Performance Profiling. In Proceedings of the First Workshop on Dynamic Analysis (WODA), 2003, 143–148.
7. Metz, E., Lencevicius, R. A Performance Analysis Tool for Nokia Mobile Phone Software. In M. Ronsse, K. De Bosschere (eds.), Proceedings of the Fifth International Workshop on Automated Debugging (AADEBUG 2003), September 2003.
8. Reiss, S., Renieris, M. Encoding Program Executions, In Proceedings of the International Conference on Software Engineering (ICSE), 2001.
9. Sitaraman, M. Kulczycki, G., Krone, J., Ogden, W., Reddy, A. Performance Specification of Software Components. In Proceedings of ACM SIGSOFT Symposium on Software Reuse (SSR '01), ACM/SIGSOFT, May 2001, 3–10.
10. Stewart, D. Measuring Execution Time and Real-Time Performance", Embedded Systems Conference (ESC'01), Spring 2001.
11. Yacoub, S. Performance Analysis of Component-Based Applications. In Proceedings of the Second Software Product Line Conference (SPLC2), San Diego, CA, August 2002, 299–315.

Establishing Extra Organizational Reuse Capabilities

Markus Voss

sd&m Research
sd&m AG software design & management
Berliner Str. 76, 63065 Offenbach, Germany
markus.voss@sdm-research.de

Abstract. Component-based software engineering (CBSE) for companies active in custom solutions development is far from being reality. To make progress more industrial research as well as accordant technology management is needed. In this contribution we introduce a classification of components in terms of component's scale and in terms of functional vs. technical concerns. From this basis we argue that only some areas of software reuse promise substantial growth in delivery efficiency and show how this is related to the extra organizational reuse approach.

1 Introduction

The idea of component-based software engineering has long been discussed and many contributions to the topic have been made (e.g. [1]). Industrial practice shows however, that the ultimate promise of plugging given components together to new systems is far from being established. Available component technologies like CORBA CCM, (Enterprise) Java Beans or Web Services are essential as a technological basis. The challenge however for software systems architects today is to be able to really leverage the power of reusing not only technical but functional elements to significantly improve productivity.

2 Component Classification

One dimension we need to address when talking about components and their specification and potential reuse is scale. Components exist from small to large and all of them need to be taken into consideration when talking about CBSE.

Whole application landscapes consist of many applications, possibly ordered in application domains (subject matter domains; one driving concept in service-oriented architecture partitioning as we e.g. pointed out in [2]). Applications themselves are comprised from application components. Application components are characterized by being elements exporting use cases and are themselves internally assembled from software objects.

The second dimension to consider is whether a component really makes a functional contribution (e.g. an application component to the application) or whether it

M. Morisio (Ed.): ICSR 2006, LNCS 4039, pp. 382–385, 2006.

makes a pure technical contribution and serves as an infrastructural basis. The former we call A-components, the later T-components.

The separation into A- and T-components is an established concept for structuring software systems [3] - an application of the concept of separation of concerns. T-components are organized in layers (presentation & integration services, business services, data services (persistence)). These layers form reference T-architectures, matching the layers of A-components and tying them together on the according levels of integration. Fig. 1 illustrates this concept.

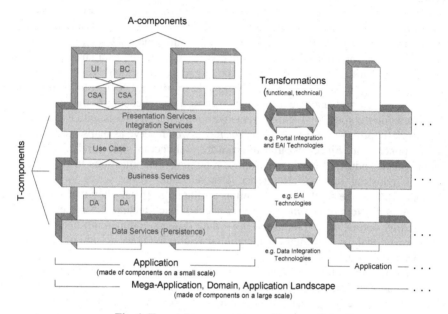

Fig. 1. T- and A-components working together

Examples for T-components on the small scale are e.g. Toplink (commercial) or Hibernate (Open Source) implementing data services or the Spring framework implementing business services. The aggregation of A-components and T-components on this small scale is called an application. An application is characterized by a special set of functionality given by the set of the use cases supported by its A-component plus a technologically homogeneous set of T-components.

Moving up the hierarchy to mega-applications, application domains or application landscapes where whole applications become A-components usually leads to heterogeneity in the T-components and redundancy in the A-components' (the applications') functionality. Therefore, the core of integrating applications – no matter whether they are custom build or off the shelf – is always based on functional and technical transformation. The corresponding T-components on a large scale are e.g. portal management, EAI solutions or data integration products.

3 Investigating the Areas of Reuse

3.1 Reuse of T-Components

Reuse of T-components - on the small as well as on the large scale - being mainly a matter of standardization is simply a prerequisite for any raise of productivity, efficiency and cost reduction in any multi-project software systems development organization. Therefore it's worth strong effort both in industrial research as well as in accordant technology management to establish this form of reuse.

Experience shows that intra organizational approaches in T-components reuse tend to be inefficient in terms of their ratio of cost and benefit and also tends to be overrun by extra organizational progress – both commercial and open source. Therefore an extra organizational reuse approach is to be preferred as a sustainable basis. T-components originating from inside the organization should very critically be judged according to its sustainability. Being able to form an open source community for the components advancement may e.g. very well be a meaningful measure.

Organizing the reuse of T-components within a company starts with establishing a framework in terms of *reference T-architectures*, which serve as maps for positioning the components on. Since research in software architecture only rarely is driven by this pragmatic industrial need, we propose reference T-architectures to be a primary focus of industrial research. Reference T-architectures make sense for structuring T-components on the small scale as well as on the large scale. They highlight central architectural clusters of *technical services* needed. Each technical service can be instantiated by one or more T-components – may they be commercial, open source or (in an exceptional case) of inter organizational origin. In [4] we go into more detail on reference architectures.

It's the responsibility of industrial research to standardize appropriate reference T-architectures. A company's accordant technology management's responsibility than is to organize an ongoing maintenance of a short list of strategic T-components (e.g. high potentials, customers' favorites) plus technical and organizational support for reusing complete proven configurations. This comprises e.g. the supply of best-practices documentation, starter kits, architectural glue code, configuration management procedures, light-weight support structures etc. The result is an increase in standardization and thus in delivery efficiency.

3.2 Reuse of A-Components

Reuse of A-components *on the small scale* is known to be extremely difficult. The reason for this is not the lack of theoretical grounding but lies within the exact fit requirement in combination with the bad ratio of cost and benefit of designing and organizing for reuse on the small scale.

From the perspective of developing a CBSE strategy we hence propose to focus industrial research not on reuse issues but on fostering standardization of the *specification* of A-components. The aspiration is to come up with a more efficient basis for the development of exact fit components. In conjunction with the standardization of their architectural framework to be plugged in, in terms of the standardization of T-components as mentioned above, highest gain in efficiency and cost optimization then is expected to come from intelligent *distribution* of the development work ("right shoring").

But progress in A-components specification also starts with an appropriate architectural approach. E.g. it has proved to be essential for a minimization of internal coupling and thus for efficient distribution of development of an application component to internally separate the business function from the channels of access to it. Having separated distinct sub-components on this note, many cuts through an application become possible. This results in being able to distribute development tasks optimally in terms of the participating development unit's special skills. The other important consequence is that it becomes clear how the interfaces look in general and individual component specification work becomes highly standardized. Since again research in software architecture only rarely is driven by this pragmatic industrial need, we propose this to be a major focus for industrial research.

Reuse of A-components *on the large scale* on the other hand is obligatory since the ratio of cost and benefit has good potential. Handling of functional redundancy and technical heterogeneity can very well pay of if integration and customizing of the components does not exceed reasonable limits.

Recent trends in further componentizing of large business software as e.g. in SAP's ESA strategy [5] may in the future shift the problem a little from the large scale to some "medium" scale. However, the challenge for industrial research to facilitate solution developers and architects will still lie in making advanced methods available for components *evaluation* in terms of functional coverage analysis, technical integration assessment, testability, and risk management procedures in terms of incorporating characteristics of different customizing patterns. To achieve progress in evaluation of A-components on the large scale (e.g. complete business software packages for potentially very different topics like e.g. ERP, order management or collaboration) needs to improve practice in exactly these processes.

References

1. Szyperski, C.: Component Software. Addison Wesley 2002.
2. Richter, J.-P.: Wann liefert eine serviceorientierte Architektur echten Nutzen? Proceedings Software Engineering 2005, Fachtagung des GI-Fachbereichs Softwaretechnik, 8.-11.3.2005, Essen, Page 231-242
3. Siedersleben, J.: Moderne Software-Architektur – umsichtig planen, robust bauen mit Quasar. dpunkt Verlag, 2004
4. Haft, M., Humm, B., Siedersleben, J.: The architect's dilemma – will reference architectures help? In: R. Reussner et al. (Eds.): Quality of Software Architectures and Software Quality (QoSA-SOQUA 2005), Lecture Notes in Computer Science 3712, pp. 106 – 122, 2005. Springer-Verlag, 2005
5. Woods, D.: Enterprise Service Architecture. Galileo Press. Bonn, 2004

Incremental Software Reuse

Juan Llorens[1], José M. Fuentes[2], Ruben Prieto-Diaz[3], and Hernán Astudillo[4]

[1] Informatics Department. Universidad Carlos III de Madrid
Avda. de la Universidad, 30 E-28911 Leganés, 28911 Madrid, Spain
llorens@inf.uc3m.es
[2] R&D Dept., The Reuse Company, Virginia, USA
josemiguel.fuentes@reusecompany.com
[3] James Madison University, Virginia, USA
prietodiaz@cisat.jmu.edu
[4] Universidad Técnica Federico Santa María, Valparaíso, Chile
hernan@inf.utfsm.cl

Abstract. Current reuse techniques disincentive their mass practice in software development organizations because of their large initial investments, the changes they required in ways of developing software, and their fragility in front of domain evolutions. We argue that the root of these problems is the poor resolution of retrieval techniques to identify candidate artifacts to utilize in new projects. We sketch an approach to reuse based on artifacts retrieval by content, which allows incremental adoption at low cost. The Incremental Reuse Method (IRM), founded on these principles, can solve the big problems of traditional reuse, allowing their application in all manner of organizations.

1 Why Isn't Software Reuse as Widespread as It Should Be?

Software Reuse is a well known concept in Software Engineering: it could be compared to the "holy grail" which has always been sought and has been impossible to reach. The reuse concept brings up strong reactions among computer industry professionals. All of us are aware that it represents a needed best practice we should know and apply within our organizations [4] but many of us also show certain level of skepticism in the success possibilities to institutionalize reuse for internal processes improvement [1].

A possible reason to understand this paradox could perhaps be found in the difficulty to balance both positive and negative effects towards its practice.

Among the benefits of practicing reuse we can mention the classical ones: Increment of productivity, reduction of time to market, reduction of project planning overheads, increment of quality, improvements in support and maintenance, better use of resources, and better tackling of system complexity.

But not everything is so promising in this vision. Many professionals, including the authors, consider that there are severe obstacles to introducing software reuse (further explained in the next section):

- Significant resources must be spent to support the reuse process.
- The investments are usually very high, so organizations must perform Return on Investment (ROI) analysis and there is high risk of failure.

M. Morisio (Ed.): ICSR 2006, LNCS 4039, pp. 386–389, 2006.
© Springer-Verlag Berlin Heidelberg 2006

- A specific Software Development Process (SDP) must be applied to produce SW, which is usually quite different from classical SDPs.
- Comprehensive training processes must be performed.
- Extra efforts must be done in identifying commonalities and variabilities (C/V). In fact, C/V identification is the core activity of the classical reuse processes.
- Extra efforts must be spent in supporting C/V knowledge.
- It is not easy to find in the market CASE applications fully supporting the reuse process.

We believe these difficulties, in addition to the fact that the retrieval technology to find artifacts by semantic content was non-existent, have been the key factors for the low impact of software reuse among software development professionals.

2   Software Reuse So Far

The literature offers more than 30 different definitions of reuse and software reuse, many of them with different shades. The 90s showed up several good definitions, like the IEEE [3]: '...a software module or other work product that can be used in more than one computer program or software system'. Ezran, Morisio, and Tully stated, in 2002 [2] that '...is the systematic practice of developing software from a stock of building blocks, so that similarities in requirements and/or architecture between applications can be exploited to achieve substantial benefits in productivity, quality and business performance'.

All of these definitions, covering nearly 40 years of experience, guide software reusers to develop new products by "finding" and using existing work-products in new projects, yet this has certainly NOT been applied in practice. Hence, the approach to reuse was transformed into coping with commonality and variability in order to define forthcoming reusable assets: this implies performing domain engineering in advance. The results of this process were pre-modeled assets: Product Lines (PLs), Generators, Frameworks... and everybody must/should (re)use them. As a consequence to this philosophy, the reuse process had to be adapted to this way of proceeding, and ROI issues appear. The investments to introduce reuse within an organization are significant and depend on forthcoming issues like how the domain is going to react in the future. Usually organizations don't like this uncertain approach, and reuse suffers from it.

3   Incremental Reuse Method (IRM)

The Incremental Reuse Method (IRM) approach minimizes the previously presented drawbacks in order to offer a very attractive set of conditions for an organization to "jump into" reuse. For us, those conditions are:

- It must be possible to introduce SW Reuse based on the argument that investment should be minimal, almost zero.

- The introduction of Software Reuse must not impact the internal Software Development Process in any significant way. The software engineers should carry on their own SDP (perhaps with slight differences).
- Introducing Software Reuse doesn't have to imply heavy training activities.
- It must be possible to introduce Software Reuse incrementally; no need to have or model anything for reuse in advance. The artifacts from the finished projects become the reusable artifacts for the new ones.
- The Software Reuse process must be robust against business dynamics (domain changes) and technology evolution.
- ROI does not have to be the most important decision factor: Organizations should be able to consider other criteria as well: Quality Improvement Issues, Time To Market, Knowledge Management, Knowledge Value as an asset in the organization.

The IRM meets these conditions.

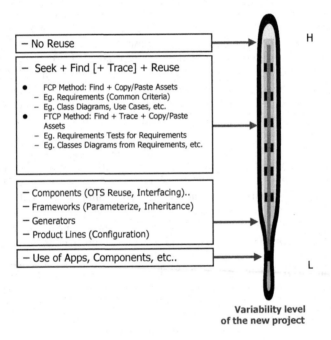

Fig. 1. C/V modeling in IRM

In IRM, the assets retrieval techniques and tools are considered essential. To succeed with this approach, a repository must be able to represent all different artifacts' contents independently of their typology, as well as provide retrieval algorithms for finding artifacts by content. In IRM, the repository representation schema is based on the RSHP meta-model [5]. Aside from enhanced semantic retrieval, IRM embraces the Commonality/Variability study as a need to provide better support to universal reuse.

The most important aspects of the C/V modeling in IRM is that it is possible to perform reuse in extremely high variability needs (including inter-domain reuse) through the Seek + Find + Trace Navigation (SFT) Reuse (See Fig 1 above).

Therefore, our working definition for reuse focuses on Retrieval and C/V Engineering:

Reuse is the use of all kinds of [known or unknown] previously created artifacts (assets) in a new project, but:

Slightly modified to fit with the problem or solution definition in the new project (e.g. a design pattern applied to my particular domain) or Which were defined to work in a different context or environment or application (e.g. a set of requirements coming from a different application project) or Which needed to be configured to fit with project requirements or specifications (e.g. a product line configured to a new product) or Where only parts of them were incorporated to the new project (e.g. An association between two UML classes coming from a previous UML Class diagram).

In order to put into practice the previous statements, the Incremental Reuse Method pretends to offer a framework for the creation of a Reuse Unit within every interested organization without huge investments. It is based on the Domain, Roles, Process and Technology.

4   Conclusions

This article has proposed a method to solve the applicability problems of classical reuse methods. The proposed process allows incremental adoption, without modifying the organization's software development process, at low cost, and with robustness to domain evolution. The Incremental Reuse Method (IRM) is based on offering retrieval and reuse of artifacts to all activities in the software development process. These artifacts are stored in a repository that is maintained through incremental indexing of all work products of an organization's projects. Its low implementation cost and minimal impact on existing SDP activities have given high success rates in actual implementation cases. We have successfully implemented IRM in several industrial settings.

References

[1] K.C. Desouza, Y Awazu, A. Tiwana: "Four dynamics for bringing use back into software reuse." Communications of the ACM, 49(1), January 2006.
[2] M. Ezran, M. Morisio, C. Tully: Practical Software Reuse. Practitioner Series, Springer 2002.
[3] IEEE Std 610.12-1990. IEEE Standard Glossary of Software Engineering (1990).
[4] I. Jacobson, M. Griss, P. Jonsson: Software Reuse: Architecture, Process and Organization for Business Success. ACM Press. Addison Wesley 1997.
[5] J. Llorens, J. Morato, G. Genova, "RSHP: An information representation model based on relationships." In: Ernesto Damiani, Lakhmi C. Jain, Mauro Madravio (Eds.), Soft Computing in Software Engineering (Studies in Fuzziness and Soft Computing Series, Vol. 159), Springer 2004, pp 221-253.

Variability in Goal-Oriented Domain Requirements

Farida Semmak and Joël Brunet

LACL, Université Paris XII, CRI, Université Paris I
{semmak, brunet}@univ-paris12.fr

Abstract. The aim of the paper is to present a framework to contribute to the improvement of requirements elicitation by reusing domain models. In our approach, a domain model gathers goals organized in goal hierarchies associated with domain rules and materialized in conceptual fragments. A conceptual fragment represents an abstract view of the specification allowing the realization of a given goal. To construct a system, the designer will extract requirements from the domain model and adapt the obtained conceptual fragments to the context of the system. Two principles are used to represent domain models: abstraction, which allows the description of common properties of a given domain, and variability, which allows the description of discriminatory properties of the domain. In our approach, variability is applied on the three levels: goal, domain rule and conceptual fragment.

1 Introduction

It is recognized that one of the main reasons of project failures lies in errors in expressing requirements, and more particularly in an erroneous interpretation of the real world. Reuse-based engineering is one of the most promise ways to increase software productivity and quality. More particularly, applying a reuse process at the requirements engineering step may contribute to improve the overall system development process [1, 2].

We present a framework to contribute to the improvement of requirements elicitation by reusing domain models. We propose to describe and organize the domain knowledge in the form of knowledge fragments [3]. The set of the knowledge fragments forms a domain model that may be made available to the designer in order to construct the future system. This domain model gathers the common properties of a class of systems as well as its discriminating properties.

2 The Domain Model

2.1 Concepts for Abstraction

The aim is to describe a set of knowledge fragments related to a class of systems in a given domain. A knowledge fragment is a triplet <goal, business rule, conceptual fragment> in which the goal represents the usage intention, the business rule a domain law with which the goal is consistent, and the conceptual fragment a behavior

M. Morisio (Ed.): ICSR 2006, LNCS 4039, pp. 390–394, 2006.

dependency between actors and objects allowing the satisfaction of the goal. Building an application by reuse consists of instantiating knowledge fragments, that is: a) to select the goals relevant for the organization; b) to select the domain rules; c) to adapt the associated conceptual fragments to the context.

The concepts allowing to describe a knowledge fragment are now presented.

Definition 1. a goal defines a potential requirement that systems might satisfy; it expresses what the end-user would wish to do.

A goal has a name and is described by a verb and at the most two parameters [4]. The verb represents an action that the user would wish to do. The first parameter represents a domain entity, which is the main object of the goal, and the second one expresses the means by which a goal may be satisfied. For instance, the goal *'To consult documents on internet'* has for verb *'to consult'*, for object *'document'* and for means *'on internet '*.

The goals form a tree structure (see figure 1) where the leaf nodes represent operational goals to which conceptual fragments are associated, while higher-level leaves represent abstract goals.

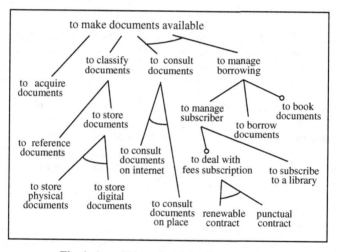

Fig. 1. A goal hierarchy of the library domain

To each goal are associated rules governing its realization.

Definition 2. a business rule defines a rule of the domain to which the goal must conform; it is described by a name and a rule expression.

Business rules are determined prior to the definition of the business process that has to be implemented for reaching a goal. They represent laws of the domain to which a goal must conform. They have an impact on the behavior of future systems, because they are taken into account in conceptual fragments.

There are of three types: ordering rules, triggering rules and safety properties. An *ordering rule* expresses the order in which the subgoals of an abstract goal must be carried out. A *triggering rule* is defined by a context that defines the situation in which the rule applies, a set of conditions and a process. A *safety property* is a rule of the domain that must always be satisfied in order to ensure the correct functioning of a system.

Definition 3. a conceptual fragment expresses some behavioral dependencies between the elements of the domain that interact in order to accomplish a goal.

A conceptual fragment expresses the materialization of a goal in accordance with the business rules. It represents the reusable knowledge, that is, the knowledge that must be adapted to obtain the model of the future system. For instance, the realization of the goal *'To acquire documents'* requires that the librarian put in orders of documents from suppliers. There are an actor (*librarian*), some domain objects (*document* and *supplier*), and some events (*document order* and *document receipt*).

A conceptual fragment can be summarized as a joint description of static and dynamic aspects. It expresses, at a generic level, a contractual relationship between domain objects and actors: its effective reuse may lead to different solutions according to the organizational context.

2.2   Concepts for Variability

The issue is to highlight the discriminatory elements between systems of a given domain. To express the variability of the domain, we adapt the *feature* concept of the method Foda [5] to the three concepts of goal, business rule and conceptual fragment.

Two types of features allow variability at the goal level:

- a *Feature* property, attached to each goal, defines its mandatory or optional characteristic (graphically represented by a small circle, see figure 1).
- a *RefinementFeature* property may be attached to a father goal to express the different ways of refining it. A set (or a subset) of child goals is related by an *inclusive OR* and is graphically represented by an arc between them. This means that the analyst must choose at least one among these child goals.

Two types of features allow variability at the business rules level:

- a *FeatureTR* property, attached to each condition of a triggering rule, is either *'mandatory'* or *'optional'*. It provides a flexible means of combining the conditions that lead to satisfying the goal. For instance, the condition *'AvailableBudget'* is mandatory while the condition *'IncreasingBorrowingRequest'* is optional, in the *'DocumentPurchaser'* triggering rule.
- a *FeatureSP* property, attached to a safety property, is either *'mandatory'* or *'optional'*. For instance, the safety property defining the maximum number of borrowed document (depending on the document type or the period) is mandatory.

The variability at the conceptual fragment level is taken into account in domain objects. As in Foda, a feature – mandatory or optional – is attached to each property of a domain object. Moreover, generalizing and parameterizing techniques are used in order to differentiate systems.

In summary, the variability principle allows to consider the elements that discriminate systems of a given domain. The degree of discrimination varies depending on the goal, business rule or conceptual fragment level. The choice of goals has a great impact on the structure of the future system, because they express requirements of high abstraction level. After choosing a goal, one must determine the business rules with which it should be consistent. Finally, the conceptual fragment associated to the goal has to be adapted to the selected business rules.

3 Related Works

Domain engineering, as a support to requirements engineering, is a process that consists, on the one hand, of eliciting the domain knowledge, structuring it, abstracting it and, on the other hand, specifying a domain model. This model must be sufficiently generic to constitute a framework to be used in the development of any system of the same domain.

In the literature, there are two categories of approaches: the first ones apprehend the requirements as objects and rules [1, 2, 5]. They use models like E/R, state diagrams, object models and so on, in order to represent the common elements for all applications of a given domain. However, each approach proposes its own solution to represent the discriminatory elements. The FORM method [5] has been the first one to propose the concept of *feature*, defined as *a prominent or distinctive user-visible aspect, quality or characteristic of a software system or systems*. The concept of feature has been widely used and extended [6]. The second ones propose the goal as a key concept for eliciting system requirements [2, 4, 7] and for reuse [2, 8]. These approaches are oriented towards the expression of problems. The model of the Elektra project [8, 9] combines the goal concept with a classification by facets[9].

4 Conclusion

In this paper, we presented a framework that allows representing knowledge fragments that may be reused for building an information system. Knowledge fragments elaboration is based upon two principles: the abstraction principle, which takes into account the common characteristics of a system class in a given domain, and the variability principle, which allows emphasizing the discriminatory characteristics of these systems. Future works will be pursued in several directions: to take into account non-functional goals, to elaborate processes for domain knowledge identification and reuse, and to implement it in a tool intended to application engineers.

References

[1] Arango G., Domain Analysis Methods, in Software Reusability, Eds by W. Schäfer, R.Prieto Diaz & M. Matsumoto, Ellis Horwood, 1994
[2] Dardenne A., Lamsweerde A., Fickas S., Goal-oriented Requirements Acquisition, Science of computer, 20(1-2) April 1993
[3] Semmak F., Brunet J., A Metamodel for Domain Requirements Elicitation, LACL technical report, may 2005

[4] Rolland C., Souveyet C., BenAchour C., Guiding Goal Modelling Using Scenarios, IEEE TSE, Special issue on scenario Management, 1998

[5] Kang K., Kim S., Lee J. et al., FORM: A Feature-Oriented Reuse Method with Domain-Specific Reference Architectures, Software Engineering, 5, 143-168, 1998

[6] Griss M., Favaro J., D'Alessandro M., Integrating Feature Modeling with the RSEB, ICSR'98, pages 76–85, Vancouver, Canada, Juin 1998

[7] Lamsweerde A. Goal-oriented Requirements Engineering: A guided tour, Proc.RE'01, 5th IEEE Int. Symposium on RE., Toronto, 2001

[8] Prekas N., Loucopoulos P., Rolland C., Grosz G., Semmak F., Brash D., Developing Patterns for Assisting the Management of Knowledge, DEXA'99

[9] Prieto-Diaz R., Freeman, P., Classifying Software for Reusability, IEEE Software, Vol. 4, No. 1, Jan. 1987

Variability Modeling in a Component-Based Domain Engineering Process

Ana Paula Terra Bacelo Blois[1, 2], Regiane Felipe de Oliveira[1], Natanael Maia[1],
Cláudia Werner[1], and Karin Becker[2]

[1] Federal University of Rio de Janeiro
COPPE/UFRJ – System Engineering and Computer Science Program
P.O. Box 68511 – ZIP 21945-970 – Rio de Janeiro – RJ – Brazil
[2] PUCRS - Catholic University of Rio Grande do Sul
Av. Ipiranga, 6681 – Prédio 30 – Bloco 4 – ZIP 90619-900 - Porto Alegre – RS- Brazil
{anablois, regiane, ntmaia, werner} @cos.ufrj.br,
{anapaula, kbecker}@inf.pucrs.br

Abstract. Domain Engineering (DE) and Component-based Development (CBD) are approaches that focus on reuse. On the one hand, DE methods emphasize variability modeling in analysis phase. On the other hand, most CBD methods gude on the development of components, with a minor focus on reusability properties. This paper presents an approach to support variability modeling, in a Component-based Domain Engineering Process.

1 Introduction

Domain Engineering (DE) aims at identifying and modeling common and variable features for an application domain, in order to generate reusable artifacts [13]. In a DE process, domain variability must be modeled throughout the whole software life cycle (i.e. analysis, design and implementation), such that domain requirements are consistently captured in artifacts that represent the domain at different abstraction levels. In general, DE methods (e.g. [8], [9], [12], [14]) offer a better support to the domain analysis phase. However, Application Engineering expects to reuse artifacts from different phases, particularly design and implementation, in the construction of a specific application. DE methods lack a proper notation for addressing domain variability in artifacts of different phases, as well as mechanisms to guarantee consistency among corresponding artifacts.

CBD (Component-Based Development) is another approach targeted at reuse. However, although CBD methods (e.g. [3], [5], [7] and [1]) provide guidance for generating components, the inherent variability of a family of applications (or domain) is rarely considered.

CBD-Arch-De is an approach that combines concepts and techniques from both DE and CBD. The striking features of CBD-Arch-De are: a) a more complete notation to variability modeling, addressing different abstraction levels and types of artifacts; b) a DE process focused on CBD; c) heuristics to support the mapping of variability throughout different domain artifacts; d) criteria to support the creation of architectural elements [2]; and, e) support for mapping technology-independent components

M. Morisio (Ed.): ICSR 2006, LNCS 4039, pp. 395–398, 2006.
© Springer-Verlag Berlin Heidelberg 2006

into technology-dependent ones using a transformation model approach, based on MDA [12]. All features are supported by the Odyssey Environment [11].

This paper discusses how CDB-Arch-De supports variability modeling during all phases of DE, and how mapping heuristics are employed to consistently generate artifacts in accordance to domain requirements. The remainder of this paper is organized as follows: Section 2 explores variability and modeling issues in CDB-Arch-DE and final considerations are addressed in Section 3.

2   Variability Modeling in CDB-Arch-DE

In order to model variability, it is necessary to represent all domain concepts and their relationships explicitly, allowing stakeholders (e.g. users, domain experts) to understand each other [10]. The Features Model is the starting point of all domain modeling activities. CBD-Arch-DE introduces the Odyssey-FEX notation for specifying a feature model, which extends the FODA notation. In Odyssey-FEX, all features must be represented according to three dimensions: category (i.e. conceptual, functional or technological), variability (i.e. variation point, variant or invariant) and optionality (i.e. mandatory or optional). This classification schema influences not only the construction of artifacts in the DE process, but the AE process as well.

In Odyssey-FEX, features are related to each other using UML relationships (e.g. association, aggregation and composition). In addition, the notation proposes the *Alternative relationship*, which is used among variation point features and their variant, as well as *composition rules* (i.e. inclusive and exclusive) with boolean operators, to represent inclusive or exclusive constraints upon features.

From the features model, other domain artifacts are derived that represent requirements at different stages of the development process, namely *Business Types*, *Use Cases* and *Components*. To capture variability in these artifacts, UML stereotypes are proposed, which are used in combination with UML relationships to preserve domain requirements semantics. In this sense, variability is represented by <<variation point>>, <<variant>>> stereotypes and optionality is represented by the <<optional>> stereotype. Artifacts that are not stereotypes are invariant or mandatory. The inclusive composition rules are represented by relationships that already exist in other notations (e.g. composition relationships among business types and required interfaces among components). On the other hand, the exclusive rules are represented by a <<XOR>> stereotype in the involved domain artifacts.

The main phases of CBD-Arch-DE process are depicted in Figure 1, together with the respective artifacts. Further details on the process workflows can be found in [2]. Each type of artifact represents domain requirements according to a point of view and abstraction level. Starting from the features models, artifacts are recursively generated one from another as a result of DE analysis, design or implementation activities. These generation activities are supported by mapping heuristics, in order to consistently propagate the variability to all domain artifacts. Heuristics were proposed for mapping: a) conceptual features into business types (BT), b) functional features into use cases (UC), c) Business Types into Business Components (BC), d) Use Cases into Process Components (PC) and e) technological features into technological components (IC and UIC). In total, 33 heuristics were proposed, some of them illustrated in Table 1.

The last phase is the Domain Implementation phase, in which Odyssey-MDA approach is used. Odyssey-MDA allows the developer to perform transformations of platform independent component models, known as *PIM* (*Platform Independent Model*), into platform specific component models, known as *PSM* (*Platform Specific Model*) (e.g. EJB) and, later, to generate code for these components. The Domain Engineer defines the desired platforms and the necessary transformations. After that, the elements of the components model are prepared with a marking mechanism (e.g. business stereotype in business component) that guides the execution of further transformations. The Domain Engineer chooses a previously defined platform. Then, a PIM is transformed into a specific model (PSM) for this platform. A representation in source-code of the PSM is generated in the selected platform programming language.

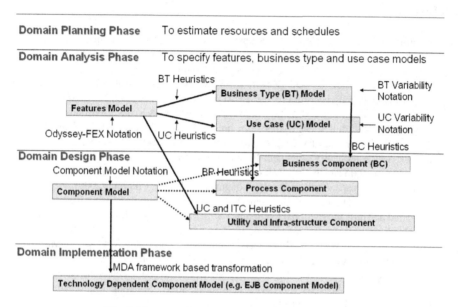

Fig. 1. Phases and Models of CBD-Arch-DE Process

3 Final Considerations

This paper presented an approach to variability modeling in DE, which is part of the CBD-Arch-DE process. The paper discussed variability modeling across artifacts of different abstraction levels, and how the DE process employs heuristics to map variability into domain artifacts of lower level abstraction levels. Other features and a systematic approach to transform PIM into PSM and criteria to group components into architectural elements (which were not discussed in this paper). Observational studies are under definition to evaluate the feasibility of all activities of the CBD-Arch-DE.

DE and CBD methods neither propose guidelines nor mechanisms to support the reference architecture construction, considering the domain variability. In this sense, the presented approach provides a supporting infrastructure that can help the domain engineer to obtain more valuable domain architectures which can be reused by domain analysts.

Table 1. Examples of Heuristics to guide de mapping through domain artifacts

Categories	Heuristics
BT	Each conceptual feature may be mapped to a business type.
UC	Each functional feature must be mapped to a use case.
BC	If mandatory and optional business types are grouped, then the resultant component must keep the mandatory property.
UC	Each domain technology feature must be mapped into a utility component.

References

1. Atkinson, C., Bayer, J., Bunse, C., Kamsties, E., Laitenberger, O., Laqua, R., Muthig, D., Paech, B., Wüst, J., and Zettel, J.: Component-based product line engineering with UML. Addison-Wesley Longman Publishing Co., Inc, Boston (2002)

2. Blois, A. P., Werner, C., and Becker, K.: Towards a Components Grouping Technique within a Domain Engineering Process. EUROMICRO, Porto, September (2005) 18-25.

3. Braga, R. M. M., Werner, C.M.L., Mattoso, M.: Odyssey: A Reuse Environment Based on Domain Models. 2nd IEEE Symposium on Application-Specific Systems and Software Engineering Technology (ASSET'99), Richardson, USA, March (1999) 50-57

4. Brown, A.: Large-Scale Component-Base Development. Prentice Hall (2000)

5. Cheesman, J. and Daniels, J.: UML components: a Simple Process for Specifying Component-based Software. Addison-Wesley Longman Publishing Co., Inc. (2000)

6. K. Czarnecki, S. Helsen, and U. Eisenecker, "Staged configuration using feature models," presented at Third International Conference Softtware Product Lines: SPLC 2004, Boston, MA, USA, 2004.

7. D'Souza, D. F. and Wills, A. C.: Objects, components, and frameworks with UML: the catalysis approach. Addison-Wesley Longman Publishing Co., Inc. (1999)

8. Kang, K. C., Cohen, S. G., Hess, J. A., Novak, W. E., and Peterson, A. S.: Feature-Oriented Domain Analysis (FODA) - Feasibility Study. Software Engineering Institute (SEI), CMU/SEI-90-TR-21 (1990)

9. Kang, K. C., Lee, J., and Donohoe, P.: Feature-Oriented Product Line Engineering. IEEE Software, Vol. 9, no. 4, Jul./Aug 2002 (2002) 58-65

10. Massen, T. V. d. and Lichter, H.: Modeling Variability by UML Use Case Diagrams. Proceedings REPL02 - International Workshop on Requirements Engineering for Product Lines, Essen, Germany, September, 2002 (2002) 19-31

11. Odyssey: Odyssey SDE. In: http://reuse.cos.ufrj.br/odyssey, Accessed in: 25/11/2005

12. OMG: MDA Guide Version 1.0.1. In: http://www.omg.org/docs/omg/03-06-01.pdf, Accessed in: 08/09/2005

13. Prieto-Diaz, R. and Arango, G.: Domain Analysis Concepts and Research Directions. In: Prieto-Diaz, R. and Arango, G. eds.): Domain Analysis and Software Systems Modeling. IEEE Computer Society Press (1991) 312

14. Riebisch, M; Böllert, K.; Streitferdt, D. and Philippow, I. "Extending Feature Diagrams with UML Multiplicities," presented at Proceedings of 6th Conference on Integrated Design & Process Technology, Pasadena,California, USA, 2002.

GENMADEM: A Methodology for Generative Multi-agent Domain Engineering

Mauro Jansen and Rosario Girardi

Federal University of Maranhão (UFMA),
Av. dos Portugueses, s/n, Campus do Bacanga, CEP 65080-040, São Luís–MA, Brasil
maurojansen@yahoo.com.br, rgirardi@deinf.ufma.br

Abstract. The generative approach is one of the most productive ways to promote the automatic reuse in software product lines. Multi-Agent Domain Engineering is a process to build multi-agent system families. This paper describes GENMADEM, an ontology-based methodology for generative multi-agent domain engineering whose main products are ontology-based domain models, domain specific languages and application generators.

Keywords: Generative Software Reuse; Multi-Agent Systems Development Methodologies; Domain Engineering; Domain Specific Languages; Generators.

1 Introduction

The generative development of software is an approach based on Software Reuse [10], Domain Engineering [2][8] and Software Generators [1][2][9], that aims the study and definition of methods that allow the production of software through the reuse of existing artifacts, in a rapid and systematized way, facilitating their maintenance and reducing their development costs.

A software product family [12] is a set of software products with similar features enough to allow the definition of a reuse infrastructure for their mass production. Domain Engineering provides this infrastructure defining a development process for reuse, collecting the knowledge about software development in a specific domain in the form of reusable software artifacts and providing support to reuse them. In this generative approach, products of Domain Engineering are Domain Models, Domain-specific frameworks, Domain Specific Languages (DSLs) and Application Generators. DSLs [3][11][14] are programming or specification languages with high abstraction level, vocabulary near to the one used by domain experts and expressive force focused on a particular domain.

In the process of Application Engineering, complementary to the one of Domain Engineering, a generator is used to map the specification of an application in a DSL to a specific application of the system family.

MADEP ("Multi-Agent Domain Engineering Process") is a process for the development of DSLs and application generators to build multi-agent system families in specific domains.

This paper introduces GENMADEM, a methodology supporting the MADEP process.

M. Morisio (Ed.): ICSR 2006, LNCS 4039, pp. 399–402, 2006.

2   The GENMADEM Methodology

GENMADEM ("Generative Multi-Agent Domain Engineering Methodology") is methodology that integrates and extends the MADEM methodology [5] and the TOD-DSL technique [7], providing a generative and ontology-based approach to Multi-agent Domain Engineering. The methodology is supported by ONTOGENMADEM, an ontology-driven tool for the specification of DSLs and design of application generators directly from domain models created in the domain analysis phase of MADEM.

Figure 1 shows the MADEP generative process of Multi-agent Domain Engineering. The process consists of six phases (domain analysis, domain design, domain implementation, pattern extraction and representation, DSL specification and DSL generator development). Based on the analysis of existent specific applications, knowledge of the domain and requirements of a family of systems, the phase of domain analysis, supported by the GRAMO technique [4], produces a domain model that represents the common and variable requirements of the systems in the domain and the dependences among them. The Domain Design phase, supported by the DDEMAS [6] technique, produces a set of models of domain-specific frameworks that are reusable multi-agent solutions to those requirements. In the Domain Implementation phase, software agents integrating these frameworks are created. The pattern extraction and representation, supported by pattern extraction and represent-tation guidelines and development experiences, produces software patterns and pattern systems that can be reused in the phases of both Domain Engineering and Application Engineering. Until this point, reuse is compositional. The phases "DSL Specification" and "Generator Development" approach the generative reuse. The DSL Specification phase, supported by the TOD-DSL technique, produces a DSL based on a set of domain models. The Generator Development phase produces an Application Generator based on the DSL and the reusable multi-agent frameworks.

GENMADEM improves the variability modeling technique initially proposed by GRAMO [4], including ideas from feature modeling [2]. The GENMADEM specification is supported by the ONTOGENMADEM tool, where all the products of GENMADEM are represented as instances of an ontology representing its develop-ment knowledge. The ONTOGENMADEM tool was designed and imple-mented as a plug-in of the knowledge-based development environment Protégé [13]. The phases of GENMADEM, listed in Table 1, are described as follows.

DSL Specification. In this phase, the vocabulary, grammar and semantics of the DSL is specified through the instantiation of the classes "DSL Vocabulary" and "DSL Grammar" of the ONTOGENMADEM ontology. The DSL specification is fully automated in ONTOGENMADEM starting from the analysis of the common and variable requirements of the family specified in a domain model. The DSL semantics is supplied by the semantic relationships among the terms of the vocabulary and the instances of the ontology. The pragmatics specification phase documents all the aspects of use of the DSL. It must include descriptions of the DSL, domain, vocabulary, syntax, generator and examples.

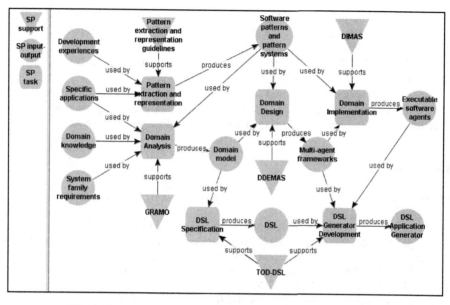

Fig. 1. The generative process of Multi-agent Domain Engineering

Table 1. GENMADEM phases and tasks

Phases	Tasks	Products
DSL Specification	Syntax Specification	Vocabulary and grammar
	Semantics specification	DSL Semantics
	Pragmatic specification	DSL documentation
Generator design	Configuration rules definition	Exigibility and mutual exclusion rules
	Mappings definition	Configuration mappings

Generator Design. The generator design includes two tasks: the definition of the configuration rules and the configuration mappings. The configuration rules are the details that identify the valid and invalid combinations among the concepts selected in a DSL program, and they are done in the form of exigibility rules and mutual exclusion rules. The mappings define the knowledge of how the generator makes the mapping of the DSL high-level abstractions for implementation-oriented abstractions in the reused domain-specific frameworks.

3   Concluding Remarks and Further Work

Generative software development is gaining importance in Software Engineering, but there are still few related works in the multi-agent system engineering community. The increasing demand of multi-agent systems turns this approach attractive, especially, when time and development cost reduction are goals and when the number of systems in the family justify the cost of the generator construct.

This paper introduced GENMADEM, a generative methodology for Multi-agent Domain Engineering that aims the development of DSLs and generators to allow generative reuse of multi-agent system families.

ONTOGENMADEM, a Protégé plug-in for the application of GENMADEM has been developed for vocabulary and code generation.

A case study is being conducted to evaluate MADEM and ONTOGENMADEM, consisting on the construction of a DSL and application generator for the development of information filtering and retrieval multi-agent applications.

References

1. Cleveland, J.C.: Program Generators with Java and XML". Prentice Hall, Inc., Upper Saddle River, NJ (2001)
2. Czarnacki, K.: Generative Programming: Principles and Techniques of Software Engineering Based on Automated Configuration and Fragment-Based Component Models. Ph.D. thesis, Technische Universität Ilmenau, Germany (1998).
3. Deursen, A., Klint, P., Visser, J.: Domain-specific languages: An annotated bibliography. ACM SIGPLAN Notices, (2000) 35(6): 26-36
4. Girardi, R., Faria, C.: An Ontology-Based Technique for the Specification of Domain and User Models in Multi-Agent Domain Engineering. CLEI Electronic Journal, V. 7, N. 1, Pap. 7. (2004)
5. Girardi, R., Lindoso, A.: An Ontology-based Methodology for Multi-agent Domain Engineering. In: 3rd Workshop on Multi-Agent Systems: Theory and Applications (MASTA 2005) at 12th Portuguese Conference on Artificial Intelligence (EPIA 2005), Ed. IEEE. Covilhã, Portugal. (2005)
6. Girardi, R., Lindoso, A.: DDEMAS: A Domain Design Technique for Multi-agent Domain Engineering. Lecture Notes in Computer Science, Perspectives in Conceptual Modeling: ER 2005 Workshops CAOIS, BP-UML, CoMoGIS, eCOMO, and QoIS, Vol. 3770/2005, ISSN 0302-9743., Ed. Springer-Verlag GmbH, pp. 141-150. Klagenfurt, Austria. (2005) 24-28
7. Girardi, R., Serra, I.: Using Ontologies for the Specification of Domain-Specific Languages in Multi-Agent Domain Engineering. In: Proceedings of the Sixth International Bi-Conference Workshop on Agent-oriented Information Systems (AOIS-2004) at The 16th International Conference on Advanced Information Systems Engineering (CAISE'04), Riga, Latvia (2004) pp 295-308
8. Harsu, M.: A Survey of Domain Engineering". Report 31, Institute of Software Systems. Tampere University of Technology. (2002)
9. Herrington, Jack.: "Code Generation in Action". Manning, Greenwich, CT. (2003)
10. Krueger, C. W.: Software Reuse., ACM Computing Surveys 24 (1992), 134-183.
11. Mernik, M., Heering, J., Sloane, Anthony M.: When and How to Develop Domain-Specific Languages. Stichting Centrum voor Wiskunde en Informatica (2003)
12. Parnas, D. L.: On the design and development of program families. IEEE Transactions on Software Engineering, SE-2(1):1-9, (1976)
13. The Protégé Project. Available at: http://protege.stanford.edu.
14. Widen, T. and Hook, J.: Software design automation: Language design in the context of Domain Engineering. In the 10th International Conference on Software Engineering & Knowledge Engineering (SEKE'98), San Francisco Bay, California (1998) pp 308-317

Product Line Architecture for a Family of Meshing Tools*

María Cecilia Bastarrica[1], Nancy Hitschfeld-Kahler[1], and Pedro O. Rossel[1,2]

[1] Computer Science Department, FCFM, Universidad de Chile, Chile
[2] Dept. Computación e Informática, Universidad Católica del Maule, Chile
{cecilia|nancy|prossel}@dcc.uchile.cl

Abstract. Meshing tools are traditionally built in a one by one basis without reusing already developed parts. However, there are several concepts within this application domain that are present in most tools. Developing software components implementing these concepts is extremely time consuming and requires highly specialized programmers. Software product lines is a way of systematically reusing assets. We propose a layered product line architecture for meshing tools. We specify it formally using xADL, and we show that it fits some already built tools.

1 Introduction

A mesh is a discretization of a domain; meshing tools generate and manage these discretizations. Meshing tools are inherently sophisticated software due to the complexity of the concepts involved, the big amount of interacting elements they manage, and the application domains where they are used. They need to accomplish specific sophisticated functionality while still having a good performance; lately, however, modifiability and flexibility have also become relevant.

There are many domains where meshing tools are used ranging from mechanics design to medicine [6], each domain requires slightly different functionality. Software engineering practices have seldom been used in meshing tool development though there have been some efforts lately mainly building general purpose libraries and using object-orientation and design patterns. In the software product line approach, the product line architecture (PLA) is reused by all software products in the family [3]. Therefore, the PLA should be carefully designed making sure it will produce software that complies with the desired requirements.

We present the PLA for a family of meshing tools that promotes flexibility and modifiability, so different existing algorithms, data structures, data formats and visualizers could be combined in different ways to produce different tools. Our PLA follows the layered architectural pattern [4]. Sometimes it is argued that layered architectures penalize performance, but we have seen that performance does not degrade significantly with the proposed PLA. We formally define the PLA using xADL 2.0 [5]; this language has shown to be appropriate to specify PLAs. We show already implemented tools as examples of our product family.

---

* The work of Nancy Hitschfeld was supported by Fondecyt N°1061227. The work of Pedro Rossel was supported by grant No. UCH 0109 from MECESUP, Chile.

M. Morisio (Ed.): ICSR 2006, LNCS 4039, pp. 403–406, 2006.

2   Product Line Architecture

Independently of the application domain, any meshing tool should provide certain general functionality: read the domain geometry and physical values, generate an initial mesh, refine, derefine or smooth a mesh according to a quality criterion, and finally store the mesh into a file.

The PLA limits the product line scope, but at the same time it should be flexible to allow designers to build all desired tools. Flexibility and interchangeability guide our PLA design, this is why we chose a layered architecture. Figure 1 shows the specification of the meshing tool PLA using ArchStudio [1]. The architecture is composed by four layers: *User Interface*, *Algorithms*, *Model* and *Input Output*. In xADL, each layer is defined as a structure; Figure 2 shows the xADL specification of the Refine module.

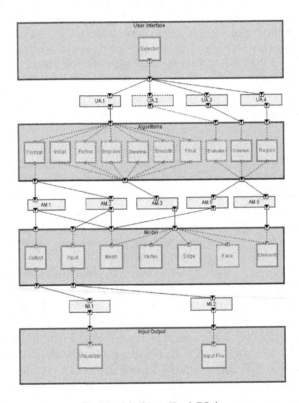

Fig. 1. Meshing Tool PLA

Refine and/or improve represent the core functionality of a meshing tool. In our PLA, both are presented as optional even though it may seem counter intuitive. The Face module in the Model layer is also optional; in 3D tools there must exist a Face module, but it is meaningless in 2D.

As we can see in Figures 1 and 2, Refine exposes two interfaces, called *Refine.Top* and *Refine.Bottom*, respectively. The former has the direction *in*,

```
- <types:component types:id="Refine" xsi:type="types:Component">
    <types:description xsi:type="instance:Description">
        Refine module</types:description>
    - <types:interface types:id="Refine.Top" xsi:type="types:Interface">
        <types:description xsi:type="instance:Description">
            Top interface</types:description>
        <types:direction xsi:type="instance:Direction"> in</types:direction>
    </types:interface>
    - <types:interface types:id="Refine.Bottom" xsi:type="types:Interface">
        <types:description xsi:type="instance:Description">
            Bottom interface< /types:description>
        <types:direction xsi:type="instance:Direction"> out</types:direction>
    </types:interface>
    + <options:optional xsi:type="options:Optional">
</types:component>
```

Fig. 2. `Refine` Module Specification

and the latter *out*; so this component can be used by any component in the upper layer, and it may use other modules in the lower layer, following the rules of the layered architectural pattern. As `Refine` is optional, its xADL specification includes the `options:optional` tag indicating optionality.

3   Product Instantiation

Designing a meshing product has two stages: component type selection and implementation selection. First, the component types are chosen; here some of the optional component types may not be included. Then, a particular implementation is chosen for every selected component type. Thus, different meshing tools may differ in their functionality or in their implementation. For example, simulating semiconductor devices using the control volume method requires to have anisotropic Delaunay conforming meshes where no part of a Voronoi region of an

Table 1. 2D control volume mesh and 3D control volume mesh

Comp. Type	Description
Selector	Allows to enter a specific improvement region and criterion, and also to choose the following algorithm to be applied (either `Improve` or `Final`)
Initial	Reads the already generated Delaunay mesh
Improve	Applies the `Delaunay_improvement_algorithm` to the specified region with a certain criterion
Final	Post-processes the mesh eliminating obtuse angles opposite to the boundary (`Non_obtuse_boundary_algorithm`)
Criterion	Improvement criteria such as `Maximum_edge_vertex_connectivity` and `Maximum_angle`
Region	Region to be improved; `Whole_geometry` is used, but it may also be `Circle`
Selector	Allows to enter a list of criteria and their associated regions, and then the whole process is invoked
Initial	Reads the geometry and generates a first coarse mesh (`Fit_Device_Geometry`)
Refine	Divides element in order to fit physical and geometric parameter values (`Refine_Grid`)
Final	Improves elements in order to fulfill the Voronoi region requirement and generates the final mixed element mesh (`Make_Irregular_Leaves_Splittable`)
Region	Regions where the refinement is applied, e.g. cuboid or rectangle, among others
Criterion	`Doping_Difference` and `Longest_Edge` as the main refinement criteria
Format	Outputs the mesh in a format understandable by the visualizer (`Write_Geometrical_Information` and `Write_Doping_Information`)

internal point is outside the domain. In 2D, this is fulfilled if there is no obtuse angle opposite to boundary/interface edges. In 3D, for each boundary face the center of the smallest circumsphere must be inside the domain. Large angles inside the domain and high vertex edge connectivity must also be avoided.

In [2], a tool for the simulation of semiconductor devices using the control volume method is described. Here the mesh is read in a format the tool is able to understand, so the `Format` component has a dummy functionality. This tool is used for improving and post-processing a mesh already generated and refined by another tool. A tool for semiconductor simulation in 3D is described in [7]. In this case, the mesh is composed of different types of elements, i.e. cuboides, prisms, pyramids and tetrahedra. The implementation is based on a modified octree approach. Even though it was not developed with SPL concepts in mind, it fits the PLA with little effort. The component types chosen and the implementations for each tool are described in the first and second part of Table 1, respectively.

4   Conclusion

We proposed a layered PLA for a meshing tool SPL and we showed that a variety of diverse meshing tools fit its structure: control volume meshes for 2D and 3D. By formally specifying the PLA using xADL, we got an architecture that was simple enough to be easily understood, while general enough to be able to capture the abstractions behind a wide variety of meshing tools. Having an integrated graphical and textual modeling tool greatly helped in this process.

References

1. ArchStudio 3. Architecture-Based Development Environment. Inst. SW Research, Univ. of California, Irvine, 2005. http://www.isr.uci.edu/projects/archstudio/.
2. María Cecilia Bastarrica and Nancy Hitschfeld-Kahler. Designing a product family of meshing tools. *Advances in Engineering Software*, 37(1):1–10, Jan 2006.
3. Jan Bosch. *Design and Use of Software Architectures*. Addison Wesley, 2000.
4. Frank Buschmann et al. *Pattern Oriented Software Architecture*. Wiley, 1996.
5. Eric M. Dashofy et al. A Comprehensive Approach for the Development of Modular Software Architecture Description Languages. *ACM Transactions on Software Engineering and Methodology*, 14(2):199–245, 2005.
6. Rod W. Douglass et al. Current views on grid generation: summaries of a panel discussion. *Numerical Heat Transfer, Part B: Fundamentals*, 41:211–237, Mar 2002.
7. Nancy Hitschfeld et al. Mixed Element Trees: A Generalization of Modified Octrees for the Generation of Meshes for the Simulation of Complex 3D Semiconductor Device Structures. *IEEE Trans. on CAD-ICS*, 12(11):1714–1725, Nov 1993.

Binding Time Based Concept Instantiation in Feature Modeling

Valentino Vranić and Miloslav Šípka

Institute of Informatics and Software Engineering
Faculty of Informatics and Information Technology
Slovak University of Technology, Ilkovičova 3, 84216 Bratislava 4, Slovakia
vranic@fiit.stuba.sk, miloslav.sipka@gmail.com

Abstract. In this paper, we address the issue of concept instantiation in feature modeling with respect to binding time. We explain the impact of such instantiation on applying constraints among features expressed in feature diagrams and as additional constraints and propose a way to validate a concept instance under these new conditions.

1 Introduction

Feature modeling aims at expressing concepts by their features as important properties of concepts taking into account feature interdependencies and variability in order to capture the concept configurability [3]. A concept is an understanding of a class or category of elements in a domain [3]. Individual elements that correspond to this understanding are called *concept instances*. While a concept represent a whole class of systems or parts of a system, an instance represents a specific configuration of a system or a part of a system defined by a set of features. Concept instances may be used for feature model validation and manual or automatic configuration of other design models or program code of specific products in a domain [2, 3].

When designing a family of systems, we have to balance between statically and dynamically bound features. In general, dynamic binding is more flexible as we may reconfigure our system at run time, while static binding is more efficient in terms of time and space. Although they often embrace the information on feature binding time, contemporary approaches to feature modeling do not consider the time dimension during concept instantiation.

This paper focuses on the issue of concept instantiation (Sect. 2) and validation of concept instances with respect to binding time (Sect. 3). The paper is closed by a discussion (Sect. 4).

2 Concept Instantiation in Time

Binding time describes *when* a variable feature is to be *bound*, i.e. selected to become a mandatory part of a concept instance. The set of possible binding times

M. Morisio (Ed.): ICSR 2006, LNCS 4039, pp. 407–410, 2006.

depend on a solution domain. For compiled languages they usually include source time, compile time, link time, and run time [1].

An instance I of the concept C at time t is a concept derived from C by selecting its features which includes the C's concept node and in which each feature f whose parent is included in I obeys the following conditions:

1. If f is a mandatory feature, f is included in I.
2. If f is a variable feature whose binding time is earlier than or equal to t, f is included in I or excluded from it according to the constraints of the feature diagram and additional constraints associated with it. If included, the feature becomes mandatory for I.
3. If f is a variable features whose binding time is later than t, f may be included in I as a variable feature or excluded from it, or the constraints (both feature diagram and additional ones) on f may be made more rigid as long as the set of concept instances available at later instantiation times is preserved or reduced.

As follows from this definition,[1] a feature in a concept instance may be bound, in which case it appears as a mandatory feature, or unbound, in which case it stays variable. Mandatory features and features bound in previous instantiations are considered as bound. A concept instance may be instantiated further at later instantiation times.

The constraints—both feature diagram and additional ones—on a variable features whose binding time is later than the instantiation time may be made more rigid as long as the set of concept instances available at later instantiation times is preserved or reduced. An example of this is a transformation of a group of mandatory or-features (Fig. 1a) into a group of alternative features (Fig. 1b).

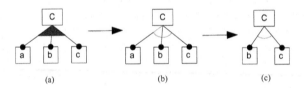

(a)   (b)   (c)

Fig. 1. Reducing the set of concept instances

Variable features with binding times later than the instantiation time are potentially part of concept instances at later binding times. Again, such features may be excluded at instantiation times earlier than their binding times as long as the set of concept instances available at later instantiation times is preserved or reduced. Consider a group of three alternative features (Fig. 1b) with run-time binding. At source time, one of these features may be excluded (Fig. 1d). However, none of the two remaining features may be excluded since preserving only one of them will force us to make it mandatory, which is illegal, or optional, which will allow an originally unforeseen concept instance to be created: the one with no features from the group.

---

[1] The definition is based on our earlier concept instance definition [7].

3   Concept Instance Validation

A concept instance is valid if its features satisfy the constraints. In general, a constraint—be it a feature diagram constraint or an additional one— may be evaluated only if all the features it refers to are bound. However, some logical expressions can be evaluated without knowing the values of all of their variables. Suppose we are instantiating a simple concept in Fig. 2a at source time (with no additional constraints). If we bind the x feature, the or-group constraint will be satisfied regardless of the y feature binding. Thus, we may omit this constraint transforming the y feature into an optional one as shown in Fig. 2b.

It is also possible to omit x. The only possibility for y is to leave it optional, as shown in Fig. 2c, but it has to be assured it will finally be bound (which can be done only at run time). For this purpose, we must add a trivial constraint to this instance: y (y has to be true, i.e. bound).

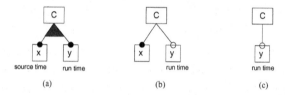

Fig. 2. Dealing with features whose binding time is later than the instantiation time

By excluding features from feature diagrams, the feature diagram constraints are gradually relinquished. After a successful concept instance validation, all additional constraints that refer to the features whose binding time is not later than the instantiation time can be safely removed from the model. All other constraints have to be postponed for further instantiation.

4   Discussion

In this paper, we presented an approach to concept instantiation with respect to binding time. We analyzed the impact of introducing the time dimension into concept instantiation on concept instance validation with respect to both feature diagram and additional constraints. We have also developed a prototype tool that supports such instantiation (available at http://www.fiit.stuba.sk/~vranic/fm/).

Concept instantiation with respect to feature binding time is similar to staged configuration of feature models proposed in conjunction with cardinality-based feature modeling [5, 6]. Although consecutive work [4] mentions a possibility of defining configuration stages in terms of the time dimension, this approach does not elaborate the issue of feature binding time with respective consequences on validation of concept specializations.

Concept instantiation with respect to binding time can be used to check for "dead-end" instances that may result into invalid configurations of a running system. Such configuration may miss some features required by other, bound features, which will lead to a system crash if such features are activated. Similarly as staged feature model configuration, concept instantiation with respect to binding time could be used for creating specialized versions of frameworks [5], which would represent a source time instantiation, and in software supply chains, optimization, and policy standards [4].

Partial validation of the constraints that incorporate unbound features may be improved by transforming them into the normal conjunctive form. This would enable to extract parts of such a constraint with bound features, while conjuncts with unbound features would be simple enough to directly determine whether they can be evaluated or not. As a further work, we plan to explore consequences of applying this approach to cardinality-based feature models [5].

Acknowledgements. The work was supported by Slovak Science Grant Agency VEGA, project No. 1/3102/06, and Science and Technology Assistance Agency of Slovak Republic under the contract No. APVT-20-007104.

References

[1] James O. Coplien. *Multi-Paradigm Design for C++*. Addison-Wesley, 1999.

[2] Krzysztof Czarnecki and Michal Antkiewicz. Mapping features to models: A template approach based on superimposed variants. In Robert Glück and Michael R. Lowry, editors, *Proc. of Generative Programming and Component Engineering, 4th International Conference, GPCE 2005*, LNCS 3676, pages 422–437, Tallinn, Estonia, October 2005. Springer.

[3] Krzysztof Czarnecki and Ulrich W. Eisenecker. *Generative Programing: Methods, Tools, and Applications*. Addison-Wesley, 2000.

[4] Krzysztof Czarnecki, Simon Helsen, and Ulrich Eisenecker. Formalizing cardinality-based feature models and their specialization. *Software Process: Improvement and Practice*, 10:7–29, January/March 2005.

[5] Krzysztof Czarnecki, Simon Helsen, and Ulrich Eisenecker. Staged configuration through specialization and multi-level configuration of feature models. *Software Process: Improvement and Practice*, 10:143–169, April/June 2005.

[6] Krzysztof Czarnecki and Chang Hwan Peter Kim. Cardinality-based feature modeling and constraints: A progress report. In *International Workshop on Software Factories, OOPSLA 2005*, San Diego, USA, October 2005.

[7] Valentino Vranić. Reconciling feature modeling: A feature modeling metamodel. In Matias Weske and Peter Liggsmeyer, editors, *Proc. of 5th Annual International Conference on Object-Oriented and Internet-Based Technologies, Concepts, and Applications for a Networked World (Net.ObjectDays 2004)*, LNCS 3263, pages 122–137, Erfurt, Germany, September 2004. Springer.

Aspects as Components

Marcelo Medeiros Eler and Paulo Cesar Masiero

Dept. of Computer Science, ICMC - University of Sao Paulo,
13560-970 Sao Carlos - SP - BR. P.O.Box 668
{mareler, masiero}@icmc.usp.br

Abstract. An adaptation of the UML Component method to design
crosscutting components is briefly presented. Such components are allowed to crosscut only the public interface of base (convencional) components. The design and implementation of crosscutting components using
the language JAsCO is discussed.

1   Introduction

Components are units of composition with contractually specified interfaces and
explicit context dependencies only [4]. Component-based software development
(CBSD) aims at decomposing software into independent modules that are easy to
manage, reuse and evolve. Several methods to support CBSD have been proposed
[1, 4, 6], which usually provide guidelines on how to encapsulate concerns into
components. However, there are crosscutting concerns such as logging, tracing
and persistence, that cannot be implemented as components using tools like
CORBA, EJB and COM. By their nature, they crosscut the component structure
within components and across the components' boundaries [3].

A way to solve this problem is to use containers but the calls to the services
provided by them are still spread along several components. Another way is to
combine CBSD with aspect-oriented software development (AOSD) to support
the implementation of crosscutting concerns as independent modules. The problem with this combination is that, by their nature, aspects may crosscut the
internal component structure thus clashing with the component opaqueness. A
solution to this is to compromise aspect expressiveness allowing aspects to operate only on the public operations exposed in the components' interfaces and
forbidding them of extending any operation through inter-type declarations [3].

We show briefly an adaptation of the UML Components method [1] to produce a component-based design that also includes aspectual (crosscutting) components, preserving the component opaqueness by allowing only crosscutting of
public operations in the interface of base components. A brief introduction to the
component architecture that is produced and to how crosscutting components
can be designed to be reused is presented.

2   Component/Aspect Architecture

We have devised a method to develop software with components and aspects.
Using this method, we produce a component/aspect architecture as the one

M. Morisio (Ed.): ICSR 2006, LNCS 4039, pp. 411–414, 2006.

shown in Figure 1 (part A) for a Hotel Reservation System (HRS) [1]. In the architecture, we have crosscuting (LoggingOpMgr) and base componentes (ReservationSystem and CustomerMgr, for example). The crosscutting component provides a crosscutting interface and requires services from business components (UserMgr and LoggingMgr). The diamond and the interface name 'ICC' prefix both indicate a crosscutting interface.

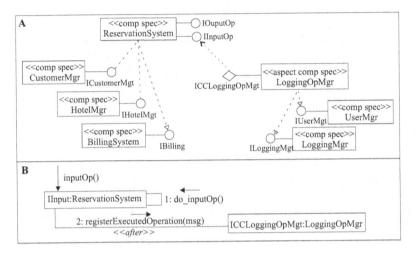

Fig. 1. Component/aspect architecture for the Hotel Reservation System [1]

The semantics for this diagram is that any operation in the interface of IInputOp will be crosscut by the crosscutting component when called by any other component and is enhanced by the behavior specified at the crosscutting interface. Following the guidelines of Clarke and Baniassad [5], the woven behavior may be represented as in Figure 1 (part B) where, for each operation crosscut (e.g. inputOp()), we create a copy of this operation in do_op1() and a new operation inputOp(). In this case, this new operation calls the original operation (do_op1()) and after that calls the crosscutting operation registerExecutedOperation().

3   Design and Reuse of Aspectual Components

There are many possible designs for an aspectual component, all of them influenced by the AOP language used and also by the intended reuse: if white box or black box. A possible way to generalize a component so that it can be reused without change of the code (black box) is to have its code prepared to be used in as many as possible advice configurations such, for example, before, after, and before followed by after. It is difficult to foresee all the possible uses of an around advice because a new behavior is to be executed instead of the original operation; but this can be done for a white box reuse. The different types of advices that are available in the component implementation have to be made clear in its documentation.

The code for the LoggingOpMgr component implemented in JAsCO [2] is shown in Figure 2 (part A). The code is prepared to be used in all three situations

```
A   class LoggingOpMgr
    {
        public void registerExecutedOperation(String msg) {
            // code of registerExecutedOperation
        }
        hook ICCLoggingOpMgt
        {
            ICCLoggingOpMgt(method(..args)) {
                call(method);
            }
            before(){
                global.registerExecutedOperation("BEFORE::"+ msg);
            }
            after() {
                global.registerExecutedOperation("AFTER::"+ msg);
            }
        }
    }
B   static connector installLoggingOpMgr
        LoggingOpMgr.ICCLoggingOpMgt ICCL =
            new LoggingOpMgr.ICCLoggingOpMgt
                    ( { * ReservationSystem.makeReservation(..),
                        * ReservationSystem.amendReservation(..),
                        * ReservationSystem.cancelReservation(..),
                        * ReservationSystem.beginStay(..),
                        * ReservationSystem.registerClient(..)});
        ICCL.before();
        ICCL.after();
    }
```

Fig. 2. JAsCo Code for the LoggingOpMgr component

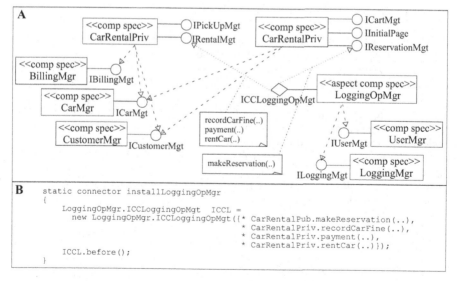

Fig. 3. Component/aspect architecture for a Car Rental System (CRS)

listed above. The connector shown (part B) is realized at the assembly phase and links LoggingOpMgr to the SystemReservation component. The connector defines the advices used (in this case, before and after, in the ICCL.before() and ICCL.after() commands) and the operations to be crosscut.

The LoggingOpMgr's code (Figure 2) is reused as it is in a Car Rental System, whose component and aspect diagram is shown in Figure 3 (part A). The notes used show that now only certain operations of the crosscutting interface have added behavior. Absence of a note means that all of the operations are crosscut. The connector's code (Figure 3, part B) shows the LoggingOpMgr being reused during the assembly phase for the CRS. The connector defines the advice (in this case, before) and the operations that will be crosscut in the interface. Note that the behavior of a crosscutting component does not change when is reused. What changes is the execution of the crosscutting behavior before, after or instead (around) the operations that will have their behavior enhanced.

4   Concluding Remarks

The approach presented also supports the design of functional crosscutting components, not shown in the example. Implementation can also be done using other languages like AspectJ, with some restrictions. For example: using JAsCO, it is possible to change a connector dinamically, what is not possible with AspectJ. Further work is going on to derive more generic designs for black box and white box reuse of crosscutting components as well for crosscutting concerns that are not fully orthogonal such as persistence.

References

1. Cheesman, J.; Daniels, J.: Uml components: A simple process for specifying component-based software. Addison-Wesley, 2000.
2. Suvee, D.; Vanderperren, W.; Jonckers, V.: Jasco: an aspect-oriented approach tailored for component based software development. In: AOSD, 2003, p. 2129.
3. Cottenier, T.; Elrad, T.: Validation of context-dependent aspect-oriented adaptations to components. In: Workshop on Component-Oriented Programming, 2004.
4. Szyperski, C.; Gruntz, G. D.; Murer, S.: Component software - beyond object-oriented programming. Addison-Wesley / ACM Press, 2002.
5. Clarke, S.; Baniassad., E.: Aspect-oriented analysis and design: The theme approach. Addison-Wesley Professional, 2005.
6. Clements, P. C.: From subroutines to subsystems: Component based software development. American Programmer, v. 6, n. 11, 1995.

Improving Reuse of Off-the-Shelf Components with Shared, Distributed Component Repository Systems

Glêdson Elias, Jorge Dias Jr., Sindolfo Miranda Filho,
Gustavo Cavalcanti, Michael Schuenck, and Yuri Negócio

COMPOSE – Component Oriented Service Engineering Group
Informatics Department, Federal University of Paraíba
João Pessoa, PB, Brazil, 58059-900, (+55 83) 3216.7093
{gledson, jjjunior, sindolfo, gustavo, michael,
yuri}@compose.ufpb.br

Abstract. The task of identifying software components that meet business requirements is a challenging issue in component-based development processes. In such a context, component repository systems can provide the means to effectively find suitable components, improving reuse of off-the-shelf software components. This paper presents a shared, distributed component repository architecture for large scale deployment of commercial and open source software components. The proposed architecture adopts a service-oriented approach in order to achieve a high degree of availability and reliability. Besides, the proposed architecture also deals with issues such as security, component certification and business models.

1 Introduction

Component repository systems have been proposed to solve problems related to discover suitable components in Component Based Software Engineering (CBSE). A component repository system acts as a process interface, where producers can register components (development for reuse) and consumers can search and retrieve them (development with reuse). Despite their contributions, present-day component repository systems [1][4][6][7] have failed in establishing a global, distributed component marketplace. Generally, such solutions adopt local and centralized approaches [5], suffering from problems related to limited accessibility, availability, reliability and scalability.

In order to overcome such limitations, this paper presents a shared, distributed component repository architecture for large scale deployment of software components. On the one hand, the proposed architecture is said to be shared because several producers can register software components in a compliant implementation. On the other hand, the proposed architecture is said to be distributed because a compliant implementation ought to be based upon a set of geographically dispersed entities who work together to provide the repository services. The proposed architecture adopts a service-oriented approach, in which a collection of loosely-coupled, self-contained services communicate and collaborate with each other in

M. Morisio (Ed.): ICSR 2006, LNCS 4039, pp. 415–418, 2006.

order to support requirements of a component repository, such as component certification, business model and component discovery.

The remainder of this paper is organized as follows. In Section 2, an overview of the proposed architecture is presented, identifying its high-level collaborating services. Then, Section 3 presents some concluding remarks.

2 Architectural Framework

The proposed architecture adopts a service-oriented approach, in which four loosely-coupled, self-contained services communicate and collaborate with each other through well-defined interfaces. Such an approach allows the design and implementation of each service to be performed in an autonomous way, provided that an agreement exists on the communication technology. Figure 1 illustrates the architectural framework.

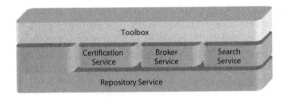

Fig. 1. High-level architectural framework

The *repository service* is a distributed component library responsible for managing the registration, storage and retrieval of software components. Components of several component models are maintained by the repository service, such as CORBA, COM, EJB and .NET. In this sense, it explores a uniform XML-based representation model, called X-ARM [2], used to describe the features of the components. These features include aspects related to naming schema, business model, certification, classification, evolution, development processes.

The repository service can interact with one or more certification services, which are implemented by distinct certification entities in order to manage the emission and validation of component and producer certificates. The component acquisition in conformance with business models specified by their producers is managed by one or more broker services. Finally, the indexing and search of components are made by search services, which can employ their own indexing algorithms and query languages. Note that certification, broker and search services can be implemented by any entity interested in provide such services. In this sense, these services must agree with a set of predefined interfaces, provided by the repository service.

The toolbox is composed of a set of reuse-driven automated tools that can be employed by producers, consumers, certification authorities and component brokers. Such tools also interact with lower-level services through well-defined interfaces and, as illustrated in Figure 2, can be categorized in development, integration and management tools.

Despite the adoption of a layered style, it is important to emphasize that the set of services follows a service-oriented approach, in which a mesh of collaborating services interact through a service bus that supports and manages the message flow between them. Figure 2 illustrates the service-oriented view of the architectural framework.

Fig. 2. Service-oriented view

As an implementation issue, the set of services can be viewed as a special-purpose middleware, in which the service bus is implemented by a communication service. By following a middleware approach, it is possible to facilitate communication and coordination, and besides, to mask heterogeneity and complexity, supporting well-defined interfaces and standard protocols [3].

The repository service is composed of a set of distributed, inter-communicating entities, called *containers*, which help to achieve scalability and support concepts of name resolution, security and persistence. Internally, each container is also designed adopting a service-oriented approach, whose services are organized into a three-layered architecture, as shown in Figure 3.

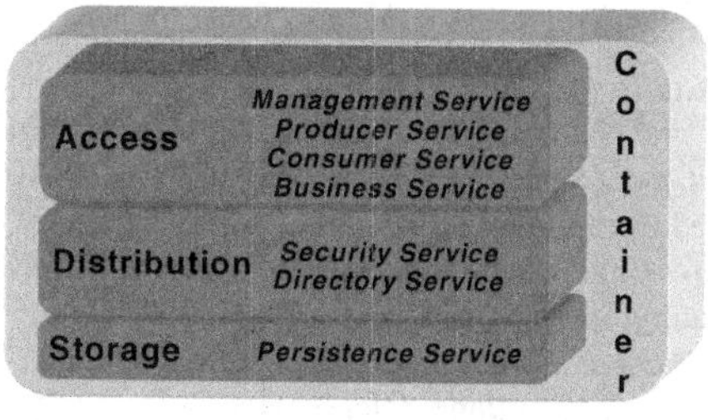

Fig. 3. Container layered architecture

The *access layer* provides services accessed by the container manager, zone administrator, consumer and broker service. These actors use such services in order to manage the container; store, change and retrieve components; retrieve free components and retrieve non-free components, respectively. The *distribution layer* is accessed by the services of the access layer and addresses distribution and security issues, making possible to transparently discover and securely retrieve stored components. Finally, the *storage layer* deals with physical storage of components.

Each container can store components of different component producers. Therefore, each producer company registered in a container has an associated zone, which stores families of products and can have several developers allowed. As the number of components can continuously grow, a zone can be divided into domains. This way, both zones and domains are able to store components and to have registered domains and subzones. The difference is that zones also store the administrative information about the producer company, including the developers authorized to manipulate the components in their zones and respective domains.

Moreover, the existence of zones and domains enables the unambiguous identification of components. In this sense, the repository service adopts a hierarchical naming schema, as suggested by Elias [8]. In such a schema, names are organized in a hierarchical tree, where the leaves are components and the internal nodes are zones and domains, representing component producers.

3 Conclusion

The proposed architecture combines various important features to the infrastructure of component repository systems, including global naming schema, distribution, scalability and security. In addition, the proposed architecture is unique since it provides facilities for dealing with component certification and business models.

This paper is a step towards the realization of the quite ambitious goals of promoting a ubiquitous and competitive component marketplace, possibly composed of an enormous quantity and variety of off-the-shelf, third-party, reusable components. It represents the preliminary results of our work, which is far from being completed. Thus, several work remains to be done, including concluding a proof of concept prototype, which is currently under laboratory work.

References

1. *Component Source*. http://www.componentsource.com. 2005.
2. Elias, G.; Schuenck, M.; Negócio, Y.; Dias Jr., J.; Mirando Filho, S. *X-ARM: An Asset Representation Model for Component Repository Systems*. SAC 2006 – The 21st ACM Symposium on Applied Computing. Dijon, France, 2006. (to appear).
3. Emerich, W. *Software Engineering and Middleware: A Roadmap*. Proceedings of the Conference on The Future of Software Engineering, 2002.
4. Inoue, K.; et al. *Component Rank: Relative Significance Rank for Software Component Search*. In ICSE, pages 14 24, Portland, OR, 2003.
5. Seacord, R. C. *Software engineering component repositories*. Technical Report, Software Engineering Institute (SEI), 1999.
6. Seacord, R.; Hissam, S., Wallnau, C. *Agora: A Search Engine for Software Components*. CMU/SEI-98-TR-011, 1998.
7. Ye, Y. *Supporting Component-Based Software Development with Active Component Repository Systems*. Phd Thesis, University of Colorado, 2001.
8. Elias, G. *SOS, A Framework for Distribution, Management and Evolution of Component-Based Software Systems over Open Networks*. Phd Thesis, CIn-UFPE, Recife, Brazil. 2002.

Support to Development-with-Reuse in Very Small Software Developing Companies

José L. Barros[1] and José M. Marqués[2]

[1] University of Vigo, CS Department, Spain
jbarros@uvigo.es
[2] Universidad de Valladolid, CS Department, Spain
jmmc@infor.uva.es

Abstract. There are a variety of specifications to represent information about reusable assets. Most of this models and specifications are complex, difficult to understand and implement in reduced environments. Small and *very small* organizations (less than 10 employees) can benefit from reuse but, they need easy to understand methodologies, processes and tools; low cost technologies and, flexible development models. We provide a flexible approach to the modelling process proposing an easy model to represent and classify reusable assets, mainly those developed inside the organization but, compliant with standards to allow the use of COTS. Our model deals with functional and non-functional properties and, it's able to represent assets from the whole software development life cycle.

1 Introduction

Industry has a variety of good, standard models to represent software components and reusable assets. Some of them, including EJB, COM and its descendants (COM+, DCOM), CORBA, UML, MOF and RAS are supported by well-known, leading organizations and tool vendors, like IBM, OMG, SUN, HP and many others [1]. Many of this models and specifications were developed thinking in big software development organizations. These organizations have a well defined environment for producing software: established methodologies, business rules and policies, consistent quality practices, and enough human and technical resources. Obviously, they also have enough economic resources for buying development tools. On the other hand, there are a lot of small and very small companies (VSC) devoted to the production of software applications. These companies have special characteristics which differentiate them from big software factories.

VSC's methods tend to be very ad-hoc. The developers worked in the way that they found most suitable, and used to change that way when new tools and/or methodologies were learned. Communication between the developers tends to be informal. They kept only one version of their product, to which they made all the changes. The development process is adapted for every new project. Work was based very much on customer requests, when a new customer was obtained additions to the product were made, if necessary, to cater for the new requirements. Little or no documentation was kept on the software, apart from the user manual [2].

M. Morisio (Ed.): ICSR 2006, LNCS 4039, pp. 419–422, 2006.
© Springer-Verlag Berlin Heidelberg 2006

Economic issues can be reduced provided that free, probably open source software tools are used. Moreover, the intrinsic benefits from reuse: reduce time to market and increase quality; should help to reduce expenses and increase benefits. Complex models to represent reusable assets can be *shortened* and *simplified* in order to adapt them to VSC's environments [3].

The paper is divides as follows: section 2 details de proposed development processes; section 3 shows the proposed model for representing reusable assets; section 4 deals with the clustering technique used to classify reusable assets and group them together into similarity sets called *finders*; finally, section 5 presents the conclusions and open issues for future research.

2   Development Processes

We focused our efforts in highlight some characteristics that we found especially interesting for VSC's, while they can be also desirable for other kinds of organizations:

- Improve development speed (**R**apid **A**pplication **D**evelopment)
- High visibility should be guaranteed (show progress)
- Allow changes on requirements along the development life cycle
- It is also desirable that a high percentage of tasks can be fully automated or at least has a sound tool support.

In order to achieve these goals we proposed methods and techniques similar to those presented in [4]. The steps to follow in the developing of new applications should be something like:

- Elicit requirements, using as many techniques as possible
- Search the Reuse Repository for reusable assets (mainly Models)
- Develop Models, adapting the retrieved ones or creating them from scratch, until the client is fully satisfied
- Automatic generation of functional deliverables (using tool support)

These steps can (and should) be repeated as many times as necessary. In our approach all the artefacts produced during software development were or can be treated as XML documents (text, models, diagrams, code, data files) allowing XML-based storing and retrieval mechanisms [5]. We enforce the use of the OpenDocument format, which can represent a variety of software [6]. All developed artefacts should be evaluated and possibly included in the repository.

3   Information Model

We need a homogeneous representation for every possible software artefact, so the same set of properties should always apply. We have divided the set of properties which represent the real artefact in two halves: functional and non-functional properties. The representation of every reusable asset will be a well-formed XML document called Reusable Asset Description (RAD). RAD documents are stored in a native XML repository [7]. The set of properties in the Administrative Description (AD) were extracted from a deep analysis of well documented component models from the Reuse arena, such as: SIB [8], REBOOT [9], MECANO [10], RSHP [11] and RAS [12]. The next figure shows valid Reusable Assets (RA).

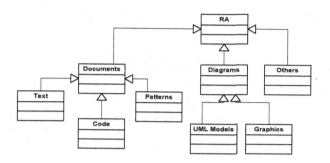

Fig. 1. Valid Reusable Assets

The Functional Description (FD) properties were similar to those proposed in [13]. A FD is an unbounded set of *features* which in turn were made of triplets *<action-object, importance>*. A FD can be seen just as a collection of properties, statically associated with a reusable component, or as a collection of requirements (a query dynamically associated to a developer). So a FD is both a classification and a retrieval mechanism. Both, A+F descriptions can be semi-automatically extracted from XML/XMI documents, produced from the original reusable asset. The next step is to classify an insert the RAD into the reuse repository.

4 Classification

In order to classify a RAD document we need to define and compute *replacement capability* between two RAD. Only the FD of the two RAD will be used for this computation. Replacement capability can be defined as the probability that the reusable asset represented by FD_1 can be substituted by the reusable asset represented by FD_2, while keeping the application requirements satisfied. FD_1 can represents a user's query or another RAD in the repository. Replacement capability is computable only by direct comparison (non-transitive, non-symmetric). The next step is to assign an incoming FD to a *finder*, the formal definition of a finder is:

"A finder is a set of similar functional descriptions"

Every finder has an associated FD (Finder Functional Description, FDD) which is constructed dynamically, adding all the features present in the FDs that belongs to that finder. This FDD can be seen as a *nucleus* or *mass centre* that represents all the functionality (without duplicates) offered by the set of FDs that belongs to the finder. When a new FD arrives we compute its similarity with respect to all the FFDs in the repository, the incoming FD is assigned to the finder whose FDD is most similar to it. A threshold value could be applied to fine tuning the granularity of the repository (number of finders) and, of the RA (mean number of DF per finder, we call this *density*).

5 Conclusions and Open Issues

The model can be expanded or configured to adapt it to the organization's needs. The FDD can be seen as a good guideline to develop new RA, from a development-for-reuse perspective. The classification space is generated automatically and, dynamoically. No human intervention is needed, reducing effort. The reuser can query the repository directly, by properties in the AD section, or using the FD, this allow users with different knowledge about the assets to use the repository. Furthermore, a user can use an UML diagram as a query, the system will retrieve all RAD related with the diagram, not only diagrams. A thesaurus can be automatically generated from FDDs, extracting its *<action-object>* pair of terms. A manual tuning of this thesaurus could be necessary.

References

1. Brereton, P., Linkman, S., Boegh, J., Thomas, N., De Panfilis, S.: "Software Components – Enabling a Mass Market", Proc. Of the 10th Int'l Workshop on Software Technology and Engineering Practice, 2002.
2. Fayad, M.E., Laitinen, M., Ward, R.P.: "Software engineering in the small", Communications of the ACM, 43(3), pp.:115-118, March 2000.
3. González, R., Meer, K.: "Standard metadata applied to software retrieval", JIS, 30(4), pp.: 300-309, 2004.
4. McConnel, S.: Rapid development. McGraw-Hill, 1996.
5. Laird, C.: "XMI and UML combine to drive product development",
6. http://en.wikipedia.org/wiki/OpenDocument_technical_specifications
7. http://www.sleepycat.com/
8. Constantopoulos, P., Dörr, M.: "Component Classification in the Software Information Base", Object-Oriented Software Composition. O. Nierstrasz and D. Tsichritzis (Eds), Prentice Hall, pp 177-200, 1995.
9. Karlsson, E.A.: "Software Reuse: A Holistic Approach", John Wiley & Sons, 1996.
10. García, F.J., Marqués, J.M., Maudes, J.M.: "Mecano: Una Propuesta de Componente Software Reutilizable", II Jornadas de Ingeniería del Software, Donostia-San Sebastián, pp. 232-244, 3-5 Septiembre, 1997.
11. Lloréns, J., Morato, J., Genova, G., Fuentes, M., Quintana, V., Díaz, I.: "RSHP: An information representation model based on relationships", In Ernesto Damiani, Lakhmi C. Jain, Mauro Madravio (Eds.), Soft Computing in Software Engineering (Studies in Fuzziness and Soft Computing Series, Vol. 159), Springer, pp. 221-253, 2004.
12. http://www.omg.org/technology/documents/formal/ras.htm
13. Barros, J., Marques, J.: Conglomerados Multidimensionales: Un mecanismo simple de organización de Elementos Software Reutilizables. JISBD'02, Madrid, Noviembre, 2002. pp.: 375-386.

A Simple Generic Library for C

Marian Vittek[1], Peter Borovansky[1], and Pierre-Etienne Moreau[2]

[1] FMFI, Comenius University, Mlynska dolina, 842 15 Bratislava, Slovakia
{vittek, borovan}@fmph.uniba.sk
[2] LORIA-INRIA, BP 239, 54506 Vandœuvre-lès-Nancy, France
moreau@loria.fr

Abstract. This paper presents Sglib, a C library freely inspired by the Standard Template Library (STL). In opposition to C++, the C language lacks any support for generic programming. Our library results from the idea to create a generic library of reusable algorithms through the C preprocessor[1].

1 Introduction

Generic libraries, like *Standard Template Library* (STL) [6, 7] define algorithms independently on particular base type. They allow to efficiently reuse non-trivial algorithms in a variety of projects. While there is a language support for generic programming in Ada, C++ or Java, the pure C seems to be incompatible with generic programming paradigm. Fortunately, the standard C preprocessor provides a limited framework allowing to define algorithms in a generic way. In this paper we present an experiment on how to build a generic library based on the preprocessor. As the result of our work we have implemented a prototype called *Sglib*, standing for *Simple Generic Library*.

A particularity of our library is that it does not operate on its own representation of data structures. Sglib provides algorithms, not data types. As explained later in the paper, for example, algorithms for sorting lists can be applied on any user defined data structure containing a pointer to the same type. Thanks to this, Sglib can be used in ongoing projects on their own existing data representations.

Sglib is not a result of a self standing research. Our interest on the subject comes mainly from the research on C/C++ source understanding and transformation systems [1, 5, 9, 10]. The idea to create Sglib comes from a combination of those knowledges with our previous interest in algebraic and term rewriting languages [4, 8], especially ELAN [2]. From the latest we know that many generic constructions are implemented via preprocessors. When working on the refactoring browser we have realized that the C preprocessor is sufficiently strong to allow implementation of a usable generic library. We have considered the idea worth of an effort also because the C language is continuously placed among the most popular languages of open source projects [3].

2 Design of Sglib

Every C programmer probably knows a macro allocating a memory cell for a given type:

---

[1] This work was supported by Agency for Promotion Research and Development under the contract No. APVV-20-P04805.

M. Morisio (Ed.): ICSR 2006, LNCS 4039, pp. 423–426, 2006.

```
#define ALLOC(X) ((X *) malloc(sizeof(X)))
```

This macro is parametrized by a type X and it expands to a call of the function `malloc` allocating as many bytes as many needed for storing the type X. The function `malloc` returns a pointer of type `void *`, and the macro also casts this result to the pointer to X.

The macro `ALLOC` is perfectly working and useful. It is a good example how to use the preprocessor in generic constructions. We can extrapolate this approach. Macros parametrized by types can be used to create a whole library of algorithms. Implementation of this idea led us to the first version of Sglib. Unfortunately, macros are too weak to implement recursive algorithms. Also for this reason, the original idea has been refined into implementation of a second part of the library, where macros are used to generate (better said instantiate) real, possibly recursive, C functions. We call those two parts of Sglib respectively the *level-0* and *level-1* user interface.

2.1   The *level-0* Interface

As pointed before, the very first idea was to implement the library simply as a collection of macros. There are several security questions which need to be posed before creating/using a library of such macros. Preprocessor macros are expanded on purely textual level. If used without moderation, they can be source of bugs. Fortunately, if macros are well written, they can eliminate majority of problems. Sglib adopts several conventions. All macro parameters are enclosed into parenthesis eliminating the danger of syntax misunderstanding. Sglib avoids multiple occurrences of macro parameters whenever possible. Finally, in order to reduce possible name clashes, all variables defined inside macros are starting and finishing with _ (underscore). As an example, let us take a macro computing the length of a list:

```
#define SGLIB_LIST_LEN(type, list, next, result) { \
  int _i_; \
  type _l_; \
  for(_i_=0,_l_=(list); _l_!=NULL; _l_=_l_->next, _i_++) ; \
  (result) = _i_; \
}
```

This implementation can be used on any user defined list data structure and there is only a small risk of wrong parsing when using it. Sglib provides a large number of macros like the one above.

2.2   The *level-1* Interface

Because macros do not permit to define recursive algorithms, we started to search an alternative design pattern for the so called *level-1* interface of Sglib. We have examined a number of design patterns for this part of the library, including *X-macros*. Finally, we have adopted a solution where Sglib defines one very large macro for each supported data structure. The macro is expanded into definitions of all functions (algorithms) operating on the given data type. For example, a macro implementing lists looks like:

```
#define SGLIB_DEFINE_LIST_FUNCTIONS(LIST_TYPE) \
  ... \
  int sglib_list_len(LIST_TYPE *list) {\
    int i = 0;\
    LIST_TYPE *l;\
    for(l=list; l!=NULL; l=l->next) i++;\
    return(i);\
  }\
  ...
```

In other words, the *level-1* interface implements all algorithms in form of functions, however, those functions are not directly a part of the goal program. They are defined inside generic macros. The program can incorporate those functions by invoking such macro parametrized by the actual data type and few additional parameters.

A small refinement of the above example is required for the final version of the library because of a problem with function name clashes. The problem appears if the user needs to use two different list types in a single program. In such case he will invoke the macro twice, which will result in two definitions of the function `sglib_list_len` (with different parameter type) causing a 'double definition' linker error. In order to solve the problem, we use the type name (supposing that it is a single identifier) and we compose it into function names using the preprocessor operator ##. For example, the final implementation of lists looks like:

```
#define SGLIB_DEFINE_LIST_FUNCTIONS(LIST_TYPE,COMPARATOR,NEXT) \
  ... \
  int sglib_##LIST_TYPE##_len(LIST_TYPE *list) {\
    int i = 0;\
    LIST_TYPE *l;\
    for(l=list; l!=NULL; l=l->NEXT) i++;\
    return(i);\
  }\
  ...
```

In the example, the NEXT parameter has the same meaning as in the *level-0* interface and the COMPARATOR parameter is a function (or macro) used to compare two elements of a list. Comparator is used by functions sorting lists, etc. Using the *level-1* interface in praxis means, that the user invokes one large macro at the beginning of his program. This macro instantiates all available functions for the given type and they can be later used in the program as regular C functions. For example an invocation:

```
SGLIB_DEFINE_SORTED_LIST_FUNCTIONS(ilist,ilist_comparator,next)
```

is expanded into functions computing the lenght of an ilist (`sglib_ilist_len`), sorting it (`sglib_ilist_sort`), etc.

At this time, Sglib implements following data structures: *lists, sorted lists, double linked lists, hashed containers* and *red-black trees*. The whole library is implemented as a single header file and it does not have any binary part. The complete list of macros and functions provided by each interface is beyond the scope of this paper. Majority of functions and macros implements operations on container data structures. For each container structure, the library provides the same basic set of functions for respectively adding, removing and finding an element and functions for iterating over elements. The uniform API allows users to easily altern between different actual implementations. Of course, for each data structure there is also a number of functions specific for given type, such as concatenation, or reverse for lists, etc.

3   Conclusion

At this moment, Sglib consists of around 2000 lines of code inside the library itself and of further 2000 lines of testing programs. The library contains also around 5000 lines of documentation. The whole library is open sourced, freely redistributable and usable in both commercial and free programs without a charge. It is available at the address *http://sourceforge.net/projects/sglib*.

References

1. Ira Baxter, Christopher Pidgeon, and Michael Mehlich. Dms: Program transformation for practical scalable software evolution. In *Proceedings of ICSE 2004: International Conference on Software Engineering*, Edinburgh, Scotland, 2004. IEEE Computer Society Press.
2. P. Borovansky, C. Kirchner, H. Kirchner, P. E. Moreau, and M. Vittek. ELAN: A logical framework based on computational systems. In *Proc. of the First Int. Workshop on Rewriting Logic*, volume 4. Elsevier, 1996.
3. A. Capiluppi, P. Lago, and M. Morisio. Characteristics of open source projects. In *Procceedings of the seventh European Conference on Software Maintenance and Reengineering, Benevento, Italy*, pages 317–330. IEEE Computer Society Press, 2003.
4. M. Clavel, F. Duran, S. Eker, P. Lincoln, N. Marti-Oliet, J. Meseguer, and J. F. Quesada. The maude system. In *Proceedings of the 10th International Conference on Rewriting Techniques and Applications*, pages 240–243, 1999.
5. A. Garrido and R. Johnson. Analyzing multiple configurations of a c program. In *Procceedings of IEEE International Conference On Software Maintenance, Budapest, Hungary*, 2005.
6. P.J. Plauger, Meng Lee, David Musser, and Alexander A. Stepanov. *C++ Standard Template Library*. Prentice Hall PTR, 2000.
7. A. A. Stepanov and M. Lee. The Standard Template Library. Technical Report X3J16/94-0095, WG21/N0482, Hewlett-Packard Laboratories, 1994.
8. Mark van den Brand, Arie van Deursen, Jan Heering, H. A. de Jong, Merijn de Jonge, Tobias Kuipers, Paul Klint, Leon Moonen, Pieter A. Olivier, Jeroen Scheerder, Jurgen J. Vinju, Eelco Visser, and Joost Visser. The asf+sdf meta-environment: A component-based language development environment. In *Proceedings of the 10th International Conference on Compiler Construction*, pages 240–243, 2001.
9. Laszlo Vidacs, Arpad Beszedes, and Rudolf Ferenc. Columbus schema for c/c++ preprocessing. In *8th European Conference on Software Maintenance and Reengineering, Tampere, Finland*, pages 75–84. IEEE Computer Society, 2004.
10. Marian Vittek. A refactoring browser with preprocessor. In *Procceedings of the seventh European Conference on Software Maintenance and Reengineering, Benevento, Italy*, pages 101–111. IEEE Computer Society Press, 2003.

Eliciting Potential Requirements with Feature-Oriented Gap Analysis*

Sangim Ahn and Kiwon Chong

Department of Computing, Soongsil University
1 Sangdo-5Dong, Dongjak-Ku, Seoul, Korea 156-743
{siahn69, chong}@ssu.ac.kr

Abstract. Software reuse has long been paid attentions as an effective way to improve software quality and productivity. In the context of Requirements Engineering (RE), a reuse approach is effective in particular because it can help to define requirements and to anticipate requirements change. We propose a feature-oriented gap analysis method to elicit potential requirements from various stakeholders. We use feature modeling, which are an important concept in software product line, to identify reusable requirements elements. To achieve our goal, we present (1) a meta-model of reusable requirements elements, (2) gap analysis between new collected requirements and reused requirements in the repository, and (3) a potential requirements elicitation process with feature-oriented gap analysis. This process is a set of sequential procedures to elicit potential requirements in addition to users' Plus minus interest (PMI).

1 Introduction

There are many reasons for project failure. The main ones related to requirements are: (1) Many users don't define correctly what they want. (2) Requirements are changing frequently. (3) There is no enough time to analyze user requirements. (4) Developers don't understand perfectly user requirements. These reasons make over time and cost of projects, and low quality of software products. Therefore, establishing good requirements is important in initial software development phase. The introduction of reuse in software development aims at reducing development costs and improving quality. More and more works try to integrate it throughout the whole cycle of production, from the phase of requirements expression to the phase of maintenance. In the context of Requirements Engineering (RE), reuse is effective in particular because it can help to define requirements explicitly and to anticipate requirements change [1][2].

We propose feature-oriented gap analysis to elicit potential requirements from various stakeholders. Since requirements specification is not suitable for representation in a computer, we use feature modeling, which are an important concept in software product line, as a reusable requirements element. The element is requirements representation formalization that can compare new collected requirements to reused requirements. New collected requirements are made based on a preliminary method such as user interview, workshops, and observing user work.

---

* This work was supported by the Soongsil University Research Fund.

M. Morisio (Ed.): ICSR 2006, LNCS 4039, pp. 427–431, 2006.

Whereas, reused requirements are stored in the repository. In this paper, we suppose that the repository is already installed and valuable requirements of many successful projects are accumulated in the repository. We define a meta-model of reusable requirements elements using feature modeling, present gap analysis between new collected requirements and reused requirements in the repository, and show a potential requirements elicitation process including users' Plus minus interest (PMI).

2   A Meta-model of Requirement Elements

The major point of our approach is to model requirements elements for representation of new collected requirements and reused requirements in the repository. Intuitively, a gap expresses a difference between these elements such as deletion, addition, and equal. In order to facilitate gap analysis, we need to define requirements elements and a set of gap types related to these elements.

A meta-model of requirements elements is drawn in Figure 2 using UML notations. These elements are composed of feature categories [3][4]. Every element has a Name and each element is characterized by a set of Property which is mapping to factors in feature categories. There are two orthogonal classifications of Element in the meta-model. The first classification makes the distinction among Capability, Operating Environment, Domain Technology, Implementation Technology Feature. The second classification is a partition of elements into Relationship and NoRelationship. The type Relationship is a connection between two elements, one being the Source and the other the Target. It means that there are semantic relationship between both of them such as dependency, association, and generalization. Elements, which are not connected, are referred to as NoRelationship [5].

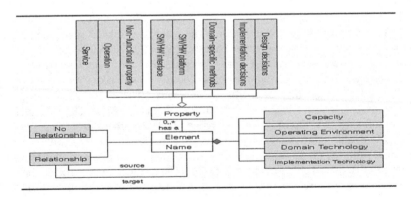

Fig. 1. The meta-model of requirements elements for gap analysis

3   Gap Analysis

There are three major types of difference: category difference, property difference, and operator difference. The gap types are composed of a set of operators applicable to elements. Each operator identifies a type of difference between new collected requirements and reused requirements in repository. For example, if Modify is an operator, it implies that there is the name difference in Service property of Capacity Element [5].

- **Element difference** is defined with the category of requirements element. They only affect the way users want to refer to requirements.
- **Property difference** is defined with the factors in one of elements. They only affect the intention that users want to refer to an element.
- **Operator difference** are the most important as they correspond to express difference of the set of elements which composes requirements.

Table 1. Gap types of elements

Element	Property	Operator	Description of operators
C.	C-Service	Add	New element is add in new collected R.E.
O.E.	C-Operation	Delete	Element is disappeared in new collected R.E.
D.T.			
I.T.	C-Non-Functio nal	Merge	Elements are merged in the repository
	O-Interface	Split	Elements are split in the repository
	O-Platform	Modify	Elements are modified in the repository
	D-Specific	Equal	Elements in the repository are same
	I-Design		
	I-Decision		

*C.-Capacity. O.E.-Operating-Environment, D.T.-Domain Technology, I.T.-Implementation Technology

The definition of each gap analysis is composed of a source and a consequence. The source identifies the status of the elements involved in the new collected requirements and in the reused requirements. The consequence is specifying difference between the new collected requirements and the reused requirements in repository. Therefore, the consequence helps user to established good requirements. After gap analysis is finished, we can get three sets of requirements such as <requirements considered>, <requirements new added>, and <requirements not considered>.

4 Requirements Elicitation Process

The potential requirements elicitation process starts with the construction of the new collected requirements. The refinement mechanism of requirements element is used as a means to analyze gaps at different levels in details. The process continues until developers and users affirm the refined requirements to be acceptable. Through the refinement process, the gap granularity issue is handled. More precisely, the process for eliciting requirements is an iterative one as follows:

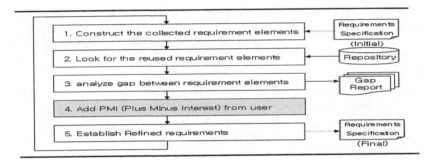

Fig. 2. The process to elict potential requirements

The five steps are carried out in a participative manner. This allows the consideration of different viewpoints with the aim of reconciling them cooperatively, in the construction of the new collected requirements' elements as well as in the refinement of gaps. Additionally, in step 4, users are given a gap report. Users can decide to add or delete elements, and put their PMI(plus minus interest) in requirements specification. Each iteration is related to activities which:

- First, system analysts gather requirements with general elicitation methods. They make an initial requirement specification. Then, they construct elements of the new collected requirements.
- Second, they look for similar elements in the reused requirement repository.
- Third, they analyze gap between the new collected requirements and the reused requirements in the repository. Then, they give users a gap report.
- Fourth, they carry out the meeting with users to check the gap report. At that time, users give analysts own opinion and analyst should reflect users'PMI(plus minus interest) in the refined requirements specification.
- Finally, system analysts establish the refined requirements specification. If the refinement is need, they carry out iteration from 1 to 5 again.

5   Conclusion and Future Works

We propose a method to elicit potential requirements from various stakeholders. To achieve our goal, we firstly presented a meta-model of reusable requirements element using feature modeling. Next, we generated requirements' element using feature categories and carried out gap analysis between the new collected requirements and the reused requirements in the repository. The gap analysis is composed of a source and a consequence. The source identifies the status of the elements involved in the new collected requirements' elements, and in the reused requirements' elements. The consequence is specifying difference between requirements' elements. Also, we presented the potential requirements elicitation process with gap analysis. This process is sequential procedures to look for potential requirements in addition to users' Plus minus interest(PMI). This can reduce requirements changes and reduce time or cost problem corresponding uncertain requirements.

We are conscious of the lack of consideration related to definition of operators and handling of complex operators such as merge and split. In addition, association conditions between elements should be analyzed in details during the gap elicitation process. These are considered in the further steps of our research.

References

[1] Ian F. Alexander and Richard Stevens, Writing Better Requirements, Addison Wesley, 2002.
[2] Ounsa Roudiks, Mounia Fredj, "A Reuse Based Approach for Requirements Engineering," IEEE, 2001.
[3] Jacob L. Cybulski1 and Karl Reed2, "Requirements Classification and Reuse:Crossing Domain Boundaries," LNCS 1844, pp. 190-210, 2000.
[4] Kyo C. Kang, Sajoong Kim, Jaejoon Lee, Kijoo Kim, Euiseob Shin, and Moonhang Huh, "FORM: A Feature-Oriented Reuse Method with Domain-Specific Reference Architectures," Annals of Software Engineering, 5, pp. 143-168, 1998
[5] Colette Rolland, Camille Salinesi, and Anne Etien, "Eliciting gaps in requirements change," Requirements Eng(2004) 9:1-15, 2004.

X-ARM: A Step Towards Reuse of Commercial and Open Source Components

Michael Schuenck, Yuri Negócio, Glêdson Elias,
Sindolfo Miranda, Jorge Dias Jr., and Gustavo Cavalcanti

COMPOSE – Component Oriented Service Engineering Group
Informatics Department, Federal University of Paraíba
João Pessoa, PB, Brazil, 58059-900, (+55 83) 3216.7093
{michael, yuri, gledson, sindolfo, jjjunior,
gustavo}@compose.ufpb.br
http://www.compose.ufpb.br

Abstract. In component-based software development processes, one of the most challenging tasks is to find reusable assets that fulfill the requirements of a particular software system under development. Over time, in the context of component repository systems, reusable asset specification approaches have been proposed to help find suitable reusable assets. As an important step forward, RAS (Reusable Asset Specification) provides a standard way to describe all kinds of software assets. However, despite its contributions, RAS suffers from problems related to fine-grain reuse. Besides, RAS does not provide representation for asset certification and business models. As another step forward, this paper presents X-ARM, an XML-based Asset Representation Model, specified as a RAS extension and organized in four hierarchical profiles. The proposed model overcomes RAS limitations, providing effective means for developing universal repository systems that can improve reuse of commercial and open source software components.

1 Introduction

The large scale adoption of Component-Based Development (CBD) is limited to the existence of an active marketplace that enables the component exchange between different system developers and component developers. Such a context is required in order to help find suitable reusable components that fulfill the requirements of particular software systems under development. In order to overcome this limitation, some open and proprietary component repository systems [1] have been proposed by industry and academia.

According to [2] and [3], repository systems must store not only software components, but also metadata describing them. Such metadata provide information used by search engines to index and classify the components and then, to allow consumers to search and retrieve the adequate components required by the construction of their applications. The component metadata must be described in a unambiguous language and can represent several kinds of component characteristics, including: the component purpose, what component model it follows, what interfaces

M. Morisio (Ed.): ICSR 2006, LNCS 4039, pp. 432–435, 2006.

it provides and depends on, what events it fires and catches, what other components compose it, what related assets it has, what is the development process in which it was generated, what quality certification it has, who has certified it, who can retrieve it, and so on.

An important initiative towards the definition of a reusable asset description model is the Reusable Asset Specification (RAS) [4]. Such model describes the assets metadata as XML documents and adopts the use of profiles, which are extensions to the core specification to represent features of particular asset types. Although it defines three profiles, they are not enough to represent all characteristics of main asset types required by a CBD-centric component repository. Moreover, RAS profiles do not focus on fine-grain reuse. For instance, interface and component specifications are not reused among different component implementations.

In such a context, this paper presents a model called X-ARM, an acronym for XML-based Asset Representation Model. It has the aim of semantically describe all kinds of software assets that can be stored in a component repository system, including software components. The proposed model is an extension of RAS, divided into four profiles that allow the description of distinct types of software assets.

The remainder of this paper is organized as follows. In Section 2, we present the X-ARM in terms of profiles and the asset types defined by each profile. Section 3 presents some concluding remarks.

2   X-ARM

A prior X-ARM version was originally presented in [5] as an independent model. However, we decided to develop a new version of X-ARM, adapting it to be a RAS extension, since RAS Default Profile defines the basic characteristics to the X-ARM goals, such as asset identification, classification, related assets and files that compose the asset [4]. Moreover, RAS is a standard proposed by OMG, adopted by important software enterprises.

X-ARM defines four profiles, created in order to separate concepts, split complexity and improve the reusability of the different asset types. In order to illustrate such types, Figure 1 presents the X-ARM asset types, categorized according to the profiles.

The *X-ARM Artifact Profile* inherits the RAS Default Profile elements. Since the other X-ARM profiles are X-ARM Artifact Profile specializations, it represents the basic features of all the asset types. In this sense, such a profile introduces elements to represent information about: the development process adopted to construct the asset, the adopted business models, the asset certification, the assets reused to construct the specified asset, and the evolution history. Moreover, X-ARM Artifact Profile describes four particular asset types. The *X-ARM XML Schema* is an asset type aimed to store XML Schemas that describe the X-ARM profiles. The *License* type represents usage licenses, which are reused by assets of other types that adopt those licenses. A *Producer certification* describes the certification of the software process adopted by specific producers. *Resources* describe any software artifacts other than the asset types represented by the remaining profiles. It is important to note that, in the case of X-ARM Artifact Profile, all asset types defined by it use the same XML elements.

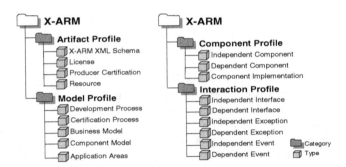

Fig. 1. X-ARM asset types

The *X-ARM Model Profile* aims to standardize the values used to represent particular features, enabling standard searches and comparisons between different assets. It allows the representation of five asset types. The first one is *development process*, which is used to specify, in terms of phases and outputs, the development processes that can be employed to construct a system and, consequently, all its compound assets. Since the component quality, reliability and functionality can be certified by certifier entities [6], a *certification process* asset is responsible to identify and describe the aspects verified by a component certification procedure and their possible concepts. The *business model* type represents, in terms of characteristics and their possible values, a negotiation model that can be adopted by distinct assets. The *component model* type is used to indicate the elements and characteristics that compose a component model, whose examples are CCM, JavaBeans and COM. Such an asset type is described in terms of properties, provided and required interfaces, and source and listener events. Specifying separate *component model* assets enables descriptions of components in accordance with any component model and avoids the creation of new *Profiles*. Finally, an *application areas* asset is employed to group a set of application areas, hierarchically organized, used by other asset types to describe and classify them.

The intent of the *X-ARM Interaction Profile* is to describe the structures used by components to communicate with other components or applications. In this sense, it defines elements to represent events, exceptions and interfaces. Each one is classified as component model independent or component model dependent. On the one hand, the model independent assets do not agree with a specific component model and, thus, can be adopted by any *independent component*. On the other hand, the component model dependent assets must attend the component model rules. For instance, a model dependent description of a CCM interface must indicate a CIDL (CORBA Interface Description Language) [7] file. This way, model dependent assets can indicate the model independent assets they derived from and can be referenced by *dependent components*.

Finally, the *X-ARM Component Profile* allows the representation of both specification and implementation of components, adding the proper elements to describe such asset types. The *independent* and *dependent component* assets describe component specifications. They differ from each other because the former does not take into account characteristics of a specific component model. Moreover, a *dependent component* can indicate the *independent component* in which it is based on. Besides, using X-ARM Component Profile it is also possible to represent *component implementations*, which represents the documentation and the executable and source codes. Such asset type must indicate the *dependent component* that it implements.

3 Conclusion

By exploring the proposed XML-based model, called X-ARM, a compliant component repository system can provide effective means to store, discover and retrieve assets with the expected functionality. X-ARM defines 18 distinct asset types in order to represent with more adequateness the particular characteristics of each type.

X-ARM allows assets to be reused under a variety of licenses and business models. The representation of the business models to acquire an asset can consider several characteristics and can indicate different license types and terms, described by distinct assets. Moreover, X-ARM allows indicating both executable and source code of components. Consequently, commercial, open source and free components may be represented.

An X-ARM compliant asset packager is currently under construction, being developed as an Eclipse plug-in. Future work should focus on the design and implementation of a compliant component repository system, including approaches for indexing mechanisms and search engines.

References

1. J. Guo, Luqui. *A Survey of Software Reuse Repositories*. 7th IEEE International Conference and Workshop on the Engineering of Computer Based Systems, April 2000, pp. 92-100.
2. Orso, A.; Harrold, M. J.; and Rosenblum, D. S. *Component Metadata for Software Engineering Tasks*. In Proc. 2nd International Workshop on Engineering Distributed Objects (EDO 2000). Springer, Berlin, 2000, 126-140.
3. Sametinger, J. *Software engineering with reusable components*. Springer-Verlag New York, Inc., NY, 1997.
4. OMG. *Reusable Asset Specification – Version 2.2*. 2005. http://www.omg.org/docs/ptc/ 05-04-02.pdf (last access on November 02, 2005).
5. Elias, Glêdson; Schuenck, Michael; Negócio, Yuri; Dias Jr., Jorge; Miranda Filho, Sindolfo. *X-ARM: An Asset Representation Model for Component Repository*. In: ACM SAC 2006 – The 21st ACM Symposium on Applied Computing, Dijon, France. (to appear)
6. Szyperski, C.; Gruntz, D.; and Murer, S. *Component Sofware: Beyond Object-Oriented Programming*. Second Edition, Addison-Wesley / ACM Press, 2002.
7. Object Management Group. *The Common Object Request Broker: Architecture and Specification*. December 2001.

Implementing Domain-Specific Modeling Languages and Generators

Juha-Pekka Tolvanen

MetaCase
Ylistönmäentie 31, FI-40500, Jyväskylä, Finland
jpt@metacase.com

Domain-Specific Modeling (DSM) languages provide a viable solution for improving development productivity by raising the level of abstraction beyond coding. With DSM, the models are made up of elements representing concepts that are part of the domain world, not the code world. These languages follow domain abstractions, and semantics, allowing developers – and depending on the domain even end-users – to perceive themselves as working directly with domain concepts. In many cases, full final product code can be automatically generated from these high-level specifications with domain-specific code generators.

This tutorial introduces DSM and looks at how it differs from modeling languages like UML that focus more on the level of the code world. This is followed by real-life examples of DSM from various fields of software product development. We will illustrate language creation by analyzing 20+ real-world DSM cases. The main part of the tutorial addresses the guidelines for implementing DSM: how to identify the necessary language constructs; how to make the metamodel to formalize language specification; and different ways of building code generation. Participants will be able to try their hand and learn these skills in practice in group exercises.

M. Morisio (Ed.): ICSR 2006, LNCS 4039, p. 436, 2006.

Metrics and Strategy for Reuse Planning and Management

Bill Frakes[1] and John Favaro[2]

[1] Computer Science Department
Virginia Tech
wfrakes@vt.edu
[2] Consulenza Informatica
john@favaro.net

Key to planning and managing a systematic reuse program is the formulation and evaluation of a competitive strategy, and subsequent monitoring and measurement of progress against the goals elucidated by that strategy.

This course provides a succinct introduction to software reuse metrics, and principles of strategic planning and economic evaluation of reuse-oriented investments. The two parts of the course provide a comprehensive overview of current practice and recent developments in reuse project planning and management.

Topics include an introduction to management of reuse projects, basic concepts and terminology in reuse measurement, principles of strategy, and fundamentals of economic evaluation of proposed investments in reuse.

This course shows senior managers, project managers, and planners,

- how and what to measure for meaningful reuse project management,
- the factors that influence a competitive strategy for reuse,
- the most effective traditional and recent approaches to economic evaluation of reuse projects.

M. Morisio (Ed.): ICSR 2006, LNCS 4039, p. 437, 2006.
© Springer-Verlag Berlin Heidelberg 2006

Building Reusable Testing Assets for a
Software Product Line

John D. McGregor

Clemson University
Clemson, SC USA 29634
johnmc@cs.clemson.edu

Testing consumes a significant percentage of the resources required to produce software intensive products. The exact impact on the project is often hard to evaluate because testing activities are distributed over the entire scope of the development effort. In this tutorial we take a comprehensive end-to-end view of the testing activities and roles that should be present in a software product line organization.

The Software Engineering Institute (SEI) identifies three areas of responsibility in a product line organization we relate these to testing:

- Organizational managers have responsibility for establishing the test strategy for the organization in general and the product line in particular. These activities are directly related to the business goals and scope of the product line.
- Technical managers have responsibility for planning the numerous test activities needed to implement the test strategy. These activities are planned in concert with the development activities to coordinate milestones and resources.
- Software engineers have responsibility for implementing the planned activities. They select the specific test cases necessary to achieve specific test coverage levels and implement any software needed to apply the test cases to the software under test.

The close relationship between developing software and testing it results in the test activities being crafted with knowledge of the chosen development process. The method engineer arranges the testing activities so that they are timely and have the appropriate perspective for their position in the development process. This tutorial considers test techniques and test process models.

M. Morisio (Ed.): ICSR 2006, LNCS 4039, p. 438, 2006.
© Springer-Verlag Berlin Heidelberg 2006

The Business Case for Software Reuse: Reuse Metrics, Economic Models, Organizational Issues, and Case Studies

Jeffrey S. Poulin

Lockheed Martin Distribution Technologies
Owego, NY 13827
Jeffrey.Poulin@lmco.com
http://home.stny.rr.com/jeffreypoulin

Successfully introducing a reuse program into an organization requires many things, such as proven processes, an organization for reuse, and management support. However, management needs to understand the value of reuse before they will allocate resources. Key to showing this value is a business case based on consistent, realistic, and easy to understand metrics. I have found that combining realistic assumptions with simple, easy-to-understand metrics often provides the incentive needed to "sell" reuse to management.

The business case for reuse has two parts. First, consider how much effort you save by reusing something rather than writing it yourself. Based on a lot of data, I have found that development savings range from 50-100% of new development (depending on the situation), with "typical" savings right around 80%. Reuse also avoids on-going maintenance costs, which further adds to this savings.

Second, consider how much it costs to write a component for reuse. Although it might cost from 0%-300% more to develop reusable components (again, depending on the situation), data shows that the "typical" additional investment lies around 50%.

In short, the business case for reuse consists of avoiding 80% of the development costs for reusing components (plus some additional maintenance savings) minus the 50% extra it cost to build the components in the first place. Using these simple metrics, it is easy to show that if you have two related projects, it will pay to base both of them on the same foundation of reusable components.

Even with conservative assumptions, the business case for reuse is overwhelming. Combined with proven "best practices" such as for organizing your team and for component management, metrics are critical to successfully rolling out reuse in any organization.

Reference

Poulin, Jeffrey S. Measuring Software Reuse: Principles, Practices, and Economic Models. Addison-Wesley (ISBN 0-201-63413-9), Reading, MA, 1997.

M. Morisio (Ed.): ICSR 2006, LNCS 4039, p. 439, 2006.
© Springer-Verlag Berlin Heidelberg 2006

Designing Software Product Lines with UML 2.0: From Use Cases to Pattern-Based Software Architectures

Hassan Gomaa

Department of Information and Software Engineering
George Mason University, Fairfax, Virginia, USA
hgomaa@gmu.edu

A software product line consists of a family of software systems that have some common functionality and some variable functionality. An important part of developing a software product line is commonality/variability analysis, during which the common and variable parts of the requirements, analysis, and design models are determined. This tutorial describes a model-driven evolutionary development approach for software product lines called PLUS (Product Line UML-based Software Engineering).

The Evolutionary Software Product Line Engineering Process is a highly iterative software process, which consists of two main phases. During Software Product line Engineering, a product line multiple-view model, product line architecture, and reusable components are developed. During Software Application Engineering, given the features for the individual product line member, the application multiple-view model and architecture are derived.

This tutorial addresses how to develop object-oriented requirements, analysis, and design models of software product lines using the Unified Modeling Language (UML) 2.0 notation. During requirements modeling, kernel, optional, and alternative use cases are developed to define the software functional requirements of the system. The feature model is then developed to capture the commonality and variability in product line requirements, and how they relate to the use case model. During analysis, static models are developed for defining kernel, optional, and variant classes and their relationships. Dynamic models are developed in which statecharts define the state dependent aspects of the product line and interaction models describe the dynamic interaction between the objects that participate in each kernel, optional, and alternative use case. The feature/class dependencies are then determined by performing an impact analysis of the optional and alternative features. The component-based software architecture for the product line is then developed, in which the system is structured into distributed components. Architectural structure patterns and communication patterns are used to help develop the software architecture. Software applications, which are members of the software product line, are developed by selecting the application features from the feature model and using this to derive the application from the product line architecture and components The tutorial is based on a book by the author, "Designing Software Product Lines with UML: From Use Cases to Pattern-Based Software Architectures", Addison Wesley Object-Oriented Technology Series, 2005.

M. Morisio (Ed.): ICSR 2006, LNCS 4039, p. 440, 2006.

Aspect-Oriented Software Development Beyond Programming

Awais Rashid[1], Alessandro Garcia[1], and Ana Moreira[2]

[1] Computing Department, Infolab21, Lancaster University,
Lancaster LA1 4WA, UK
{awais, garciaa}@comp.lancs.ac.uk
[2] Departamento de Informática, Universidade Nova de Lisboa, 2829-516
Lisboa, Portugal
amm@di.fct.unl.pt

Software systems and the concerns addressed by them are becoming increasingly complex hence posing new challenges to the mainstream software engineering paradigms. The objectoriented paradigm is not sufficient to modularise crosscutting concerns, such as persistence, distribution and error handling, because they naturally crosscut the boundaries of other concerns. As a result, these broadly-scoped concerns cannot be systematically reused and evolved. Aspect-oriented software development (AOSD) [1] tackles the specific problem of managing crosscutting concerns throughout the software development lifecycle. It supports a new abstraction – the *aspect* – and new composition mechanisms to facilitate developers to modularise, analyse and reason about crosscutting concerns in a system. Its potential benefits include improved comprehensibility, reusability, evolvability and maintainability of the system.

Although AOSD is founded on the concepts of aspect-oriented programming (AOP) [4], AOSD is not just about programming. In fact, several aspect-oriented techniques for preliminary development stages (collectively referred to as Early Aspects approaches [2]), such as requirements engineering and architecture design, have been proposed in order to provide systematic treatment of crosscutting concerns throughout the software lifecycle and not just at the programming stage. Hence with the emergence of AOSD techniques, reuse of crosscutting concerns is no longer limited to the context of code artifacts.

In this context, the focus of this tutorial is on providing attendees with a sound knowledge, rooted in concrete examples based on real-world scenarios, on how to employ AOSD beyond the programming stage of the software development life cycle. The tutorial covers how to use AOSD techniques to systematically treat crosscutting concerns in a reusable fashion during requirements engineering, architecture design and detailed design as well as the mapping between aspects at these stages. The discussion is based on concrete methods, tools, techniques and notations drawn from the state-of-the-art in Early Aspects, e.g., [3, 5, 6]. With a clear focus on reusable composition, modelling, trade-off analysis and assessment methods, the tutorial imparts an engineering ethos to be translated into day-to-day AOSD processes and practices.

M. Morisio (Ed.): ICSR 2006, LNCS 4039, pp. 441–442, 2006.

References

[1] AOSD, "Aspect-Oriented Software Development", http://aosd.net, 2006.

[2] E. L. A. Baniassad, et al., "Discovering Early Aspects", IEEE Software, 23(1), 2006.

[3] A. Garcia, et al., "Modularizing Design Patterns with Aspects: A Quantitative Study ",Proc. AOSD Conf. 2005, ACM, pp. 3-14.

[4] G. Kiczales, et al., "Aspect-Oriented Programming", Proc. ECOOP 1997, pp. 220-242.

[5] A. Moreira, et al., "Multi-Dimensional Separation of Concerns in Requirements Engineering", Proc. Requirements Engineering Conf. 2005, IEEE CS, pp. 285-296.

[6] A. Rashid, et al., "Modularisation and Composition of Aspectual Requirements", Proc.AOSD Conf. 2003, ACM, pp. 11-20.

Author Index

Lecture Notes in Computer Science

For information about Vols. 1–3907

please contact your bookseller or Springer